SPECIAL
INDIAN
EDITION

Corporate Information Strategy and Management

Text and Cases

Seventh Edition

D1316321

Corporate
Information Strategy
and Management

Text and Cases

Seventh Edition

Corporate Information Strategy and Management

Text and Cases

Seventh Edition

Lynda M Applegate

Robert D Austin

F Warren McFarlan

All of the Harvard Business School

Tata McGraw-Hill Publishing Company Limited
NEW DELHI

McGraw-Hill Offices

New Delhi New York St Louis San Francisco Auckland Bogotá Caracas
Kuala Lumpur Lisbon London Madrid Mexico City Milan Montreal
San Juan Santiago Singapore Sydney Tokyo Toronto

Tata McGraw-Hill

CORPORATE INFORMATION STRATEGY AND MANAGMENT: TEXT AND CASES

Indian Adaptation done by arrangement with The McGraw-Hill Companies, Inc., New York

Sales Territories: India, Pakistan, Nepal, Bangladesh, Sri Lanka and Bhutan

First reprint 2007
RZZCRRXYRAYRA

Tata McGraw-Hill Edition 2007

ISBN 0-07-063584-6

Published by the Tata McGraw-Hill Publishing Company Limited, 7 West Patel Nagar, New Delhi 110 008, and Typeset at Script Makers, 19, A 1-B, DDA Market, Paschim Vihar, New Delhi 110 063 and printed at India Book Binding House, Sector 65, Noida

Cover Printer: De-Unique

The McGraw·Hill Companies

Dedicated to our colleague and mentor of many years,
James L McKenney

Preface

Corporate Information Strategy and Management examines how information technology (IT) enables organizations to conduct business in radically different and more effective ways. The commercialization of the Internet has created a seismic change in the business environment. New channels of supply and distribution are emerging. New electronic marketplaces and exchanges are being created. The infrastructures of firms and the industries within which they operate have been permanently altered.

This is a fast-moving and global phenomenon. For established companies, the resulting challenges have been deep and pervasive. In many cases, the changes have threatened not just a firm's competitiveness but also its survival. Executives bear an enormous burden as they attempt to understand the challenges, keep abreast of events, and make intelligent decisions and plans.

The objective of this book is to provide readers with a better understanding of the influence of twenty-first-century technologies on business decisions. The book discusses today's challenges from the point of view of the executives who are grappling with them. It recounts stories of success and failure, focusing on the issues faced and the decisions made by executives in companies around the world.

The 18 cases and readings presented here are organized in an Introduction, three modules, and a Conclusion. The first module is aimed at understanding the impact of IT on industries, markets, and organizations. It discusses issues of strategic positioning and explains how twenty-first-century IT provides opportunities to alter market/industry structure, power, and relationships. New technologies also enable new organizational capabilities and management/leadership principles. The second module turns the reader's attention to operational issues at the interface of business and technology as it examines approaches to designing and managing open-standard, networked technology infrastructures. The third module concentrates on leadership and management of IT activities, focusing on the issues that arise at the boundary as four key constituents—business executives, IT executives, users, and IT partners—work together to leverage technology to create a sustainable advantage. The Conclusion summarizes key frameworks, insights, and themes. Additional cases are provided in the final section that enable discussion of the integrated issues that twenty-first-century executives must address.

The material presented here is the outgrowth of field-based research we have conducted at the Harvard Business School since the early 1970s. To Deans John McArthur and Kim Clark we express our appreciation for making the time and resources available for us to complete this work.

We are particularly indebted to the executives who provided so much time and insight during the course of our research. All the cases in this book are based on observations of strategic decision making and action in real organizations. Without the cooperation of many executives, the preparation of this book would not have been possible.

We are grateful as well for the many valuable suggestions and insights provided by our Harvard Business School colleagues, especially Jim Cash, Alan MacCormack,

Andrew McAfee, Jim McKenney, Richard Nolan, Kash Rangan, and David Upton. In addition, we acknowledge the valued work of our doctoral students, fellows, and research assistants. Our heartfelt thanks go to Nancy Bartlett, Alastair Brown, Elizabeth Collins, Mark Cotteleer, Melissa Dailey, Brian Delacey, LeGrand Elebash, Cedric Escalle, David Lane, Marc Mandel, Felipe Monteiro, Beth Rochefort, Tom Rodd, Mary Rotelli, Deb Sole, Erin Sullivan, George Westerman, and Fred Young. We also acknowledge the support of the directors of Harvard Business School research centers, including Christina Darwall of the California Research Center; Gustavo Herrero, Director of the Latin America Research Center; Camille Tang Yeh, Director of the Asia Pacific Center; and Carin Knoop, Executive Director of Global Research. Thanks go to Alan Murray, a superlative friend and former colleague, who provided important reviews of technical details, especially in the chapter on computer security. Finally, we express our appreciation to our editor, Tom Cameron, and to Jennifer Chalfin, Maureen Donovan, Zoya Omartian, Brooke Spangler, and Maurie SuDock, who provided administrative support.

Lynda M. Applegate
Robert D. Austin
F. Warren McFarlan

Contents

Introduction: Challenges of Managing in a Networked World

Information technology (IT) has always been a wildcard in business, a source of opportunity and uncertainty, of advantage and risk. Business executives often view IT with apprehension, as the province of technocrats primarily interested in new features that may have little relevance to real-world business problems. Technology executives often consider business managers to be shortsighted, lacking the vision to exploit all that technology has to offer. Both struggle as they attempt to implement increasingly complex systems in the face of rapid change in business and technology.

And yet we have, since the inception of business computing, tightened our embrace of IT—and for good reason. Despite exasperating moments, technology has become embedded in the way we define and execute strategy, in how we organize and lead businesses, and how we define a unique value proposition.

Indeed, the pace of IT change has been both dramatic and disconcerting. The co-evolution of technology, work, and the workforce over the past 40 years has dramatically influenced our concept of organizations and the industries within which they compete. No longer simply a tool to support "back-office" transactions, IT has become a strategic part of most businesses, enabling the redefinition of markets and industries and the strategies and designs of firms competing within them. Today's global communication networks carry information around the world in seconds. Distance and time have become much less significant determinants of market and organizational structures and processes.[1] Moreover, information has become a

---

[1] R. Miles and C. Snow, "Organizations: New Concepts for New Forms," *California Management Review* 28 (1986), pp. 62–73; T. Malone, J. Yates, and R. Benjamin, "Electronic Markets and Electronic Hierarchies: Effects of Information Technology on Market Structure and Corporate Strategies," *Communications of the ACM* 30, no. 6 (1987), pp. 484–497; R. Johnston and P. Lawrence, "Beyond Vertical Integration—the Rise of the Value-Adding Partnership," *Harvard Business Review,* July–August 1988; W. Powell, "Neither Market nor Hierarchy: Network Forms of Organization," *Research on Organizational Behavior* 12 (1990), pp. 295–336.

major economic good, frequently exchanged in concert with, or even in place of, tangible goods and services.

The 1990s added considerably to the mystique and the magic of IT. Something dramatic happened to technology, although it is probably too early to discern the full impact. Many of us remember the first time we opened a browser and gained access to the World Wide Web (WWW). For some executives who had lived their lives avoiding technology, a light went on, and they glimpsed the potential of what previously had lain deep within the silicon switches that processed data in the basement of the organization. Others ventured forth only to become mired in a sea of useless information and broken links that convinced them that, although the technology was more appealing to the eye, the same old flaws remained.

Then came the boom of the late 1990s, when the capital markets caught the fever. Stories of "20-something" billionaires who only a few years earlier had plotted their business ideas on napkins grabbed our attention. Stories of investors who pushed entrepreneurs to take more money and spend it more quickly challenged our view of the blood, sweat, and tears that used to define how a new business was built from the ground up. Stories of newly public firms with market capitalizations in the billions of dollars, yet with no discernible path to profitability, caused us to question the fundamental economic principles that guided how we built and managed companies.

As the new century dawned, the speculative "bubble" burst. The tech-heavy Nasdaq lost more than half its value within months and spending for IT equipment and services dropped. The world economy headed into a downward spiral that continued for several years. As we write in early 2005, welcome signs of economic recovery are thawing the deep freeze that had settled over IT activities. Unlike the mad growth we saw during the bubble, recent growth appears sustainable, catalyzed by real business models and profitability.

Indeed, some things are becoming clear. The world is forever changed. IT has burst forth from the basement. Business executives have begun to wrest control from IT executives who have failed to step up to the challenge of entering the boardroom. Technology has become a core enabler and, in some cases, the primary channel through which business is done. The world is smaller and the "global village" is quickly becoming a reality. Borders and boundaries, ownership and control have become less rigid. The last decade has offered examples of IT-enabled "virtual" organizations, in which many small, independent firms band together as nodes on an information network to achieve dramatic increases in scope and scale. Such arrangements challenge both our legal and social definitions of an organization as business practice outpaces legal and regulatory policy—especially in areas like international competitiveness and trade, intellectual property, privacy, security, family, community, education, and culture. And, yet, there are still new frontiers to explore, new challenges to meet, and new magic in store.

Because so much has changed so quickly, because the ups and downs have come in such a short interval, now is a difficult time to engage in sense-making. Yet, that is precisely what we are doing in this book. We're attempting to relate what we know from decades of study to what we are learning from those who are creating the future. The last decade has provided the richest vein of potential learning we have ever been positioned to mine. It has been a period of intense experimentation. Many new models were tried. Many of them failed. We would be remiss if we did not attempt to understand it all—the successes and the failures.

Our objective is to help business executives take important steps on the path of IT-enabled transformational change. At the same time, we wish to help IT executives assume leadership positions, not just in defining and executing technology strategy, but also in defining and executing business strategy. As we work toward these dual objectives, we draw on years of research and experience, much of it in the field with executives that have accepted the challenge and are venturing forward into uncharted waters. This book is filled with their stories, captured in case examples and full-length case studies. We hope you enjoy the book as you attempt to leverage the opportunities and address the challenges of managing in a networked economy.

Case I.1

Li & Fung (A): Internet Issues

"I'm not an Internet guy, I'm a business guy," quipped William Fung, managing director of Li & Fung Trading Co. Clad in his chinos and black American Eagle T-shirt, Fung looked much more like a new economy entrepreneur than the self-described offline, "old economy relic": "I'm 51, I'm more than a grey hair in Internet terms, I'm a fossil."[1] Nor did lifung.com, his elder brother Victor's new online company, resemble a typical Internet start-up, particularly with a 96-year-old parent born at the end of the Qing Dynasty. In August 2000, the day before beta launch of the new business-to-business (B2B) e-commerce portal, William described the challenges facing Li & Fung:

> About three or four years ago, Victor and I discussed the Internet and how it impacts us. Our starting point was a defensive posture: Would the Internet disintermediate us? Would we get Amazoned[2] by someone who will put together all of the information about buyers and factories online? After a lot of research we realized that the Internet facilitates supply chain management and we weren't going to be disintermediated. The key is to have the old economy know-how and yet be open to new economy ideas.

With a press conference the following day, William was confident of the Group's performance and lifung.com's prospects. But he knew that important issues remained unresolved: Was there any chance of channel conflict or cannibalization between the offline business and the start-up? How would the market react to the start-up once it was launched the following year? And how specifically would e-commerce ultimately transform his family's century-old company?

Company Background[3]

Li & Fung was founded in 1906 by William's grandfather, Fung Pak-Liu and his partner, Li To-Ming in Guangzhou, China as an export trading company selling to overseas merchants. In the 1920s and 1930s the company diversified into warehousing and the manufacture of handicrafts. Shortly after Fung Pak-Liu passed away in 1943, his son Fung Hon-Chu assumed charge of the company. Two years later, silent partner Li To-Ming retired and sold his shares to the company. The company retained Li's surname, a homophone

(HBS #301-009) Professor F. Warren McFarlan and Senior Researcher Fred Young from the Asia-Pacific Research Center, 2000.

[1] Rahul Jacob, "Inside Track: Traditional Values at the Click of a Mouse," *Financial Times*, August 1, 2000, p. 14.

[2] Online bookseller Amazon.com transformed the book industry forcing traditional book retailers to respond.

[3] Some information in this section comes from previous Harvard Business School Case Studies: "Li & Fung: Beyond 'Filling in the Mosaic'"—1995–98," (HBS Publishing No. 398-092) Michael Y. Yoshino, Carin-Isabel Knoop, Anthony St. George; January 1, 1998; and "Li & Fung (Trading) Ltd.," HBS Publishing (No. 396-075) Gary Loveman, Jamie O'Connell, October 26, 1995.

for "profit" in Chinese, which, along with "Fung," a homophone for "abundance," had an auspicious ring when combined.

Li & Fung relocated permanently to Hong Kong at the end of World War II, expanding its operations to include toys, garments, plastic flowers, and electronics. In the early 1970s, both Fung brothers had just returned from the United States: William had earned his MBA from Harvard Business School and returned to the business in 1972. Victor had recently completed his PhD in economics at Harvard University and, following a two-year stint teaching at Harvard Business School, rejoined the business in 1974. Their return heralded Li & Fung's transition from a family-owned business to a professionally managed firm, with a planning and budgeting system in place for the first time. William and Victor, the third generation to run the company, felt that the next logical step in growing the company was to go public. In 1973, Li & Fung became the holding company for the Group and was listed on the Hong Kong Stock Exchange (HKSE). Throughout the 1980s, Li & Fung expanded its regional network of offices throughout the Asia-Pacific region as more sources of supply emerged in the rapidly industrializing Asian economies. In 1988 the Group was privatized and streamlined, incorporated in Bermuda in 1991, and its trading activities were again listed on the HKSE in July 1992. With the 1995 acquisition of Inchcape Buying Services (formerly Dodwell), Li & Fung expanded its customer base in Europe while simultaneously shifting its sourcing network beyond East Asia to include the Indian subcontinent, the Mediterranean, and Caribbean basins.

By 2000, Li & Fung was a $2 billion global export trading company with 3,600 staff worldwide, sourcing and managing the global supply chain for high-volume, time-sensitive consumer goods. (Exhibit 1 shows recent Li & Fung financial data.) By 2000, 69 percent of Li & Fung's sales were in the United States and 27 percent in Europe. Key customers included The Limited, Gymboree, American Eagle, Warner Brothers, Abercrombie & Fitch, and Bed Bath & Beyond. Tesco, Avon Products, Levi-Strauss, and Reebok had become customers within the last two years; Royal Ahold, GUESS? jeans, and bebe had signed on in 2000.

Li & Fung's product mix included hard and soft goods. Soft goods referred to apparel, including woven and knit garments for men, women, and children. Hard goods included fashion accessories, festive or holiday products, furnishings, giftware, handicrafts, home products, fireworks, sporting goods, toys, and travel goods. Hard goods provided higher margins than soft goods because, despite a generally lower item value per unit, they required higher value-added services for orders that were also usually much smaller than soft goods orders. Hard goods items such as watches, shoes, suitcases, kitchenware, or teddy bears required an inspector for quality control evaluation for even the smallest batch order, thereby greatly increasing what Li & Fung could charge. Margins for soft goods were roughly 6 percent to 8 percent, while

EXHIBIT 1   Li & Fung Consolidated Income Statement (December 31, 1999), in HK$*

	2000 (HK$ thousands) (June 30)	1999 (HK$ thousands) (December 31)	1999 (HK$ thousands) (June 30)	1998 (HK$ thousands) (December 31)
Turnover	10,267,606	16,297,501	6,583,730	14,312,618
Cost of sales	(9,262,171)	(14,585,881)	(5,895,432)	(12,891,709)
Selling expenses	(191,616)	(354,124)	(143,136)	(287,524)
Administrative expenses	(87,741)	(867,842)	(56,436)	(747,725)
Profits before taxation	328,943	613,861	208,936	471,098
Taxation	(29,805)	(36,638)	(14,536)	(16,425)
Profit after taxation	299,338	577,223	194,400	454,673

*In August 2000, US$1 = HK$7.78.

EXHIBIT 1 (continued)
Li & Fung Consolidated Balance Sheet (December 31, 1999), HK$

Source: Company documents.

	1999 (HK$ thousands)	1998 (HK$ thousands)
Fixed assets	1,161,808	1,145,056
Investment securities	86,484	51,389
Current assets		
Inventories	110,014	72,267
Trade and bills receivable	1,488,780	1,089,011
Cash and bank balances	1,029,373	904,581
	2,961,634	2,234,490
Current liabilities		
	2,976,829	1,976,958
Net current (liabilities)/assets	(15,195)	257,532
	1,234,339	1,466,767
Financed by:		
Share capital	64,765	63,761
Reserves	749,346	1,030,295
Shareholders' funds	814,111	1,094,056
Minority interests	4,460	(24,595)
Long-term liabilities	414,868	397,058
Deferred taxation	900	248
	1,234,339	1,446,767

margins on hard goods ranged anywhere from 10 percent to 30 percent, depending on the degree of complexity involved in sourcing raw materials. As a result, Li & Fung attempted to expand its sale of hard goods. In 1998 soft and hard goods contributed 77.5 percent and 22.5 percent of total sales, respectively, while the proportion of hard goods sales grew to 25 percent in 1999 and was projected to increase to 27 percent in 2001 and 29 percent in 2002.

Holistic Supply Chain Management

Although Li & Fung described itself as a trading company, by 2000 it was far more sophisticated than a typical Hong Kong import-export trading company and had come a long way from its roots in matching Chinese manufacturers with Western buyers:

We have been changing. Now we're orchestrating a whole production process that starts from raw materials all the way through to finished product. If you look at the old days, language skills could guarantee you margins better than we have now. My grandfather used to

charge 15 percent or more, basically to be an interpreter. Those days are over.[4]

With 48 offices in 32 countries, the company provided value-added services across the entire supply chain in a so-called borderless manufacturing environment (see Exhibit 2). A down jacket's filling, for example, might come from China, the outer shell fabric from Korea, the zippers from Japan, the inner lining from Taiwan, and the elastics, label, Velcro, and other trim from Hong Kong. The garment might be dyed in South Asia, stitched in China, then sent back to Hong Kong for quality control and finally packaged for delivery to The Limited or Abercrombie & Fitch. Victor explained:

Say we get an order from a European retailer to produce 10,000 garments. We determine that, because of quotas and labor conditions, the best place to make the garments is Thailand. So we ship everything from there. And because the customer needs quick delivery, we may

[4] Gren Manuel, "Technology Journal: Historic Trader Keeps Its Cool—Li & Fung Says It's Found a Place in the Internet Economy," *The Asian Wall Street Journal,* March 27, 2000, p. 15.

EXHIBIT 2
Li & Fung
Total Value-
Added Services

Source: Company
documents.

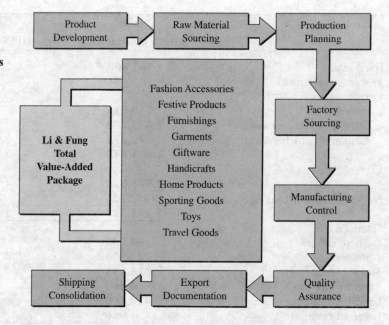

divide the order across five factories in Thailand. Effectively we are customizing the value chain to best meet the customer's needs. Five weeks after we received the order, 10,000 garments arrive on the shelves in Europe, all looking like they came from one factory.[5]

Li & Fung clients benefited in several ways: supply chain customization could shorten order fulfillment from three months to five weeks, and this faster turnaround allowed clients to reduce inventory costs. Moreover, in its role as a middleman, Li & Fung reduced matching and credit risks, and also offered quality assurance to its customers. Furthermore, with a global sourcing network and economies of scale, Li & Fung could offer lower cost and more flexible sourcing than its competitors. In addition, through acquisitions and global expansion, Li & Fung was extending this knowledge base to sub-Saharan Africa, Eastern Europe, and the Caribbean. Finally, Li & Fung provided up-to-date fashion and market trend information to clients. As a

result of its Camberley acquisition in 1999, it started offering clients virtual manufacturing or product design services.

According to Victor, "Li & Fung does not own any of the boxes in the supply chain, rather we manage and orchestrate it from above. The creation of value is based on a holistic conception of the value chain." In recent years, however, Li & Fung had begun to improve operations by controlling or owning strategic links in the chain. In some cases, Li & Fung offered raw material sourcing. In the past when clients placed an order, Li & Fung would determine the manufacturer best suited to supply the goods, and that factory would source its own raw materials. But Li & Fung understood its clients' needs better than its manufacturing plants did, so by offering raw materials to its suppliers, the company both ensured greater quality control and bought larger and thus more cost effective amounts of raw materials, thereby producing cost savings for each manufacturer. In such cases, Li & Fung also earned revenue by charging its factories a commission on each raw material purchase they made. By mid-2000, nearly 15 percent of Group sales involved Li & Fung's raw material sourcing service.

[5] Joan Magretta, "Fast, Global, and Entrepreneurial: Supply Chain Management, Hong Kong Style, An interview with Victor Fung," *Harvard Business Review,* September–October 1998, p. 106.

Corporate Culture and Compensation

From the 1992 privatization on, the division of labor between the Fung brothers was clear-cut: as Group chairman, Victor was primarily concerned with the Group's strategic issues and long-term planning; as Group managing director, William attended to everyday operations of the publicly listed trading arm, or as he joked in a recent interview, "Victor is the deep thinker, and I just make the money."[6] In another interview, Victor joked that "William calls me the visionary, meaning that I don't really know what's going on."[7] But both brothers lived in the same apartment building as their mother and sisters and conversed every day to keep abreast of developments at Li & Fung. The duo created a strong synergy that was described by the CEO of the Group's e-commerce venture as

> A combination of both thought leadership and execution, with the unique relationship between Victor and William cementing the entire organization. They create a very particular kind of culture that blends pragmatism and, at the same time, a recognition of and openness to innovation.

According to Victor, once the business was successful, it was essential to keep an open mind and rather than resting on their laurels, that the challenge was to move past success and look forward. Furthermore, Victor held that it was imperative to cultivate a corporate culture that not only tolerated but encouraged diversity, or in his words, "keep the culture so that it remains humble, agile, and responsive all the time and keep the people externally focused." Biannual retreats were held in Hong Kong, senior management meetings attended by division-level managers in order to foster communication across the Group.

Li & Fung's 3,600 employees were spread around the globe in offices ranging in size from 6 staff in Saipan to 1,100 in the Hong Kong head office. Five of the 48 offices were hubs—Hong Kong, Taiwan, Korea, Thailand, and Turkey. Each

(except the Hong Kong office) had 200 to 300 employees. Li & Fung was entrepreneurial, allowing senior managers to run 90 small, worldwide management teams as separate and individual companies. These dedicated teams of product specialists focused on the needs of specific customers and were grouped under a Li & Fung corporate umbrella that provided centralized IT, financial, and administrative support from Hong Kong. This decentralized corporate structure allowed for adaptability and rapid reaction to seasonal fashion shifts.

As a meritocracy, performance-based promotion and compensation were cardinal principles. Each of Li & Fung's top executives negotiated individual compensation packages. In contrast to companies that restricted executive bonuses to a fixed percentage of salary, Li & Fung bonuses were based on profits with no ceiling.

> It's not every company that calls its executives "little John Waynes." But for Li & Fung, the image captures perfectly the drive, dedication, and independence of the company's far-flung managers. As Li & Fung extended its geographic reach, it also expanded its mix of cultures. And to manage the mix it uses a simple formula: give managers the freedom to work as they see fit, so long as they get the job done.[8]

Tripartite Growth Strategy

In 2000 Li & Fung saw its future growth coming from a combination of organic growth, expansion through acquisition, and extension of its supply chain to new markets via the Internet.

Organic Growth

Since 1995, the Group had grown organically by receiving more orders from existing clients and by securing new mandates from strategic clients. Li & Fung further extended its network and diversified its sourcing around the globe with new offices in places as diverse as Bangladesh, sub-Saharan Africa, and Manchester, England (see Exhibits 3 and 4).

---

[6] Louis Kraar, "The New Net Tigers," *Fortune Magazine*, May 15, 2000, p. 310.

[7] Joanna Slater, "Masters of the Trade," *Far Eastern Economic Review*, July 22, 2000, p. 10.

[8] Joanna Slater, "Corporate Culture," *Far Eastern Economic Review*, July 22, 1999, p. 12.

EXHIBIT 3   Li & Fung's Global Network

Source: Company documents.

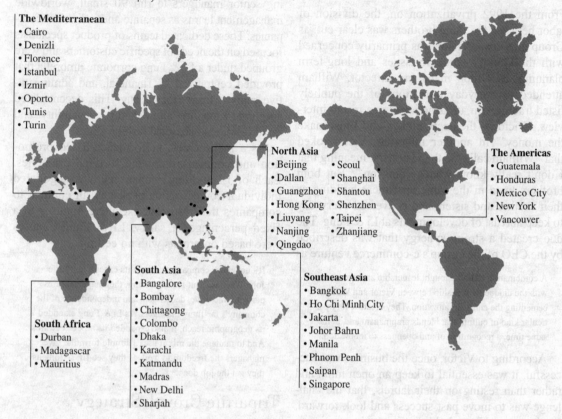

The Mediterranean
- Cairo
- Denizli
- Florence
- Istanbul
- Izmir
- Oporto
- Tunis
- Turin

North Asia
- Beijing
- Dallan
- Guangzhou
- Hong Kong
- Liuyang
- Nanjing
- Qingdao
- Seoul
- Shanghai
- Shantou
- Shenzhen
- Taipei
- Zhanjiang

The Americas
- Guatemala
- Honduras
- Mexico City
- New York
- Vancouver

South Asia
- Bangalore
- Bombay
- Chittagong
- Colombo
- Dhaka
- Karachi
- Katmandu
- Madras
- New Delhi
- Sharjah

Southeast Asia
- Bangkok
- Ho Chi Minh City
- Jakarta
- Johor Bahru
- Manila
- Phnom Penh
- Saipan
- Singapore

South Africa
- Durban
- Madagascar
- Mauritius

EXHIBIT 4
Li & Fung
Sourcing
Markets (Q1
and Q2, 2000)

Source: Company
documents.

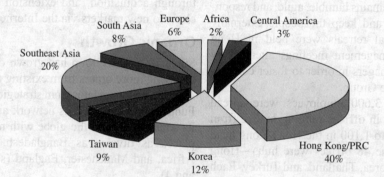

South Asia
8%

Europe
6%

Africa
2%

Central America
3%

Southeast Asia
20%

Taiwan
9%

Korea
12%

Hong Kong/PRC
40%

In 1996 Li & Fung adopted a "three-year plan" system, one which William described as having been adopted directly from the economic planning system of the Chinese Communist Party, that "allows the company to look ahead, but not too far ahead." William elaborated:

> We thought that the Chinese had a neat system. They have five-year plans, fixed; we have three-year plans, fixed. We don't want moving goalposts, we want set goals. At the beginning of every three-year plan we sit down and look at the business from its fundamentals. We use backwards planning, we recognize where we want to be in three years time, identify the gaps between that and where we are now, and see what we have to do to get there.

During its first three-year plan (FY1993–1995), entitled "Filling in the Mosaic," Li & Fung focused on filling in the gaps in its network of offices to cover new sourcing markets. The second three-year plan (FY1996–1998), "Margin Expansion," was launched immediately after the Inchcape acquisition to increase its profitability. A third three-year plan "Doubling Profits" (FY1999–2001), established the goals of doubling profits every three years and achieving $3 billion in annual sales.

Investors liked the results: Li & Fung outperformed the Hang Seng Index by over 75 percent in 2000. The reward was inclusion in the Morgan Stanley Country Index for Hong Kong in May 2000, subsequent inclusion in the HSI in August 2000 and on the FTSE World Index Hong Kong Section in September 2000. With a market capitalization of $6.6 billion, by mid-2000 Li & Fung was the nineteenth largest Hong Kong stock trading with a company record price to earnings (P/E) ratio of nearly 60×. A local newspaper declared:

> It is difficult to find a bad word [about Li & Fung]. It could be a poster-child for shareholder value, with a return-on-equity of 60.2 percent at the end of last year. The firm is well positioned to benefit from the opening of the mainland market and Beijing's accession to the World Trade Organization, with 40 percent of sourcing on the mainland and Hong Kong.[9]

---

[9] David Wilder, "Internet Key to More Gains for Li & Fung," *South China Morning Post,* September 4, 2000, *Business Post,* p. 1.

Acquisitions

Li & Fung's acquisition strategy was based on buying rival sourcing companies, thereby gaining new client accounts, integrating their operations, and eventually bringing the operating margins of these acquired units up to Li & Fung levels. In 1995 Li & Fung acquired Inchcape Buying Services, a 100-year-old company roughly the same size as Li & Fung and its closest competitor. The Dodwell acquisition brought access to sourcing markets on the Indian subcontinent and European export markets. This acquisition took nearly three years to be fully absorbed into Li & Fung's operations. Within three years, Dodwell's operating margins increased from 0.8 percent to 3 percent, primarily through the provision of Li & Fung value-added services to Dodwell customers.

In December 1999, Li & Fung acquired the export trading operations of the Swire Group, Swire & Maclaine and Camberley, which were Li & Fung's next two largest Hong Kong–based competitors, and in the process became the only listed supply chain management company in Hong Kong. Like Li & Fung, Camberley did not own its factories. Instead, it provided "virtual manufacturing" in the form of in-house design, pattern and sample making, and raw material sourcing. Manufacturing was subcontracted to factories in China. Through Camberley, Li & Fung gained access to the design process—another link in the value chain—as well as access to new clients such as the Asia buying offices of Laura Ashley and Ann Taylor. As it had with Inchcape, Li & Fung expected to bolster its own bottom line by raising the operating margins of these two companies. With a robust cash flow and the solid financial performance of past acquisitions, Li & Fung was in position to continue growing its business by further acquisitions.

By August 2000, Li & Fung was nearly five times the size of its two closest local competitors, William E. Connor and Associates and Colby International, which had twice postponed the IPO of its B2B portal in 2000.

E-Commerce

A core element of Li & Fung's three-year planning system included an introspective look at "whether we are still relevant, including whether or not we are going to be disintermediated." Part of its response was an Internet initiative of its own. In 1995 Li & Fung launched an intranet to link the Group's offices and manufacturing sites around the world, thereby expediting and simplifying internal communications. The progress of orders and shipments could be tracked in real time, and digital imagery allowed for online inspection and troubleshooting. For example, past quality problems with Bangladeshi production would require an on-site Li & Fung inspector to send physical samples to Hong Kong by express mail, whereas the intranet now allowed a high-resolution digital photo to be sent via the intranet for real-time response and remedy.

In 1997, Li & Fung launched secure extranet sites. Each site linked the company directly to a key customer and was customized to that customer's individual needs. By 2000, 10 such extranets were in place, each taking nearly 6–9 months to fully implement, from design to testing of the user interface. Through each site, Li & Fung could carry out online product development as well as order tracking, obviating much of the cost and time necessary to send hard copies of documents back and forth. Furthermore, with Li & Fung as the key link between manufacturers and retailers, the extranet provided a platform for the two to interface, thus streamlining communications as the order moved through the supply chain. Customers could track an order online just as it was possible to track a UPS delivery. This monitoring of production also promoted quick response manufacturing. Until the fabric was dyed, the customer could change the color; until the fabric was cut, the customer could change the styles or sizes offered, whether a pocket or a cuff would be added, and a number of other product specifications. According to William, some customers went as far as connecting their entire ERP (enterprise resource planning) system to Li & Fung's extranet system.

Li & Fung's IT division had 60 people, all based in Hong Kong, but software development of both the intranet in 1995 and its extranets in 1997 was outsourced.[10] Successful implementation of these systems provided the initial building blocks of Li & Fung's e-commerce solution and with them in place, the Fungs became further aware of the extent to which integration of Internet technology enhanced internal efficiency and improved communication between Li & Fung divisions and customers and began to consider extending the organization's online presence.

Competitive Threats

The Fung brothers said that they decided to go online to avoid being disintermediated. But a closer examination of local B2B portals and online exchanges led Victor to conclude that the online threat to their offline business was far less than first imagined. "People from the first wave were so far out and garbled in their thinking that we felt that there was no immediate threat," he noted. "Therefore, we needed to think through e-commerce properly, to formulate a proper response."

In Victor's words, B2B exchanges were "a molecule thick and a mile wide," based on many depthless relationships. Li & Fung preferred "narrow and deep" relationships nurtured with fewer customers and including value-added services. As William professed, "The same reason why we were not disintermediated by the offline guys is going to be the reason why we're not going to be disintermediated by the online guys."

However, William discovered on a 1999 visit to the United States that Li & Fung's old economy retail customers felt seriously threatened by Internet pure plays. At first this hype did not make much sense:

> I asked my friend at Toys 'R' Us, "Why are you concerned about eToys? It does about $28–$30 million in sales whereas you do $11 billion, and it loses as much as its entire turnover? How can you worry about them?" And the first lesson I learned was that it's not their size that is the threat but the fact that investors are throwing money at them.

---

[10] See Appendix A for more details on the intranet and extranet.

William discovered that Internet companies could use the money that was pouring in to damage offline competitors, often by acquiring them or their key people. "They can hire away all of the talent that you have. The biggest weapon is the money they have. At one point, they could have hired away my entire management."

Other possible threats came from online companies acquiring an old economy trading company, or from offline companies like Japanese trading companies or local sourcing firms that could partner with a dot-com and become a competitor overnight. William hinted that the Swire & Maclaine acquisition was a defensive move to preempt acquisitions by new economy companies.

William gave his view of the Internet revolution:

> I started off saying that the Internet is just another technology that affects the way information is transferred and people communicate with each other. It has a very dramatic impact, more dramatic than the fax. But for me it's yet another in a series of technological changes that affects our business that we have to be keenly aware of. It may be the most important change until now, but it is probably not the last.

According to Victor,

> The Internet is a revolutionary technology, but new technology is nevertheless still technology. Li & Fung always has been aggressive in adopting new technologies. When the telephone came along, my grandfather was shocked. When the fax came around, the technology changed our turnaround time into just days. With Internet technology, now we get answers within hours. When broadband and WAP comes online, there will be even less lag.

"Bubble In"

Once the Fungs determined that Li & Fung needed an e-commerce strategy, the remaining question was how and in what shape it would emerge, how specifically e-commerce would eventually add value to Li & Fung, and whether it would use the existing IT department of 60 or absorb a new team of "entrepreneurs." Victor felt strongly that their e-commerce strategy should come from within the company, not outsourced as the intra- and extranets were, or as he phrased it, "bubble in, *not* bubble out." According to

Victor, only if the solution was an internal one could he be certain that "the technology would pervade the entire Li & Fung organization." Neither did Victor care to start a brand-new entity separate from the parent:

> I'm not interested in starting a dot-com division, getting a high valuation with, a $13 million cash flow, and then spinning it off. I want Li & Fung to be around for another 100 years, not just 5 or 15. To start a pure Internet division is as equally absurd as starting a fax division, a division that exclusively uses faxes.

To better grasp the fundamentals of embarking on a new IT venture, Li & Fung added two new technical directors to its board, one a technology company CEO, the other an academic. According to William:

> The one thing certain about our business is that it will be constantly changing, so we need to install a mechanism for monitoring external environmental changes that impact our business. We decided a long time ago that we were an information and knowledge-based services company, so anything to do with information technology is crucial to us. We keep up with what's happening with board members who can help us scan the horizon.

Enter Castling

In 1997, Michael Hsieh (HBS '84), president of LF International Inc., Li & Fung's venture capital arm and 15-year Li & Fung veteran, received a telephone call from John Suh (HBS '97), CEO of Castling Group, an Internet start-up company that, like the chess move allows you to defend your king and simultaneously position your rook for attack, used the Internet to both defend the offline, old economy companies against online companies' threat to their markets while simultaneously extending their own online presence. The two met in San Francisco to discuss how a focused combination of technology and supply chain reform could transform retail.

Hsieh, well aware that Li & Fung was working on its own e-commerce strategy, noted:

> As a VC, I see numerous business plans that say that with Li & Fung behind an online exchange, we create significant value and therefore offer you 5 percent if you join us. However most of the plans do not make sense. They offer

very little value and the founders lack either industry or technology expertise. John had the right blend of technology and business sense, the right mix of right and left brain.

Like the Fungs, Hsieh favored a "bubble in" approach. He compared outsourcing e-commerce implementation to a third-party consultant for a $10 million fee as "putting the fox in the chicken coop." It created a risky dependency on outsiders, particularly if future design changes were required and also provided outsiders with proprietary information, strategy, and the entire business model. Finally, Hsieh remarked: "As a venture capitalist, I always have to think about the strength of the management team and what could go wrong with the venture. Can they deliver? Do they know the industry? Is this a credible business proposition? What if there is a negative reaction?" By late 1999, the time was right to act on their initial meeting. Hsieh commented that "both the evolution of Castling from B2C to B2B and Li & Fung's needs complemented each other nicely; John had a real appreciation for the supply chain and a record for building successful e-commerce models." In December 1999 Hsieh joined Castling's board and LF International invested in Castling. They subsequently co-invested in an initial round of financing for lifung.com, and Castling committed key managerial staff to lifung.com. Suh described Li & Fung as "the perfect strategic partner. They have an entrepreneurial philosophy rooted at the core of their system. They've got an aggressive and visionary leadership team at the forefront of supply chain management. And they're ready to operate according to the rules of the new economy."

In one fell swoop, San Francisco-based lifung.com's management team was immediately staffed with Castling's professionals, serving as vice president of Business Development, vice president of Operations, director of Marketing, and CTO (Chief Technology Officer). Suh stepped down as CEO of Castling, retaining the position of non-executive chairman, and signed on as CEO of lifung.com. Apart from Suh and CTO Derek Chen, 20 percent of lifung.com's initial staff came from Castling, amounting to an in-house e-commerce incubation team that represented a slight twist on

Victor's "bubble in" strategy. Suh and Chen, the latter formerly of Andersen Consulting's Advanced Network Solutions Group, brought along their experience from Castling e-commerce strategy projects for jcrew.com, hifi.com, giftcertificate.com, and ferragamo.com. The rest of the team came from either within Li & Fung (e.g., the senior vice president of Merchandising) or from outside the Li & Fung organization (e.g., the vice presidents of Sales and of Marketing). To facilitate the integration of the new online entity into the Li & Fung fold, a senior manager was tasked to provide an interface between the two groups. By Q3 2000, lifung.com had 40 full-time professionals and 25 consultants, with 80 full-time staff expected by year's end. For B2B ventures, moving first and fast was often a prerequisite for dominance. Scarcely a year had passed since the initial meeting with Castling and its first round of financing. According to Suh, there were three stages of launching an online venture: the business strategy, the design-build-test phase, and then actual execution. "Moving quickly," Suh remarked,

Requires a fundamental trust in an organization that best arises from the experience of a team that has built things together, with members who know each other's strengths and weaknesses. We do a lot of team building, because without trust you cannot move at the speed required. There are certain elements critical to the success of a dot-com . . . openness and constant communication are essential because there are so many skills and inter-functional dependencies that must be navigated for a successful launch. At lifung.com, we have a great mix of people, individuals with 30 years of merchandising experience, a deep operations staff, seasoned technologists and wonderkids, rounded out by newly minted MBAs. It's truly a mix of old and new, but what's united through this mix is the culture and that's what makes me most proud of our team.

However, before Li & Fung fully embarked on its e-commerce venture, William reminded analysts at a press conference that, "Although the Group is developing along the lines of the new economy, we're still using an old economy mindset." At this juncture, William felt that it was essential to complete some traditional market research, something that most dot-coms simply did not do: "We cannot assume," he said, paraphrasing Kevin Costner in

Field of Dreams, "that if you build it they will come. In building lifung.com we have to have a balance of the two mentalities, both old and new, there needs to be a happy medium. So let's do some top-down old economy market research first to find out how big the target market is, some bottom-up focus group research to identify retailers' real needs, and then we'll see whether or not they will come."

SME Target Market: "B to small b"

Market research was well received by industry analysts, who unanimously endorsed Li & Fung's preliminary research of its target SME (Small and Medium-sized Enterprise) market. Given the proliferation of B2B portals in early 2000, it was important to foster initial investor confidence in the lifung.com business model. Li & Fung defined its target SMEs in the United States as primarily retailers with annual sales under $100 million and wholesalers with turnover of less than $50 million. According to William, 15 to 20 SME focus groups told him that the Li & Fung brand was well known as "the guys who work with the Gap and The Limited." More importantly, the market research pinpointed SME needs and determined the extent of demand for a "B2b" portal like lifung.com. According to William, "One of the beauties of B2B is the finite number of customers. You don't have to take out Super Bowl advertising time or plaster the New York subway system with ads. By and large, we knew just whom to target, we know the names and addresses of these retailers, we know how to reach them since they all read the same trade publications and go to the same trade shows."

Li & Fung's research determined that 20,000 retailers and 2,800 wholesalers in the United States with a total market size of $54 billion were potential customers, not including the more fragmented markets of Europe and Japan. Because SME orders were small and lacked economies of scale, SMEs traditionally had to pay importers high margins, ranging anywhere from 25 percent to 30 percent of the total order, compared with the 6–8 percent commission Li & Fung charged its key clients for apparel and 10–12 percent average commission for hard goods. Not only did the SMEs pay the most, but they were also served the least: These smaller firms were typically only offered a limited range of options in product specifications and were frequently overlooked by suppliers more concerned with serving larger clients. Furthermore, SMEs often lacked current information and lagged far behind large retailers in identifying fashion trends (see Table A). William summarized: "Not surprisingly, the small guys want what the big guys want, a differentiated product line at good prices. However, the SMEs do not have many options and have been poorly serviced in the past."

Historically it had not been cost effective for Li & Fung to trade with SMEs since orders were small and often below factory minimums. But by aggregating their smaller orders via its B2B portal, the Fungs projected that they could profitably offer SMEs an array of products with the option of limited mass customization. In other words, Li & Fung could offer a differentiated product to SMEs despite the small order size, providing them with the limited amount of customization that they required. Explained William, "The idea is to capture economies of scale by concurrently manufacturing the aggregated orders while giving SMEs

TABLE A
Needs and Realities for SMEs

Source: Li & Fung analyst presentation.

	Needs	Realities
Product	Differentiation of product at competitive price	No purchasing power
Service	Reliable procurement	No supplier leverage, no logistics for direct sourcing
Information	Up-to-date news, information	Starved for information

TABLE B
SMEs'
Sourcing
Possibilities

Source: Li & Fung
analyst
presentation.

	Product Differentiation	Competitive Price	Reliable Procurement	Information Flow
Importer	Poor	Poor	Strong	Poor
Small agent	Fair	Fair	Poor	Poor
Small buying office	Fair	Fair	Poor	Fair
Internet exchange	Poor	Fair	Poor	Fair
lifung.com	Strong	Strong	Strong	Strong

enough differentiation of embellishment choice (i.e., color, pockets, label) to enable them to each have a different product."

Lifung.com planned to charge SMEs a 10–15 percent commission, far less than what these small retailers were used to paying. Limited mass customization represented a further extension of Li & Fung's supply chain customization and innovation, critical in the Internet age in which customers expected even greater speed and reliability of order fulfillment. With lifung.com's limited customization, a given China-sourced item might be available in one shape but with 10 different patterns and 15 different colors. The possible permutations were infinitely greater than what other online and offline competitors could efficiently offer (see Table B).

In addition, by not requiring a minimum order, Li & Fung added further value by allowing SMEs to reduce their inventory levels and use the system for replenishment buying. This made it easier for them to respond to changing market conditions and fashion trends. If, for example, orange polo shirts were fashionable one season and light blue the next, orders could be placed in small quantities each month to avoid being stuck with a surplus inventory of orange polo shirts.

"B2B³" Parameters

On March 27, 2000, Li & Fung announced 1999 final results and the creation of B2B portal lifung.com, as well as the start-up's management team. Li & Fung also acknowledged that it was committing $200 million to build the online business and proceeded to outline how the start-up would achieve $2 billion in sales by 2004 by targeting SME clients. The next day Li & Fung raised

$250 million by placement of 60 million shares through underwriter Goldman Sachs to fund the new online venture, fortuitously timed just before the mid-April 2000 dot-com crash in the U.S. stock market. According to Li & Fung management, $200 million of these funds were slated for lifung.com with the remaining $50 million devoted to acquisitions in the core business start-up.

William remarked on the old economy-style financing of lifung.com:

> Besides market research, the second atypical thing for Internet companies that we did was the way we approached financing: The typical way of financing Internet start-ups is that first you have some entrepreneurs who decide on a great idea. They have a lot of sweat equity in the beginning and don't want that diluted unless the value increases a lot. Consequently they finance themselves very short, up until the next stage where they have something new to show. However, they don't think about how much financing required to make this a viable business.
>
> Our approach has been completely different: We come from a traditional background and don't want to think about that kind of financing at all, particularly since we are building this as part of our total business. Therefore, we want to know what it's going to cost us to take it all the way to the end. And that's why we went out into the market for $200 million and got $250 million.

Furthermore, according to the Fungs, two of the three guiding principles behind lifung.com referred to as "B2B³" were old economy standards: the online company would adopt a "business-to-business" model that took a "back-to-basics" approach by implementing Li & Fung's supply chain management know-how to SMEs on a "back-to-back" order basis, in other words, with no inventory risk for Li & Fung.

While its initial contribution to Group earnings were likely to be minimal for the first two years, lifung.com was expected to bolster earnings by an operating margin of roughly 6 percent, or 14 percent of total revenue. Li & Fung expected that by 2004 the online division would contribute as much as $2 billion in sales, or nearly up to one-third of the Group's total revenues, with 1,000 new SME clients in the United States targeted for sales of $2 million each. As lifung.com gained credibility over time and its value proposition became known among SMEs, Li & Fung expected its operating margins to increase to 7 to 8 percent.

Located near Silicon Valley, lifung.com would not only be close to the heart of Internet culture, but also close to its SME clients in the United States. Neither was lifung.com a prodigal start-up that would be allowed to run at a loss for long; like the parent company, there was an unspoken mandate from the top which decreed that it would follow the three-year planning system with attention focused clearly on the bottom line. According to Suh, lifung.com was steeped in the pragmatic culture of Li & Fung Trading, which was "How does it affect my bottom line? What are the commission rates?" William dismissed the risk of channel conflict between the SMEs and key client business:

> The biggest conflict that our existing customers fear is us working in an old fashioned way with their direct competitors. In other words, if I am Abercrombie & Fitch and you also work with American Eagle, which is a direct competitor, I normally should have a problem. But if you are big enough, like Li & Fung is, you can compartmentalize these customers, you put walls between them, which is also how banks work with clients who are competitors. We have a system of dedicated accounts and management to segregate the two. Our large customers' first concern will not be the SME competitors but large direct competitors.

E-Commerce Execution

Lifung.com[11] offered a wide array of customization options to its clients. For example, with polo shirts, users could choose on-screen from a limited variety of specifications such as pockets, collars,

and buttons including that customer's own logo. The Web site would display a high-definition, rotating image of a polo shirt (see Exhibit 5), which the user could customize. When satisfied with its appearance, the user could then place an order online, 24 hours a day. Lifung.com used Sun Microsystems for its hardware platform; Selectica for online configuration of products; Oracle for its database software; Broadvision for its transaction system; an interface to CIT to evaluate credit risk; an interface to Danzas AEI, a bulk freight specialist, to allow door-to-door tracking; and Andersen Consulting, a leading systems integrator, to "wrap" the entire package for a seamless experience.

Moreover, lifung.com was developed and operated independently of Li & Fung's IT department, particularly since the two were based on separate continents. From time to time, four or five programmers from Li & Fung's IT department traveled to lifung.com in San Francisco in order to map the connection between the two units and to ensure that the order placement and fulfillment processes functioned seamlessly. In practice, lifung.com was designed to interact with Li & Fung in the same way as one of the Group's key customers, with orders placed through an extranet. However, as part of Li & Fung Trading, lifung.com would enjoy a far closer interaction with its parent.

If there was any concern that it would be difficult to integrate an online venture into the corporate culture of a 96-year-old trading company, Victor was determined to "demystify" the technology among the offline staff with internal training courses and daily exposure to the new technology. Victor noted:

> The Internet is not black magic, there is no need to be afraid of it. Yes, it is a disruptive technology, but so what? I want to ensure that the technology pervades the entire organization, mainly because it is a technology that will be adopted sooner or later, and the sooner we do, everyone will be the wiser. Disruption comes from the real world, not cyberspace. For example, if the whole world goes into a trade war or China doesn't gain entry into the WTO, now those are real world issues I worry about. Li & Fung has always been at the forefront of adopting new technology, and that's why we are ahead of the game.

---

[11] On August 17, 2000, lifung.com was rebranded as StudioDirect.com (http://studiodirect.com).

EXHIBIT 5   Limited Mass Customization (Web Page Sample)

Source: Company documents.

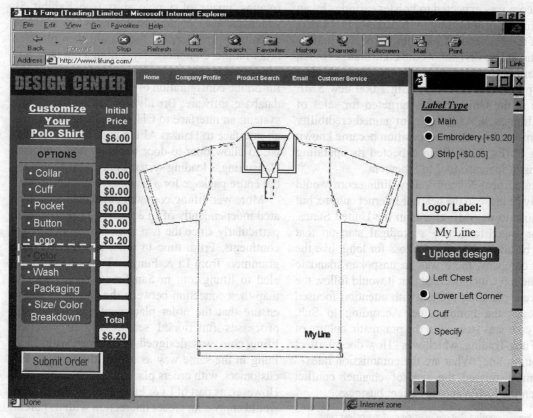

Just as Castling's e-commerce solution prescribed, lifung.com was not only a defensive move, protecting the traditional markets of Li & Fung from local online sourcing companies such as GlobalSources.com and Alibaba.com, but also offered an offensive thrust at new markets that these B2B pure plays were aiming for (see Exhibit 6). The Fungs believed that B2B exchanges did not constitute a tangible threat since they only offered a trading platform matching buyers and sellers. They could not add value in the same way that Li & Fung could through back-end logistics infrastructure, reliable procurement, market knowledge, and brand reputation; neither could they provide product differentiation. Referring to Li & Fung's historical

relationships with suppliers, William believed that it would be difficult for any B2B portal to effectively compete with lifung.com: "You couldn't just have four recent MBAs put this all together."

Future Ventures

William indicated that Li & Fung was exploring ways in which the Internet could draw on the company's traditional strengths to enhance Li & Fung's existing business. Lifung.com was only the beginning. By 2001 Li & Fung planned to expand its online B2B penetration with a new platform known as "Electronic Stock Offer." Whereas lifung.com aspired to aggregate the orders of

EXHIBIT 6   **Li & Fung Competitive Positioning**

Source: Tristan Chua and Wui Kiat Heng, "Li & Fung," *Goldman Sachs Global Equity Research,* June 21, 2000, p. 10.

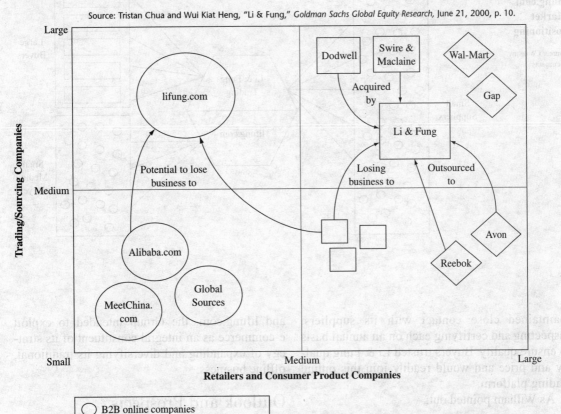

retailers, Electronic Stock Offer, code-named "eSO," would target the other side of the butterfly model (see Exhibit 7) and attempt to aggregate suppliers to post surplus inventory for sale on the Internet. According to William:

> What we've done on the buyer side, we're now doing on the supply side. We thought about what business we should be in with the suppliers that we haven't been in before that would actually help our business. Because we're in the quick response fashion business, a business where there is very little machinery, we generate a lot of stock and this creates seconds for orders that are can-

celled because of untimely delivery. What can the Internet do more efficiently than what we do now? We view these stock problems as a nuisance and have a handful of buyers such as Value City, Ross Stores, and TJ Maxx and who do nothing but specialize in buying these goods.

In particular, eSO was aimed at creating an efficient system for reaching out into Li & Fung's supplier base and posting surplus stocks on the Internet. This, in turn, would provide a more efficient and cost-effective platform from which Li & Fung could sell to buyers primarily interested in purchasing seconds. Li & Fung

**Exhibit 7
lifung.com
Market
Positioning**

Source: Company
documents.

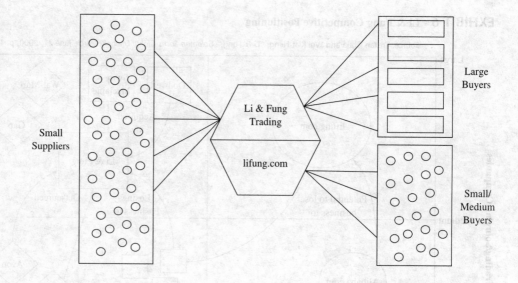

maintained close contact with its suppliers, inspecting and certifying each on an annual basis to ensure quality. Buyers trusted Li & Fung quality and price and would readily join this online trading platform.

As William pointed out:

> Because of our old economy history and our network, we can inspect suppliers' goods much easier. Buyers don't have confidence to buy from anonymous suppliers that they don't know. We think we can bring the two together within the Li & Fung network, we can build a business using the Internet to aggregate suppliers on their stock positions. You go back to the butterfly shape: We feel it's far too ambitious to create a virtual exchange inside this middle space that tries to be a clearinghouse for both sides. All I need to do is interpose Li & Fung and we can intermediate the whole process. This is the mirror position of what we are doing at lifung.com, using the Internet to aggregate thousands of small suppliers around the world and then have them post whatever stock they have available.

In contrast with vertical B2B portals, exchanges that proposed to match suppliers with buyers, Li & Fung aimed to add value to the e-commerce transaction by virtue of its old economy network, brand, and reputation. Through online ventures such as Electronic Stock Offer

and lifung.com, the Group intended to exploit e-commerce as an integral constituent of its strategy of expanding and diversifying its traditional, offline business.

Outlook and Prospects

Thanks to robust macroeconomic conditions in the United States and Europe, the trend towards casual wear in the American workplace, and the rapid growth of private label in United States and Europe, the Group was expected to enjoy strong top-line growth for at least the next few years. A survey by Levi-Strauss indicated that over half of the American white-collar workforce now wore casual apparel to work every day.[12] The trend towards casual wear in the American workplace offered considerable upside for retailers of polo shirts and khakis and thus for sourcing agents such as Li & Fung. Even a downturn in the U.S. economy promised potential upside, as retailers would consolidate and turn to outsourcing to minimize costs and

[12] "Retailing: General Industry Survey," *Standard & Poors,* May 25, 2000, p. 13.

remain competitive. An increasing number of Li & Fung's key clients as well as SMEs had already begun outsourcing in order to minimize costs, which along with the rapid growth of private label in United States and Europe provided lifung.com with a fertile market for limited mass customization.

"What if we do build it and no one comes?" William wondered. In other words, what if the 1,000 SMEs projected to procure customized goods through lifung.com and provide $2 billion in sales over the next four years did not flock to the B2B portal? If the online venture had a negative impact on share performance, at what point would Li & Fung cut its losses and shut it down? Suh had remarked in his presentation that "Beta means never having to say you're sorry." The soft beta launch was intended to highlight bugs in the system. The company was on the verge of beta-testing with a select few American clients, but if the beta launch was a failure, would that undermine investor and SME confidence in the model?

When asked about competition, Suh pledged that "We're going to run like we don't know who is chasing us."[13] But was there, in fact, a risk Li & Fung would not be able to see who was chasing them, such as a copycat old economy sourcing company that would see the success of lifung.com and mimic its well-publicized model?

Finally, what was the chance that Li & Fung's offline operations would eventually migrate online after lifung.com had proven itself as a reliable and established model? This could potentially reduce many of the offline costs and enhance operating margins. But what of possible channel conflict? Although the online venture was based in San Francisco, how would its integration into the Group be perceived by old economy Li & Fung veterans? What would be the future of the in-house e-commerce team once lifung.com was online? Would Li & Fung eventually spin off the clicks-and-mortar hybrid and take it public, or would it remain within the Group?

[13] L. R. Scott, "Chess and the Wired Age," *Global Partnerships* 5, no. 2, p. 1.

Appendix A

What the Fungs created is a hybrid system. Today, the company maintains Internet-based communications with its major customers. Almost 75 percent of those are large retailers in the United States including Avon, The Coca-Cola Co., and Disney, all of which rely on Li & Fung for promotional items. Its largest customer in the United States, Kohl's Department Store chain, accounts for 13 percent of Li & Fung's sales.

For these large customers, Li & Fung has created extranet sites dedicated to them. Information about the products they've ordered comes from Li & Fung's Electronic Trading System, now in its fifth generation of refinement and known as XTS 5.

Li & Fung's XTS is also linked to its own network of offices, where it has 5,000 people supervising the manufacturing of customer items. The nature of its electronic connections varies depending on the sophistication of a country's telecommunications system. In more advanced countries, a Li & Fung local office can be linked immediately to headquarters in Hong Kong. The branch office can tap the company's central databases and send digital photos of fabrics or products back and forth. The geeks at Li & Fung call that a "thick" connection. In cases where telecommunications are more primitive, however, the company depends on e-mails and e-mail attachments, using Lotus Notes. That's a "thin" connection.

Li & Fung uses Hewlett-Packard and Compaq computers and Oracle database software to manage information and store the data, but has largely designed and written the software that makes up its XTS. "The important part is what we do with the technology," Fung says. Altogether, the system currently holds a very respectable 1.5 terabytes of data, which is equivalent to 1.5 million books.

The company's most important tech initiative is working with Microsoft's Biztalk software to better connect front-end orders from all customers—from the biggest to the smallest—with the back-end order processing system. That will enhance the supply chain's efficiency and make the system more transparent to customers. But Fung points out that the Internet applies only to certain segments of the supply chain. At other points, there is no substitute for human expertise, such as in the designing of products or allocating a single big order to four different factories to get the job done quickly.

The company doesn't connect its system to the thousands of manufacturers who make its products, partly because communications systems aren't advanced enough in China, the Philippines, Bangladesh, and other Asian countries, not to mention Africa and the Caribbean. Li & Fung relies on personal visits, phones, faxes, and couriers to keep in touch.

The other reason manufacturers aren't linked to Li & Fung's system, however, is that it wants its own employees to make sure that materials have arrived, that production has been scheduled, and shipping arrangements have been made. If it depended on manufacturers to directly enter that information, the quality of its data would be "like raw sewage," says Fung. A manager in Pakistan could say, "Sure, we've started production—pay us," even if nothing was happening. Li & Fung personnel also have to be on the ground to make sure manufacturers comply with a customer's standards in terms of how they treat labor.

For all those reasons, it's unlikely the Internet will ever connect the complete supply chain. "Technology is an enabler," says Fung, a 53-year-old marathon runner who needs stamina for the 150 days a year he spends on the road. "You have to be clear on what you want to achieve."

Module

1

Business Impacts

Lynda M. Applegate

Between 1997 and 2001, an estimated $2.5 trillion was spent on IT in the United States—nearly double the amount for the previous five years.[1] The same pattern was seen around the world. Fueled, on the one hand, by the excitement and experimentation that accompanied the commercialization of the Internet and, on the other, by the need to overhaul an aging IT infrastructure in preparation for the turn of the century (the "Y2K problem"),[2] this spending highlights both the search for opportunity and the avoidance of operational risk that accompanies the ever-increasing dependence on and impact of IT. Exploiting these opportunities, while avoiding the pitfalls, requires vision, sound execution, and the ability to respond quickly. It also requires a deep understanding of how industries, markets, and organizations are built and managed for optimal performance.

The chapters and cases in this module enable discussion of approaches executives use, decisions they make, and issues they face as they attempt to leverage IT to create business advantage and avoid risk. The module discusses issues of strategic positioning and alignment, business design, and investment decision making. Four cases and one article are available at the end of this module.

[1] B. Temkin, "Tech Recovery Update: Coming Off the Bottom," *Forrester Research*, March 2002. IT spending declined in 2001 and 2002, but began growing again in 2003. See A. Bartels, "Projected U.S. IT Growth Edges up to 6% in 2004," *Forrester Research*, June 4, 2004.

[2] Traditional approaches to coding software often used the computer date as part of the control logic. The shift from the 1900s to the 2000s threatened to cause older software (often called "legacy systems") to perform erratically or fail. During the late 1990s, massive global IT investments were directed at fixing the Year 2000 (Y2K) problem.

Charles Schwab in 2002

Charles Schwab Inc. was long admired as an innovator that creatively used IT to develop a unique and differentiated position within the highly competitive financial services industry. The Charles Schwab case traces the history of the firm from its founding in the mid-1970s through its sustained growth during the 1980s and its meteoric rise in the late 1990s. The case ends in late 2002 as the company struggles to reinvent itself and the industry during a period of global economic decline that threatened even the strongest firms in the financial services industry. The case enables a deep understanding of fundamental principles and frameworks that guide strategic decision making and action as executives leverage IT to create sustainable business advantage.

Learning from LeapFrog

Since its founding in 1995, LeapFrog, Inc. exploited innovative technology and sound educational principles to "leap" to the number 3 position in the highly competitive global toy industry in 2002. Only Mattel (number 1) and Hasbro (number 2) were larger—a remarkable feat for so young a company. The case explores the evolution of the company's strategy and business design from idea to business launch to profitability and acclaim. In 2003, CEO and founder Mike Wood struggled to protect and preserve the creative spirit at LeapFrog, even as the company grew to challenge the industry giants. LeapFrog's future depended on successfully balancing the excitement, energy, and spontaneity of the creative process with the rigor, accountability, and formal structures a large company required. The organizational challenges are accentuated as the company responds to Mattel's launch of a competitive offering.

Wyndham International: Fostering High-Touch with High Tech

Wyndham International Corp. was founded in 1999 to consolidate the core assets of Patriot American Hospitality—a failing Real Estate Investment Trust (REIT). By late 2000, Wyndham International had been reorganized as a lodging company that focused on three branded products: Wyndham Hotels & Resorts, Wyndham Luxury Resorts, and Summerfield Suites by Wyndham. In May 2000, Wyndham International hired its first Chief Technology Officer (CTO) and tasked him with "insourcing" IT and prioritizing investments to support the company's core strategy and operations. Early efforts focused on creating a centralized Property Management System to streamline operations and a Customer Relationship Management System that would enable a single view of Wyndham's customer relationships across all three of its global brands. In February 2001, Wyndham launched a $30 million advertising campaign promoting its new brand and, at the same time, announced an innovative customer loyalty program called Wyndham ByRequest. The case permits an in-depth discussion of the business impact of IT and provides detailed data on early results from the rollout of a new IT-enabled customer loyalty initiative. As such, the case enables debate on the practical issues that executives face as they attempt to prioritize IT investments and implement IT-enabled strategic initiatives.

Global Healthcare Exchange

Founded in March 2000 at the height of the dot-com bubble, Global Healthcare Exchange (GHX) was one of 90 online marketplaces in the health care industry. The company's founders were among the largest suppliers in the industry, including Johnson & Johnson, GE Medical, Abbott, Baxter, and Medtronic. At the time of the case (spring 2003), GHX was the largest of the three remaining online health care supply chain marketplaces and ownership had expanded to include the leading players across all parts of the value chain, including suppliers, health care providers, managed care organizations, group purchasing organizations, and distributors. At the time of the case, executives confronted key strategic issues, including integrating the company's latest merger, defining a fair pricing strategy for all members, determining the pace of global expansion, and prioritizing among competing IT-enabled business investment opportunities that addressed the needs of its diverse stakeholder groups. The case provides an excellent summary of the strategic and operational decisions that executives of small, resource-constrained businesses must make as they attempt to leverage emerging technologies to create sustainable and profitable businesses that deliver value to all stakeholders.

IT Doesn't Matter

In 2003, an article entitled, "IT Doesn't Matter," appeared in the *Harvard Business Review* (HBR). Priding itself on bringing important new ideas, insights, and research to its business readers, HBR editors sought to involve its readers in what they believed would be an important debate. As such, the editors were thrilled with the passionate response to the Nicholas Carr article. We took "one side of an argument that's undeniably urgent and important to its business readers," Tom Stewart, HBR's managing editor explained. The article and selected letters to the editor are reprinted at the end of the module to facilitate continued debate and dialogue.

CHAPTER 1

IT and Strategy[1]

Companies that have deployed Internet technology have been confused by distorted market signals, often of their own creation. It is understandable, when confronted with a new business phenomenon, to look to marketplace outcomes for guidance. But in the early stages of the rollout of any important new technology, market signals can be unreliable. New technologies trigger rampant experimentation, by companies and their customers, and the experimentation is often economically unsustainable. As a result, market behavior is distorted and must be interpreted with caution.[2]

Have you ever watched young children play football (or soccer as we refer to it in the United States)? The referee blows the whistle to start the game and, immediately, all the players on both teams jump on the ball. Similarly, executives often use this "jump on the ball" approach to formulate strategy. In fact, during the dot-com era, this approach became so popular that many lost sight of the fundamental principles for how to build sustainable businesses. The results were predictable. Few of these businesses survived. How do you distinguish "hair-brained schemes" from "strategic coups"? In stable times, executives often rely on the intuition that comes from experience. When the rules of the game are changing, however, this experience may steer you wrong and new logic has yet to be developed. Peter Drucker cautions that:

> In turbulent times, an enterprise has to be able to withstand sudden blows and avail itself of unexpected opportunities. This means that in turbulent times the fundamentals must be managed and managed well.[3]

An enterprise's business model frames these "fundamentals" and can be used to guide strategic analysis and decision making. This chapter begins by providing an overview of the concept of a business model and then discusses other key frameworks that can be used to understand the forces that shape strategy. The chapter ends with guidance on how to use IT to create sustainable business advantage.

[1] This chapter is adapted from papers and materials from Professor Applegate's *Building Businesses in Turbulent Times* course. The correct citation is L. M. Applegate, *Building Businesses in Turbulent Times* (Boston: Harvard Business School, 2004), available on request from the author.

[2] M. Porter, "Strategy and the Internet," *Harvard Business Review*, March 2001.

[3] P. Drucker, *Managing in Turbulent Times* (New York: Harper & Row, 1980).

Understanding the Forces That Shape Strategy

"Business model" was one of the great buzzwords of the Internet boom, routinely invoked, as the writer Michael Lewis put it, "to glorify all manner of half-baked plans . . ." Many people—investors, entrepreneurs, and executives alike—bought the fantasy and got burned. And as the inevitable counterreaction played out, the concept of a business model fell out of fashion . . . That's a shame. For while it's true that a lot of capital was raised to fund *flawed business models,* the fault lies, not with the concept of a business model, but with its distortion and use. A good business model remains essential to every successful business.

Joan Magretta[4]

While many believe that the idea of a business model emerged with the Internet, the concept can be traced to early management thinking. Published in the 1960s, Chandler's *Strategy and Structure* provided an important foundation for the concept of a business model.[5] This path-breaking book describes how the alignment of strategy with the environment within which a company operates and the resources and capabilities required to execute that strategy drives growth and creates value for all stakeholders. Chandler's work, combined with a large body of increasingly sophisticated twentieth century management research, laid out the theory of the Industrial Economy business models that guided management practice through much of the twentieth century.[6] In today's global, Network Economy, new business models are emerging to guide management practice in the twenty-first century. These new models are discussed in more detail later in this book. While the details of these new models may change, the underlying framework remains the same. Figure 1.1 summarizes the relationship among key components of a business model.

A business model defines how an enterprise interacts with its environment to define a unique strategy, attract the resources and build the capabilities to execute it, and, in the process, create value for all stakeholders. A successful business model aligns an organization with its environment. The strategy defines the revenue and growth potential of the organization. It focuses attention and resources on a specific set of goals and the projects required to achieve them. Capabilities are built to achieve the goals in the least costly way while also responding quickly and effectively to change. As such, the capability dimension of a successful business model defines the cost model of an organization that, when combined with the revenue model, specifies how an organization generates profitable growth and efficient return on assets. These profits fuel the engine that enables executives to evolve the strategy, build new capabilities, and drive increasing returns. Economists call this cycle of innovation, productivity, and increasing returns

---

[4] J. Magretta, "Why Business Models Matter," *Harvard Business Review,* May 2002.

[5] A. Chandler, *Strategy and Structure* (Cambridge, MA: MIT Press, 1990).

[6] For a summary of the strategy research that formed the backbone of business model research, see H. Chesbrough and R. Rosenbloom, "The Role of the Business Model in Capturing Value from Innovation," *Industrial and Corporate Change,* June 2002.

FIGURE 1.1
Components of a Business Model

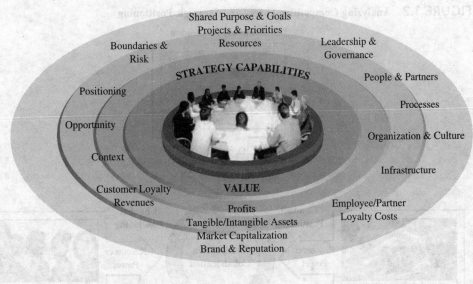

a "virtuous cycle." In contrast, a poorly aligned business model can create a "vicious cycle," causing a business to spin out of control and destroy value.[7]

This chapter focuses on the strategy dimension of the business model. Future chapters in this module discuss the capabilities and value dimensions. We begin with a discussion of the components of a strategy audit and then discuss how IT can be used to influence the different components. The chapter ends with a discussion of strategy execution and risk management.

Conducting a Strategy Audit

Michael Porter stresses that successful strategies define how a company plans to achieve a ***distinctive and unique*** position that "woos customers from established players or draws new customers into the market."[8]

Strategic positions are the result of choices in four areas (see Figure 1.2).

- *Market/Channel* positioning determines the choice of customers to serve, the needs and expectations that will be met, and the channels to reach those customers.
- *Product* positioning determines the choice of products and services to offer, the features of those offerings, and the price that will be charged.
- *Value chain/Value network* positioning determines the role an organization plays and the activities it performs within an extended network of suppliers, producers, distributors, and partners.

[7] A summary of the theory of "virtuous" and "vicious" cycles can be found in C. Shapiro and H. Varian, *Information Rules: A Guide to the Network Economy* (Boston: Harvard Business School Press, 1998).

[8] M. Porter, "What Is Strategy?" *Harvard Business Review*, November–December 1996.

FIGURE 1.2 Analyzing Competitive Forces and Strategic Positioning

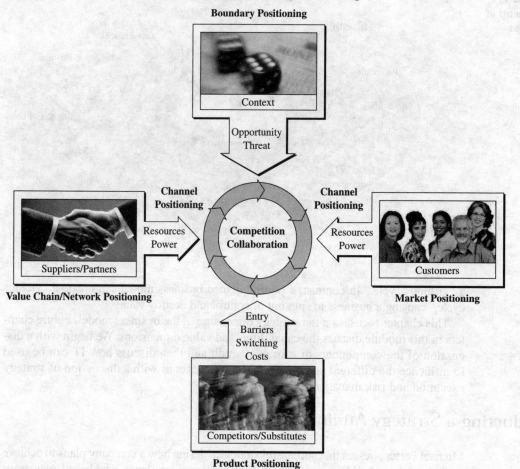

- *Boundary* positioning determines markets, products, and businesses you will NOT pursue.

Successful strategic positions often attract imitation. **Sustainable advantage** occurs when barriers exist that make it difficult for competitors to imitate and/or customers to switch. For example, an established player may be forced to launch products or services that cannibalize existing offerings, implement tough organizational changes, or acquire scarce and expensive resources. Successful new entrants often actively seek out strategic positions that enable them to gain a foothold "under the radar" of established competitors and then quickly evolve their strategic position into areas that would require competitors to make tough trade-off decisions. For example, in 1975, when Charles Schwab first entered the brokerage industry with his "discount broker" strategy, he positioned his business to serve underserved markets that were under the radar of established full-service brokerage firms such as Merrill Lynch. He then

TABLE 1.1   The Customer Audit Approach

Customer Audit Approach	Sample Questions
• Talk with current and potential customers. • Visit and watch them perform activities that product/service offerings support (or will support). • Collect market research. • Conduct focus groups. • Involve customers in product design or improvement.	• What are the pressing problems ("pains") that customers face? • How well are customer needs and expectations being met today? • How much are customers willing to pay to get their needs met? • What is the current (and future) size of the customer base? • Are customer markets large and growing? Which segments are growing (or could grow) most rapidly? (Measure growth in terms of revenues, units sold, customer visits, number of customers/users, pricing, etc.) • Which of our current product/service offerings do our customers use today and how much revenue do we generate from each customer (or customer segment)? • What product/service offerings would our customers like us to offer? • What market share do we have today? What "share of wallet" do we have? • What can we do to increase market share and share of wallet?

provided differentiated product/service offering that met the needs of this underserved market at a price that could not be matched by full service brokers. He used emerging technologies of the day to keep his costs low while offering a unique value proposition to his customers. The technology also made it difficult for new entrants to entice customers to switch.[9]

A strategic audit begins with a thorough understanding of the *customer.* The more a company knows about its customers, the better it can develop product and service offerings that meet their needs.

Once a company understands what customers want, analysis should turn to the alternatives they have for meeting their needs. These alternatives include competitive offerings, substitute products, or customers may simply choose to leave the need unmet. *Competitor analysis* includes traditional rivals, potential new entrants, and substitute products and services. Michael Porter's Five Forces Industry Analysis is a frequently used framework to analyze traditional rivalry, bargaining power, and competitive intensity.[10]

Once customer expectations, needs, and alternatives are well understood, it's time to make the choices and trade-offs needed to develop a *unique product/market position.* Figure 1.3 illustrates the product/market positioning of key competitors in the traditional retail financial services market and how the market is changing to provide solutions rather than targeted offerings.

Once product/market position is established, identify the activities, resources, and capabilities required to design, produce, market, sell, and service the products for the target market. Determine which of these activities your firm will perform, which capabilities and resources you will own, and which will be sourced. This analysis

[9] L. M. Applegate, *Charles Schwab in 2002*, Boston: Harvard Business School Publishing (No. 803-070).

[10] M. Porter, *Competitive Advantage: Creating and Sustaining Superior Performance* (New York: Free Press, 1998).

TABLE 1.2 The Competitor Audit Approach

Competitor Audit Approach	Sample Questions
• Identify traditional rivals, potential new entrants, and substitutes. • Benchmark current or potential new offerings. • Ask potential customers why they use alternatives, what needs are not being met, and what would cause them to switch. • Collect industry data. • Talk to experts.	• Who are our competitors (including substitute products and services) and how do they differentiate their offerings? • What prices do they charge and what margins do they get? • How sustainable are their positions? • Can their customers easily switch to other offerings? • How easy (or hard) would it be for competitors, new entrants, or substitutes to enter our market and steal share? • What market share and share of wallet do key competitors/substitutes have? What potential approaches could competitors take to increase market share and share of wallet? What approaches could *we* take to preserve your differentiated position? • How powerful are competitors and how might they respond to changes we might make?

enables an organization to define its position within a value chain or value network of *suppliers and partners.*

Traditional business logic states that activities should be performed inside an organization if: (1) they are considered core to the strategy and value proposition of the firm; (2) the organization is able to build or acquire the expertise and infrastructure at less cost and higher quality than if the activity is sourced; and (3) the costs and risks of coordinating and controlling the activity inside the organization are significantly

FIGURE 1.3
Product/Market Positioning in the U.S. Retail Financial Services Industry, 1990

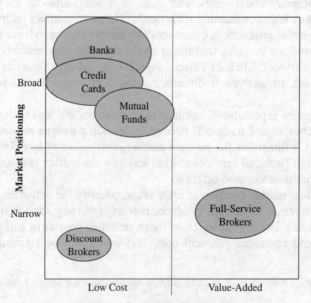

Note: The size of the circle represents market size.

TABLE 1.3   **Product/Market Positioning Audit Approach**

Product/Market Positioning Audit Approach	Sample Questions
• Choose markets to serve, product/service offerings, and channels to reach markets. • Decide which markets, products, channels, and businesses you will NOT pursue. • Identify basis for differentiation. • Define messages to develop and communicate brand.	• Which markets will we serve? • What products and services will we offer and how will we differentiate our offerings? • How will the features of our offerings compare with available alternatives? • How will the prices we charge compare with available alternatives? • What channels will we use to reach our markets? • How sustainable is our position and the business model needed to achieve and support that position? • What are our options for growing our business in the future? • What opportunities will we not pursue?

less than the costs and risks of coordinating and controlling them on the outside.[11] In the past, the cost and risk of coordinating and controlling all but the most routine activities caused executives to choose to locate the majority of activities inside the firm. Eastman Kodak, for example, followed this path even into the 1980s.[12] Founded in the 1800s on the principle of commitment to quality, the firm established its own laundry to ensure that cloth for wiping film was of the highest quality; it built its own foundry to make its machines and built all of its own parts. Having defined the company's strategy around quality, Kodak executives believed that the costs and risks associated with managing these activities on the outside were greater than the benefits that would be achieved through sourcing. Over the past few decades, IT has significantly lowered the costs and risks of sourcing even core activities by providing access to a common infrastructure for sharing information needed to coordinate and control the flow of information and goods across organizational and value chain boundaries.

The final category of analysis in a strategic audit is the ***business context***—political, societal, regulatory, legal, and economic factors that affect (or could affect) a business today and in the future. In analyzing the business context, it is important to, not just take a static snapshot, but also to look both backward and forward, assessing relative stability and the sources of instability and turbulence. Interestingly, factors that threaten to disrupt the status quo within a business environment may be viewed as a significant threat by some players while others view those same factors as the source of tremendous opportunity. In fact, entrepreneurs often seek out unstable industries experiencing disruption such as new technologies, regulations, or the entry or exit of a major competitor, finding these business environments to be ideal for spawning new businesses.

---

[11] O. Williamson, *Markets and Hierarchies* (New York: Free Press, 1975); O. Williamson, "Comparative Economic Organization: The Analysis of Discrete Structural Alternatives," *Administrative Sciences Quarterly* 36 (1991), pp. 269–296; W. Powell, "Neither Market nor Hierarchy: Network Forms of Organization," *Research in Organizational Behavior* 12 (1990), pp. 295–336.

[12] L. M. Applegate and R. Montealegre, *Eastman Kodak Co.: Managing Information Systems through Strategic Alliances*, Harvard Business School Publishing (No. 192-030).

TABLE 1.4 Value Network Audit Approach

Value Network Audit Approach	Sample Questions
• Identify activities, resources and capabilities needed to execute product/market/channel strategy and assess current status. • Determine what you will do and what you will source. • Visit current and potential suppliers and partners and assess capabilities and infrastructure.	• What activities, capabilities, and resources are required to execute strategy? • Which will my company perform and which will we source from the outside? • For the activities we outsource, how will we coordinate and control activities with key suppliers and partners? • How does the quality and cost of outsourced resources and capabilities compare to what we could provide inside? • How powerful are the individuals and organizations that control key activities, capabilities, and resources required to execute our strategy? • What is the source of their power? For example, does demand outpace supply or vice versa? Are there high barriers to entry or exit or high switching costs? • What relationships do we have with powerful individuals and organizations?

Strategic Shifts: Evolution and Revolution

Strategy is a journey—not a destination. As such, the strategic audit described above should provide a continuous flow of information on current strategy and performance and on future opportunities and threats. But information is not enough; the *strategy process* must also engage executives, employees, customers, suppliers, and partners in an ongoing dialogue to enable them to make sense of the information they collect as they analyze current performance and identify opportunities and threats.

There are four key approaches executives can take to evolve an organization's strategy. Each of these approaches can be applied to one or more of the four strategic positions to create an opportunity profile as shown in Figure 1.4.

- *Enhancements* involve incremental changes to an existing product, market, channel, or value network. For example, an existing product can be improved to make it easier to use or to add new functionality. A new marketing program can be

TABLE 1.5 Context Audit Approach

Context Audit Approach	Sample Questions
• Identify relevant political, regulatory, legal, societal, and economic factors and trends that will either positively or negatively influence strategy. • Define key strengths, weaknesses, opportunities, and threats. • Develop approaches to build on strengths and eliminate or manage weaknesses and threats. • Determine which opportunities to pursue and the sequence.	• How favorable (or unfavorable) is the business context within which we operate today and what changes do we anticipate? • How turbulent is the environment within which we do business? Have there been disruptive changes that would signal entry opportunities or threats to our existing strategy? • Which factors in the business environment help us achieve our goals? Which hinder us? • What are the key things we must do well? • What are the key threats and risks and their implications for our success and survival? • What are the key strengths we can leverage and the weaknesses we must overcome to position ourselves for success?

FIGURE 1.4 Options for Evolving Strategy

	Enhance	Expand	Extend	Exit
Product	Improve quality, lower cost, increase ease-of-use, add features	Add new products or services	N/A	Drop a feature, a service, or a product
Market	Attract new customers within existing market through advertising, etc.	Expand into new markets, segments, or geographies	N/A	Exit a market, segment, or geographic region
Channel	Improve quality, cost, or capacity of a current channel	Add new channels	N/A	Exit a channel
Value Chain/ Network	Improve operations and/or relationships with current suppliers, partners, etc.	Add new suppliers or partners; outsource an activity	N/A	Stop doing business with a supplier or partner; insource an activity
Business Model	Improve the alignment or economics of current business model	Add new revenue streams	Extend into a new business or adopt a new business model	Exit a business or business model

implemented to improve the ability to attract an existing market; a sales training program can be developed to increase the productivity of a direct sales channel; or a new supplier can be added to improve product quality.

- *Expansions* involve the launch of new products or product categories, entry into new markets, or the launch of a new channel (e.g., an online channel to market) to complement existing channels. Finally, a network can be expanded by the decision to outsource an activity to a new partner.

- *Extensions* involve the launch of a new business or business model.

- *Exits* involve decisions to drop a product or product category, exit a market, and/or close a channel or business.

Many strategic shifts—for example, the decision to enhance or expand a product, market, or channel—are evolutionary. At times, however, an organization may take a less evolutionary approach and decide to either enter or exit—not just a product, market, or channel—but an entire business. These revolutionary shifts change an organization's strategic boundaries and often require radical changes to the existing business model or even the adoption of a new business model.

An example of these evolutionary and revolutionary shifts in strategy can be seen in the case of Charles Schwab. The company was founded in 1975 as a discount broker. Charles Schwab spent the next 25 years evolving the company's strategy and business model, enhancing, expanding, and exiting products, markets, and channels. Between 1975 and 1995 Schwab dominated the discount broker segment of the retail financial services industries (refer back to Figure 1.3), offering his products through multiple channels, including branch offices, call centers, and proprietary online channels. But, in the late 1990s, online Internet brokers entered the market with deeply

FIGURE 1.5
Categories of
Strategic Risk

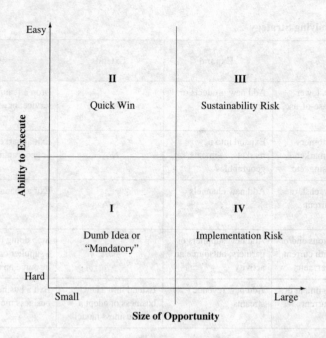

discounted fees. At the same time, full-service brokers also discounted their fees. Soon Schwab was no longer a discount broker nor was it a value-added service provider. Instead, the company was caught in the middle struggling to differentiate itself. In June 2000, Schwab's purchase of U.S. Trust, a full-service financial advisory and brokerage firm that served wealthy investors, represented a radical shift in strategic direction. With this decision, Schwab changed its strategic boundaries and entered a new line of business that required dramatic changes to its business model. Between 2000 and 2004, the company continued to enter and exit businesses as it struggled to redefine its business model during one of the worst economic downturns to hit the financial services industry in decades.

Strategic opportunities are implemented through ***initiatives and projects*** that signify a company's ***strategic intent.*** Assess your project portfolio. Is it tightly aligned with your organization's strategy and long-range goals? Have you allocated the resources and support needed? Do you have the capabilities you need to execute? A risk profile frames the risk involved in pursuing new projects and initiatives based on their impact on core strategy and ability to execute (see Figure 1.5).

Assessing IT Impact and Alignment

Research shows that cyclists expend significantly less energy when properly positioned to draft off of one another. Similarly, geese can travel 70 percent farther when aligned in a "V" formation. Businesses, too, achieve similar benefits when they are well aligned. But increasingly, businesses are suffering from a lack of alignment.[13]

[13] C. Benko and F. W. McFarlan, *Connecting the Dots* (Boston: Harvard Business School Press, 2003), p. 1.

The ability to achieve alignment among the environment, strategy, and capabilities is central to creating a successful business model that delivers value to all stakeholders. Yet this is easier said than done—especially in today's earnings-driven, turbulent economy. And, the difficulty of achieving business alignment increases significantly when IT enters the picture.

Long considered a tool to automate back-office activities—for example, payroll and accounts receivable—only recently has IT become an important tool for defining new strategic opportunities and building the capabilities needed to execute them. Evidence suggests, however, that, in the United States alone, a staggering 40 percent of IT investments fail to deliver their intended return each year. This number becomes even more significant when we consider that in 2003, on average, companies spent approximately 4 percent of revenues on IT.[14] In the United States alone during 2003, over $148 billion was spent on purchased software, an additional $40 billion on custom-built software for use inside the organization, and $46 billion for software that would be used by outside parties.[15] Worldwide, the IT services market was expected to reach $621 billion in 2005.[16]

Two key frameworks, which are discussed below, can be used to guide strategic decision making and action as executives attempt to align IT and business strategy. The first, the Strategic Grid, was developed by Warren McFarlan to assist executives with analysis of their organizations' portfolio of IT projects.[17] The second, the Strategic Alignment Model, was developed by John Henderson and N. Venkatraman, to assist executives with the ongoing alignment of IT and business strategy and operations.[18]

The Strategic Grid

Examination of the project portfolio of an organization provides a glimpse into its priorities and strategic intent. Indeed, it is through initiatives and projects that organizations translate strategy into reality. In an ideal world, the allocation of resources (e.g., money, people, time, attention) to projects is tightly aligned with goals and performance targets and fuels the innovation, productivity, increasing returns business cycle. Finally, an organization's project portfolio can become an important agent for organizational change.

With this in mind, McFarlan suggests that an organization's portfolio of IT initiatives and projects be assessed along two key dimensions: (1) the impact on business operations; and (2) the impact on strategy. Categorization of investments along these dimensions enables executives to assess the alignment of IT with the strategic goals of the firms and then to ensure that the approaches for organizing and managing IT are appropriate given placement on the strategic grid.

[14] B. Gomolski, "IT Spending and Profitability: What the Numbers Show," *Gartner Group Research*, May 21, 2003.

[15] A. Bartels, "Industry Profiles of Software Spending," *Forrester Research*, July 22, 2004.

[16] K. Hale, et al., "2Q03 Update: IT Services Forecasts, 2002–2005," *Gartner Group Research*, July 2003.

[17] F. W. McFarlan, "Information Technology Changes the Way You Compete," *Harvard Business Review*, May 1984.

[18] J. C. Henderson and N. Venkatraman, "Strategic Alignment: Leveraging Information Technology for Transforming Organizations," *IBM Systems Journal* 32, no. 1 (1993).

The first dimension assesses the impact of IT on business operations. In firms like the Nasdaq Stock Exchange and PSA (previously called the Port of Singapore Authority prior to its privatization), reliable, zero-defect operation of IT is essential for performing critical activities inside each firm and across the extended network of customers, suppliers, and partners. In Nasdaq's case, failure for even a few seconds can bring the entire securities industry to its knees. In PSA's case, failures can halt or seriously hinder global shipping, affecting—not just PSA's operations—but also those of global shippers, freight forwarders, carriers, and customers. In each firm, a significant portion of investments and resources are directed toward projects and initiatives that ensure improved quality, functionality, and 99.9999 percent reliability of the IT-enabled operating core.

In other firms, for example some law firms, the impact of an IT failure of several hours would be much less immediate and severe. In these firms we see the majority of investments are often related to expanding the number of legal professionals and increasing their billable time, expanding the scope of legal services offered, and/or expanding into new markets. While IT may be used to support these strategic initiatives, we would expect to see a much smaller portion of the investment directed toward IT. In addition, leadership and governance of IT would rarely be found at the board level.

The second dimension of the strategic grid assesses the impact of IT on the strategy of a firm. In firms like Charles Schwab, a discount brokerage firm, a steady stream of technology innovations drove strategy evolution through much of the firms' existence. At Schwab, IT development activities are inextricably linked to the strategy of the company and IT investment decisions are made in the boardroom by those charged with assuring business success and survival. In fact, David Pottruck, CEO and chairman of Schwab during the 1990s, publicly stated that he considered Schwab "an IT firm that happens to be in the financial services business."[19]

In some firms, the impact of IT on the portfolio of initiatives and projects that drive strategy is low. IT development priorities are targeted toward incremental, operational improvements that may improve a firm's cost profile but do little to change its position or power in the industry.

The strategic grid (depicted in Figure 1.6) uses these two dimensions to define four categories of IT impact that help determine the approach used to identify opportunities, define and implement IT-enabled business initiatives, and organize and manage IT assets and professionals.

Projects and initiatives that fall squarely within the *Support* quadrant of the grid have little impact on an organization's core strategy or operations. The goals of this type of project are often targeted toward local improvements and incremental cost savings. This type of project is often designed, implemented, and managed by IT specialists in partnership with local end users.

IT projects that fall within the *Factory* quadrant are designed to reduce costs and improve performance of the core operations of an organization. While the goals of projects in this quadrant may be targeted toward cost and quality benefits, the magnitude

[19] See L. M. Applegate et al., *Charles Schwab in 2002*, Boston: Harvard Business School Publishing (No. 803-070).

FIGURE 1.6
McFarlan's
Strategic Grid

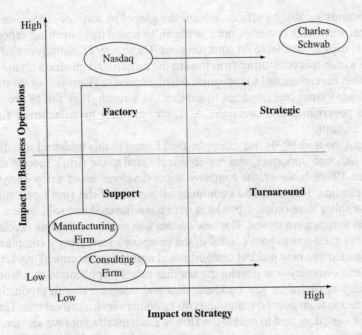

of the operating impact and risk requires that projects be designed, implemented, and managed by business unit executives in partnership with IT executives.

IT-enabled projects in the *Turnaround* quadrant are designed to exploit emerging strategic opportunities. They are often designed, implemented, and managed through partnerships between business executives (often those involved with business development), IT executives, and emerging technologies groups. At times, technology partners may be added to the team to bring the necessary technology expertise.

Firms that have moved into the *Strategic* quadrant have made a commitment to use IT to enable both core operations and core strategy. In these firms, IT initiatives are often defined, implemented, and managed at the top levels of the corporation.

Analysis of IT projects and investments at a given point in time enables assessment of the alignment of individual IT projects with business operations and strategy. It also enables assessment of the *portfolio* of IT projects and initiatives and the approach to organizing and managing the IT function as a core enabler of its business model. Finally, the strategic grid can be used to benchmark a company's IT project and investment portfolio with other firms in the industry and to *assess changes over time*.

As mentioned above, until recently, the impact of IT on the core operations and strategy of most professional services firms (e.g., law firms and consulting firms) was quite low. For example, despite a consulting company spending $30 million in the early 1990s to equip each of its 2,000 consultants with laptop computers, consultants in the firm were able to continue serving the needs of their clients during a major IT failure of over 24 hours. In addition, IT had little impact on strategic projects and decisions (e.g., the decision to close one consulting practice and expand into another). By the late 1990s, however, this picture had changed. The same consulting firm had begun to use IT to connect its global customers to virtual teams of consultants located in offices around the globe. In addition, the company increased market share and revenues once it began to make its consulting reports and "intellectual capital" available on Amazon.com. These new IT initiatives shifted the impact of IT within this consulting firm toward the turnaround quadrant on the strategic grid.

Often executives fail to recognize when a specific IT project or set of projects shift a company from one quadrant to another. As a result, they fail to provide the appropriate governance and oversight. A rapidly growing manufacturing firm provides a good example.

Until the mid-1990s, for example, the IT used in this midsized manufacturing company, although important, was not absolutely vital to the firm's success and survival. In the late 1990s, however, the company began development of a new IT system designed to streamline, integrate, and coordinate all aspects of the firm's operations, including how supplies were ordered, products were manufactured and sold, orders were fulfilled, and customers were served. The new system was required to enable executives and local business managers to gain control of the company's increasingly complex operations as it expanded into new product categories and multiple international markets. At the same time, the company was developing another new IT application that would enable the company to centralize key customer data and integrate it with production scheduling information from over 60 plants and two customer service call centers. These new applications were designed to enable the firm to dramatically improve service, sharply lower administrative costs, and significantly decrease the cost of operations.

With the launch of these new projects, the company entered the factory quadrant of the strategic grid. As it did, the approach to running the IT function changed. A senior business unit executive was appointed as Chief Information Officer (CIO), and the firm's business unit and IT executives formed an IT Council that met monthly to provide oversight and governance of strategic IT-enabled business initiatives and projects. Over time the company's position shifted to the strategy quadrant.

As we enter the twenty-first century, most executives recognize that IT is an essential component of current and future strategy and operations. Going forward, banks, insurance companies, auto manufacturers, and major retail chains have embedded IT in their core operations and core strategy. Within strategically IT-dependent firms, leadership and governance of IT becomes deeply embedded in the leadership and governance of the business.

The Strategic Alignment Model

Given the growing strategic impact of IT, Henderson and Venkatraman developed the Strategic Alignment Model to assess business and IT alignment across all components of the business model. Figure 1.7 presents the Strategic Alignment Model, modified to fit with terminology used in the business model framework.

The strategy domain assesses alignment in terms of context, purpose, positioning, projects, and goals. The capabilities domain assesses alignment in terms of leadership, people/partners, processes, organization, and infrastructure. The model specifies the need for two types of alignment. The first, represented by dotted arrows, is alignment between corresponding IT and business domains. The second, represented by solid arrows, is alignment of IT and business strategy and capabilities. Value is created through alignment across all four domains.

FIGURE 1.7
Strategic
Alignment
Model

Source: Adapted from
J. C. Henderson and
N. Venkatraman,
"Strategic Alignment:
Leveraging
Information
Technology for
Transforming
Organizations," *IBM
Systems Journal* 32,
no. 1 (1993).

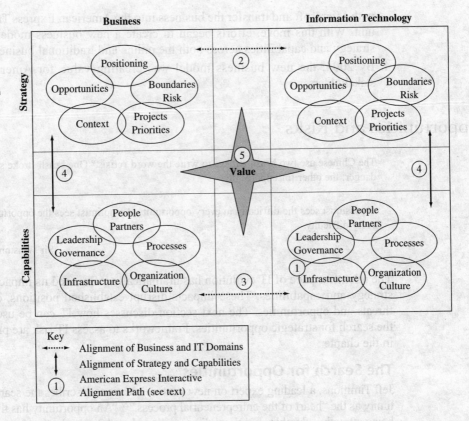

The evolution of American Express Interactive—a new online travel service—from the time it was introduced in 1995 to its integration within American Express Travel in 2001, shows how the Strategic Alignment Model can be used to trace the path through which alignment is achieved over time.[20] This path is represented on Figure 1.7 by circled numbers.

1. Motivated by the commercialization of the Internet, IT and business executives at American Express worked together to identify potential new opportunities for IT-business strategy alignment. An online travel service for business customers was chosen as the introductory product position with the expectation of follow-on business opportunities.

2. To gain access to the necessary IT capabilities, the commercialization of the new online service was initially built as an independent joint venture with Microsoft. The new venture brought together executives and employees from American Express and Microsoft to align IT and business capabilities.

3. Executives soon learned, however, that the real power of the new business model could only be achieved through the alignment of the online and traditional travel service businesses. In June 2001, the decision was made to exit the joint venture

[20] L. M. Applegate, *American Express Interactive*, Boston: HBS Publishing (No. 802-022).

with Microsoft and transfer the business into the American Express Travel Services unit. With this move, efforts began to create a new business model that aligned strategy and capabilities across both the online and traditional businesses.

4. By 2004, the new business model was creating value for American Express stakeholders.

Opportunities and Risks

The Chinese use two brush strokes to write the word "crisis." One brush stroke stands for danger; the other for opportunity.

A pessimist sees the difficulty in every opportunity. An optimist sees the opportunity in every difficulty.

Sir Winston Churchill[21]

The relentless pace of IT evolution has dramatically influenced its impact on business strategy and capabilities. These impacts disrupt established positions, creating both threats and opportunities. The next section discusses how IT can be used to support the search for strategic opportunities. Frameworks to assess IT risk are presented later in the chapter.

The Search for Opportunities

Jeff Timmons, a leading expert on new venture creation, describes the search for opportunity as the "heart of the entrepreneurial process."[22] "An opportunity has the qualities of being attractive, durable, and timely," he continued, and it must be "anchored in a product or service that creates or adds value for the buyer or the end user." Paul Maeder, founder and managing general partner of the Boston-based venture capital firm, Highland Capital Partners, explained the evaluation criteria he used to evaluate opportunities:

When we invest in [early-stage start-up] businesses, [we always ask]: Is this a unique value proposition? Do we have a real shot at being first in the market? . . . Is this a compelling enough business that people are going to be drawn to it, [initially employees and] managers and ultimately customers? Are there barriers to entry that we can erect so that when other people see our good ideas they don't pile in? Finally, can we build it with a reasonable amount of capital in a reasonable period of time? If the answers to those questions are satisfactory, we'll typically fund it.[23]

As can be seen from the above quotes, while the search for opportunities often begins with a creative idea-generation process, opportunity identification requires a more analytically driven evaluation of the viability of the business model. This analysis uses frameworks discussed in this chapter on strategy and in Chapters 2 and 3 on building capabilities and creating value, respectively. Below, we list five key questions that can be

---

[21] Quotations are from Famous Quotations (www.famous-quotations.com; downloaded July 2004).
[22] J. Timmons, *New Venture Creation: Entrepreneurship for the 21st Century* (New York: McGraw Hill, 1995), pp. 3–11.
[23] Author interview with Paul Maeder, March 14, 2000.

used to guide executives as they search for opportunities to use IT to support and drive strategy in their search for value-creating opportunities. Questions to assess the impact of IT on capabilities and value are presented in later chapters in this module.

- Can IT change the basis of competition?
- Can IT change the nature of relationships and the balance of power among buyers and suppliers?
- Can IT build or reduce barriers to entry?
- Can IT increase or decrease switching costs?
- Can IT add value to existing products and services or create new ones?

Can IT Change the Basis of Competition?

At its core, IT is used to automate activities—whether they take place inside an organization or across its boundaries. But, as it automates, IT can also be used to both *inform* and *transform*.

In the 1950s and 1960s, when IT was first introduced for commercial use, the primary target of IT applications was to automate routine, information-intensive back-office transactions (e.g., payroll processing, accounting, and general ledger postings). The primary goal was to increase efficiency and productivity.

Businesses quickly learned to apply these same benefits to front-office activities that involved transactions with suppliers, distributors, customers, and other value chain participants. Benefits increased dramatically when businesses learned to use IT, not just to automate, but also to inform and transform—especially across business boundaries. A streamlined and integrated value chain helped businesses eliminate redundancies, reduce cycle time, and achieve even greater efficiency and productivity. Information, a by-product of automation, also enabled executives, employees, partners, and other stakeholders to better understand fast-cycled operations. Moreover, timely—even real-time—information could be used to drive new benefits, including improved coordination and control; personalized products and services; enhanced strategic positioning and differentiation of existing products and services; and, finally, the creation of IT-enabled products and services that attracted new market participants and generated new revenue streams.

American Hospital Supply Corporation (AHSC) and American Airlines (AA) were two early examples of how IT could be used to reengineer value activities and transform the basis of competition.[24] The story began during the late 1960s when an entrepreneurial sales manager at AHSC created a system that enabled hospital purchasing clerks to order supplies across telephone lines using punch cards and primitive card-reading computers. At about the same time, enterprising sales managers at AA were also paving new ground by giving large travel agencies computer terminals that allowed them to check airline schedules posted within American's internal reservation systems. Indeed, from these entrepreneurial actions grew two legendary strategic IT applications that changed the basis of competition in their respective industries.

[24] See J. L. McKenney and D. G. Copeland, *Waves of Change* (Boston: HBS Press, 1995); and L. M. Applegate, "Electronic Commerce," in *The Technology Management Handbook*, ed. Richard C. Dorf (Englewood Cliffs, NJ: CRC Press 1999), for an in-depth discussion of the evolution of early strategic systems.

Both AHSC and AA built their strategic systems upon internal systems that were originally designed to automate back-office transaction processing. AHSC, for example, first installed computers to manage internal inventory and order processing activities; AA used computers to manage their internal reservation process. In both cases, the value of these early systems came from the ability to structure, simplify, and coordinate internal operations. But, once they had simplified and structured activities inside the firm, both AHSC and AA recognized that they could allow customers to self-serve without fear of reducing quality. Because each firm had built its systems using proprietary technology, AHSC and AA owned the platform upon which business was conducted—and they also owned the information flowing from the automated transaction systems. This information enabled executives and frontline workers, in both firms, to coordinate and control activities whether they took place inside the firm or outside. And, by harnessing the power of the information, both firms were able to differentiate existing services and to offer new information-based services.

The benefits of conducting business online were so great that AHSC gave hospitals the card readers required to do business electronically and taught hospital supply clerks how to use them. AHSC even helped hospital personnel redesign their internal purchasing processes to fit with the new online process. AA did the same thing when they gave travel agents the computer reservation system terminals. Neither AHSC nor AA charged their customers for the computer equipment or the training. Why? The benefits to AHSC and AA from online purchasing, whether it was hospital supplies or seats on an airplane, more than offset the cost of giving away the terminals. For example, by 1985, AHSC saved over $11 million per year through online ordering and generated $4 to $5 million per year in additional revenue.

The AHSC and AA examples demonstrate how two firms used IT to fundamentally alter the basis of competition in their respective industries. This occurred when executives implemented strategies that radically changed both the cost structure for the industry and, at the same time, differentiated their product/service offering and strategic positions, causing massive shifts in market share and demand.

The Charles Schwab case, presented at the end of this module, provides another example of how a firm built upon existing capabilities and technology infrastructure to radically transform the financial services industry. Founded in 1975, Schwab accomplished this feat—not once but twice. Initially Schwab executives placed a bet that a growing number of individual investors would prefer to save money and time by using low-cost local branch office brokerage services rather than high-priced full-service brokers. Committed to delivering the levels of trust and responsiveness of a full-service broker but at a dramatically reduced cost, Schwab turned to IT. For example, by the late 1970s, the company had launched an IT-enabled 24 × 7 call center and customer relationship management system that quickly became the channel of choice for Schwab customers. In the mid-1980s and early 1990s, Schwab pioneered online trading capabilities—well before the Internet simplified adoption. Indeed, by 1997 revenues for Schwab's discount brokerage business—a new market segment that Schwab had started, built, and dominated for over 20 years—had reached $2.3 billion.

When the commercial Internet appeared in the mid-1990s, Schwab was poised again to segment the market. Already routine customer service requests (quotes, balances, positions) had migrated from Schwab branches to the call center and, to a lesser extent, to its proprietary online service. Indeed, at the time it launched its Internet online brokerage in January of 1998, only 5 percent of routine customer service was handled at a brokerage office—with the majority handled by phone. The Web-based service provided access to online and offline brokerage services for a single fee of $29.95 per trade (compared to an average $80 per trade for full-service brokerage commissions). Within less than one year, sales were up 19 percent. And, since the online self-service business dramatically lowered costs, profits were also up 29 percent.

The Charles Schwab case provides an excellent example of how, between the mid-1970s and late 1990s, this technology innovator aligned business and IT strategy and capabilities to redefine the basis of competition in the retail brokerage segment of the financial services industry. The case ends in late 2002 as Schwab struggles to redefine its business model yet again as the financial services industry reels from the one-two-three punch of a dramatic erosion of investor trust, economic recession, and regulatory reform.

Can IT Change the Nature of Relationships and the Balance of Power in Buyer-Seller Relationships?

As mentioned above, AHSC rose to power within the hospital supplies industry by streamlining channels, dramatically decreasing cost, improving order accuracy, and increasing speed of fulfillment between suppliers (e.g., Johnson & Johnson, Baxter, and Abbott) and hospital buyers. Initially, AHSC used traditional offline processes to buy supplies from manufacturers and to store them in AHSC-owned warehouses. But, once it succeeded in getting a large number of customers to buy online, AHSC sought to further streamline the supply chain. Sensing they were at risk from being excluded from the market and lacking the money, expertise, and time to respond, suppliers succumbed to the pressure to put their catalogs online and join the electronic market. Once electronic links to suppliers had been established, AHSC customers could order directly from supplier inventory, which enabled further reduction in cost and cycle time for all members of the online market.

Customers encouraged channel consolidation; they recognized the value of a multivendor marketplace but were unwilling to put up with the problems of using multiple different supplier systems to conduct business. Within a short time, AHSC became a powerful supply chain services provider within the hospital supply industry, controlling both the physical and information channels for conducting business. In fact, this neutral, third-party distributor created such a significant shift in the balance of power toward the channel that, in 1985, it was bought by Baxter Healthcare Corporation, a hospital supplier in the industry. A few years later, responding to pressure from market participants, Baxter was forced to spin out the supply chain business it had purchased to ensure neutrality.

Initially, many believed that the Internet might similarly shift power from suppliers (e.g., manufacturers and service providers) to channel players (e.g., wholesalers, distributors, and retailers) and buyers. Indeed, during the late 1990s, Internet-based channel players flooded the market in an attempt to gain the position of power in this new online channel.

By 2004, however, many of the independent Internet marketplaces were struggling or had closed. As neutral, independent channel players faltered, established players rushed in—initially to defend their turf and later to drive efficiencies as the economy worsened. Once again, the health care industry provided an excellent view into the changing nature of relationships and shifting power dynamics.

In March 2000, five of the largest health care suppliers—Abbott, Baxter, GE Medical, Johnson & Johnson, and Medtronic—launched the Global Healthcare Exchange, LLC (GHX).[25] GHX promised to eliminate inefficiencies in every step in the health care supply chain, from placing orders to tracking delivery. These inefficiencies accounted for an estimated $11 billion in unnecessary purchasing costs.[26] The five founding companies supplied over 70 percent of all products and services purchased by hospitals and did business with over 90 percent of potential buyers. Within months of the announcement of GHX's formation, more than half of the emerging independent health care Internet marketplaces disappeared as venture capital investors pulled back their funding and support in recognition that chances for success were slim given plummeting stock markets and the eroding economy.

Consolidation of the industry continued as the majority of the health care marketplaces joined forces with GHX. By mid-2003, GHX's board of directors and investors included representation by the largest buyers, distributors, and suppliers in the health care industry. As one of only two remaining large online supply chain marketplaces, GHX enabled over 1,400 health care buyers and distributors to transact over $2 billion in business with over 100 suppliers.

The GHX case, located at the end of this module, provides a rare glimpse into the evolution of relationships and power dynamics in an industry as key participants in the value network work together to drive efficiencies for all. When the Internet burst on the scene, it was initially believed that power would shift to independent channel players as they disintermediated traditional buyer-supplier relationships and fragmented industries. By 2000, the view had shifted as established players regained power and sought ways to consolidate it even more. The evolution of GHX as a trusted, neutral *collaborative* marketplace committed to creating value and efficiencies for all players provides yet another view—one that is being replicated in the highly competitive auto industry; in 2003, a struggling Covisint—the online supplier marketplace formed by the large auto manufacturers—was sold to Compuware—a neutral IT services provider.

Can IT Build or Reduce Barriers to Entry?

Companies erect entry barriers by offering customers and other market participants attractive products and services at a price and level of quality that competitors cannot match. Before the rise of the commercial Internet, first movers like AHSC and AA spent hundreds of millions of dollars over decades to establish a dominant position within electronic markets. The sheer magnitude of the investment to build and operate proprietary networks, transaction systems, and databases created significant barriers to entry. For example, American Airlines and archrival United Airlines each spent hundreds of millions of dollars during the late 1970s and early 1980s to build the proprietary

---

[25] For a thorough discussion of GHX, see L. M. Applegate, *Global Healthcare Exchange*, Harvard Business School Publishing (No. 804-002). This case is also available at the end of Module 1.

[26] R. Winslow, "Baxter International, Others Plan Net Concern for Hospital Purchases," *Wall Street Journal Interactive*, March 30, 2000.

networks and computer systems required to launch and run online customer reservation systems. By the time other airlines recognized the opportunity—and threat—they were forced to tie into these two dominant online channels or risk being cutoff from customers.[27]

Over time, however, these technology-based advantages decreased. The more sustainable advantage came from second order barriers to entry created by exploiting the value of information generated by the technology and the value of the loyal community of suppliers, customers, and partners that did business using the company's proprietary digital infrastructure.

Initially, many believed that the overall impact of Internet technologies would be to lower entry barriers for all players in online markets.[28] This belief arose from the fact that Internet technologies dramatically lowered the cost of participating in an electronic market. In addition, the shared, nonproprietary nature of the Internet made it easy for market participants to link to a common, shared platform for conducting business online and, more importantly, to sever ties with one firm and link to another.

Indeed, it has been shown that the Internet's low cost and ease of penetration decrease the benefits to any one participant *unless people within the firm are able to:*

- Learn and respond more quickly and more effectively than others.
- Build proprietary capabilities that are not easily replicable.
- Create a large, loyal community that remains committed and engaged despite the availability of seemingly comparable alternatives.

As we saw in the past, these capability and community barriers provide a sustainable entry barrier—even within open standard electronic markets. In most cases, we see that incumbent firms with large investments in proprietary infrastructure and channels to market are at a particular disadvantage relative to new entrants when attempting to create and quickly deploy second order barriers to entry.

Amazon.com, one of the most celebrated new entrants of the dot-com era, provides an example of how new technology can lower entry barriers in an established industry. But, as we will see, while entry barriers were initially low, Amazon's business model required the company to take ownership of physical inventory. This, in turn, required significant investment in building an online/offline retail infrastructure. While building and deploying the infrastructure delayed profitability, the company eventually found ways to capitalize on the infrastructure they had built, the community they had connected, and what they had learned to turn a profit during fourth quarter 2001—*and build significant entry barriers to subsequent entry.*[29]

---

[27] During the late 1980s and early 1990s, new entrant Southwest Airlines offered a regional service that offered a significant decrease in price and a corresponding increase in the number of flights to popular destinations within a local area. This niche market strategy enabled them to achieve a sustainable competitive advantage without tying into online reservation systems. By early 2000, Southwest was able to offer their own online reservation system that enabled customers to bypass travel agents and buy directly from Southwest.

[28] M. Porter, "Strategy and the Internet," *Harvard Business Review,* March 2001.

[29] See L. M. Applegate and M. Collura, *Amazon.com 2000,* Harvard Business School Publishing (No. 801-194); and L. M. Applegate, *Amazon.com Update: January 2001–July 2002,* Harvard Business School Publishing (No. 801-392).

In July 1995, Jeff Bezos, Amazon's CEO and founder, launched his online bookstore from a 400-square-foot warehouse (about the size of a one-car garage) with only a few servers and a high-speed connection to the Internet. The company quickly became the number 1 online bookstore. Just two years after launch, sales had reached $148 million and the number of customers exceeded 2 million.

During its third year, Amazon executives demonstrated that the initial success in quickly dominating the online book market could be repeated. During the summer and fall of 1998, Amazon opened new online music and video "stores," and achieved the number 1 position in online music sales within four months and the number 1 position in online video sales within a record 45 days.

At this point, Amazon's success was due to the fact that the Internet had lowered entry barriers to the detriment of established players. But there was a deeper lesson here. Established competitors, such as Barnes & Noble, Borders, and Bertelsmann (in Europe), were not blind to Amazon's early success; they invested heavily but were unable to catch up. Why? Many erroneously believed that Amazon's dominance came from its first-mover advantage. While this was important, in other instances first movers were quickly crushed. CDNow, for example, was overtaken by Amazon.com in short order.

The secret to Amazon's success in entering and dominating multiple industries were the capabilities that it built *behind its Web site* to execute strategy. During 1999 and 2000, Amazon executives spent over $500 million building a sophisticated, Web-based order fulfillment capability that enabled the company to fulfill orders for over 31 million units during the six-week 2000 holiday period from mid-November to the end of December. Over 99 percent of orders arrived on time.

Like the success stories from the 1980s, the automated transaction infrastructure generated valuable information that, in Amazon.com's case, was fed into a sophisticated knowledge management infrastructure that allowed executives and employees at all levels to develop a real-time understanding of the dynamics of the marketplace and of the needs of individual consumers and business customers. Amazon used this knowledge to coordinate and control operations—not only inside the firm but also across organizational boundaries. More importantly, it used its growing understanding of customer preferences to personalize its online services in a way that could not be matched by competitors and to feed valuable information to suppliers. The number of loyal customers increased quickly and by late 2000, over 25 million people shopped on Amazon. These *proprietary* capabilities (which united people and technology) enabled Amazon to develop powerful barriers to entry that, to date, competitors have been unable to match. In Bezos' words:

The Amazon.com platform is comprised of brand, customers, technology, distribution capability, deep e-commerce expertise, and a great team with a passion for innovation and serving customers well . . . We believe that we have reached a "tipping point," where this platform allows us to launch new e-commerce businesses faster, with a higher quality of customer experience, a lower incremental cost, a higher chance of success, and a clearer path to scale and profitability than perhaps any other company.[30]

[30] Amazon.com Annual Report, 1999.

By mid-2001, however, many wondered whether these proprietary advantages would be enough. After the rapid decline in the price of Internet stocks during 2000 and the loss of investor confidence in online business models, the company found that sources of financing had dried up. Amazon executives altered the company's strategy and business model away from a dependence on retail product sales and toward a services model in an effort to reach profitability more quickly. This new strategy paralleled the approach used by AHSC and AA during the 1980s, to shift from selling products to selling capabilities and expertise.

By early 2004, Amazon had successfully attracted a number of established "brick-and-mortar" retailers that wished to tap into online markets while avoiding the risk and time required to develop, deploy, and manage equivalent capabilities. These firms signed multiyear outsourcing contracts that, over time, began to shift the Amazon.com business model from an e-retailer to an online/offline logistics services provider—and one of the few profitable and growing survivors from the dot-com era.

Can IT Raise or Lower Switching Costs?

To provide a sustainable source of revenues, an IT system should ideally be easy to start using but difficult to stop using. Customers drawn into the system through a series of increasingly valuable enhancements should willingly become dependent on the system's functionality. Once use of the system becomes ingrained within day-to-day activities, switching to another system becomes difficult and costly.

In the past, when proprietary technologies were the norm, switching costs were high because switching usually required buying into different proprietary networks and systems owned and operated by an online service provider, such as American Airlines in the travel industry, American Hospital Supply in the hospital supplies industry, or Wal-Mart in the retail industry. On the public Internet, however, the cost of a simple connection is relatively low and the technologies required to participate are not proprietary. Switching costs are, therefore, substantially reduced. For example, the cost to a customer of switching from shopping at Amazon.com to shopping at Barnes & Noble's online store is merely a few keystrokes effort. Easy switching also makes for easy price comparisons, which led many to believe that it would be difficult to achieve strong customer loyalty.

While there appears to be a certain inevitability to this logic, savvy executives, for example, Scott Cook at Intuit, have identified ways to exploit the power of the Internet to increase, rather than decrease, switching costs. Launched in 1983, Intuit provided low-cost financial services software (Quicken, TurboTax, and QuickBooks) designed to be easy to use by individuals with little to no background in finance or technology. Initially, the products "hooked" the user by providing a much simpler and easier way to complete time-consuming and repetitive tasks. By also providing a simple way to store personal information, which would have to be re-entered if a customer switched to a different product, the company kept users hooked over time. Intuit quickly became the market leader for individual and small business financial software with over 80 percent market share across its product line and over 90 percent retention rates. Throughout the 1990s, the company continued to maintain this position despite aggressive competition by software giant Microsoft.

A decade after launching its first software product, the company launched an online financial services portal, Quicken.com, to complement and extend its packaged software offerings. By linking its Internet business to the company's traditional desktop software, Intuit was able to transition users from its desktop product line to a less costly Internet product line while also offering an even easier to use and more useful set of services. By 2001, consumers and small business owners could pay bills and bank online, calculate and pay taxes, and manage a portfolio of investments. Small business owners could also manage payroll, inventory, and customer accounts, and could purchase supplies. As these features were added to the service, and as customers benefited from their ease of use and convenience, switching became more difficult. Changing an online bill paying service, for example, involved setting up relationships between the new online bill paying service and each company to be paid.

Intuit used the lessons learned from its successful software business to guide the launch and evolution of its Internet business. Careful attention was paid to create a service offering that provided a unique value proposition for customers and that hooked them to the company by providing a simple and easy to use way to complete time-consuming and repetitive tasks. And, once users invested the effort to store personal information and to set up online transaction relationships, it became much harder to switch. Using these principles, within less than one year of launch, Intuit's online version of its TurboTax software gained over 80 percent market share in the highly competitive market for online tax preparation and filing.

Can IT Add Value to Existing Products or Services or Create New Ones?

In addition to lowering cost, improving quality, and changing power dynamics, IT can also add value to existing products or services and create new ones. For example, grocery stores used to be in the business of selling packaged goods and fresh food. But, now they are also in the business of selling information. Many market research firms purchase scanner data on consumer shopping behavior from large supermarket chains, analyze it, and then sell it back to the supermarkets along with aggregate competitor, industry, and demographic data from a wide variety of sources.

The information content of existing products has also increased markedly. Many are unaware that, by 2000, there were more computer chips in a late-model car than were in the entire U.S. Department of Defense in 1960. Not only do these chips control everything from a car's internal air temperature to the braking system, they also provide valuable information to service mechanics and auto manufacturers to guide after-sales service and future product design, and most importantly, to consumers who can now tap into General Motor's OnStar service to get driving directions, make dinner reservations, contact police and rescue personnel, and even open the car door to retrieve keys inadvertently left inside.

Finally, IT can alter or even completely transform a product from an analog to a digital form. Products particularly well-suited to digitization include books, magazines, music, video, and games.

Strategic Risk

Interestingly, the more successful a company is, the easier it is to forget about risk. "It's in good times that managers need to be most watchful for signs of impending danger," warns Bob Simons.[31] "[Success] has an uncanny way of setting a company up for trouble, if not impending attack. And, not just from outside sources, such as competitors and regulators, but, just as important, from within the organization itself." While the previous section of this chapter focused on the impact of IT on the search for opportunities, this final section discusses IT impact on strategic risk. Below are key questions that executives can use to frame their analysis of the strategic risk of IT. Later chapters will deal with implementation and project management risk.

- Can emerging technologies disrupt current business models?
- Are we too early or too late to exploit an IT opportunity?
- Does IT lower entry barriers?
- Does IT trigger regulatory action?

Can Emerging Technologies Disrupt Current Business Models?

Clay Christensen describes the challenges that established firms face when confronted with disruptive technologies.[32] When do we classify an emerging technology as a disruptor? Key features of *disruptive* technologies include:

- The technology evolves significantly faster than the evolutionary path of the dominant technology in the industry (e.g., the pace of evolution of the performance/price ratio of personal computer technology in the 1980s was significantly faster than the evolution of well-established mainframe technology).
- The technology enables new products, services, pricing, or business models that change the basis of competition in ways that are difficult for established players to match (e.g., Internet securities brokers offer deep discounts that can't be matched by either full-service brokers, like Merrill Lynch, or traditional discount brokers, like Schwab).
- The emergence of the technology coincides with regulatory changes or significant customer dissatisfaction with the status quo that dramatically influence the competitive power of established players to respond (e.g., Department of Justice restrictions against Microsoft coincide with customer dissatisfaction and the emergence of Linux as a commercially viable alternative).

Interestingly, while executives in established firms often view disruptive technologies as a threat, entrepreneurs recognize that these disruptors are a source of opportunity. Indeed, as can be seen in Figure 1.8, the disruptive process often begins when an entrepreneur—whether he or she is creating an independent start-up or is exploiting a new opportunity within an established firm—begins experimentation and eventually enters the market, in this case with a new technology. While the performance/price ratio of the new technology may initially be well below the established technology (T1 on Figure 1.8), disruptive technologies are characterized by an evolutionary path that is much steeper.

---

[31] R. Simons, "How Risky Is Your Company," *Harvard Business Review*, May–June 1999, p. 85.
[32] C. Christensen, *The Innovators Solution: Creating and Sustaining Successful Growth* (Boston: Harvard Business School Press, 2003).

FIGURE 1.8
Analyzing Disruptive Technologies

Source: Adapted from C. Christensen, *The Innovators Dilemma* (Boston: HBS Publishing, 1997).

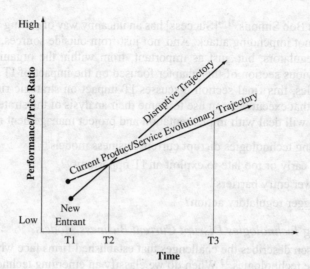

Initially established players may not be concerned about the new entrant, believing that the technology is inferior to what current customers expect and value. Indeed, that is the scenario that entrepreneurs and venture capitalists are anticipating. In fact, the tight alignment of an established player's current product positioning with its established customer base often ties the company into a product/service trajectory that makes it tough to introduce new offerings that make use of emerging technologies.

The history of IBM provides an excellent example of the challenges incumbent players encounter when attempting to respond to disruptive technologies. IBM faced its first significant disruptive technology threat when new entrant, Digital Equipment Corporation (DEC), launched its first smaller scale server in the 1970s; at the time these midrange computers were called minicomputers. In fact, at the time, IBM's ability to respond aggressively to new entrants was complicated by legal and regulatory concerns as the company repeatedly responded to lawsuits and threatened sanctions as new entrants accused IBM of abusing its monopoly power to restrict competition.

Having created the first commercially successful mainframe computer in the late 1960s, IBM owned the market and had strong relationships with its large corporate customers. Close contact between IBM's technologically sophisticated salespeople and product design engineers, and the technologically sophisticated data center managers of the day ensured tight alignment between the mainframe's evolution in performance, features, and price with its customers' expectations and interests.

But the evolutionary trajectory of the new entrants in the 1970s progressed at a much faster rate than the mainframe trajectory and, as the performance/price ratio approached the mainframe's (T2 on Figure 1.8), IBM executives began to worry. At what point should they attempt to enter the minicomputer market when doing so would cannibalize mainframe sales. In addition, the data center managers who purchased mainframes strongly resisted the IBM's entry into the smaller scale computer market as the customers for these smaller minicomputers inside large corporations, engineering departments and factory managers, were outside of the data center manager control.

Despite data center manager protests, as the performance/price ratio of the mini-computer exceeded that of the mainframe (T3 on Figure 1.8), IBM hastened to wrest control back from the increasing powerful "upstarts." But the tight alignment of its mainframe business model kept IBM from responding *effectively.* The launch of the IBM 9370, designated as the "VAX-killer," was a case in point: an IBM executive explained:[33] "It was a mainframe-based thought in a midrange market. We used main-frame thinking, in terms of pricing and cost structures, and tried to launch it in the middle market—and it bombed."[34] In the end, IBM ceded the smaller scale server mar-ket to DEC and subsequent new entrants, such as Sun Microsystems. That same main-frame thinking also blinded IBM to the much faster evolutionary path of the personal computer (PC) in the early 1980s.

Having learned from the DEC VAX experience, IBM was determined to enter early and aggressively into the PC market. Indeed, with its on-time launch in 1981, the IBM PC became the most successful technology introduction of its time; its sales of almost 250,000 units *in a single month* shortly after launch exceeded the company's *five-year forecast*.

While successful, however, the PC was always considered a "stepchild" of the real money-making machine—the mainframe. Rather than push low-margin PCs through IBM's traditional field sales force, it became the first product to be sold through third-party retailers, distributors, and value-added resellers (VARs). While it was aggressive in its launch, once again, IBM's mainframe-based business model kept the new busi-ness from living up to its potential. "Just about every vendor [did] a better job of mar-keting PCs than IBM [did]," said the CEO of one IBM customer. "No one ever looked at the IBM PC as being inferior, but IBM [did] nothing to sell it. Meanwhile, in the early '90s, Compaq stole IBM's PC market with the right price and the right message. Now it's Dell. IBM [was] a sleeping giant losing its golden egg."[35]

By the late 1980s, IBM was, as one executive put it, "very much in denial about client-server."[36] Among IBM's customers, the need to interconnect mainframe, midrange, and increasingly mobile PCs with distributed data sources and applications led to fewer and fewer purchases of mainframes, the source of almost half of IBM's revenues during the mid- to late 1980s, and 70 percent to 80 percent of its profits. Between 1980 and 1989, IBM was *the* most profitable company in the world, gener-ating over $51 billion in profits for its shareholders. In 1990, the company was the sec-ond most profitable company in the world, generating $6 billion in profits. In 1991, however, the years of difficulty in responding to the relentless stream of disruptive technologies caught up with the "most admired company in the world"; between 1991

[33] The "VAX" was a Digital Equipment Company midrange computer that was introduced in the 1970s but gained wide-scale popularity in the 1980s. The VAX family of computers, from high end to low end, were based on the same architecture and were much easier to interconnect than the main-frame computers of the day. This degree of "interoperability" was unusual at the time the VAX was introduced, and provided a flexible and cost-effective alternative to mainframes for many applications.

[34] R. Austin and R. Nolan, "IBM Corporation: Turnaround 1991–1995," Harvard Business School Publishing (No. 600-098), p. 5.

[35] J. Stafford, "IBM's Plan to Win VAR 2000," *VarBusiness*, May 24, 1999.

[36] L. M. Applegate et al., "IBM's Decade of Transformation: A Vision for On Demand," Harvard Business School Publishing (No. 805-018).

and 1993 IBM lost $16 billion and the board of directors and senior executives began the painful process of breaking up the company to sell the pieces at fire sale prices. In the process, they found a new CEO who immediately saw the value of "One IBM" and set out to transform the company to lead—rather than follow—the next disruptive technology wave. A new case study, written by the authors, tells this remarkable story of the rise, fall, and rebirth of IBM.

The IBM story provides a compelling example of the challenges that disruptive technologies pose for established players. As discussed earlier, the tight alignment of strategy, capabilities, and value creates a "virtuous cycle" of innovation, productivity, and increasing returns. When the environment changes, however, that same tightly aligned business model can prove a company's downfall. Strong leadership and a sense of crisis are often needed to catalyze effective change in the face of rapidly evolving disruptive technologies. In the absence of crisis, Christensen recommends, and executives, like those at American Express, agree that it is helpful to build the new business model as a separate new venture. In fact, the IBM PC was built as a separate business and its successful launch attests to the potential of sidestepping the tightly aligned current business model. However, both IBM and American Express also learned that it's no easy feat to integrate the new venture with the established business later on if integration is necessary to exploit the full power of the technology and business opportunity. If necessary to capture the full value, savvy executives are learning that they must manage the integration of new and old business models much as they would the integration of an acquisition or merger.

Are We Too Early or Too Late to Exploit an IT Opportunity?

The above discussion on disruptive technologies highlights the challenges that established players face as they attempt to determine when and how to adopt a new technology or technology-enabled business model. Enter too early, and you increase the risk that a new technology may never live up to its early promise. Alternatively, standards may change midstream and early adopters may find that their investments are worthless. Adopt too late, and you increase the risk that the market closes before you have a chance to establish your position and reap the value. Clearly, the IBM example shows that the pace of technology evolution is an important factor to consider. So too, is your organization's capability to respond quickly and effectively—to build an organization that has the power, resources, efficiency, and reach of a large firm, while also having the speed, passion, and agility of an entrepreneurial venture. We will address the required capabilities in the next chapter. Here we will provide an approach for balancing opportunity and risk when making decisions on when to adopt a new technology.

Figure 1.9 provides a framework for comparing the windows of opportunity for two technologies with markedly different evolutionary paths—the mainframe and the PC. Figure 1.9(a) shows a basic cash flow curve for comparing all business opportunities. Note that the curve begins with a period of investment and risk that can be modeled by analyzing the level of the investment required in terms of time to generate positive cash flow and time to break even. Once the break-even point is reached, the return can be modeled by analyzing the maximum return at the point where growth slows, plateaus, and then declines. As we saw with the investment model, the pace of evolution at each stage strongly influences the risk/reward profile.

FIGURE 1.9(a)   Analyzing the Cash Flow Curve

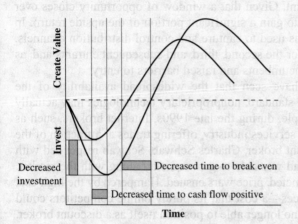

FIGURE 1.9(b)   Comparing Cash Flow Curves and Windows of Opportunity (As Represented by Ovals)

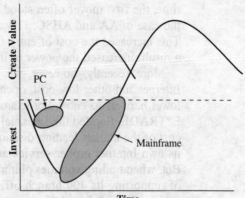

Figure 1.9(b) compares the cash flow curves for both the mainframe and PC during the 1980s and adds in a hypothetical window of opportunity. It is important to note that the window changes in response to changes in assumptions concerning the level and timing of risk and reward. Notice how the much deeper investment and slower pace of evolution of mainframe technology innovations when compared to the emerging PC technology influences both the size of the window of opportunity and the speed within which new innovations must be exploited. This model helps clarify why "mainframe thinking" and "mainframe business models" were ineffective when attempting to exploit PC opportunities.

The LeapFrog case at the end of this module provides an example of the challenges that the entrepreneur/founder faced when attempting to create a new technology platform upon which this innovative new educational toy was based and then bring it to market. After reading the case, take time to plot the cash flow curve and the window of opportunity for the company's initial product. Data in the case enable you to create a rough model of the investment, the time to break even, and the return for the initial product. The company's decision to acquire Explore Technologies changed the cash flow curve. Once again, the case enables you to create a rough model of how the acquisition of a new technology platform created new business opportunities. Finally, at the end of the case, the company is attempting to enter a new market—the primary and secondary school market with new products that customize and reposition its consumer toys for the needs and expectations of the new market. Once again, the window of opportunity and the cash flow curve are influenced—this time by the change in business model.

Does IT Lower Entry Barriers?

Earlier in this chapter, we described how IT was used to raise barriers to entry in many industries. In situations where extensive investment in hardware and software is obligatory for all participants, the investment required for exploiting the technology and entering the market is also increased. This seriously influences the cash flow curve's risk/return profile and serves as a powerful barrier to entry if a similar investment must be made by each new entrant. Given that a window of opportunity closes over time, the first mover often stood to gain a significant portion of the upside return. In the case of AA and AHSC, IT was used to capture and control distribution channels. This increased the cost of entry for the second, third, and subsequent entrants and, as a result, increased the power of incumbents and raised barriers to entry.

More recently, however, we have seen that the widespread availability of the Internet and other low-cost, open standard, nonproprietary technologies may actually lower barriers to entry. For example, during the late 1990s, Internet brokers, such as E*TRADE, flooded the financial services industry, offering trades at a fraction of the cost of the market leading discount broker, Charles Schwab. Schwab responded with its own Internet broker service and was able to grow quickly along with the market. But, when trading volumes plummeted, price wars ensued. Hampered by the high cost of supporting its 400 branch offices—a cost that its purely online competitors could avoid—Schwab found that it was no longer able to position itself as a discount broker. In fact, in 2002, Schwab's price per trade of $29.95 was equal to the price charged by full-service broker Merrill Lynch.

As can be seen in the case at the end of this module, Charles Schwab anticipated the impact of the Internet on barriers to entry and responded quickly to minimize the risk. The company continues to struggle, however, as it attempts to redefine the basis of competition to avoid being caught in the squeeze between deep-discount Internet brokers and multichannel full-service brokers in an industry where market size has shrunk dramatically along with the cost and time required to enter and extract value from a new technology-enabled innovation.

Does IT Trigger Regulatory Actions?

At times an IT advantage can be too successful and eventually gives rise to claims of unfair competition and cries for government regulation. In the past, outcomes of these success stories included forced divestiture, costly litigation that diverted management attention and harmed the firm's reputation, and limitations on future strategic options.

The regulatory actions that limited the competitive impact of the airline reservation systems of the mid-1980s illustrate this danger. So too, does the forced spinoff of Baxter's hospital supplies business shortly after its acquisition of AHSC. More recently, the U.S. Department of Justice (DOJ) investigated claims that Microsoft used the pervasive adoption of its Windows operating system to unfairly restrict competition. At the same time that the DOJ rulings limited Microsoft's strategic options, competitors banded together to support the "Open System" movement to commercialize Linux as a viable competitor to Windows.

The Global Healthcare Exchange case at the end of this module provides a detailed analysis of these changing power dynamics. It also provides an alternative model within which traditional suppliers, buyers, and channel players develop a neutral, third-party channel upon which all transactions and information can flow. The need for clear delineation of how ownership and control of infrastructure, applications, and information is apportioned among members of the extended supply chain and the design of a *collaborative* governance structure provides an excellent example of alternatives to government regulation.

Summary

Exploiting IT opportunities, while avoiding risk, requires vision, sound execution, and the ability to respond quickly. It also requires imagination—and a lot of creativity. This chapter has presented frameworks for analyzing the strategic impact of IT. An understanding of strategic opportunities must be combined with an understanding of strategic risks. Risks increase when executives (1) have a poor understanding of sources of competitive dynamics in the industries within which their firm competes; (2) fail to fully understand the long-term implications of the risk/return profile; (3) launch a system that brings on litigation or regulation to the detriment of the innovator; and (4) fail to account for the time, effort, and cost required to ensure user adoption, assimilation, and effective utilization—especially as this is compared to the window of opportunity.

When an organization invests in a new technology, it is important to candidly assess whether the investment will result in a sustainable advantage or whether it will simply maintain the current industry and.competitive dynamics and market share. Finally, the movement of IT personnel between firms often results in rapid proliferation of strategic ideas. This puts pioneering firms under pressure to keep innovating and evolving IT-enabled strategies and business models. The following questions can be used by executives to assess IT-enabled business opportunities and risks:

1. What business are we in? Who are our customers, suppliers, and business partners? What value do we provide to these key constituencies (including employees and owners)? What are the competitive dynamics and balance of power within the industry? Can IT be used to create value and to change the basis of competition?

2. Who are our biggest competitors today? Who will they be in the future? How easy (or difficult) is it for new players to enter our markets, offering a unique value proposition and/or substitute products and services? How easy (or difficult) would it be for customers, suppliers, or partners to switch?

3. How efficient and effective are our core operating activities and processes? How easy (or difficult) is it for customers, suppliers, and partners to do business with us? How easy (or difficult) is it for us to continuously improve our products and services and the way we do business?

4. Are there any disruptive changes looming on the horizon? Are we in a position to capitalize on these changes? What is the risk/return profile and the window of opportunity? Do we want to lead the industry or be a fast follower?

5. Will changes in related industries (or even in unrelated industries) influence our industry? Can we not just enhance what we do today, but also expand into new products or markets and extend into new businesses?

6. Have we accurately identified the strategic risks that we face today and in the future? Do we have the systems and processes in place to understand and manage risks?

CHAPTER 2

IT and Organization[1]

If the old model of organization was the large, hierarchical organization, the new model that is considered characteristic of the New Competition is a network of lateral and horizontal interlinkages within and among firms. (Nohria and Eccles 1992, p. 2)[2]

Today's executives are both fascinated by—and often skeptical of—the new business models that they read about in the business press. Some academics and business futurists argue that we are in the midst of an economic transition from the industrial economy to a global network economy that promises to be just as profound as the transition from the agrarian economy to the industrial economy during the latter half of the nineteenth century.[3] Others prefer to avoid such far-reaching predictions. But, no matter what their position, most agree that traditional organizational designs are inadequate for coping with today's turbulent and increasingly networked world. Executives in large, established firms increasingly find that their organizations must become much more agile, innovative, and entrepreneurial while not losing the efficiency, power, and reach that comes with size and scale. And entrepreneurs and executives in small firms find that they must tap into an extended network of partners to achieve the scale and power needed to succeed in industries dominated by large, global players.

[1] This chapter is adapted from a previously published article: L. M. Applegate, "In Search of a New Organizational Model: Lessons from the Field," in *Shaping Organizational Form: Communication, Connection, and Community* (Thousand Oaks, CA: Sage Publications, 1999).

[2] The above quote references a model of New Competition that was defined by Best as networks of small entrepreneurial firms and geographic "competitive clusters" such as those in Silicon Valley, California and the *keiretsu* model popularized in Japan. M. Best, *The New Competition* (Cambridge, MA: Harvard University Press, 1990).

[3] During the late 1980s and early 1990s, academics and business futurists predicted the demise of the hierarchy and the rise of a more networked, intelligent, and agile organizational model. For examples, see Drucker, "The Coming of the New Organization," *Harvard Business Review,* January–February 1988; W. Powell, "Neither Market nor Hierarchy: New Forms of Organization," *Research on Organizational Behavior* 12 (1990), pp. 295–336; F. Ostroff and D. Smith, "The Horizontal Organization," *McKinsey Quarterly* 1 (1992), pp. 148–168.

As they attempt to build lean yet agile businesses, these executives are finding that they can no longer rely on gut instinct alone. Neither can they simply copy organizational models that worked in the past. Instead, they must understand how organizational and design choices influence operational efficiency and flexibility and, even more important, how to best align the organization with the environment and the strategy chosen to quickly and effectively "sense and respond" to opportunities and threats.

This chapter examines the capabilities required to build businesses that can survive and prosper in today's fast-paced and uncertain environment. The challenges of preserving the advantages of a big company while responding as quickly and innovatively as a small company are not new. Indeed, the insights presented in this chapter have emerged from over 20 years of work with hundreds of executives and entrepreneurs as they struggled to build businesses that could cope with the demands of a rapidly changing, increasingly networked global economy.[4] The insights from this research suggest that IT is an important enabler for developing the best-in-class capabilities required for success.

The Need for New Capabilities

Executives spent much of the twentieth century building and perfecting hierarchies— and the last few decades attempting to tear them down. During the 1980s and 1990s, downsizing, delayering, and re-engineering swept through large companies. Rigid intra- and inter-firm boundaries were shattered to enable firms to focus on core competencies while also delivering customized solutions in global markets. Strategic partnerships and alliances were formed to ensure access to capabilities and expertise that could not be efficiently and effectively built and managed inside and, in the extreme, networked consortia of independent firms emerged.

The vision of eliminating hierarchy was compelling, and the change initiatives— many of them enabled by emerging information technologies—shook business markets and the organizations within them to their foundations. But take a walk around most large, established firms, or talk with executives from established industries, and it soon becomes clear that the "hierarchy" is far from dead. Yet, when asked what their companies or industries should look like, most executives call immediately for new capabilities that enable them to work more effectively and efficiently within more diffuse and fluid business networks that are popularly called "ecosystems."[5] The problem confronting these executives, they report, is that they do not wish to sacrifice

---

[4] L. M. Applegate, "In Search of a New Organization," in *Shaping Organizational Form: Communication, Connection and Community,* eds. G. DeSanctis and J. Fulk (Newbury Park, CA: Sage, 1999); L. M. Applegate, "Time for the Big-Small Company," *Financial Times Mastering Information Management,* April 1999.

[5] Applegate (1999) describes the features of early attempts at building intra-firm collaborative community. Also see Applegate (1994) for results of a survey of business executives who were asked to describe changing governance models during the early 1990s and expectations for future changes. L. M. Applegate, "Business Transformation Self-Assessment—1992–1993," Harvard Business School Publishing, 1994 (No. 194-013). L. M. Applegate, "Time for the Big Small Company," *Financial Times Mastering Information Management Series,* March 1, 1999.

FIGURE 2.1
The Organization Design Challenge

Adapted from: *Nolan Norton Research Report*, 1988.

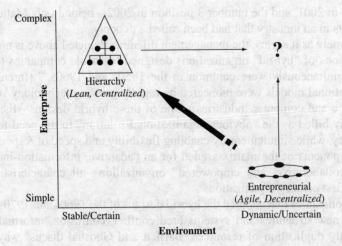

efficiency for speed; neither can they abandon authority and control as they empower others—be they employees, partners, or other loosely connected network members—to make decisions that directly influence real-time customer needs and business performance.

In the mid-1990s, Jack Welch, CEO of General Electric (GE) at the time, summarized the dilemma his company faced. "Our dream and our plan well over a decade ago was simple," he said. "We set out to shape a global enterprise that preserved the classic big company advantages while eliminating the big company drawbacks. What we wanted to build was a hybrid enterprise with the . . . power, resources, and reach of a large firm and the hunger, spirit, and fire of a small one."[6] This was not just a U.S. point of view: Percy Barnevik, CEO of Switzerland-based Asea Brown Boveri (ABB), was one of many in other countries who echoed Welch's comments. "ABB is an organization with three internal contradictions," he explained. "We want to be global and local, big and small, and radically decentralized with centralized reporting and control. If we resolve those contradictions, we create real competitive advantage."[7] Figure 2.1 summarizes the dilemma that drove these executives and countless others to search for new organizational solutions.

Today, it's not just large established companies that are coping with this challenge. Small companies also struggle with the problems that come from doing business within a global network of partners. Take for example, LeapFrog, the educational toy company.[8] Founded in 1995, executives outsourced manufacturing to seven Chinese factories and shipping and distribution to global logistics firms that, by 2002, were shipping LeapFrog product to Toys "R" Us and Wal-Mart retailers located in over 28 countries. Operating as the creative design and marketing hub of its global network of partners, LeapFrog rose from its position as the number 15 toy company in 2000, to the number 4

[6] J. Welch, "Managing in the 90s," *GE Report to Shareholders*, 1988.

[7] R. Simons and C. Bartlett, "Asea Brown Boveri" Harvard Business School Publishing (No. 192-139).

[8] L. M. Applegate, et al., "Learning from LeapFrog: Creating Educational and Business Value," Harvard Business School Publishing (No. 804-062).

position in 2001, and the number 3 position in 2002—behind only Mattel and Hasbro, the giants in an industry that had been called a duopoly.[9]

As timely as it seems, the management dilemma depicted above is not new. In fact, descriptions of "hybrid" organizations designed to enable companies to be lean and agile simultaneously were common in the 1950s and 1960s.[10] (Interestingly, these organizational models were pioneered by rapidly growing technology start-ups in the aerospace and computer industries.) One of these hybrid designs—the matrix—was originally billed as the "obvious organizational solution" to the need for control and efficiency, while simultaneously enabling flexibility and speed of response.[11] Decades ago, proponents of the matrix argued for an "adaptive, information-intensive, team-based, collaborative, and empowered" organization—all characteristics of today's twenty-first century organizations.

But companies that adopted the hybrid designs of the 1960s and 1970s soon learned that the new structures and systems bred conflict, confusion, information overload, and costly duplication of resources. Bartlett and Ghoshal discuss why many firms adopted the matrix only to abandon it several years later: "Top-level managers are losing control of their companies. The problem is not that they have misjudged the demands created by an increasingly complex environment and an accelerating rate of environmental change, nor that they have failed to develop strategies appropriate to the new challenges. The problem is that their companies are organizationally incapable of carrying out the sophisticated strategies they have developed. Over the past 20 years, strategic thinking has outdistanced organizational capabilities."[12]

Is History Repeating Itself?

Given such problems, we might legitimately ask, "If these hybrid organizations failed in the past, why are we trying them again?" Interestingly, one of the major sources of difficulty with the matrix was the dramatic increase in the need for timely information to manage it successfully.[13] While the hierarchy managed complexity by minimizing it, the matrix demanded that managers deal with complexity directly. Product managers had to coordinate their plans and operations with functional managers. Country managers had to coordinate activities with headquarters. And senior managers,

---

[9] A *duopoly* is an industry controlled by two large competitors. In the U.S., the Sherman Antitrust Act prevents one player from gaining monopoly control.

[10] T. Burns and G. M. Stalker, *The Management of Innovation* (London: Tavistock, 1961); J. Woodward, *Industrial Organization, Theory and Practice* (London: Oxford University Press, 1965); J. D. Thompson, *Organizations in Action* (New York: McGraw-Hill, 1967); P. Lawrence and J. Lorsch, *Organization and Environment* (Boston: Harvard Business School Press, 1967, 1986); L. Greiner, "Evolution and Revolution as Organizations Grow," *Harvard Business Review* 50, no. 4 (1972), pp. 37–46; J. Galbraith, *Designing Complex Organization* (Reading, MA: Addison Wesley, 1973).

[11] C. Bartlett and S. Ghoshal, *Managing across Borders: The Transnational Solution* (Boston: Harvard Business School Press, 1991).

[12] Ibid.

[13] Research in the mid-1960s suggested that successful firms operating in uncertain and complex environments developed systems to improve vertical and lateral information processing in the firm. See J. Galbraith, *Designing Complex Organizations* (Reading, MA: Addison Wesley, 1973); and P. Lawrence and J. Lorsch, *Organization and Environment* (Boston: Harvard Business School Press, 1986).

FIGURE 2.2
**Building Lean,
Yet Agile,
Enterprises**

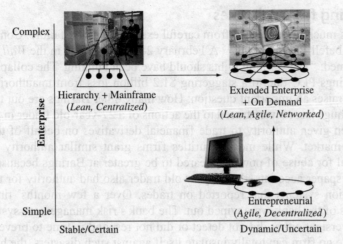

attempting to reconcile overall organization performance and plan corporate strategy, were faced with a dizzying array of conflicting information.

In the large hierarchical companies of the 1960s and 1970s, paper-based and word-of-mouth information moved slowly and channels of communication were limited. While the mainframe computer systems of the day helped process some of this information, they were designed, like the hierarchy itself, to support centralized decision making and hierarchical communication. The microcomputer revolution of the 1980s provided tools to decentralize information processing—which helped improve local decision making—but the technology to support both local and enterprisewide information sharing and communication was inadequate.

Only recently has information technology (IT) become capable of meeting the information challenge inherent in the organization design challenge discussed above (see Figure 2.2). The "networked IT revolution," which began in the 1980s and picked up speed with the commercialization of the Internet and related innovations, has made possible new approaches to communicating and sharing information that redefine organizational possibilities. IBM CEO, Sam Palmisano, termed this new approach: "Business On Demand" and has focused IBM's over 300,000 employee workforce and its global network of partners on making it a reality for IBM and its customers. He describes an On Demand enterprise as one that "unites information, processes, and people to create an enterprise in which end-to-end processes are integrated across a company, an industry, and globally to enable it to respond with speed and flexibility to any customer demand, market opportunity, or external threat."[14]

How can executives exploit the power of emerging IT infrastructures to enable organizations to act big and small simultaneously? Technology is not enough. New approaches to organizing and managing are required.

---

[14] L. M. Applegate, et al., "IBM's Decade of Transformation (B): A Vision for On Demand," Harvard Business School Publishing (No. 805-131), p. 1.

Learning from Mistakes

There is much to be learned from careful examination of a failure. Consider the disaster that befell Barings Bank.[15] A February 28, 1995, article in the *Wall Street Journal*, proclaimed: "The warning lights should have been blinking. The collapse of 233-year-old Barings PLC due to a staggering $1.2 billion loss from unauthorized derivatives trading raises an important question: How many other Barings are out there?"[16]

The huge losses were traced to the actions of a 27-year-old trader in Singapore who had been given authority to trade financial derivatives on behalf of the firm on the futures market. While most securities firms grant similar authority to traders, the potential for abuse of power appeared to be greater at Barings because, according to the newspaper accounts, the 27-year-old trader also had authority for the back-office transaction systems that reported on trades. Over a few months' time, the capital reserves of the bank were wiped out. The bank's risk management systems and executive oversight either did not detect or did not respond in time to prevent disaster.

While no firm can totally insulate itself against such disasters, the hierarchy specifies a number of structures and systems that help to safeguard a large firm.[17] Authority systems limit decision making and actions by strict *segregation of responsibility and duties, standardization of jobs, direct supervision,* and *restricted access to information and assets everywhere but the very top of the firm.* In theory, the hierarchy is designed so that, short of sabotage, no single employee or work unit can make a decision or take an action that can immediately threaten the entire organization. Even at the top of a firm, the CEO is responsible to a board of directors that includes external members representing shareholder interests.

Similarly, hierarchical control systems are designed to ensure tight control of operating processes through multiple intersecting checks and balances. At lower levels, control systems are based on *action controls*—employees are told exactly what they are supposed to do and supervisors watch to see that they do it.[18] As one moves up in the hierarchy, managers are evaluated and compensated based on their ability to meet predefined performance criteria; these *results controls* help focus managerial attention and actions on organizational priorities and ensure coordination of actions and decisions across functional boundaries. *Personnel controls* ensure that the right people with the right skills are recruited, hired, developed, motivated, and retained. Finally, *transaction controls*—accurate and complete documentation of financial and legal transactions with regular review by senior executives, the board of directors, and external auditors—ensure risk and asset management.

Current "new age organization" buzzwords exhort executives to empower their people and expand their areas of responsibility; to wipe out middle management ranks and create self-managing teams. *But they do not specify how control and authority are to*

---

[15] R. Stevenson, "Markets Shaken as a British Bank Takes a Big Loss," *New York Times,* Feb. 27, 1995; G. Millman, "Barings Collapses: Financial System Bears Up Well," *Wall Street Journal,* Feb. 28, 1995.

[16] S. Lypin and G. B. Krecht, "How Many Other Barings Are There?" *Wall Street Journal,* Feb. 28, 1995.

[17] In small, privately held firms, authority for most decisions is retained by the CEO/founder, and controls are based on direct oversight and supervision.

[18] K. Merchant, *Rewarding Results* (Boston: Harvard Business School Press, 1989); R. N. Anthony, *The Management Control Function* (Boston: Harvard Business School Press, 1988).

be maintained once the traditional systems have been disrupted. Executives often learn important lessons about the complexity of organizational control and authority systems as they embark upon these change initiatives. Unfortunately some—like the executives at Barings Bank—learn their lesson too late.

Analysis of both failure and success has clarified several important lessons for designing organizations that can develop the "sense and respond" capabilities required of today's fast-paced, complex, and volatile business environment.

- **Speed Counts, but Not at the Expense of Control.**   When the business environment is unstable, speed counts. New products must be introduced ever more quickly; order fulfillment cycles must be cut dramatically; and executives are exhorted to create organizations that can turn on a dime. But we know that taking one's time has its advantages. A driver racing along the freeway at 55 miles per hour is much more vulnerable to serious injury if something unexpected happens. Decisions must be made quickly; there is no margin for error. Skill and expertise—especially in dealing with unforeseen circumstances—are critical. Constant vigilance is necessary. In short, the faster we go, the more important it is—and the harder it is—to keep control of our car. Executives of fast-cycled organizations face the same dilemma. The faster the pace, the greater the need to monitor business operations and clearly define and enforce the rules of the road.

- **Empowerment Is Not Anarchy.**   When asked to define the term *empowerment,* some executives describe vague efforts to "push decision making down the line." Others equate empowerment with "getting rid of (or bypassing) middle management." Most have a hard time describing exactly who will make what decisions and fail to recognize that decisions concerning who has *authority and accountability* to make a decision, take action, or commit resources on behalf of the firm are tightly linked to a more complex set of organization design features. These features include structure (how people are grouped into units and how those units coordinate activities to develop and deliver products and services to customers); reporting relationships and power (both formal and informal); and incentives and performance management (compensation, evaluation, and measurement systems). Many learn the hard way that isolated efforts to empower employees can lead to disaster when not accompanied by a more comprehensive redefinition of authority and control throughout the organization. For example, in an empowered organization, senior executives must be *more* involved, not less; and organizational boundaries and value systems must be more clearly communicated, closely monitored, and consistently enforced.

- **Transforming an Organization Requires More Than Just Changing the Structure.**   It is not enough to simply take out layers or redraw boxes on an organization chart. The resulting organizational confusion from structure changes can help to shake up an entrenched organization and create the "conditions" for change, but structure change alone cannot harness the energy of the workforce to recreate an organization with a common purpose and direction. Nor can simple changes in structure promote the alignment of people, processes, and information needed to make decisions and take actions in a complex and volatile business environment.

These three key lessons from the field suggest that building the capabilities required to execute strategy in a fast-paced, uncertain business environment requires that managers adopt a comprehensive approach to organization design that includes analysis and realignment of capabilities within five key areas of business model design: processes, people and partners, organization and culture, infrastructure, and leadership and governance. Improved access to information and high capacity networked communication systems are core elements of redesign in all five areas.

Information, Organization, and Control

> Organizations are information systems. They are communication systems. And they are decision-making systems . . . If one thinks about it, every aspect of organizational functioning depends on information processing of one form or another.[19]

We have long known that organizations are information processing systems.[20] As such, limitations in vertical and horizontal information processing capacity directly influences the range of organizational choices available to managers as they attempt to execute strategy. We also know that the ability to align and adapt an organization's strategy and capabilities to the demands of a turbulent business environment is essential for building a high performance organization.[21]

Earlier in this chapter, we described that executives spent the past two decades searching for a new organizational model that would enable their organization to survive and prosper in an increasingly volatile, complex, networked environment. Executives faced two key organizational design challenges as they attempted to design organizations and build the capabilities. As we see below, success in addressing these two challenges requires that we break through previous information processing capacity limitations.

Organizing for Innovation and Execution

As executives struggle to build a lean, yet agile, organization we see them making a common mistake; they make changes to portions of their operations without considering the impact on other parts of the organization or on partners, suppliers, or even customer organizations and are surprised when the results fall short of their goals. For example, a consumer products firm attempted to accelerate the rate of new product development without ensuring that the supply chain, manufacturing, and order fulfillment processes could handle the increased complexity. They failed to view their organization as a set of integrated, horizontal operating processes that must be redesigned in concert. Not surprisingly, chaos resulted.[22] Suppliers could

---

[19] G. Morgan, *Images of Organizations* (Thousand Oaks, CA: Sage Publications, 1997), p. 78.

[20] P. Lawrence and J. Lorsch, *Organization and Environment* (Boston: Harvard Business School Press, 1966); J. Galbraith, *Organization Design* (Reading, MA: Addison-Wesley, 1977).

[21] R. Miles and C. Snow, "Organizations: New Concepts for New Forms," *California Management Review* 28 (1986), pp. 62–73; M. Hammer and J. Champy, *Reengineering the Corporation* (New York: Harper Business, 1993); J. Collins and J. Porras, *Built to Last* (New York: Harper Business, 1994).

[22] It is important to note that the consumer products firm did make changes to isolated functional activities, but no attempt was made at end-to-end process redesign.

not handle the demand, manufacturing defects rose, and inventory piled up in the warehouses.

Having failed in their first process redesign attempts, the consumer products firm executives launched a second project—this time to integrate their new products development process with their supply chain, manufacturing, and order fulfillment processes. They eliminated bottlenecks and squeezed excess time and cost out of end-to-end operations. Yet they still fell short of intended goals.

This example highlights two common problems: (1) failure to redesign end-to-end processes; and (2) failure to realign operations with other components of the organization design (e.g., organization structure, control, authority systems, incentives, culture). Both problems cause failures of execution. The consumer products firm ran headlong into the first problem when executives attempted to accelerate new product development without consideration for the end-to-end process. They increased the number of products and product variations, the rate of new product development, and the number of marketing campaigns and promotions. These actions dramatically increased operating complexity. Plans created by product managers and approved months in advance were being revised by field sales employees attempting to respond to local customer needs and competitive response. At the same time, marketing managers began offering promotions within targeted customer accounts. But, neither manufacturing nor logistics were in on the decision nor were they informed in a timely enough manner to adjust supply and production schedules. Not surprisingly, within a short time, the company was out of control.

The problems during the second project were traced to the fact that the executives had failed to change the way the newly streamlined and integrated processes were aligned with control, authority systems, and so on. As a result, the real-time business intelligence and early warning systems needed to make decisions and take actions in these faster time frames were not in place. Opportunities were missed and problems went undiscovered.

The consumer products firm learned several important lessons from the series of problems they encountered. "I don't think any of us fully appreciated how highly leveraged and integrated our business truly was until the abortive attempt at accelerating new product development," the CEO explained. "The problems were so abrupt and severe that it made a lasting impression on all of us. Two major lessons came from this situation. First, it became very clear that we needed to recast our vision for change as an enterprisewide initiative rather than just a change within a specific function. Despite our functional organization, our operations were highly integrated. We couldn't make a change in one area without causing problems somewhere else. Second, we became aware that as we sped up our processes we needed to provide much more timely information to the people on the line that were being asked to respond more quickly within a much more complicated and less structured role. Finally, we needed to bring functional managers together as teams, which we called area operating teams, and provide them with the authority and accountability to coordinate and control these end-to-end processes."

When attempting to build the capabilities to sense and respond quickly and effectively, executives like those at the consumer products firm discussed above are finding that it is important to recognize that organizational control is determined by two

FIGURE 2.3 Streamlining Operating and Management Process

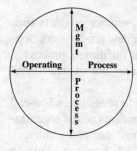

1. **The business cycle is composed of two types of processes:**

   Operating Processes: The activities through which an organization designs, produces, markets, delivers, and supports its products or services.

   Management Processes: The activities through which an organization *manages* the design, production, marketing, delivery, and support of its products or services.

2. **Many companies attempt to streamline the business cycle by streamlining operating processes without a corresponding streamlining of management processes.**

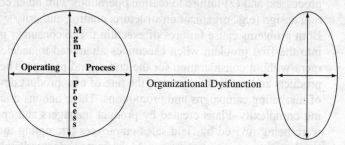

Organizational Dysfunction

3. **The key is to streamline, integrate, and "time synchronize" both operating and management processes.**

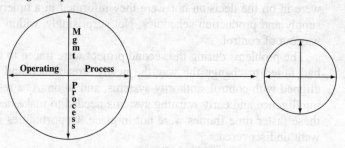

tightly integrated sets of processes. Operating processes are the series of activities that define how a firm designs, produces, distributes, markets, sells, and supports its products and services. Management processes are activities that define strategic direction, and coordinate and control operations. As executives attempt to respond to a much faster business cycle, both operating and management processes must be—not only streamlined—but also *integrated and synchronized* (see Figure 2.3). The ability to design a firm that is innovative and responsive, while also "in control" also requires a fundamental redesign in management processes.

A traditional hierarchy focuses on standardization of jobs and direct supervision—a "compliance" model of control. The emerging organizational model for a fast-cycled, more complex global network economy requires a "learning" model of control that preserves flexibility and fosters commitment.[23] Systems thinking—the ability to see a situation or problem in its totality is at the heart of learning. It demands an understanding

[23] R. Walton, *Up and Running* (Boston: Harvard Business School Press, 1988).

FIGURE 2.4   **Redefining Control Systems**

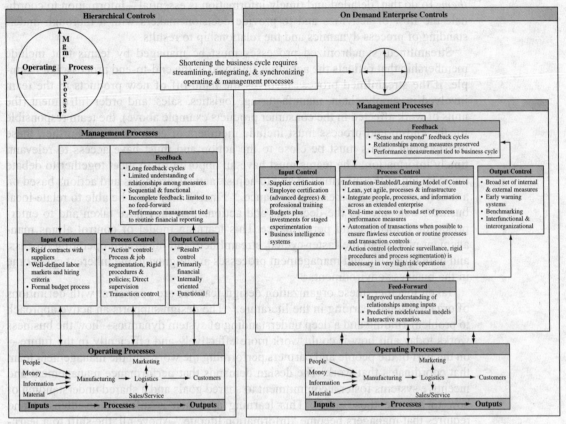

of the causal relationships between individual components of a system and the whole; this understanding of causal relationships must then be linked to the performance of the system in accomplishing goals[24] (see Figure 2.4).

A learning model of control is founded on a deep understanding of core operating processes. Reminiscent of Frederick Taylor's compulsion to define the most efficient means of turning out a product of 100 percent consistency, it begins with streamlining and synchronizing operating processes.[25] But there the similarity ends. Rather than segregate

[24] P. Shrivastava, "A typology of organizational learning systems," *Journal of Management Studies* 20 (1983), pp. 7–28; Walsh, and Ungson, "Organizational Memory," *Academy of Management Review* 16 (1991), pp. 57–91; H. Simon, "Bounded Rationality and Organizational Learning," *Organization Science* 1 (1991), p. 133; P. Senge, The *Fifth Discipline: The Art and Practice of the Learning Organization* (New York: Doubleday, 1990); D. Garvin, "Building a Learning Organization," *Harvard Business Review,* July–August, 1993.

[25] The principles of scientific management, which specified the careful analysis and design of operations to achieve maximum efficiency and consistency, were an important foundation for the design of hierarchical organizations. F. Taylor, *The Principles of Scientific Management* (New York: Harper and Row, 1911).

and structure those processes, executives seek to *integrate and continuously improve them*. To do that, detailed and timely information is essential—information to coordinate the flow of activities and to provide decision makers with a thorough understanding of process dynamics and the relationship to results.

Streamlined, synchronized processes must be managed by teams that include membership that reflects the activities involved in the end-to-end process. For example, if the streamlined process involves the hand-off of new products to the team involved in supply chain, manufacturing, logistics, sales, and order fulfillment (the units of work affected in the consumer products example above), the team responsible for the end-to-end process must include members of each function. Further, these management teams must be close to the action and must have access to relevant, timely information. The teams must have an opportunity to meet together to debate the meaning of the information and to adjust tactical strategies and actions based on a timely review of business performance.[26] Finally, they must be able to relate local business outcomes to the decisions and actions that they have taken and to enterprisewide priorities and performance. This learning model of control aligns management process to the faster-cycled, streamlined, and integrated operating process, and both operating and management processes are aligned to the inherent cycle time in the business environment.

Taken together, these organization design features are consistent with definitions of organizational learning in the literature.[27] The design supports an active approach to problem-finding and a deep understanding of system dynamics—how the business works today and how it could work more effectively and efficiently in the future—on the part of the people and partners performing the work and the management team that coordinates that work. The design demands that performance management and incentive systems foster a commitment to shared goals and a shared understanding of how to achieve those goals. This learning approach is information-intensive and requires that managers become "information literate." Above all, the shift to a learning model of management when combined with flawless execution of end-to-end processes requires that we resolve the paradox between tight control and flexibility and between organizing for execution and organizing for innovation. (Appendix 2A summarizes design features of the hierarchy, entrepreneurial, and an on demand network organization.)

Organizing for Accountability and Collaboration

Empowerment, teams, and collaborative organizations—these modern-day buzzwords describe different facets of organizational authority structures and systems: the formal and informal structures, coordinating mechanisms, responsibilities, and incentives that define the distribution of power and accountability within a firm.

---

[26] While IT can support the more intense nature of communication and information sharing, face-to-face dialog remains at the heart of a learning model of control in complex, turbulent, and uncertain business environments. See R. Simon, *Levers of Control* (Boston: Harvard Business School Press, 1995) for an excellent description of the design and implementation of "interactive" control systems.

[27] Refer back to citations in footnote 20.

FIGURE 2.5   **Redefining Authority Systems**

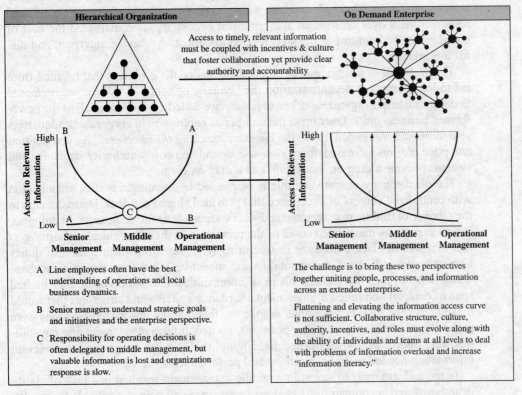

Hierarchical Organization	On Demand Enterprise

Access to timely, relevant information must be coupled with incentives & culture that foster collaboration yet provide clear authority and accountability

A Line employees often have the best understanding of operations and local business dynamics.

B Senior managers understand strategic goals and initiatives and the enterprise perspective.

C Responsibility for operating decisions is often delegated to middle management, but valuable information is lost and organization response is slow.

The challenge is to bring these two perspectives together uniting people, processes, and information across an extended enterprise.

Flattening and elevating the information access curve is not sufficient. Collaborative structure, culture, authority, incentives, and roles must evolve along with the ability of individuals and teams at all levels to deal with problems of information overload and increase "information literacy."

Traditionally, the formal distribution of authority within an organization has been viewed as a trade-off between centralization and decentralization (see Figure 2.5). Organizations were considered networks of relationships among principals (owners and senior executives) and self-interested "agents."[28] In hierarchical organizations, the cost and risk of coordinating local operations and aligning individual interests was minimized by centralizing decision making, structuring operations, and developing a deep hierarchy so that operations were executed efficiently and according to clearly defined procedures. This approach assumed that centrally located executives and decision makers had access to the information they needed to understand local business dynamics. It also assumed that they had the time and expertise to analyze the information to ensure that decisions optimized the best interests of the corporation with the best interests of local decision makers.

As the complexity, uncertainty, and volatility in the business environment intensified, it became increasingly difficult to satisfy these assumptions. During the 1990s,

---

[28] M. Jensen and W. Meckling, "Theory of the Firm: Managerial Behavior, Agency Costs, and Ownership Structure," *Journal of Financial Economics* (1973), pp. 305–360; E. Fama, "Agency Problems and the Theory of the Firm," *Journal of Political Economics* (1980), pp. 288–307.

the solution adopted by many executives was to decentralize decision making to increasingly more focused and autonomous profit centers—favoring speed and responsiveness over centralized authority. But decentralization increased the cost of coordination and control as the staff needed to collect, synthesize, interpret, and distill information.

The president of a large, global oil company called the problems that resulted from his failed attempts at decentralization the "tyranny of control." "When we attempted to decentralize our organization," he recalled, "we added controllers in all of the newly formed business units. Over time, the number of controllers in corporate headquarters also increased. We ended up having *checkers checking the checkers!*" As competition and price erosion increased, these slow-to-respond and costly authority structures and systems became a drag on innovation and a drag on earnings.

The oil company executives initially responded by creating a matrix organization with centralized centers of excellence that provided shared services. Dramatic cuts in the number of middle management and staff were made at the same time. In doing so, the oil executives maintained some of the principles of the hierarchical authority system that was in place before the restructuring (e.g., functional segregation of duties and authority, individual accountability and incentives), but they unwittingly abandoned others (e.g., hierarchical chain of command, direct supervision, and limited span of control) and failed to implement alternative systems and structures that would make up for the loss. For example, despite the fact that the downsized positions were primarily information processing positions, no new information processing capabilities were added. Employees in the field found that they no longer had the relevant information needed to make decisions and performance suffered.

In the end, attempts to streamline middle management resulted in a lack of clarity in authority and accountability. Local managers were still held accountable for results, but so too were group executives. As we have learned in studies of complex organizations, when "everyone is accountable, no one is accountable."[29]

As executives attempt to design organizations for both innovation and execution, we must rethink the nature of authority. No longer can it be viewed as a simple, linear trade-off between individual authority and collaboration. Instead, managers must clearly identify authority and accountability yet, as discussed earlier, must simultaneously ensure that executives accountable for various activities within an integrated process get together to analyze timely, relevant information on process performance and results. How is this reflected in changes in organization design? Authority continues to be vested in a single individual, while an executive team, similar to the governing board of directors of a public company, share accountability for end-to-end process performance. Not only must teams ensure that effective decisions can be made and executed, they also represent the important "checks and balances" that help guard against organizational failure when employees are empowered with broad authority and accountability.

Shared incentives (e.g., team-based incentives and employee stock ownership plans) augment and reinforce shared authority and help align individual, team, and

[29] S. Snook, *Friendly Fire: The Accidental Shootdown of U.S. Blackhawks over Northern Iraq* (New Jersey: Princeton, 2002).

organizational priorities. Since personal accountability must still be maintained, however, performance evaluations and incentives must also recognize performance against individual goals in addition to team and organizational goals. At the organizational level, stretch targets help intensify effort, clarify priorities, focus attention, and support a commitment to collaborate among independent divisions.[30]

As such, while it no longer directs how the organization operates, the hierarchical chain of command—albeit flatter—still remains to ensure clear lines of accountability and authority. And in many firms, functional units are still in place, but are becoming centers of functional excellence and career development.

In general, authority for operating strategy development and its execution is moving from corporate headquarters to the field. Interfunctional (and at times interorganizational) operating teams are being inserted into the middle of the firm, where they are granted broad authority for defining operating strategy and the processes, systems, and organizational arrangements to carry out and manage it. They are being held accountable for profitability, stakeholder satisfaction, operating process design, and continuous improvement. They coordinate their businesses (both inside and outside their organizational boundaries) using face-to-face and IT-enabled information sharing, networked communication, and ad hoc adjustment. Work teams are being formed at the line, and broader authority for defining work and the specific activities to carry it out are being pushed down from the middle to the line.

[30] "Stretch" targets are performance goals that exceed the level of output that can be predicted based on historical data. The degree of "stretch" and policies for how to manage the failure to achieve performance targets are discussed in more detail in "Designing and Managing the Information Age Organization," Harvard Business School Publishing (No. 196-003).

APPENDIX 2A   Characteristics of the Hierarchy, Entrepreneurial, and Networked Organization

Characteristic	Hierarchy	Entrepreneurial	Networked
Process integration and synchronization	• Process activities segregated into distinct tasks managed by functions. • Activities are synchronized during yearly planning sessions.	• Process activities defined on an ongoing basis by the people doing the work. • Activities synchronized through ad hoc discussion (face-to-face, e-mail, phone).	• Process activities integrated and synchronized through the flow of information in IT systems. • Changes discussed and planned through frequent interactions among those doing the work (face-to-face, e-mail, phone). • In the case of unstructured and uncertain activities, teams may meet daily or weekly to plan activities.
Process cycle time	• Operating cycle time based on organization's management cycle time. • For highly structured, routine, automated processes (e.g., factory operations), cycle time can be shortened. • In unstructured situations, time and inventory buffers used to manage uncertainty.	• The operating cycle time based on the cycle time of changes in the business environment. • Operating activities not structured, as a result, all activities managed in the same, unstructured way.	• Information on the market, industry, and operations available and acted on in real time. • The cycle time of operating activities approaches the cycle time of changes in the business environment.
Process complexity	• The inherent complexity of the business environment minimized through structure and slow response to change. • Standard products and services mass produced for mass markets to reduce business complexity. • Processes structured to reduce operating complexity.	• Start-up firms offer a limited product set to a limited market. • Within this simple business environment, significant customization provided to ensure that products meet the requirements of individual customers.	• Despite significant business complexity, real-time information and sophisticated analytical tools enable products and service to be customized for increasingly smaller customer segments. • At the limit, a company can personalize for a "market of one."

Characteristic	Hierarchy	Entrepreneurial	Networked
Management cycle time	• Defined around yearly planning and budgeting systems. • Yearly and quarterly performance monitoring and reporting dictated by country-level regulations for public and private firms.	• Management processes defined by the founder, often ad hoc. • Direct involvement of the founder in most decisions and activities cause the management cycle time to be timed directly to the business cycle.	• Real-time information and sophisticated analytics enable a large firm to manage complexity directly rather than managing through complexity reduction. • Real-time information and reporting enables the management cycle time to be tied directly to the operating cycle, which, in turn, has been timed to the inherent cycle time of the business environment.
Scope and granularity of business understanding	• Understanding of business limited to specific job an employee is hired to do. At operating levels, scope is limited to a specific task. Only top management team understands business dynamics across scope of enterprise but depth of understanding of any one portion of the business limited. • Employees at all levels unable to link specific decisions and actions to the firm's overall performance. • Planning targets and goals set on a yearly basis and monitored and adjusted quarterly. This results in quarterly cycles of feedback/feedforward. • Understanding business dynamics predicated on the organization operating as originally structured.	• Because of their direct involvement in all activities and decisions, founders, and employees have an in-depth understanding of the business. • Business performance monitored and communicated in real time, enabling founders and employees to link actions to performance in a real-time cycle of feedback/feedforward. • Operations continually adjusted and refined in an ad hoc manner.	• Detailed information on the market, industry and business performance, and operations enables operating teams (which may include customers, suppliers, and business partners) to refine and adjust goals and activities *within the scope of their authority*, based on changes in the business environment. • Operating teams, rather than individuals, have authority over a broader set of business activities (processes), and senior management, like the founders in an entrepreneurial venture, take a more active role in monitoring business operations and participating in high-risk decisions.

(continued)

APPENDIX 2A Characteristics of the Hierarchy, Entrepreneurial, and Networked Organization (Continued)

Characteristic	Hierarchy	Entrepreneurial	Networked
Information and business literacy	• Employee understanding of business dynamics and information limited to specific assigned tasks.	• Employees and founders have access to all information required to run the company and are expected to use that information to solve problems, make decisions, and take actions to accomplish firm's goals.	• Employees at all levels have access to information on business goals and operations across a wide range of activities, and, working in teams within the scope of their collective authority, are expected to use that information to make decisions and take actions to accomplish firm's goals. • As decision authority pushed down, shared values become an important component of strategic control.
Boundaries and values	• Activities and authority segmented so that no one individual has the power or authority (short of sabotage) to cause irreparable harm to company. (Even the CEO reports to a board of directors.) • In areas of high risk, special security precautions (e.g., restricted access, direct supervision) prevent sabotage. • Since broad decision-making authority limited to upper levels of management, companywide value systems not as crucial.	• Boundaries and values created in real time and transmitted directly by founders. • Founders directly involved in most decisions and actions. • The size of the company limits risk to the founders and a small number of investors.	
Units of work and chain of command	• Work highly segregated by function with duplication of resources within each operating unit. • Deep chain of command who report through business unit heads to corporate headquarters.	• Simple, functional chain of command. • Flat chain of command (3 or less) with functional managers reporting directly to the founder.	• Flat, team-based chains of command. • Market-focused operating teams composed of functional managers report to business unit managers, which report to corporate headquarters. • Broad chains of authority with work teams reporting to operating management teams.

Characteristic	Hierarchy	Entrepreneurial	Networked
Span of management	• Each manager supervises 5–7 direct reports.	• Varies with the size and stage of development. Spans of more than 10 are common.	• Spans of 30 or more are common.
Corporate headquarters	• Large corporate headquarters staff assume major responsibility for planning, budgeting, and performance management. • Large staff of analysts required to plan, monitor, and coordinate work.	• Single site for headquarters and operations. • Little formal planning, budgeting, and performance monitoring. • Operations planned, coordinated, and managed by those who do the work.	• Small corporate headquarters with minimal responsibility for planning, performance monitoring, and organizationwide resource management. • While formal planning, budgeting, and performance monitoring still take place, planning, coordinating, and managing operating activities take place in operating units.
Coordinating mechanisms	• Work is primarily coordinated through direct supervision and the chain of command.	• Work is coordinated through ad hoc adjustments by those directly involved in the work.	• Work coordinated through the integrated flow of information. • Routine work coordinated through real-time feedback and adjustment. • Important decisions and actions coordinated through meetings of operating managers and employees who analyze real-time operating information to continually adjust and refine goals and their execution.
Roles	• Except at top levels of firm, roles, and accountability defined in formal job descriptions. • Roles based on functional expertise and skills.	• Minimal to no formal specification of roles. • Emphasis on hiring innovators ("pioneers").	• All organizations, regardless of size, require innovators ("pioneers") and operators ("settlers"). • Senior executives must be skilled at leading and engaging.

(continued)

APPENDIX 2A Characteristics of the Hierarchy, Entrepreneurial, and Networked Organization (Continued)

Characteristic	Hierarchy	Entrepreneurial	Networked
Career progression	• Employees advance through functional hierarchical progression. • Seniority is as important as (and in some organizations is more important than) expertise and performance as a criteria for advancement.	• Career progression is often lateral. • In a rapidly growing firm, employees may move down in rank as senior managers are hired to ensure the leadership required by the more complex organization. Original employees may leave at this point.	• Self-managing work teams define work and how it gets done. • Minimal opportunities for advancement within flat hierarchical chains of command. • Innovators may have an opportunity to launch and grow new businesses. • Expanded jobs, increased lateral movement, and ownership incentives make work environment more challenging and rewarding.

Summary   Executives made significant efforts during the past decade to reorganize to meet the challenges of operating in a more dynamic, hyper-competitive world. But as we entered the twenty-first century it became clear that even more radical change is required. As the Internet transforms markets, industries, and the organizations that compete within them, executives are forced to respond even more quickly, deliver higher quality and more customized products and services, and cut costs even more deeply. In large companies, layers of management have been cut and spans of authority increased to the point where many executives worry that their organizations would spin out of control. Entrepreneurial start-ups must grow and expand their products and markets without losing their agility, speed, and responsiveness to local needs. In short, the assumptions behind traditional organizational models, such as the hierarchy and the entrepreneurial model, were pushed to the limit and found lacking.

It has been shown time and time again in history that crisis is a precondition for the emergence of a new theory or model.[31] But when presented with crisis, most people do not immediately reject existing models. Instead, they attempt incremental adjustments that, over time, begin to blur the fundamental structure and assumptions upon which the old models were based. Practitioners are often the first to lose sight of old models as the familiar rules for solving problems become ineffective. At some point, total reconstruction is required. During the transition, however, there is frequently an overlap between the problems that can be solved by the old and new models. But no matter which is used, there is a decisive difference in the modes of solution.

This appears to be the point at which we now find ourselves. A crisis, largely driven by a fundamental mismatch between environmental demands and organizational capabilities, has called into question many of the assumptions of traditional organizational models. Academic thinking in this area is being led by practice. The lessons from managers in the field suggest that a new organizational model is emerging that harnesses the power of today's technologies in the hands of a more knowledgeable workforce to create networks of organizations that can act big and small at the same time. But these new models and capabilities are built on design principles we already know. The steps below can be used to guide you as you build the capabilities to execute strategy in the face of high levels of environmental turbulence and uncertainty.

The following questions can be used to guide organizational design decisions as executives attempt to leverage emerging networked IT that expand information processing capacity to enable "business on demand":

1. Have we identified the key activities and decisions needed to complete our projects and initiatives and reach our goals?

2. Do we have, or can we acquire, the resources (people and expertise, information, technology, equipment and supplies, capital) we need to be successful?

3. Have we correctly identified the activities and decisions that should be performed inside our organization and those that should be sourced from the outside?

4. Have we correctly grouped people and partners into teams and units that enable them to coordinate and control streamlined and integrated end-to-end processes?

[31] T. Kuhn, *The Structure of Scientific Revolution* (Chicago: University of Chicago Press, 1970).

5. Have we provided clear direction and the resources, support, and incentives to enable individuals, teams, and units to meet realistic stretch targets?

6. Have we designed and implemented the systems and structures required to coordinate and control activities, people, and partners to ensure efficient, high quality, best-in-class operations?

7. Do we have the systems, structures, and expertise needed to access, interpret, and communicate relevant, timely information and then respond quickly and successfully to opportunities and threats?

8. Have we effectively developed, organized, and leveraged the creativity and full potential of our people and partners?

9. Have we created a culture of shared values and behaviors that unite the organization and its partners around a common shared purpose and the achievement of both personal and shared goals?

CHAPTER 3

Extending the Enterprise[1]

A fundamental shift in the economics of information is underway—a shift that is less about any specific new technology than about the fact that a new behavior is reaching critical mass. Millions of people at home and at work are communicating electronically using universal, open standards. This explosion in connectivity is the latest—and for business strategists, the most important— wave in the information revolution . . . Over the next decade, a new economics of information will precipitate changes in the structure of entire industries and in the ways companies compete.[2]

Technology can sometimes catch us off guard. When Rutherford B. Hayes, the 19th president of the United States, saw a demonstration of the telephone in the late 1800s, he reportedly commented that, while it was a wonderful invention, businessmen would never use it. Hayes believed that people had to meet face-to-face to conduct substantive business affairs; and he was not alone in his assessment. Few of his contemporaries could foresee the profound changes that the telephone and other technologies of the day—including production machinery, transportation, electricity, and the telegraph— would bring. The shift from an agricultural to an industrial economy; the exodus of people from rural to urban areas; the shift from craft-based work to mass production; and the decline of small, owner-operated firms in favor of large, vertically integrated multinationals—these radical changes evolved incrementally and were most clearly understood when viewed retrospectively.

One such technology that has recently galvanized our attention is the Internet. Many consider the Internet a revolutionary technology that, like the telephone a century

---

[1] This chapter is adapted from L. M. Applegate, "Building Inter-Firm Collaborative Community: Uniting Theory and Practice," in *Collaboration and Community: Redefining the Role of Trust in 21st Century Business,* eds. C. Heckscher and P. Adler, Oxford University Press, (forthcoming 2005); and L. M. Applegate, "E-Business Models: Making Sense of the Internet Business Landscape." In *Information Technology and the New Enterprise: New Models for Managers,* eds. Gary W. Dickson and Gerardine DeSanctis (Upper Saddle River, NJ: Prentice-Hall Inc., 2001).

[2] P. B. Evans and T. S. Wurst, "Strategy and the Economics of Information," *Harvard Business Review,* September–October, 1997.

before, will radically change the way companies do business in the future. But, like most so-called revolutionary technologies, the Internet really represents the integration of a number of core technological innovations that evolved gradually over a period of years. Similarly, its impact on business and society will be a product of many evolutionary changes that have transformed organizations and the industries within which they compete. This chapter focuses on the impact of IT on industries and the organizations that do business within them. In Chapter 2 the focus was on building IT-enabled capabilities within firm boundaries. In this chapter, we examine the challenges of doing business across firm boundaries. As such, our focus is on the analysis of *business networks,* popularly called *ecosystems,* within which people and partners work together to achieve shared goals.

Understanding Business Networks

Companies need not trade off flexibility for integration in critical cross-company processes. By managing the activities of and relationships with suppliers as networks rather than production lines, companies can swap their tightly coupled processes for loosely coupled ones, thereby gaining much needed flexibility and improving their performance in the bargain.[3]

At the most basic level, organizations and the industries and markets within which they operate can be defined as networks of specialized nodes (units) that work together to achieve a common purpose.[4] As discussed in Chapter 2, organizational solutions enable these specialized units to manage interdependencies as they work together on tasks that require coordinated efforts. Chapter 2 examined IT-enabled organizational solutions among units inside a firm. This chapter extends that discussion to include organizational solutions among units that cross firm boundaries.[5] Two overarching design goals must be considered in the design of business networks, whether those networks are inside an organization or cross organization boundaries.[6]

- *Differentiation* defines how individuals, groups, and organizations are subdivided into specialized work units (nodes). This differentiation may include horizontal division of work into specialized "operating units," vertical division into power/authority levels, and spatial division into geographic or product groups. Differentiation enables a network to manage complexity, develop specialized expertise and assets, and focus attention and resources on accomplishing specific goals and tasks.

---

[3] J. Seely Brown and J. Hagel, "Loosening Up: How Process Networks Unlock the Power of Specialization," *McKinsey Quarterly,* Special Edition (2002), pp. 59–69.

[4] McEvily et al. "Trust as an Organizing Principle," *Organization Science* 14, no. 1 (1998), pp. 91–103.

[5] W. Baker, "Network Organizations in Theory and Practice," (ed. Nohria et. and Eccles), *Networks and Organizations: Structure, Form and Action* (Boston: Harvard Business School Press, 1992).

[6] Pioneering work on differentiation and integration as core organizational design principles was developed by P. Lawrence and J. Lorsch, *Organization and Environment: Managing Differentiation and Integration* (Boston: Harvard Business School Press, 1968); and J. Galbraith, *Designing Organizations: An Executive Guide to Strategy, Structure and Process Revised* (New York: Jossey Bass, 2001), among others. Baker (1992) applied these principles to the design of intra-firm and inter-firm business networks.

- *Integration* defines the relationships and links between nodes that are required to unite specialized individuals, units, and organizations to enable them to achieve a common purpose and create shared value. Three types of network relationships must be considered.[7]

  - *Task-based relationships* unite individuals, groups, or organizations that work together or sequentially to perform one or more activities in a process that creates economic output.

  - *Information- or expertise-based relationships* unite individuals, groups, or organizations that provide information or expertise required by the network.

  - *Social relationships* unite individuals, groups, or organizations to enable them to develop strong bonds of affiliation and identity.

Sociologists have found that stronger, deeper network relationships are required in environments characterized by increased complexity, uncertainty, and turbulence—especially when the network contains a large number of highly differentiated nodes that must work closely together to achieve a common goal.[8] Stronger, deeper relationships are also required in the presence of:

- Increased task interdependence secondary to the need to:
  - Produce customized products or deliver shared services.
  - Develop and deliver innovative and creative products, services, and solutions.
- Increased information/expertise interdependence secondary to the need to:
  - Share large amounts of real-time information.
  - Unite the perspectives of various actors to make sense of the information to support decisions and actions.
- Increased social interdependence secondary to:
  - A large number of divergent subcultures that must develop shared beliefs and a sense of trust to work together.
  - Incentives that reward cooperation and collaboration across highly differentiated subunits.
  - Leader preferences for shared vision and values.

While network relationships tend to be stronger among people and groups who are in close physical contact and are most "like" one another (e.g., within a single highly differentiated unit such as a functional unit within a hierarchy), network performance in complex, uncertain, and turbulent environments usually requires a dense network of diverse specialized assets (physical products and services, information and expertise, etc.) and the ability to quickly and effectively deploy those assets to create value for all members and the network as a whole.[9] This is balanced, of course, by the cost of

---

[7] M. Granovetter, "Economic Action and Social Structure: The Problem of Embeddedness," *American Journal of Sociology* 1 (1985), pp. 451–510; R. Burt, *Structural Holes: The Social Structure of Competition* (Cambridge: Harvard University Press, 1992).

[8] See Granovetter (1985) in footnote 7.

[9] See Burt (1992) in footnote 7.

developing and maintaining a diverse network of interdependencies and relationships. As such, redundant relationships that lead to the same resources may help to mitigate risk and increase the speed with which resources and assets can be leveraged and used, but they do so at an increased cost. One core proposition of this book is that shared, open-standard networked IT infrastructures and systems can support new approaches to managing and organizing the end-to-end flow of activities and information that greatly improve the ability of large, diverse networks—whether inside or outside an organization—to achieve short-term goals while also innovating for the future.

Executives face three key categories of decisions as they attempt to design high performance inter-firm business networks. These include decisions related to (1) network differentiation and unit groupings, (2) network integration and interdependencies, and (3) network ownership.

Framing Decisions Concerning Network Differentiation and Unit Groupings

Differentiation refers to the logic behind the choices that executives make when combining different activities, resources, and capabilities into unit groupings.[10] Unit grouping decisions are frequently tied to *functions* that need to be performed, *products* or *services* that need to be developed, and/or *customer* or *geographic markets* that need to be served.[11] Key decisions include:

1. What are the key capabilities and resources required to execute strategy and achieve our goals?
2. What activities must be performed to acquire or build those capabilities and resources?
3. How should these activities be grouped within specialized units (network nodes and subnets) to focus attention and resources on the development of best-in-class proprietary capabilities and to most efficiently and effectively accomplish goals?

As can be seen in Table 3.1, decisions concerning unit groupings are based on decreasing the cost and risk of coordinating and controlling activities *within* a specific unit grouping (node of a network) by enabling groups of people performing the same tasks and using the same resources to work closely together. Within a single unit, individuals may set goals and coordinate and control work through direct, face-to-face communications and actions or through a combination of face-to-face and technology-mediated communications and actions. More complex units (e.g., a division or organization) may use more formal organizational solutions that involve process design and authority, planning, budgeting, performance management, and incentive systems. These formal organizational solutions may involve both face-to-face and technology-mediated communications and actions.

---

[10] See P. Lawrence and J. Lorsch (1986), and J. Galbraith (2002) in footnote 6.

[11] D. Collis and C. Montgomery, *Corporate Strategy* (New York: McGraw-Hill/Irwin, 1997), p. 214.

TABLE 3.1 Options for Designing Differentiated Unit Groupings

Unit Groupings/Context	Design Logic	Design Goal
Functional Best suited to delivery of standardized products to mass markets within relatively stable, simple business environments.	Create units containing specialized activities required to perform a common function (e.g., marketing, R&D, manufacturing).	Focus attention and resources to enable efficient and effective execution of a common task. Build task expertise and related proprietary assets. Minimize coordination and control cost and risk related to task performance.
Product or Service Best suited in business environments characterized by rapid growth and evolution in the number or complexity of products and services.	Create units containing all activities required to design and build related families of products or services. In complex but stable environments, large product/service organizations may be formed at upper levels of a corporation or as stand-alone companies within an industry. Simple functional unit groupings are often present within these large product organizations. In dynamic environments, small product groups coordinate multifunctional teams that deliver customized solutions in niche markets.	Focus attention and resources to enable efficient and effective delivery of current products and services and to support the design, development, and launch of new products, services, and businesses.
Customer or Geographic Market Best suited in business environments characterized by rapid expansion into new customer segments, geographies, and/or rapidly changing expectations among small, but powerful, customer groups.	Create units containing all activities required to market, sell, and deliver customized products, services, or solutions to specific market segments. In complex, widely dispersed but stable markets, large marketing and sales organizations may be formed at the upper levels of a corporation or as stand-alone companies within an industry. Within these large organizations, simple, functional units may sell to a specific market. In dynamic, uncertain environments, small multifunctional market-facing groups may be needed to deliver customized solutions in niche markets.	Focus attention and resources to increase loyalty and lifetime value of key customers, market segments, and niches.

Framing Decisions Concerning Governance of Interdependencies

Once decisions have been made to define the ideal unit groupings, a second set of decisions must be made to determine the interdependencies and relationships among nodes. While many believe that these decisions are made in an orderly, linear sequence, in fact, the process is much "messier," with insights from one decision influencing decisions made earlier and later in the process. Key decisions include:

1. What are the key task, information/expertise, and affiliation/identity interdependencies that must be managed between specialized units located inside and outside the organization?

2. What organizational solutions are needed to coordinate and control key areas of interdependence among specialized units?

3. What configuration of organizational solutions should be used to ensure alignment and fit with the business environment and strategy to enable the network to fulfill its common purpose, achieve shared goals, and create value for all stakeholders?

An enduring principle of network design states that the choice of organizational solutions for integrating, coordinating, and controlling interdependencies and relationships among differentiated units depends on the context within which an organization operates.[12] During the twentieth century, three key interorganizational governance models—markets, hierarchies, and partnerships—emerged to meet the integration, coordination, and control challenges associated with different contexts. The design logic associated with these three governance choices is summarized in Table 3.2.

Market models of governance involve the simple exchange of goods, services, and payments, usually during a specific time period and with limited interaction or information sharing between the parties involved. While bonds of affiliation and identity may develop among members of the network, this affiliation and identity is related primarily to repeated purchase, use, and experience with a product or service—not to strong direct face-to-face interactions between suppliers and customers. The interaction between a consumer product manufacturer, such as Procter & Gamble, and the consumers that use its products is an example of a market transaction.[13]

In *hierarchical* models of governance, formal contracts and authority define the activities to be performed, the products or services to be provided, the price to be paid by each party, and the length of the relationship. These contracts are well-defined at the start and are clearly documented. The formal "terms of the contract" become the

---

[12] T. Burns and G. M. Stalker, *The Management of Innovation* (London: Tavistock, 1961); J. Woodward, *Industrial Organization, Theory and Practice* (London: Oxford University Press, 1965); J. D. Thompson, *Organizations in Action* (New York: McGraw-Hill, 1967); P. Lawrence and J. Lorsch, *Organization and Environment* (Boston: Harvard Business School Press, 1967, 1986); L. Greiner, "Evolution and Revolution as Organizations Grow," *Harvard Business Review*, 50, no. 4 (1972), pp. 37–46; J. Galbraith, *Designing Complex Organization* (Reading, MA: Addison Wesley, 1973).

[13] Inside a corporation, market-oriented governance models can be implemented by allowing independent units the freedom to either buy from an internal unit at a "market" price (often called a transfer price) or buy from external suppliers.

TABLE 3.2 Options for Designing Inter-Firm Governance

	Market	Hierarchy	Partnership
Business Context	Simple, short-term; best suited for discrete transactions with low levels of interdependency.	Stable, certain, structured; best suited for complex, but routine work.	Complex, uncertain, turbulent, hypercompetitive; best suited for creative, knowledge-based work and customized solutions.
Task Interdependency	Low; emphasize exchange of goods, services, and payments; no expectation that relationships continue over time.	Low to moderate; interdependencies are "hardwired," highly structured, and difficult to change; length of task relationship is specified by contracts.	High; requires frequent interaction and shared ethic of contribution; expectation that relationship will last beyond short-term contracts and projects.
Information/ Expertise Interdependency	Low; information and expertise needed to make decisions is readily available and non-proprietary; focus is on mass market; low levels of customization.	High *within* units; low *across* units; formal hierarchy tends to segregate info and expertise within diversified, specialized units.	High; extensive exchange of rich, detailed information; dynamically changing; customizable; nature of the work and problem requires that expertise be integrated across multiple specialized disciplines.
Affiliation/ Identity Interdependency	Low; short-term.	Low to moderate; structured based on position and reporting relationships; loyalty based on self-interest (although local work units can engender loyalty).	High; requires shared purpose and goals, shared beliefs and values—especially those related to the attainment of goals and toward the success of others; long-term affiliation and identity extend beyond loyalty to the institution; high levels of trust based on mutual expectations and confidence in the "behaviors and values" of others.
Coordination and Control	Supply and demand determine market price for a product/service offering with a specific bundle of features.	Formal contracts define job positions (or activities to be performed), procedures (how activities will be performed), information sharing, monitoring, and reporting.	Flexible, dynamic, and organic structure, processes and relationships enable agility and creativity; high levels of commitment required.

basis for defining responsibilities and obligations of each party, and for coordinating and controlling the exchange of goods, services, payments, and information and for managing interdependencies throughout the length of the contract. Joint ventures, in which two or more firms become an equity owner of a legally defined entity are another form of interorganizational hierarchical governance.

Partnership governance models are required when the interdependencies among specialized units are complex, uncertain, and critical to the success of the firms involved. As a result, neither market nor hierarchy governance models are sufficient. Partnerships require shared goals, complementary expertise and skills, high levels of trust among the parties, and networked integration of processes and work across organizational boundaries. The exchange of goods and services is ongoing, and the interactions and relationships must adapt to the changing priorities, needs, and expectations of the parties involved. Long-term partnerships often require significant investments in interactive governance systems (for example, joint boards, product councils, operating committees, and information and performance monitoring systems) these systems are used to carry out, coordinate, and control densely networked and interdependent activities. While features of a hierarchical and market form of governance may be used to support a partnership model of governance, the distinct feature of partnership-style governance is the frequent one-on-one personal interactions and trust that develop over time. This hybrid form of governance is discussed in more detail in the next section of this chapter.

Framing Decisions Concerning Network Ownership

While a complex business network may exhibit a wide variety of ownership models within subnets, the three dominant forms include:

- The majority of specialized units may be located inside a *corporation* or other legally defined organization.
- An *alliance* may be formed between two (or a small number of players).
- A diverse *community,* also called an ecosystem, of players representing different roles (e.g., suppliers, distributors, buyers) may work together to achieve shared goals.

Figure 3.1 provides a framework for categorizing business networks based on ownership and governance. As seen in Figure 3.1(a), within the industrial economy business environment of the first half of the twentieth century, executive decision making favored corporate ownership of all but the most simple, transactional activities that could be easily governed through market mechanisms or structured contracts.

During the late 1980s and early 1990s, executives began to break up deep hierarchies and shed noncore activities. Alliances were formed to manage activities across organizational boundaries, and these alliances were often supported by information systems that enabled electronic data interchange (EDI) and the coordination and control of transactions across firm boundaries. Depending on the level of uncertainty and the type of interdependence, hybrid forms of governance emerged and features of a partnership-style of governance became much more prevalent.

Given that EDI and interorganizational transaction processing systems were often needed to support the hybrid forms of governance—and given that, in the 1980s and early 1990s, these systems were built using proprietary technology—alliance membership

FIGURE 3.1   Emerging IT-Enabled Extended Enterprise Models

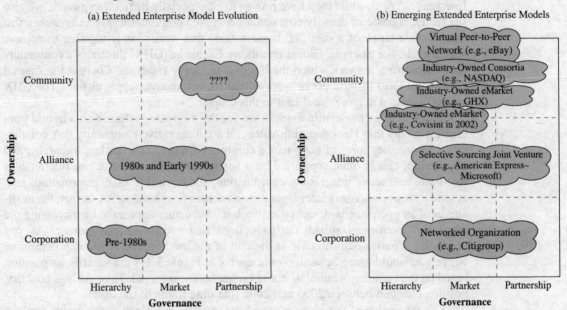

(a) Extended Enterprise Model Evolution   (b) Emerging Extended Enterprise Models

was limited to those organizations that adopted the same proprietary technology. Yet, despite these limitations, by the mid-1980s a few well-known examples of electronic communities had emerged in the travel industry (American Airlines SABRE system), the health care supply industry (American Hospital Supply), and in the securities industry (NASDAQ Securities Exchange). These examples became a model that executives used as they sought to exploit the Internet as an open, nonproprietary platform for sharing information and conducting business during the late 1990s.[14] Appendix 3A provides a taxonomy for classifying the emerging network business models of the late 1990s.

Initially many believed that widespread adoption of open-standard Internet technologies would cause business networks to evolve toward community forms of ownership governed by either trust-based partnerships or transaction-based market mechanisms. As seen in Figure 3.1(b), however, the emerging network business models of the twenty-first century represent a wide range of ownership and governance structures. We see the increasing importance of large, vertically integrated corporations—especially in industries that deliver information-based products and services, such as publishing and financial services. For example, the merger of Travelers Group and Citicorp to form Citigroup, created what many have called a "universal bank"—an intraorganizational business network composed of differentiated product, market, and geographic units that provides a one-stop shop for retail and commercial financial services.[15] In other industries, we see the increased importance of IT-enabled alliances,

[14] L. M. Applegate, "E-Business Models: Making Sense of the Internet Business Landscape," in *Information Technology and the New Enterprise: New Models for Managers,* eds. Gary W. Dickson and Gerardine DeSanctis (Upper Saddle River, NJ: Prentice-Hall, Inc., 2001).

[15] See L. M. Applegate, et al., "Citigroup 2003: Testing the Limits of Convergence (A) and (B)," Harvard Business School Publishing (Nos. 804-041 and 804-131) for a discussion of the Citigroup business model.

such as the one formed by American Express–Microsoft to develop American Express Interactive.[16] And, while they have proven to be especially difficult to govern, we also see the emergence of densely connected networked communities, or ecosystems, that unite a wide range of specialized organizations that work closely together to achieve shared goals. For example, Global Healthcare Exchange (GHX) illustrates a community form of business network within the health care supply chain and Covisint illustrates a community form of business network within the automotive supply chain.[17] The GHX case is discussed in more detail later in this chapter.

Across all three ownership models, we see the increasing reliance on a hybrid governance model that Hecksher and Adler call a collaborative community.[18] A collaborative community form of governance combines features of a market, hierarchy, and partnership, and is often supported by a sophisticated IT infrastructure that enables real-time, interactive integration, coordination, and control of task, information, and, at times, even relationship interdependencies across firm boundaries. In fact, the availability of an open standard, shared network infrastructure appears to be increasing the intra- and interorganizational design options that executives may pursue. As you review the Charles Schwab case at the end of the module, see if you can determine where you would place Schwab on the matrix in Figure 3.1. First identify its position based on the company's initial discount broker business model. Then analyze how that position changed between 2000 and 2002 (the time frame of the case).

The next section of this chapter provides a more detailed look at the design features and evolution of collaborative community governance models. The NASDAQ Securities Exchange provides a model for analyzing the emergence of collaborative community within the U.S. securities industry.

Designing Hybrid Governance Models

Neither the market nor the hierarchy is the ideal form of organization. Instead, each form of organization has its costs and each has its benefits . . .[19]

Traditional economic theory framed governance decisions as a choice between markets and hierarchies. In the former, principles of supply, demand, and pricing are used to coordinate and control the flow of goods and services across legally defined entities. In the latter, structure, systems, and authority are used to coordinate and control the flow of goods and services inside a legal entity—which can be a legally constituted organization, a joint venture, or a contractual relationship.

Transaction cost theory—so named because it focuses on transactions among discrete nodes on a network as the basic unit of analysis and the associated costs and risks

[16] See L. M. Applegate, "American Express Interactive" HBS (No. 802-022).

[17] L. M. Applegate and E. Collins, "Covisint (A): Building an Automotive Supply Chain Exchange," HBS (No. 805-110) addresses the challenges that the company faced in attempting to build a collaborative community within the hierarchically-structured automotive supply chain. A second (B) case is available to discuss the company's approach during 2004 and 2005 to address those challenges.

[18] C. Heckscher and P. Adler, *Collaboration and Community: Redefining the Role of Trust in 21st Century Business* (Oxford University Press, forthcoming, 2005).

[19] D. Collis and C. Montgomery, *Corporate Strategy, Resources and Scope of the Firm* (Chicago: Irwin, 1997), pp. 105 and 113.

of these transactions—argues that market forms of governance lead to greater efficiency and effectiveness *unless the cost and risk of using market mechanisms to coordinate and control interdependencies are higher than the cost and risk of hierarchy.*[20] Conditions that increase the cost and risk associated with market forms of governance include the (1) need to duplicate costly, proprietary assets that cannot be easily leveraged and shared across organizational boundaries; (2) need to settle frequent disputes among parties in a transaction; (3) increased cost and effort related to access and validation of information concerning transactions and price; and (4) need to join with others to increase market power.

Hierarchical models of governance provide an alternative form that can be used when the conditions for market failure are high.[21] Key to its power is the simple fact that executives within a legal entity have been vested with the authority to determine shared purpose and goals; define activities needed to accomplish goals; hire, compensate, and fire employees; and monitor, coordinate, and control activities, assets, and resources. Unified ownership and authority help to focus attention and resources on the pursuit of a common goal (e.g., maximization of corporate profits). Hierarchical forms of governance can be more efficient and effective than the market when high levels of uncertainty or inequalities in power increase the risk of market failure—especially when parties in a transaction must interact frequently to perform a task, share information, innovate, and develop expertise. In summary, while markets optimize lateral information processing among peers, hierarchies optimize vertical information processing.

But the hierarchy can also fail. The model works well to reduce uncertainty and opportunism when a business is operating within a stable, mature business context. Indeed, the hierarchy can be highly efficient and effective when structure, standardization, incentives, and supervision can be designed to ensure that each individual and unit acts in the best interests of executives and owners to achieve corporate goals. But, as was discussed in Chapter 2, the hierarchy often fails in turbulent, uncertain, hypercompetitive business contexts.

As discussed in the previous chapter, during the latter half of the twentieth century, evolving information technologies were a key driver of the turbulent, hypercompetitive conditions that destabilized traditional power bases and led to failure of the market and hierarchy in their pure form.[22] At the same time, increasingly more powerful information technologies dramatically increased both vertical and lateral information processing capacity to enable a new approach to coordinating and controlling intra- and inter-firm interdependencies that relied on learning and commitment rather than compliance. These new IT-enabled governance models provide a new business logic that enables executives to reevaluate decisions concerning which activities to own and which to source. They also enable the emergence of a new governance model that artfully combines features of a market, hierarchy, and partnership—often supported by state-of-the-

[20] R. Coase, *Essays on Economics and Economists* (Chicago: University of Chicago Press, 1995); O. Williamson and S. Winter. The *Nature of the Firm: Origins, Evolution, and Development* (Oxford: Oxford University Press, 1992).

[21] Collis and Montgomery, *Corporate Strategy,* provide an excellent discussion of the theory framing decisions concerning market, hierarchy, and trust forms of governance.

[22] C. Shapiro and H. Varian, *Information Rules: A Strategic Guide to the Network Economy* (Boston: Harvard Business School Press, 1998).

art information and communication systems. This emerging governance model—whether used to control intra- or inter-firm relationships—has been termed *collaborative community*.[23] The key features that distinguish collaborative community are:

- Shared purpose and values stress an ethic of contribution that replaces the uneasy coexistence of loyalty and individualism in traditional intra- and inter-firm business networks.

- Organizational configurations and solutions support horizontal relationships among peers, yet, as we see below, these peer-to-peer horizontal relationships do not preclude the existence of interdependent vertical, authority-based relationships and market-based transactions.

- Development of an interdependent form of identity that motivates and engages active participation and affiliation over time.

Because the collaborative community model has been designed to maximize high performance in complex, uncertain, turbulent, and hypercompetitive business environments, it appears to be well-suited to business networks of various size, age, and purpose.[24] In addition, it appears to be appropriate for managing interdependencies inside an organization, among parties entering into an alliance, and in more diffuse ownership structures that we call communities. The following section provides an example of one such online collaborative community—the NASDAQ Stock Exchange—that was launched in the 1960s and has survived to the current day. The Global Healthcare Exchange case, located at the end of Module 1, enables analysis of the challenges and opportunities for building twenty-first century collaborative communities. Other online collaborative communities frequently discussed in the literature include Visa's credit card network[25] and Li & Fung's global trading network. The Li & Fung case is featured in the Introduction to this book.

NASDAQ Securities Exchange: A Collaborative Community in Action

NASDAQ mission: To facilitate capital formation in the public and private sectors by developing, operating, and regulating the most liquid, efficient, and fair securities market for the ultimate benefit and protection of the investor.

NASDAQ vision: To build a worldwide market of markets built on a worldwide network of networks . . . assuring the best possible price for securities at the lowest possible cost.[26]

NASDAQ was created in 1971 by the National Association of Securities Dealers (NASD) as an online securities market that enabled a widely dispersed network of independent broker-dealers to trade securities on behalf of individual and institutional investors.

---

[23] C. Heckscher and P. Adler, *Collaboration and Community: Redefining the Role of Trust in 21st Century Business* (Oxford University Press, 2005).

[24] See Adler and Heckscher, *Collaboration and Community.*

[25] P. Chutkow, *Visa: The Power of an Idea* (New York: Harcourt Press, 2001).

[26] Background for the discussion of the NASDAQ Stock Exchange is from two cases and a note. See Perold, 2002 and Applegate, 2002. This quote is taken from The NASDAQ Stock Market, Inc. case, p. 2.

By early 2005, NASDAQ listed over 22.5 billion shares of stock compared to 100 in 1971. These shares were offered by over 3,000 issuers (companies that list on the NASDAQ exchange) and were traded by over 500 broker-dealers. During the 1990s, NASDAQ expanded its network to link to competitive securities exchanges in the United States (e.g., NYSE and AMEX) and to stock exchanges around the world (e.g., the securities exchanges in Tokyo and London).[27]

The mission and vision that unites NASDAQ's business network is to be a worldwide *market of markets* built on a worldwide *network of networks*. Unlike a physical trading floor, the NASDAQ Stock Market is not located in a single place, neither is it owned by a single entity. Instead, it is a diffuse, interdependent network; success requires that everyone participate and strictly adhere to the policies and procedures required to ensure a fair, transparent, and orderly market that delivers value to all members. Over the years, NASDAQ has adopted a complex governance model that combines features of market, hierarchy, and partnership and has become a model of a collaborative community that has survived and prospered for over three decades. While recent events have caused the NASDAQ Securities Exchange to struggle, there is much to learn from deeper examination.

Laying the Foundation

The core operating process of a securities exchange involves the buying and selling of securities and the clearance and settlement of the transaction. The activities that need to be performed to accomplish this process are organized within the following specialized units: The companies that list on the NASDAQ and offer shares of securities that can be bought and sold are called *issuers*; individuals and institutions (e.g., pension funds, mutual funds, corporations, governments) that buy and sell securities are called *investors*; individuals and investment companies that trade stocks on behalf of investors are called *broker-dealers*; and *clearance and settlement* firms (e.g., banks, electronic funds transfer firms) ensure that payments are made and credited and that ownership rights are transferred. Figure 3.2 summarizes the roles of each member of the NASDAQ extended enterprise.

The automation of the end-to-end securities trading and clearance and settlement process provides the foundation for NASDAQ's extended enterprise governance model. By streamlining and integrating activities performed by specialized units, NASDAQ ensures efficiency, consistency, and reliability of its day-to-day operations. In addition, information is generated to enable NASDAQ members around the world to make decisions about securities to buy and sell and the price to be paid. The governance process that is used to coordinate and control these routine end-to-end processes is primarily market-based.

By tapping into a common network infrastructure and by agreeing to common standards that are embedded within automated end-to-end operating processes, the NASDAQ network gains tremendous efficiency and stability. Yet this same infrastructure enables dynamic reconfiguration of the network to meet the real-time needs of buyers and sellers.

---

[27] In some cases, issuers dual-listed their stock on more than one exchange. More frequently, electronic linkages allowed investor to trade stocks listed on exchanges around the world.

FIGURE 3.2 NASDAQ Extended Enterprise

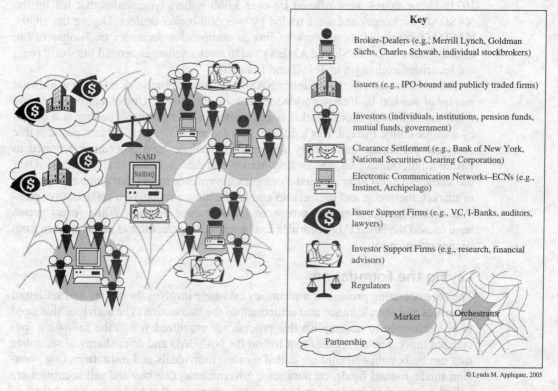

Key

Broker-Dealers (e.g., Merrill Lynch, Goldman Sachs, Charles Schwab, individual stockbrokers)

Issuers (e.g., IPO-bound and publicly traded firms)

Investors (individuals, institutions, pension funds, mutual funds, government)

Clearance Settlement (e.g., Bank of New York, National Securities Clearing Corporation)

Electronic Communication Networks–ECNs (e.g., Instinet, Archipelago)

Issuer Support Firms (e.g., VC, I-Banks, auditors, lawyers)

Investor Support Firms (e.g., research, financial advisors)

Regulators

© Lynda M. Applegate, 2005

Broker-dealers play the role of "network orchestrators"[28] uniting buyers and sellers to enable them to achieve the best price and to complete the transactions in the shortest time.

Because the transactions take place online, the NASDAQ market is able to capture information on each transaction in real time, package it, and then distribute relevant, timely information to investors, stock brokers, and other members of the NASDAQ community. The information is also made available to those who have authority for the integrity and performance of the end-to-end securities trading process to ensure that, despite the speed and complexity with which transactions take place, the widely dispersed global network remains in control. Thus the NASDAQ provides an excellent example of an extended enterprise version of the *on demand, learning model of control,* discussed in Chapter 2.

From Flawless Execution to Innovation

While the buying and selling of securities is the core operating process of a securities exchange, other processes are also in place to support innovation and growth of the network. In addition to the issuer, investor, broker-dealer, and clearance and settlement roles discussed above, other members of the NASDAQ business network include *issuer*

[28] J. Seely Brown and J. Hagel, "Loosening up: How process networks unlock the power of specialization," *McKinsey Quarterly*, Special Edition (2002), pp. 59–62.

support firms (e.g., investment banks, accountants, lawyers, and public relations firms) help issuers prepare public offerings of stock, set the initial price at which the shares will be sold, and then market the securities to broker-dealers and institutional investors; and *investor support firms* (e.g., financial planners, information providers, and research firms) provide information and advice to investors to help them decide whether to buy or sell a given security at a given price and also help them manage their overall portfolio of investments to increase personal wealth. NASDAQ works in partnership with these information and service providers to ensure growth of the network while also ensuring a secure, transparent, and fair market.

While the routine buy-sell transactions are primarily governed through market-based governance mechanisms, the knowledge-based and creative processes related to issuer support and investor support take place in highly interactive, self-managing teams. These teams help determine the new firms that will go public on NASDAQ and provide the information and support to both increase the value and determine the market price of those companies over time. Innovation also occurs through activities of the Technology Advisory Council (TAC)—an advisory board that meets regularly to help define market and product innovations and support their introduction into the market. The TAC is made up of operating executives from organizations representing issuers, investors, broker-dealers, issuer support, and investor support. These self-managing teams and the TAC depend primarily on a partnership form of governance model, although all operate within a legislative framework defined by NASD and various other regulatory agencies and groups (examples of hierarchical forms of governance).

Role of IT in Operating and Governing the NASDAQ Securities Exchange

As mentioned above, IT forms the foundation for NASDAQ's operating and management processes. Within the NASDAQ electronic market, the standards and rules for buying and selling stock and for clearance and settlement of transactions are embedded within the automated transaction processing systems that all members use. These standards and rules are clearly communicated, closely monitored, and consistently enforced through mandatory information reporting. Information is created as a byproduct of the automated systems used in securities trading and clearance and settlement. This information enables all NASDAQ members to self-monitor transactions to ensure the market is operating according to agreed-upon standards and rules and the information is used to create reports that form the foundation of the hierarchical authority system.

NASDAQ's *information transparency* not only promotes consistency and confidence in the repeated interactions among members—a necessary precondition to the development of trust[29]—but it also enables members to learn how the dynamics of the market link to positive or negative outcomes. As a result, common data standards and information transparency also enable both individual and team learning—a necessary precondition to creativity and innovation. Closely aligned and synchronized, interdependent end-to-end operating and management processes are key to the success of the NASDAQ ecosystem over time.

[29] L. Zucker, "Production of Trust: Institutional Sources of Economic Structure, 1840–1920," *Research on Organizational Behavior* 8 (1986), pp. 63–111; D. McKnight, et al., "Initial Trust Formation in New Organizational Relationships," *Academy of Management Review* 23 (2003), pp. 473–490.

Many suggest that the simple act of embedding standards and procedures into the information systems used to process day-to-day routine transaction and control systems automatically leads to vertical distribution of power and an unequal distribution of value (as we would expect in the evolution to a hierarchical form of governance). Yet NASDAQ has been able to embed standards and procedures into its routine operations while also supporting horizontal peer-to-peer transparency and trust. As a member-based organization, NASDAQ was granted the authority by its members to provide a shared platform (infrastructure, information, supporting processes) to enable all parties to self-manage interdependencies in real time. NASDAQ works with members to define agreed-upon standards and processes and embeds them within the technology platform. NASDAQ's authority was granted *by network members* and the value created is *delivered back to those members*. When functioning well, government regulation and oversight ensure that the needs and interests of all network members (and society) are protected.

Linking IT to the Evolution of Partnerships and Trust

The organizational solutions adopted by the NASDAQ business network enable examination of the link between design choices and the development of trust among members of an inter-firm business network. Zucker (1986) suggests three different approaches for building trust in business networks:

1. *Process-based trust* emerges from recurrent transactions as parties manage task interdependencies.
2. *Affiliation-based trust* rests on strong feelings of identity within a specific group.
3. *Institution-based trust* is tied to formal organizational and social structures.[30]

Stewart (2003) shows that trust can be transferred from a trusted party to an unknown party.[31] The willingness to transfer trust from one person or institution to another has been shown to be important when deciding how much, if at all, to trust an unknown other. Key approaches used in trust transfer include (1) developing a relationship with a trusted party who will vouch for the unknown party; and (2) providing verifiable evidence (including direct observation, monitoring, and information) of trustworthiness.[32] As shown below, NASDAQ executives drew upon these approaches to building trust as their governance model evolved over time.

NASD was formed by its broker-dealer member-owners to enable them to work together to buy and sell securities on behalf of investors. As such, the *shared purpose and mission of NASD was set by its broker-dealer members and provided the foundation for affiliation-based trust.*

---

[30] See Zucker, "Production of Trust . . . "

[31] K. Stewart, "Trust Transfer on the World Wide Web," *Organization Science* 14, no. 1 (2003), pp. 5–17.

[32] See Uzzi, "The Sources and Consequences of Embeddedness for the Economic Performance of Organizations, *Sociological Review* 61 (1996), pp. 674–698; R. Milliman and D. Fugate, "Using Trust Transfer as a Persuasion Technique," *Journal of Personal Selling and Sales Management* 8 (1998), pp. 1–7; and P. Strub and T. Priest, "Two Patterns of Establishing Trust," *Sociological Focus* (1976), pp. 399–411.

NASD was granted authority by its members to work on their behalf to develop, perform, and oversee the licensing process that would enable all members to trust that broker-dealers involved in a transaction were reputable and knowledgeable. NASD was also granted power by its members to develop and monitor the procedures and information sharing standards required to price and trade securities, and the clearance and settlement systems that ensured that ownership and payments were correctly transferred. As such, *the authority, duties, and obligations of NASD were defined and granted by its members and provided the foundation for institution-based trust.*

NASD granted NASDAQ the authority to embed these agreed-upon processes, information-sharing standards, and controls in technology systems that all members of the industry would use to do business. As such, *NASD transferred its authority, duties, and obligations to NASDAQ along with the trust of its members; and NASDAQ created institutional structures, standards, and safeguards that further increased willingness to trust.*

Once everyone was connected and business was being conducted online, information was generated that enabled the *development of a reliable market that consistently met the expectations* of members. Further, market transparency enabled all members to *access real-time information that confirmed and strengthened perceptions of trustworthiness.* As such, NASDAQ was able to develop *process-based trust,* which, in turn, provided the *foundation for a collaborative community, hybrid form of inter-firm governance that includes features of market, hierarchy, and partnership grounded in trust, shared authority, and learning.*

The NASDAQ case illustrates the design features of an inter-firm collaborative community. As a cooperative, NASDAQ's members sought to promote collective action through shared identity that stressed an ethic of contribution and collective action. Organizational solutions were designed from the outset to support horizontal processes among peers. Given that NASDAQ was originally formed as an industry cooperative, it does not enable us to study the challenges of transforming established industries toward a collaborative community model. The Global Healthcare Exchange (GHX) case at the end of this module discusses the challenges of building a collaborative community form of governance within a hypercompetitive industry context. As you read the case, consider the lessons from the NASDAQ example and from other executives that have struggled to define interorganizational collaborative communities.

Building Collaborative Community: Lessons from the Field

Cutting-edge companies are swapping their tightly coupled processes for loosely coupled ones, thereby gaining much-needed flexibility and improving their performance . . . and [they are] handling critical cross-company processes as though they were networks rather than production lines. The key role in a loosely coupled business network is the central coordinator or "orchestrator."[33]

Throughout the second half of the twentieth century, advances in IT—coupled with the rapid evolution of management theory and tools (e.g., total quality management, business process reengineering, self-managing teams, and networking and negotiation

[33] See J. Seely Brown, et al., "Loosening up . . ." p. 59.

skills)—made it increasingly easier for *independent* companies to coordinate *interde-pendent* activities. Consultants championed the rise of the "virtual corporation"—a network of focused businesses that would come together as free agents to design, build, market, sell, and support products and services within a wide variety of old and new economy industries.[34] The proposed benefits—greater efficiency, increased respon-siveness, the ability to share specialized assets (including physical assets, knowledge, and relationships), and to tap into high-powered market incentives. Indeed, the busi-ness literature has provided numerous examples of virtually integrated firms, like Dell, that outperformed much larger vertically integrated competitors and rose to the number one position in the industry.[35]

But the same factors that make virtual business networks so powerful can also leave them vulnerable. Increased inter-firm coordination costs can destroy hoped for effi-ciency gains; self-interest and opportunism can lead to free riding; and lack of trust can delay adoption of the shared standards and horizontal processes required to enable collective action. The NASDAQ and GHX cases provide insight into how these prob-lems arise. They also show how they can be addressed through IT-enabled organiza-tional solutions that enable coordination of interdependencies, alignment of interests, and development of trust. Key insights from the field are summarized below.

Key Insight: Hybrid Forms of Governance Are Emerging That Unite Hierarchy, Market, and Partnership

For decades, academics have recognized the power of hybrid forms of governance that unite hierarchy, market, and partnerships.[36] The NASDAQ case shows that emerging hybrid governance models do not need to eliminate hierarchy or market for partner-ship models to become a distinctive and dominant governance model. Instead, GHX and NASDAQ show that *market and hierarchy can actually facilitate and enable collaborative capacity and trust*. These cases highlight how standards, policies, and procedures—all governance mechanisms typically associated with hierarchy—can be embedded in transaction processing systems that enable market-based trans-actions to take place consistently, reliably, and efficiently. More important, these automated transactions capture information on each transaction and, when linked to outcomes, enable self-monitoring to occur which increases trust.

While routine transactions are governed primarily through market transactions, the information about transactions can also be captured and made available to other parties. At NASDAQ we see that this information could be used to support routine reporting to regulators that ensure compliance with policies and laws (a hierarchical governance feature and a requirement in any stable community). We also see that the same

---

[34] See J. Seely Brown, et al., "Loosening up . . ."

[35] See M. Dell and J. Magretta, "The power of virtual integration: An interview with Dell Computer's Michael Dell," *Harvard Business Review,* March 1998. This article is available at the end of Module 2.

[36] See J. Bradach and R. Eccles, "Price, authority, and trust," *Annual Review of Sociology* 15 (1989), pp. 97–118; W. Powell, "Neither market nor hierarchy: Network forms of organization," *Research on Organization Behavior* 12 (1990), pp. 295–336; and P. Adler, "Market, Hierarchy, and Trust: The knowledge economy and the future of capitalim," *Organization Science* 12, no. 2 (2001), pp. 215–234.

information can be made available to teams of experts from many disciplines that join to develop highly customized, knowledge-based solutions and product innovations. These self-managing, highly creative teams can form anywhere on the network and can unite multiple independent agents. An example is the team of investment bankers, lawyers, accountants, advertising agencies, NASDAQ listing agents, and issuer executives that come together to complete an initial public offering (IPO). All share common information, all submit to common standards and procedures, yet the output is highly creative and innovative. And, unless team self-interest overpowers network interests, value can be created—not just for the members of the team working on the deal—but also for all members of the NASDAQ business network. Thus partnership features increased the innovative and collaborative capacity by building on a foundation of hierarchical and market governance.

Key Insight: A Network Orchestrator Role Is Emerging to Coordinate Inter-Firm Interdependencies within Business Ecosystems, Like NASDAQ and GHX

Given the complexity of the transactions carried out and the sheer number of highly differentiated yet interdependent parties involved, a network orchestrator was required to coordinate task, information, and affiliation interdependencies within the business ecosystems discussed in this chapter. Within the securities industry, NASD—an industry cooperative—launched NASDAQ to fulfill the orchestrator role. Within the health care industry, suppliers, distributors, and health care providers launched GHX to fulfill the network orchestrator role.

Both GHX and NASDAQ built collaborative communities that were owned and governed by industry members involved in both the buy- and sell-side of the transaction. The founders of these consortia believed that shared ownership was critical to ensuring active commitment to collective action and participation. They also believed that a "cooperative" association membership model would best align member interests and contributions to value created and received.

Key Insight: Network Orchestrators Design Organizational Solutions That Reflect the Interests of All Parties

The NASDAQ case provides an initial view of how a network orchestrator ensures that all interests in a buy-sell transaction are represented. The identification of obligations and responsibilities begins with the board of directors responsible for defining direction, setting priorities, and overseeing the actions taken to ensure that the collective interests of the members are supported. NASDAQ received its legitimacy to act on behalf of its members from NASD—an industry association that represented the interests of the broker-dealer community. Given that broker-dealers bought *and* sold stocks on behalf of investors, NASD was in a unique position to represent both the buy-side and the sell-side of the market transaction.

In contrast to the NASDAQ case, which looks back in time, the GHX case provides the rare opportunity to observe first-hand the emerging design of collaborative communities that represented the complex—and often competing—interests within an industry. Unlike NASDAQ, GHX was originally launched to support only one position in the buy-sell transaction—the supplier side. Executives soon learned that they would need to broaden their base of support to effectively represent the interests of all parties in the transaction and gain the necessary participation.

Initially GHX attempted to link its network of suppliers to independent networks of buyers. The case details how this approach enabled routine transactions to take place, but there was little progress in developing the common standards and horizontal processes required to drive out costs while also enabling the technological innovation needed to improve the quality of care delivered. To reach this deeper level of collaboration, GHX merged its operations and organizations with networks that represented the interests of distributors and health care providers. These mergers provided the foundation upon which process-based trust and a collaborative community model of governance could be built. Through the mergers, all stakeholders in a securities transaction became owners and gained a seat at the table where policy and strategy decisions were made.

Key Insight: Collaborative Community and Trust Co-evolve Over Time

The GHX case provides a detailed analysis of how months of face-to-face negotiation among senior executives enabled five of the most powerful competitors in the health care industry to achieve a common understanding and "hammer out" the governance framework that would serve as the foundation for collective action in this supply chain collaborative. Recognizing that most legal agreements were inadequate, the founders had the foresight to capture not just their legal obligations, but also the purpose and goals that united them in seeking a collective solution to problems that plagued the industry.

The intent and governance processes were formalized in legal agreements that united supplier, distributor, and health care provider interests. These agreements contained Guiding Principles and Data Standards that were used to frame decision making and action and became a clear statement of the shared values that all members were expected to uphold.

As we saw with NASDAQ, standards, policies, and values were also embedded within IT-enabled processes that integrated task interdependencies within the GHX business network. These automated processes supported and coordinated collective actions among GHX members. These IT systems provided the information transparency needed for each member to participate fully and the self-monitoring required for the development of "process-based trust" among all members.

The GHX case also provides deep insight into the interplay between the evolving governance model and evolving trust. Trust initially developed within a small team of individuals as they engaged in months of face-to-face negotiation around the initial launch of GHX. These individuals became the governing board that represented the interests of their respective companies in the GHX consortium. Once interests and benefits were aligned at the board of directors level, GHX formed a product council made up of operating managers that mirrored the membership of the board of directors and the interests of the broad-based constituency. The board transferred authority for product strategy and its execution to the product council, and the council worked with all members to develop the common standards and processes required to coordinate interdependencies. These standards, procedures, and rules were then embedded in a shared platform and common IT-enabled processes.

Summary

Today's executives are faced with a myriad of organizational and industry design choices. They may continue to operate within industries and organizations with clearly defined boundaries and relationships. Alternatively, they may operate within a business network in which boundaries and relationships are becoming increasingly fluid. If executives choose the latter, they must have a much better understanding of how to design and build successful business networks and the hybrid governance models required to operate and manage them. The emerging hybrid governance model unites features of a market, hierarchy, and partnership to create a collaborative community founded on trust and cooperation.

Many believe that the ability to conduct business electronically, integrating supply and distribution channels, and extending enterprise boundaries would eventually give rise to virtually integrated communities that are popularly called ecosystems. Indeed, we presented two examples of emerging collaborative community models in this chapter. Yet similar collaborative community business networks can also be found inside vertically integrated corporations and within alliances of one or more specialized businesses.

The lessons from the history of electronic commerce and this glimpse into the future help frame the questions executives ask and the solutions sought as they design twenty-first century "on demand" network businesses.

1. What are the key activities that make up the core operating process in your business network? How have you organized those activities into specialized units and how do you coordinate and control task, information/expertise, and affiliation interdependencies?

2. What decisions have you made concerning which activities you will own and which you will source? What were the cost, risk, and benefit trade-offs that you considered? Is it time to revisit any of these decisions?

3. Can IT and the information it delivers be used to simplify, streamline, and better manage end-to-end processes within your business network? Are you harnessing the power of information generated by end-to-end business processes to enable specialized units and the individuals within them to sense and respond to internal and external customer demands?

4. Are you building the collaborative communities that will be required to do business in the future? Are you delivering value to each member of the community to ensure engagement and commitment to shared goals and to ensure loyalty today and in the future?

5. Have you selected partners wisely? Do you have a shared vision and common purpose? Do you bring equal, and complementary, power and resources to the relationship? Are you and your partners financially viable, and is the relationship financially and competitively sustainable? Have you defined shared systems of authority, accountability, and learning to ensure that all members of your business network work together to deliver value?

6. Is the technical infrastructure you have in place the right one to enable the types of electronic commerce you are considering? Are you maintaining the appropriate balance between experimentation and control as you move to emerging on demand business architectures? Have you instituted appropriate levels of privacy, security, and control?

Appendix 3A

Emerging Network Business Models

During the 1980s, pioneers like American Airlines, American Hospital Supply, Li & Fung, Wal-Mart, and America Online blazed new trails and changed the economics of their industries. These new economics laid the foundation for the network business models that were further refined by Internet pioneers of the late 1990s, like Amazon.com, eBay, and Rakuten. This chapter provides a framework that begins by separating the business models into two primary categories (see Figure A3.1).

First are *businesses being built and launched on the Internet*. Here, most of the action is taking place in the channel where powerful new models are emerging that link members of a business network. These *network businesses* include business-to-consumer models (Amazon.com and Landsend.com); consumer-to-consumer models (eBay); consumer-to-business models (Priceline.com); and business-to-business models (Free-Markets, Global Healthcare Exchange, and American Express Interactive).

The second category encompasses *businesses that provide the digital infrastructure*. Here, most of the action is from vendors and service providers that provide IT infrastructure products and services directly to business customers and consumers. Models in this category include computer and network equipment providers (IBM, Hewlett-Packard, Cisco, and Lucent); software firms (Microsoft and Oracle); and custom suppliers (Dell for equipment, Accenture for software, and IBM Global Services for emerging business process outsourcing and on demand business services).

As discussed in this section, as the Internet and related network technologies penetrate to the very core of how firms do business, the distinctions between these two categories—digital businesses and infrastructure providers—is beginning to blur. But rather than complicate the picture, this appendix provides an overview of selected models and how each one drives revenues, costs, and assets—the financial performance metrics that flow from the choice of a strategy and the capabilities that are built to execute the strategy. (Note: Refer back to Chapter 1 to recall how the *strategy of a firm defines the revenue model* of a firm while

FIGURE A3.1

Classifying Network Business Models

Create and package products, services, and solutions   Enable buyers and sellers to connect, communicate, and transact business

Create and package technology-based products, services, and solutions   Enable technology buyers and sellers to transact business   Enable consumers and businesses to access online services and information

the *capabilities define the cost and asset models* and how the linkages among strategy, capabilities, and values define the business model of a firm.)

Businesses Built on the Internet

Emerging network business models can be categorized based on the primary industry role performed. *Producers* package the work of creators into products, services, and solutions that meet a market need. They may sell and maintain the product or may share that role with others in the value chain.[37] *Distributors* enable buyers and sellers to connect, communicate, and transact business. *Portals* aggregate products, services, and/or information for use by members of the community.

Because the Internet initially functioned primarily as a channel, many of the earliest businesses that leveraged the Internet were launched to transform channels to market, channels to suppliers, or both. These included Focused distributors—for example, eRetailers, eMarkets, Aggregators, Exchanges and Infomediaries—and Portals.

Focused Distributors

Focused distributors provide products and services related to a specific industry or market niche. For example, InsWeb is a focused distributor offering products and services within the insurance industry; Landsend.com is a focused distributor for clothing and accessories; and, at the time of launch, Amazon.com was classified as a focused book distributor. Answers to the following questions can help differentiate different focused distributor business models.

- Does the business assume control of inventory?
- Does the business sell online?

- Is the price set outside the market or is online price negotiation and bidding permitted?
- Is there a physical product or service that must be distributed?

eRetailers

eRetailers, for example, Amazon.com's online bookstore (www.amazon.com), assume control of inventory, set a nonnegotiable price to the consumer, and sell physical products online.[38] Therefore, the primary revenue model is based on product/service sales and the cost model includes procurement, inventory management, order fulfillment, and customer service (including returns). Because online retailers assume control of physical goods, their ratio of tangible to intangible assets often is much higher than would be found in a firm that does not assume control of physical inventory. How would you expect the eRetailer business model to perform as Amazon.com quickly expanded into new product categories (e.g., toys, lawn, and garden) during the late 1990s? Clearly, logistics complexity increased dramatically as Amazon's physical warehouse space expanded to house the growing inventory of lawn chairs, gas grills, bikes, and other bulky, hard-to-ship items. Soon Amazon.com executives recognized that the company's pure "clicks" eRetail model was limited. In early 2000, Amazon.com adopted a new business model that emphasized its core capabilities as a retail software and online direct marketing company and shifted its business model accordingly. Today, while Amazon.com's online book and music stores still operate as eRetailers, its primary business model is as an eLogistics Web services provider. A two-part case series that details Amazon.com's business model transition is available.[39]

---

[37] These roles first emerged within traditional industry value chains that did business in a linear fashion, receiving inputs and value from those downstream in the chain and delivering inputs and value to upstream members. Today, the simple linear relationships are giving way to a complex "value web" of relationships, which we term a collaborative community or business ecosystem.

[38] See L. M. Applegate, "Amazon.com: 1994–2000" (HBS No. 801-194).

[39] The "Amazon.com: 1994–2000 case" (HBS No. 801-194) provides a detailed look at the evolution of the Amazon.com business model during the late 1990s. The "Amazon.com: January 2001–July 2002" case (HBS No. 801-392) updates the business model evolution through July 2002.

eMarkets

eMarkets, for example, Global Healthcare Exchange (www.ghx.com), link buyers and sellers allowing them to compare and purchase products online.[40] Unlike eRetailers, eMarkets do not take control of physical inventory. As a result, the revenue model includes a commission or transaction fee on each sale. Because sales transactions take place online, eMarkets must electronically link to supplier databases and order fulfillment systems to ensure that transactions can be completed and revenue recognized. Business-to-business (B2B) eMarkets, like GHX, often establish electronic linkages to buyer and seller databases and to order fulfillment (sell-side) and purchasing (buy-side) systems—although browser-based purchasing from electronic catalogs is also available. Direct linkages to supplier and/or buyer databases and transactions systems can provide a second revenue stream related to system integration consulting and custom software development. With the addition of this system integration revenue stream, an eMarket launches a second business model, which is classified as an infrastructure services business model. This infrastructure services business model comes with very different economics as the company must hire the system engineers and consultants needed to perform these costly and time-intensive system integration consulting services. Unless these costs are covered by customers willing to pay, the system integration services business model can serve as a drag on earnings. In summary, since eMarkets do not take control of physical inventory, the physical distribution and logistics costs are lower than those of eRetailers. But the addition of a system integration services business model may make the eMarket business model more costly and higher risk—especially when compared with the eAggregator business model discussed next.

eAggregators

eAggregators, for example, InsWeb (www.insweb.com), provide information on products or services for sale by others in the channel. Companies adopting this model often provide electronic catalogs and comparisons of features and pricing—but do not enable the customer to complete the final sale transaction. Instead, they pass the customer through to the supplier to complete the sale. The revenue model for these sites is often based on referral fees and advertising. Because the transaction is not completed online, some aggregators find that consumers use the site to comparison shop then go offline to make the purchase. As a result, aggregators often lose referral fees and must depend heavily on advertising and other supplemental revenue sources. It is no surprise that only a few large focused eAggregators survived the dot-com meltdown during 2000 and 2001. InsWeb, an eAggregator for the insurance industry, was an example of an eAggregator that was launched and went public during the late 1990s when dot-com fever was at its highest. But, unlike most eAggregators, InsWeb was still independent in early 2005. While executives were attempting to change the business model to an eMarket, InsWeb continued to depend heavily on its eAggregator model and had yet to become cash flow positive, posting a loss of $8.9 million on revenues of $14.1 million during 2004.[41] If successful with the launch of its online Term Life Agency business, InsWeb insurance agents would begin selling policies online and the business model would shift to an eMarket.

Infomediaries

Infomediaries, for example, Internet Securities (www.securities.com), are a special class of eAggregator that unites sellers and buyers of information. Because no physical product is involved, the transaction can be completed online. Infomediaries—especially those that cater to business professionals—may charge individual users a subscription fee for the service. B2B infomediaries, like Internet Securities, often charge a company a corporate subscription fee that may provide either unlimited or limited usage. B2C infomediaries often provide the information free to consumers and make money based on

---

[40] See L. M. Applegate, "Global Healthcare Exchange" Harvard Business School Publishing (No. 804-002).

[41] InsWeb Investor Relations, 4th Quarter 2004 financial performance, downloaded April 1, 2005.

advertising revenues collected from sponsors or affiliates. Because information is available elsewhere and the cost of packaging and delivering the information is relatively low, barriers to entry are also low. As a result, infomediaries often seek to quickly evolve from simply brokering information. Some, like Internet Securities, choose to develop unique, value-added content and analytical tools; others, like InsWeb, choose to extend their business by allowing customers to complete transactions online. Within limits of privacy, ethics, and regulation, infomediaries must also leverage the economic value of the information they collect on how individuals use information to make decisions and take actions. Over time, these intangible information assets can become a major source of differentiation and sustainability.

Exchanges

Exchanges, for example, NASDAQ, eBay, and FreeMarkets, may or may not take control of inventory—the tendency is to try and avoid assuming inventory carrying costs whenever feasible—and may or may not complete the final sales transaction online. The key differentiating feature of this model is that the price is not set; it is negotiated by the buyer and seller at the time of the sale. The revenue, cost, and asset models vary depending on whether the online exchange assumes control of inventory and completes the transaction and the level of human facilitation required. B2B auction exchanges, such as FreeMarkets, charge transaction fees and supplement revenues with fees for consulting services. B2C and C2C exchanges often supplement transaction revenues with advertising revenues.

Portals

The *American Heritage Dictionary of the English Language* defines the term *portal* as "a doorway or gate—especially one that is large and imposing." To many this definition seems a fitting description of the portal business model that has emerged on the Internet. Although the term *portal* became popular during the late 1990s, the earliest online consumer portals (for example, America Online and CompuServ) emerged in the

1980s with the adoption of the personal computer.[42] Built upon proprietary technology, these pre-Internet portals provided limited access. In fact, in late 1993, AOL's proprietary consumer portal had only 500,000 members. By early 2005, about 30 million people around the world were AOL members, and those members sent roughly 450 million e-mails per day and about 1.5 billion instant messages per day; nearly 170,000 chat rooms were open on AOL.com every day.[43]

Early Internet portals emerged to help consumers gain access to an ever-increasing amount of content available on the World Wide Web. They served as gateways and provided the tools needed to connect to the Internet, to browse through its contents, and to provide directory and search services (for example, Google.com). By 2005, the portal model had evolved and was considered the interface of choice for delivering information inside and across extended enterprises. As such, a portal has become a recognized channel through which users can access information and services provided within a focused area (vertical channels) or across a wide range of content, similar to the broadcasting channels on television or radio channels.

Producers

Although the focus of our discussion is primarily on distributor models, it is helpful at this point to comment on the evolution of producer business models. Producers design, produce, and distribute products and services that meet customer needs. They include:

- Manufacturers (e.g., Ford Motor Company, PepsiCo, Procter & Gamble) that use the Internet to design, produce, and distribute physical products.

[42] See L. M. Applegate, F. W. McFarlan, and J. L. McKenney, "Electronic Commerce: Trends and Opportunities," *Corporate Information Systems Management* (New York: McGraw-Hill/Irwin 1999).

[43] AOL Web site (www.corp.aol.com/who_timeline.html), downloaded April 1, 2005.

- Service providers (e.g., American Express, Citigroup, Avis, American Airlines) that produce and deliver a wide range of online information products and services.
- Educators (e.g., Harvard Business School, University of Phoenix, McGraw-Hill, Knowledge Universe) that create and deliver online educational offerings.
- Advisors (e.g., Accenture, Booz Allen) that provide online consulting and advice.
- Information and news services (e.g., Internet Securities, *The Wall Street Journal* Interactive) that create, package, and deliver online information.

During the first half of the twentieth century, large, vertically integrated producers had the upper hand in most industry value chains. While these established players initially approached the Internet with caution, most have now embraced the Internet as a fundamental component of their business strategy and operations. As they do, savvy producers are defining powerful new roles. For example:

- Citigroup has linked its strong brand-name "brick and mortar" retail financial services within portals that go direct to consumers and provides a similar offering for its business customers. Over the past decade, this financial services powerhouse has become what many are calling a "universal bank," offering a broad range of financial services offerings that provide a one-stop-shop for consumer and business financial services that are sold through portals and a broad range of physical channels.[44] The flexibility to sell in multiple channels is a hallmark of success in times of uncertainty and rapid industry transition.
- Throughout the first half of the twentieth century, the automakers led the world into the era

of mass manufacturing. Now these same players want to repeat their trailblazing role. For example, GM now embeds its OnStar wireless Internet services into many of its cars, providing consumers and fleet operators with mobile Internet access, e-mail, global positioning, and much more. In addition, Ford, GM, and DaimlerChrysler banded together in early 2000 to launch Covisint—an eMarket, similar to GHX, that enables auto industry suppliers and buyers to conduct business anywhere and any time.

Digital Infrastructure Providers

As mentioned earlier, digital business models have been part of the business landscape since digital computers and communication networks were introduced in the 1950s, 1960s, and 1970s.[45] Recall the pioneering digital business models introduced by American and United Airlines, McKesson, American Hospital Supply, and Wal-Mart in the mid-1980s. Until recently, however, there was a distinct separation between network businesses and the providers of the digital infrastructure—the latter of which were often grouped together within the "high tech industry."

Yet businesses in the twenty-first century increasingly find that the digital infrastructure has become embedded within the very fabric of how the firm creates, produces, and distributes products and services. As a result, it has become increasingly difficult to clearly categorize a firm as a "pure play" high tech firm. David Pottruck, CEO of Charles Schwab until 2004, emphasized this point:

[Charles Schwab] is a technology company that just happens to be in the brokerage business. Everything we think about as we run our business has technology in the center

---

[44] A. Cairns, J. Davidson, and M. Kisilevitz, "The Limits of Bank Convergence," *McKinsey Quarterly,* March 22, 2002; G. Stein, "Goldman vs. Citi Showdown Tests "Big is Best" on Wall Street," Bloomberg News Service, August 25, 2003.

[45] While the first commercial computers were sold to firms in the 1950s, it was not until the 1960s that the penetration of digital computers reached critical mass in companies. Similarly, while analog communication networks—for example, early telephone and telegraph networks—became available in the late 1800s, it was not until the mid-1970s that AT&T installed its first digital telecommunications networks.

of it with the goal of engineering costs down and service up . . . If you want to constantly increase service while decreasing the cost structure and the cost of service, then technology is the play. You have to be great at it. If we are going to be successful [against our competitors], it is going to have to be that technology is built into our DNA in a way that's different.[46]

Digital infrastructure provider business models are classified using the same producer/distributor categorization scheme that was used to classify digital businesses built on the Internet. Once again, powerful channel players—horizontal infrastructure portals (e.g., Cingular Wireless, Comcast Broadband) and vertical infrastructure portals (e.g., Sales.com)—are emerging. Focused distributors include high tech eResellers (e.g., Tech Data, Ingram Micro) that take control of hardware and software inventory and complete the sales transaction with the customer.

But unlike their slower-to-respond digital business counterparts, high tech producers—including digital equipment and software manufacturers (e.g., Cisco, Microsoft, Intel, IBM) and custom suppliers (e.g., Dell)—were early adopters of direct-to-customer online models. Given space constraints in this chapter, we limit discussion of digital infrastructure provider business models to a short description of emerging infrastructure portals.

Infrastructure Portals

Infrastructure portals are firms that provide consumers and/or businesses with access to a wide range of network, computing, and application hosting services. Prior to the commercialization of the Internet, many large firms developed and ran their own networks and data centers—often leasing telephone services and data lines from network service providers—called common carriers or value-added network services (VANs) providers. Small- to midsize businesses often bought low-end computers and packaged software from local retailers, national distributors, or from a network of value-added resellers (VARs). In the network

era of the twenty-first century, a new option has emerged; an increasing number of small to midsize firms—and even large firms—are choosing to plug in to a sophisticated global data network and business software application infrastructure. Under this model, firms rent their digital infrastructure hosted by an infrastructure portal player rather than leasing or buying it.

Infrastructure portals—like their digital business portal counterparts—are either horizontal or vertical. They are differentiated by the following characteristics.

- Does the firm provide "gateway access" to a complete set of network, data center, and/or Web hosting services?
- Does the firm provide access to hosted vertical application services?

Horizontal Infrastructure Portals include Internet service providers—also called—ISPs (e.g., Comcast Broadband Services, AOL.com), Network Service Providers (e.g., AT&T, MCI, Sprint) and Web Hosting Service Providers (e.g., IBM Global Services). These firms provide gateway access to a wide range of network (cable, voice, Internet), data center, and Web site/online business hosting services. The revenue model includes access and maintenance fees, subscription services, and, at times, transaction fees. If combined with an online content business (e.g., Yahoo!), the portal may also generate advertising revenues. The key costs include data and network center operations, software development and maintenance, system integration consulting and software development, marketing, sales, and administration.

Digital infrastructure *Vertical Portals* are often referred to as application service providers (ASPs). Rather than sell software applications, an ASP hosts and maintains a software application, enabling businesses and individuals to log in and conduct business online. Examples of ASP vertical portals include Salesforce.com (www.salesforce.com), IBM's Business Transformation Outsourcing, and Oracle On Demand's application services. Because ASPs

[46] Presentation by David Pottruck in a Harvard Business School executive program, October 22, 1999.

often operate as a business portal, advertising is often not a significant source of revenue. Instead, application service providers typically generate revenues through hosting and maintenance fees, consulting fees, and system integration fees. Key costs are similar to those incurred by horizontal portals.

Charts summarizing revenue, cost, and asset options and the characteristics of emerging network business models are provided next.

Sample Revenue Options

Commerce Revenues	
Revenue Category	**Description**
Product Sales	Sell or license physical or information-based products.
Commission, Service, or Transaction Fees	Charge a fee for services provided; can be a set fee or a percent of the cost of a product or service.

Content Revenues	
Revenue Category	**Description**
Subscription Fees	Charge for receipt of updated information on a particular topic or a broad range of topics for a specified period of time (e.g., annual).
Registration or Event Fees	Charge a fee for attendance at an online event, workshop, or course.

Community Revenues	
Revenue Category	**Description**
Advertising, Slotting, Affiliate, and Referral Fees	Collect a fee for hosting a banner advertisement or special promotion. Collect a fee for an exclusive or nonexclusive partnership relationship. Collect a fee each time a visitor clicks through from your site to another company's site.
Membership Fees	Charge a fee to belong to a private group or service.

Infrastructure Revenues	
Revenue Category	**Description**
Software/Hardware Sales	Sell or license a technology product.
Installation and Integration Fees	Charge either a set or variable fee for services provided; large-scale fixed-price projects are often broken into a series of discrete projects with well-defined time frames and deliverables; variable fees are often based on time, materials, and expenses incurred while working on a project.
Maintenance and Update Fees	Charge a fee for software/hardware maintenance and updates.
Hosting Fees	Charge a fee for hosting a software application, Web site, data center, or network.
Access Fees	Charge a fee for providing access to a network and/or to an Internet service.

Sample Cost Categories

Cost Category	Description
People and Partners	Cost to acquire, develop, and retain skills and expertise needed to execute strategy.
Marketing and Sales	Cost of offline and online advertising, marketing, and sales.
Business Development	Cost of designing and launching new businesses, developing alliances and acquiring partners, mergers, acquisitions, and spinouts.
Materials and Supplies	Cost of physical materials used in production of products and delivery of services; includes general purpose and specialized supplies and components.
Specialized Equipment (excluding IT)	Cost of equipment—especially capital equipment—used in design, production, delivery, and distribution.
Research and Development	Cost of designing and developing products and services; may overlap with business development and, in the case of network business, with IT infrastructure costs.
Physical Facilities and Infrastructure	Cost of corporate and regional headquarters, sales offices, factories, warehouses, distribution centers, retail stores, service centers, etc.
Information Technology	Cost of computers and equipment (e.g., printers, data storage devices).
(IT) Infrastructure	Cost to operate and maintain data centers. Cost to design, develop, implement, and maintain software. Cost of voice, data, and video network equipment (e.g., physical cables, routers). Cost to design, operate, and maintain networks.

Sample Asset Categories

Current Assets	
Asset Category	**Description**
Financial Assets	Accounts receivable. Cash and convertible notes.
Marketable Securities	Investments made as part of a cash management program.

Tangible Assets	
Asset Category	**Description**
Property, Plant, and Equipment	Physical facilities. Fixed assets required to produce goods and services.
Inventory	Assets held for sale.

Investments	
Asset Category	**Description**
Securities	Stock held by a firm to enable joint control over shared business activities. Stock held by a firm in anticipation of a return at some time in the future.
Real Estate	Investment in property in anticipation of a future return.

Intangible Assets	
Asset Category	**Description**
Relationships	Breadth and depth of relationships with customers and the business community. Loyalty and commitment of customers and business community members.
Strength of Online and Offline Brand	Strong brand recognition among business and consumer communities (includes corporate brand, business unit brands, product brands, and global brand). Ability to generate strong personal identification with brand. Reputation and image.
Knowledge and Expertise	Experience, skills, and intellectual capabilities of employees and partners (asset value depends on loyalty and retention). Technical and business skills and experience. Understanding of market and business dynamics. Scope and granularity of stored information and expertise. Flexibility and ease of accessing, customizing, and distributing information. Information literacy.
Agility and Responsiveness	Ability to quickly recognize and act on new opportunities and threats ("sense and respond on demand"). Ability to access and efficiently utilize resources required to execute strategy. Ability to capture the attention and mobilize the commitment of customers and members of the business community to implement new strategies.
Intellectual Property	Patents, copyrights, etc., for which an objective measure of value can be assessed.
Goodwill	Value of an acquired company over and above current and tangible assets. The value of an acquired company's "franchise"—e.g., loyalty of its customers, the expertise of its employees—that can be objectively measured at the time of a sale or change of control.

Focused Distributor Business Models

Model and Examples	Model Differentiators				Likely Revenues	Likely Costs
	Own Physical Inventory	Sell Online	Price Set Online	Physical Product or Service		
eRetailers Landsend.com Staples.com	Yes	Yes	No	Yes	Product/service sales	Advertising and marketing; physical facilities, inventory and customer svc.; R&D; IT infrastructure
eMarkets GHX	No	Yes	No	No	Transaction fees; service fees; commissions	Advertising and marketing; R&D; IT infrastructure
eAggregators InsWeb.com	No	No	No	Possibly	Referral fees; advertising and marketing fees	Advertising and marketing; R&D; IT infrastructure
Infomediary Internet Securities	No	Yes	Yes	No	Subscription fees; advertising fees	Advertising and marketing; R&D; IT infrastructure; content acquisition
Exchange eBay.com Freemarket.com	Possibly	Possibly	Yes	Possibly	Depends on model	Advertising and marketing; staff support for auctions (especially B2B); inventory and logistics if inventory control; R&D; technical infrastructure

Focused Distributor Business Model Trends:
- Focused distributors that do not allow customers and the business community to transact business online have lost power.
- Aggregators have evolved to eMarkets and/or vertical portals.
- Multiple business models increase flexibility and sustainability.
- Focused distributors are aligning closely with vertical and horizontal portals or are evolving their model to become vertical portals.

Portal Business Models

Model and Examples	Model Differentiators			Likely Revenues	Likely Costs
	Gateway Access	Deep Content and Solutions	Affinity Group Focus		
Horizontal Portals Google (www.google.com) Yahoo! (www.yahoo.com)	Yes	Through partnerships with vertical and affinity portals	Possibly; often through partnerships	Advertising, affiliation and slotting fees; possibly subscription or access fees	Advertising, marketing, and sales; content/info asset mgmt.; R&D; IT infrastructure
Vertical Portals WebMD.com Small Business Administration (SBA.gov)	Limited	Yes	No	Transaction fees; commissions; advertising, affiliation and slotting fees	Advertising, marketing and sales; content/info asset mgmt.; R&D; IT infrastructure; legacy system integration to support transactions
Affinity Portals Women's Financial Network (WFN.com)	Possibly	Focused on affinity group	Yes	Referral fees; Advertising, affiliation and slotting fees; transaction fees	Advertising, marketing, and sales; content/info asset mgmt.; R&D; IT infrastructure

Portal Business Model Trends:

- Horizontal and vertical portals are emerging as gateways to a wide variety of content and services on the global public Internet and on company or extended enterprise intranets.
- Horizontal portals are joining forces with horizontal infrastructure portals to provide, not just access to content and services, but also access to network and hosting services.
- Large media and entertainment portals that represent convergence of data, telephone, television, and radio networks are emerging in the consumer space. These portals unite content development, packaging, and distribution components of the value chain.
- B2B portals provide both horizontal access to business networks and vertical industrywide solutions.

Producer Business Models

Model and Examples	Model Differentiators			Likely Revenues	Likely Costs
	Sell Physical Product/Service	Sell Information-Based Product/Service	Customization		
Manufacturers Ford Motor Co. Procter & Gamble	Yes	Possibly	Low to Moderate	Product sales; service fees	Advertising, marketing, and sales; content/info asset mgmt.; R&D; IT infrastructure
Service Providers Singapore Airlines (www.singaporeair.com) Avis (www.avis.com)	Yes	Possibly	Moderate to High	Commission, service, or transaction fees	Advertising, marketing, and sales; content/info asset mgmt.; R&D; IT infrastructure
Educators University of Phoenix (www.phoenix.edu)	Possibly	Possibly	Moderate to High	Registration or event fee; subscription fee; hosting fee	Content/info asset mgmt.; R&D; IT infrastructure
Advisors Booz Allen (www.boozallen.com) Accenture (www.accenture.com)	Yes	Yes	Moderate to High	Service fee; registration or event fee; membership fee; commission, transaction, or subscription fee	Content/info asset mgmt.; IT infrastructure
Information and News Services Dow Jones (www.dowjones.com) Euromoney (www.euromoney.com)	Yes	Yes	Moderate to High	Subscription fee; commission, transaction, or service fee	Content/info asset mgmt.; advertising, marketing, and sales; IT infrastructure
Producer Portals Citigroup (www.citi.com)	Possibly	Yes	High	Transaction or service fee; subscription or membership fee; consulting and integration fee; hosting fee	Content/info asset; IT Infrastructure and R&D; software development; logistics

Producer Business Model Trends:
- Producers often augment offline product, market, and channel positioning with online channels.
- Some vertically integrated producers, like American Express and Citigroup in the financial services industry and Time Warner in the entertainment and media industry, are offering the one-stop-shop, customized solutions required by some customers. These are offered through company-owned portals and also through a wide variety of distribution agreements that further expand customer options.

Infrastructure Distributor Business Models

Models and Examples	Model Differentiators				Likely Revenues	Likely Costs
	Control Inventory	Sell Online	Price Set Online	Physical Product or Service		
Infrastructure Retailers Dell (www.dell.com) Oracle (www.oracle.com) Microsoft (www.microsoft.com)	Yes	Yes	Not usually	Yes	Product sales; service fees	Advertising and marketing; physical facilities, inventory, and customer svc.; R&D; IT infrastructure
Value-Added Resellers (VARS) & Distributors Ingram Micro (www.ingrammicro.com) Tech Data (www.techdata.com)	Usually	Yes	Not usually, but may be customized	Yes	Transaction fees; service fees; commission; channel assembly fee	Advertising and marketing; R&D; IT infrastructure
Infrastructure Aggregators CNET (www.cnet.com)	No	No	No	Possibly	Referral fees; advertising and marketing fees	Advertising and marketing; R&D; IT infrastructure
Infrastructure Exchanges Converge Global Trading Exchange (www.converge.com)	Possibly	Possibly	Yes	Yes	Depends on model	Advertising and marketing; staff support for auctions (especially B2B); inventory and logistics if inventory control; R&D; technical infrastructure

Infrastructure Distributor Business Model Trends:

- The speed of obsolescence of the technology, coupled with the complexity of customer solutions and the slim margins for technology products/components, has forced massive consolidation in network and computing technology channels. For many, service revenues are driving profitability.
- Those distributors that take ownership of inventory are searching for inventory-less, just-in-time business models.
- Distributors that have the capability for custom configuration of products and services are gaining power.

Infrastructure Portal Business Models

Models & Examples	Model Differentiators		Likely Revenues	Likely Costs
	Internet/Network Access and Hosting	Hosted Applications and Solutions		
Horizontal Infrastructure Portals AOL.com British Telecom (www.bt.com) IBM Global Solutions (www.ibm.com)	Yes	Through partnerships with noninfrastructure portals and ASPs	Access fees; commission, service, or transaction fees; subscription fees; hosting fees	R&D; IT infrastructure; advertising, marketing, and sales
Vertical Infrastructure Portals Salesforce.com Oracle On Demand (www.oracle.com) IBM Transformation Outsourcing (www.ibm.com)	Often through partnerships with horizontal infrastructure portals	Yes	Licensing fees; service and transaction fees; maintenance and update fees; hosting fees	Advertising, marketing, and sales; content/info asset mgmt.; R&D; IT infrastructure

Infrastructure Portal Business Model Trends:

- Horizontal infrastructure portals (ISPs, network service providers, and Web hosting providers) are merging or partnering with horizontal content portals to increase value created through intangible assets such as information, community, and brand.
- Horizontal content portals such as AOL are vertically integrating with horizontal infrastructure providers, such as Time Warner Cable. (Note: Prior to the AOL Time Warner merger, AOL was both a horizontal portal and a horizontal infrastructure portal.)
- Convergence of voice, data, and video channels and global acceptance of a common set of standards is leading to global industry convergence at the content and infrastructure levels.
- Aggressive pursuit of a growing market for hosted application services is leading to confusion as players with markedly different business models converge on a common competitive space.
- Two competing Vertical Infrastructure Portal (ASP) models are emerging: producer-ASPs (e.g., Oracle, Siebel, SAP) provide online access to Internet-enabled versions of their brand-name software; distributor-ASPs (e.g., US Internetworking and Jamcracker) offer application hosting of many software brands.

Infrastructure Producer Business Models

Models & Examples	Model Differentiators				Likely Revenues	Likely Costs
	Manufacture Equipment	Develop Software	Services/ Consulting			
Equipment/ Component Manufacturers IBM Sony Cisco Intel	Yes	Possibly	Possibly		Product license or sales; installation and integration fees; maintenance, update, and service fees	R&D; advertising, marketing, and sales; production; physical facilities and infrastructure; specialized equipment, materials, and supplies; IT infrastructure
Software Firms SAP Siebel Oracle Microsoft	Rarely	Yes	Possibly		Product license or sales; installation and integration fees; maintenance, update, and service fees	R&D; advertising, marketing, and sales; production; physical facilities and infrastructure; specialized equipment, materials, and supplies; IT infrastructure
Custom Software and Integration Service Providers Accenture Ingram Micro	Possibly	Possibly	Yes		Commission, service, or transaction fee	Access to specialized talent; professional development and training; travel
Infrastructure Services Federal Express (logistics) Hyperion (business intelligence)	Rarely	Possibly	Yes		Commission, service, or transaction fee; hosting fee	Content/info asset mgmt.; R&D; IT infrastructure

Infrastructure Producer Business Model Trends:
• Many hardware and software producers were early adopters of online commerce, selling directly to Internet-savvy customers and through online distributors. For example, in 1999, over 80% of Cisco's sales were through online channels—most of which was through online distribution partners.

CHAPTER 4

Making the Case for IT[1]

We continue pumping $2 trillion annually into information technology to pursue competitive advantage and spur productivity. But extracting strategic value and productivity from IT has become increasingly challenging.[2]

In spring 2003, Nicholas Carr published a controversial article entitled, "IT Doesn't Matter."[3] Following on the heels of the dot-com meltdown and subsequent global economic recession, the article quickly became a best seller as business executives challenged their chief information officers (CIOs) to explain—and sometimes defend—their IT budgets and requests for support of new IT investments.

Carr's argument (see Figure 4.1) is built upon the premise that, in the past, IT applications were developed in-house with each application representing millions of dollars worth of investment and years of effort. Given the investment and time required, economists considered these IT applications a "scarce resource"—something that your firm could do or had access to which others did not. When targeted toward strategic differentiation, *proprietary* IT applications could deliver *proprietary* advantage to a firm.

Today, Carr argued, many of the IT applications in use within firms are widely available from vendors and service providers. Others are built using development tools that dramatically decrease development cost and effort and, as a result, can be easily copied. Since strategic positioning defines what makes a company unique, Carr believed that IT no longer conferred proprietary advantage. Instead, he argued, IT should be considered a commodity—part of the infrastructure upon which a firm does business.

Carr's second premise builds upon the first. While proprietary technologies are more valuable when they are owned and exploited by a single company, infrastructure is more valuable when shared. As hardware, and increasingly even software, become part of the shared infrastructure for doing business, a greater percentage of IT investment dollars is used to build infrastructure. While Carr admits that an infrastructure owner

---

[1] This chapter is adapted from papers and materials from Professor Applegate's *Building Businesses in Turbulent Times* course. The correct citation is L. M. Applegate, *Building Businesses in Turbulent Times* (Boston: Harvard Business School, 2004), available on request from the author.

[2] "Wringing the Real Value from IT," *Harvard Business Review OnPoint* (No. 5135).

[3] N. Carr, "IT Doesn't Matter," *Harvard Business Review*, May 2003.

FIGURE 4.1
**Key Premises
of Nicholas
Carr's
Argument**

Carr's Key Premises

➤ IT is ubiquitous, not scarce.

➤ IT is infrastructure, not proprietary.

➤ The Internet is accelerating the rate of
    commoditization of new IT applications.

can gain proprietary advantage in the early phases of an infrastructure build-out when access is limited, the mistake most executives make, he says, is that they think the advantage continues indefinitely and are not prepared when rapid commoditization causes prices to drop before the infrastructure investment delivers the expected returns. Alternatively, executives may sink money into risky investments in infrastructure that never gain widespread acceptance.

Carr's third premise is that the widespread adoption of Internet-based technology standards—when coupled with the dramatic increase in network speed and capacity and the tendency to develop applications that cross firm boundaries—has provided the perfect channel for quickly disseminating IT applications throughout an industry. As a result, new value-creating IT applications are quickly commoditized. In addition, while modular IT architectures enable rapid customization, the ease of entry and lower switching costs mean that even these customized applications quickly become commoditized. Rapid commoditization means that the window of opportunity for creating value from IT often closes before proprietary advantages can be fully exploited.

Given the above premises, Carr concludes that executives should (1) spend as little as possible on IT; (2) concentrate IT investments on driving cost savings; (3) follow rather than lead when adopting new IT, allowing others to bear the risk and cost of testing new technologies; and (4) concentrate on managing risk, rather than searching for IT opportunities.

When Carr's article hit the streets, the letters to the editor began pouring in. While some criticized Carr's entire article, thoughtful readers recognized that—while the title was designed to be provocative—the basic premises could not be totally dismissed. Many executives *are* spending too much on IT believing that the technology itself conveys proprietary advantage. Many firms have been investing to build new infrastructure that duplicates what could have been bought much more cheaply. And, the increased pace of innovation and speed with which commoditization occurs has caused the windows of opportunity within which a new technology innovation must be exploited to shrink. John Seely Brown, former chief scientist at Xerox Parc, and John Hagel, a management consultant, captured the mood of many letters.[4]

---

[4] See "Does IT Matter? An HBR Debate," *Harvard Business Review*, June 2003, p. 2.

Businesses have overestimated the strategic value of technology. They have significantly overspent on technology in the quest for business value. They need to manage large portions of their infrastructure more rigorously to reduce capital investment and operating expenses. As companies become more dependent on IT for their day-to-day operations, they must focus on potential vulnerabilities and more aggressively manage for reliability and security.

But Seely Brown and Hagel go on to argue that:

. . . such ideas are not inconsistent with the view that IT remains a profound catalyst for the creation of strategic differentiation . . . IT may be ubiquitous but the insight required to harness its potential [is not] . . . The gap between IT potential and business realization of that potential has not narrowed. Instead it has steadily widened over the past several decades. This gap creates enormous instability in the business world. Wherever there is so much potential for instability, there is also fertile ground for new strategies.

Vijay Gurbaxani, professor and director of the Center for Research on IT and Organization at the University of California at Irvine, agrees: "The scarce resource never was technology; it was always the set of managerial capabilities needed to create value with that technology."[5] Paul Strassman, executive advisor at NASA, goes further:[6]

Easy availability of information technology is what makes IT increasingly valuable . . . I spent 40 years of my career implementing information technologies; for the first 30 years, that was a great pain. The technology was expensive, faulty, insecure, hard to manage, and unstable. I finally see the advent of an era in which low-cost ownership of information technologies is possible . . . Carr's logic is defective because his examples deal exclusively with capital intensive goods. Capital investments in machinery do indeed exhibit diminishing returns as markets saturate and the difference between marginal costs and marginal revenues disappears, but information goods are not subject to such effects.

Indeed, Carr's arguments seem to be based on the traditional mainframe-base and client-server approach to building IT infrastructure. These approaches led to IT infrastructures that were costly to build, costly to maintain, and provided limited opportunity for rapid leverage to drive insight and innovation. Today's flexible, open standard and ubiquitous IT infrastructures are designed to be shared and, as Carr has argued, actually become more valuable when shared. This new breed of IT infrastructure has dramatically increased the range of business building opportunities that can be pursued while also dramatically decreasing the cost and time required to launch new IT-enabled strategic initiatives. IBM executives call this new IT design and the business opportunities it opens up—Business On Demand. And, as will be seen later in this chapter, the shift to On Demand at IBM enabled executives to exploit the immediate cost savings and asset productivity that come from sharing a common infrastructure while also exploiting the dramatic increase in "strategic options" for pursuing opportunities that drive profitable growth and proprietary advantage. And, unlike securities

---

[5] See "Does IT Matter? An HBR Debate," *Harvard Business Review*, June 2003, p. 14.
[6] See "Does IT Matter? An HBR Debate," *Harvard Business Review*, June 2003, p. 7.

options, these IT options were exercised over and over to create what economists refer to as a "virtuous cycle" of innovation, productivity, and increasing returns.[7]

Executives that fail to recognize the new economics of emerging On Demand IT infrastructures can quickly find themselves at a serious disadvantage. The design implications of an On Demand, shared, network IT infrastructure are discussed in more detail in Chapter 6. An executive familiar with the emerging On Demand IT architecture model explained their impact:[8]

> I would argue that the commoditization of technology is the very thing that enables innovation in what many industry leaders now call an "On Demand" world. An On Demand enterprise is one that leverages standards-based, componentized technology to support integrated and flexible business processes. In a world where customer needs and global market forces are more dynamic than ever, it is these component-based technologies and flexible business processes that enable organizations to sense and respond to new opportunities and threats and to turn on a dime to meet new challenges. While technological innovation continually provides us with more powerful and efficient tools that do become commoditized and ubiquitous, strategic innovation using the technology—how we put the hardware and software together to solve pressing business problems and create competitive advantage—is very much alive and well.

This chapter presents frameworks, approaches, and examples that executives can use to create a compelling business case for exploiting the power of IT to create value inside the firm and for customers, suppliers, and partners.

Building the Business Case for IT

It is little wonder that there is confusion over how to exploit IT to create business value. Most executives continue to view technology as a budgeted expense to be managed on a project-by-project basis within traditional budgeting cycles. This approach is a throwback to the mainframe era when IT infrastructure was composed of large stand-alone computers, housed within a single data center, and was tightly managed and controlled by a centralized group of IT professionals that were dedicated to keeping the technology running. Using this approach, decisions on IT infrastructure investments—for example, in mainframe computers, networks, and facilities—were made along with other capital budgeting requests and ongoing maintenance and operations were managed through the annual budgeting process.

Value-creating IT applications that were built to run on traditional mainframe infrastructures were funded as stand-alone projects. Each application performed a specific task and delivered well-specified benefits—usually involving cost savings that would come from increasing the efficiency of a structured, paper-intensive back-office process. Once deployed, the application became part of the operating environment and routine operations and maintenance costs were factored into the annual operating

---

[7] D. Farrell, "The *Real* New Economy," *Harvard Business Review*, October 2003; C. Shapiro and H. Varian, *Information Rules: A Strategic Guide to the New Economy* (Boston: Harvard Business School Press, 1998).

[8] Author interview, July 2004.

budget. Since most applications could only be used for a single purpose and were tightly coupled to a highly structured task, the ability to reuse (or share) applications was limited.

Exceptions to this norm were widely publicized, which increased executive awareness of strategic IT systems that could transform an organization and an industry, generating significant proprietary advantage. For example, American Airlines legendary computer reservation system (SABRE) was built on its internal reservation system that was running in the company data centers. While the internal system had been built in the 1960s to lower the cost and improve the efficiency of the internal reservation process, insightful marketing executives soon recognized that a new front-end could be added to enable the airline's travel agent partners to book reservations directly. Given that the SABRE system was a fundamental component of the firm's business strategy to lock in travel agents, the system and strategy were tightly intertwined and evolved in tandem creating proprietary advantage. As will be seen later in this chapter, this ability to leverage an existing IT application that generated cost savings and efficiency as a platform to create a new strategic IT application is at the heart of the IT value proposition for today's open standards, networked IT infrastructures.

Over the years, IT has become ever more tightly intertwined with business operations and strategy. Indeed, by the early 1990s, forward-thinking executives had begun to search for new investment models. But the proliferation of incompatible computers, operating systems, and applications within and across organization boundaries impeded the adoption of investment models that recognized the dual role of IT to both create operating efficiencies while also driving business insight, innovation, and proprietary advantage.

The commercialization and rapid adoption of the Internet proved to be the "tipping point."[9] Rapid penetration and adoption of Internet standards for packaging, storing, accessing, and sharing information in all of its forms—voice, video, data, and graphics—catalyzed convergence of multiple technology platforms and a commitment to develop and adopt common standards. By 2005, the stage was set for providing a shared infrastructure that would enable a dramatic decrease in the total cost of ownership and the speed with which new value-creating IT applications could be developed and deployed across an organization, an industry, and the world.

More importantly, building on these industry standards, new approaches to system design and development now enabled large, complex applications to be built from reusable modules linked together through shared "middleware" services and common interfaces. This approach dramatically increased the ability to reuse data, information, and applications and to share a common infrastructure, which further increased the flexibility and speed with which new value-creating IT-enabled business initiatives could be launched and globally deployed. Thus while infrastructure alone can't convey *sustainable* proprietary advantage, businesses that remain chained to a "legacy" of incompatible and inflexible *proprietary* infrastructures find themselves at a significant strategic disadvantage as they attempt to keep pace with increasingly shorter cycles of innovation, productivity, and returns.

---

[9] C. Kim and R. Mauborgne, "Tipping Point Leadership," *Harvard Business Review*, April 2003 (HBR #3353).

FIGURE 4.2
IT Value
Framework

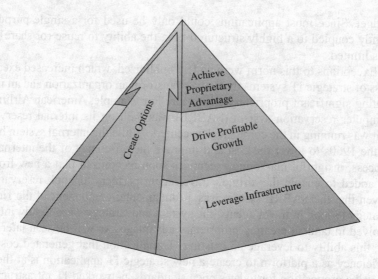

A Web services approach to building and deploying IT infrastructure and applications demands a very different approach to investment decision making. Given that large portions of an IT investment involve shared infrastructure that serves as a platform upon which multiple business building, value-creating applications can be deployed, IT can no longer be considered an expense that is managed on a project-by-project basis. Instead, we must think of business-building IT opportunities as a string of investments that must deliver value today and in the future. The value of these future uses can be thought of as the "options value" of IT, which will be discussed in more detail below.

The IT Value Framework, see Figure 4.2, identifies three categories of benefits that can be used to define the business case for IT: (1) investments in reusable, *value-enabling* infrastructure lower costs, improve asset efficiency, and create strategic options for future growth; (2) investments in *value-creating* IT applications drive profitable growth through further cost reductions and, more importantly, through revenue generation; and (3) *value-sustaining* IT applications and infrastructure provide strategic differentiation and proprietary advantage that can be measured in terms of increased market share, improved brand value, and increased market capitalization.[10] Table 4.1 provides examples of IT projects and metrics within each category that drive business value. The IT Value Framework is discussed in more detail below.

Leveraging Infrastructure and Creating Options

IT infrastructure includes two key components—*IT operations* (e.g., data center, network, and call centers) and *supporting enterprise processes* (e.g., procurement, enterprise resource planning, finance, and human resources). This infrastructure forms the foundation for delivering business value. When IT infrastructure is designed to optimize

[10] This framework was first introduced in L. M. Applegate, "Making the Case for IT," *Financial Times Mastering Information Management Series,* March 29, 1999.

TABLE 4.1 **IT Investment Categories, Examples, and Metrics**

IT Investment Category	Examples of Projects and Initiatives	Sample Metrics
Achieve Proprietary Advantage	Differentiate products (e.g., information value-added; price). Enter new markets or increase market spend from existing customers. Launch new IT-enabled businesses. Increase barriers to entry or switching costs.	Increased market share. Increased brand value and awareness. Increased market capitalization.
Drive Profitable Growth	Improve new product development process to increase speed to market and effectiveness of new product launches. Improve customer-facing processes to increase customer satisfaction, loyalty, lifetime value, and demand. Develop information and support for business analytics. Improve customer segmentation and personalization. Enhance the speed and improve performance of acquisition integration.	Increase IT contribution to net income. Increase IT contribution to revenues while holding constant or decreasing expenses. Shift expenses ratio from fixed to variable. Add new revenue streams from current customers.
Leverage Infrastructure	Leverage shared services, centers of excellence, offshoring, and outsourcing to ensure delivery of a best-in-class lean, yet flexible, infrastructure (includes data centers; networks; personal computers and devices; and supporting processes such as ERP, HR, finance, etc.). Create IT development, deployment, and operating processes that decrease the cost, time, and effort needed to launch value-creating and value-sustaining IT applications. Develop best-in-class security and risk management systems.	Decrease total cost of ownership of current infrastructure and operations. Improve asset productivity ($ of sales generated by each $ of infrastructure assets). Decrease IT infrastructure and operations costs as a percent of revenues. Decrease IT headcount costs as a percent of sales.
Create Options	Identify opportunities to decrease the time and cost of pursuing future value-enabling, value-creating, and value-sustaining opportunities.	Metrics depend on the type of option.

efficiency, speed to market, and flexibility, companies can drive down costs while also dramatically increasing IT asset productivity and future options value. Given that the IT infrastructure in most established companies is far from "best-in-class" in terms of being lean, yet flexible, significant value can be created through investments to modernize infrastructure.

Indeed, most large, established companies have a long way to go to achieve best-in-class status in their IT operating environment. Most companies assembled IT infrastructure in a piecemeal fashion over the past 20 to 30 years. New technologies were adopted as they became available with little consideration for how the different technologies might need to work together in the future. By the mid-1990s, this "legacy" IT infrastructure had become a hodgepodge of incompatible and inefficient technologies that were costly and difficult to manage and maintain. Given the state of IT infrastructure in most established firms, it is not surprising that massive investments have been required to simply keep critical systems up and running. In fact, most executives are shocked to learn that, at the height of the economic recession in 2002 when IT spending had already dropped precipitously, most established firms continued to spend over 50 percent of their capital budgets on IT equipment and projects. Globally, IT expenses in 2002 topped $2 trillion.[11] Even more shocking was the fact that the cost of maintaining and managing IT infrastructure often represented 80 percent or more of the yearly IT budget, leaving few resources to be directed towards creating proprietary business value.

Given that investments in infrastructure are more valuable when shared, some firms are turning their infrastructure over to specialized shared services providers (for example, IBM Global Services, EDS, CSC) that can deliver best-in-class, asset efficient, yet flexible, global IT shared services. Recognizing that each outsourcing decision needed to also be paired with a local business process reengineering project, in 2002, IBM bought Price Waterhouse's strategy and process reengineering consulting group to ensure that its outsourcing customers did not fall into the trap of saving money on technology while simultaneously driving up the cost of doing business and putting revenues at risk.

Other large, global firms prefer to build their own best-in-class shared services IT infrastructure, often *offshoring* IT shared services (for example, data centers, call centers, and even enterprise applications such as enterprise resource planning) in company locations in India, China, Brazil, or other emerging markets where they can take advantage of lower cost, yet highly skilled, labor markets. Savvy executives have learned to manage the business risks of implementing of these shared services initiatives by factoring in the cost and risk of reengineering intra- and inter-firm processes and the potential business disruptions that could occur.

But, no matter which approach is chosen to modernize IT infrastructure, executives are beginning to understand that they cannot sacrifice flexibility in their quest for efficiency. The "options value" that networked, flexible IT infrastructure can provide can no longer be ignored in companies where survival depends on being both lean and agile. See the text box, *Comparing Securities Options with IT Options*.

Analyzing the Options Value of Investments in IT Infrastructure

The series of cash flow curves presented in Figure 4.3 help frame how investments in value-enabling infrastructure create IT options that can deliver value today and in the future. As you review the curves, recall Nicholas Carr's key arguments supporting his contention that "IT Doesn't Matter." Assume that a colleague has just dropped a copy

---

[11] N. Carr, "IT Doesn't Matter," *Harvard Business Review*, May 2003.

Comparing Securities Options with IT Options

In financial terms, a *securities option* gives the owner the right (as distinct from the obligation) to buy a security at a fixed, predetermined price (the exercise price) on or before some fixed date (the maturity date). Important features of securities options that determine value include (1) the nature of future benefits (risky projects often generate the highest returns); and (2) the length of time you have to exercise the option (the longer the time frame the greater the value of the option).

Using this same logic, an *IT option* provides executives with the right (as distinct from the obligation) to pursue value-added IT-enabled business opportunities at a lower cost, more quickly, and with less inherent risk throughout the useful life of the technology. Features of an IT option that determine value include (1) the cumulative value from business opportunities that could potentially be pursued (the value of these benefits depends upon the number, type, and range of business opportunities); (2) the ability to pursue riskier opportunities where there is a higher potential return (as we will see below, the IT option "cuts off the downside risk for future investments"); and (3) the length of time for capturing value (keeping in mind that IT options can be exercised over and over again throughout the useful life of the technology).

of the article on your desk and asked: "What do you think of this?" Can you use the IT value framework and the discussion of cash flow curves below to frame your response? We will return to this question at the end of the chapter.

When faced with an investment decision, executives frequently perform a pro forma analysis of anticipated future revenues and expenses. The results of the analysis can be used to plot the expected cash flow curve for the future investment. Figure 4.3(a) represents an investment that executives of a medical device company are considering as they evaluate a business plan to launch a new Internet-enabled remote patient monitoring business. Patients with cardiac pacemakers would be able to place an external device over the pacemaker to collect data on cardiac rhythm, volume of blood pumped with each beat, and other clinical data. Data in the device could then be sent from the patient's home by Internet to their physician, family, and other interested health care providers, thus reducing the cost of monitoring the disease for the patient, family, and health care providers while also improving clinical outcomes. The cash flow curve suggests that executives will need to invest $300 million over five years to develop the monitoring device, the associated IT infrastructure (customer and provider databases, networks, call centers) and remote monitoring applications, and then to launch it into the market and begin to generate revenues. The business is expected to begin generating positive cash flows in five years, to break even two years later, and to generate over $2 billion in revenues by year ten. This scenario is represented by the solid line on Figure 4.3(a). Assuming that this is a risky new business, however, and that the device maker would be the first mover, the executives know that they must model, not just the most likely scenario but also alternative scenarios, which are represented by the dotted lines in Figure 4.3(a).

Now let's compare the cash flow curves of two investments—one by executives in MedCo A (as discussed above) and one by executives in MedCo B. See Figure 4.3(b). Assume that MedCo A executives plan to spend the first two years and $150 million of investment in the remote monitoring business developing customer and provider databases, networks, and call centers. During the next 18 months, the proprietary remote monitoring business applications and user interface will be built for an additional

123

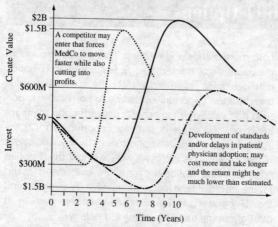

FIGURE 4.3(a)   Comparing Three Cash Flow Scenarios for MedCo Patient Monitoring Investments

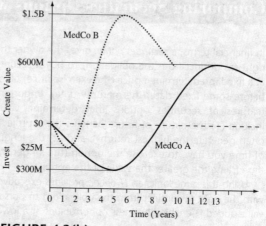

FIGURE 4.3(b)   Comparing MedCo A and MedCo B Patient Monitoring Investments

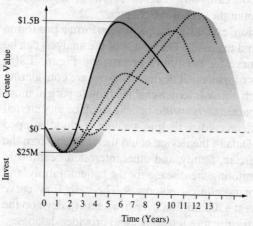

FIGURE 4.3(c)   MedCo B Leverages Infrastructure and Exercises Options

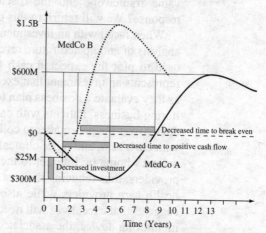

FIGURE 4.3(d)   The Value of Leveraging Infrastructure and Exercising Options

$25 million. The final 18 months and $125 million will be spent doing custom installation at early adopter physicians' offices, connecting patients and families, and rolling out the new offering. Finally, assume that the high cost of custom integration at each physician office and customer site increases operating costs and limits adoption resulting in cash flow of only $600 million by year 13. Clearly, most executives would not jump at the chance to invest in this business.

MedCo B executives were able to leverage existing IT infrastructure (e.g., customer and provider databases, networks, and call centers) built for other applications to launch the remote monitoring business in two years at a cost of $25 million. Also, by leveraging the shared browser-based, public Internet, custom integration was minimized and roll out to patients, families, and clinicians was faster and cheaper. Finally, while proprietary advantage only lasted for three years from launch, cash flows approached $1.5 billion due to the dramatically lower cost to acquire, connect, and serve customers.

Now suppose that the same network, database, call center, and remote monitoring infrastructure could also be leveraged to pursue other value-creating IM business opportunities. See Figure 4.3(c). For example, information captured by the patient monitoring application and stored in customer and provider databases could be used to provide outcome data that could be sold to health care providers and could be used by MedCo for future pacemaker enhancements and for new products. A new Web-based subscription service could be sold to concerned children who were an integral part of their elderly parents' care regime. Finally, remote monitoring for other disease states could also be pursued—all leveraging existing infrastructure and capabilities. The cost—and risk—of pursuing each of these "strategic options" would be much lower and the revenue-generating productivity of the shared IT asset would increase.

The shaded area below the break-even dotted line in Figure 4.3(d) represents the cumulative investment in IT applications and infrastructure over the life of the patient monitoring business and the shaded area above the line represents the cumulative value created by business applications built on the infrastructure. While each follow-on investment, representing the decision to exercise an IT-enabled strategic option, requires some additional development cost, the ability to leverage reusable infrastructure enables new applications to be built better, faster, and cheaper, increasing the productivity of the IM asset. In addition, reusable infrastructure decreases the risk involved in implementing a new application and improves innovative capacity.

Driving Profitable Growth

With a lean, flexible IT infrastructure in place, companies like MedCo B are poised to pursue opportunities to drive profitable growth. While cost control efforts can increase profits, opportunities in this category are characterized by the ability to *increase revenues*. There are two key categories of IT-enabled revenue-generating opportunities that can be pursued. First, revenue-generating capabilities can be enhanced. Second, IT-enabled product/service or business offerings can be launched.

While back-office enterprise processes (e.g., procurement, HR, finance) can be considered part of a firm's infrastructure—supporting but not directly influencing revenue growth—efforts to improve customer-facing processes and the performance of employees directly responsible for revenue generation (e.g., employees associated with new product or business development, marketing and sales, customer service) can have a direct impact on revenue generation. Examples of IT projects that directly influence revenue-generating capabilities include systems that provide timely, actionable information (e.g., marketing or sales analytics, competitor) to knowledge workers and executives whose performance is measured based on the ability to drive revenue growth; customer relationship management systems that increase the productivity of salespeople; and reengineering of product and/or business development processes that enable executives to identify business-building opportunities, speed time to market, and evolve product/market channel positioning. These intra-firm revenue-generating capabilities can be enhanced even further when a company uses IT to extend its revenue-generating capabilities across firm boundaries.

IT-enabled or information-enabled products and services are another example of revenue-generating IT initiatives. The remote monitoring application developed by MedCo and the follow-on IT-enabled revenue-generating business opportunities are examples of this second class of value-creating IT applications designed to drive profitable growth.

Achieving Proprietary Advantage

While many use the term "strategic" to refer to any IT system that is remotely related to business strategy, the metrics for measuring proprietary advantage are much more strict. It is not enough to simply cut costs, drive revenues, or increase profits and asset efficiency. To achieve *proprietary advantage,* executives must also *change competitive positioning* as measured by (1) successful entry into a large and growing market or exit from a shrinking one; (2) achieving the number one or number two position in an attractive industry and providing evidence that the company can sustain that position over time; and (3) attracting loyal investors that pay a premium, as measured in price/earnings (P/E) ratio and other capital market measures, over other players in a company's industry or even across industries.

Today it is hard to identify companies that have achieved *sustainable* proprietary advantage over time—with or without IT. It is even more difficult to find a company that has been able to climb back to the top of its industry from a near death experience. The next section describes how IBM fought back from the brink of extinction to take back its position as a global IT market leader. It was a core component of the turnaround. A three-case sequence, available from the authors, provides a compelling story of value creation and turnaround leadership.[12] Below, we excerpt from the case to highlight the short-term and long-term benefits that were gained by leveraging IT shared infrastructure to create strategic options, drive profitable growth, and to reestablish itself as a market leader, setting the pace for the industry.

IBM's Decade of Transformation: A Case Study in Turnaround Leadership and Delivering IT-Enabled Business Value[13]

In 1990, IBM was the second most profitable company in the world and was completing a transformation that was designed to position it for success in the next decade. For the world leader in an industry that was expected to keep growing spectacularly, the future looked promising. But all was not well within IBM and its senior executives realized it. "In 1990, we were feeling pretty good because things seemed to be getting better," one executive remarked. "But we weren't feeling great because we knew there were deep structural problems." Those structural problems revealed themselves sooner than anyone expected and more terribly than anyone feared. Beginning in the first quarter of 1991, IBM began posting substantial losses. Between 1991 and 1993, IBM

---

[12] L. M. Applegate, et al., *IBM's Decade of Transformation (A), (B), and (C)* Harvard Business School Case (Nos. 805-130, 805-131, 805-132), 2005.

[13] The IBM case study is discussed in more depth in L. M. Applegate, et al., *IBM's Decade of Transformation (A), (B), and (C)* Harvard Business School Case (Nos. 805-130, 805-131, and 805-132). The case series provides a more detailed discussion of the IBM turnaround, including how the company leveraged infrastructure, created options, drove profitable growth, and achieved proprietary advantage.

lost a staggering $16 billion. In April 1992, John Akers, IBM CEO from 1985 to 1993, vented his frustrations during a company training program. His comment "people don't realize how much trouble we're in," made its way from company bulletin boards to the press, shaking employee and investor confidence.

In April 1993, Lou Gerstner took charge. While many wondered how an executive with no technology background could rescue IBM, insiders knew that Gerstner was brought in—not to rescue the company—but to break it up for sale. In no time, however, Gerstner learned from customers, analysts, and employees that IBM's value was not in its pieces. Reversing direction, he rallied support for saving IBM.

By 1995, the company was back on solid financial footing. Catalyzed by the Internet boom and the massive technology spending needed to ready businesses for the new millennium, IBM began growing again. By 2003, one decade after Gerstner set out to rescue IBM, the company had once more become the industry leader firmly holding the number one market share position in its IBM Global Services and Server businesses and number two in market share in its software business (behind Microsoft). After losing $4.9 billion on revenues of $64 billion in 1992, IBM generated $7.6 billion in profits on over $89 billion in revenue in 2003 with almost half of those revenues generated by IBM Global Services.

How did Gerstner turn around IBM? IT played an important role. Infrastructure was leveraged and processes were reengineered to reduce costs and improve asset efficiency as the company struggled to stem the bleeding. Having stemmed the bleeding in 1995, IBM executives began to cash in on the options value of its investments in infrastructure to drive profitable growth and achieve proprietary advantage.

Leveraging Infrastructure and Creating Options

When it became clear that he would fight to save the company, Gerstner acted quickly to reverse the company's plunging profits and stock price and to keep customers from leaving in droves. He hired Jerry York, a former Chrysler CFO, and charged him with getting costs under control. Upon taking charge, York launched a benchmarking study to determine how IBM's costs in each of its businesses compared with those of competitors. The results were daunting: The expense to revenue ratio (42 percent in 1993) needed to be reduced by 9 percent. This meant that the company's expenses needed to be cut by at least $7 billion.

Despite its prior leadership position in the IT industry, IBM's internal IT infrastructure, like that of many of its customers, was out-of-date, inflexible, and costly to maintain. As a result, this poorly performing asset became a lightning rod for restructuring. When the dust cleared, IBM's internal IT organization had contributed *over $2 billion per year* to the $7 billion per year cost reduction required. In fact, between 1994 and 1997, the cost of operating and running IT operations was cut in half. Key savings came from reducing the number of data centers from 155 to 3 regional "megacenters" fed by 11 "server farms," and a 60 percent reduction in headcount. IT leadership was centralized; 128 CIOs were reduced to 1. IBM's 31 incompatible networks were converted to 1 common protocol Internet (TCP/IP) network.[14] The system

---

[14] TCP/IP (Transport Control Protocol/Internet Protocol) is the standard used to communicate and share information on the Internet.

TABLE 4.2
Leveraging
Infrastructure
at IBM: IT
Operations

IBM Sample Projects and Value Drivers	Sample Financial Metrics
Leverage Infrastructure: IT Operations	
• Decreased data centers from 155 to 11, which feed into three "megacenters." • Developed a single global Internet network to replace 31 incompatible networks, reducing network operating costs by over 50% while dramatically increasing network accessibility, functionality, and reach. • Shifted to "open source," common standards for information processing (Linux) and from proprietary to industry standard enterprise applications (SAP, PeopleSoft, Siebel). • Redesigned system development processes to enable modular design and reuse. • Decreased number of global applications from 16,000 to 5,200. • 60% reduction in IT professional headcount; 128 CIOs to 1.	• 50% reduction in total cost of ownership for data center and network operations and internal enterprise application development and maintenance. • Direct cost savings in internal IT expenses of over $2 billion per year beginning in 1997. • IBM spent $100 million between 1994 and 1996 to reengineer its IT infrastructure processes; ROI on the investment in infrastructure was less than one year.

development process was also reengineered and IT applications that were deemed to be "underperforming assets" were retired. Within two years, the number of internal applications that needed to be operated and maintained decreased from 16,000 to 5,200. See Table 4.2.

As cost-cutting got underway, Gerstner also focused on reengineering back-office processes. In late 2003, he assigned each member of the corporate executive committee the responsibility for a functional reengineering project (e.g., procurement, product development, sales). He set two priorities for these projects: (1) get cost out as quickly as possible; and (2) "clean sheet" the process and redesign it for global use. The redesigned processes would form the foundation for sustained cost competitiveness and best-in-class operations as the company embarked on the growth phase of its transformation. An IBM executive explained how procurement, logistics, and fulfillment processes were standardized and streamlined."[15]

In 1995, each of our key brands handled its own procurement, logistics, and fulfillment activities. As a result, we had silos of these activities all over the company. During 1994 and 1995, we began to reengineer and standardize activities. If there was someone on the outside that could perform the activity better, faster, and cheaper than us, we outsourced the physical activity and kept the strategy, planning, and management. For example, in logistics, we now handle all of the planning and management centrally but we outsource all of the warehousing and distribution to a third-party partner. In addition, given our decision to move away from competing with enterprise application software vendors, we decided to partner with SAP, PeopleSoft, and Siebel and use the same software internally as our customers used.

[15] Author interview, January 2004.

TABLE 4.3 **Leveraging Infrastructure at IBM: Enterprise Support Processes**

IBM Sample Projects and Value Drivers	Sample Financial Metrics
Leverage Infrastructure: Enterprise Support Processes	
• Streamlined, integrated, and centralized IT-enabled enterprise processes (e.g., procurement, enterprise resource planning, human resources, payroll, finance). • Selectively outsourced activities and processes where IBM was not best-in-class (e.g., HR, physical warehouse, inventory management, selected logistics). • Decreased the number of financial centers from 67 to 8 and financial applications from 145 to 55. • Decreased the cycle time for accounting close from 187 to 7 days. • eEnabled then decreased the number of suppliers to 33,000; electronic purchases reached 95%. • Centralized and integrated the supply chain and outsourced to IBM Global Services; 19,000 employees managed procurement, inventory, and logistics for over $47 billion in parts, equipment, and services. • Decreased maverick buying from >35% to <0.2%. • Supplier quality increased from <85% to >99%. • Purchase order processing time decreased from >30 days to <1 day. • Ability to "sense and respond" to customer demand enabled IBM to quickly meet unexpected rise or fall in demand for products. • Supplier, employee, and partner satisfaction scores doubled. • Winner MIT Process Improvement Award and Purchasing Magazine Medal of Excellence.	• $7 billion in direct savings + $2 billion in cost avoidance per year from supply chain improvements. • Cash generation increased by $8 billion from supply chain cost savings. • HR, payroll, finance process costs reduced over 50%, representing almost $1 billion in direct cost savings per year. • Purchasing expense/revenue ratio decreased from 3.2% to 1.5%.
Create Options	
• Transferred internal IBM shared services and centralized process reengineering infrastructure and expertise to IBM Global Services where it became the basis for new service offerings, including business transformation outsourcing. • Leveraged end-to-end IT-enabled processes to deliver real-time, actionable information to internal IBM decision makers and to customers, suppliers, and business partners. • Enabled continuous improvement and organizational learning.	• See metrics associated with profitable growth and proprietary advantage.

Within one year of reengineering procurement processes, costs were down 20 percent and the time needed to complete and confirm supply orders had decreased from an average of 48 hours to 2.5 hours. By 2000, 94 percent of goods and services, representing $4.3 billion were procured online from 24,000 worldwide suppliers at a cost saving of over $370 million annually. And, even as year-over-year growth in procurement volume increased by 60 percent between 1999 and 2000, no new staff were added. (See Table 4.3 for a summary of benefits due to cost-cutting and reengineering or back-office support processes.)

Driving Profitable Growth

In addition to using IT to support reengineering of enterprise support processes, IBM executives also redesigned customer-facing processes to lower costs while also improving revenue generating capabilities. Research and new product development processes were among the key revenue-generating processes targeted for improvement when benchmark studies indicated that, in over 85 percent of new product launches, IBM's time to market was at least $1.25\times$ slower than best-in-class competitors and that the development expense to revenue-generation ratio was over $2\times$ higher than best-in-class.

By 1995, IBM executives had streamlined and integrated the new product development process to reduce time to market and lower development costs: Abandoned project expense were decreased by over 90 percent, the warranty expense to revenue ratio decreased by 25 percent, and time to market for new products improved 67 percent. Overall, product development expenses were decreased by 50 percent, generating over $1.6 billion per year in cost savings and, more importantly, driving increased revenues from the increased rate of new products that entered the market much faster. In 2003, for example, of 22 new businesses that had been launched within the previous two years, four were already generating over $1 billion in revenues per year and another three were experiencing double-digit revenue growth.

In addition to reengineering revenue-generating processes, IBM also leveraged the Internet to develop Web-based portals and tools designed to provide timely, actionable information to support business decision making. IBM Global Services consultants used the tools to quickly develop a Web-based knowledge-sharing portal for consultants in its rapidly growing and increasingly more complex services business. At a cost of only $25,000 invested over several weeks, the consultants launched the portal and within one year had decreased consultant engagement times by 40–80 percent, increased revenues per consultant by 20 percent, and improved contribution margin per consultant by 400 percent. In addition, the Web was also used to shift a significant portion of its eLearning training programs online, saving $350 million in training costs per year.

While the initial return to profitability and a positive return on equity were driven by cost savings and improved asset efficiency, during the late 1990s, IBM turned the corner and began to grow revenues. But at only 5.7 percent average growth per year, IBM lagged others in the industry that were experiencing double-digit revenue growth rates.

IBM Global Services (IGS) leveraged the data center expertise and partnerships that it used in running IBM's internal global data centers and reengineering to augment its outsourcing services and to expand its service offerings. Leveraging its acquisition of Price Waterhouse Consulting (PWCC), in 2002 and 2003, IGS launched two new services offerings: Business Consulting Services (which leveraged the 30,000 business consultants from PWCC) and Business Transformation Outsourcing (BTO), which offered consulting and outsourcing services for HRM, finance, procurement, supply chain management, and customer relationship management enterprise processes.

In September 2003, Procter & Gamble (P&G) signed a 10-year, $400 million BTO agreement with IBM to outsource their payroll processing, benefits administration, compensation planning, expatriate and relocation services, travel expense management, and human resources data management for over 98,000 P&G employees in over 80 countries around the world.[16] In doing so, P&G gained access to partnerships that IBM had established with Fidelity, ADP, and Ceridian—leaders in HR outsourcing and partners in providing HR services to internal IBM employees. IBM expected that the global market for BTO services would exceed $100 billion in revenues by 2006.[17] In fourth quarter 2003 alone, IBM signed over $3 billion in BTO agreements that would provide ongoing revenues for years to come. Table 4.4 summarizes how IBM leveraged the best-in-class, lean, yet flexible, infrastructure to begin cashing in on options to return IBM to double-digit revenue growth during an improving, but still sluggish, economy.

Achieving Proprietary Advantage

The launch of its BTO service offering, when coupled with the launch of 22 unique new technology products, in late 2002 and early 2003, marked the turning point in IBM's transformation from profitable revenue growth to proprietary advantage. The new generation of products and services were developed using IBM's proprietary assets (including proprietary IT assets) that would be exceedingly difficult to replicate. These scarce resources came from the integration of IBM's broad technology research and product leadership, its 60,000 business strategy and technology consultants, and its world-renowned research capabilities. The ability to deploy these assets around the world further enhanced IBM's proprietary advantage.

Building on the unique differentiation and proprietary advantage provided by its BTO services offering, in 2004, IBM launched another new offering that demonstrated the "options value" of the infrastructure, capabilities, and assets that IBM had built over the previous decade. This new offering, called IBM Business Innovation Services, leveraged IBM's unparalleled strength in technology and analytical research with its product specialists, strategy consultants, and service providers to help customers solve tough problems. An IBM executive from the Mathematical Sciences Research unit, explained:[18]

> When you add tremendous advances in processing speed to the fact that we can now harness the capacity of hundreds of processors connected within an "On Demand" network and can access real-time "On Demand" data from anywhere in the world, the analytical power becomes staggering. This is why access to researchers that can develop new analytical models to solve complex real-world problems is such a huge competitive differentiator for us. The tougher, messier, and more important the problem, the more value we can add for our customers.

Another IBM executive went on to state that adding direct customer contact with IBM researchers differentiated IBM's product/service offerings three key ways.

> First, our customers believe that having direct access to IBM's distinguished scientists to solve their tough problems is a huge differentiator that has helped our Business Consulting

---

[16] IBM Press Release, September 9, 2003.

[17] IBM Annual Report, 2003, p. 7.

[18] Author interview, January 2004.

TABLE 4.4 Driving Profitable Growth at IBM

IBM Sample Projects and Value Drivers	Sample Financial Metrics
Drive Profitable Growth: Revenue Generating Capabilities	
• Benchmarked new product development process and found slow time to market (85% of projects at least 1.25× longer than best-in-class) and development expense ratio that was over 2× higher than best-in-class. • Redesigned hardware/software research and new product development processes to reduce time to market and lower development costs.	• Abandoned project expense decreased by over 90%. • Warranty expense to revenue decreased by 25%. • New product development cycle time: 67% faster time to market. • Decreased product development expense ratio by 50%, generating cost savings of over $1.6 billion annually.
Drive Profitable Growth: Actionable Information and Business Analytics	
• Developed knowledge management, content, collaboration, and Web portal infrastructure and tools to enable knowledge workers to develop personalized knowledge sharing and business analytics • IBM Global Services developed a Web-based knowledge sharing portal to leverage its consultants' expertise during period of rapid growth. • Partnered with Siebel to reengineer Customer Relationship Management (CRM) processes and link to intranet portals. • 68% of employees rank the intranet as preferred channel for doing business.	• Consultant intranet led to decreased consulting engagement time by 40–80%, increased revenues per consultant by 20%, and improved consulting margins by 400%. • eLearning saves $350 million per year on employee education (12% YOY savings). • Internal intranet, content management, and collaboration tools become products and generate double-digit revenue growth in 2003.
Drive Profitable Growth: IT-Enabled Product/Service Offerings	
• Leveraged shared services infrastructure and expertise to deliver services to internal IBM customers and to offer significant enhancements to its data center outsourcing business. • Launched new offerings related to business transformation outsourcing, e-business, and Web services. • Leveraged partnerships with best-in-class software and services firm (e.g., Fidelity in pension fund administration, ADP in HR, SAP in enterprise resource planning, and Siebel in customer relationship management) to launch Business Transformation Outsourcing (BTO) services business. • By 2003, 22 of 25 new business offerings had transitioned from new ventures to high-growth businesses.	• IBM Global Services revenues exceeded $46 billion in 2004, up from $15 billion in 1992 and $36 billion in 2002. • Linux-based (open standard) server market revenues grew at 35% per year. • Server revenues grew at 32% and contribution margin increased to 31%. • Software revenue increased to $14.2 billion in 2003, up from $11.1 billion in 1992. • Four new product offerings generated over $1 billion in revenues annually and three additional new businesses doubled their revenues. • In total, IBM revenues grew from $64 billion in 2002 to over $96 billion in 2004. • Profits increase from $3 billion in 2002 to over $8 billion in 2004.

Services group win consulting projects like a sophisticated logistics scheduling project with BostonCoach. Second, we can bring inventions to the market that can become new products and also can spur new services revenues. For example, our research lab in Zurich built a new advanced security architecture that BCS consultants are using in a project with the French organization that handles land deeds. Third, we bring deep, specialized expertise in a wide range of areas that a typical consulting organization cannot access. For example, prior to its merger with IBM, PWCC was working with a transportation logistics firm on the reengineering of its core logistics process. The proposed process and system would have met the client's stated requirements but could not address a pressing problem that everyone agreed could not be solved using current technology. After the PWCC/IBM BCS merger, researchers became involved in the project and brought the sophisticated optimization modeling expertise needed.

Spurred by double-digit growth in revenues and profits from its services business and strong growth from new products from its hardware and software units, by 2004, IBM had begun to outperform its competitors. Proprietary advantage was not achieved through any single strategic coup but was instead created by IBM's ability to leverage infrastructure and capabilities from across its global organization and its extended enterprise of partners. The Business Transformation Outsourcing and Business Innovation Services offerings were examples of new differentiated offerings that could be quickly launched and grown to drive profitable growth and create competitive advantage.

In one short and tumultuous decade the "dinosaur" that had faced extinction had once more assumed a position of leading the industry, having achieved number one position in Global Services and Servers, number two in software, and number three in hardware. The success confirmed what Gerstner had heard from customers when he first took charge of the failing company and sought advice on how to complete its breakup.[19]

> [Our customers] said repeatedly, "We don't need one more disk drive company, we don't need one more database company or one more PC company. The one thing that you guys do that no one else can do is help us integrate and create global solutions."

By late 2003, the "One IBM" vision became a reality. Table 4.5 summarizes how IBM leveraged its resources and capabilities to create proprietary advantage.

No longer an IT company, by 2004, IBM had transformed into a shared infrastructure and services provider that enabled businesses and industries to participate in the Business On Demand vision that had transformed IBM. This first-hand experience at driving massive organizational, cultural, and strategic change inside IBM became just as much of a foundation for its new differentiated offerings as the IT infrastructure and global processes that had been created to enable IBM's transformation. The story of IBM's transformation provides a compelling example of how a firm embedded IT within a series of strategic initiatives designed to create and then leverage a best-in-class, lean, yet flexible, infrastructure to drive profitable growth and create proprietary advantage. The case demonstrates the use of the IT Value Framework and provides examples of actions taken at each step in the company's evolution and the value delivered at each stage.

---

[19] R. Austin and R. Nolan, *IBM Corporation: Turnaround 1991–1995* HBS (No. 600–098), p. 20.

TABLE 4.5
Creating Proprietary Advantage at IBM

IBM Sample Projects and Value Drivers	Sample Financial Metrics
Achieve Proprietary Advantage	
• Built IBM Global Services into the number 1 global IT services provider. • Launched unique BTO service offering in 2002 (e.g., P&G signs a $400 million/multiyear contract; Sprint signs a multibillion/5-year contract). • Launched unique Business Innovation Services offering in 2004 and closed several high profile, multimillion dollar client engagements. • BTO and Business Innovation Services provides proprietary advantage and strategic differentiation.	• Worldwide Global Services market estimated to reach $14 trillion in 2010; BTO market estimated to exceed $100 billion in 2006. • Market share: number 1 in services and servers; number 2 in software (behind Microsoft). • 2003 market capitalization = $159 billion (second to Microsoft); P/E ratio = 4.42 (number 1 in the industry).

Nicholas Carr Revisited

The IBM case example provides a compelling example that helps frame a response to the Nicholas Carr argument that IT doesn't matter. Clearly Carr was considering the IT legacy that has chained an organization and an industry to both a strategy and operating model that resists attempts at innovation and insight. The IBM case demonstrates that emerging lean, yet flexible, IT-enabled business infrastructures can become a value engine that creates strategic options and then decreases the cost and time of pursuing those options and cashing in on their value.

The Strategic Grid Framework, discussed in Chapter 1, helps put the lessons from the IBM case in perspective (see Figure 4.4). Carr is correct when he claims that efforts should be made to create a best-in-class lean and asset efficient infrastructure.

FIGURE 4.4
Nicholas Carr's Argument as Framed on the Strategic Grid

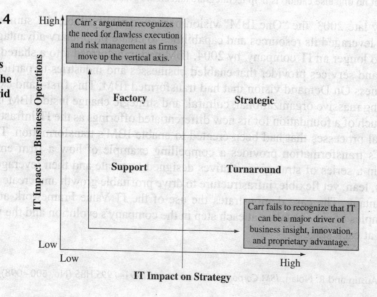

Every effort should be made to leverage an infrastructure to share costs and improve asset productivity—as long as the decision to centralize or outsource does not disrupt business operations or future revenue-generating potential elsewhere in the firm or with partners, customers, or suppliers. Risk management becomes essential as the importance of IT to business operations increases. Failure to deliver flawless execution as a firm's position on the strategic grid moves up the vertical axis can threaten a firm's (and an accountable executive's) survival.

But Carr failed to recognize that emerging networked IT infrastructures have dramatically changed our ability to shift position on the horizontal axis of the grid. As a firm harnesses the power of lean, yet flexible, IT infrastructure to cash in on the strategic options value, IT-enabled scarce resources and proprietary advantage can be created and sustained.

Summary

As we enter the twenty-first century, excitement concerning the potential of IT to transform business and drive improved performance has never been higher. But, the fascination with IT business innovation comes at a time of significant uncertainty and change as entrenched players and new entrants struggle to define a sustainable proprietary position for success in the turbulent twenty-first century. While most agree that Internet-based technologies have progressed at lightning speed since they were introduced to the business world in the early to mid-1990s, developing common standards and robust commercial technologies takes time. The challenge of integrating new technologies into the "legacy" of computers, networks, and systems already in place within companies adds to the problem. To achieve the grand vision of the Network Economy, a new approach to building businesses and measuring performance is needed.

This chapter explored the challenges that executives face as they attempt to develop the business case for digital business in the context of increasing volatility and uncertainty. Executives should consider the following questions as they attempt to forecast the value of digital business strategies and the ability of their organizations to execute them.

1. How well do you understand the linkages among your strategies, the capabilities and infrastructure built to execute those strategies, and the value that can be created for all stakeholders (e.g., customers, suppliers, partners, employees, investors)?

2. Is your business infrastructure best-in-class in terms of asset efficiency and strategic flexibility? How can IT be used to improve your ability to leverage infrastructure and assets to drive profitable growth and create strategic options for the future?

3. How well do you understand the key factors that drive business performance in your organization and industry? What must be done well to reduce costs, grow revenues, and improve asset efficiency? How can IT be used to drive profitable growth and achieve proprietary advantage?

4. Conduct an audit of your digital business infrastructure. How much are you spending to run and maintain current IT operations? On average, how long does it take and how much does it cost to implement a new IT-enabled business product, service, or strategy? What are key bottlenecks that slow down the IT-enabled business innovation process and the key activities that increase the cost?

5. Create a list of IT-enabled business strategies and the solutions that could be developed that would leverage an open standard networked infrastructure. Are there opportunities to:

   a. Improve internal operating efficiency and quality?

   b. Improve knowledge worker performance and enhance organizational learning?

   c. Increase employee satisfaction, engagement, and loyalty and attract and retain top talent?

   d. Increase customer/supplier satisfaction, engagement, and loyalty?

   e. Attract and retain high value-added customers, suppliers, and partners?

   f. Add "information value" to existing products and services or create new information-based products and services?

   g. Streamline and integrate channels to market, create new channels, and integrate multiple online/offline channels?

6. From the above list, identify one or more simple, yet powerful, "big wins" where IT could significantly improve business performance. What are the realistic business goals you expect to achieve? Define measurable performance improvements that can be achieved quickly (usually within one year) and the follow-on benefits that will accrue as you pursue strategic options. How will these performance drivers link to financial and capital market performance? Validate your analysis by talking with others who have implemented similar systems. Ask for lessons learned and areas of high risk that must be managed closely. Collect benchmark data on the benefits that can be expected.

7. Do you have the resources, expertise, and skills required to successfully complete these projects? Can outside partners be identified when the organization's resources are not sufficient?

8. Do you have the political support required to ensure that the project can be completed quickly and effectively? Do project leaders have the resources, authority, and accountability required to get the job done?

9. Have you considered ways to limit the scope of the project? Keep in mind the "80/20 rule": you can often achieve 80 percent of the benefit with 20 percent of the effort. Don't push to include hard-to-implement features and functions that are not critical to overall project success.

10. Has an effective change control process been implemented? Can you ruthlessly manage "project creep" while not losing sight of the good ideas that emerge during implementation? To assist with the latter task, create two task forces to search for follow-on "options" benefits. One task force can be charged with identifying new IT-enabled business building opportunities to drive profitable growth and build scarce resources and capabilities. The second task force can be charged with searching for ways to continuously enhance infrastructure performance to ensure that the organization achieves and maintains best-in-class status—through partnering or internal development.

Case 1-1

Charles Schwab in 2002

We face enormous competition. We're getting deeper into the business of giving advice, and that means we are competing with everyone, from deep discount brokers to traditional full-service firms. But, we compete with significant advantages. First, we have enormous scale: Schwab is the world's largest online brokerage, the largest service provider to independent investment managers, and a leading distributor of over 3,100 third-party mutual funds. Second, I believe we are unmatched at meshing people and technology to keep costs low and the level of service high. We can deliver a great experience regardless of how we work with clients. It could be face-to-face at one of Schwab's nearly 400 offices or through our Web site, the telephone, or wireless connection. Or we can refer investors to an affiliated independent investment manager or to one of more than 30 [company-owned] U.S. Trust offices. All this makes Schwab a very powerful competitor, but we are not nearly as good as we can be and plan to be.[1]

David Pottruck, Co-CEO and President, Charles Schwab, 2002

On May 16, 2002, Charles Schwab Corporation, the nation's largest discount broker, announced that it had expanded and restructured its service offerings to provide brokerage services and professional financial advice to three classes of investor: *self-directed investors,* who wanted unbiased information and tools but preferred to manage their investments on their own; *validators,* who also wanted to manage their own portfolios but wanted some consultation; and *delegators,* who wanted someone else to manage their portfolio for them. These new services were designed to meet the needs of Schwab's evolving customer base, which now included its traditional discount broker clients along with both emerging affluent and high-net-worth investors with over $500,000

to invest. The two new services it announced were its Schwab Private Client offering, which was targeted toward validators, who wished to manage their own portfolio with only minimal consultation; and the Schwab Advisor Network, which was targeted toward delegators, who wanted someone else to manage their portfolios for them.

Founded in the mid-1970s, for most of its history Schwab functioned primarily as a discount broker. But during the late 1990s, the company found that its customers and their requirements were changing. With the self-service model of the Internet, new investors flooded the market.[2] An increasing number of them began using online brokerages to trade and to learn how to manage their growing equity portfolios. They became hooked on the excitement of watching their wealth accumulate and watched in horror as their wealth—and dreams—evaporated when the bubble burst. As they watched their wealth decline, many sought the services of professional investment advisors. Recognizing that its investors

This case was developed from published sources (Boston: Harvard Business School Publishing, 2000) and portions of the case are based on a preview case series by Nicole Tempest and F. Warren McFarlan, "Charles Schwab Corporation (A) and (B), Harvard Business School Case Nos. 300-024 and 300-025 (Boston: Harvard Business School Publishing, 2000).

This case was prepared by Professors Lynda M. Applegate and F. Warren McFarlan and Research Associate Jamie Ladge. Copyright © 2002 Presidents and Fellows of Harvard College. Harvard Business School Case No. 803-070.

[1] Charles Schwab 2001 Annual Report (San Francisco: Charles Schwab, 2001), p. 5.

[2] During the 1996–1998 period, investors began rapidly moving their accounts to online brokerage firms in an effort to take advantage of the low-cost commissions and convenient point-and-click investing. Arthur Thompson and John Gamble, *Competition in the Retail Brokerage Industry in 2000* (New York: McGraw-Hill, 2000), p. C-225.

would need additional guidance, in 2000, Schwab purchased U.S. Trust, a well-respected wealth management firm for high-net-worth investors.

As it positioned itself to compete with full-service investment firms such as Merrill Lynch and Morgan Stanley, Schwab and a group of other online brokers bought equity in Epoch Partners, an online investment banking firm. Schwab also considered using its U.S. Trust subsidiary to develop proprietary research capabilities. A press release at the time of the acquisition quoted Schwab co-CEO and president David S. Pottruck as saying: "For our investment manager and affluent clients at Schwab, we are also working with U.S. Trust to develop a new research offering and planning the development of administrative trustee services. Moving forward, we will leverage the capabilities and strengths of both firms to create new service offerings for investment managers and for self-directed investors growing in affluence."[3]

But events in late 2001 and early 2002 caused Schwab to embark on a different tack. On June 14, 2001, Schwab sold its interest in Epoch. And on May 16, 2002, Schwab announced the rollout of a third new service—the Schwab Equity Rating System—which could be used by clients of all of its service offerings. The Equity Rating System enabled individual investors to tap into a sophisticated stock performance analysis model that Schwab marketed as "an objective, conflict-free system for rating over 3,000 U.S. stocks." An article in *Business 2.0* evaluated Schwab's new equity rating system:[4]

> . . . what's good about Schwab's system—its objectivity—is also a drawback. Picking stocks involves being subjective. It requires factoring in intangibles, like the management team, products, and competition. [Also, Schwab] isn't being all that forthcoming about just what

inputs go into the stew that spits out the grades. It seems Schwab doesn't want the secret sauce explained.[5]

Pottruck commented on the rationale for the company's introduction of the three new service offerings:

> Today, with the introduction of Schwab Equity Ratings, Schwab Private Client, and Schwab Advisor Network, we set a new standard in the world of personalized financial advice, in a unique way that is true to our vision: expert, objective, and not driven by commissions or hidden investment banking interests. Our new full-choice advice and relationship services are built on the same premise as our past successes in discount brokerage, online brokerage, and mutual fund investing—namely, find a way to serve individual investors better than they are currently served by breaking down the barriers and striving to avoid the conflicts that inhibit their success. Today, more than ever, investors need an alternative, and now they have it at Schwab.[6]

While Schwab saw its portfolio of service options as a seamless "full-choice" offering for customers—no matter how much they wished to invest—others believed that the new offerings would lead to channel conflict, particularly between the independent advisors in the Schwab Advisor Network and the company-owned advisors within its U.S. Trust subsidiary. Pottruck emphasized that these services were complementary, not competitive with one another. The company's goal was to provide the full range of services that its customers required.[7]

Even if the company was successful in creating a seamless, integrated multichannel offering, it would still face massive organization changes to develop the capabilities and culture required to

---

[3] "Schwab and U.S. Trust Complete Merger; Close of Deal Launches New Model for Serving the Affluent Investor," Schwab Press Release, June 1, 2000.

[4] Adam Lashinsky, "Schwab Gets an E for Effort," *Business 2.0* on the Web, May 20, 2002, www.business2.com, accessed October 10, 2002.

[5] Schwab complemented its Equity Ratings System with third-party research from Goldman Sachs PrimeAccess Research and other financial information services providers such as Standard & Poor's and First Call.

[6] "Schwab Gives Individual Investors a New Alternative to Wall Street Investment Research and Advice," *Business Wire*, May 16, 2002, available from Factiva, http://www.factiva.com, accessed October 2, 2002.

[7] Charles Schwab 2001 Annual Report (San Francisco: Charles Schwab, 2001), p. 7.

implement its new business model. Many believed that the company had proven itself capable of reinventing itself and the industry. Indeed, the company had earned a top spot on *Fortune*'s list of the "Most Admired Companies" in 2000, 2001, and 2002 and had been ranked number three across all companies and all industries for its ability to successfully innovate.

But the shift to its new business model came at a time when Schwab's core discount brokerage business was in sharp decline, leaving few resources available for innovation—not the least of which was the attention of its management. In 2001, Schwab's revenues fell 25 percent and net income fell 72 percent as average daily trades declined 34 percent. The company took drastic measures to cut costs. Restructuring in 2001 reduced operating expenses by $570 million, and a restructuring in August 2002 further trimmed another $250 million in operating expenses. Employee headcount was expected to be reduced to 17,000 by year-end 2002, down 36 percent from peak levels.[8] The company also closed several of its international operations including those in Japan, Australia, and Canada. From year-end 2000 to 2001, Schwab's stock price fell over 41 percent, from $26.06 to $15.47. By October 2002, the stock price had reached a three-year low, with prices ranging between $7 and $10 per share.

To execute its new strategy and business model, Schwab would have to reinvent itself, competing with industry heavyweights such as Merrill Lynch, Citigroup, and Morgan Stanley Dean Witter. Since its founding, Schwab had proved on multiple occasions that it could reinvent itself quickly and successfully—most recently by its early and aggressive entry into online brokerage. At that time, however, the financial markets were growing at a record pace. The question in fall 2002 was: Could Schwab do it again, particularly as the financial services markets and the global economy spiraled downward and existing players competed for a piece of a much smaller pie?

Company Background[9]

Our vision is to be recognized by our service quality, market wisdom, and client relationships as the most trusted firm in the financial services business.

To be fair, empathic, and responsible.

To support our colleagues in the spirit of teamwork.

To be worthy of our clients' trust.

To constantly strive to improve and innovate.

Charles Schwab Annual Report, 2001

Founded in 1975, Charles Schwab pioneered the development of the first discount brokerage firm just months after the U.S. Securities and Exchange Commission (SEC) eliminated fixed-rate commissions on brokerage trades. Schwab believed that there was an inherent conflict of interest when brokers were paid a commission on every trade. Driven to create a brokerage business that focused on the customer, Schwab built his company upon the fundamental principle of providing high-quality customer service at an affordable price. He wanted to empower investors with the information and tools needed to make informed investment choices, and he wanted to keep his costs low so that he could offer these services at a deeply discounted price. Traditional full-service investment firms (e.g., Merrill Lynch, Morgan Stanley) employed a network of highly paid investment professionals who actively managed client accounts and proactively made investment recommendations. These full-service firms also employed financial analysts and researchers who developed proprietary investment research for clients of the firm. In contrast, Schwab's discount brokerage provided customers with third-party investment research and ease of access at a much lower cost structure.

Schwab's focus on satisfying customers who wished a more self-directed style of investing led

[8] G. Maszkowski, "The Charles Schwab Corporation," Salomon Smith Barney Investment Research, November 25, 2002. Available from Investext Group www.investext.com, accessed February 8, 2003.

[9] Portions of this section are from N. Tempest and F. W. McFarlan, *Charles Schwab Corporation (A) and (B)*, HBS Nos. 300-024 and 300-025.

the firm to focus on ease of access and simplification of transactions as key components of its value proposition, long before service quality became fashionable. In 1975, Schwab was the first discount broker to open a branch office and to offer access 24 hours per day and 7 days per week (24×7). By the mid-1980s, customers could access Schwab in person at local branch offices during office hours, by phone day or night, or through a variety of automated channels, including a telephone voice-recognition quote and trading service and an innovative proprietary online network. Recognizing that some customers required more sophisticated financial advice than could be offered by Schwab's customer service representatives and brokers but not wishing to raise its cost structure, Schwab developed a specialized service offering for independent financial advisors that enabled them to manage their customers' assets using Schwab's sophisticated transaction systems and analytical software.

Its focus on satisfying customers also caused Schwab to rethink the traditional commission structure. While most full-service brokerage firms paid their brokers commissions on each trade, Schwab paid all of its employees, including its branch office and call center brokers, a salary plus a bonus that was calculated based on overall job performance. The bonus was tied to attracting and retaining satisfied customers and achieving productivity and efficiency targets. The desire to be the "most useful and ethical provider of financial services" was a founding principle of the company.

While Schwab initially attracted customers who felt they had been "burned" by traditional full-service brokers, by the early 1980s the company had begun to enlarge the market for brokerage services by attracting new investors who were less affluent and more value conscious. By 1982, the company had generated $54 million in revenues and had attracted the attention of BankAmerica. In 1983, BankAmerica acquired Schwab for $57 million. But Schwab's entrepreneurial culture clashed with the conservative style at BankAmerica and, in 1987, Schwab bought back his company in a $280 million management-led buyout. Just months later,

Schwab took the firm public and raised over $450 million.

Fresh on the heels of its IPO, Schwab pursued an aggressive growth strategy through product innovation and a national advertising and marketing campaign. Key messages that Schwab communicated were (1) its full range of high-quality, easy-to-use brokerage services; (2) its emphasis on putting individual customers in control of their investments; (3) the value delivered (at that time Schwab trades cost 30 percent less than those of full-service brokers); and (4) its commitment to provide a trusted, conflict-free place for individuals to trade.

Building on a History of Innovation

We view them [Schwab] as perpetually having next year's model. They see trends early, execute well, and get in [quickly] with a sizable market position.

U.S. Banker, 1998[10]

After pioneering the concept of a discount brokerage with 24×7 multichannel access, Schwab continued to develop innovative new products and services. Given Schwab's focus on keeping costs down while offering innovative services and improved access, coupled with the fact that the company was headquartered near Silicon Valley's rapidly growing high-tech industry, it was not surprising that much of this innovation exploited new and emerging technologies. Pottruck explained:

At its core, Schwab is really a technology company that happens to be in the financial services business. We have a culture that embraces technology as the core of our business. To us, technology is not a channel; it's the air we breathe. We think about our business as a human-technology partnership.[11]

[10] "Doing it the Schwab Way," *U.S. Banker*, July 1998, p. 47. As quoted in Tempest and McFarlan, "Charles Schwab Corporation, HBS No. 300-024," *Creating Business Advantage in the Information Age*, eds. L. M. Applegate, R. D. Austin, and F. W. McFarlan (New York: McGraw-Hill, 2002), p. 11.

[11] Ibid.

Schwab's emphasis on a high-tech, high-touch approach to achieve high-quality customer service and superior productivity dated back to the 1970s. When the company first launched, Schwab brokers placed trades by phone, waited for another phone call to get trade confirmation, and then called the customer to complete the loop. The process was slow and costly. It quickly became apparent that technology could put Schwab brokers in direct contact with the exchanges to allow immediate confirmation of a trade while the customer was still in the office. Shortly after launch, the company sought out a technology services provider to implement a system to automate trade clearance and settlement. The new system simultaneously improved the trading process from both its customers' and Schwab's perspectives.

Recognizing the strategic value of the clearance and settlement system and the future "strategic options" that it made possible, in 1979 Schwab decided to bring its entire trade-clearing system in-house, thus breaking ranks with the rest of the financial services industry, which was still outsourcing this function from a third-party vendor. This "bet the company" investment, which cost $500,000, was made at a time when the net worth of the company was only $500,000.

In the mid-1980s, Schwab began leveraging its technology infrastructure to develop innovative new service offerings. In 1985, Schwab pioneered online trading with the introduction of Equalizer—a software application that was distributed to customers on a set of diskettes. After installing the software application on a personal computer (PC), Schwab customers could use a modem to dial in to Schwab's internal trading and information systems to access up-to-date information (including news, stock quotes, and company information), to conduct trades, and to manage their portfolios and accounts. Schwab generated three revenue streams from its Equalizer PC software: First, the software was sold to customers for $199; second, customers paid a subscription fee for dial-in access to third-party financial information (e.g., Standard &

Poor's Marketscope, Dow Jones news, and company reports); and, third, customers paid a transaction fee for each trade.

In 1989, Schwab launched Telebroker, an automated voice-response telephone brokerage service offering trades at a 10 percent discount.[12]

In 1993, Schwab introduced a more full-featured online trading service that ran on the newly launched Microsoft Windows operating system. Named StreetSmart, the PC software was fully integrated with the popular personal money management software, Quicken, which was available from Schwab's Silicon Valley neighbor, Intuit. Having experienced firsthand that online trading increased customer loyalty, Schwab lowered the cost of the StreetSmart software to $59 and offered customers a 10 percent discount off the standard transaction fee for each trade conducted online. By the end of 1995, 6 percent (approximately 200,000) of Schwab's 3.4 million accounts were trading online using StreetSmart.

While the StreetSmart program was well received, it was a costly endeavor for Schwab, as customer service representatives needed to spend a significant amount of time helping customers install and configure the trading software and modem. This unexpected cost was in addition to the cost of running the dial-in network service.

By 1995, Schwab executives had become aware of several important trends that caused the firm to begin to seriously evaluate newly emerging Internet technologies as a potential platform for its growing online trading business: (1) Customer response to StreetSmart was strong, yet the cost structure made the business unsustainable; (2) Schwab's client base was both willing and able to trade online; (3) Online services, like America Online, were growing rapidly; and (4) There was growing excitement in Silicon Valley about the potential of the Internet as a channel for doing

---

[12] By 1997, Telebroker averaged 5.7 million calls per month and accounted for 13% of Schwab's trading volume.

business online. In spring 1995, Pottruck formed a special project team to develop an Internet online-trading offering. The "skunk works" project team reported directly to Pottruck. Dan Leemon, chief strategy officer at the time, explained:

> The decision was made at a senior level that, if we were really going to develop an online business, we couldn't have it buried in retail where it would have to compete for funds with new branches because, on a net present value basis, branches would always come out on top. Instead, the senior management team decided that the online project should be raised to the level of all other business units so that it would get the management attention and funding it needed.[13]

In 1996, Schwab introduced its e.Schwab Internet brokerage service, pricing it at $39.95. Within months it had lowered the price to $29.95, which was still significantly higher than E*TRADE, which had priced its offering at $14.95. (See Exhibit 1 for a comparison of commission rates in 2001.) While the Internet had been touted as a low-cost platform upon which to offer an online service, Schwab executives were initially discouraged by the economics. Pottruck explained: "The migration to Internet trading happened much faster than we thought, but the elasticity we were expecting came more slowly than we thought. So people were paying less and not trading significantly more. As a result, the costs hit faster than we thought, and the benefits were slower to accrue."[14]

By 1998, the cannibalization of its established business model had begun to take its toll. After revenue growth of 6.5 percent over the previous four quarters, revenues declined by 3 percent during the first quarter of 1998. Investors reacted immediately, and Schwab's stock declined from $40 per share in January 1998 to $33 per share in June 1998. However, by the end of 1998, the online bet began to pay off. Between December

entive

1997 and December 1998, Schwab's online accounts rose from 1.2 million to 2.2 million, which represented 40 percent of the company's accounts. The average number of daily trades during this same period rose 49 percent to 115,300, with online trades accounting for 61 percent of the trading volume. As the assets under management and volume of trade increased, so too did revenues, which grew 19 percent during 1998. More importantly, once sufficient volumes had been achieved, the efficiency of the Internet channel resulted in a 29 percent growth in pretax profit margin, which surprised even senior executives. At scale, executives found that online transactions cost one-fifth as much as those conducted with Schwab employees in branch offices or via telephone. As a result, Schwab was able to cut its trading costs by $439 million in 1999 alone.[15] Schwab also found cost-avoidance benefits; no new branch employees had to be hired, and no new call centers had to be built to handle the additional transaction volume.

As Schwab's performance improved and investors became more enamored of Internet business models, investor confidence skyrocketed. Schwab's stock price rose by 158 percent between June 1998 and December 1998. Riding the wave of the Internet bubble, by year-end 1998 the company's market value was $25.5 billion, edging out the number one full-service broker, Merrill Lynch, which was valued at $25.4 billion. By 2000, Schwab had over 13 million online accounts and estimated that it was saving over $100 million per year from its online trading service.

In February 2000, Schwab.com won *CIO* Magazine's prestigious Enterprise Value Award.[16] The annual award honored organizations that had used information technology to bring about a "fundamental change, not just marginal improvements,

[13] As quoted in Tempest and McFarlan, "Charles Schwab Corporation (A), HBS No. 300-024," p. 12.
[14] Ibid., p. 25.

[15] E. Cummings, "In Search of Excellence: CIO Enterprise Value Awards," *CIO*, February 1, 2000.
[16] Ibid.

EXHIBIT 1 **Comparison of Full-Service and Discount Broker Commission Rates, 2001**

Source: "2002 Broker Survey," *SmartMoney*, August 2002.

Full-Service Broker	Market Order			Stop/Limit Order			20 options at $8
	100 Shares of $20 stock	501 Shares of $20 stock	1,001 Shares of $20 stock	100 Shares of $20 stock	501 Shares of $20 stock	1,001 Shares of $20 stock	
American Express	$95.00	$248.33	$388.23	$95.00	$248.33	$388.23	$80.00
Charles Schwab	$69.00	$119.07	$159.04	$69.00	$119.07	$159.04	$97.70
Edward Jones	$65.00	$230.00	$392.83	$65.00	$230.00	$392.83	N/A*
AG Edwards	$65.55	$219.10	$401.24	$65.55	$219.11	$401.24	$351.40
Fidelity	$45.00	$45.05	$67.55	$50.00	$50.05	$72.55	$80.00
Merrill Lynch	$71.00	$238.62	$374.07	$71.00	$238.62	$374.07	$367.00
Morgan Stanley	$66.13	$232.39	$426.26	$66.13	$232.39	$426.26	$339.81
Prudential	$71.58	$252.91	$444.32	$71.58	$252.91	$444.32	$358.98
Salomon Smith Barney	$65.02	$247.73	$435.91	$65.02	$247.73	$435.91	$387.00
UBS PaineWebber	$75.69	$249.03	$437.19	$75.69	$249.03	$437.19	$419.52

(continued)

* Broker does not offer options.

EXHIBIT 1 Comparison of Full-Service and Discount Broker Commission Rates, 2001 (Continued)

Discount Broker	Market Order			Stop/Limit Order		
	100 Shares of $20 stock	501 Shares of $20 stock	1,001 Shares of $20 stock	100 Shares of $20 stock	501 Shares of $20 stock	1,001 Shares of $20 stock
American Express	$19.95	$19.95	$19.95	$19.95	$19.95	$19.95
Ameritrade	$8.00	$8.00	$8.00	$13.00	$13.00	$13.00
Bidwell	$12.00	$12.00	$12.00	$15.00	$15.00	$15.00
Brown & Co.	$5.00	$5.00	$5.00	$10.00	$10.00	$10.00
Charles Schwab	$29.95	$29.95	$29.98	$29.95	$29.95	$29.98
Cititrade	$24.95	$24.95	$24.95	$24.95	$24.95	$24.95
Datek	$9.99	$9.99	$9.99	$9.99	$9.99	$9.99
Empire Now	$5.00	$5.00	$5.00	$10.00	$10.00	$10.00
E*TRADE	$14.95	$14.95	$14.95	$19.95	$19.95	$19.95
Fidelity	$25.00	$25.00	$25.02	$30.00	$30.00	$30.02
Firstrade.com	$6.95	$6.95	$6.95	$9.95	$9.95	$9.95
Harris (formerly CSFB)	$20.00	$20.00	$20.02	$9.95	$20.00	$20.02
JB Oxford	$14.50	$14.50	$14.51	$9.95	$19.50	$19.51
Merrill Lynch	$29.95	$29.95	$29.98	$9.95	$29.95	$29.98
Muriel Siebert	$14.95	$14.95	$14.97	$9.95	$14.95	$14.97
MyDiscountBroker	$12.00	$12.00	$12.00	$9.95	$12.00	$12.00
Quick & Reilly	$23.95	$23.95	$23.95	$9.95	$23.95	$23.95
Scottrade	$7.00	$7.00	$7.00	$9.95	$12.00	$12.00
T. Rowe Price	$19.95	$19.95	$19.95	$24.95	$24.95	$24.95
TD Waterhouse	$14.95	$14.95	$14.95	$17.95	$17.95	$17.95
USAA	$24.00	$24.00	$24.02	$24.00	$24.00	$24.02
Vanguard	$20.00	$20.00	$20.02	$20.00	$20.00	$20.02

in the way they do business; in doing so, they raised the bar" for others in their industry. Dawn Lepore, vice chairman and chief information officer (CIO), explained: "I can't think of anything, other than our online brokerage systems, that has had more business impact. Schwab's ability to foster an innovative and collaborative working environment between our technology organization and our customer-focused enterprises enabled us to broaden the investing experience quickly and efficiently with the launch of e.Schwab."[17]

As more and more Schwab customers demanded access to online trading services, Schwab determined that it needed a more sophisticated technology infrastructure. In early 2000, Schwab acquired CyberTrader, a direct-access broker specializing in electronic trading and brokerage services. Formed in 1995 as a trading technology company, CyberTrader began by licensing its sophisticated software to trading rooms. In 1998, CyberTrader changed the focus of its business model to include providing online brokerage services to individual investors. CyberTrader witnessed phenomenal growth, capturing a substantial share of the active online trader market. Upon its acquisition by Schwab, CyberTrader became a wholly owned subsidiary of the company.[18] The CyberTrader software provided an easy-to-use, point-and-click advanced-execution platform with access to nine ECNs[19] and over 450 market makers and exchanges (for example, NASDAQ and NYSE). After the acquisition, CyberTrader software became the engine powering StreetSmart Pro, Schwab's expanded trading platform for the active trader market, which was launched in March 2001.

Defining a New Market

As investors shifted more of their wealth to Schwab, the company found that they needed and wanted more advice than could be provided by Schwab's branch office consultants. At the same time, the company began to identify a new, underserved segment of the investment services market. (See Exhibit 2 for demographic information on this emerging market segment.) Pottruck explained:

> The baby boomers are emerging as a dominant wealth segment in the United States. They bring with them a desire for a high degree of control, a willingness to embrace technology for their investing needs, and an unwillingness to compromise. Many of these investors will demand wealth management services—supported by the unique strengths of the Internet—that offer them more control and information than has ever been available before. At the same time, we believe that these investors are underserved—no one has garnered a truly significant share of this expanding market; no one has developed a comprehensive wealth management service especially for the needs of the emerging affluent investor.[20]

To address this opportunity, on June 1, 2000, Schwab completed the purchase of U.S. Trust, a full-service investment firm headquartered in New York City that catered to high-net-worth individuals. Founded in 1853, U.S. Trust provided investment management and consulting, fiduciary services, financial and estate planning, and private banking to affluent individuals and families. U.S. Trust also provided a full range of services to institutional clients. "Through U.S. Trust, we will be able to provide the trust, financial and estate planning, and private banking services that are so crucial to wealth management," Pottruck explained. "Our investment manager clients have told us repeatedly that trust and private banking services are absolutely essential in order to serve affluent clients well."

Under the terms of the agreement, U.S. Trust shareholders received 3.427 shares of Schwab stock for each share of U.S. Trust stock. Based on

[17] Charles Schwab Press Release, February 11, 2000.

[18] Visit the CyberTrader Web site at www.cybertrader.com.

[19] An Electronic Communications Network (ECN) provides an online platform that brings together buyers and sellers to trade stocks. In 2001, well-known ECNs included Instinet, Island (which was acquired by Instinet in 2001), and Archipelago.

[20] "About Schwab—Press Room, January 13, 2000," Charles Schwab Web site, http://www.businesswire.com/schwab, accessed September 23, 2002.

EXHIBIT 2   Demographics in the Emerging Market Segment

Source: Adapted from Booz Allen Hamilton, *Insights* Newsletter 4, no. 1 (May 2001).

The Emerging Affluent Consumer	
Demographics	
Age	55 and under
Annual income	$100,000 +
Investable assets	$500,000 +
Characteristics	Entrepreneurial, technologically savvy, high risk tolerance, self-directed, financially active
Investment manager expectations	High degree of expertise and competency, become loyal when satisfied
Segment growth	Doubled from 10.8 million households in 1994 to over 20 million in 2000
Representation of total population	Represent 18% of total U.S. households; control 80% of the nation's $18.1 trillion in investable assets
How they made their fortune	90% earned their wealth themselves—most are business owners
Education	Highly educated and smart, technologically and financially savvy, and want to use technology to obtain quick results

Affluent households generate more than $50 billion in revenues annually for the financial services industry. These revenues are growing at a rate of 10%–15% annually as the number of affluent households increases.

Schwab's closing stock price as of January 12, 2000, the transaction valued each U.S. Trust share at $129, resulting in a total transaction value of approximately $2.7 billion.

While some felt that Schwab paid too high a price for U.S. Trust,[21] Schwab executives maintained that the acquisition was central to the company's mission to provide a trusted environment for investors who wished to preserve and maximize their wealth. Many analysts agreed with Morgan Stanley that the acquisition strengthened Schwab's business model:

This is an increasingly important [acquisition] for Schwab, given that 10% of the company's customers have $1 million or more in investable assets . . . It gives Schwab greater institutional order flow [as] Schwab would be the beneficiary of some percentage of [U.S. Trust] commissions that had previously been doled out across Wall Street . . . It lowers Schwab's dependence on trading revenues . . . Key to this is the 100 basis points that U.S. Trust earns on its $74 billion in assets under management . . . [This is] a revenue-creation story rather than an expense-saving one . . . Management has indicated that it can get $80 to $100 million in revenue enhancements from this deal.[22]

After the announcement on January 13, 2000, Schwab's stock rose from approximately $36 to

[21] A report from CIBC World Markets said that its analysts believed "that Schwab paid a high price for a premium asset. Schwab will be paying about a 63.5% premium for U.S. Trust, or about 31x UTC's 2000 consensus EPS estimates of $1.04."

[22] Henry McVey, Morgan Stanley Dean Witter, "Charles Schwab, Moving Right Along," January 14, 2000, available from Investext Group, http://www.investext.com, accessed September 23, 2002.

$40 per share, while U.S. Trust's stock rose from approximately $83.50 to $133 per share. When the merger was completed on May 31, 2000, the price per share of the combined entity rose to approximately $33.50 per share after a 3-for-2 stock split. Upon completion of the merger, Schwab had combined shares outstanding of 1,262,547 and a market value of approximately $42 billion. At year-end 2001, U.S. Trust operated 34 client offices employing 1,900 financial advisors and had $93 billion in assets under management[23]

Indicative of the success of its diversification strategy, by 2001 Schwab had captured top honors as both a discount and full-service broker. In its 2001 Annual Broker Survey, *SmartMoney* Magazine ranked Schwab as the number one discount broker, while also ranking it as the number three full-service broker.[24] "Being recognized as a premium provider for both self-directed investors and those who want more advice and education is particularly gratifying," said Steve Scheid, Schwab vice chairman and president of Retail.[25]

As events unfolded after the merger, customers' demands for professional advice increased dramatically. By the middle of 2000, the stock market had entered a free fall decline, and the supercharged economy began to falter. The devastating attacks on the World Trade Center and the Pentagon on September 11, 2001 heightened investor anxiety and uncertainty.

In early November 2001, a Harris poll was commissioned by Schwab to measure its customers' sentiments related to the economy and protection of assets.[26] The survey indicated that nine out of ten Schwab clients "believe we are already in or are entering a recession," while eight in ten "believe that the recession will last at least six months." Nearly one-fifth of respondents (18 percent) reported that, as a result of the market downturn,

they would have to delay their retirement. Going forward, 59 percent of clients believed that "looking for investments that are relatively safe is more important than looking for higher returns." As they looked for ways to diversify their portfolios, an overwhelming number stated that they would seek the help of professional advisors. A follow-up survey, conducted in early February 2002, summarized the top five ways investors had changed their behavior between 2000 and 2002: "I avoid companies I don't understand" (33 percent); "I do more research" (31 percent); "I diversify more" (27 percent); "I pay more attention to financial advisors" (22 percent); "I worry more" (15 percent).[27]

Schwab, 2002

By year-end 2001, Schwab was the sixth-largest public financial services firm in the United States.[28] The company served three major segments of the financial services industry—individual investors, institutional investors, and capital markets. (See Table A.)

The individual-investor segment represented the largest of Schwab's segments. The segment included retail services, online services, active trader services, and international. Retail services catered to walk-ins at Schwab's 395 branches and provided additional service via call centers and automated voice-response service. Online services catered to 4.3 million Schwab clients who maintained their accounts online through the Schwab Web site.[29] For highly active traders, Schwab offered real-time electronic trading technology and online brokerage services. In the late 1970s, 95 percent of Schwab's business was done through branch walk-ins or telephone calls to branch office personnel; by 1998, only 5 percent of Schwab's business was done in branch offices. In 2002, nearly 83 percent of trades at Schwab were

[23] Charles Schwab Annual Report, 2001.

[24] "2001 Annual Broker Survey," *SmartMoney*, August 2001.

[25] Charles Schwab Press Release, August 6, 2001.

[26] Schwab Press Release, November 15, 2001.

[27] Schwab Press Release, March 13, 2002.

[28] "Top Participants Financial Summary: Investment Services," OneSource Information Services, Inc., http://www.onesource.com, October 22, 2002.

[29] The 4.3 million accounts represented 83% of Schwab's total trading volume. As of March 2002, Schwab.com averaged over 40 million hits per day.

TABLE A   Schwab Services, June 2002

Investor Type	Services for Individual Investors
Self-Directed	Schwab Signature Client™ offered the most comprehensive services for investors who wanted to make their own investment and trading decisions. Access to research and analytical tools was available online. The monthly fee was $45 for accounts under $10,000 and $30 for accounts valued between $10,000 and $49,999. Accounts over $50,000 were free.
Validators	Schwab Private Client™ provided an ongoing, one-on-one relationship with a Schwab Private Client consultant who provided advice, but clients were expected to manage their own portfolios. Once a plan was in place, the advisor would periodically call on the investor to provide market updates or make suggestions regarding attractive opportunities. The fee was 0.6% of assets or a minimum of $1,500 per year. The minimum investment was $500,000. In 2001, Schwab pilot tested its Private Client service and attracted 1,000 existing customers with $1.5 billion in assets, of which $225 million was new money.
Delegators	Schwab Advisor Network™ which was a network of independent professional financial advisors who had access to Schwab's trading systems, information, and tools. Schwab clients that wanted a full-service broker were referred to a financial advisor in this network. The minimum investment was $500,000. In 2002, there were over 300 independent financial advisors participating in the network and 1,900 company-owned U.S. Trust financial advisors. Average assets under management for U.S. Trust clients was $5 to $10 million.

Investor Type	Services for Registered Investment Advisors
Financial Services Professionals	Services for Investment Managers™ provided access to Schwab's trading systems, information, and tools to a much more extensive network of registered investment advisors (RIAs). The key difference between an RIA and a member of the Schwab Advisor Network was that Schwab actively referred clients to members of the Schwab Advisor Network but did not refer clients to the independent RIAs. In spring 2001, Schwab's 5,800 RIAs contributed approximately one-third of Schwab's $858 billion total assets.[a]

Investor Type	Services for Institutional Investors
Institutional Investors	The Capital Markets group executed trades and provided trading, clearance and settlement, research, and support services for institutional clients. This group also ran the trading systems and services used by active investors, Schwab RIAs, and the Schwab Advisor Network. Schwab's Capital Markets group owned or leased 21 seats on seven major stock exchanges and had a strong presence in the options trading market. Schwab Capital Markets was responsible for making markets in over 5,000 over-the-counter securities and accounted for 4.5% of NASDAQ's 2001 volume. Other services offered through Schwab Capital Markets included extended-hours trading and fixed-income services. Major institutional clients included money managers, pension managers, mutual fund companies, and other financial institutions.[b]

[a] Guy Moszkowski, Salomon Smith Barney, "The Charles Schwab Corporation," December 17, 1999, available from Investext Group, http://www.investext.com, accessed September 23, 2002.
[b] "Organizational Groups: Schwab Capital Markets," Charles Schwab Web site, http://www.schwab.com, accessed October 4, 2002.

EXHIBIT 3   Leading Full-Service Investment Management Firms

Source: Adapted from Global OneSource, accessed October 23, 2002. All data is current as of October 4, 2002, unless otherwise noted.

	Merrill Lynch	Citigroup SSB	Goldman Sachs	Morgan Stanley Dean Witter	Charles Schwab
Key Numbers					
2001 Total Net Revenues ($M)	21,880	80,057	15,811	21,896	4,353
Employees	57,402	268,000	20,647	61,319	19,600
Market Value ($M)	25,981	141,605	29,880	34,006	10,687
Brokerage Market Share	9.6%	7.7%	10.1%	6.9%	5.5%
Assets under Management ($M)	1,300	994	351	595	725
Profitability Margins					
Operating Profit Margin (2001)	3.6%	33%	11.9%	13%	8.2%
Net Profit Margin (2001)	2.0%	21%	7.4%	8.1%	4.6%
Return on Equity (2001)	4.1%	19.6%	13.3%	18%	4.7%
Return on Assets (2001)	.2%	1.4%	.8%	.8%	.5%
Valuation Ratios					
Price/Earnings	113.85	9.12	15.62	11.06	60.70
Price/Sales	.88	2.32	1.38	1.05	2.56
Price/Book Value	1.22	1.70	1.55	1.60	2.47
Price/Free Cash Flow Ratio	11.54	7.26	9.25	10.69	18.56

conducted via online trading, compared with 48 percent in 1998 and 28 percent in 1997.[30]

With its acquisition of U.S. Trust, Schwab expanded its coverage of the individual investor market segment to include affluent clients. Analysts at Morgan Stanley commented: "If management executes on what it has laid out, it will have services for straight retail, emerging affluent, and high-net-worth [market segments] that address all the key 'sweet spots' in the retail food chain."[31] (Refer to Exhibit 3 for a comparison of

retail financial services firms that compete in the full-service investment management sector.)

Both independent advisors and U.S. Trust professionals paid Schwab a fee for referrals and additional fees for selected Schwab services. Schwab's Web site stated "Schwab investment consultant compensation is structured so that they have no incentive to refer clients to U.S. Trust over other advisors."[32]

Schwab's Value Proposition

Schwab's effective integration of multiple service channels, its strategic use of advanced technologies, and its track record for successful innovation were key elements of Schwab's value proposition. An analyst at Bear Stearns commented: "In our view, Schwab's leading technology yields significant efficiencies, particularly as measured

[30] Arthur Thompson and John Gamble, *Competition in the Retail Brokerage Industry in 2000* (New York: McGraw-Hill, 2000), p. C247.

[31] Henry McVey, Morgan Stanley Dean Witter, "Charles Schwab, Moving Right Along," January 14, 2000, available from Investext Group http://www.investext.com, accessed September 23, 2002.

[32] "Schwab Business Practices," Charles Schwab Web site, www.schwab.com, accessed September 23, 2002.

by revenue per employee. . . . Revenue per average employee is nearly 150% higher than that of the national full-line investment firms and almost 40% above the industry average."[33]

Schwab's use of technology to provide innovative service offerings and to provide its customers with multiple, easy-to-use channels through which to do business with Schwab was widely recognized as a benchmark for the industry. The company was consistently ranked the number one online broker by Gomez. (See Exhibit 4.) Another key element of the Schwab value proposition was its brand and reputation. According to a 2001 ranking of U.S. brands based on media expenditures, Schwab was ranked number 84, close behind number 78 Merrill Lynch.[34] (See Exhibit 5 for additional detail on rankings of financial services industry brands.) In 2001, *Fortune* Magazine ranked Schwab number one as the "Most Admired Company" in the securities industry and number five as the "Best Company to Work for in America." Companies that made the "Most Admired Company" list were selected by industry peers and analysts, who were asked to rate companies in their respective industries on the basis of innovativeness, employee talent, use of corporate assets, social responsibility, quality of management, financial soundness, long-term investment value, and quality of products/services.

Companies that made the "Best Company to Work for in America" list were selected based on employee responses to the "Great Place to Work Trust Index," a survey instrument measuring the quality of workplace culture. The ranking was also based on company responses to a "Culture Audit."[35] In 2002, Schwab's rank on the "Best

Company to Work For" list dropped to 46. The drop was due largely to the massive layoffs Schwab had instituted. (See Exhibit 6 for rankings of Schwab and other financial services firms in the *Fortune* surveys. See Exhibit 7 for a list of all the awards and recognitions Schwab received in 2000, 2001, and 2002.)

Financial Performance

As of year-end 2001, Schwab reported annual sales of $4.3 billion, with annual assets under management of over $40 billion. Schwab's individual investor segment represented the largest portion of revenues, at 58.5 percent, while the Institutional, Capital Market, and U.S. Trust segments represented 19.1 percent, 7.3 percent, and 15.1 percent, respectively. From 2000 to 2001, Schwab's revenues had decreased by approximately 25 percent, while pretax income dropped by 89 percent. During the first two quarters of 2002, Schwab announced massive job cuts and lower-than-expected earnings, causing its stock price to fall. Between December 31, 2000 and October 4, 2002, Schwab's stock price fell nearly 79 percent, from $26.06 to $7.83. (Exhibits 8a, 8b, and 8c provide detailed financial statements, Exhibit 8d provides stock price history, and Exhibit 8e outlines key financial results within each of Schwab's business segments.)

Schwab was not alone in its struggles to keep financially afloat while continuing to satisfy customers in an increasingly challenging economic environment. While many hoped for a recovery, the bleak picture became even worse during early 2002. A reporter for *SmartMoney* Magazine explained:

These days investors are very nearly apoplectic over the disastrous news that's been whacking them in the face day after day and week after week. Bankruptcies. Earnings manipulation. Insider trading. Companies moving to Bermuda for tax reasons. Enron, Adelphia, WorldCom, Arthur Andersen, Tyco, Global Crossing, and ImClone. Did we forget to mention the imminent possibility of war: in the Middle East; between Pakistan and India; between the U.S. and unknown, untamable terrorists? The list gets longer and longer with each opening bell of the New York Stock Exchange . . . No wonder the Standard & Poor's 500 is down 17% over the past year, while the NASDAQ has

---

[33] Daniel C. Goldberg, Bear Stearns, "The Charles Schwab Corporation," September 12, 2002, available from Investext Group http://www.investext.com, accessed September 23, 2002.

[34] "America's Top 2001 Brands," www.brandweek.com/brandweek/features/superbrands/top2000_01a.jsp, accessed October 23, 2002.

[35] "Fortune's Lists," *Fortune,* http://www.fortune.com/lists, accessed October 2, 2002.

EXHIBIT 4 Gomez Rankings of Online Brokerages

Source: Adapted from Gomez Advisors, www.gomez.com, accessed October 29, 2002.

Firm Name	Ameri-trade	HARRIS direct	Brown & Co.	E*TRADE	Datek	Fidelity	TD Water-house	Quick & Reilly	Merrill Lynch	Charles Schwab	Index Average
Average GPI Transaction Performance (sec.)	6.1	6.6	7.4	7.8	8.3	12.4	13.5	14.3	14.8	17.3	10.8
GPI Transaction Success Rate (%)	100%	88.4%	99.3%	98.6%	99.5%	98.9%	100%	97.4%	99.5%	99.9%	98.1%
GPI Transaction Utility Rating	34.9%	40.5%	29.0%	75.8%	51.6%	43.2%	49.2%	51.6%	48.0%	56.3%	47.6%
Homepage Unique Visitors (000s)*	857	125	n/a	750	502	1,275	710	n/a	340	667	921
Dial-up User Homepage Performance** (sec.)	7.0	10.6	15.6	35.9	16.0	17.9	23.9	n/a	23.1	32.5	20.3
# of Active Online Accounts Q2 2002 (in Mil)	1.92	n/a	n/a	3.65	n/a	4.46	2.62	n/a	n/a	4.30	—
# of Online Trades Q2 2002 (in Mil)	4.63	n/a	n/a	n/a	n/a	5.22	n/a	n/a	n/a	4.30	—
Online Assets Q2 2002 (in Bil)	n/a	n/a	n/a	$38.0	n/a	$288.0	n/a	n/a	n/a	$308.2	—
GPI Transaction Consistency Rating ***	★★☆	★☆☆	★★★	★★★	★★☆	★★★	★★★	★★☆	★★☆	★★★	—
Last Biweekly GPI Performance Ranking	1	2	3	4	5	6	7	8	9	10	—

Period = (Mon.–Fri., 9:00 AM to 4:00 PM, market trading days).

* Unique visitor traffic metrics for the month of September 2002 generated by ComScore.

** Dial-up user homepage performance metrics generated by Porivo.

*** Consistency ratings are based upon standard deviation for the defined period.

The following key applies:

★★★ = 1 Standard Deviation <= 2.4 seconds

★★☆ = 1 Standard Deviation > 2.5 <= 3.5 seconds

★☆☆ = 1 Standard Deviation > 3.5 seconds

Note : GPI = Gomez Performance Index; ranking of 10 represents the highest rank among all online brokers.

EXHIBIT 5   **Ranking of Financial Services Industry Brands**

Interbrand Survey—Best Global Brands by Brand Value				
2002 Rank	Brand	2002 Value ($ billions)	% change from 2001	Country of Origin
13	Citibank	$18,066	−5%	U.S.
15	American Express	16,287	−4%	U.S.
25	Merrill Lynch	11,230	−25%	U.S.
26	Morgan Stanley	11,205	n/a	U.S.
29	Goldman Sachs	7,194	−9%	U.S.

Source: Adapted from "The Best Global Brands," *BusinessWeek Online*, August 5, 2002, www.businessweek.com/magazine/content/02_31/b3794032.htm.

Interbrand used the following methodology for calculating brand value. The $ value of revenues for products and services that carry the brand is calculated. All direct costs and indirect costs are identified. A deduction is made for taxes, and the opportunity cost for use of tangible assets (e.g., property, plant, equipment, working capital) is assessed. This provides a base return on tangible assets that is used to calculate Economic Value Added (EVA), which reflects earnings over a five-year period discounted to the present value.
Visit the Web site for more detail, www.brandchannel.com/interbrand/test/WMVBFAQ_Rank.pdf.

Brandweek Survey—U.S. Financial Services Brands by Media Expenditure in 2001 (in $ millions)			
2001 Rank	Brand	2001 Total Media Expenditures	2000 Total Media Expenditures
13	Bank of America	$109,632.1	$ 72,505.5
78	Merrill Lynch	94,076.5	60,594.8
84	Charles Schwab	87,941.3	135,853.1

Source: Adapted from "America's Top 2001 Brands," Brandweek.com, June 17, 2002, www.brandweek.com, accessed October 23, 2002.

dropped more than 26% . . . [Investor sentiment] has sunk by nearly half since the tech boom of late 1999 and early 2000, according to a monthly investor optimism survey conducted by UBS and Gallup. Meanwhile, another poll by *The Wall Street Journal* and NBC News found that some 57% of Americans say they do not trust corporate executives or brokerage houses to provide honest information. "Who are you going to trust out there?" asked Thomas Baker, a retired restaurateur from West Palm Beach, Fla.[36]

Retail Financial Services Industry

You almost wouldn't know it for all the obsessive talk about the market outlook recently, but finance history was made last week. After some two decades of debate, Congress and the Administration have reached agreement on repealing the outdated Depression-era Glass-Steagall laws that kept the banking, insurance, and securities businesses separate. True, each industry has been invading the others' turf for years, but in a haphazard, piecemeal fashion. Regulation will finally recognize that all three are essentially in the same business: managing society's savings.

BusinessWeek *Online, 1999*[37]

An appreciation of the challenges facing Schwab and other financial services players in 2002 requires an understanding of the impact of deregulation on the financial services industry during the past two decades. Until the mid-1980s, the financial services industry was divided into a

[36] L. Young, "Who Can You Trust?" *SmartMoney*, August 5, 2002.

[37] "The Internet and Financial Services," Morgan Stanley Dean Witter Equity Research, August 1999.

EXHIBIT 6 *Fortune* Magazine Rankings in 2002

Source: Adapted from http://www.fortune.com/lists/mostadmired/snap_1346.html.

Fortune Magazine: Most Admired Companies: Securities Industry

						Criteria				
Rank	Company	Overall Score	Innovation	Employee Talent	Use of Corp Assets	Social Resp	Quality of Mgmt	Financial Soundness	Long-Term Investment Value	Quality of Products/Svcs
1	Charles Schwab	7.43	1	2	1	1	1	2	4	2
2	Goldman Sachs Group	7.17	2	1	3	5	2	1	1	1
3	Morgan Stanley	6.91	3	3	2	3	3	3	2	3
4	Merrill Lynch	6.41	4	5	7	4	5	4	3	5
5	A.G. Edwards	6.19	10	6	4	2	4	5	5	4
6	Lehman Brothers Hldgs.	6.19	6	4	6	9	6	7	5	6
7	Bear Stearns	5.88	7	7	5	7	7	8	7	9
8	Franklin Resources	5.73	9	8	8	8	9	6	8	7
9	Raymond James Financial	5.58	8	8	9	6	8	9	9	8
10	E*TRADE Group	4.15	5	10	10	10	10	10	10	10

Source: Adapted from http://www.fortune.com/lists/mostadmired/attributes_list.html.

Fortune 1000 Most Innovative Companies

Rank	Company	Attribute Score
1	Minnesota Mining & Mfg.	8.8
2	Intel	8.6
3	Charles Schwab[a]	8.5
4	Texas Instruments	8.5
5	AOL Time Warner	8.4
6	Nike	8.3
7	Applied Materials	8.1
8	Citigroup	8.1
9	Medtronic	8.1
10	Johnson Controls	8.0

[a] Charles Schwab ranked number one within the financial services segment.

EXHIBIT 7   List of Awards/Recognition

Source: Adapted from Schwab.com.

2002
- Gomez.com—Ranked first on Gomez's Internet Brokerage Scorecard for the sixth consecutive period
- *Barron's* Magazine—Ranked number one with a four-star rating in seventh annual Online Brokerage Review

2001
- Gomez.com—Schwab maintains number one position on the Gomez Internet Brokerage Scorecard
- *Working Women* Magazine—Ranked number two of the Top Twenty-Five Companies for Executive Women
- *Worth* Magazine—Reader's Choice Award: Most popular brokerage
- *SmartMoney* Magazine—Ranked best brokerage for independent investors
- *Forbes* Magazine—Schwab.com is recognized among "Best of the Web"
- *PlanSponsor* Magazine—Rated Top Provider for fourth consecutive year
- *Fortune* Magazine—Number Five of the Hundred Best Companies to Work for in America

2000
- Gomez.com—Ranked number one overall online broker
- *BusinessWeek* Magazine—Ranked number fourteen on list of fifty Best Performers
- *CIO* Magazine—Winner of the Enterprise Value Award, which recognizes companies that use information technology to achieve business objectives
- *Fortune* Magazine—Ranked number sixteen on list of the World's Most Admired Companies
- CRESTCo—Charles Schwab Europe Brokerage Operations Division—Rated Best in U.K.
- Forbes.com—Schwab.com recognized among the "Best of the Web"—September 2000
- *Internet Week* Magazine—Ranked number one in financial services on list of hundred e-businesses
- *Forrester* Magazine—Ranked number one in Forrester Power Ranking of Online Brokers
- *Worth* Magazine—Selected the best full-service brokerage as well as best discount and online brokerage by Readers' Choice Survey
- *WE* Magazine—Named to list of Top Ten Companies to Work for in the U.S. for People with Disabilities
- *Computer Weekly* E-Business Excellence Awards—Charles Schwab Europe won the "E-Commerce Award" for the best use of e-business technology to sell products to customers
- *Information Week* Magazine—Dave Pottruck and Dawn Lepore named Chiefs of the Year

number of distinct segments that included commercial banks, insurance companies, consumer financial services (e.g., credit services, such as credit cards), investment services, real estate services, and savings and loans. Schwab operated primarily in the investment services sector—specifically, the security brokers and dealers subsegment. (See Exhibit 9 for an overview of traditional financial services segments and key players within each segment.)

This highly segmented structure dated back to the passage of the Glass-Steagall Act of 1933, which erected a wall between commercial banking and investment management. The act barred banks from investing in shares of stocks, limited them to buying and selling securities as an agent, and prohibited them from underwriting and dealing in securities as well as from being affiliated with any organization that was "engaged principally" in underwriting or dealing in securities. Securities firms were not permitted to accept deposits.

But the Glass-Steagall Act left cracks in the walls. For example, commercial banks were granted permission to underwrite and deal in selected "bank eligible" securities. In addition, the vague wording of the act left it open to question what level of activity would be necessary to state that a firm was "engaged principally" and/or "primarily engaged" in underwriting and dealing securities. In the mid-1980s and 1990s, a series of legislative changes provided clarification while also relaxing restrictions. But "firewalls" were also set up to restrict information flow and prevent conflicts of interest.

As the cracks in the walls opened, successive mergers among leading players within the financial services industry created vertically integrated financial services holding companies. By 1997, 40 U.S. financial services bank holding companies had subsidiaries conducting limited investment activities, and some had successfully challenged Glass-Steagall. For example, in 1996, two of the top 10 underwriters of U.S. corporate debt (by dollar volume) and two of the top 10 underwriters of municipal bonds were affiliated with banking organizations.[38]

On November 1, 1999, Congress passed, and President Clinton signed into law, the Gramm-Leach-Bliley Act, which eliminated many of the federal and state legal barriers to affiliations among banks and securities firms, insurance companies, and other financial services providers.[39] Furthermore, the legislation provided financial organizations with flexibility in structuring these new financial affiliations through either a holding company structure or a business subsidiary (with certain limitations on activities and appropriate safeguards).[40] Major competitors emerged immediately, particularly from the commercial banking industry, where firms such as Citigroup and Deutsche Bank quickly began offering a one-stop shop for financial services with a full complement of banking and investment management offerings. Major consumer financial services firms, like American Express, also entered the market and began providing a full range of investment management services and administered pensions and other employee benefit plans.

Many of these firms anticipated the legislative changes. For example, Citigroup was formed in 1998 through the merger of Citicorp, which delivered a wide range of commercial and merchant banking, lending, and credit services; and Travelers Group, which was formed through a series of mergers in the late 1980s and 1990s that brought together Travelers Insurance, Primerica, Smith Barney, Drexel Burnham Lambert, Shearson Lehman Brothers, and Salomon Brothers. By year-end 2001, the top 10 financial services holding companies controlled the industry and 50 percent of industry revenues. The next 15 firms controlled 26 percent of the revenues, and the remaining 7,700-plus firms controlled 24 percent of industry revenues.[41]

As competitors in the financial services industry fought to dominate this newly deregulated industry, they were forced to contend with an economy that was spiraling downward and taking the industry with it. Between year-end 2000 and early October 2002, U.S. securities firms cut over 32,000 jobs—nearly 9 percent of their workforce—and were preparing for additional belt-tightening as the bear market showed little sign of easing.[42]

Despite the grim outlook, the market opportunity for financial services firms that could weather the current economic downturn was huge. Bank of America reported that, in 2001, there were between $16 trillion and $21 trillion in investable assets, based on income from U.S. households. Baby boomers represented a large portion of the market, as they were expected to inherit $7 trillion of wealth in the next 10 years.[43]

[38] "Cracking the Glass-Steagall Barrier," Federal Reserve Bank of San Francisco, March 21, 1997, available at http://www.frbsf.org/econrsrch/wklyltr/el97-08.html.

[39] A detailed discussion of the Gramm-Leach-Bliley Act of 1999 can be found at http://www.senate.gov/~banking/conf.

[40] The Gramm-Leach-Bliley Act preserved the role of the Board of Governors of the Federal Reserve System (the "Federal Reserve Board" or the "Board") as the umbrella supervisor for holding companies and incorporated a system of functional regulation designed to utilize the strengths of the various federal and state financial supervisors. Finally, the legislation defined policies and procedures that would be used to approve new bank financial activities and to restrict banks from participating in the new financial affiliations if they were not "well capitalized and well managed."

[41] "Standard & Poor's Industry Surveys: Investment Services," published by OneSource Information Services, Inc., http://www.onesource.com, May 2, 2002.

[42] "Wall Street Braces for Deepest Job Cuts Yet as Market Remains Depressed," *Dow Jones Newswire,* October 8, 2002.

[43] *Flow of Funds Accounts of the United States,* Board of Governors of the Federal Reserve System, September 16, 2002.

Implementing the New Schwab

> Schwab had an enviable business model for a long time, but it's no longer a small company and may not be able to deliver the growth associated with its historically high multiple . . . If they really want to be serious and compete with the Merrill Lynches of the world, it's going to cost them a lot of money to do that, and that's going to hinder their earnings growth going forward.
>
> *Newbridge Partners, 2002*[44]

In February 2002, the head of Schwab's retail business resigned, and Pottruck announced he would temporarily step in to fill the void.[45] He faced one of the most challenging times in the company's history. Yet, Schwab had proven time and again that it could deal with challenging times and use the chaos and uncertainty as a catalyst for reinventing itself—and the industry. In the past, however, Schwab's strategy was designed to entice new categories of investors into the market while nibbling away at the edges of the established industry players' markets. The strategy launched in spring and summer 2002 changed all that as Schwab stepped into the ring to do battle with industry heavyweights such as Citigroup, Merrill Lynch, and Morgan Stanley. Pottruck immediately went on the offensive with a series of hard-hitting print and TV ads designed to capture the attention of the most profitable clients. "We're promoting a model that's different from all of those other firms," said Pottruck, "and we won't be shy about promoting it."[46]

While analysts believed that Schwab's new strategy was necessary to stabilize its revenue stream and reduce dependence on its faltering discount brokerage business, they were also quick to point out that the company was straying far from its roots. "Employees hired mainly as order takers are finding that they're underqualified as Schwab strives to upgrade its branch staff with more experienced—and more expensive—financial advisors," one analyst said.[47] In addition, the company's relationship with the almost 5,000 RIAs that used Schwab's technology and services to manage their client assets was also being tested. Finally, even if it solved these problems, Schwab faced a massive culture change at a time when employee morale had been severely tested. A Bear Stearns analyst explained:[48]

> Schwab has completed three restructuring programs in the past year and a half, taking charges of more than $450 million . . . The firm is currently reviewing its options with the intention of cutting operating expenses by an incremental $200 million annually. Though we firmly believe these restructuring activities are necessary in light of the changing market environment, we question whether Schwab management has gone a bit too far. Besides some concern about the firm's ability to fully participate in any recovery in the equity markets, we also wonder if its strong culture and employee cohesiveness may be damaged.

The new strategy positioned the company to capture market share in what all agreed would be a huge, rapidly growing market. "Global high-net-worth assets are expected to grow to a staggering $38 trillion by 2006," an analyst stated. "As important, this client segment typically generates relatively high profit margins. Still, we caution that these very same factors could also eventually attract increased competition, which could penalize profit growth over time. As such, we think the firms that choose to specialize in this arena will ultimately enjoy the greatest success."[49] Schwab's announcement that, contingent upon regulatory approval, it planned to commence banking operations in 2003 led some to question whether the firm was losing sight of its specialist focus. While concerns were voiced, most agreed that it would be foolish to count this aggressive and innovative competitor out.[50] A reporter commented:

> Pottruck clearly has to execute a delicate balancing act.
> The company's ambitious financial targets for this year

---

[44] E. Maronak, Newbridge Partners, as quoted in "Schwab Fails to Convince Investors on Growth Rebound (Update 3)," *Bloomberg News Service*, October 5, 2002.

[45] Schwab Press Release, February 20, 2002.

[46] "L. Lee and E. Thornton, "Schwab vs. Wall Street," *BusinessWeek*, June 3, 2002, p. 65.

[47] Ibid, p. 67.

[48] D. Goldberg, "The Charles Schwab Corporation," Bear Stearns Equity Research, September 12, 2002, p. 8.

[49] Ibid, p. 9.

[50] Lee and Thornton, p. 65.

don't leave him much room to maneuver—requiring him both to cut costs and bag significant new revenues. Schwab is targeting operating profit margins of 12%–14% by year-end and aiming to boost revenue per employee to $300,000 in 2003, up from $190,000 in 2001. In addition, it hopes to garner $125 billion in net new assets, a considerable jump from the $74 billion added in 2001—all the while nurturing the new Private Client Service . . . But, it would be dangerous for Wall Street to assume that Schwab's [new strategy] will fall flat. Time and again Chuck Schwab's rivals have pooh-poohed his ideas as impractical or unnecessary; time and again his ideas have wrought major changes in the way Wall Street operates.

EXHIBIT 8a   Income Statement, 1995–2001 ($ millions)

Source: Schwab 10-K statements.

	2002	2001	2000	1999	1998	1997	1996	1995
Revenues								
Commissions	1,206	1,355	2,294	1,875	1,309	1,174	954	751
Asset management and administration fees	1,761	1,675	1,583	1,220	559	428	311	219
Interest, revenues, net	841	929	1,237	820	476	354	255	211
Principal transactions	184	255	570	500	287	258	257	191
Other[a]	143	139	104	71	105	86	74	48
Total revenues	4,135	4,353	5,788	4,486	1,427	2,300	1,851	1,420
Expenses								
Compensation & benefits	1,854	1,875	2,414	1,888	1,162	962	766	594
Other compensation—merger retention program	22	56	39					
Occupancy & equipment	471	490	415	307	206	154	131	111
Communications	262	339	353	279	201	182	165	129
Depreciation & amortization	321	338	255	169	155	129	98	69
Advertising & market development	211	246	332	248	138	125	84	53
Professional services	177	193	255	184	88	70	52	41
Commissions, clearance, & floor brokerage	71	92	138	100	83	92	81	77
Goodwill amortization		66	53	12				
Merger related			69					
Restructuring and other charges	373	419						
Other[b]	144	104	234	200	126	137	80	69
Total expenses	3,967	4,218	4,557	3,387	2,159	1,851	1,457	1,143
Pretax income	168	135	1,231	1,099	−732	447.3	369	277
Income tax provision	71	57	513	433	228	177	160	105
Net income (before extraordinary charges)	109	199	718	666	−960	270.3	234	173
Weighted average common shares outstanding	1,375	1,399	1,404	1,373	411	409	404	178
Earnings per share—basic	.08	0.14	0.53	0.51	0.88	0.69	0.60	0.97
Earnings per share—diluted	.07	0.14	0.51	0.49	0.85	0.66	0.58	n/a

[a] Other revenues include retirement plan services fees, account fees, and wire fees.
[b] Other expenses include a $39 million charge related to NASD litigation.

EXHIBIT 8b Balance Sheet, 1997–2001 ($ millions)

Source: Schwab 10-K statements.

December 31,	2002	2001	2000	1999	1998	1997
Assets						
Cash & equivalents	3,114	4,407	4,876	2,079	1,155	797
Investments	21,005	17,741	9,425	8,466	10,242	6,774
Receivables from brokers, dealers, & clearing orgs.–net	222	446	348	482	335	267
Receivables from customers—net	6,845	9,620	16,332	17,060	9,647	7,752
Loans to banking clients	4,555	4,046	3,147			
Securities owned—at market value	1,716	1,700	1,618	340	242	283
Property plant & equipment, other	868	1,058	1,133	598	397	343
Intangible assets—net	603	628	605	45	46	55
Other assets	777	818	670	229	200	210
Total assets	39,705	40,464	38,154	29,299	22,264	16,481
Liabilities						
Deposits from banking clients	5,231	5,448	4,209			
Drafts payable	134	396	544	468	324	268
Payable to brokers, dealers, and clearing orgs.	1,476	833	1,070	1,749	1,422	1,123
Payable to customers	26,401	26,989	25,715	23,422	18,119	13,106
Accrued expenses and other liabilities	1,302	1,327	1,277	931	618	478
Borrowings	508	578	1,109	455	352	361
Total liabilities	35,694	36,301	29,715	27,025	20,835	15,336
Shareholders' equity						
Preferred stock	0	0	0	0	0	0
Common stock	14	14	14	8	4	3
Additional paid-in capital	1,744	1,726	1,588	539	213	241
Retained earnings	2,769	2,794	2,713	1,795	1,255	956
Treasury stock	(465)	(295)	—	—	(1)	(35)
Unearned ESOP shares	(33)	(39)	(71)	(71)	(43)	(3)
Unamortized restricted stock compensation	(18)	(37)	(14)	(1)	—	(17)
Foreign currency translation adjustment	(0)	(0)	(0)	4	1	
Total shareholders' equity	4,011	4,163	4,230	2,274	1,429	1,145
Total liabilities + shareholders' equity	39,705	40,464	33,945	29,299	22,264	16,481

EXHIBIT 8c Statement of Cash Flows, 1997–2001 ($ millions)

Source: Schwab 10-K statements.

Year ended December 31,	2002	2001	2000	1999	1998	1997
Cash flows from operating activities						
Net income	109	199	718	666	348	270
Adjustments to reconcile net income to net cash provided by (used for) operating activities:						
Depreciation and amortization	321	338	255	169	138	125
Goodwill amortization	61	66	53	12		
Compensation payable in common stock	27	32	82	35	28	24
Deferred income taxes	4	(79)	(27)	(3)	(62)	(290)
Tax benefits from stock options exercised and other stock-based compensation	4	37	330	215		
Non-cash restructuring and other charges	42	80				
Net gain on sale of an investment		(26)				
Extraordinary gain on sale of corporate trust business, net of tax	(12)	(121)				
Other	(1)	22	8	12	47	30
Net change in:						
Cash and investments segregated and on deposit for federal or other regulatory purposes	(3,302)	(8,334)	(942)	1,563	(3,466)	(457)
Securities owned (excluding securities available for sale)	105	14	(54)	(98)	40	(155)
Receivables from brokers, dealers, and clearing organizations	220	(89)	131	(154)	(66)	(37)
Receivables from brokerage clients	2,745	6,709	727	(7,419)	(1,894)	(2,742)
Other assets	7	(35)	(94)	(28)	16	(26)
Drafts payable	(261)	(150)	75	144	56	44
Payables to brokers, dealers, and clearing organizations	643	(335)	(662)	329	298	245
Payables to brokerage clients	(527)	1,291	2,329	5,317	5,010	1,936
Accrued expenses and other liabilities	(16)	(203)	(13)	334	209	153
Net cash provided by (used for) operating activities	169	(584)	2,916	1,094	718	268
Cash flows from investing activities						
Purchases of securities available for sale	(1,147)	(1,025)	(545)	(466)		
Proceeds from sales of securities available for sale	636	473	93	10		
Proceeds from maturities, calls, and mandatory redemptions of securities available for sale	415	611	227	414		
Net increase in loans to banking clients	(705)	(835)	(458)	(518)		
Purchase of equipment, office facilities, and property—net	(160)	(301)	(705)	(370)	(185)	(139)
Cash payments for business combinations and investments, net cash received		(52)	(35)	(26)	(1)	(1)
Proceeds from sale of an investment		49				
Proceeds from sale of corporate trust business	26	273				
Net cash used for investing activities	(739)	(807)	(1,423)	(956)	(187)	(141)

(continued)

EXHIBIT 8c   Statement of Cash Flows, 1997–2001 ($ millions) (Continued)

	2002	2001	2000	1999	1998	1997
Cash flows from financing activities						
Net increase in deposits from banking clients	(217)	1,139	4	790		
Net increase in short-term borrowings	(70)	224	198			
Proceeds from long-term debt	100		311	144	30	111
Repayment of long-term debt	(214)	(40)	(59)	(45)	(40)	(34)
Dividends paid	(60)	(61)	(62)	(61)	(43)	(37)
Purchase of treasury stock	(299)	(368)		(54)	(150)	(18)
Proceeds from stock options exercised and other	34	30	85	66	31	15
Net cash provided by financing activities	(726)	924	477	840	−173	37
Effect of exchange rate changes on cash and cash equivalents	3	(2)	(4)	2	0	0
Increase (decrease) in cash and cash equivalent	(1,293)	(469)	1,966	980	358	164
Cash and cash equivalent at beginning of year	4,407	4,876	2,910	1,930	797	633
Cash and cash equivalent at end of year	3,114	$4,407	$4,876	$2,910	1,156	797

EXHIBIT 8d   Schwab Stock Price History

Source: Quicken 5-Year Stock Chart, http://www.quicken.com, accessed October 29, 2002.

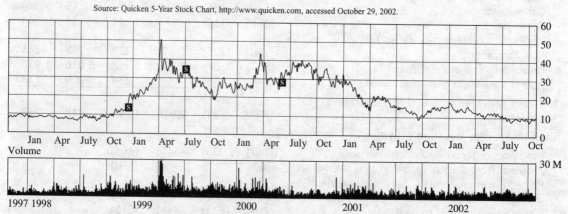

Period: Oct-29-1997 – Oct-29-2002

Note: Based on Schwab closing prices.

EXHIBIT 8e Annual Business Segments: Total Revenues and Pretax Income

Source: "Charles Schwab Corp. One Stop Report," Global OneSource, accessed October 2, 2003.

Total Revenues and Pretax Income (in $ millions)

	12 Months Ending 12/31/2002		12 Months Ending 12/31/2001		12 Months Ending 12/31/2000		12 Months Ending 12/31/1999	
Revenues								
Individual investor	$ 2,392	57.8%	$ 2,531	58.5%	$ 3,645	63%	$ 2,762	61.6%
Institutional investor	833	20.1%	827	19.1%	861	15.9%	632	14.1%
Capital markets	259	6.3%	315	7.3%	640	11%	551	12.3%
U.S. Trust	651	15.7%	654	15.1%	643	11.1%	542	12.1%
Segment total	4,135	100%	4,327	100%	5,788	100%	4,486	100%
Other	0		26		0			
Consolidated Total	$ 4,135		$ 4,353		$ 5,788		$ 4,486	
Pretax Income								
Individual investor	$ 256	40.7%	$ 245	37.9%	$ 837	60.3%	$ 690	63.8%
Institutional investor	240	38.2%	272	42%	297	21.4%	175	15.9%
Capital markets	16	2.5%	18	2.8%	96	6.9%	106	9.7%
U.S. Trust	117	18.6%	112	17.3%	157	11.3%	128	11.6%
Segment total	629	100%	647	100%	1,388	100%	1,098	100%
Other	(461)		(512)					
Consolidated Total	$ 168		$ 135		$ 1,231		$ 1,098	

EXHIBIT 9   Overview of Traditional Financial Services Segments

Source: Casewriter.

Industry Segment	Description	Key Players
Banks	Companies that extend credit and make loans to individuals and businesses.	Citigroup, Bank of America, Bank One, Wells Fargo
Consumer Financial Services	Credit card and consumer services: Companies that extend credit and make loans to individuals through credit cards, installment loans, student loans, and other consumer credit instruments.	American Express, MBNA, Citifinancial
Insurance	The insurance sector includes, life, health, property, casualty, and title insurance companies, as well as insurance brokers and reinsurance companies.	AIG, Berkshire Hathaway, Allstate
Investment Services	Full-service investment firms and discount brokers offering a wide variety of financial services, including investment banking, underwriting, brokerage, and research and advisory services to corporate and individual clients.	JP Morgan, Goldman Sachs, Merrill Lynch, Morgan Stanley, Bear Stearns, Schwab, E*TRADE
Real Estate Services	Companies engaged in originating, purchasing, selling, and servicing home mortgage and equity loans.	Fannie Mae, Freddie Mac, First Mortgage Corporation, E-Loan Inc.
Savings and Loans	Regionally based banks, savings & loans, and other savings institutions located in Puerto Rico and other U.S. territories and protectorates.	First BanCorp, Oriental Financial Group Inc., Popular Inc.

Case 1-2

Learning from LeapFrog[1]

My kids actually ask to stay in from recess to play with their LeapPads! It's the best educational investment we've ever made.

An early childhood specialist, Oakland, California

Mike Wood, CEO of LeapFrog Enterprises, hustled through the narrow aisles of his cavernous corporate headquarters, a former warehouse located in a scrappy industrial zone in Emeryville, California. LeapFrog, since its founding in 1995, had leapt to the number three ranking among U.S. toy manufacturers in 2002. With revenues that year of $532 million, only the venerable industry powerhouses, Mattel (number one) and Hasbro (number two), were larger, a remarkable achievement for so young a company.

Wood paused as he rounded a corner, his attention caught by a small group crowded outside one of the cubicles that covered the building's main floor. The group, members of the product-development team for a future LeapFrog offering, had gathered to look over the newest prototype created by one of the company's model makers. LeapFrog's explosive growth trajectory made such hallway meetings necessary, as conference rooms had been sacrificed to provide space for the firm's many new hires.

LeapFrog, in fact, was one of the very few bright lights in the otherwise dismal Bay Area economy of the new millennium, which was still struggling in 2003 to wring out the excesses of the dot-com craze of the late 1990s. Surveying the former warehouse decked in trademark colors of

brilliant purple and green and now home to 700-plus LeapFrog staff, one could see many such gatherings taking place—an advertising campaign being planned on the floor of a cubicle, a product team gathered in the kitchen debating voice talent for a new interactive book, a design group huddled in a corner over sketches of the company's Leap™ characters. All these efforts were aimed at further solidifying LeapFrog's position as one of the nation's largest toy companies—and one of its largest publishers of children's books.

Wood spotted Jim Marggraff, LeapFrog's executive vice president for worldwide content, at the center of the group, holding a small foam model of its latest new product. Marggraff turned it over, pushed its pretend buttons, and examined it with an eye toward its ergonomics, its attractiveness, and its general ability to engage a child's attention. He then passed it along to the others to try. One by one, members of the group offered their comments: A former teacher, now an artist for the company, approved of the model's bright color scheme; a product manager commented on the positioning of the speakers; a writer, also a former educator, asked a software programmer if the screen display offered sufficient real estate for the planned content. The comments swirled as the team tested the mock-up against their vision of what this product might become.

A meeting like this was just one step in the highly iterative process of taking a LeapFrog product from concept to finished product. The model under study was the culmination of months of collaborative effort by dozens of people. More months, and many more such meetings, would be required before the final product would find its

This case was prepared by Professors Lynda M. Applegate, Harvard Business School, and Christopher Dede, Graduate School of Education, and Research Associate Susan Saltrick. Copyright © 2003 President and Fellows of Harvard College. Harvard Business School Case No. 804-062.

[1] Professor Lynda M. Applegate prepared this case solely as the basis for class discussion. Cases are not intended to serve as endorsements, sources of primary data, or illustrations of effective or ineffective management.

way to the shelves of LeapFrog's retailers and from there into children's hands in homes and schools across the globe.

Wood listened attentively to the exchange, which reflected the group's hard work, expertise, and passion. He, too, examined the model with care, imagining it in the hands of his own children, then addressed the team. "From your comments, I think we're on the right track here, but something is still missing," he said, then, asking the question he was known for asking, "What can be done to make this product, not just great, but spectacular?"

In response to the question, a new round of comments bubbled up from the group. Wood directed a few more questions, made a couple of suggestions, then took his leave, mentally noting, with some pleasure, that the group's ideas had advanced to a new level. Finding time to interact in such sessions was a top priority of Wood's; it was perhaps the part of his job he loved the most—and he was widely recognized to have a certain genius at it. But with the wildfire growth of the company, his day was more and more filled with the details of running a half-billion dollar company. His energy and tenacity were already the subject of company legend, but there were still just 24 hours in a day.

Wood was absolutely committed to protecting and preserving the creative spirit at LeapFrog, even as the company grew, David-like, to challenge the industry giants. LeapFrog's future depended on successfully balancing the excitement, energy, and spontaneity of the creative process with the rigor, accountability, and formal structures a large company required. Many young companies had foundered trying to steer this middle course. Would LeapFrog do the same, or would it continue to "leapfrog" its competitors, jumping ever higher, from one success to the next? Other challenges lay ahead as well. LeapFrog was one of the very few firms to have succeeded in building a consumer brand upon the educational claims of its products. But would those claims hold up under rigorous research? Were LeapFrog's products promoting real and longlasting learning gains? More specifically, what would the coming year bring as LeapFrog encountered its first real competition from industry leader Mattel? His thoughts racing, Wood hustled off to his next meeting.

Building LeapFrog

LeapFrog is an educational company selling things that look like toys.

Sean McGowan, toy industry analyst

From Inspiration to Incorporation

LeapFrog Enterprises began operations in 1995, but the origins of the company date to 1990 to an epiphany Wood, then a partner at a major San Francisco law firm, experienced while playing with his son, Mat, then three years old. (For LeapFrog executive team bios, see Exhibit 1.) Using a wooden ABC puzzle, Wood was attempting to help Mat recognize that letters have both names and sounds, for example, that the letter "A" is named "A" but it sounds like "ahh." This concept is of central importance to the development of *phonemic awareness,* "a conscious perception of the sounds of language; that is, the recognition that what we may hear or think of as a single utterance or sound, such as a word, is actually made up of a string of smaller sounds, or phonemes."[2] According to educational researchers, children who can detect these small units of sound are more likely to be successful readers. Like most young children, though, Mat could recall the *name* of each letter but had difficulty correctly associating its corresponding *sound*. Wood, in a flash of insight, thought of making a set of 26 squeezable plastic letters, each equipped with a small sound chip (similar to those used in singing birthday cards) that would "say" the letter's sound when pressed.

[2] Linda Bevilacqua, "Did Someone Say Phonemic Awareness?" *ProTeacher,* http://www.proteacher.com, accessed July 9, 2003.

EXHIBIT 1   2003 Executive Team

Source: LeapFrog 2002 Annual Report.

Michael Wood, CEO since March 2002 and President and Vice Chairman of the board of directors since September 1997. CEO of LeapFrog RBT, LLC (LeapFrog Enterprises' predecessor limited liability company) from its inception in 1995 until 1997. Before founding LeapFrog, Wood served as partner at Cooley Godward LLP, a national law firm where he specialized in venture capital and technology law. Serves on the board of directors of Sangamo BioSciences, Inc. His B.A. is from Stanford University, his J.D. from University of California, Hastings College of the Law, and his MBA from University of California, Berkeley.

Thomas Kalinske, Chairman since March 2002. Chairman and CEO from September 1997 to March 2002. Since 1996 President of Knowledge Universe. From 1990 to 1996, President of Sega of America. From 1987 to 1990, President and CEO of Universal Matchbox Group. Prior to that, President and Co-CEO of Mattel, Inc. Has served as Chairman of the Toy Manufacturers Association of America and, in 1997, was inducted into the Toy Industry Hall of Fame. Member of the board of the Millken Family Foundation, the National Foundation for the Improvement of Education, and the RAND Education Board. His B.S. is from the University of Wisconsin and his MBA from the University of Arizona.

Paul Rioux, Vice Chairman since January 2001 and Acting Chief Operating Officer since October 2002. Worked as an independent consultant from June 1999 to December 2000, and worked almost exclusively for LeapFrog from August 2000 to December 2000. Former President of Universal Studios New Media Group from May 1996 to May 1999. Prior to that worked at Sega of America from 1989 to 1996, most recently as Executive Vice President. COO of Wonderline Toys from 1986 to 1988. Worked at Mattel from 1973 to 1985, most recently as Senior Vice President. His B.S. and M.S. are from California State University–Northridge.

James Curley, Chief Financial Officer at LeapFrog since December 2001. Former CFO of Open Table, Inc. from October 2000 to August 2001. From January 1998 to December 2001, founded and served as CEO of Four Green Fields, a specialty retailer. From July 1992 to January 1998, Senior Vice President and CFO of Gymboree. From 1989 to 1992, Vice President and CFO of Huffman-Koos, a furniture retailer. A CPA, his B.B.A. is from Texas A&M University.

Timothy Bender, President Global Consumer Group since January 2002, served as Senior Vice President of Sales and Marketing from July 1999 to December 2001 and as Senior Vice President of Sales from November 1997 to June 1999. Former Director of National Accounts at Yes! Entertainment, a toy and entertainment company, from October 1994 to January 1997 and Senior Vice President from February 1997 to October 1997. From 1984 to 1994, he was at Lego Systems, most recently as Senior National Accounts Manager. His B.S. is from Bradley University.

Robert Lally, President LeapFrog SchoolHouse Division since March 1999, Executive Vice President of Education and Training Group since January 2002, and co-founder of LeapFrog RBT. From March 1995 to February 1999, CFO. From July 1992 to March 1995, he was CFO and Vice President of Operations at the Republic of Tea, and was a manager at Price Waterhouse from 1983 to 1991. His B.S. is from the University of Oregon and his MBA from The Wharton School at the University of Pennsylvania.

L. James Marggraff, Executive Vice President Content, since January 2002. From March to December 2001 served as independent consultant to Leapfrog focusing on new products and software. From September 2000 to February 2001, President of Ubiquity LLC, established to investigate market opportunities for NearTouch™ technology. From August 1999 to August 2000, President of LeapFrog's Internet division and from July 1998 to July 1999 Vice President of Content. Co-founder, President, and Vice-President of Marketing and Sales of Explore Technologies from September 1995 to July 1998. From 1984 to 1992 co-founder and Manager of Marketing and Sales of StrataCOM, Inc. His B.S. and M.S. are from the Massachusetts Institute of Technology.

(*continued*)

EXHIBIT 1   2003 Executive Team (Continued)

Mark Flowers, Chief Technology Officer, Executive Vice President and Chief Technology Officer since January 2002. Previously Vice President of Technology from January 2001 to December 2001 and Vice President of Engineering from July 1998 to December 2000. Prior to that Vice President of Hardware Engineering and Director of Explore Technologies, Inc. from September 1995 to the acquisition of Explore in July 1998. From 1990 to 1995, independent consultant in Silicon Valley. Prior to that Director of Hardware Engineering at Telebit Corporation. His B.S. and M.S. are from the Massachusetts Institute of Technology.

So taken was he by this idea that he invested $15,000 to file a patent and, on the advice of a friend in the toy industry, held a professionally organized focus group with mothers to test the product's marketability. Of the 20 mothers he assembled, all 20 loved the concept. His hopes were dashed, however, when all 20 said they would buy the product at a $50 price point, but only two would do so at $100. As the product design at the time required a separate chip in each letter, the cost of those 26 chips would have necessitated a selling price near $100. Wood abandoned the notion of manufacturing the product at that time but continued to brainstorm the idea with his friends and work associates.

Recalling that early experience, Wood noted:

The parents in that focus group taught me a valuable lesson, one that's stayed with me over the years. Whenever I'm considering a new product or innovation, I always ask myself four questions: (1) Does this product reflect a fundamental learning need? (2) Does it reflect best practice in teaching? (3) Does the technology truly enhance the learning process? (4) Do parents want to buy this at the price that we must sell it to make money? If I can say "Yes" to all these, I know we've got a fair chance at success, but if even one of them is "No," it's back to the drawing board.

We iteratively test our products throughout their development with four groups. We want teachers to tell us, "This is the way I want it taught." We want kids to say, "This is the way I want to learn, and I want to learn this way again and again." We want parents to say, "This is important, and I'll buy it at this price." And, finally, retailers have to say, "I'll give you shelf space for this product."

For four years after that initial focus group, Wood continued to explore new designs and new technology. As a partner in a law firm specializing in venture capital and technology law, he was well-positioned to come into contact with innovative technologies and product designs. Finally, after much tinkering, by 1994 the design had evolved to require just one battery, one speaker, and one chip. Wood felt he was close, at last, to building a product he could sell at a price parents were willing to pay.

His next step was to ensure the soundness of the product's underlying phonics system. He called on Dr. Robert (Bob) Calfee, a reading specialist, then a professor at Stanford University's School of Education,[3] who confirmed that Wood's instincts about phonics instruction were on target. Calfee commented, "Kids don't hate to read, they hate not being able to read. Here was a product that had the potential to help kids crack the code of reading."

Not only did Wood and Calfee concur on the educational value of the nascent product, but the men found themselves compatible professionally. Wood was impressed with Calfee's emphasis on the positive: "Bob saw that his 30 years of work in phonemic awareness and phonics was going to be on the shelves at Wal-Mart. And he didn't see it as a degradation of his expertise. In fact, he was thrilled at the prospect of getting all these kids

---

[3] Calfee was named Dean of the School of Education at the University of California–Riverside in 1998.

started off on the right foot." Shortly thereafter, Wood asked him to be the primary educational advisor to his soon-to-be-created company. Calfee recalled his thoughts about Wood: "From time to time, entrepreneurs had come to me to ask my advice on the educational value of their products. Mike, though, especially impressed me with his ideas and energy. He listened carefully to what I had to say, took careful notes, and then went away. I never expected to see him again, but he surprised me by coming back, just a month later, having completely redesigned the product for the better." Showing his strong predilection for protecting intellectual property, Wood patented his effort as "The Phonics Learning System," thus creating what would become one of LeapFrog's core intellectual assets.

That same year, on a flight from Hong Kong, Wood was musing over the ways kids play and the notion of helping kids advance. The game of leapfrog came to mind, exemplifying both the notion of leaping ahead and the sense of play that Wood wanted to instill in his products. And so LeapFrog got its name. Reflecting on its core values, Wood noted: "When interacting with our products, we wanted to make sure kids never get the message that they are doing something wrong. The feedback they receive must always be positive and never discourage them from attempting new things." Calfee noted, "It is easy to offer encouragement when the program promotes success." He elaborated, "The key was to keep it simple and focus on the essential rules of phonics. We wanted kids to see that the basic syllabic unit is like a sandwich, with the consonants as the bread and vowels as the filling."

Working with Calfee and technologists from Sandia National Labs, Wood further refined his one-chip design into a product that could be sold at a $50 price point. In 1995, he showed a prototype of what he called *The Phonics Desk* to a Toys "R" Us buyer, who promptly ordered 40,000 units for the holiday season. With a $2.4 million order under his belt and $800,000 in start-up capital from angel investors, Wood left his law practice, and the company was launched.

(For a timeline of key events in the company's history, see Exhibit 2.) Despite his connections with the venture capital world, Wood shunned VC funds and obtained start-up capital from family and friends. In contrast to many technology firms that were springing up in the over-exuberant climate of the late 1990s, LeapFrog made a retail product on which it would generate a real revenue stream—or not. "There's no halfway," Wood noted in a *Fast Company* article. "You execute and you get to do next year's plan. You fail, and next year's plan is irrelevant."[4]

According to Sean McGowan, a toy industry analyst and senior vice president at Manhattan-based research firm Harris Nesbitt Gerard,[5] "Launching a new toy is not necessarily harder than launching other consumer products. It's a very trend-driven business, so the barriers to entry are relatively low. Retailers are willing to give a new company a try if they like the product, but if delivery dates or execution slips, that company won't get a second chance. While the barriers to entry are low, the barriers to exit are even lower."

In its first year, LeapFrog retained a consulting engineer to secure the services of a reputable agent to represent the company to manufacturers in China. The agent sourced factories, contracted for quality assurance, and arranged shipping, receiving in return a percentage fee based on the value of the goods produced. As a start-up, the company was not able to secure manufacturing at the biggest and most reliable factories. Robert Lally, cofounder and COO at the time, recalled that he, Wood, and other executives paid frequent trips to the manufacturing sites in an effort to keep the production line running. Yet despite a LeapFrog presence on-site about 80 percent of

---

[4] Bill Breen, "LeapFrog's Great Leap Forward," *Fast Company*, June 2003.

[5] In July 2003, McGowan's firm, formerly known as Gerard Klauer Mattison, was acquired by a division of the Bank of Montreal. The firm is now known as Harris Nesbitt Gerard.

EXHIBIT 2 Company Timeline

Source: LeapFrog corporate fact sheet, casewriter.

KNOWLEDGE UNIVERSE

LeapFrog SchoolHouse™

NYSE
New York Stock Exchange

T.O.Y.™

1995	1997	1998	1999	2000	2001	2002	2003
LeapFrog Enterprises launches first product, Phonics Desk™, which integrates technology with research-based learning model for phonics instruction.	Knowledge Universe acquires 85% of LeapFrog Enterprises; KU President Tom Kalinske joins LeapFrog as CEO.	Product line expansion: Little Leap™, Explorer Globe, and Twist and Shout® (later renamed TurboTwist™). July: LeapFrog acquires Explore Technologies, Inc. (holders of NearTouch™ technology).	LeapPad® Learning System launched, which integrated new patented technology with research-based learning model.	Mike Wood reassumes CEO role; Tom Kalinske moves to chairman. SchoolHouse division is launched; company expands international sales efforts.	LeapFrog extends product lines to reach infant, toddler, and 'tweens markets.	IPO executed in July (most successful IPO of the year); LeapPad and its accompanying books are the #2 and #1 (respectively) best-selling U.S. toys.	LeapFrog wins Educational Toy of the Year award for 3rd year in a row.

that first year, the company encountered frequent production delays. To offset their impact, LeapFrog would rely on costly air freight to ship its products from Asia. Lally stated, "Of the initial $800,000 in start-up capital, $350,000 went to air freight. That essentially consumed our gross margin and made it necessary to raise another $1.2 million in capital in the fall of 1995. Fortunately, our investors—mostly drawn from Mike's [Wood's] family, friends, and law partners—had faith in what we were doing. The products were showing strong results at the retail stores."

Lally commented that the company ran lean, air freight notwithstanding, in contrast to many start-ups in the late 1990s. Their first office was 1,000 square feet and featured used furniture. Executives flew coach, even on long-haul flights to Asia. Recalling those start-up days, he noted: "We were tenacious in our belief in the products and were completely committed to what we were doing. We were blind to failure."

Independent manufacturers' representatives, working on straight commission and representing many lines, pitched the products to the major retail buyers. With their reputation on the line, manufacturers' reps were critical first "buyers" of The Phonics Desk and other stand-alone products built on the same phonics learning model. Fortunately, the products were a hit, resulting in bookings that first year of $6 million. Unfortunately, LeapFrog had to cancel almost half those orders as they were unable to manufacture enough products in time to meet demand. Still, with $3.5 million in revenues that first year, LeapFrog began to attract the notice of competitors—and investors.

Acquiring Capital—and Being Acquired

LeapFrog's second year was much smoother, with far fewer production kinks and sales of $10.5 million, yet Wood realized he would need a major capital infusion to take it to the next level. Tom Kalinske, former CEO of Mattel and Sega of America, now LeapFrog's chairman and one of the most respected figures in the toy industry, recalled: "As president of Knowledge Universe,[6] I was very interested in LeapFrog, as we had an exact meshing of mission. We had capital and were looking to invest in educational technology; LeapFrog had educational technology and needed capital." In September 1997, Knowledge Universe acquired 82 percent of LeapFrog.

The acquisition brought LeapFrog $50 million in much-needed growth capital, and just as valuable, Kalinske, assuming the CEO role, brought his 30-plus years of industry expertise and connections. He played a key role in reestablishing a relationship with Wal-Mart, which had dropped LeapFrog after its first year to focus on a competitor with a then-larger product line. It was Kalinske who was behind LeapFrog's successful guerrilla marketing campaign, in which they posted a large LeapFrog billboard outside Wal-Mart's Bentonville headquarters and sponsored the local county fair. And it was Knowledge Universe that brokered a meeting between LeapFrog and a small educational toy company, Explore Learning, developers of an interactive children's globe. It was a meeting that would have dramatic consequences for both companies—and, indeed, for the toy industry at large.

Marggraff, then with Explore Technologies, subsequently in various LeapFrog management positions from 1998 to 2001 and executive vice president of content for LeapFrog since January 2002, told the story:

> In 1996, Explore Technologies launched a high-end children's globe which featured a technology we'd developed called NearTouch™. The interior of the globe was sprayed with a special conductive paint. When a point on the globe was touched with a special stylus, it triggered audio feedback, stored on a sound chip, corresponding to that point. Essentially, NearTouch™ technology and our passion for innovative learning spawned paper-based multimedia.

[6] According to the company Web site, www.knowledgeu.com, "Knowledge Universe (KU) is the parent of a diverse group of operating companies with a common theme of building human capital by helping individuals and businesses to realize their full potential." The educational holding company was founded by Larry Ellison, founder of Oracle, and Michael Millken.

EXHIBIT 3 LeapFrog Product Platforms

Source: Author based on LeapFrog 2002 Annual Report.

Learning System	Educational Objectives	Interactivity	Content Library
LeapPad U.S. Launch: Summer 1999 Ages: 4 to 8 48% of 2002 sales	Teaches 4 skills levels: reading and math readiness, phonics, reading comprehension, and vocabulary; math, science, music, logic	Based on proprietary NearTouch technology; child touches words, numbers, and pictures with stylus to receive audio feedback that guides skills development.	• Over 45 titles • Available in English, French, Italian, Spanish, Japanese • Library is divided into 4 age-appropriate Leap Levels • Reading activity sheets available through Never-Ending Learning Club via Mind Station • Accompanying *Pond* magazine published by LeapFrog, features content from Time for Kids • Features Leap characters as well as licensed material such as Winnie-the-Pooh, Scooby-Doo, and Arthur
Imagination Desk U.S. Launch: Summer 2001 Ages: 3 to 5	Introduces essential preschool skills	Children color on activity sheets; pressure of the crayon activates audio feedback to guide skill development.	• 10 titles • Available in English, French, Spanish • Weekly curriculum updates available through Never-Ending Learning Club (via Mind Station) • Features Leap characters as well as licensed material such as Winnie-the-Pooh
My First LeapPad U.S. Launch: Summer 2001 Ages: 3 to 5	Teaches prereading and premath skills, vocabulary, science, social studies, safety, community awareness	Based on NearTouch technology; child points to words, numbers, and pictures with stylus to activate audio feedback to guide skill development.	• 8 titles • Available in English and Japanese • Features Leap characters as well as licensed material such as Dora the Explorer, Winnie-the-Pooh, and Thomas the Tank Engine
TurboTwist Handhelds U.S. Launch: Summer 1999 1st through 6th grades	Reinforces spelling, math, vocabulary, and social studies concepts learned in school	Children twist, pound, and press handheld devices to display questions; audio feedback guides skill development; program self-adjusts to accommodate learning level of individual child.	• Available in English, French, Italian, and Spanish • Via Mind Station, scores can be uploaded and new content downloaded • Weekly curricula for spelling and math for 1st through-5th grades available to Never-Ending Learning Club subscription via Mind Station • Additional content cartridges available • Brain-Quest edition features licensed content

Product	Focus	Technology/Description	Content/Features
Quantum Pad U.S. Launch: Fall 2002 3rd through 5th grades	Focuses on subjects learned in school, such as science, social science, complex reading comprehension, math, and the arts	Employs the same technology and interactivity as LeapPad, but in a form factor more appropriate for an older child.	• 15 titles • 3 different content types: grade-based and curriculum-based content, complex reading skills, introduction to enrichment topics such as arts and music
iQuest Interactive Handheld U.S. Launch: Summer 2001 5th through 8th grades and high school	Assists students with test taking	Correlated with over 200 major textbooks used in 5th through 8th grade social studies, science, and math classes, this handheld device displays questions, then provides audio feedback based on the child's response to promote content mastery.	• Preloaded content includes 40,000 word version of Merriam-Webster Dictionary and 1,000 basic fact questions created in consultation with Princeton Review • Device can store phone numbers, addresses, and class schedule data • Through Never-Ending Learning Club, via Mind Station connection, subscribers are able to download 7,000+ test questions and chapter outlines from over 200 major textbooks; this content is also available via cartridge at retail • SSAT/SAT/PSAT/ACT test prep content, licensed from Kaplan, is available via the Mind Station connection, or via cartridge at retail
Stand-Alone Products For infants, toddlers, and children	Teaches a variety of fine motor as well as cognitive skills	Products, which numbered 35 in 2003, include:	• LeapStart Learning Table: introduces motor and developmental skills to toddlers • Leap's Phonics Railroad: a train set that teaches the alphabet and phonics • Pretend and Learn Shopping Cart: teaches young children colors, math concepts, and food facts • Explorer Globe: for older children, an interactive touch-sensitive globe that utilizes NearTouch technology to teach geographic facts. Also available in a Junior Explorer version for younger children. • Learning Friends, Learning Drum, Learning Hoops Basketball: toys for infants and toddlers that encourage development of cognitive skills

While the globe was a limited commercial success, the technology and Marggraff's vision for "paper-based multimedia" had caught the attention of investors, including Kalinske of Knowledge Universe. He arranged for a meeting with Wood and Calfee. Calfee recalled, "I saw Jim's demonstration of the prototype LeapPad and thought, 'This is it! This has the potential to bring paper to life. Now, we can create a book that can read itself to kids.'"

LeapFrog acquired Explore Technologies in 1998, and Marggraff and the NearTouch technology came to LeapFrog, as well as Explore engineers who formed the nucleus of LeapFrog's hardware and software development unit. Building on the product ideas discussed in that initial meeting, the LeapPad product emerged, aimed at the three- to seven-year-old age group. The LeapPad hardware featured a stylus and audio playback base unit, into which the "software," a removable audio cartridge and a spiral-bound book about 20 pages in length, was inserted. Children used the stylus to touch various points on the book's pages and received audio feedback to guide them through the product's learning activities. (For more on the LeapPad and other LeapFrog platforms, see Exhibit 3.)

LeapPad: The Separation of Platform and Content

Key to the product's design was the separation of the content (the book and its audio cartridge) from the platform itself (housing the speakers, batteries, stylus, and base). Launched into the market in 1999, LeapPad won the prestigious Toy Industry Association's People's Choice Educational Toy of the Year Award for 2000 and became the top-selling toy for that year. As LeapFrog's core product, LeapPad again gained the top industry sales rank in 2001. It missed a "three-peat" in 2002 only because LeapPad books took the number one toy sales slot, while the LeapPad platform came in at number two. In total, LeapPad and its related titles

accounted for 48 percent of the company's total 2002 revenues.[7]

By making the platform and content separate, LeapFrog gained the advantages of the classic razors-and-blades marketing strategy. Unlike razors, though, which were often sold close to cost to drive sales of consumable blades, LeapFrog platforms were sold at a marked-up price ($29.99 to $59.99 suggested retail price), thus delivering gross margins of 30 percent on newer platforms, rising to 50 percent-plus margins for more mature platforms as economies of scale kicked in. But even better, margins of 50 percent to 60 percent were to be made on the sales of book/cartridge content, which sold at $9.99 to $14.99. What's more, these add-on sales helped smooth the highly seasonal sales pattern of the typical toy, as parents bought titles throughout the year, not just at holiday time. In 2002 alone, over 18.5 million interactive books and cartridges were sold for use with various LeapFrog platforms. That same year, the company announced that over 8 million LeapPad systems had been sold since the product's introduction in 1999.

LeapFrog Goes to School

LeapFrog's products did not escape the notice of teachers in the classroom, many of whom purchased LeapPads from retailers for use with their students. Writing in by the hundreds, offering suggestions, and asking for product modifications to better suit the classroom environment, these teachers inspired Wood to establish the company's SchoolHouse division in June 1999. (For more details on the division, see Exhibit 4, LeapFrog business unit highlights.) Sales were first broken out from the U.S. consumer unit in 2000. Lally, LeapFrog's cofounder and first COO, assumed the presidency of the division upon its creation. Said Lally in mid-2003:

> To date we've invested close to $20 million to customize
> our content for the classroom. This content has to be a lot

[7] Figures from analyst Howard Block's report for Banc of America Securities, Equity Research, "LeapFrog Enterprises, Inc.: A Toy for All Seasons," December 20, 2002.

EXHIBIT 4 **LeapFrog Business Unit Highlights**

Source: LeapFrog 2002 Annual Report, company records.

U.S. Consumer Division	International Consumer Division	SchoolHouse Division
• More than 65 learning products	• LeapFrog products available in 30+ countries and in 5 languages	• SchoolHouse products in over 14,000 schools
• As of 2002, 6 learning platforms, with 3 new ones announced for 2003	• First international office established in the U.K. in 2000	• Over 20 awards for SchoolHouse products since launch of division
• Over 120 interactive software titles	• At end of 2002, 33 employees on international sales team	• Targets pre-K through 5th-grade classrooms, teacher supply stores, and catalogs
• 15 new stand-alone products in 2003	• By 2003, LeapFrog sales offices also in Canada and France	• 99 employees in sales, marketing, content development, and operations, many of them former teachers, learning and child development specialists
• Over 200 industry awards, with over 40 in 2002	• Manufacturing coordination office in Hong Kong	
• Educational Toy of the Year awards in 2000, 2001, 2002	• In 2002, Sega Toys and Benesse Corp. of Japan begin distribution of cobranded adaptation of LeapPad platforms, and related content, for home and school markets	• 35 dedicated company field reps, plus about 20 independent sales reps
• Numerous awards from retail partners	• Learning Center retailing strategy expanded in 2003 to U.K. and Canadian retailers	• Secured placement on 8 state-approved adoption lists (100% of those applied for)
• Over 8 million LeapPads sold (worldwide)	• In 2003, a partnership is announced with Stadelbauer, a leading German-language distributor	• Over 200 books and 267 skills cards created for SchoolHouse platforms

more granular, because teachers may be teaching the "th" sound for four days and need a book just on that concept. We need to deal, too, with the fact that the overall requirements are different for schools. With home products we're competing with Nintendo, sports, and TV for a kid's time; in the schools we're competing against worksheets. So we have to build things that are exciting enough to engage kids and get them focused and learning, but not so much they get giddy.

We have also developed a special version of the LeapPad for the school market—you might say it's "rugged-ized." It's got rubber corners, high-quality headphones, and AC adapters. Batteries are fine for 18 to 20 hours of home use, but not if you're a teacher and you've got 20 LeapPads in the classroom.

SchoolHouse faced not just different product requirements but also a very different decision process for school materials than for toys. Lally

commented, "You can show buyers at a mass market retailer, 'Here's a prototype and it's going to work like this,' and they'll place an opening order and see how it sells. But schools are different. They say, 'Alright, when it's finished, we'll buy one and try it out for a while.' The cycles are much longer and the decisions much slower and more cautious."

Competitors in the school market were different, too, as LeapPad went up against mainstream traditional educational publishers such as Harcourt, Houghton Mifflin, McGraw-Hill, Pearson, and Scholastic, as well as electronic publishers such as Knowledge Adventure, LightSpan, and Riverdeep. In the assessment area, it faced established test-prep competitors such as Sylvan, Princeton Review, and Kaplan (the latter was also a licensor of content for the iQuest platform).

EXHIBIT 5
LeapFrog 2002
Sales by
Segment

Source: Company
records.

LeapFrog 2002 Segment Results ($ millions)				
	U.S. Consumer	International	U.S. School	Total
Net Sales	$458.0	$53.3	$20.1	$531.8
(% of Total)	*86%*	*10%*	*4%*	*100%*
Gross Profit	$237.1	$23.3	$11.6	$272.0
Gross Margin	*51.8%*	*43.5%*	*57.6%*	*51.2%*
Operating Income	$72.7	$7.6	($9.0)	$71.4
	15.9%	*14.2%*	*—*	*13.4%*

The rapid top-line growth that characterized U.S. consumer sales had eluded SchoolHouse. According to the company's annual report in 2002, "The division, which is accounted for under our Education and Training Segment, has generated limited sales and has incurred substantial losses," contributing only 4 percent of total 2002 revenues. (See Exhibit 5 for LeapFrog 2002 sales by segment.) The report further noted that substantial losses were expected to continue into the foreseeable future. As of December 31, 2002, $3.2 million in content development costs for the division had been capitalized, with another $0.9 million of capitalization planned in early 2003. But optimism for the group still ran high, with 2002 revenues increasing 129 percent to $20 million versus those of 2001, with 21 new products launched that year. And at an investor's conference in May 2003, Wood pointed out that first-quarter results for 2003 were up 67 percent, to $5.9 million from $3.6 million in 2002's first quarter.[8] Noting that the overall supplemental educational market was estimated at $4.7 billion for 2003, Wood indicated there was plenty of room to grow.

Lally provided another reason for entering this complicated market: "The company was making these huge investments in technology, so we wanted to find ways to leverage that investment into other markets. We really wanted our brand to be perceived, not as a toy company, but as a company people look to for learning solutions." As the SchoolHouse division leveraged the technology and design talents of the consumer division, the company also leveraged the research expertise of the SchoolHouse group as a resource for companywide use, guiding development of all products to ensure that they were appropriate for each target age or grade level.

LeapFrog Goes International

LeapFrog, like other U.S. toy companies, saw an opportunity to grow its presence internationally and launched its first international subsidiary in the United Kingdom in 2000. American culture was highly exportable. As analyst McGowan noted: ". . . the continued influence of American television, movies, and other content will spur more toy sales." He went on to note that Toys "R" Us in 2002 operated 507 toy stores in 28 countries, including 282 licensed and franchised stores, and enjoyed its best year ever.[9]

LeapFrog planned to accelerate its international growth by establishing additional subsidiaries and using a combination of direct sales to retailers and distribution arrangements.

[8] Michael Wood, presentation to US Bancorp Piper Jaffray 23rd Annual Consumer Conference, July 11, 2003, New York.

[9] Sean McGowan, "Toy Manufacturing and Retailing," analyst report issued for Gerard Klauer Mattison, October 2002.

EXHIBIT 6

Comparative Revenue Growth: LeapFrog, Mattel, Hasbro, and GDP

Source: Company reports, Bureau of Economic Analysis, Banc of America Securities LLC estimates.

	1998	1999	2000	2001	2002
LeapFrog	$31	$72	$160	$314	$532
% Growth	*83.1%*	*130.9%*	*122.8%*	*95.9%*	*69.4%*
Mattel	$4,782	$4,503	$4,566	$4,688	$4,885
% Growth	*1.1%*	*5.8%*	*1.4%*	*2.7%*	*4.2%*
Hasbro	$3,304	$4,232	$3,787	$2,856	$2,816
% Growth	*3.6%*	*28.1%*	*(10.5%)*	*(24.6%)*	*(14%)*
GDP ($ billions)	$8,782	$9,724	$9,825	$10,082	$10,446
% Growth	*5.6%*	*5.6%*	*5.9%*	*2.6%*	*3.6%*

Special partnerships were sought in countries where distribution and/or educational circumstances called for local expertise. In Japan, for instance, the company entered into relationships with both Sega and Benesse to develop customized versions of its platforms and content for both school and home markets. LeapFrog's 2002 international results were $54 million, or about 10 percent of total sales.

Tim Bender, LeapFrog's president, Global Consumer Group, commented on LeapFrog's global strategy: "We're trying to develop a product and market lifecycle that supports our international expansion. We want to build a global brand so that, whether we're in France or China or the U.S., the product is consistent with the educational standards of that country." (For more on LeapFrog's international efforts, refer back to Exhibit 4, LeapFrog business unit highlights.) Second-quarter 2003 results for the division showed a sales increase of 94 percent from second-quarter 2002, with a higher gross margin (44.2 percent) than in the comparable period in 2002 (38.2 percent).

LeapFrog Goes Public

The year 2002 was a banner year for LeapFrog. Sales of $532 million, a 69 percent increase in revenues over the prior year, took the company to the third position among U.S. toy company rankings. The fast-growing library of titles for LeapPad and other LeapFrog platforms made the company one of the nation's largest children's publishers. LeapFrog totally dominated two product categories it had essentially created, preschool electronic learning aids (ELA), in which it held a 77 percent market share, and nonpreschool ELA (for ages six to nine), with a 68 percent market share. With no long-term debt, top-line sales growth, and a strong balance sheet, LeapFrog's management team felt well-positioned to capitalize on the opportunities and challenges that lay ahead. (For more on LeapFrog's financial performance, see Exhibits 6 and 7. Financial statements from the company's 2002 annual report can be found in the Appendix.)

On July 25, 2002, in the midst of a grim capital market, LeapFrog (NYSE: LF) successfully issued 9 million shares in its initial public offering (IPO) at $13 per share, raising $115 million for the company. Share prices rose that day to close at $15.85. Shares continued their upward trend, peaking at just over $35 per share in December of 2002, making it the most successful IPO of 2002, before falling to a low in the mid-teens in February 2003 as earnings estimates were reduced in the climate of uncertainty prior to the Iraq war. Share prices rebounded in the general market upswing of spring 2003, and by mid-July 2003, were trading in the $30 range, around 26 times earnings.

EXHIBIT 7
LeapFrog Sales Growth

Source: Company records.

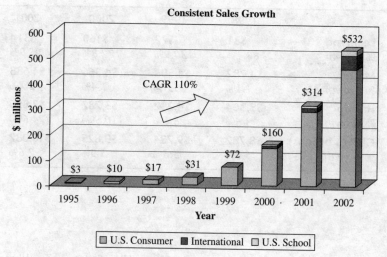

Barbara Miller, an analyst for The Federated Kauffman Fund, offered an investment perspective in mid-July 2003:

> LeapFrog has built a strong brand in a short period of time. While their top-line growth is impressive, it's good to see earnings growth occurring at an even higher rate. They are efficiently managing their operating costs, and their lack of debt shows they are able to fund their growth organically. The company has consistently outperformed expectations and has defied a difficult economic environment. I consider their P/E ratio of 26 to be fair for a growth company. Looking ahead, I would want to see the company demonstrate continued improvement in managing inventory, sales gains in the international sector, and movement into secondary retail channels, while maintaining share of shelf with the major retailers.

Background on the Toy Industry

LeapFrog's unique dual nature—as both toy company and educational company—required that the young company meet the challenges inherent in not just one, but two sectors. In 2002, the global toy market was valued at approximately $70 billion according to industry estimates, with the North American market share almost half the total ($31 billion) despite there being fewer children in North America than on the other major continents. Average North American toy expendi-

tures of $328 per child, driven largely by U.S. household figures of $405 per child, were 10 times the world's per capita average of $32.[10] (See Exhibit 8 for global toy market figures.) As one expert noted, "Only 2% of the world's children reside in the U.S., yet those kids consume nearly half the world's toys."[11] Totaling $25 billion in 2001 sales, the U.S. market was also mature, with a compound annual growth rate of just 2 percent.[12] Long considered "a duopoly, with two large companies [Mattel and Hasbro] controlling almost one-third of the industry,"[13] toy industry rankings had shifted to accommodate LeapFrog's dramatic rise from 15th place in 2000, to 4th in 2001, to 3rd in 2002.

Toy industry analyst McGowan noted that despite the challenging economic environment of

---

[10] NPD Group Worldwide, Banc of America Securities LLC estimates.

[11] M. Eric Johnson, "Learning from Toys: Lessons in Managing Supply Chain Risk from the Toy Industry," *California Management Review*, 43, no. 3, Spring 2001.

[12] NPD Funworld figures, as cited in Sean McGowan, "Toy Manufacturing and Retailing," analyst report issued for Gerard Klauer Mattison, October 2002.

[13] Sean McGowan, "Toy Manufacturing and Retailing," analyst report issued for Gerard Klauer Mattison, October 2002.

EXHIBIT 8   Global Toy Market

Source: NPD Group Worldwide, Banc of America LLC estimates, as found in "LeapFrog Enterprises, Inc.: A Toy for All Seasons," an equity research report from Banc of America Securities, December 20, 2002; and NPD Funworld as reported in Sean McGowan, "Toy Manufacturing and Retailing," analyst report issued for Gerard Klauer Mattison, October 2002.

Percentage of Population of Children <18 years

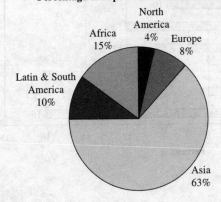

North America 4%
Europe 8%
Africa 15%
Latin & South America 10%
Asia 63%

Percentage of Worldwide Toy Sales

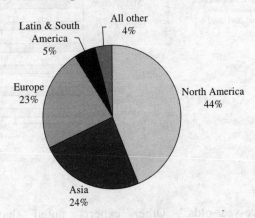

Latin & South America 5%
All other 4%
Europe 23%
North America 44%
Asia 24%

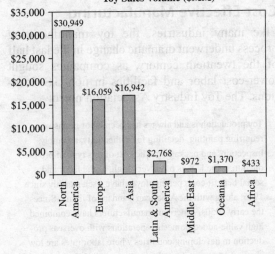

Toy Sales Volume ($MM)

North America $30,949
Europe $16,059
Asia $16,942
Latin & South America $2,768
Middle East $972
Oceania $1,370
Africa $433

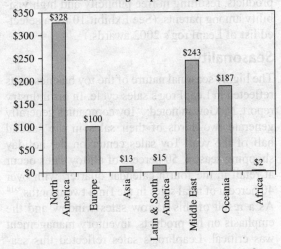

Annual Average Expenditure per Child ($)

North America $328
Europe $100
Asia $13
Latin & South America $15
Middle East $243
Oceania $187
Africa $2

the early 2000s, toys had proven themselves to be rather recession proof. Yet, toy spending was difficult to predict, as the category, according to McGowan, was ". . . rather elastic, as hot products, such as Trivial Pursuit, in a given year may pull in discretionary dollars from consumers who are not typically toy buyers. Once that product ceases being hot, though, those dollars do not show up in

the category again the following year." (See Exhibit 9, toy sales by product category.)

According to another toy industry expert, Chris Byrne, CEO of Byrne Communications, "Toys are a lot like the fashion business. There's a huge emphasis on what's hot, what's trendy, and a lot of importance is placed on brand, although obviously brand matters more to parents than to

EXHIBIT 9

Total Toy Sales by Product Category 2000

Source: Adapted from *Toy Industry Fact Book:* 2001–2002.

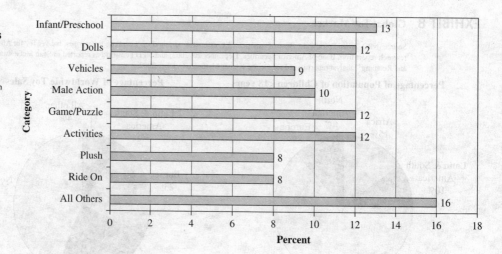

five-year-olds." Other experts noted that LeapFrog had been savvy in seeking awards for its products, resulting in free publicity and high visibility among parents. (See Exhibit 10 for a selected list of LeapFrog's 2002 awards.)

Seasonality

The highly seasonal nature of the toy business was reflected in LeapFrog's sales cycle. In his industry report, McGowan noted: "Toy companies generally generate two-thirds of their sales in the second half of the year. Toy sales center on the holiday shopping season; 50 percent of all toy sales occur at retail in the fourth calendar quarter, with over 40 percent of total sales in the final two months."[14] As a result of this narrow sales window and the emphasis on hit products, inventory management was critical. LeapFrog's sales reflected this seasonal pattern, with approximately 81 percent of its 2002 U.S. sales occurring in the third and fourth quarters. The industry's concentration of sales into the narrow holiday window was expected to increase as retailers moved to increasingly sophisticated just-in-time inventory management systems,

thus shifting risk to their suppliers and lessening their inventory exposure.

Cost-Effective Manufacturing

Like many industries, the toy manufacturing process underwent dramatic change in the last half of the twentieth century, as companies sought lower-cost labor and facilities in non-U.S. locations. The Toy Industry Association noted:

Toy production is and always has been labor intensive, requiring painting, detailing for authenticity, assembly, inspection, and packaging. The cost of this type of production in the U.S. is often very high, as the labor and social benefit costs per employee have risen steadily since 1945, along with the American standard of living. Since the early 1950s, American manufacturers have combined high value-added domestic operations with overseas production in developing countries where labor rates are low in an effort to significantly decrease costs. It is estimated that 80% of the toys, including video games, sold in the U.S. are manufactured either wholly or in part overseas. In 2000, U.S. toy imports totaled $15.1 billion of which $10.7 billion represented toys produced in China.[15]

Analyst McGowan commented, "Very few toy 'manufacturers' actually make their own products.

---

[14] Sean McGowan, "Toy Manufacturing and Retailing," analyst report issued for Gerard Klauer Mattison, October 2002.

[15] *Toy Industry Fact Book: 2001–2002*, Toy Industry Association, viewed at http://www.toy-tia.org/industry/publications/fbcurrent/review.htm.

EXHIBIT 10 Selected LeapFrog Awards

Source: Company Web site.

Discovery Ball® Learning System	• Seal of Approval, The National Parenting Center
iQuest™ Handheld	• Recommended Award Winner, Parents' Choice 2002
	• Seal of Approval, The National Parenting Center
	• Toy Wishes All Star, Education & Learning Category
	• What's New in 2002, Popular Science
Learning Drum™ Educational Toy	• Seal of Approval, The National Parenting Center
	• "Toys of the Year," Parenting.com
	• "Editors' Choice Toys of the Year," Baby Talk
	• 20 Toys, KTVU-TV (Fox) Great American Toy Test, San Francisco
Learn to Read Phonics Desk® System	• Toy Wishes All Star, Education & Learning Category
LeapStart™ Learning Table	• Top 10 Best Selling Toys Sold in Specialty Stores (PlayDate)
	• Toy Wishes All Star, Infant Category
	• All Star Award, Children's Software Revue
LeapPad® Learning System	• #1 Best Selling Toy Sold in Specialty Stores and Top 10 Best Selling Toy Overall (PlayDate)
	• Winner, Oppenheim Toy Portfolio, Gold Seal Award
	• T.O.T.Y. Educational Toy of the Year Award, 2000
	• People's Choice Toy of the Year, 2000
My First LeapPad Learning System	• Educational Toy of the Year, 2001
Pretend & Learn™ Shopping Cart	• Approved Award Winner, Parents' Choice
	• Toy Wishes All Star, Preschool Category
	• Seal of Approval, The National Parenting Center
	• Family Fun Toy Awards, Active Toys Category
	• All Star Award, Children's Software Revue
Quantum Pad™ Learning System	• Toy Wishes Hot Dozen
	• Wishes All Star, Education & Learning Category
	• Educational Toy of the Year, 2002
TurboTwist(® Handheld BRAIN QUEST® Edition	• Recommended Award Winner, Parents' Choice 2002
	• Seal of Approval, The National Parenting Center
TurboTwist® Vocabulator Handheld	• Winner, Silver Honor Award, Parents' Choice 2002

Toy companies, essentially, are marketing companies, creators of IP [intellectual property]." LeapFrog mirrored the industry in this regard, with virtually all its products produced by seven contract manufacturers in Guandong province in China. One of these manufacturers, Jetta Company Limited (the sole manufacturer of LeapPad), supplied 45 percent of LeapFrog products sold in 2002, while the top three man-

ufacturers supplied 58 percent of the total. Retail customers took title to one-third of LeapFrog products sold in 2002 directly from manufacturing facilities in China, while the remaining two-thirds were shipped to the company's contract warehouse in Ontario, California, for distribution to retailers.

This concentration of manufacturing, while efficient, could have its downside. The 11-day

West Coast dockworkers strike of September 2002 cost the company $3 million in additional freight charges. Fortunately for the company, the SARS health crisis, which seriously disrupted Asian trade in the spring of 2003, did not unduly affect LeapFrog operations as the outbreak did not coincide with a peak shipping period.

Given the vagaries of long-distance manufacturing and the narrowness of its key sales season, supply chain management was a critical factor in the toy industry. While generally contract manufacturers assumed responsibility for sourcing parts, LeapFrog took on the sourcing of some key long-lead-time parts to better manage its supply chain. Tim Bender, president, Global Consumer Group, commented:

> Sometimes those parts have a 12 to 14 week lead time, yet they might cost only a quarter, while the wholesale value of the total product might be $35. We'll assume a bit more risk so that if we need to get that part to our manufacturer in a hurry, we can. The beautiful thing is that, as a result, we've become one of the largest integrated circuit purchasers in the world. And so we get some of the best pricing in the world on one of our key product components.

Shifting Demographics

The market for toys, like many consumer segments, experienced significant transformation in recent years—largely stemming from changing demographics, the impact of technology, the rise of new retail channels, and shifts in distribution methods. Although birth rates in the first years of the new millennium continued to decline in the United States and many other developed countries, overall demographics favored the industry, as the trend toward older parenting generally meant more disposable income to spend on children. LeapFrog was well poised to take advantage of these demographic shifts. As the U.S.-based Toy Industry Association expressed in its *Toy Fact Book 2001–2002,* the 88 million children of the consumer-heavyweight baby boomer generation had very different characteristics from those of their parents:

Here's how *Advertising Age* describes children of this generation (nicknamed "millennials"): "Tech-savvy and educated; multicultural; bombarded by media messages; accustomed to sex and violence; growing up in an affluent society; and [they have] big spending power." Add to that the description from *The Economist*: "These millennials are technologically precocious, growing up with a rattle in one hand and a computer mouse in the other."

As a result of this new phenomenon in our society, the toy industry has discovered a whole new category of toys that integrate technology and play, called "Smart Toys." By combining learning, play, and technology, sales in this category increased by 98% in 2000, and they are rapidly approaching the $1 billion mark, according to The NPD Group's retail tracking service. The significant increase in this category represents a "revolutionary change" that is occurring in America, influenced by a number of factors including parents' concern with the state of education in public schools across our nation and partly due to the growing pressures for children to excel. Whatever is causing the shift, the results are worth taking note. For the first time in our nation's history, an educational product—namely, a toy called LeapPad by LeapFrog, designed to help kids read—was the best-selling product during the 2000 holiday season.[16]

Jim Silver, publisher of *Toy Wishes* magazine, cited another attribute of today's sophisticated child-consumers: "Many in the toy industry are paying close attention to a market phenomenon we call 'age compression.' The reality today is that toys appeal to kids at earlier ages than they did a few years ago, and kids outgrow their toys faster than ever before." Or as McGowan put it, "Kids are getting older younger." Age compression can result in reduced toy revenues, as narrower age ranges mean fewer potential customers. Kalinske, though, noted that LeapFrog was reversing that trend: "With our Little Touch and Leapster products in 2003, and our existing iQuest and Quantum Leap platforms, we are expanding successfully beyond the age range of

---

[16] Ibid.

EXHIBIT 11   **2000 Worldwide Toy Sales by Channel of Distribution 2000**

Sources: *Toy Industry Fact Book: 2001–2002,* and Sean McGowan, "Toy Manufacturing and Retailing," analyst report issued for Gerard Klauer Mattison, October 2002.

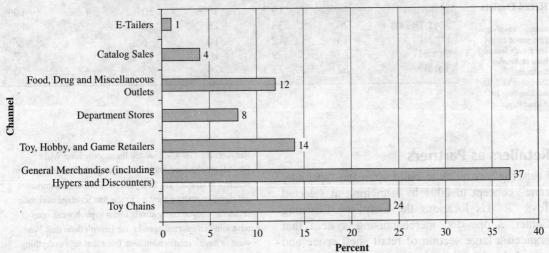

our core LeapPad product to reach toddlers and infants, as well as 'tweens and teens."

The Changing Retail Landscape

By the end of the twenty-first century, the local toy shop was an endangered species in the retail landscape. (See Exhibit 11 for toy sales by distribution channel.) Independent toy stores had long been losing market share to chains. Initially, independent toy stores lost business to specialty chains such as Toys "R" Us, but in the late 1990s, both independent and chain toy stores were losing ground to the generalist discount retailers such as Wal-Mart. The latter trend showed some signs of reversal, as McGowan noted in his 2002 industry analysis: "Chain retailers . . . are again picking up share, but from local independent competitors as well as from the bankruptcies of Ames and Kmart. We expect this trend to continue for the foreseeable future, as independent retailers continue to weaken, with the biggest battle for share to be one that pits the discounters like Wal-Mart and Target against the toy chains

like Toys "R" Us and KB."[17] Noting that Wal-Mart took over the leading toy retailer slot from Toys "R" Us in 1998, McGowan explained that discounters held a 37 percent share of the total U.S. toy market in 2001: "The ability to expand and contract the toy section as demand dictates, creating a loss-leading category in the holiday months to drive traffic, is a big reason for the success of discounters in toy retailing." However, with a 24 percent share, the toy chains were still attracting plenty of customers since toy chains offered a wider selection of toys year-round and better customer service, the latter especially important for educational toys. For example, Toys "R" Us, the largest U.S. toy retailer, hoping to entice consumers seeking "the total toy experience" had created special sections in its stores for educational toys.

[17] Sean McGowan, "Toy Manufacturing and Retailing," analyst report issued for Gerard Klauer Mattison, October 2002.

EXHIBIT 12
Top Four
LeapFrog
Retail Outlets

Source: "LeapFrog
Enterprises, Inc.: A
Toy for All Seasons,"
Banc of America
Securities,
December 20, 2002;
and LeapFrog 2002
Annual Report.

	LeapFrog's Top Retailers (% of Total Sales)				Toy Industry Sales	
	1999	2000	2001	2002	1999	2000
Wal-Mart	16%	19%	30%	30%	17%	19%
Toys "R" Us	20	33	28	28	16	17
Kmart	14	12	10	6	7	7
Target	7	9	10	11	7	7
Total	57	73	79	75	47	50

Retailers as Partners

LeapFrog was quick to build upon the "specialty zone" concept in 2001 by launching at selected Toys "R" Us locations the LeapFrog Learning Center, a one-stop merchandising system that branded a large section of retail shelf space and provided interactive signage to guide the consumer (and the chain's shelf stockers) through the full array of age-appropriate LeapFrog products. Company executives hoped to expand the Learning Center strategy, already in place at over 5,000 stores by the end of 2002, to additional stores and with other retail partners to gain an additional 40 percent of shelf space in 2003.[18]

LeapFrog also gathered sophisticated point-of-sale reports from retailers. According to Bender, "We manage our shelf space to the inch. By Tuesday morning of every week, we know what the sales were for the previous week. We're doing a constant trend analysis to determine where our business is going." This sales data proved useful not only for LeapFrog's internal inventory management purposes but also for managing relationships with its key retailers. Bender explained, "We believed that if we became experts in our retailers' businesses and could tell them how they could better manage their own business, they would look to us as leaders and come to us first when opportunity presented itself." He continued:

Retailers trust us when we tell them something. Mike [Wood] emphasized integrity and long-term commitment to retailers from our very first year. Sometimes as companies get significant share they try to use that leverage over their retailers—maybe using strong items to push weak ones or advancing an internal agenda. We haven't done this. We want to have a relationship with them that says everything we do should work for both of us in the long term.

(See Exhibit 12 for more on LeapFrog's top four retailers.)

LeapFrog's efforts seemed to be paying off. In May 2003, the company announced it had received "toy vendor of the year" awards from four top retailers in the United States—the Fred Meyer "Toy Vendor of the Year" award for the second year in a row, the ShopKo Stores "Toy Vendor of the Year," a Toys "R" Us "Vendor of the Year," and the coveted "Supplier of the Year" from Wal-Mart Stores.[19]

Online Retailing

While online toy retailing had been expected to become a dominant force in the industry, the collapse of early entrants, such as eToys in 2001, proved those expectations premature. Yet, by 2002 the online leaders, including toyrus.com and KB Toys (purchasers of the eToys brand), reported robust sales growth. McGowan's analysis indicated that specialty toy stores would do better online

[18] Michael Wood, presentation at US Bancorp Piper Jaffray 23rd Annual Consumer Conference, June 11, 2003, New York.

[19] LeapFrog corporate press release, May 14, 2003, viewed at http://www.leapfroginvestor.com/phoenix.zhtml?c=131670&p=irol-nrtext&t=Regular&id=412110&.

EXHIBIT 13
Online Toy and Video Game Sales

Source: Adapted from Sean McGowan, "Toy Manufacturing and Retailing," analyst report issued for Gerard Klauer Mattison, October 2002.

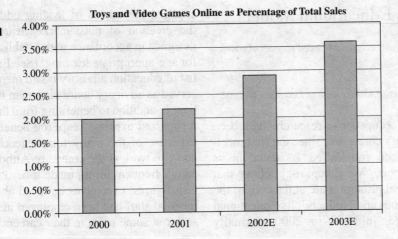

Toys and Video Games Online as Percentage of Total Sales

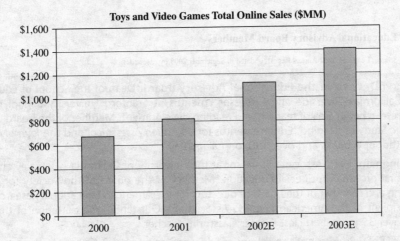

Toys and Video Games Total Online Sales ($MM)

than the chain stores, as destination sites had fared better online than one-stop discounters. He further predicted steady growth in the sector but still not exceeding single-digit percentages of total sales through 2003.[20] (See Exhibit 13 for a comparison of online versus traditional retail channels.)

LeapFrog's Internet retailing strategy shifted as the sector cooled in the aftermath of the dot-com meltdown. Although no platforms or prepackaged content were available for sale from its Web site, purchasers of the company's Mind Station connection could download LeapPad content to rewriteable cartridges and print activity sheets. Users of LeapFrog's TurboTwist (a handheld quizzing product) were able to upload scores, view assessment reports, and get individualized recommendations for additional content to download. A six-month subscription was offered free with the purchase of the Mind Station. However, LeapFrog found most of its consumers preferred to purchase prepackaged content at retail and tailored its product development and marketing strategies accordingly.

[20] Sean McGowan, "Toy Manufacturing and Retailing," analyst report issued for Gerard Klauer Mattison, October 2002.

LeapFrog's Educational Model

"LeapFrog is the only consumer-branded provider of educational products."

Howard Block, Banc of America analyst, December 20, 2002

Educators, and educational research, had been part of LeapFrog's core assets since the first meeting between Wood and Calfee. As noted in its 2002 annual report, "We [LeapFrog] believe that sound educational principles are at the core of the value of our brands and products." Its Educational Advisory Board, initiated in 2000, formally engaged the talents of leading educators toward the creation of mass-market learning products designed in accordance with established standards for age-appropriate learning. (See Exhibit 14 for a list of education advisory board members.) Calfee served as advisory board chairman from its inception. In addition to benefiting from these nationally recognized experts, LeapFrog benefited from the expertise of the many former teachers who had come to work at the company. Although the company's frequent hiring made it hard to obtain precise figures, executives believed about a third of the total staff had been employed in the education sector at some point in their careers.

EXHIBIT 14 **Educational Advisory Board Members**

Source: LeapFrog 2002 Annual Report, updated in September 2003 by casewriter.

Robert Calfee, PhD, Chair of the Educational Advisory Board. Dean of the School of Education at the University of California—Riverside and Professor Emeritus at Stanford University School of Education. Distinguished researcher in area of reading and reading development. Member of the board of the Society for the Scientific Study of Reading. Editor emeritus for *Education Assessment* and the *Journal of Educational Psychology*. Author of 8 books and over 150 journal articles.

Anne E. Cunningham, PhD. Associate Professor at the University of California—Berkeley and Director of the Joint Doctoral program in Special Education. Member of the board of the Society for the Scientific Study of Reading and member of the board of directors for the American Educational Research Association Division C. Recipient of the American Reading Association's Outstanding Dissertation of the Year Award and author of over 35 journal articles. Former classroom teacher.

Karen C. Fuson, PhD. Professor at the School of Education and Social Policy at Northwestern University. Mathematics educator and cognitive scientist focusing on children's mathematical understanding. Contributing editor of the *Journal of Mathematical Behavior*, editorial board member of *Mathematical Cognition, Mathematical Thinking and Learning*. Serves on the National Science Foundation's Mathematics Learning Council. Author of over 100 articles.

Scott G. Paris, PhD. Graduate Program Chair of the Department of Psychology at the University of Michigan, Site Coordinator for The Center for the Improvement of Early Reading Achievement. Member of board of directors of the National Reading Conference, and the editorial boards of *Journal of Educational Psychology*, *Child Development*, *Journal of Cognitive Education*. Author of 10 books and over 70 journal articles.

P. David Pearson, PhD. Dean of the Graduate School of Education at the University of California–Berkeley. Previously John A. Hannah Distinguished Professor of Education in the College of Education and the Co-director of the Center for the Improvement of Early Reading Achievement at Michigan State University, and Dean of the College of Education and Co-director of the Center for the Study of Reading at the University of Illinois, Urbana-Champaign. Past President of the National Reading Conference and the National Conference on Research in English, served on board of directors of the American Association for College for Teacher Education. Author of 12 books and over 100 journal articles.

Public Concerns about Education

LeapFrog's focus on education mirrored growing concern over the effectiveness of public education, an issue that had gained national attention with the publication of the U.S. Department of Education's report *A Nation at Risk* in the early 1980s. Underscoring the concern were frequent reports showing the lackluster performance of U.S. children on math and reading tests, especially when compared with results in other developed economies, such as those in Asia. Fears that a poorly educated workforce would reduce global competitiveness drove parents, politicians, and employers to demand increased accountability of the educational system.

Public interest in phonics was heightened as well, due in part to publicity about the "reading wars," a policy debate that raged in the 1980s and 1990s over various approaches to reading instruction. The phonics curriculum espoused by LeapFrog had emerged over time as a leading method, and its essential underpinning of phonemic awareness was a core tenet of the second Bush administration's literacy policy. Phonics was in the news, and LeapFrog was ready with products to help kids learn it.

Furthermore, LeapFrog's kid-friendly use of technology appealed to parents who wanted their children to enjoy the benefits of multimedia. They appreciated, too, that LeapFrog's products were priced dramatically lower than a home computer system and accompanying software. Increasingly, tech-savvy parents were aware that the interactivity afforded by new technology made it possible for learning to be more individualized, more engaging, and more fun. And again, LeapFrog's products promised to do just that.

"No Child Left Behind"

Looking ahead, SchoolHouse executives, in particular, were focused on the No Child Left Behind (NCLB) accountability mandates with their emphasis on "scientifically based research."[21]

The U.S. Department of Education, drawing on the example of medical research, had announced its intent to "provide strong incentives for the widespread use of educational practices proven effective in randomized controlled trials," that is, "studies that randomly assign students to treatment and control groups." The department further noted that instances of proven effectiveness are rare because randomized trials are uncommon in educational research. [22]

Many educators argued that the educational environment was subject to far more variables than a clinical trial, and further that the high costs of such trials put this sort of research beyond the reach of most school systems. Nonetheless, the research requirement was now federal policy, and content providers were forced to scramble to validate their products accordingly. Calfee, LeapFrog's educational advisory board chair, suggested that NCLB's more stringent requirements offered an opportunity for greater input by the board into SchoolHouse's research activities. The division's Literacy Center (an integrated system providing direct instruction in phonemic awareness for pre-K, K, and grade one) was positioned as meeting the "Reading First" requirements of the act. Pilot studies employing control groups were commissioned by the company, with results generally showing greater improvements in reading scores for those children using the LeapFrog systems than those using other supplemental materials.[23]

Language First!, LeapFrog's English-as-a-second-language system for pre-K through grade two, was aimed at the needs of the many non-English-speaking children entering U.S. schools. Perhaps the company's most ambitious product was LeapTrack, an assessment system for grades K through five launched in August 2002. The

---

[21] For more on the No Child Left Behind Act (NCLB), see www.nclb.gov.

[22] "Report on Scientifically Based Research Supported by U.S. Department of Education," U.S. Department of Education press release, November 18, 2002, viewed at http://www.nclb.gov/media/news/111802.html.

[23] "Effectiveness Study Series, Northern California, Summer 2000 Research Report," LeapFrog document, March 13, 2001.

LeapTrack system offered teachers and administrators a means of assessing student skills and developing customized interventions. Employing the LeapPad and iQuest platforms as assessment mechanisms for students, the systems also enabled teachers to use the same devices as reporting, tracking, and prescriptive tools. Data recorded on these platforms was uploaded to personal computers and then aggregated to school or district servers. Customized learning plans were developed to address the individualized student learning needs uncovered in the assessment process. Priced at just under $3,000, a LeapTrack classroom kit included management software, 24 student cartridges, 12 LeapPads or Quantum Pads, 100-plus assessment books, 250-plus skill cards, 20-plus interactive books, instructor guides, and one year of toll-free system support. Volume discounts were also available.

With many educators expressing deep concerns over the frequency of data collection—and the attendant expense—required by the NCLB legislation, LeapFrog had high hopes that the low-cost and ease-of-use features of the LeapFrog platforms would provide a competitive advantage over alternative PC or handheld solutions. A leading educational technology expert noted that, if LeapTrack's claims were true, this represented a truly innovative approach in the educational market—and an interesting blurring between a product and a service offering. He further wondered if the SchoolHouse business model could sustain the ongoing costs of providing refreshed content and 24×7 maintenance and support.

On July 23, 2003, LeapFrog announced net sales for the SchoolHouse division had increased over second-quarter 2002 results by 151 percent (a 117 percent increase for the first half of 2003 when compared with the first half of 2002). LeapTrack system sales accounted for 20 percent of that total. Gross profits for the division were up as well, to 63.9 percent over 53.8 percent for the same quarter in the prior year. Wood, in the analyst call that accompanied the second-quarter press release, stated that the company anticipated SchoolHouse would break even in 2003.

Driving LeapFrog's Growth . . .

"I've had the good fortune in my career to work with two industry visionaries—Sam Walton in the early days of Wal-Mart, and now here at LeapFrog with Mike Wood. Both share the leadership quality of having a very clear sense of where they want their company to go and know how to marshal the appropriate people and resources to get there."

Tom Prichard, Senior Vice President of Marketing

LeapFrog had definitely made its mark on the toy industry in just a few short years, and its classroom efforts were being watched closely by teachers, parents, and competitors. But early success, of course, did not guarantee future results. How would the company sustain its growth?

. . . Through IP Creation and Product Extension

In Wood's mind, the company's key growth engine was the creation of intellectual property—that is, the turning of ideas about learning into marketable educational solutions. (See Exhibit 15 for LeapFrog's content development highlights.) Bucking the current corporate trend for outsourcing, LeapFrog elected to keep all its research and development (R&D) and content development in-house. A team of some 70 software and mechanical engineers based in a Los Gatos office custom-designed the ASIC chips at the technological heart of LeapFrog's products. Wood, commenting on the decision not to outsource, said, "When you have a group really focused and dedicated, they will in the long run do a lot better than if you are outsourcing to people who don't have your spirit and dedication."

"What we do differently," Marggraff elaborated, "is combine new technology with learning methods and concepts. We experiment as actively with new technology as any Silicon Valley firm, but we then apply that technology to enhance the learning process. By designing chips specifically for our purposes, we can achieve the greatest efficiency and make the biggest breakthroughs. And I like big breakthroughs."

EXHIBIT 15 R&D Highlights

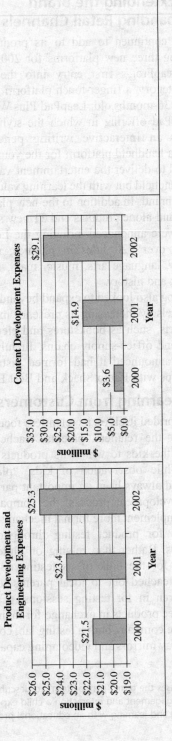

Source: LeapFrog 2002 Annual Report.

Hardware and Software Development	Content Development	Intellectual Property
• 61 employees, located in Los Gatos, CA facility	• 221 employees in content development, content production, and Internet groups	• 17 utility and design patents issued by U.S. Patent Office, 21 issued internationally
• Innovations in areas of touch detection technology, speech compression, music synthesis, and content generation	• Content reflects LeapFrog's pedagogical approach based on established educational standards	• 16 domestic and foreign patents related to LeapPad platform, not to expire before 2011
• Group participates in all phases of product development—from concept through manufacturing launch	• Most staff have experience in education, entertainment, video game, or educational software industries	• Over 76 pending patent applications
• Internal expertise in hardware design, hardware synthesis, custom ASIC chip design, real-time embedded systems, software design, tools for packaging and compiling product content and mechanical engineering	• Developed content development process and standards	• 36+ trademark registrations in U.S., 60+ internationally
	• Some content is licensed (e.g., characters, Kaplan, Inc. test prep, and BrainQuest for TurboTwist products)	
	• Developer's Studio, launched in July 2001, dedicated team to create software tools to turn content into interactive books and activity sheets—also license toolset to third-party developers	
• One of the world's largest purchasers of mass programmable ROM	• Internet group develops interactive content for download via Mind Station to TurboTwist and iQuest platforms	

Content Development Expenses

Year	$ millions
2000	$3.6
2001	$14.9
2002	$29.1

Product Development and Engineering Expenses

Year	$ millions
2000	$21.5
2001	$23.4
2002	$25.3

... By Extending the Brand and Expanding Retail Channels

LeapFrog continued to add to its product mix, announcing three new platforms for 2003: Little Touch, LeapFrog's first entry into the infant-toddler category, a finger-touch platform for children 6- to 36-months old; LeapPad Plus Writing, a new LeapPad offering in which the stylus functioned as an interactive writing pencil; and Leapster, a handheld platform for the young child that aimed to deliver the entertainment value of a gaming handheld but with the learning value of the LeapFrog brand. In addition to the new platforms, 15 new stand-alone products and 31 new software products were announced, bringing the LeapFrog library to over 120 titles in phonics, reading, vocabulary, language arts, music, math, science, geography, and history.

LeapFrog also looked to expand beyond its current channels by increasing its presence in nontoy retail outlets, such as bookstores and electronics retailers, and office-supply chains. In July 2003, LeapFrog announced it had formed distribution relationships with Radio Shack and Best Buy.

... By Learning from Customers

LeapFrog prided itself on its relentless focus on its customers—the retailers, parents, teachers, and especially the kids to whom its products had to appeal. While observation of kids' "play patterns"[24] had always been an important part of the product-development process, the company had begun to implement more formal mechanisms and procedures for product testing throughout the early 2000s. Rather than relying on children of employees for the bulk of its testing audience, LeapFrog reached out to local parents to bring their children in for testing sessions. (Children received free products in exchange for their time.) In 2002, the company built a testing lab, complete with one-way mirrors and videotaping capacity, so that researchers could observe children's play patterns and assess their overall user experience and product satisfaction. From these efforts, design practices were emerging to guide further product development.

Marggraff commented on the company's growing expertise in codifying what it learned from its close observation of children at play:

> Some years ago, I first observed something we now call "The Seven-Second Rule." This finding applies to paper-based multimedia. It states that a child must engage visually or kinesthetically within any seven-second period of audio or the child will cognitively disengage from the learning experience. If at the end of a seven-second stream of audio the child's eyes haven't been directed to a specific location or she hasn't touched a spot in the art, she will disconnect. This, and hundreds of other rules relating to interactivity with different platforms and forms of interactive media, drive our content design at LeapFrog.[25]

In combination with LeapFrog's internal hardware and software development efforts, these new research initiatives resulted in R&D costs of approximately 10 percent of 2002 sales, in contrast with those of Mattel, which spent only 3.3 percent of 2002 net revenues ($4.9 billion). When the capitalized costs associated with creation of its new book products were added in, LeapFrog's total R&D costs were actually closer to 15 percent of sales. (See Exhibit 16 for expense comparisons between LeapFrog and its two main competitors.)

... Through Aggressive Brand Management

"My primary task in the three years since I joined LeapFrog has been to build the brand," said Tom Prichard, LeapFrog's senior vice president of marketing (see Exhibit 17).

> Consistency is the key—we use the same logo; the same tagline, "Learn Something New Every Day"; and the same color green on all our products, ads, communications.

---

[24] LeapFrog uses the term "play pattern" to describe the pattern of engagement and interaction a child experiences when playing and learning with an educational product or toy.

[25] The value of engaging children's attention in short bursts has been made by many in the children's media business, including Children's Television Workshop (the creators of *Sesame Street*).

EXHIBIT 16   2002 Expense Comparisons: LeapFrog, Mattel, and Hasbro

Sources: LeapFrog, Mattel, and Hasbro 2002 Annual Reports.

Please note that cost of goods and R&D expenses may be accounted for differently among the three companies.

all #s in MMs	Net Sales	Gross Margin	Advertising	R&D	SG&A	Operating Income	Net Income
LeapFrog	**$532**	**$272.0**	**$56.7**	**$54.41**	**$80.9**	**$71.4**	**$43.4**
% of net sales	*100%*	*51.2%*	*10.7%*	*10.2%*	*15.2%*	*13.4%*	*8.1%*
Mattel	**$4,885**	**$2,360**	**$553**	**$159**	**$1,050**	**$733**	**$230**
% of net sales	*100%*	*48.3%*	*11.3%*	*3.3%*	*21.4%*	*15.0%*	*4.7%*
Hasbro	**$2,816**	**$1,717**	**$297**	**$154**	**$657**	**$219**	**($171)**
% of net sales	*100%*	*60.9%*	*10.5%*	*5.4%*	*23.3%*	*7.8%*	*(6.1%)*

EXHIBIT 17   LeapFrog's Marketing and Advertising Highlights

Source: Company records and 2002 Annual Report.

Advertising and Marketing	Sales and Distribution U.S. Consumer	SchoolHouse Division Sales and Marketing
• 2002 expenditures: $56.7 million, largely on TV and ads in holiday season	• 39 U.S. retail sales and sales support staff	• 10 in-house customer service reps
• 57 full-time employees	• Sales to Wal-Mart, Toys "R" Us, and Target > 75% of net sales in this segment	• 20 employees in retail sales service team, provides point-of-sale analysis for forecasting and inventory management purposes
• Network and cable TV campaign "Learn Something New Every Day" launched in fall 2001, to continue through 2003	• Sales team works in conjunction with store buyers from key retailers to forecast demand, plan store footprint, secure retail shelf space, and agree upon pricing (including cooperative ad allowances)	• Customer service center operates 24X7 November through January (peak), 14 hours weekdays and 9 hours on Saturday during off-peak
• Print advertising campaign "Learn Something New Every Day" launched in 2002 in national magazines such as *People, O!, Parents, Parenting,* and *Good Housekeeping*	• Chains provide a preliminary forecast of their purchases of LF products—estimates revised continuously, retailers issue purchase orders throughout the year as product is needed	• Toll-free phone support provided to educators, consumers, and retailers
• Cooperative print ads in local newspapers with key retail chains such as Toys "R" Us, Wal-Mart, Kmart, and Target	• Direct sales to customers through subscription-based Never-Ending Learning Club; small amount of online sales	

Everyone here is aware of the value of this brand—that it's LeapFrog spectacular, that we don't just meet expectations, we exceed them. I want to establish LeapFrog as not just one of the best-known brands in the toy arena, but one of the best-known brands in the world.

The results seemed to show his efforts had paid off. Prichard commissioned his first brand equity study in December 2000 and found, when consumers were asked, "When I say 'educational toy company,' what comes to mind?" only 1 percent responded "LeapFrog." Three years later, that top-of-mind percentage had soared to 42 percent, a shift Prichard said was unparalleled in his experience.

. . . Finding the Right People

By mid-2003, LeapFrog was the toy company to watch as it won numerous awards, developed imaginative products, and implemented innovative sales and marketing strategies. Yet, its executives stressed again and again that all the awards of the past were worthless without great people to win new ones in the future. "The core challenge is finding the right people," said Marggraff. "Sometimes we hire based on history and experience because we need that expertise applied to a particular position. Every company has those slots and needs good people to fill them. But if you want to make big breakthroughs, you need people who are nimble and flexible in their problem solving, people who can step into the unknown."

Bender elaborated:

Someone asked me last week, "Are we going to hire so-and-so?" I asked him, "Are you going to lose sleep tonight if this person goes to our competitor? No? Then don't hire him." This is the time in our company when we have to get great people. There's a learning curve here. You may have been a superstar at your last company, but here you are part of a team; you have to collaborate. What may have been great at your last company isn't good enough here. Our standards are higher.

. . . Facing Competition

At the February 2003 Toy Fair, Mattel's Fisher Price division announced the PowerTouch platform for preschoolers, aimed squarely at the LeapPad platform. Toy industry expert Silver expected Mattel to give LeapFrog its "first real taste of competition," noting that the Fisher Price division was one of Mattel's most profitable brands and had forward momentum from 2002, one of its best years ever.

Prichard commented on the competition:

Toys are all about buzz, about what's hot right now. What we're fighting right now is the fact that education is perceived as hot, it is the buzz of the toy industry. A lot of people are rushing into this category, sometimes with inferior products, creating a lot of confusion for the consumer and for the retailers. Education is not a fad for us; it's what we do every day. We believe that the brand-building efforts we've instituted over the past three years will see us through—that moms and retailers who've come to trust us over the years will continue to do so.

. . . Managing Two Business Models

As a company with a dual identity—that of a toy company and an educational publisher—LeapFrog had taken on two business models with vastly different profiles. As a toy company, LeapFrog focused sales on four key retailers with highly efficient purchasing and inventory management systems. Risk in this sector centered around accurate planning, fulfillment execution, and product acceptance by the consumer. The SchoolHouse division, by contrast, catered to an educational market that was highly fragmented, highly diverse, and highly regulated, with a plethora of overseers and stakeholders. While the overall market was huge, school district budgets were tight and getting tighter, and decision makers were risk adverse and slow to innovate. Recent legislation was certainly causing customer pain, on which LeapFrog hoped to capitalize. To grow as both a toy manufacturer and an educational supplier, LeapFrog would need to wage a competitive battle on two highly divergent fronts—and would need to pursue two very different strategies to succeed.

. . . Sustaining the Vision

LeapFrog's success to date had itself brought challenges to its leaders. With the exception of the engineering team and a handful of staff located in the company's worldwide marketing and distribution offices, most of the company's employees were housed in its 100,000-square-foot, hangarlike headquarters in Emeryville. LeapFrog's furious growth rate, though, increasingly made colocation a challenge. Some staffers had moved offices as frequently as seven times in four years. Both privacy and common space were in short supply in the warren of cubicles that made up the corporate headquarters. But Wood saw value in keeping the bulk of the company under one roof. As quoted in a *Fast Company* article, he noted, "There's a lot of institutional wisdom that gets passed around when all of us are working in the same space . . . By collectively yoking people's passion and energy, we raise the art of the possible."[26] By mid-2003, plans were well under way to add another 30,000 square feet to the Emeryville facility.

Managing the company's explosive growth also competed for time with the creative process that had made the company so successful in the first place. Marggraff commented, "As we've grown, it's been essential that our senior management has been completely dedicated to our vision and our creative spirit. We've continued to touch the product. Not doing so was not an option. It's who we are." At the same time, executives had to focus on closely managing their fast-growing web of relationships with suppliers, distributors, retailers, investors, educators, parents, and kids. Prichard noted:

> It's all about trust—about underpromising and overdelivering. I'm from the Midwest, and for me, it's about those

[26] Bill Breen, "LeapFrog's Great Leap Forward," *Fast Company*, June 2003.

good old-fashioned values of doing what you say you're going to do. We are not in the "hits" business, we are not in the game to maximize short-term goals. In fact, since we've gone public, there's been even more of an emphasis on building our brand, on establishing this company for the long term.

Wood stated, "Our people are idealistic. They're constantly leapfrogging themselves so that the next piece of content reflects and improves on what they did before." He continued:

> One thing I want is for 10 percent of the products we make to fail. Let me explain, I don't want us to fail because we made a less-than-spectacular product, or because we didn't do our customer homework, or because we ticked off a retailer. That sort of failure is inexcusable. The kind of failure that's good is the kind that keeps us pushing the envelope, that keeps us working on the edge of what's possible. If we fail one out of ten times because we pushed past our limits, then I'll know we're on the right track.

Keeping the spirit of fun and creativity alive at LeapFrog while managing the rigors of a complex and global business strategy—and while keeping its educational mission foremost—this was the course Wood had set for the company. On July 23, 2003, the company released its second-quarter results, showing strong top-line sales growth, up 57 percent companywide over second-quarter 2002, as well as improvements in gross margins.

Looking ahead, would LeapFrog meet its ambitious goals? Would it continue to leapfrog not only the competition but its own best efforts of yesterday? Only time would tell, but the company was sure to "learn something new every day" in the attempt.

Case 1-3

Wyndham International: Fostering High-Touch with High-Tech

Points are pointless. We differentiate ourselves by saying: "Points are for tomorrow, how can we offer satisfaction and gratification today?" Rather than giving guests a commodity that they can trade for airline miles, we are going to give them something that they enjoy.

Ted Teng, Wyndham International president and COO

Systemwide execution . . . There are companies that can store guest history on particular customers who stay at their property . . . How do you deliver that same information to every property in your company portfolio and be able to deliver on it consistently?

Mark Hedley, Wyndham International CTO

In early February 2001, Wyndham International launched a $30 million advertising campaign featuring "the King" himself, Elvis Presley. In the award-winning commercial series formally launching the Wyndham ByRequest guest-recognition program, the company prompted its prospective guests to "request the things that make your room your room" and asked: "What's your request?" The advertising campaign was part of Wyndham's effort to become the lodging brand of choice for business and leisure travelers in the upscale and high-upscale segments of the market. Achieving such a goal was no small mission for the rapidly expanding chain. It required Wyndham to successfully complete a three-year transformation into a "world-class branded hotel operating company."[1]

Between 1999 and 2001, Wyndham divested many "nonstrategic" assets—such as the midpriced hotel brand Sierra Suites—and reinvested the proceeds into growing the Wyndham brand. As a result, the number of hotel properties flying the Wyndham flag doubled. But achieving its strategic goal also required Wyndham International to break into a

market dominated by entrenched competitors. Ted Teng summarized the challenge that lay ahead, "What can we do to build a recognized brand, change the rules of engagement, and carve a profitable niche that we can defend?" The ByRequest program was a cornerstone of the Wyndham strategy, and the executive team pondered its future growth and its potential for delivering a sustainable competitive advantage.

Wyndham's Background

In 1981, renowned builder Trammel Crow, president of Trammel Crow Company (TCC), founded Wyndham Hotels to manage and franchise the Wyndham brand. The first Wyndham Hotel opened its doors to guests in 1982 in Dallas, Texas. TCC charged Wyndham's management with running the hotels it developed and owned. Soon after, Wyndham Hotels began to manage properties owned by other developers as well. By 1985, there were 14 upscale properties in the Wyndham portfolio, and the chain continued to grow steadily, reaching a total of 66 hotels and resorts in 1996, when the firm filed for its initial public offering. At the time of its IPO, the firm managed 17,398 rooms in 22 states, the District of Columbia, and four Caribbean islands. TCC retained a 47 percent ownership interest.

In early 1997, Wyndham Hotels entered into a definitive agreement to be acquired by Patriot

This case was prepared by Professors Lynda M. Applegate, Harvard Business School, and Gabriele Piccoli, Cornell University. Copyright © 2002 President and Fellows of Harvard College. Harvard Business School Case No. 803-092.

[1] Wyndham letter to shareholders, March 2001.

American Hospitality Inc. for $1.10 billion in cash, stock, and assumption of debt. Wyndham held considerable appeal for Patriot American Hospitality—a paired-share real estate investment trust (REIT) actively looking for an operating company with an established brand as a vehicle for further growth. (See the Appendix for more information about the paired-share REIT structure and its implications.) At the time the acquisition was finalized, Wyndham Hotels owned or managed 106 hotels and resorts that, with the 52 properties already owned by Patriot American Hospitality, created the United States's largest hotel REIT—surpassing Phoenix-based Starwood Lodging Trust.

Patriot American Hospitality Inc., founded in 1991 by real estate lawyer Paul Nussbaum as a REIT, grew through steady acquisitions until it went public in 1995. Following its successful IPO, the largest IPO of any REIT, the Dallas-based company started an aggressive acquisition campaign and assembled a portfolio of 45 upscale hotels, operated under the DoubleTree, Hilton, Hyatt, Marriott, and Radisson brands, by the end of 1996. At the same time, Patriot American Hospitality became one of only four REITs enjoying paired-share status after acquiring the California Jockey Club and the Bay Meadows Operating Company and reverse merging into them in order to assume their structure. The paired-share REIT structure allowed Patriot American Hospitality not only to own real estate under the corporate tax-exempted REIT classification, but also to operate its properties—and receive tax-sheltered rental income—through a paired operating company. The acquisition of Wyndham Hotels Corporation—renamed Wyndham International after the acquisition—completed the puzzle by giving Patriot American Hospitality an established lodging operating company with an existing brand.

Upon acquiring the paired-share REIT structure, Patriot American Hospitality and Wyndham International started an aggressive acquisition campaign, focusing on smaller companies such as Williams Hospitality, Carefree Hospitality, and Summerfield Suites. In 1997, they acquired Interstate Hotels Corporation, adding 217 hotels to the portfolio with the intention of converting many to the Wyndham brand. While Interstate was later spun off as an independent management company—Interstate Hotel Management Inc.—Patriot American Hospitality retained ownership of the properties. Patriot and Wyndham also acquired Summerfield Hotel Corporation, with a portfolio including 37 upscale all-suite owned and leased properties.

The growth of Patriot American Hospitality during the three years after going public was nothing short of explosive. In 1995, the company went public with just $350 million in properties. By mid-1998, however, Patriot had leveraged its paired-share REIT status to achieve a market capitalization of $7 billion, including debt. At the height of its growth, Patriot American Hospitality's portfolio numbered 472 lodging properties. But as the company achieved these heights, the paired-share REIT structure came under increasing federal regulatory scrutiny. Competitors, such as Marriott International and Hilton Hotels, complained that the structure provided its holders with an unfair advantage that allowed them to pay considerable premiums for lodging properties and other real estate.

As it became clear that the U.S. Congress would repeal the tax benefits enjoyed by paired-share REITs, a decision finalized in the 1999 federal budget, Patriot American Hospitality's stock price began to slide. Moreover, its use of equity forward instruments[2] as the stock price continued to decline contributed to its deteriorating financial situation. In declining financial health, Patriot, to reduce debt pressure, sold some assets that did not fit its branding strategy. In addition, it increased its focus on operations and converted many existing properties to the Wyndham flag. This focus on operations prompted Nussbaum to pronounce that

---

[2] In an equity forward, the borrowing company receives the money immediately but has the option of issuing stock in the future to pay for it. In essence, it is betting that its stock price will increase in the future and it will require fewer shares to pay off the equity forward.

Patriot viewed itself as a lodging company first, rather than a REIT. "This is a lodging company that owns a lot of its real estate," he was quoted as saying.[3]

In early 1999, Patriot American Hospitality's stock was trading around $5, a drop of over 80 percent from its all-time high. Under increasing pressure from creditors, the company dropped its REIT status and converted to a C-corporation under the name Wyndham International Corporation. As part of its restructuring plan, Wyndham International accepted a $1 billion equity investment and a related $2.45 billion restructuring of debt (see Exhibit 1 for Wyndham's financials). The company's executives believed that the financial restructuring provided significant breathing room, with no significant payments required before 2004. As part of the reorganization plan, Nussbaum left the company. Nonstrategic assets—those assets that could not be rebranded to Wyndham because of long-term franchise or management agreements or a lack of appropriate quality—were sold, and resources were focused on running premier-brand full-service hotels and resorts. Reflecting its new focus on operations and hotel management, a number of senior executives with significant experience and deep knowledge of operations were brought in to rebuild Wyndham's executive team around chairman and CEO Fred J. Kleisner and president and COO Teng (see Exhibit 2). Eloquently summing up the reorganization effort, Kleisner stated: "I wasn't hired because I am a great investment banker or deals guru. I was hired because I have spent my life creating profitable hotels and groups of branded properties. And what was needed was someone with the skill set to make that happen here."[4]

As it began its third year in the restructuring plan, Wyndham International focused on its three branded products: Wyndham Hotels & Resorts, Wyndham Luxury Resorts, and Summerfield Suites by Wyndham (see Exhibit 3 for portfolio composition information).

The Lodging Industry

The large percentage of properties flying the Wyndham flag that were owned and operated by Wyndham International represented an anomaly among large lodging brands (see Exhibits 3 and 4).[5] The industry's complex structure was a product of the trend toward the separation of real estate ownership and hotel management, significant consolidation in the U.S. lodging market, and the aggressive growth strategy pursued by many brands.

In a typical franchising agreement, the brand would contract with a management company and contribute its name, its advertising, its specifications for the characteristics of the property (e.g., room size, approved vendors), and its operating procedures. Distribution infrastructure was one of the key assets the brand contributed. Generally, this asset included a computerized reservation system (CRS),[6] a central reservation office (CRO) and call centers, relationships with distribution partners (e.g., airlines' global distribution systems, travel agents), and relationships with major accounts (e.g., large corporations, associations). In return, the management company paid an initial franchise fee for the right to join the franchise. Generally, the yearly royalty fee that covered the right to use the brand was between 3 percent and 7 percent of room sales. The management company, which also paid operator systems reimbursement expenses (e.g., fixed reservation fees, transaction fees, sales and marketing fees, training fees, publication fees), was accountable for running the

---

[3] Neal Templin, "Patriot American is Planning to Sell Some U.S. Property," *The Wall Street Journal*, June 11, 1998.

[4] "People, Trends, Ideas: Fred Kleisner's Plan to Resurrect Wyndham," *Hotels*, June 2000.

[5] The term "the brands" or "the flags" is commonly used to refer to firms that brand national lodging chains (e.g., Marriott, Hilton, Starwood, Wyndham). Many of these companies manage only a subset of the properties that fly their flag and enter into franchise agreements with independent management companies and real estate owners.

[6] The CRS is the computer application that supports electronic distribution of room inventory. Reservations coming in through the Web site, call center (i.e., 1-800 number), travel agents, and other channels flow to the CRS.

EXHIBIT 1 **Financials—Annual Income Statement (thousands)**

Source: U.S. 10-K History, 2001 Thomson Financial.

Fiscal Year Ending	12/31/98	12/31/99	12/31/00	12/31/01
Net sales	2,041,448	2,484,079	2,467,631	2,095,174
Cost of goods	1,403,411	1,776,591	1,747,601	1,557,985
Gross profit	638,037	707,488	720,030	537,189
Sell gen & admin exp	109,325	178,039	97,766	101,901
Inc bef dep & amort	528,712	529,449	622,264	435,288
Depreciation & amort	231,233	302,890	304,785	254,209
Non-operating inc	−149,884	−364,667	−468,638	−85,671
Interest expense	260,103	353,227	371,855	308,524
Income before tax	−112,508	−491,335	−523,014	−213,116
Prov for inc taxes	17,122	571,421	−205,912	−96,438
Minority inc (inc)	−3,224	−625	7,569	10,060
Invest gains/losses	NA	NA	NA	NA
Other income	NA	NA	NA	NA
Net inc bef ex items	−126,406	−1,062,131	−324,671	−126,738
Ex items & disc ops	−31,817	−9,838	NA	−12,202
Net Income	**−158,223**	**−1,071,969**	**−324,671**	**−138,940**
Outstanding shares	213,522	167,194	167,416	167,848

Annual Assets	12/31/98	12/31/99	12/31/00	12/31/01
Cash	158,954	246,813	150,530	251,634
Receivables	194,583	186,321	188,381	120,283
Inventories	23,583	23,304	21,211	17,742
Other current assets	35,346	450,190	1,208,568	102,499
TOTAL CURRENT ASSETS	412,466	906,628	1,568,690	492,158
Prop, plant & equip	5,838,196	4,984,185	3,515,223	4,399,256
Accumulated dep	252,580	NA	NA	NA
Net prop & equip	5,585,616	4,984,185	3,515,223	4,399,256
Invest & adv to subs	146,912	165,663	104,814	77,619
Other non-cur assets	119,737	42,653	48,976	50,385
Deferred charges	428,078	362,815	108,377	75,876
Intangibles	679,863	495,437	443,281	424,622
Deposits & oth assets	42,998	46,109	277,538	248,155
Total Assets	**7,415,670**	**7,003,490**	**6,066,899**	**5,768,071**

(continued)

property in a manner consistent with the brand specifications. While they provided an appropriate vehicle for rapid growth with limited capital expenditure and limited assumption of risk, franchising agreements also presented significant challenges. Teng explained: "When I was with another brand, we suffered major schizophrenia about franchising. Franchising was the 'f' word. They loved the income it brought, did not like the quality, but it was too big of an income to get rid of it and the dilemma was: are we in or are we out?"

Some challenges associated with a franchising strategy were evident in regard to decision making and responsibility for information technology (IT) expenditures. IT was a critical tool supporting

EXHIBIT 1   (continued)

Annual Liabilities	12/31/98	12/31/99	12/31/00	12/31/01
Accounts payable	313,657	322,195	210,592	213,596
Cur long-term debt	1,274,918	129,700	155,728	117,484
Other current liab	26,392	70,963	544,779	66,520
Total current liab	1,614,967	522,858	911,099	397,600
Deferred charges/inc	123,637	671,707	437,905	297,617
Long-term debt	2,582,603	3,482,345	2,737,386	3,298,070
Other long-term liab	7,919	NA	NA	73,490
Total liabilities	4,329,126	4,676,910	4,086,390	4,066,777
Minority int (liab)	483,507	188,918	186,322	113,073
Preferred stock	90	103	111	119
Common stock net	4,270	1,672	1,674	1,678
Capital surplus	3,024,540	3,753,235	3,828,900	3,912,656
Retained earnings	−405,509	−1,591,307	−2,018,526	−2,279,104
Other equities	−20,354	−26,041	−17,972	−47,128
Shareholder equity	2,603,037	2,137,662	1,794,187	1,588,221
Total Liabilities & Net Worth	**7,415,670**	**7,003,490**	**6,066,899**	**5,768,071**

Cash Flow Provided by Operating Activity	12/31/98	12/31/99	12/31/00	12/31/01
Net income (loss)	−158,223	−1,071,969	−324,671	−138,940
Depreciation/amortization	265,769	343,686	332,606	278,330
Net incr (decr) assets/liabs	−42,576	10,490	−28,074	8,250
Cash Prov (used) by disc oper	31,817	9,838	NA	12,202
Other adjustments, net	147,706	910,257	266,977	−1,483
Net Cash Provided by Operating Activities	**244,493**	**202,302**	**246,838**	**158,359**

Cash Flow Provided by Investing Activity	12/31/98	12/31/99	12/31/00	12/31/01
(Incr) decr in prop, plant	−2,136,112	−289,186	114,712	−82,955
(Acq) disp of subs, business	NA	16,086	−67,372	−1,001
(Incr) decr in securities inv	1,474	−15,468	−38,551	1,638
Other cash inflow (outflow)	27,415	−67,996	28,483	18,891
Net Cash Provided by Investing Activities	**−2,107,223**	**−356,564**	**−37,272**	**−63,427**

Cash Flow Provided by Financing Activity	12/31/98	12/31/99	12/31/00	12/31/01
Issue (purchase) of equity	279,947	860,907	−9,775	−5,909
Issue (repayment) of debt	NA	NA	NA	NA
Incr (decr) in borrowing	1,889,399	−223,320	−308,176	45,081
Dividends, other distribution	−135,915	−15,607	−29,248	−14,624
Other cash inflow (outflow)	−92,796	−440,091	−36,198	−6,414
Net cash prov (used) by finan	1,940,635	181,889	−383,397	18,134
Effect of exchg rate on cash	2,749	−6,379	7,414	176
Net Change in Cash or Equivalent	**80,654**	**21,248**	**−91,873**	**113,242**
Cash or Equiv at Year Start	**42,431**	**123,085**	**144,333**	**52,460**
Cash or Equiv at Year End	**123,085**	**144,333**	**52,460**	**165,702**

**EXHIBIT 2
Organizational
Structure**

Source: Wyndham
International.

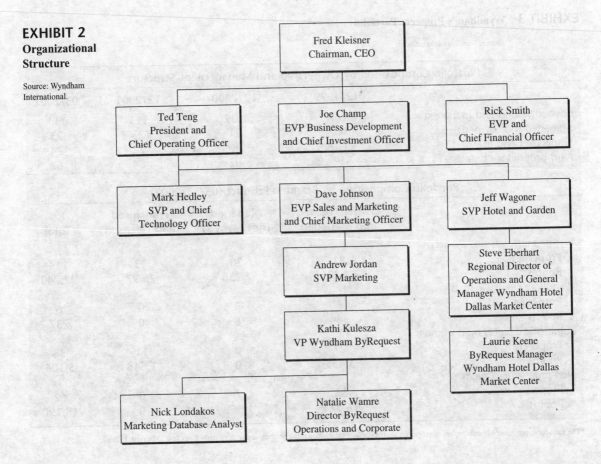

Fred Kleisner
Chairman, CEO

Ted Teng
President and
Chief Operating Officer

Joe Champ
EVP Business Development
and Chief Investment Officer

Rick Smith
EVP and
Chief Financial Officer

Mark Hedley
SVP and Chief
Technology Officer

Dave Johnson
EVP Sales and Marketing
and Chief Marketing Officer

Jeff Wagoner
SVP Hotel and Garden

Andrew Jordan
SVP Marketing

Steve Eberhart
Regional Director of
Operations and General
Manager Wyndham Hotel
Dallas Market Center

Kathi Kulesza
VP Wyndham ByRequest

Laurie Keene
ByRequest Manager
Wyndham Hotel Dallas
Market Center

Nick Londakos
Marketing Database Analyst

Natalie Wamre
Director ByRequest
Operations and Corporate

day-to-day operation of hotel properties (e.g., checking guests in and out, maintaining and distributing room inventory, managing supplies) and providing management with important information and decision-making support. But IT purchases were traditionally regarded as physical asset purchases or capital expenditures and, as such, fell within the realm of responsibility of the owner. Thus owners performed periodic need assessments. Typically, these assessments were undertaken during the annual budgeting process, when the management company contributed information on what new equipment or renovations were needed and the owner accepted or rejected them.

A significant lack of standardization of IT plagued the lodging industry. Most hotel chains ran an assortment of hardware/software platforms, computer applications, and interfaces. Large chains ran multiple versions of the property management system (PMS)[7] on multiple operating systems and from multiple vendors. Lack of a standardized computing infrastructure was due to the complex structure of the lodging industry, its high degree of fragmentation, and the conflicting interests of the parties involved in making technology purchasing decisions. The absence of a

[7] The PMS is the "brain" of hotel operations. The software is used to maintain current room inventory (e.g., available rooms, occupied rooms, unchanged—or dirty—rooms), to check guests in and out, to consolidate charges from various systems (e.g., minibar, restaurant systems, call accounting), and to produce the guest folio (i.e., invoice).

EXHIBIT 3 Wyndham's Property Portfolio

Source: Wyndham International.

Portfolio Composition by Ownership and Management Structure

	12/1999	12/2000	12/2001	03/2002
Owned/leased and managed	N/A	109	111	111
Managed (not owned)	N/A	21	23	23
Franchised and licensed	N/A	30	22	24
Non-proprietary brands*	98	82	64	62

Portfolio Composition by Branded Product (03/31/2002)

	Owned/Leased and Managed	Managed (not owned)	Franchised and Licensed	Total
Wyndham Hotels and Resorts				
Properties	81	20	13	114
Rooms	22,785	7,258	2,697	32,740
Wyndham Luxury Resorts				
Properties	3	3	0	6
Rooms	354	383	0	737
Summerfield Suites by Wyndham				
Properties	27	0	11	38
Rooms	3,458	0	1,648	5,106
Non-proprietary Brands				
Properties	55	7	0	62
Rooms	16,521	1,669	0	18,190

*The term "non-proprietary brands" refers to properties that Wyndham International is operating under third-party flags (e.g., Marriott, Hilton).

dominant vendor of hospitality IT and the relative frequency with which properties were reflagged compounded these problems. The growing complexity of the technology infrastructure of large lodging companies, many of which had hundreds of different legacy systems supporting their operations, spurred trends toward increasing standardization. For example, Marriott International, traditionally a leading user of IT in the hospitality industry, announced plans for standardizing and consolidating its legacy systems into an integrated portfolio of applications designed to provide guest profile information, consolidated inventory and rate management, guest management, yield management, and marketing program support. At the property level, the plan called for the consolidation of over 15 systems supporting front-office operations—including five different PMSes, sales and catering systems, and food and beverage systems.[8]

Sources of friction in the relationship between brands, owners, and operators were not limited to technology expenditures and standardization decisions. With the recent focus on customer relationship management (CRM) and the realization that the guest information traditionally collected by properties could be of significant value, a number of questions about the ownership of the data awaited answers. For example, who owned the guest information? Was it the property owner?

[8] "Marriott Focusing on Technology Application Upgrades," *HotelBusiness*, March 13, 2002.

EXHIBIT 3   Geographical Distribution of Wyndham International Properties in the
United States *(continued)*

Source: Authors' research.

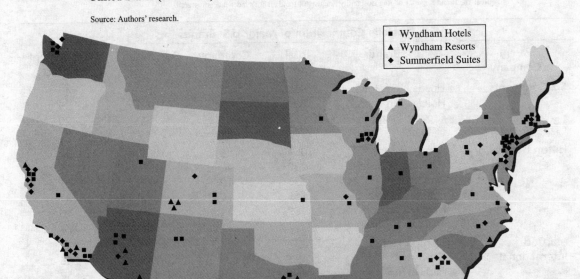

In the words of an industry observer: "Without a hotel for the guest to go to, there would be no guest data." Was it the brand—whose advertisement efforts and distribution infrastructure may have made the guest aware of the existence of the property? Was it the management company, whose work in providing the guests with a positive experience strengthened the brand and kept guests coming back? Lodging companies and individual properties had spent significant amounts of money and resources collecting guest preferences and data. But, as an industry observer noted: "Effectively utilizing all this data remained a challenge. Many hotels spend millions of dollars acquiring data, but it just sits there. It is easy to generate great databases, but what do you do with them?"

These difficulties were indicative of the traditionally complicated relationship between IT and hospitality operations. Many operators harbored strong negative feelings toward technology and believed that technology depersonalized the relationship with guests. They subscribed to the old adage that hospitality was "high-touch, not high-tech" and that no technology should get between the guest and the hotelier. Yet, through the introduction of CRS and electronic reservations, the lodging industry had been among the electronic commerce pioneers long before the advent of the commercial Internet and e-commerce buzzwords.

Wyndham's IT Infrastructure

Prior to the arrival of Mark Hedley in the role of chief technology officer in May 2000, Wyndham had outsourced its IT operations to a subsidiary serving the needs of both Wyndham and TCC. But the growing portfolio of properties and the new

EXHIBIT 4 **The Structure of the Lodging Industry**

Source: The Brand Report, Lodging Hospitality, August 2001 and author's independent research.

Portfolio Composition of Major U.S. Brands					
Parent Company	U.S. Brands	Total Properties	Company Owned	Franchised, Licensed	Management Contract
Six Continents	Holiday Inn Hotels	1056	5	1004	47
	Holiday Inn Express	1083	0	1078	5
	Crowne Plaza	77	6	51	20
	Total	*2216*	*11*	*2133*	*72*
Hilton Hotels Corp.	Hampton Inns	1094	1	1081	27
	Hilton Inns/Hotels	230	40	171	15
	Doubletree	153	10	49	59
	Embassy Suites	155	6	75	57
	Homewood Suites	89	14	59	16
	Total	*1721*	*71*	*1435*	*174*
Marriott International	Marriott Hotels	277	4	39	234
	Courtyard	493	1	236	256
	Fairfield Inn	464	0	412	52
	Residence Inn	362	0	242	116
	Renaissance	53	0	22	31
	Total	*1649*	*5*	*951*	*689*
Starwood Hotels and Resorts Worldwide	Sheraton	189	40	105	44
	Westin	57	22	10	25
	Four Points	105	6	84	15
	Total	*351*	*68*	*199*	*84*
Hyatt Hotels Corp.*	Hyatt Hotels	120	18–36	4	80–98

*Hyatt Hotels Corp. is privately owned, and a precise classification of ownership is not available. Range estimates were provided directly by company representatives.

focus on operations highlighted the need for a hotel-oriented IT function that could provide a strong vision. Hedley was charged with insourcing IT and creating an IT infrastructure that could support Wyndham International's new strategy.

Hedley was a big proponent of a centralized IT infrastructure to serve the needs of Wyndham's three branded products. In early 2002, Wyndham was in the process of centralizing its operational systems starting with the PMS followed by the call-accounting system, with future plans possibly including revenue management and the point-of-sale (POS) system as well. Wyndham used an

application service provider (ASP)[9] model to deliver the software applications. With the applications in place, Wyndham became the first company to use the PMS in a centralized environment. Describing the centralized infrastructure, Hedley remarked:

> In late 2000, we started a strategy of integration of the PMS to the CRS and with ByRequest. We found that it

[9] When software applications are delivered using an ASP model, they are not installed on the computers at the property. Rather, the applications are centralized and accessed by remote users on the Internet through a Web browser.

EXHIBIT 4   (continued)

Source: The Brand Report, Lodging Hospitality, August 2001 and author's independent research.

Portfolio Composition of Major U.S. Management Companies

Parent	U.S. Brands	Properties	Parent	U.S. Brands	Properties
Six Continents	Holiday Inn/Crowne	21	Six Continents	Holiday Inn/Crowne	8
Hilton	Embassy Suites	6	Hilton	Embassy Suites	1
	Hilton Inns/Hotels	35		Hilton Inns/Hotels	4
	Hampton Inns	6		Hampton Inns	38
	Doubletree	9		Doubletree	0
	Homewood Suites	6		Homewood Suites	5
Marriott	Courtyard	9	Marriott	Courtyard	10
	Fairfield Inn	2		Fairfield Inn	6
	Marriott Hotels	5		Marriott Hotels	14
	Residence Inn	2		Residence Inn	13
	Renaissance	0		Renaissance	2
Starwood	Sheraton	16	Starwood	Sheraton	1
	Westin	3		Westin	2
Wyndham	Wyndham	4			
Others	Multiple Brands	59	Others	Multiple Brands	34
	Total	183		Total	138

Meristar Hospitality Corp. | | | *Interstate Hotels Corporation* | | |

Parent	U.S. Brands	Properties	Parent	U.S. Brands	Properties
Six Continents	Holiday Inn/Crowne	62	Six Continents	Holiday Inn/Crowne	16
Hilton	Hilton Inns/Hotels	4	Hilton	Hampton Inns	36
	Hampton Inns	2		Homewood Suites	7
	Doubletree	1			
Marriott	Courtyard	8	Marriott	Courtyard	18
	Fairfield Inn	5		Fairfield Inn	113
	Marriott Hotels	1		Residence Inn	32
	Residence Inn	2			
Starwood	Four Points	3			
Others	Multiple Brands	21	Others	Multiple Brands	112
	Total	109		Total	334

Lodgian Inc. | | | *Tharaldson Property Management, Inc.* | | |

made sense to take the PMS and centralize it. We were trying to minimize the number of disparate systems we had in the field. All Summerfield Suites properties are now centralized; as capital allows, we will continue the centralization until all properties in our portfolio are on the centralized infrastructure.

Centralization not only allowed standardization of service but also more segmentation. For example, the call-accounting system allowed telecommunication plans to be tailored to company accounts, ByRequest members, or other individual guests. In June 2002, this ability allowed the company to offer free faxing, local, and long-distance calls to the portfolio of ByRequest amenities. After the centralization efforts, a typical property-level computing infrastructure for smaller hotels required 10 to 12 networked personal computers. Needed applications then could be accessed directly from the company's Dallas data center. Discussing the benefits of the model, Hedley said: "If you centralize all your server, networking, and application technologies, you can have a core set of technology people versus having people in remote locations. When implementing application upgrades, hotels that are online receive a new version of the code literally overnight versus sending somebody out to every single site to install something physical."[10]

As users became increasingly familiar with computer applications (largely due to widespread adoption of the Internet) and computer applications became increasingly intuitive and relatively easy to use, an information systems infrastructure with no property-level specialists appeared a reality for many operators. In 2002, Wyndham's IT function numbered 67 professionals who developed, supported, and managed the centralized infrastructure.

At the height of its expansion as a REIT, Wyndham maintained a number of different back-office systems and up to four different PMSes with four separate interfaces to process reserva-

tions. Wyndham began its standardization program in early 1998 with the development of a custom-developed software application designed to extract guest folios directly from each property's PMS. The initiative was designed to consolidate guest-stay information, determine booking sources, and offer travel buyers the opportunity to access folio data electronically. These early tests showed that chainwide PMS standards, including consistent data fields, were needed to make the data usable. In the absence of consistency and standardized applications across properties, it took an estimated six months to add a property to the program.

Wyndham executives felt that a centralized IT infrastructure was a viable alternative for the company. Hedley remarked, "It is very easy for us to centralize our IT infrastructure. To obtain the capital required we have one approval cycle to go through, whereas the 'selling' process is much longer for nonowned assets."

Teng added, "We control 85 percent of our distribution. So, when we want to implement brand standards, we can very quickly do it, while a bigger company must talk to the franchisees and owners of managed hotels. Being integrated gives us an advantage in terms of consistency."

Competing for Guests

Wyndham International targeted the upscale and luxury traveler. More specifically, Wyndham Hotels & Resorts offered full-service accommodations aimed at attracting business and leisure travelers in metropolitan areas and resort markets. Summerfield Suites by Wyndham targeted the business traveler on longer-term assignments and offered upscale, all-suites, extended-stay accommodations. Wyndham Luxury Resorts, a portfolio of five-star-quality properties distinguished by unique settings and exceptional service, focused on the affluent luxury guest. To become a dominant player in these market segments, Wyndham had to lure customers away from entrenched incumbents. Competitors included the dominant hotel chains serving the upscale U.S. market—Marriott Hotels Resorts and Suites,

[10] "Face-to-Face with Mark Hedley," *Hospitality Upgrade,* Spring 2002.

EXHIBIT 5

Operational Performance Measures

Source: Companies' Annual Reports.

Operational Measures Comparison				
Hotel	Year	Rev PAR ($)	ADR ($)	Occupancy (%)
Marriott Hotels and Resorts	1997	104.35	128.64	77.7
	1998	107.60	137.95	78.0
	1999	109.22	140.86	77.5
	2000	116.95	149.50	78.2
	2001	100.62	142.96	70.4
Hilton Hotels and Resorts	1997	94.58	145.33	74.6
	1998	90.54	127.19	71.2
	1999	92.34	130.60	70.7
	2000	98.62	135.75	72.6
	2001	88.48	131.13	67.5
Hyatt Hotels and Resorts	Private company does not release data.			
Starwood Hotels and Resorts	1997	94.04	133.86	70.3
	1998	97.18	138.38	70.2
	1999	101.99	142.28	71.7
	2000	115.01	161.59	71.2
	2001	101.98	156.73	65.1
Wyndham International	1997	79.54	112.32	70.8
	1998	84.35	119.57	70.5
	1999	90.61	127.63	70.9
	2000	95.12	130.22	73.0
	2001	103.88	114.64	71.8

Hilton Hotels, Hyatt Hotels and Resorts, Sheraton, and Westin (the latter two owned by Starwood Hotels and Resorts Worldwide Inc.). Competition also came from smaller chains and independent upscale properties in local urban markets and popular vacation destinations (see Exhibit 5 for a comparison of these brands' recent operational performance).

Following its reorganization, Wyndham became particularly attentive to the needs of business travelers. When it launched its Wyndham's "Room That Performs" initiative, Wyndham became the first national hotel brand to offer high-speed Internet access and cordless phones in every room. The "Room That Performs" initiative also featured redesigned rooms that provided significant workspace and the Herman Miller Aeron ergonomic desk chair to help business travelers stay productive on the road. In early 2001, Wyndham International also became the first

hotel chain to enable reservations and access to guest-loyalty programs via wireless devices (e.g., cell phones and personal digital assistants).

Wyndham International was particularly devoted to meeting the needs of women business travelers through the "Women On Their Way" program. A section of the Wyndham.com Web site was expressly designed to foster a community of women who traveled on business. It provided tips, a newsletter, editorials, and articles of interest to women and support for discussions and feedback. As part of the initiative, Wyndham also sponsored various women's associations and events.

One of the main challenges faced by Wyndham was the low brand recognition of the Wyndham name among business and leisure travelers. In 2000, the Wyndham name did not appear in the National Business Travel Monitor's preferred brands list of the top 20 most recognizable brands to business travelers (see Exhibit 6).

EXHIBIT 6   Brand Preferences and Business Travel Decision Process

Source: The YP&B Yankelovich Partners National Business Travel Monitor (2000 and 2002).

Preferred Hotel/Motel Brands (unaided, by income differences)					
	Year 2002			Year 2000		
	$100K+	$50K+	$30K–$49.9K	$100K+	$50K+	$30K–$49.9K
Marriott	52%	44%	32%	53%	43%	33%
Holiday Inn	32	38	43	36	41	38
Hilton	30	26	20	27	22	21
Hyatt	18	15	5	17	15	7
Sheraton	18	14	10	6	10	7
Embassy Suites	12	11	9	14	12	12
Hampton Inn	11	9	8	16	10	5
Radisson	9	11	7	5	6	7
Comfort Inn	9	9	14	13	12	16
Ramada	7	11	12	13	16	16
Westin	6	4	0	8	4	0
Best Western	5	13	19	17	20	16
Days Inn	4	5	12	5	8	14
Doubletree	4	5	3	0	0	0
Wyndham	2	2	0	0	0	0
No preference	5	5	3	2	1	3

Hotel Selection Decision Elements Influential in %	2002	2001	2000	1999
Location	91	89	83	86
Previous experience with hotel	89	94	84	86
Value for the price	82	86	76	72
Reputation of hotel/chain	82	80	74	71
Room rate	72	81	75	62
Recommendation of friend/associate	69	70	68	68
Likelihood of upgrade to better accommodation	63	N/A	N/A	N/A
Brand name	59	53	62	66
Gives both airline mileage and points	51	52	N/A	N/A
Airline mileage	37	44	26	25
Recommendation of travel agent	34	35	40	34
Frequent-guest points	29	42	31	26

Primary Decision Maker for Business Trips	2002	2001	2000	1999
Business traveler	60%	56%	63%	58%
Travel manager/company travel office	18	19	15	19
Business associate	12	12	7	9
Secretary	5	7	5	7
Travel agent	2	5	5	4
Other	3	1	5	3

EXHIBIT 6   (continued)

Source: The YP&B Yankelovich Partners National Business Travel Monitor (2002).

What Business Travelers Are Looking for in a Hotel and Motel Experience		
Attributes Considered Extremely/Very Desirable (%):	2002	2001
Mastery of Basics:		
Clean/well-maintained rooms	98	99
Friendly, efficient service	95	97
Safe place to stay	92	95
Electronic door locks on guest rooms	69	70
Availability of an in-room safe	53	55
Pricing/Value:		
Free local phone calls	80	85
No long-distance access charge	80	85
Complimentary breakfast included with the nightly room rate	73	71
Free in-room movies	56	65
Streamlining/Simplification:		
Offer express check-in and check-out	85	88
Complimentary shuttle service to and from the airport	75	76
A complimentary area shuttle service other than to the airport	68	69
Baggage check-in and ticketing for the airline you are flying	62	70
Check-in for your flight at the hotel	62	65
24-hour room service	54	62
Automated airline arrival and departure information system in the lobby	53	59
Offer personalized information through television	51	52
Offer access to information through PDAs	44	45
Cordless telephone in room	36	35
Business Services/Command Center Concept:		
Free access to the Internet from guest room	65	N/A
Business services (e.g., copying, faxing, etc.)	62	60
Computer data port in room	56	57
Personal service enabling send and receive faxes from laptop	56	N/A
Computer in room	55	53
Voice mail	54	53
High-speed Internet access in room	54	53
VCR in room	37	42
Printer in room	37	41
Fax in room	36	35
Cordless telephone in room	36	35
Multi-line telephone in room	32	29

EXHIBIT 6   Brand Preferences and Business Travel Decision Process (continued)

Number of Business Trips Taken*		
	2002	**2001**
1–3	59%	57%
4–5	13	13
6–9	9	8
10+	19	22

* Only travelers taking at least one trip.

Average Business Trip Duration	
Number of Nights	**1998**
0	14%
1	15
2–3	35
4–9	28
10+	8

Source: *The 2001 Travel and Tourism Market Research Handbook.* Richard K. Miller & Associates.

Direct competitors, such as Marriott, Hilton, Hyatt, Westin, and Sheraton, were well positioned, particularly in the most affluent segment—coming in 1st, 3rd, 4th, 10th, and 11th, respectively. Wyndham faced similar challenges with the leisure travel audience.

For lodging companies, becoming a recognized brand was all the more important, as many feared that hotel products competing in the same segment were becoming indistinguishable in the customers' eyes. This "commoditization of the hotel product" or "brand erosion" was a major concern for many hotel executives and operators. Many observers believed that for some time hotel chains had been offering increasingly similar products, thereby making their value propositions indistinguishable and leading to within-segment competition increasingly focused on price. Andrew Jordan, Wyndham's senior vice president of marketing, explained: "Consumers are pretty smart. They see that companies buy a property, change the flag, and nothing different happens." The rapid spread of Internet technologies and the increasing

customer access to information, some argued, accelerated the commoditization process by decreasing the costs that travelers incurred when searching for and selecting a suitable hotel room. Services such as Priceline.com that treated hotels within the same category as interchangeable and prevented customers from explicitly selecting a brand were believed to contribute to further brand erosion. Industry observers suggested: "If the [lodging] industry continues to see itself primarily as a provider of hotel accommodations—competing on price—the move to commoditization will be unstoppable . . . To avoid the threat of commoditization, firms must develop inimitable and sustainable differentiators and know their customers intimately."[11] While the merits of commoditization fears remained uncertain, the issue significantly raised executives' attention to the value their lodging product offered to a traveler population with rapidly increasing options and more sophisticated taste.

Guest-recognition and CRM programs were seen as a possible solution to the commoditization threat. Proponents of these initiatives and observers in the popular press suggested:

Hotels will be able to pamper their guests so subtly, so easily, and knowingly that management will appear to be omnipotent and omnipresent, creating in those visitors a sense of loyalty so strong they will always want to return to any property within the brand's system. Gone will be the fear of commoditization spurred by impersonal auction Web sites where rooms are sold at rock-bottom prices.[12]

Guest-recognition or guest-loyalty programs had been a fixture in the lodging industry since the introduction by Holiday Inn of the Priority Club in 1968 (see Exhibit 7). Marriott International recently

[11] "An executive summary of key technology trends surfaces from the IH&RA's annual Technology Think Tank," *Hotels* Magazine, available at http://www.hotelsmag.com/0800/0800hra.html.

[12] R. Terrero, "Technology Raises the Bar on Customer Service Level Expectations at Hotels," *Hotel Business Technology Trends,* November 7–20, 2000.

EXHIBIT 7 **Comparison of Guest Recognition Programs**

Source: Authors' research.

Total Membership by Brand		
Brand Program	**Established**	**Total Members***
Marriott Rewards	1983	15.5
Starwood Preferred Guest	1986	15
Hilton HHonors	1987	12.7
Hyatt Gold Passport	1987	10

* In millions (including active and nonactive members)

Program Characteristics by Brand			
Brand Program	**How Points Are Earned**	**Approximate Number of Participating Properties**	**Number of Points for Free 3-Day Vacation*****
Marriott Rewards	10 points per dollar spent*	2,100	50,000
Starwood Preferred Guest	2 points per dollar spent**	700	21,000
Hilton HHonors	10 points per dollar spent	2,100	65,000
Hyatt Gold Passport	5 points per dollar spent	363	36,000

* Only room rate at Courtyard, Fairfield Inn, and SpringHill Suites

** 3 points for higher status members

*** Estimated

announced the addition of the 15 millionth member of its program—Marriott Rewards. According to Marriott's own research, program members—who earned airline miles or points that could be redeemed against a holiday in a Marriott property or merchandise—were twice as likely to stay at a Marriott hotel as other guests. All major chains in the upscale segments offered rewards programs based on the point system and differentiated their programs by offering specials and minimizing restrictions. In 2002, Starwood's Preferred Guest program was voted program of the year by a panel of frequent travelers:

Travelers have once again lauded Starwood Preferred Guest for the program's continued efforts to aggressively reward and recognize its members. The program made headlines when it launched in 1999 with a breakthrough policy of no blackout dates and no capacity controls, meaning members can redeem free nights anytime, anywhere. Starwood Preferred Guest members have also cited the program's hassle-free award redemption,

outstanding customer service, and innovative promotions and benefits for elite members.[13]

While guest-loyalty programs helped steer the frequent traveler toward branded properties, recent marketing research showed that the primary elements driving selection decisions by business travelers were location and their previous experience with the hotel property. Natalie Wamre, director of ByRequest operations and corporate guest services, explained:

What we heard from our customers during our early research efforts was: "When I am in Chicago, I stay at the Sheraton because Bob at the front desk takes care of me, but when I am in Dallas, I stay at a Wyndham because I had a good experience." But with the ByRequest technology

[13] "Starwood Preferred Guest Wins Freddie Awards Hotel Program of the Year," *Hotel Online* Special Report, http://www.hotel-online.com/Neo/News/PR2002_2nd/Apr02_Freddie.html.

EXHIBIT 7 (continued)

Source: Wyndham International.

Frequent Guest Rewards Programs Comparison					
	Wyndham ByRequest	Marriott Rewards	Starwood Preferred Guest	Hilton HHonors	Hyatt Gold Passport
Cost of membership	Free				
Personalized room	Y	N	N	N	N
Welcome amenities	Y	N	N	N	Y
Express check-in	Y	N	Y	N	Y
Frequent flyer miles	Y	Y	Y	Y	Y
Free 800 calls	Y	N	N	N	N
Free high-speed Internet access	Y	N	N	N	N
Best available room on day of arrival	Y	N	N	N	Y
Free weekday newspaper	Y	N	N	Y	Y
Late check-out	Y	N	Y	Y	Y
Stay history online	Y	Y	Y	Y	Y
Dedicated manager	Y	N	N	Y	N
Special offers	Y	Y	Y	N	Y
Dedicated reservation service	Y	N	N	Y	Y
Express check-out	Y	N	N	Y	Y
72-hour guarantee	Y	N	N	Y	Y
Special e-announcements	Y	N	Y	N	Y
Instant awards	Y	N	Y	N	N
Spouse stays free	N	N	N	Y	N
Free nights using points	N	Y	Y	Y	Y
Free flights using points	N	Y	Y	Y	N
Monthly statement	N	N	N	Y	Y
Different level of membership	N	Y	Y	Y	Y
No blackout dates	N	N	Y	N	N
Guaranteed room availability	N	N	Y	N	N
Usable currency	N	N	Y	N	N

and the dedicated managers, we can provide a personalized experience across the brand.

In the list of decision criteria, location and previous experience with individual properties were closely followed by price/value perceptions and the reputation of the hotel/chain. About one in three survey respondents considered frequent-guest points and airline miles important decision-making criteria. Once at the property, three drivers of customer expectations clearly stood out, with over 90 percent of respondents considering them extremely or very desirable: a clean and well-maintained room, friendly and efficient service, and a safe place to stay (see Exhibit 6). Speaking about guest-recognition programs, Jordan remarked: "We spent a lot of time talking to travelers, and it became clear that points programs were not all that they were built up to be. We could hear a lot of dissatisfaction and frustration. There was the expectation that we knew a lot more about our guests than we really did. Moreover, how many people do redeem points? Very few, I believe."

Steve Eberhart, regional director of operations, added, "Starwood's big selling feature is no black-out dates. Now, when you have the Superbowl in New Orleans, are you going to let someone stay for free just because they stayed in Omaha for 50 nights? I am sure that general manager is not too happy, especially when you are talking about hotels that are franchised or managed for other owners."

Some brands also focused on creating incentives for travel arrangers and recognized that they were often responsible for making the reservations (see Exhibit 7). The most prominent example was Carlson Hospitality's patented "Look To Book" program. Look To Book automatically awarded bonus points to travel agents who booked a Carlson property (e.g., Radisson, Regent International Hotels). The bonus points were redeemable for merchandise, electronic products, and other goods. ByRequest was exclusively directed to the traveler, but the company had evaluated whether it should be extended to travel arrangers. Jordan explained:

We grapple with that to some degree, but since the business traveler is the core target of ByRequest, this is less of an issue. We are fairly confident that the administrative assistants and travel agents are not making the brand decision. We feel that they are just executing the traveler's decision. So we don't have a "secretaries' version" of ByRequest. We have done some education in an effort to communicate to travel agents that ByRequest is not attempting to steal their customers. We also try to educate those that make travel arrangements that they must provide the member number once they make the reservation.

Wyndham ByRequest —

At the heart of Wyndham's new strategic positioning was a novel guest-recognition program named Wyndham ByRequest. Introducing Wyndham ByRequest, Jordan defined the program as "a guest-service philosophy that is the heart and soul of the brand." He added, "We said, OK, we are going to reinvent the Wyndham brand. We are going to say: 'We are all about personalized service.' We are going to say: 'We are the brand who really recognizes that guests are individuals, we

know you have specific needs, quirks—you tell us about them one time and we are going to remember them.'"

More than just a guest-recognition program, ByRequest was a strategic initiative that defined the Wyndham brand. The centrality of the ByRequest initiative was apparent in subsequent letters to shareholders. In March 1999, Wyndham first briefly introduced its use of information systems to enhance guest recognition: "We have established four priorities that we believe will drive shareholder value . . . Our second priority is to develop greater equity in our core brands . . . We are working to be able to reward customers with real-time recognition through enhanced information systems."

Prefacing the 1999 annual report, in March 2000, the letter to shareholders formally introduced Wyndham ByRequest:

Technology, which has helped the industry to improve operating efficiency, is also redefining what customers expect from a hotel . . . Our investment in technology allowed Wyndham Hotels & Resorts to introduce a new customer loyalty program that differs from the competition because of its high level of personalization. Wyndham ByRequest provides popular perks, including virtually registration-free check-in, room upgrades, late check-out, free telecom services, and complimentary products—all to the guest's preferences.

The 2000 annual report featured the ByRequest initiative on its very first page, asking the familiar question "What's your request?" and further explaining: "Built on individual customization and a technology foundation, Wyndham ByRequest is the vehicle to create a comfortable and memorable guest experience." The letter to shareholders, cosigned in March 2001 by Kleisner and Teng, reported early success: "Wyndham ByRequest, our new, unique guest recognition program, is energizing the Wyndham brand. The first program of its kind for an upscale chain, Wyndham ByRequest is a brandwide focus on providing customers with the highest level of customization available during their stay."

While Wyndham ByRequest offered perks similar to those of many other recognition programs, such as airline miles with the major carriers, the program was fundamentally different. The most important component of the program was that it allowed guests to convey exactly what they wanted in their hotel stay, while also empowering managers at the property to take better care of the guest and allowing the company to implement the initiative chainwide. As Kathi Kulesza, vice president of Wyndham ByRequest, put it: "With delays and inconveniences, traveling can be stressful. It makes a difference when you can come to a Wyndham and find the comforts of your home, from your favorite bottle of wine or a pair of your favorite slippers."[14] Executives also felt that ByRequest continued Wyndham's tradition of innovation. Kleisner explained: "Through the years, we have led the charge to respond to the needs of our guests, from being the first to offer in-room hair dryers and irons to standards such as high-speed Internet access in every room. Wyndham ByRequest continues this tradition of innovation while truly raising the bar for the entire category."[15]

The essential characteristic differentiating Wyndham ByRequest from other reward-and-recognition programs was its focus on customization rather than points. Wyndham promised its guests that they could expect to find a room that would fit the preferences they stated in their profile. The program required prospective members to complete a comprehensive profile of their travel and stay preferences by providing substantial information—including recurrent booking information, preferred room configuration and location, preferred welcome snack and drinks, newspaper, and so on (see Exhibit 8). ByRequest members received many free amenities, including automatic upgrades based on availability, free Internet access, and free complimentary snacks, drinks,

and reading material according to their profile. Providing guests who stayed more often with more complimentary amenities and choices and refreshing those amenities more often during their visit served to reward a guest's loyalty. Additionally, ByRequest allowed Wyndham to be responsive to customers' changing preferences. Wamre explained: "In the profile we have options and 'other' fields. We analyzed the profiles of all guests who filled the 'other' field, and when we found that so many people wanted a certain amenity, we added it. Things like reading material, later check-outs, guaranteed room availability are examples of perks we added because our guests asked for them."

Delivering Wyndham ByRequest

Hedley was convinced that chainwide execution and the ability to consistently serve any guest who chose to join the program were the critical success factors of the initiative. He remarked: "Integration was fundamental because the timely delivery of information on arrivals and the pairing of that information with profiles was paramount to ByRequest managers' ability to deliver the guest experience consistently across the brand. If we can't do it brandwide, we don't want to do it at all." Wamre added: "Execution is the biggest challenge. It is very easy to make the promise, but once you make it, you have to deliver. From a technology standpoint, if we don't have the member number with the reservation, we are going to fall short because the ByRequest managers cannot prepare for the guest arrival. Training guests to provide their member number when they make a reservation is fundamental."

The ByRequest program was built on a centralized IT infrastructure. The ByRequest data warehouse married guest profiles with guest-stay information extracted from the PMS. The software, custom developed by the Wyndham IT group, could be accessed from any property through a standard Web browser (see Exhibits 9 and 10). Wyndham officials believed that this design ensured that all affiliated properties could access the system at any time and that the interface was

---

[14] "Wyndham International Appoints New Director of ByRequest," Wyndham International News Release, February 2001.

[15] "Profile: Wyndham ByRequest[SM] Personalization and Technology Redefines the Guest Experience," *LRA Worldwide News*, Vol. 3, Issue 2, 2001.

**EXHIBIT 8
Wyndham
ByRequest
Web Site**

Source: Wyndham
International.

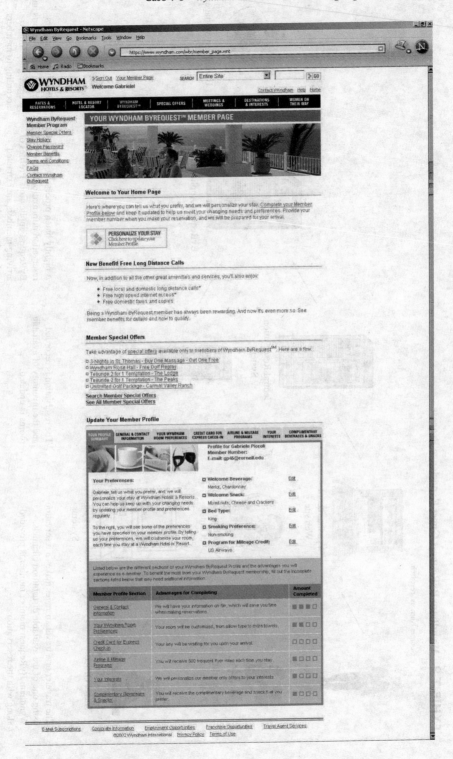

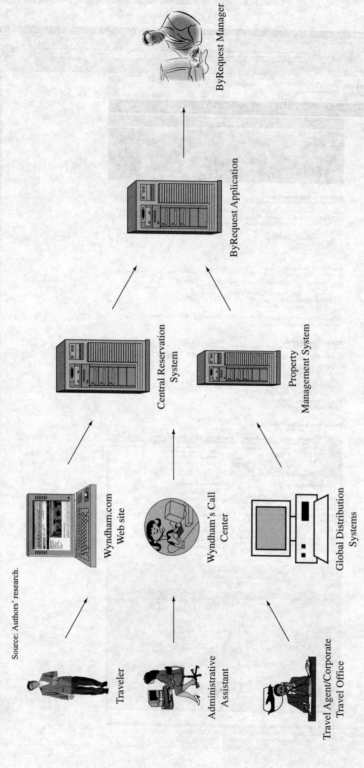

EXHIBIT 9   Wyndham ByRequest Guest Experience Process

Source: Authors' research.

Traveler

Administrative Assistant

Travel Agent/Corporate Travel Office

Wyndham.com Web site

Wyndham's Call Center

Global Distribution Systems

Central Reservation System

Property Management System

ByRequest Application

ByRequest Manager

The traveler or a travel arranger makes a reservation using one of the available distribution channels. Wyndham ByRequest member number is provided along with the reservation.

The reservation is recorded and the inventory of available rooms is updated.

A nightly batch process downloads reservation information to the ByRequest application. Profiles of arriving members are extracted and made available to ByRequest managers.

ByRequest managers retrieve arrival reports and prepare guestrooms according to members' preferences.

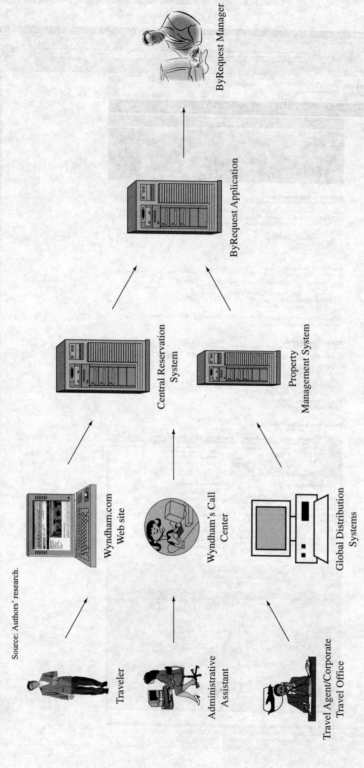

212

EXHIBIT 10
Wyndham ByRequest Information Architecture

Source: Authors' research.

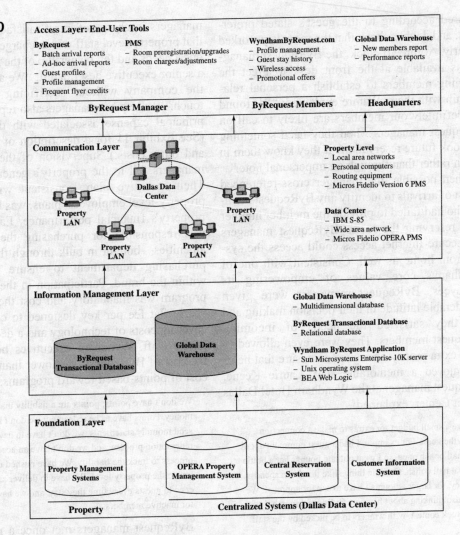

Access Layer: End-User Tools

ByRequest	PMS	WyndhamByRequest.com	Global Data Warehouse
– Batch arrival reports	– Room preregistration/upgrades	– Profile management	– New members report
– Ad-hoc arrival reports	– Room charges/adjustments	– Guest stay history	– Performance reports
– Guest profiles		– Wireless access	
– Profile management		– Promotional offers	
– Frequent flyer credits			

ByRequest Manager · **ByRequest Members** · **Headquarters**

Communication Layer

Dallas Data Center

Property LAN · Property LAN · Property LAN · Property LAN

Property Level
– Local area networks
– Personal computers
– Routing equipment
– Micros Fidelio Version 6 PMS

Data Center
– IBM S-85
– Wide area network
– Micros Fidelio OPERA PMS

Information Management Layer

ByRequest Transactional Database · Global Data Warehouse

Global Data Warehouse
– Multidimensional database

ByRequest Transactional Database
– Relational database

Wyndham ByRequest Application
– Sun Microsystems Enterprise 10K server
– Unix operating system
– BEA Web Logic

Foundation Layer

Property Management Systems · OPERA Property Management System · Central Reservation System · Customer Information System

Property · **Centralized Systems (Dallas Data Center)**

sufficiently user friendly so that few barriers to chainwide adoption existed. Each participating property had a Wyndham ByRequest manager in charge of execution of the program who reported directly to the general manager. Hedley explained:

Each night, our proprietary ByRequest software extracts an arrival list from the PMS, matches up the profiles, and identifies for the managers which Wyndham ByRequest members are checking into the hotel for the upcoming day. Managers also have the ability to go online at any time so they can identify people who have made reservations the

same day. At the same time, all the consumption data are extracted and transferred back to ByRequest so that folios are available electronically for ByRequest members and for us to analyze.

After identifying the incoming ByRequest members, the manager preblocked all the rooms and preregistered the guests in the best available rooms for the arrival date. They passed a list of special requests to housekeeping (e.g., extra pillows, extra towels) so that the housekeeper could service each room appropriately while cleaning it, deliver the amenities, ensure that the room was prepared according to the guest's stated preferences, and double-check that the room key worked properly. At three o'clock, the ByRequest manager was available at the front desk to greet the incoming members to establish a personal relationship with them. Wamre explained: "We found that definitely our members are likely to call on ByRequest managers when they need something and book future reservations if they know them in person rather than through an impersonal note."

When possible, the manager cross-referenced the list of arrivals to identify any ByRequest member who had failed to provide the member number when reserving the room. ByRequest managers with secure Internet access could access the system from home as well. Consistent with one of Wyndham's core values of empowering its employees, ByRequest managers were given considerable latitude in their decision making and how they satisfied the needs of incoming ByRequest members. They were even allowed to spend extra money on a guest to ensure that he or she enjoyed a memorable stay. Laurie Keene, ByRequest manager at the Wyndham Hotel Dallas Market Center, explained:

> I have a small budget for extras to make a connection with the guest. For example, I had a guest comment about my nail polish once, so I went out and bought her a bottle of that nail polish. On little things like that I can spend money, for larger amounts I have to ask for approval. We are also thinking about having a ByRequest member of the week contest, with winners to be picked by the staff.

ByRequest managers were also in charge of training staff and instilling in employees the importance of the program and its underlying philosophy. A big part of the ByRequest manager's role was signing up new members. Eberhart explained: "We have a sign-up program consisting of giving to qualified guests a sampling of the program and then helping them sign up. This requires considerable coordination with the sales team in selecting good prospects—those with high potential for repeat travel."

While technology played a fundamental role in supporting the Wyndham ByRequest initiative, company officials believed that having ByRequest managers in charge of guest satisfaction ensured that property-level staff was in charge of fulfilling guest needs and felt ownership of the initiative. As a senior executive described it: "We are digitizing the company without sacrificing the human touch." ByRequest managers also represented the principal expense associated with the program. (See Exhibit 11 for a description of the position and other costs.) Supervision of the ByRequest managers fell to the property's general manager. Their incentive plan, consistent with standard property-level employees' plans, was based on the property's financial performance. Each property was responsible for purchasing the free guest amenities—bought in bulk through the corporate purchasing department to ensure consistency within the brand. Participation in the ByRequest program was mandatory and cost the property a yearly flat fee per key designed to contribute to covering costs of technology and a dedicated corporate staff. Wyndham executives believed that the cost of ByRequest was lower than the typical cost of points-based reward programs:

> We don't have points; points are a liability that cost money. Points have to be redeemed; we don't have to send monthly statements, we don't have to have a redemption process, and we don't have an accounting process to track the liability. We have pushed those dollars to the property level. We have to deliver an experience to guests every time they stay, and we have no cost for inactive members.

ByRequest managers met once a month with the corporate staff to discuss new initiatives and the progress of the program. The meetings took place through PC-based Web conferences software and always ended with question-and-answer sessions recorded for future access. Support for knowledge sharing among the ByRequest managers was also built into the ByRequest software. Managers were required to call the guest prior to departure and ask for feedback. They had the ability to record their observations about a guest's preferences, characteristics, or experience in a field of the guest's profile visible only to other ByRequest managers. This information was then available in real time to ByRequest managers at

EXHIBIT 11
ByRequest
Program:
Manager Job
Description
and Cost
Drivers

Source: Wyndham
International.

WYNDHAM HOTELS & RESORTS

ByRequest Manager	*JOB DESCRIPTION*

DIVISION: Gardens, Grand Heritage, Hotel/Resort
DEPARTMENT: Rooms
REPORTS TO: General Manager/Rooms Director
STATUS: Exempt

JOB SUMMARY

The ByRequest manager is responsible for on-property management of Wyndham's frequent guest program, *Wyndham ByRequest*, including the coordination of all departments involved in the service of member/VIP guests. He/she will be responsible for updating the guest infor- mation database, training employees, managing local inventory of program collateral, and pro- viding every VIP guest with a personalized and memorable stay.

QUALIFICATION STANDARDS

Education & Experience:
- At least 5 years of progressive experience in a hotel or a related field, or a 4-year college degree and at least 1 year of related experience, or a 2-year college degree and 3 or more years of related experience.
- Previous supervisory experience perferred.
- Must be proficient in Windows, company-approved spreadsheets, Internet Web browsers like Microsoft Explorer, email, and word processing.
- Internal candidates must have a minimum of an above average score on most recent performance appraisal.

DUTIES & FUNCTIONS

- Approach all encounters with guests and employees in an attentive, friendly, courteous, and service-oriented manner.
- Maintain regular attendance in compliance with Wyndham standards, as required by scheduling which will vary according to the needs of the hotel.
- Convey ideas clearly through written communication to members including proper spelling, grammar, penmanship, and personalization.
- Maintain high standards of personal appearance and grooming, which include wearing the proper uniform and nametag when working.
- Maintain an attentive, gracious, and friendly demeanor at all times.
- Maintain the guest profile information system, updating it as necessary to reflect current preferences (i.e., newspapers, smoke sensitivity, dining reservations, cultural interests, etc.). Ensure preferences are communicated to central database as necessary.
- Prior to the arrival of all members/VIPs confirm their reservations, transportation needs, room type, requests/amenities, and social reservations.
- On the day that members/VIPs arrive determine that everything is ready for them including: reservation information, transportation, key packets, room accommodations, welcome note, amenities, and special requests.
- Assist all departments with the implementation and maintenance of the standard frequent guest program, including conducting training sessions as necessary.
- Produce welcome letter/packet for member/VIP arrivals.

(continued)

EXHIBIT 11
(coutinued)

> **DUTIES & FUNCTIONS** (cont.)

- Produce daily information sheet to include: hotel facilities, local attractions, concerts, museum events, meetings, meeting rooms, and evening dinner specials, etc.
- Attend and provide input at the PM rooms meeting (Daily Line Up) for all guest service agents, supervisors, bell staff, and door staff.
- Work with human resources/training manager to coordinate the delivery of all customer service training programs (including Be the Brand) to all employees. Become a certified customer service/Be the Brand trainer.
- Understand the preparations required for the Scoop Sheet and provide necessary input.
- Work on training related projects such as Training Standard of the Week.
- Greet arriving guests and assist members/VIPs with check-in.
- Meet with MOD to review arrivals/evening business.
- Call all members/VIPs departing the following day to offer assistance with departure arrangements; follow up with transportation requests.
- Develop rapport with return guests while maintaining a professional attitude and image.
- Meet with PM supervisor/MOD to review remaining member/VIP arrivals.
- Ensure guest privacy and security by correctly following Wyndham SOP.
- Maintain a presence in the lobby during peak check-in and/or check-out times to assist with guest requests.
- Operate radios and pagers efficiently and professionally when communicating with other departments.
- Maintain a professional working relationship and promote open lines of communication with other managers, employees, and departments.
- Ensure implementation of all Wyndham policies and house rules.
- Work with property accountant/credit manager to arrange special billing for members/VIPs if applicable.
- Respond to all member/VIP guest requests, situations, complaints, and accidents in an attentive, courteous, and efficient way.
- Comply at all times with Wyndham standards and regulations to encourage safe and efficient hotel operations.

Property Level Costs for Participation in ByRequest	
Item	**Amount**
Participation cost	N/A
ByRequest manager salary	$24,000–$40,000 (yearly)
Amenities	$4.37 per occupied room per day (estimate)
Airline miles	$10.25 per 500 miles
Free faxing and calling	Variable

any other Wyndham property. Hedley summed up the essence of ByRequest and the role of the IT group: "ByRequest is not a technology; ByRequest is a culture of Wyndham. The technology infrastructure allows the delivery of an experience, an experience that was described by people in marketing and people in operations. We have to produce technology that allows them to execute it efficiently and effectively, no matter which hotel a guest comes into."

Early Results

As Wyndham entered the third and last year of its planned transformation into a branded hotel operating company, the Wyndham ByRequest initiative was beginning its second year of operation.

(The year 2000 was considered a pilot year during which the program was not heavily advertised.) Wyndham had gained increased recognition for its use of IT as well as for its innovative advertisement. The company won the prestigious *CIO* 100 Award two years in a row for its successful fast-track development of wireless access to Wyndham ByRequest and for its integration efforts. It won the Hospitality Technology Lodging Award and the *InformationWeek* 500 Award for its IT initiatives in wireless reservations, wireless check-in, and the ByRequest guest-recognition program. Wyndham also won the 2001 Hospitality Sales & Marketing Association International's "Best of Show" Award for "the success of its integrated marketing and advertising campaign showcasing Wyndham ByRequest, the company's unique guest recognition program."[16] Commenting on these accomplishments, Jordan remarked:

> Importantly, we are getting a lot of recognition in the industry, not from a technology standpoint, not from a marketing standpoint, but from a customer service standpoint. This visibility is reinforcing that what we are doing is really different. This is a huge goal for ByRequest, to show that this category is sort of beige and everyone is the same, but we are unique.

The impact of the program on revenues was still small but expected to grow substantially. Teng explained: "Wyndham ByRequest contributed only about $60 million in revenue in 2001. It is not a big part of the revenue yet. It's going to grow very fast, but what's so special about it is that people know us by it. It defines our brand."

Overall membership in the program, having recently passed the 600,000 members mark, was still a fraction of the more dominant programs, but the number of new members joining Wyndham ByRequest was increasing steadily (see Exhibit 12). With the program still relatively new, the company was limiting its focus on analysis. Kulesza explained:

16 "Wyndham International Wins the Prestigious HSMAI 'Best of Show' Award for Excellence in Advertising," *HospitalityNet*, http://www.hospitalitynet.org/news/4011058.html.

How many people we signed up last month is my main concern right now. We are conducting limited historical analyses, and we are not collecting the typical demographic data like age, income, etc. We have plans to do this, but our focus right now is on growing the membership. We want people to experience ByRequest because once they do, we believe, they will return and seek out a Wyndham property in their future stays . . . which is exactly what we want.

While actively pursuing membership growth, the company was also attentive to recruiting members that fit the target profile. Teng explained: "We want to make sure the program is executed well and consistently and that we are finding the right people to sign up as members to achieve quality of market share, not just quantity." While still too early to draw definite conclusions, Wyndham International executives were optimistic and believed that results were beginning to show. Jordan remarked:

> We are targeting the average upscale traveler who, on average, takes 12 to 14 trips a year. We have targeted the right travelers with ByRequest. ByRequest members spend 25 percent more on a per-stay basis than nonmembers, they stay at about 20 percent more Wyndham, and their average length of stay is shorter. All of our members are active because there is no benefit to being an inactive member. Brand awareness is up about 40 percent, trial numbers are very strong. Brand loyalty, as measured by repeat guests visits, has doubled versus just 18 months ago. For corporate travelers particularly, ByRequest is a really good program because it increases compliance with company policy and negotiated rates. We even bulk sign up all employees from corporate accounts.

Wyndham was seeing some early signs of success, both in terms of guest satisfaction and financial returns, and executives believed that ByRequest provided Wyndham with a competitive advantage. As he pondered the future of the firm, Teng considered some key questions: How could the competitive advantage built by ByRequest be sustained over time? How could Wyndham continue to provide significant value for ByRequest members? How could the relationship with ByRequest members be leveraged and expanded?

EXHIBIT 12 **Early Results of ByRequest Program**

Source: Wyndham International.

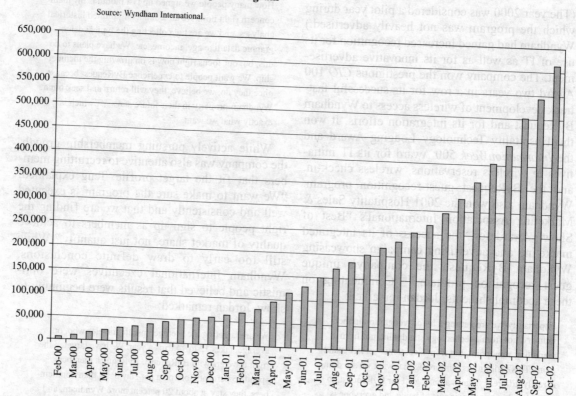

Membership by Number of Stays[a]

Number of Stays	Percentage
0–1	76%
2	4
3–5	13
6–11	3
12–18	3
19+	1

[a]One-year data as of April 2002. Note: The data is incomplete because a number of properties were unable to communicate members' stay frequency to the central data warehouse for a large portion of the year.

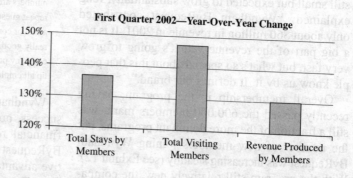

First Quarter 2002—Year-Over-Year Change

Appendix

A REIT is a corporate structure and tradable security backed up by ownership of real estate. In the 1960s, the U.S. Congress passed the U.S. Real Estate Investment Trust Act introducing the REIT structure. It allowed the creation of "mutual funds of real estate" with the intent of providing smaller investors with access to real estate investments.

The REIT benefits from special tax treatments when complying with certain requirements. The most important and interesting benefit REITs enjoy over C-corporations is their exemption from corporate taxes. To enjoy these benefits, among its requirements the REIT has to be organized as a corporation or trust, has to have 75 percent of its total assets invested in real estate, and must derive 75 percent of its gross income from rents, mortgage interest, or real estate sale gains—the "qualified income." Moreover, a REIT must distribute in excess of 90 percent of its taxable income to its shareholders.

Since hotel net income does not qualify as rents, hotel REITs are generally not allowed to operate hotels and instead lease the real estate they own to independent operating companies. The operating company pays rent to the REIT.

There are several variations of the basic REIT structure. One such variation, the paired-share model, essentially allows a REIT to operate its portfolio of properties. In the paired-share model, the REIT shares are paired with those of an operating company and they trade together. When a REIT enjoys paired-share status, its sister operating company can run the properties while paying significant rents, thereby sheltering a significant portion of its operating income from corporate taxation. Starwood Lodging Trust and Patriot American Hospitality Inc. were two of only four U.S. firms that enjoyed grandfathered paired-share status (the creation of new paired-share REITs was stopped in 1984). The U.S. Congress curtailed the benefits of the paired-shared model in 1999. It accepted the critics' argument that paired-share status allowed firms holding such status to be able to pay significant premiums for real estate—premiums that C-corporations could not afford—thus granting them an unfair advantage inconsistent with the original intent of the U.S. Real Estate Investment Trust Act.

Case 1-4

Global Healthcare Exchange

We have continued to stay consistent with our goals. We must (1) hit our financial targets; (2) build the offerings and capabilities required to deliver value to all of our members; and (3) gain critical mass. We've been consistent in our message and strategy about our priorities, and we've executed to achieve these three goals. What separated us from many other dot-com start-ups was that we had very experienced leaders and employees who understood how to build a company that could achieve these three goals. We were able to hit our financial and strategic targets, which enabled us to build credibility with our investors and our members. We also stuck by our Guiding Principles, which enabled us to build and maintain the trust of everyone involved.

Mike Mahoney, CEO of Global Healthcare Exchange, L.L.C., 2003

In May 2003, Mike Mahoney, CEO of Global Healthcare Exchange, L.L.C. (GHX), put the finishing touches on a presentation he was scheduled to make to the 18 members of the company's board of directors. GHX was at an inflection point in its development. Established in early 2000, the company was designed to provide a "worldwide online, open, and independent electronic trading exchange to facilitate the real-time transfer of information, money, goods, and/or services in the worldwide medical equipment, products, and services industry."[1] Its founders included the biggest names in health care, including Johnson & Johnson (J&J), GE Medical Systems, Baxter Healthcare, Abbott Laboratories, and Medtronic. James T. Lenehan, vice chairman and president of J&J, explained the motivation for these fierce competitors to come together to form GHX. "Every health care system around the world is under enormous pressure to create efficiency and take out costs. This exchange is a big part of the solution, providing access to state-of-the-art supply chain management and clinical content [while dramatically lowering the cost of doing business]."[2] Miles White, CEO and chairman, Abbott

Laboratories Inc., continued: "For more than 40 years, Abbott has invested in and maintained a world-class distribution infrastructure designed to provide high-quality, low-cost, flexible distribution options to our customers. Today, as a founding member of the Global Healthcare Exchange (GHX), Abbott is enhancing our customers' options once again, this time utilizing the power of the Internet to move information, drive down supply chain costs, and deliver the highest level of customer service."[3] Jeff Immelt, president and CEO, GE Medical Systems at the time that GHX was formed,[4] stressed that: "Health care requires the speed of the Internet and the staying power of trusted, experienced industry leaders. This venture combines both and is a perfect extension to our long-standing customer relationships."[5] Curt Selquist, company group chairman, J&J Medical Devices and Diagnostics, and chairman of GHX, emphasized the importance of maintaining direct relationships with customers: "During 1999 and early 2000, there was a flood of new entrants that launched business-to-business (B2B) health care supply chain marketplaces. We viewed this with concern. We didn't want anyone to come between us and our customers."

This case was prepared by Professor Lynda M. Applegate and Research Associate Jamie J. Ladge. Copyright © 2003 President and Fellows of Harvard College. Harvard Business School Case 804-002.

[1] Global Healthcare Exchange Limited Liability Company Agreement, August 25, 2000.

[2] Global Healthcare Exchange, News Desk, March 29, 2000.

[3] Abbott Laboratories Web site (www.abbott.com), accessed June 27, 2003.

[4] Immelt assumed the position of CEO and chairman of General Electric upon the retirement of former CEO and chairman, Jack Welch, in September 2001.

[5] Medtronic press release, April 18, 2000.

Indeed, by early 2000, over 90 Internet health care marketplaces had been formed. But, decreased investor confidence in unprofitable Internet businesses followed by worldwide economic declines caused many of the new entrants to fail. Founded on the principle of providing a trusted, fair, and transparent marketplace, GHX was "committed to creating customer value, not market value." In fact, the Limited Liability Company Agreement that its founders signed emphasized that the company did not plan to register an initial public offering (IPO) with the Securities and Exchange Commission.[6]

Not long after the announcement of GHX's formation, more than half of the emerging independent health care Internet marketplaces disappeared as venture capital investors recognized that the chances for success were slim given the commitment of the established suppliers to fund a neutral, third-party exchange. In an open letter to customers, Harry Kraemer, CEO and chairman of Baxter, stressed: "With more than 400 years of combined experience in the health care industry, this new company combines our proven record of quality and trust with the agility of an Internet technology company."[7] Consolidation continued during 2001 and 2002 as GHX convinced many of the remaining health care marketplace competitors to join forces. GHX's November 2001 acquisition of HealthNexis and its December 2002 acquisition of Medibuy, coupled with alliances with Neoforma, AmeriNet, and Broadlane, united the leading participants of the health care supply chain (see Exhibit 1).

At the time of the Medibuy merger in late 2002, GHX connected over 80 health care suppliers and 739 buyers while Medibuy connected 39 suppliers and 561 buyers. Once the two companies' infrastructures and operations were connected, the merged company, which would continue under the GHX name, would enable over 1,400 buyers to transact business with over 100 suppliers. Annual

[6] Global Healthcare Exchange Limited Liability Company Agreement, August 25, 2000.

[7] Open Letter to Customers, March 29, 2000, Baxter Corporation Web site (downloaded on June 27, 2003).

EXHIBIT 1 **Key GHX Acquisitions, Mergers, and Alliances**

Source: GHX Web site and company press releases.

Date	Company	Event
September 27, 2000	CentriMed	Acquisition
August 28, 2001	Neoforma	Alliance
November 11, 2001	AmeriNet	Alliance
November 26, 2001	HealthNexis	Merger
June 26, 2002	Broadlane	Alliance
December 30, 2002	Medibuy	Merger

transaction volume for the merged company was $1 billion in 2002. By July 2003, the company had achieved $1 billion in transaction volume, and it was expected that the annual volume for 2003 would be $2 billion and by the end of 2004 $4 billion.[8]

But, even as he celebrated the company's success, Mahoney recognized that 2003 presented new challenges. Not the least of these was the need to quickly integrate GHX's and Medibuy's operations and cultures. The merger came at a time when GHX was already reorganizing to achieve greater discipline and customer focus in the face of the company's rapid growth.

As he pondered the company's organizational challenges, Mahoney also recognized that the new organization would need to align with the evolution of the company's strategy (see Exhibit 2). Prior to the Medibuy merger, GHX was primarily focused on achieving a critical mass of buyers and suppliers and providing them with connections and the basic content and transaction support to allow them to do business online. As GHX entered 2003, however, its members were pressing for new value-added services. To meet these needs, the company needed to shift from a "product-centric" to a "customer-centric" organization. Given this, new capabilities and skills would be required. Finally, GHX's investors were concerned that these strategic and organizational goals would not deter the company from achieving cash flow break even by year-end 2003.

[8] Company documents.

EXHIBIT 2   GHX Strategy: 2003

Source: Company documents.

Value-Added Products/Capabilities

- Strong Customer Satisfaction
  - Reliability/Value-Added
  - Supplier Benchmarking
- Medibuy Transition Excellence
- Deliver on Value-Added Services Roadmap
  - Content Services
  - Requisition Processing Services
  - Reporting
  - Contracting Services
- Reduce Cycle Time for Member Integration

Critical Mass

- Become the Recognized Industry Utility
- Win strategic IDNs
- 2,000 Providers and 115 Suppliers Connected by the end of 2003
- Enhance Technology Partner Relationships

Organizational Capabilities

Critical Mass

2004

GHX
Global Healthcare Exchange

Financial Execution

Financial Execution

- EBITDA Positive in 2003
- Non Equity Revenue Growth ... $7M
- All Stakeholders Pay for Value ... No Capital Calls

GHX has built critical mass and a winning business model
Key focus for 2003 is to implement value-added products and capabilities that drive greater ROI for members

Industry Overview

As information and biotechnology converge to provide enhanced medical technology, and as that medical technology is moved from product development to standard of care, it is clear that one company may not possess all the requisite skills to ensure success. As a result, the most successful growth companies will increasingly pursue enhanced partnering. In fact, this trend will result in some very interesting alliances, and perhaps some very strange bedfellows."[9]

Art Collins, CEO and Chairman, Medtronic, 2002

In 2002, U.S. health care expenditures contributed over 13 percent, or approximately $1.3 trillion, to the U.S. gross domestic product (GDP), up 8.9 percent in 1980 and 12.2 percent in 1990. The industry's major leading sectors included health care equipment manufacturers and suppliers,

pharmaceuticals, biotechnology, health care providers, health care distributors, and managed care. As of February 2003, sales for the health care industry represented approximately 15 percent of the Standard & Poor's (S&P) 500, with pharmaceuticals making up nearly 9 percent[10] (refer to Exhibit 3a for leading companies within each sector).

Key Participants in the Health Care Industry

The increased complexity and cost of medical care coupled with increased consumer demands and regulatory constraints contributed to increasing inefficiencies in the health care supply chain. The first of these factors, the rise in U.S. health care costs, was due largely to the greater availability of medical products and services. Sales of prescription drug pharmaceuticals played a major role, rising from $12 billion in 1980 to

[9] Art Collins, Keynote Address: Georgia Tech-Parker H. Petit Institute Distinguished Lecture Series, November 14, 2002.

[10] Phillip M. Seligman, S&P Industry Survey: "Healthcare: Facilities," December 19, 2002.

EXHIBIT 3a Leading U.S. Health Care Companies by Sector ($ in billions)

Source: Company annual reports and Web sites; Hoovers.com N/A = Not available.

Company	2002 Revenues	2002 Net Income	No. of Employees	Ownership Status
Sector: Health Care Facility Providers: Market Size (U.S. $ Revenue) = $342 billion				
HCA, Inc.	19.7	.83	178,000	Public
Tenet Healthcare	13.9	.78	113,877	Public
Ascension Health	7.6	.11	83,412	Private
Triad Hospitals	3.5	.14	33,000	Public
Sector: Pharmaceuticals: Market Size (U.S. $ Revenue) = $179 billion (Note: Also participate in the Equipment & Supplies sector.)				
Merck & Co.	51.8	7.1	N/A	Public
Johnson & Johnson	36.3	6.6	108,000	Public
Pfizer, Inc.	32.3	9.1	90,000	Public
Abbott Laboratories	17.7	3.2	70,000	Public
Bristol Myers Squibb	18.1	1.9	46,000	Public
Sector: Equipment & Supplies: Market Size (U.S. $ Revenue) = $175 billion				
GE Medical Systems	9.0	N/A	27,500	Subsidiary
Baxter International	8.1	.78	55,000	Public
Tyco Healthcare Group	7.9	N/A	40,000	Subsidiary
Siemens Medical	7.5	N/A	31,000	Subsidiary
Medtronic	6.4	.98	28,000	Public
Becton Dickson & Co.	4	.48	25,200	Public
Guidant Corp.	3.2	.68	10,000	Public
Fisher Scientific	3.2	.51	9,100	Public
C. R. Bard	1.3	.15	7,700	Public
Boston Scientific Corp.	.8	.13	14,000	Public
B. Braun	N/A	N/A	N/A	Private
Sector: Managed Care/Payors: Market Size (U.S. $ Revenue) = $20 billion				
Blue Cross/Blue Shield	N/A	N/A	N/A	Private
Aetna, Inc.	19.9	−.25	28,371	Public
Cigna Corp.	19.3	−.39	44,600	Public
United Health Group	25	1.3	30,000	Public
WellPoint Health Networks	17.3	N/A	16,500	Public
Sector: Biotechnology: Market Size (U.S. $ Revenue) = $26 billion				
Amgen, Inc.	5.5	1.39	7,700	Public
Genetech, Inc.	2.25	.06	5,252	Public
Biogen, Inc.	1.15	.24	1,992	Public
Chiron Corp.	.97	.18	4,044	Public
Other Relevant Industry Players				
Distributors				
Cardinal Health	51.1	1.0	50,000	Public
McKesson	50	.42	24,000	Public
AmeriSource-Bergen	45	.34	13,700	Public
Retailers				
Wal-Mart	244	8.0	1,383,000	Public
Walgreen	28.7	1.02	141,000	Public
CVS	24.1	.72	105,000	Public
Online Marketplaces				
Neoforma	.073	−.082	196	Public
GHX	.039	−.035	210	Private
Broadlane	N/A	N/A	180	Private

over $122 billion in 2000. By 2011, prescription drug costs were expected to rise to $414 billion. An additional strain was the growing number of older individuals eligible for Medicare (approximately 12 percent of the population). According to a 2002 S&P report, "In 2030, when the last of the 'baby boomer' cohort attained age 65, an estimated 77 million Americans, or 18 percent of the projected population, would be beneficiaries." Total U.S. health care expenditures were expected to grow to $2.8 trillion by 2011.

As costs rose, the demands for quality care and customer service also increased. Both providers and patients expected the right products be available to them at the right time and at an affordable price. Given that health care was considered a "public good" and that errors could cost people their lives, government regulation added significant cost and time to the development of new drugs, devices, and care routines. The regulatory cost and complexity increased for companies that did business globally, as each country had different requirements.

To offset the growing costs in health care and increased competitive pressure, the industry had consolidated. Mergers and acquisitions led to mega-health care manufacturers, wholesalers, and providers[11] (refer to Exhibit 3b for key terms).

In November 1996, an independent study commissioned by CSC Consulting titled "Efficient Health care Consumer Response" (EHCR) identified some $11 billion in potential improvements in health care supply chain processes throughout the industry. The medical device sector was targeted as a key area of inefficiency. The study went on to state that information technology (IT) enabled supply chain redesign could reduce costs from $23 billion to $12 billion.[12]

The EHCR study proved a rallying cry for the industry. It also motivated dot-com entrepreneurs who were searching for opportunities to apply emerging Internet technologies to improve supply chain efficiencies and create value. But, by early 2003, only a few health care marketplaces had survived the inevitable consolidation; the key competitors included Broadlane, Neoforma, and GHX. Brief descriptions of Neoforma and Broadlane are provided below. GHX is discussed in more detail in the next section of the case.

Neoforma, based in Santa Clara, California, was launched in 1996 and, in late 2002, was the only health care marketplace that operated as a publicly traded company. Neoforma offered supply chain solutions for hospitals, group purchasing organizations (GPOs), and distributors. In March 2000, Neoforma entered into a strategic alliance with Novation, formed through the merger of Voluntary Hospitals of America (VHA) and University Healthsystem Consortium (UHC)—two of the largest integrated delivery networks (IDNs). Neoforma's relationship with Novation enabled the company to rapidly expand its installed base of customers and transaction volume. In 2001, $24.6 million of the firm's reported $27.8 million in transaction revenue was contributed by Novation.[13] It was estimated that, in 2002, over 95 percent of the company's $73.7 million in revenues came from Novation, with VHA contributing $55 million.[14] "Not only does Novation own approximately 60 percent of Neoforma's stock," a Bear Stearns analyst reported, "but VHA, the hospital network that founded and runs Novation (along with UHC), is also Neoforma's largest lender."[15] Curt Nonomaque, an executive vice president at VHA, was reported to have said that he considered the payments to Novation for Neoforma to be an outsourcing fee rather than a subsidy. "We're comfortable paying outsourcing fees to Neoforma

[11] Phillip M. Seligman, S&P Industry Survey: "Health care: Facilities," December 19, 2002.

[12] Computer Science Corp. press release, "Health care Industry Study Reveals $1 Billion in Potential Supply Chain Savings: Study Also Shows How EHCR Can Help Improve Quality of Care," December 18, 1996 (downloaded July 2003).

[13] C. Becker, "Baby Steps Toward Profitability: Neoforma," *Modern Healthcare*, April 29, 2002 (downloaded from OneSource Business Browser, June 2003).

[14] R. Falci, J. Gurda, and A. Weinberger, "Neoforma," *Bear Stearns Equity Research*, January 8, 2003.

[15] Op. Cit, Falci, "Neoforma."

EXHIBIT 3b   **Health Care Industry Key Terms**

Source: Author.

Key Terms	Definitions
Group Purchasing Organizations (GPOs)	A GPO is an organization that enables health care providers to realize savings and efficiencies by aggregating purchasing volume and using leverage to negotiate discounts with manufacturers, distributors, and other vendors. The largest GPOs in Jan. 2002 are listed below. ["U.S. top 11 hospital group purchasing organizations and their e-commerce/Internet partners ranked by number of member hospitals," Nelson Publishing, January 1, 2002 (available on OneSource Business Browser)].

GPO (No. of Member Hospitals)	GPO (No. of Member Hospitals) cont.
Novation (2,300)	Joint Purchasing Group (611)
AmeriNet (1,900)	Shared Services Healthcare (570)
Premier Inc. (1,600)	InSource (500)
MAGNET (775)	Consorta (400)
HSCA (700)	Health Trust Purchasing Group (345)
Managed Healthcare (632)	MedAssets (N/A)

Key Terms	Definitions
Integrated Delivery Networks (IDNs)	IDNs aggregate health care providers (e.g., hospitals, clinics, medical groups) and provide integrated management systems and operations to enable increased efficiency and expanded access to specialized patient care services across previously independent institutions.

IDN (No. of Member Hospitals)	IDN (No. of Member Hospitals) cont.
HCA (179 hospitals in U.S., London, and Sweden)	Community Health Systems (63 hospitals)
Tenet (116 hospitals in the U.S. and 1 in Spain)	Health Management Association (41 hospitals)
Triad (49 hospitals, 14 surgery centers)	LifePoint Hospitals (28 hospitals)
Universal Health Service (34 hospitals, 38 behavioral health centers)	Province Healthcare (56 hospitals; 20 owned by Province)
Kindred Healthcare (65 hospitals, 285 nursing centers, rehab, and pharmacy)	Veterans Health Services (2,200 community health care hospitals and other providers)
Ascension Health (67 hospitals)	University Healthsystem Consortium (87 academic health centers)

Key Terms	Definitions
Managed Care Organizations (MCOs)	Managed Care is a method of delivering and paying for health care through a system of provider networks. MCOs are organizations and affiliated networks that are accountable for providing and financing health care services. Managed Care plans include Health Maintenance Organizations (HMOs), Preferred Provider Organizations (PPOs), Point of Service Plans (POS), and similar coordinated plan networks.

because it's core to our business."[16] In late 2002, Neoforma reported a net loss of $82.2 million.[17] The company stated that it had 196 employees and more than 1,200 customers, including 287 suppliers and 929 hospitals. With over 4,000 connections between hospitals and suppliers, the company reported 300,000 transactions per month and $5 billion in transaction dollars annually.

Broadlane was formed in 1999 as a joint venture between Tenet HealthSystems and Nexprise Corporation. Tenet, one of the largest health care systems in the United States, operated 114 acute care hospitals and related businesses in 16 states. Nexprise, (formerly Ventro), was a holding company that operated Internet marketplaces such as Chemdex (a marketplace for specialty chemicals, biochemicals, and reagents), ProMedix (a marketplace for specialty medical supplies), Industria (a marketplace for energy and chemical plant supplies), Amphire (a marketplace for the food industry), and MarketMile (a marketplace selling supplies and services to small to midsize companies).[18]

Broadlane, which evolved from Tenet HealthSystems' corporate purchasing department, operated as a GPO. Its customers included leading hospital groups such as its founder, Tenet, Kaiser Permanente, and Universal Health Services. By 2002, Broadlane had 180 employees with offices in San Francisco, Oakland, Dallas, and New York. The company had 290 health care providers linked to its systems and handled an estimated $1.2 billion in transaction dollars annually.[19]

Two other electronic marketplaces—Health-Nexis and Medibuy—had also played a significant role in shaping the health care industry supply chain. By late 2002, both had merged with GHX.

HealthNexis was founded in April 2000 by four of the largest U.S. health care distributors: AmerisourceBergen Corporation, Cardinal Health Inc., Fisher Scientific International Inc., and McKesson Corporation. HealthNexis provided information and technology solutions to health care suppliers, providers, distributors, and GPOs. The company's core offering consisted of a transaction clearinghouse, product data manager, contract manager, and associated data services. HealthNexis was acquired by GHX in November 2001.

Medibuy, which was also formed in 2000, was an independent venture-backed health care marketplace that, by the time of its merger with GHX, had received over $120 million in funding from several large venture capital firms. Its key customers included IDNs/managed care organizations (MCOs) and GPOs, such as Premier Inc., HealthTrust Purchasing Group (HPG), and Hospital Corporation of America (HCA). The decision was made to merge (rather than simply form an alliance) to enable both companies to rapidly achieve scale across the health care industry value chain, to leverage operating synergies, and to broaden product scope. "Over the past several years, both GHX and Medibuy have been working on parallel tracks to deliver on the same market promise: a more efficient health care supply chain," said Selquist. "GHX and Medibuy each provide valuable technology solutions. Together, they have an opportunity to eliminate redundancy and improve business processes for all participants."[20] One of Medibuy's key customers, HCA, agreed. "Medibuy's products and services played a significant role in the achievement of HCA's supply chain efficiency objectives over the past few years, and we anticipate that the combined resources of the new company will deliver even greater value," said Jim Fitzgerald, senior vice president, contracts and operations support for HCA. "HCA hospitals have

[16] C. Becker, "Baby Steps Toward Profitability: Neoforma," *Modern Healthcare*, April 29, 2002 (downloaded from OneSource Business Browser, June 2003).

[17] Sales are based on pro forma figures, net income is based on GAAP. Adapted from Neoforma, Inc., News and Events "Neoforma Reports Fourth Quarter and Full Year 2002 Results; Begins 2003 with Strong Momentum," February 13, 2003.

[18] See L. M. Applegate and M. Collura, "Ventro: Builder of B2B Businesses" (HBS Publishing No. 801-042) for more information on the Ventro business model at the time that Broadlane was formed.

[19] Broadlane, Inc, "About Us," and "Broadlane Finds Connection to Suppliers," Broadlane Web site, http://www.broadlane.com, accessed February 2003.

[20] GHX Press Release, December 11, 2002.

utilized the Medibuy's Reqs™ software to stream-line the requisitioning process. Now, as a result of the merger, HCA will be able to improve the accuracy of their purchase orders by using product data, maintained and verified by suppliers, in the GHX AllSource™ catalog [and Content Intelligence™]."[21] (See Exhibit 4 for a summary of GHX and Medibuy products before the merger.)

[21] Op. Cit., GHX Press Release.

EXHIBIT 4   **GHX Software Offerings (Before Medibuy Merger)**

Source: Company records.

Product Category	Description
Transaction Engine	
GHX MemberSource™ Exchange Platform	The MemberSource exchange platform can fully manage the flow of information and transactions among a large and broad range of members and was built upon high standards for reliability, security, and scalability.
Connectivity Options	
GHX Connect™	GHX Connect enables providers to use their existing ERP systems to place orders, which are then routed through GHX's exchange platform to GHX's broad supplier membership.
GHX Advantage™	Through a "channel partner" relationship, GHX links with independent ERP and MMIS (materials management information system) vendors (including Lawson, Omnicell, and Ormed) to create integrated connectivity for hospitals, IDNs, and MCOs. GHX automatically passes updates and enhancements directly through the channel partner to the end user.
GHX Axiom™	Health care providers with little or no ERP or MMIS functionality can connect to GHX using GHX's stand-alone browser interface. GHX Axiom provides searching capabilities, generation and electronic submission of purchase requisitions and orders, order status, and other features.
Value-added Products and Services	
GHX AllSource™ Catalog	Online standards-based product catalog containing normalized data owned, verified, and maintained on an ongoing basis by suppliers. GHX AllSource catalog facilitates electronic communication between buyers and sellers, thereby reducing errors that can cost both time and money for all involved.
Report Source	GHX members have access to real-time data related to their specific health care purchases. Report Source is designed to, among other things, identify pricing, product item number, and unit of measure inaccuracies; alert participants to actions that need to be taken to expedite transactions; and summarize transactions for planning purposes.
GHX Content Intelligence™	This product functionality automatically reviews purchase orders for incorrect product data, electronically notifies buyers of any such errors, inserts a correction using the most up-to-date product data from suppliers, and makes a record of the change for future purchases.
Capital Equipment and Contract Management	GHX is currently developing products that improve efficiencies associated with the purchase of capital equipment and consignment products, as well as the management of health care purchasing contracts.

(continued)

EXHIBIT 4 Medibuy Product Offerings (Before Medibuy Merger) (Continued)

Source: Company records.

Medibuy Access

Access Integration Platform and Tools enabled members to search catalogs and complete transactions. Features included:

- Enhanced order cycle management replaced phone and fax ordering
- Integrated new XML technology with current EDI technology
- Expanded networks of health care providers and suppliers
- Single point of contact for procurement
- Seamless business process automation
- Simplified maintenance and support via online technology upgrades

Reqs™: Requisition to Purchase Order Workflow Application

Reqs™ integrated directly with a hospital's medical management information systems (MMIS) and enterprise resource planning (ERP) systems to create a requisition and manage all aspects of the requisition to purchase order process. Features included:

- Requisition creation
- Automated approval routing
- Requisition process monitoring and management with real-time status reporting and information
- Automatic acknowledgment and order tracking
- Full requisition reporting

In addition to the online marketplace competitors, many GPOs and distributors were also providing supply chain software and services. For example, **McKesson Information Solutions** provided enterprisewide patient care; clinical, financial, supply chain, managed care; and strategic management software solutions, as well as outsourcing and other services to health care organizations throughout the United States and selected other countries. (McKesson was an equity owner of HealthNexis and thus became an equity owner of GHX at the time of the HealthNexis acquisition.)

AmeriNet was founded in 1986 as a GPO. By 2002, it served a network of over 14,000 acute and nonacute health care service providers and offered a catalog for obtaining a group purchasing discount on supplies and capital equipment. The catalog was available online and on CD-ROM. GHX formed a strategic alliance with AmeriNet in November 2001. Finally, **MedAssets HSCA,** headquartered in St. Louis, Missouri, was one of the largest GPOs in the country, serving more than 16,000 health care providers nationwide (with purchasing power approaching $7 billion in gross throughput). By early 2003, 2,200 of its hospital members were connected to MedAssets' online marketplace platform. In April 2003, GHX strengthened its position with providers yet again by forming an alliance with MedAssets.[22]

Finally, several software vendors and service providers sold supply chain solutions to health care industry participants. In late 2002, the key players included (1) enterprise resource planning (ERP) software firms such as SAP, J.D. Edwards, Oracle, and PeopleSoft; (2) procurement software firms such as i2 and Manugistics; and (3) supply chain and ERP vendors offering customized vertical industry solutions within the health care industry such as Lawson, Cerner, Eclipsys, IDX, and Siemens Medical Solutions. (Siemens was an equity investor in GHX.) A 2002 Forrester report predicted that, on average, U.S. firms would spend

[22] GHX Press Release, April 10, 2003.

$4.8 billion per year through 2008 on supply chain management initiatives.[23]

GHX

> GHX was started for four very important strategic reasons. First, we wanted to avoid third parties getting in between existing supplier and provider relationships. The second reason was to have input on the fees being charged to suppliers, which represented 3% to 5% of sales. Third, we wanted to play a role in standardizing data in the industry. Lastly, we wanted to build a utility model that would improve the efficiency and effectiveness of the supply chain for both providers and suppliers.
>
> *Curt Selquist* [24]

The vision for GHX originated during discussions between senior executives at J&J and GE Medical Systems that took place between 1999 and early 2000. Shortly after talks began, J&J and GE Medical decided to approach other suppliers with the goal of forming a consortium of founding investors. By the time the company was formally announced on March 29, 2000, J&J, GE, Baxter, Abbott, and Medtronic had joined together as founders. C. R. Bard, Becton Dickinson, Boston Scientific, Guidant, and Tyco joined two weeks later. Siemens joined as an equity investor in spring 2001. B. Braun Medical Inc. joined in June 2002.

Initially GHX was considered the "supplier exchange." However by 2003, after several mergers and acquisitions, GHX had become one of the leading Internet-based health care marketplaces—and the only one with equity ownership by key participants representing health care providers, manufacturers, distributors, and GPOs. By year-end 2002, GHX managed 800,000 transactions and had revenues of $120 million (including revenues from Medibuy). In addition to its Westminster, Colorado headquarters, GHX had offices in Europe and

Canada. With the Medibuy merger, the company added offices in Nashville, Tennessee.

Defining the Concept and Launching the Company

The initial concept for GHX was defined through discussions among the senior executives of the five founding investors. One of the initial challenges that the founders faced was to prove that it was possible for competing organizations to work together collaboratively. Initial discussions helped clarify a common vision, mission, and goals. The vision, which remained as a guiding force in 2003, was "To grow as the global leader in business-to-business supply chain management solutions and services for the health care industry, providing superior member satisfaction, delivered by energized employees who are driven to meet commitments."[25] The company's mission clarified its long-term goals and provided the foundation for its business model. These goals included "To transform health care by dramatically improving the efficiency of health care delivery through information exchange and by maximizing efficiencies in the supply chain; and to facilitate continuous improvement in the relationship between all stakeholders in the health care supply chain resulting in collaborative communication, reduced costs, and better patient care."

To formalize the nature of the relationship, wording was added to the Global Healthcare Exchange Limited Liability Corporation (L.L.C.) Agreement that specified the motivation for and purpose of the partnership and the intent of the founders. In addition, specific clauses were inserted to cover key negotiated agreements. For example, the L.L.C. Agreement explicitly stated that the company did not plan to pursue an IPO. Instead, the firm would seek to generate revenue and distribute excess profits back to its investing members and its customers through fee reductions. Given that the company did not plan an IPO, the L.L.C. Agreement also specified that each

[23] Navi, Radjou, Forrester Research, "SCM Processes Replace Apps: 2003 to 2008—Analysis," December 2002.

[24] Company group chairman, Johnson & Johnson, and member of the Global Healthcare Exchange board of directors.

[25] Global Healthcare Exchange, "Company Vision," www.ghx.com, accessed March 15, 2003.

founder would be issued "Membership Units," with each unit equivalent to $1 of capital contributed by a founding member during the Initial Capital Call. Subsequent equity investors were issued Membership Units at a price per unit that was determined by the board based on the value of the company. The Membership Units were used to determine voting rights, decision authority, and distribution of profits and loss. Finally, the L.L.C. Agreement also specified other governance issues, for example, the composition of the board of directors, change of control, and so on.

(See Exhibit 5 for a summary of key areas covered in the L.L.C. Agreement and Exhibit 6 for the composition of the board of directors.) John Gaither, GHX general counsel, explained:

> The initial L.L.C. Agreement formalized many hours of discussion among the founders. We tried to provide a legal framework for corporate governance and for the partnership that would protect all members yet be flexible enough to deal with uncertainty. A key area of uncertainty in the beginning involved the eventual equity ownership structure. For example, the initial L.L.C. Agreement only considered the interests of suppliers since, at the time, we

EXHIBIT 5   **Summary of GHX (Third Amended and Restated) Limited Liability Agreement: Table of Contents (November 19, 2001)**

Source: Company records.

Preliminary Statements

Definitions and Interpretations

Organization (Formation, Company Name, Purpose)

Members (Initial Members, Admission of Additional Members, Authority & Liability, IPO; Change of Control Events)

Capital Contributions (Capital Contributions and Capital Accounts, Membership Units; Issuance of Membership Units, Optional Additional Cash Contributions, Capital Accounts)

Allocations and Distributions (Distribution of Profits and Loss, Limitations on Loss, Interest in Profits)

Transfer Restrictions (Transfer of Membership Units, Admission of Transferee as Member, Corporate Combinations of Members, Resignation of a Member)

Meetings (Place and Notice of Meetings, Voting, Conduct)

Management of the Company (Management of the Company and Business, Board of Directors, General Powers of the Board, Limitations on the Board, Resignations, Standard of Care and Liability, Conversion to Corporate Form)

Officers (Appointment of Officers, Resignation/Removal/Vacancies, Delegation of Authority, Authority and Duties, Limits on Power of Officers, Employees, and Agents, Litigation and Claims, Nature and Validity of Transactions with Members and Affiliates)

Ownership of Company Property

Fiscal Matters, Books, and Records (Company Bank Accounts/Investments, Records Required, Right of Inspection, Access to Information, Fiscal Year, Taxes)

Dissolution and Winding Up

Dispute Resolution

Indemnification of Directors, Officers, Employees, Agents, Insurance

Miscellaneous

Exhibit 1: Members, Capital Contributions, Membership Units, Membership Interests

Exhibit 2: Guiding Principles and Data Ownership Statement

EXHIBIT 6 **Composition of the Board of Directors (January 2003)**

Source: Company records.

Composition of the Board

7 GHX Investors (Closely mirrored equity ownership)
- 5 of the 6 Majority Owners: J&J, Abbott, GE, Medtronic, Siemens (Baxter was scheduled to rotate onto the board and one of the members would rotate off in 2004)
- 1 of the HealthNexis Distributors: Fisher Scientific (AmeriSourceBergen, Cardinal, and McKesson were scheduled to rotate onto the board over the next few years)
- 1 of the 5 Minority Owners: B. Braun (Becton Dickinson, Boston Scientific, C. R. Bard, Guidant, and Tyco were scheduled to rotate onto the board over the next few years)

3 Medibuy
- 1 HCA
- 1 Premier Executive
- 1 Premier Hospital Executive

GHX Executives
- CEO

Four additional *independent* directors were added to the board in early 2003. Independent directors were selected based on consensus between GHX and Medibuy to provide "strategic value and industry expertise."

Member	Ownership (%)
Premier, Inc	16.83%
HealthNexis, LLC	12.85
Baxter Healthcare Corporation	9.90
Johnson and Johnson Health Care Systems	9.90
Abbott Exchange Inc.	9.73
GE Medical Systems	9.23
Medtronic USA, Inc.	9.23
Siemens	9.23
HCA (BNA Holdings, Inc)	7.21
Becton, Dickinson and Company	1.41
Guidant Corporation	1.39
C. R. Bard, Inc.	1.36
Tyco Healthcare Group LP	1.36
B. Braun	0.21
Boston Scientific Corporation	0.15
Total	**100%**

did not anticipate that we would have nonsupplier equity owners. We soon realized, however, that it would be more difficult than we expected to gain the trust of distributors, GPOs, and health care providers. This was essential to gaining the critical mass needed to become the industrywide exchange we envisioned. This led us to become more open to broader equity ownership from the key industry participants. In February 2001, we finalized a deal to acquire HealthNexis—an exchange owned by the leading distributors in the industry. During the discussions leading up to the acquisition, HealthNexis owners stated three basic strategic risks that they wanted us to address. First, they wanted us to agree that GHX would not become a distributor or a GPO. They also wanted us to state that we wouldn't aggregate demand and that we wouldn't try to influence pricing. These concepts were very consistent with our intent, and we thought that it was a great idea to formalize our Guiding Principles and to include statements covering these areas as an Exhibit in the L.L.C. Agreement.[26]

Bruce Johnson, VP of sales and marketing continued:

The Guiding Principles also evolved over time as we learned more about the needs and expectations of our expanding membership base and ownership structure. They provided a tangible statement of these shared expectations and became a powerful tool for marketing and selling the exchange to new members.

(Exhibit 7 contains the Guiding Principles and the Data Ownership Statement—both of which were included as exhibits in the L.L.C. Agreement.)

Early in the formation of the company the founders also needed to avoid challenge by antitrust regulators.[27] To ensure compliance with antitrust regulations, a lawyer experienced with antitrust rules was hired and all board meetings started with a reading of the guidelines that specified what could be discussed and what could not. Antitrust lawyers attended key meetings and Congressional hearings during the formation of the company. While discussions of each firm's strategy, products, cost structure, and pricing was prohibited, the investors were able to discuss issues related to developing and delivering GHX strategy and offerings.

The L.L.C. Agreement provided a strong statement to investors, members, and potential members that GHX was committed to creating and governing the organization as a trusted, neutral platform upon which all members of the industry

could conduct business. By December 2000, GHX had signed on 35 nonequity owner members. While the majority were health care suppliers, one was a large health care provider (Long Island Jewish Health System) and another was a distributor (The Burrows Company). In addition, an alliance with Neoforma in August 2000 enabled access to a larger pool of health care providers, GPOs, and distributors.

With the vision and mission in place, the investor team set out to elect a board chairman and recruit a senior management team. Curt Selquist, company group chairman of J&J's Medical Devices and Diagnostics Group, was elected as chairman of the board of GHX. He and other members of the board then set out to recruit key executives. Michael Mahoney, a long-term executive at GE Medical Systems, was selected as CEO in spring 2000. (See Exhibit 8 for profiles of the senior management team in early 2003).

While he was involved with the development of the vision and concept from the beginning, Mahoney officially joined GHX as president and CEO in May 2000. Other senior officers were Kevin Ruffe, formerly of J&J, who joined GHX as vice president of operations; Patrick Egan, former director of human resources at Medtronic, who joined GHX as vice president of human resources; Richard Hunt, former vice president of corporate audit at Baxter, who joined GHX as chief financial officer; Bruce Johnson, former general manager of sales and marketing at GE Medical Systems, who joined GHX as vice president of sales and marketing; and John Gaither, former vice president corporate development and deputy general counsel at Baxter, who joined GHX as general counsel.

Building and Launching the Initial Product/Service Offering

The senior team quickly turned their attention to getting the talent needed to build and launch the first product offerings. To ramp up quickly, they "borrowed" employees from the five founding member firms, with about equal representation from each. These employees stayed on with their

---

[26] Global Healthcare Exchange, L.L.C., Amended and Restated Limited Liability Company Agreement, February 22, 2001.

[27] In the U.S. and across the world, antitrust rules prohibited collusion among competitors.

#3

EXHIBIT 7   GHX Guiding Principles in 2003

Source: Company records.

1. The strategic mission of GHX is to create an open and neutral supply chain utility for the health care marketplace. GHX will be open to membership from all participants and will treat its members with neutrality. The objective of the Exchange is to reduce supply chain costs and to improve efficiencies for all its members.

2. The Exchange will focus on health care supply chain customers, especially on purchases in the following areas: medical/surgical supplies and equipment, pharmaceuticals, dietary needs, and other services. A Product Council composed of an equal number of supplier and purchaser representatives will determine specific functionality that is consistent with the approved budget.

3. The Exchange financial model is designed to reduce supply chain costs to its members. The Exchange will implement pricing and business models that will generate revenues sufficient to cover its operating and capital needs. Excess revenues beyond the anticipated operating and capital cash needs will be used to reduce the future pricing structure to all participants.

4. As a supply chain utility for the health care industry, the Exchange will seek to charge all participants fair value for the benefits received. The Exchange will not charge members who are distributors duplicate fees for products manufactured by members who are suppliers.

5. The Exchange will not manufacture, package, or distribute health care products.

6. The Exchange will not intentionally influence the terms of any contracts (e.g., pricing incentives, auctions, and promotions between users). The Exchange will use commercially reasonable efforts to present competing products in a neutral manner, except as otherwise requested by a purchaser. The Exchange will not intentionally influence the distribution channel of any product.

7. The Exchange will implement appropriate security to ensure the confidentiality of pricing, product availability, and purchase information between buyer and seller.

8. The Exchange will not aggregate demand or otherwise become a Group Purchasing Organization.

9. The Exchange will follow data ownership guidelines as detailed in the "Data Ownership Statement."

10. The Exchange will work to promote the adoption of industry standards (e.g., UPN, HIN, UNSPSC, ECRI).

Data Ownership Statement

- The parties to each transaction own the data relating to that transaction.
  - The parties are the buyer (e.g., hospital) and seller (e.g., manufacturer).
  - If a distributor is legally an agent, then its rights to data are governed by its agreement with the seller.
  - If a distributor is legally the seller, then the manufacturer's rights to data are governed by its agreement with the distributor.
- The Exchange will not disclose transaction-specific data to anyone without the consent of the buyer or seller.
- The Exchange may sell aggregated data.
  - Aggregate data may not disclose participants.
  - Aggregate data will only include data from buyers and sellers who consent.

EXHIBIT 8 Profiles of Senior Management Team

Source: Company records.

Executive	Background
Michael F. Mahoney, CEO	Before joining GHX, Mahoney held positions of increasing responsibility at GE Medical Systems, most recently as general manager of sales and marketing, integrated imaging solutions. During his tenure at GE Medical Systems, he gained expertise in leading start-up, growth-oriented IT businesses, sales management and training, and nuclear/CT medical products.
Roger Morgan, GM, Europe	Prior to joining GHX, Morgan served 21 years with Becton, Dickinson and Company, most recently as vice president for its global SAP implementation.
Richard W. Hunt, CFO	Before joining GHX, Hunt served as a vice president of corporate audits for Baxter Inc. During his 19 years with Baxter/American Hospital Supply, Hunt held leadership positions in corporate finance, business development, manufacturing, and distribution.
John F. Gaither, Jr., VP, General Counsel	Before joining GHX, Gaither was vice president for corporate development for Baxter International Inc. and was also responsible for Baxter's international strategy. Prior to that, he held a variety of positions at Baxter including senior attorney, corporate secretary, and deputy general counsel, as well as vice president, law/strategic planning, for Baxter Diagnostics, Inc. and Baxter's medical technology businesses.
Bruce Johnson, VP, Sales & Marketing	Before joining GHX, Johnson served as America's marketing manager, integrated imaging solutions, for GE Medical Systems. He had nine years of previous experience with the company, including tenure as magnetic resonance imaging product marketing manager and product line sales representative.
Kevin Ruffe, VP, Operations	Before joining GHX, Ruffe spent nine years in the information management division of Johnson & Johnson Health Care Systems, most recently as director of account and contract management. Before his work with Johnson & Johnson, Ruffe served for four years as the manager of applications development for McNeil Specialty Products, New Brunswick, NJ.
Jeff Cunningham, VP, Professional Services	Before joining GHX, Cunningham served in key leadership positions with Medibuy, primarily focused on product strategy, development, and operations. Cunningham came to Medibuy through the merger with Premier Health Exchange, where he was a founding member of the senior management team. In previous roles, Cunningham was a partner in Computer Science Corporation's National eBusiness Consulting Practice.
Patrick Egan, VP, Human Resources	Prior to joining GHX, Egan was director of human resources at Medtronic, Inc. Egan worked at Medtronic for 11 years, holding a variety of human resource positions. Most recently, he was responsible for the domestic sales organization, implementing performance management systems, succession planning, and creating compensation and organization design strategies.

respective companies but were expected to spend the majority of their time building GHX. Mahoney commented:

It was a great show of commitment on behalf of the founding companies that they would give up a significant

number of their best employees to get this initiative off the ground. However, it was difficult to form a cohesive culture because the employees were all from aggressive competitors. In addition, these employees were considered to be "on loan" to GHX and continued to hold their original positions. So while it was a great idea and got us started, those early years were a bit chaotic. By December 2000, it was clear that we really needed to get our own team in place, and we went through our list of "employees" and determined which were really needed and, more importantly, which were committed to the GHX vision, mission, and Guiding Principles. The remaining employees went back to the founder companies.

Egan continued:

> When the company was first announced in March 2000, we thought of it more as a project than an actual company. Each of the original founding firms loaned people to work on building GHX and continued to pay their salaries. The arrangement we had with the board was that we could work on the project on loan from the parent for about 6 months and then we could renew once for another 6 months. After 12 months we needed to make a decision whether to return to the parent firm or quit and work for GHX. The purchase of CentriMed and the decision to move corporate headquarters to Colorado were defining moments. We all knew that it was time to make a decision. By that time I had developed compensation, benefit, and payroll systems so we had the infrastructure in place. Once we had a corporate headquarters with offices, HR systems in place, and the beginnings of a business model, people began to think of GHX as a company and it was much easier to sign on officially. After the move to Colorado, we hired over 70 people in less than 6 months.

As they shifted from a "borrowed" workforce to a permanent one, GHX established a compensation and rewards structure suitable for a privately held company. In addition to a base salary, employees were given a yearly performance bonus plus they were promised an additional bonus if they stayed with the company for three years. While the base pay and bonuses were consistent with "market rates," the long-term incentives were very different from those offered by other technology firms at the time. According to Ruffe:

> We had developers who wanted to make $120,000 plus stock options. But this wasn't appropriate for a company that did not plan to go public. Instead, we offered a base salary and a bonus. After the dot-com meltdown, many of the prospective employees to whom we had made offers but who had declined came back to GHX and said, "Well, the options didn't work out for us so now we want that base salary." Instead of trying to follow what everyone else was doing in the market, we did what made sense for

our business. I think this helped us build an organization that was aligned with the vision, mission, and strategy.

To quickly get to market, GHX didn't have time to build its own technologies, so it sought the expertise of third-party supply chain solution vendors. Originally, GHX negotiated with i2, IBM, and Ariba, who had been working together to build B2B exchange software for use across multiple global industries. But the partnership among the software vendors was strained, and GHX was forced to find a new solution. In September 2000, GHX acquired CentriMed, a Colorado-based company with a software product that could run online global supply chain markets.[28] Initially, the founder and several of the executives of CentriMed took over senior positions at GHX, including the role of chief technology officer. But most left within the next year to pursue other interests. According to Ruffe:

> CentriMed gave us an immediate presence in the marketplace. They had an Internet browser-based online catalog that could be used to load each supplier's product catalog. Given that most of the major suppliers in the industry were GHX investors, we got the buy-in up front to transfer their catalogs to the CentriMed engine. The more difficult piece was to integrate the CentriMed system with the IT systems used by suppliers, health care providers, and distributors. While CentriMed's solution enabled customers to browse an integrated supplier catalog and obtain product descriptions, pricing, and order details, without connections to suppliers' and customers' internal systems transactions could not be fully automated.

During late 2000, GHX developed the functionality and features required for members to connect their internal systems to the GHX online transaction engine. In December 2000, GHX announced that it had successfully completed online transactions with its first pilot hospital. By February 2001, 26 IDNs representing 207 hospitals had joined GHX and were in the process of integrating internal supply chain systems and procedures to enable them to do business on the GHX platform. To encourage buyers

[28] Global Healthcare Exchange, News Desk, "Global Health Care Exchange, L.L.C. to Acquire CentriMed," August 14, 2000, accessed February 2003.

to sign on, GHX did not charge them for joining its marketplace, neither did it charge for each transaction.

Growing and Evolving the Business

Initially, it was planned that the GHX marketplace would be funded entirely by suppliers. However, it soon became clear that expanded ownership would be needed to get the full buy-in and participation of other value chain participants. In August 2001, GHX entered into an alliance agreement with Neoforma, which at the time had 514 hospitals signed up to its health care marketplace. The partnership enabled each member to tap into the other's platform. According to Hunt:

> Neoforma's biggest owner was Novation, a large GPO. As a result, the deal with Neoforma gave us direct access to healthcare providers that purchased through Novation. A hospital could connect to Neoforma, which then passed the request for information to GHX. The GHX

marketplace enabled the hospital to access the supplier catalogs and place an order and then passed the information back to Neoforma, which delivered it to the hospital. In essence, we established a connection between the Neoforma and GHX marketplaces which ran in the background.

The merger between GHX and HealthNexis in November 2001 expanded not just participation but also equity ownership. In addition, it added several large distributors to its member base, including AmeriSourceBergen, Cardinal Health Inc., Fisher Scientific International Inc., and McKesson Corporation. Initially, distributors were concerned that the suppliers were attempting to bypass them and link directly to customers. Mahoney explained:

> The partnership deals we did early on with AmeriNet, Neoforma, and large health care providers and GPOs provided us with the credibility we needed to bring HealthNexis to the table. However, we still had to deal with the issue of trust. We needed to prove to the distributors that our goal was to work with them, not against

EXHIBIT 9   **Summary of the GHX/Medibuy Merger**

Source: Adapted from company records.

Strategy/Mission

- Merged entity retains the GHX name and brand.
- All 18 strategic investors in Medibuy (e.g., Premier, HCA) and GHX retain ownership in the merged entity.
- Purpose of the merger is to create critical mass within all categories of the value chain and to improve the value proposition for all.
- The Guiding Principles provide the strategic framework.
- Sufficient checks and balances in place to ensure neutrality, openness, and fairness.

Financial

- Significant cost-reduction benefits for all stakeholders as a result of the merger.
  - 50% reduction in fees for Premier members to utilize GHX.
  - 30% to 50% reduction in 3-year fees paid by all the other owners.
- Future revenues will be generated at levels to cover GHX operating expenses and those investments approved by equity members.
  - All supply chain participants pay fair prices.

Operational

- Headquarters remain in Colorado.
- Single technology platform and service offerings combine the best from GHX and Medibuy.
- Transition will not impact functionality of existing Medibuy and GHX customers.

them. Developing mutual understanding and trust was a long process, but eventually we were able to strike a deal that was beneficial to the industry.

The merger with HealthNexis led to several key wins in member recruitment. For example, in April 2002, GHX signed an agreement with Allegiance, a large distributor and a subsidiary of Cardinal Health.[29] In June 2002, GHX entered into a multiyear agreement with Broadlane that enabled GHX to connect to 292 participating health care providers that were enrolled in Broadlane's BroadLink marketplace. The relationship with Broadlane, when combined with its alliance with Neoforma, helped GHX to make substantial progress in penetrating the buy side.

In 2001, GHX began talking with Medibuy about a possible merger to strengthen its access to buy-side members. After nearly 18 months of discussion, the two came to a mutual agreement and closed the deal in December 2002 (see Exhibit 9). According to Mahoney:

> This was a watershed event for GHX that led to three significant milestones. First, it allowed hospitals and GPOs to become owners of GHX, making us the first utility owned by hospitals, suppliers, distributors, and GPOs. Second, it enabled us to secure three-year revenue commitments from our 18 equity owners. This was quite a big deal for GHX because, in the past, suppliers had paid us annually based on equity capital calls. Now they would provide up-front revenue commitments, which gave us demand visibility. Third, because it was no longer necessary to pay for two online marketplace infrastructures, the Medibuy merger immediately lowered the overall cost for all of our members by 30% to 40%, while also increasing the functionality provided by our combined marketplace. Thus, the Medibuy deal enabled us to shift the economic curve, which reduced the on-going funding requirements for all of the equity

owners, decreased the costs for all members and, at the same time, it made it much easier for us to penetrate the buy side.

Evolving the Product Offering

While most companies in the dot-com era were trying to extend their influence and dominate all positions in the value chain, we chose a very different approach. We knew we would never try to take over the system operations *within* our customers, manufacturers, or distributors—nor did we want to. What we could offer was a complementary set of offerings that would serve as a nerve center, connecting all parties but stopping at the doors to their organization. This was consistent with our Guiding Principles that stated that the members would own their own information.

Kevin Ruffe

When it was first launched, GHX simply provided a secure online catalog for each supplier's products. Using a standard Web browser and a secure Internet-based virtual private network (VPN),[30] buyers could access those catalogs, store their order preferences, and communicate with suppliers. Consistent with its vision and mission, each supplier "owned" its product data and the buyer and supplier jointly "owned" data on their respective transactions. GHX did not provide search aggregation services that enabled comparison of product features and pricing on the same page, neither did it support auctions.

During 2001, GHX developed the online applications that allowed buyers to connect their internal purchasing and billing systems with each supplier's internal order fulfillment and billing systems. They also provided system integration

---

[29] Allegiance was originally named American Hospital Supply. It was acquired by Baxter in the mid-1980s, spun out as a separate company, and subsequently acquired by Cardinal Health. The history of American Hospital Supply as one of the early pioneers in electronic commerce is discussed in L. M. Applegate, "Creating Business Advantage with IT," *Corporate Information Strategy and Management* eds. L. M. Applegate, R. D. Austin, and F. W. McFarlan (New York: McGraw-Hill, 2002).

[30] A virtual private network (VPN) provides the additional security and network performance required for companies to do business electronically. A VPN network can use the Internet protocol or it can use another network protocol (e.g., ATM) to enable communications, transactions, and information sharing. By creating its marketplace on an Internet protocol VPN, GHX was able to provide standardized network access to all participants and to enable browser-based or computer-to-computer communications.

EXHIBIT 10 GHX/Medibuy Integration Plan (as of May 2003)

Source: Company documents.

Transition Phases and Deliverables	
Current State: Separate GHX and Mediby Marketplaces	
Phase 1: Common Connection for Customers **Projected Completion Date:** *June '03* Deliverables: • Link GHX and Medibuy marketplaces • Start migration to common connection • Adopt standardized integration technology for providers	
Phase 2: Combine Components into New Exchange **Projected Timing:** *July–Aug. '03* Deliverables: • Medibuy & GHX critical components move to GHX data center in Plano • Medibuy customers gain access to GHX services and suppliers	
Phase 3: Migrate Customers to New Exchange **Projected Timing:** *July–Sept. '03* Deliverables: • Incorporate best products from both exchanges into a common exchange • All transactions available in ReportSource • All providers can access all suppliers	

consulting services to help implement the online connections.

During 2001 and 2002, GHX also developed the applications needed to connect alliance partner marketplaces and integrated the GHX and HealthNexis marketplaces. In 2003, GHX planned to integrate the GHX and Medibuy technology infrastructure and product offerings (see Exhibit 10). It would also begin developing and delivering new value-added offerings. (Exhibit 11 provides an overview of the GHX online marketplace in 2003.)

Developing industry standards was an immediate priority that needed to be addressed to enable GHX to move beyond simply providing connectivity to become a flexible "engine" for delivering value-added industry solutions. To push this agenda forward, a number of industry players had formed the Coalition of Healthcare Standards (CHeS). Prior to the merger, GHX and Medibuy had joined the coalition along with several large GPOs and technology vendors. Based in Ann Arbor, Michigan, CHeS's purpose was to adopt and promote uniform health care industry data standards for supply chain transactions over the Internet. Ruffe commented:

Today, not everyone agrees on the same product identifiers. Distributors, manufacturers, and providers still

EXHIBIT 11
GHX Online Marketplace

Source: Company records.

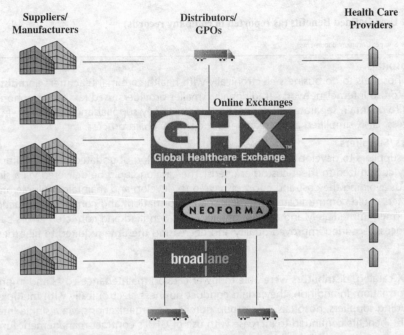

Suppliers/ Manufacturers

Distributors/ GPOs

Health Care Providers

Online Exchanges

GHX Product/Service Offerings

Source: Company Web site (downloaded July 8, 2003).

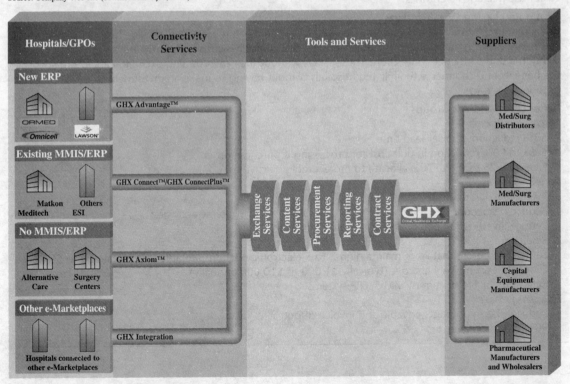

EXHIBIT 12   User-Defined Benefits (as reported in company records)

Source: Company documents.

Providers/Hospitals

GHX enabled hospitals to do business electronically with health care manufacturers and distributors via a single, easy-to-use Internet network. Traditionally, smaller providers used fax and telephone and large providers had to maintain separate EDI connections for each key supplier and distributor. In addition to enhanced access, GHX simplified and streamlined the supply chain process.

Manufacturers/Suppliers

GHX enabled suppliers to develop and maintain an online catalog of updated product information that could be easily customized to meet customer needs. The catalog could be delivered via a single Internet connection thus avoiding the cost and effort of having to develop and maintain multiple online links. Buyers and sellers could communicate via e-mail, share information, and complete transactions, which could be confirmed immediately and tracked online. GHX identified and corrected errors early in the purchasing process, ensuring improved quality and decreasing the time required to fill orders and receive payments.

Distributors

Using the GHX catalog, distributors were able to lower catalog maintenance costs and improve accuracy of product information. In addition, they could conduct business electronically with multiple trading partners, including suppliers, hospitals, and group purchasing organizations, via a single Internet connection. The benefits continued to increase with use of GHX's contract management functionality that helped reduce errors, which lead to delays in payment of customer invoices and supplier rebates. Further, with more up-to-date purchasing information, distributors were able to better help hospital customers manage inventories.

Group Purchasing Organizations

GPOs that had formed their own online marketplaces could link to GHX and provide hospital customers and members with the ability to conduct business electronically with significantly more suppliers through a single Internet connection. Those GPOs without their own trading exchange could provide the benefits of e-commerce to affiliated hospitals without having to make an investment in developing a proprietary service.

Benefits for All User Groups

Purchasing Process
   50% reduction in order lead time
   60% to 90% reduction in unit cost for processing a purchase order
   Free up 0.25 to 0.65 FTE—allocate to more strategic activities

Receiving Process
   90% reduction in errors
   Reduce headcount by 1 purchasing FTE—allocate to more strategic activities
   Reduce investigation and analysis of disputed invoices

IT Resources
   Same IT resources that were maintaining 2 to 5 electronic relations are able to maintain 20 to 50+
   Eliminate existing VAN charges (typically $1,000 to $10,000 annually)
   Extend useful life of current MMIS/ERP systems

Payment Process
   Reduce FTEs in accounts payable and invoice disputes
   90% reduction in errors

refer to identical products by different numbers. There is also no agreement on how customers should be identified since every supplier, GPO, and distributor has their own unique customer identifiers. Agreement on these two standard identifiers alone would have a major impact on our ability to deliver value-added industry solutions. Agreement on transaction standards for common processes such as placing purchase orders, sending invoices, and electronically transferring funds would further simplify our ability to develop value-added industry solutions—lowering the cost for the entire industry. The delay in reaching agreement on standards to date is that everyone is waiting for someone else to go first. Hospitals won't push the issue because manufacturers aren't, and manufacturers won't push the issue because their customers aren't. Until now, no one has had the critical mass to break through the obstacles. However, with the Medibuy acquisition, we're in a great position to accelerate the adoption of standards. We recently formed a Product Council, composed of representatives from the supplier, distributor, GPO, and provider communities. The Council will meet regularly to provide input on the design of GHX product offerings. This will be a great forum to help us discuss standards that can be embedded in our product offerings.[31]

In 2002, health care providers reported that using GHX reduced the cost and improved the quality of supply chain processes for all members of the health care value chain. To date, members reported returns on investment (ROI) benefits of up to 30 percent. (Exhibit 12 summarizes how GHX has helped to drive ROI improvements for its value chain members to date.) According to Hunt:

> The benefits delivered to an individual member depend on the company, the state of its internal technology and processes, and the degree of penetration and use of GHX. Our members have reported anywhere from 0% ROI for those with limited penetration and use of GHX to 30% ROI for those with heavy penetration and use. One of our strategic goals for 2003 is to increase the value delivered to all members. As a first step in achieving this goal, we plan to administer a survey to all members during 2003 so that we can gain a deeper

understanding of the value we are delivering today. We will then develop a set of best practices that we can use to show all of our members how they can achieve 30% ROI or greater.

Evolving the Organization

In September 2000, GHX opened its U.S. headquarters in Westminster, Colorado, and later that year opened European headquarters in Brussels and Canadian headquarters in Toronto. By early 2003, the company had approximately 180 full-time equivalent (FTE) employees worldwide (148 in the United States, 28 in Europe, and 4 in Canada) and had undergone significant organization changes. (See Exhibit 13 for an organization chart.) By May 2003, less than 3 percent of the company's transaction volume was generated outside the United States (1.3 percent from Canada and 1.4 percent from Europe). As mentioned in Exhibit 3, while international sales were an important source of growth for health care industry suppliers, it was unclear how fast European markets would evolve to critical mass.

GHX was a company that blended multiple business models and cultures: It was a technology company, a service company, and a health care supply chain and logistics company; it was an entrepreneurial start-up, yet was owned by the largest established firms in the health care industry. One of the key challenges that GHX faced was in developing its own unique business model and culture that would unite these various perspectives while preserving the advantages. According to Ruffe:

> I think we faced many of the same challenges that all new companies face, but the complexity was much greater. We needed to figure out our business concept and business model, develop a unique set of product offerings, and get customers and suppliers engaged and connected as we brought together all of the different cultures and organizations of our founders. So it wasn't only that the marketplace was moving fast, but the individuals inside the company were also in a constant state of flux as we tried to build a shared culture and organization. Tensions were high because we were trying to achieve all of this while

---

[31] "GHX is on a Roll," *Repertoire Magazine*, February 2003.

EXHIBIT 13   GHX Organization Chart (as of 3/30/03)

Source: Author interpretation based on GHX documents.

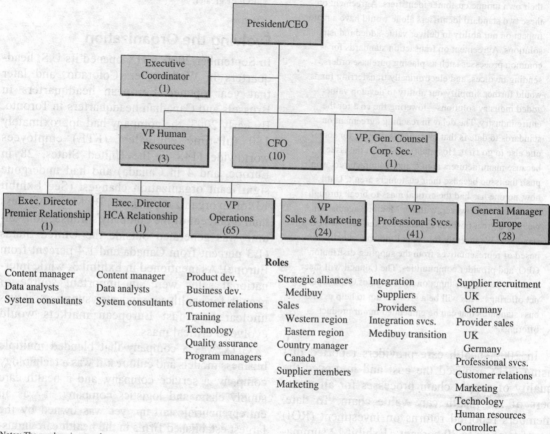

Roles

Exec. Director Premier Relationship	Exec. Director HCA Relationship	VP Operations	VP Sales & Marketing	VP Professional Svcs.	General Manager Europe
Content manager	Content manager	Product dev.	Strategic alliances	Integration	Supplier recruitment
Data analysts	Data analysts	Business dev.	Medibuy	Suppliers	UK
System consultants	System consultants	Customer relations	Sales	Providers	Germany
		Training	Western region	Integration svcs.	Provider sales
		Technology	Eastern region	Medibuy transition	UK
		Quality assurance	Country manager		Germany
		Program managers	Canada		Professional svcs.
			Supplier members		Customer relations
			Marketing		Marketing
					Technology
					Human resources
					Controller

Notes: The numbers in parentheses represent headcount. Four employees (not included in the above headcount) supported GHX Canada. Executives in shaded boxes comprise the Leadership Team.

the dot-com world was falling apart. The good news is—we survived. We have people in place now that are comfortable with operating in the midst of chaos and know how to put structure in place that provides stability and control yet is able to adapt quickly. This past year, we finally hit our stride. We've proved ourselves in the marketplace *and inside our organization.*

Early on, GHX senior executives made a decision that they would not be pressured to become a dot-com and adopt the approach being advocated to build and grow an Internet company. Instead, the company focused on achieving solid financial discipline and on building an organization that aligned with its strategy, vision, and mission. On one hand, the executives maintained the business practices and approaches that had enabled them to run large, established firms. At the same time, they developed new capabilities that would enable the company to innovate and adapt as quickly and flexibly as an entrepreneurial organization.

The small size of the company—when combined with the large size of its network of partners (many of whom were owners)—fostered a

EXHIBIT 14   **Levels of Board Approval for Key Decisions**

Source: Company records.

1. *The Guiding Principles* set the strategic direction and parameters to guide key decisions. Any changes in the Guiding Principles required Super Majority shareholder approval (see below).

2. *Ultra/Super Majority Shareholder Approval* decisions required greater than 95% approval of all shareholders with equity interests greater than 5%. The decision to become a public company (IPO) was an example of a decision that required this level of approval.

3. *Super Majority Shareholder Approval* decisions required greater than 85% approval of equity shareholders. Examples of decisions that required this level of approval included changes to Guiding Principles, liquidation, mergers, and alliances.

4. *Majority Shareholder Approval* decisions required greater than 50% approval of equity shareholders. Examples of decisions that required this level of approval included capital calls and issuance or redemption of stock.

5. *Majority Board Approval* decisions required greater than 50% approval of the board of directors. Board members approved budgets, contracts, expenditures over a specified amount, executive compensation, auditor selection, and the launch of new lines of business that fell within the Guiding Principles.

"big-small" organizational model. In essence, GHX was a network of networks uniting stakeholder networks across the industry and eventually across the world. Only a small number of GHX employees were needed to build and provide services to this network as the company was able to leverage the infrastructure, capabilities, and customer base of its members. Open and frequent communication among the board of directors, the executive team, and the employees on the front line enabled everyone to understand the link between strategy, operations, and performance in real time. For example, in the beginning, the board met monthly, and senior executives were in constant touch with frontline employees and the marketplace. Throughout, the vision, mission, and Guiding Principles provided the framework for making tough decisions.

Given the network structure, the board of directors served a key "boundary spanning" role. Each member of the board represented the interests of a key constituency, and the L.L.C. Agreement specified the formal structure of network roles,

authority, and governance. The L.L.C. Agreement also specified a formal process for decision making (see Exhibit 14).

Going Forward

When the GHX-Medibuy integration was complete and all members had been connected to the new platform, the company would connect over 1,400 providers (750 from GHX and 550 from the Medibuy merger) to over 100 of the largest suppliers and distributors. This reach would enable GHX to leap ahead of Neoforma in terms of members connected (see Exhibit 15). During 2002, average monthly transaction volume had grown at a rate of 30 percent to reach a $1 billion postmerger annualized run rate. By July 2003, transaction volume had already reached the $1 billion mark and the annual transaction volume was expected to reach $2 billion for 2003 and $4 billion for 2004. Since its inception, the company had made significant, yet necessary, shifts in its strategic vision (see Exhibit 16) and was now focused on two key core capabilities:

connectivity and value-added services. Mahoney commented:

> In addition to the immediate need to integrate Medibuy and GHX, we also need to think more strategically about how to offer more value to all members of the health care supply chain. To date, we've focused on achieving connectivity. Now it's time to focus on our customers and to determine how we can significantly increase the value we provide them. But, we must do this without compromising the financial discipline we have established. We have committed to becoming cash flow break even in 2003 and to achieving $7 million in "non-equity-owner" revenues in 2003. Total 2003 revenue is forecasted at $46 million compared to $39 million in 2002.

Johnson continued:

> You can't have a viable marketplace with only one side participating and you can't have a viable business with only investors paying. One of our key challenges in 2003 is to create a viable business model with a pricing model that is fair to everyone. This is complicated by the fact that people have come to expect that online marketplaces won't charge them. Initially, GHX needed to attract buyers so we didn't charge the buyers and Medibuy needed to attract suppliers so they didn't charge the suppliers. Now we are positioned to complete the business model. In 2003, we need to have a pricing structure where all members share in the benefits and pay a fair price for those benefits. We have a number of provider and supplier members who are coming up for renewal, converting them to this new pricing model will be the test that determines if we have been successful in creating a fair pricing model.

Analysts were optimistic about the company's ability to achieve its goals. "GHX is on a roll," a *Repertoire* reporter wrote in early 2003. "The acquisition of Medibuy makes GHX the clear leader in the e-commerce sweepstakes." The article quoted Gartner Inc. vice president, Michael Davis:

> We see [the GHX-Medibuy merger] as a very good event . . . that will move health care forward. You can't have all these different marketplaces . . . [Now], instead of different companies writing different interfaces, we have one company writing all of them. The acquisition

of Medibuy will eliminate some competition, but that might be a good thing for the industry. We always said that GHX was a model that could work. It's nonprofit[32] and totally controlled by its members—manufacturers, suppliers, and many providers. So you have a board of people who will make sure that all the issues, all the business problems, will be looked at from several different perspectives.[33]

As Mahoney packed up for the evening to go home, he reviewed the presentation he had created. One slide in his presentation showed GHX's key milestones (see Exhibit 17). In 2000, GHX had started as a team of "on-loan" employees with a vision and Guiding Principles. By early 2003, the company was well positioned to become the leading online marketplace for the health care industry. The next phase of the company's evolution would be challenging, but Mahoney believed that GHX had the capabilities and drive to move to the next level. But, he still admitted to some sleepless nights. "What keeps me up at night?" he said:

> Successful integration of Medibuy is central to our ability to stabilize our operations and achieve critical mass. It is also necessary to achieve our customer satisfaction goals. Finally, we can't move forward with our value-added offerings until we have the platform in place. We've committed to an aggressive 90-day transition schedule and to ensuring that the transition will not impact our customers. The technical challenge is huge, but the organizational and cultural challenges are even bigger. We have a dedicated team in place that can "cross train" each other on all aspects of the technology. The team is experienced with the technology and with projects of this size. We have developed a clear and detailed project plan with measurable goals, and the senior executives and team review progress daily. Clearly this is our most strategic and highly visible project. If it takes

---

[32] As mentioned earlier, technically, GHX was structured as a Limited Liability Corporation that had a clause in its L.L.C. Agreement that stated it did not intend to register for an IPO. Its Guiding Principles provided that it would only implement pricing and business models designed to generate revenues sufficient to cover its operating and capital needs.

[33] "GHX Is on a Roll," *Repertoire Magazine*, February 2003.

longer or costs more, we won't be able to meet our financial commitments for the year and will slow down our momentum at gaining critical mass and delivering value-added offerings.

But, even while I devote tremendous energy and focus to the merger integration, I also find myself worrying about how long it will take and the level of resources that will be needed to build critical mass in Europe. Europe is key to the growth strategy for some of our large investor suppliers. They would like us to move faster to connect to European health care providers. Other investors want us to concentrate on dominating U.S. markets for now. Our budget is tight and we don't have the money to pour into Europe right now. We've been successful to date because we were able to combine strong financial discipline and controls with the creativity and flexibility of a start-up.

Clearly, 2003 should be another exciting year!

EXHIBIT 15   **GHX (post Medibuy acquisition) and Neoforma Comparison**

Source: GHX Company Records, Neoforma, 10K, 2002.

	Neoforma		GHX	
	2002A	**2003E**	**2002A**	**2003E**
Investor-related revenues	69.5	70.0	37.7	39.0
Third-party revenues	4.3	30.0	1.8	7.0
Total revenue* ($M)	73.9	100.0	39.5	46.0
Operating expenses ($M)	73.7	65.0	53.5	42.0
GHX/Medibuy integration ($M)				3.5
No. of hospitals integrated to marketplace (U.S.)	639	N/A	1200	1700
No. of suppliers integrated to marketplace (U.S.)	167	N/A	45	65
No. of employees (U.S.)	225	N/A	193	193

*In its 2002 Annual Report, Neoforma stated that $69.5 million of what it had previously considered as revenues were paid by VHA and UHC through the purchase of stock. As a result, the company restated its revenue to reflect third-party revenues of $4.3 million.

EXHIBIT 16 **GHX Evolution**

Source: Company records.

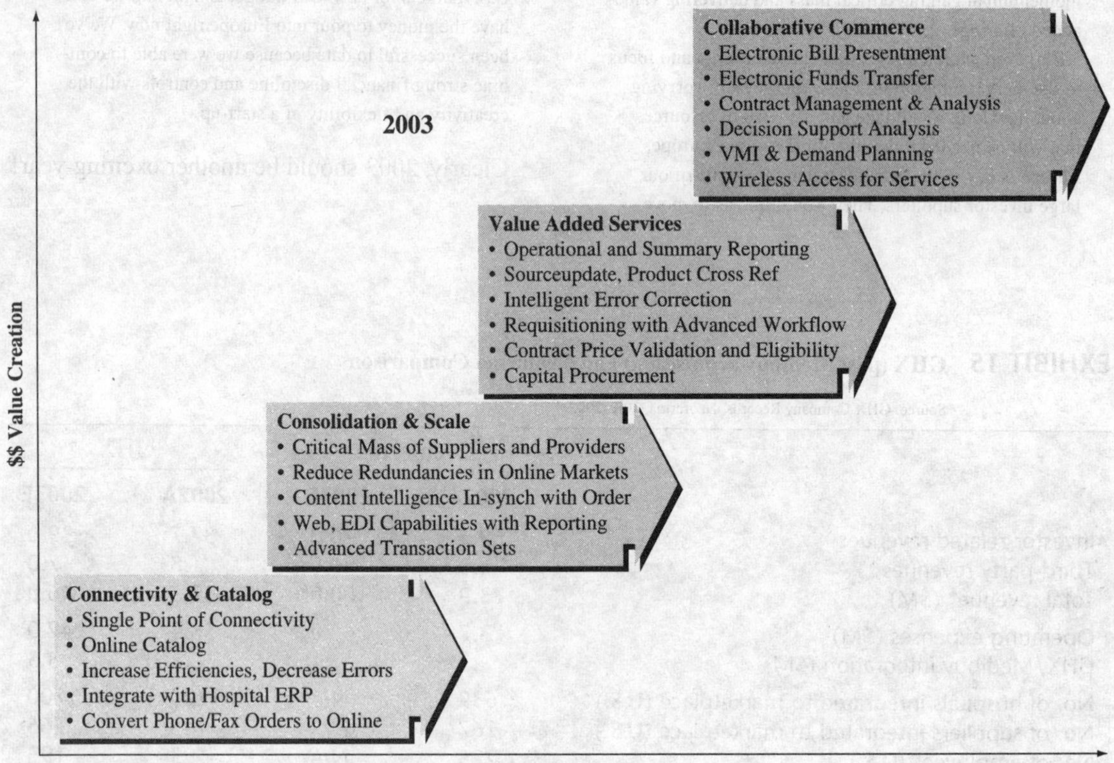

2003

$$ Value Creation

Connectivity & Catalog
- Single Point of Connectivity
- Online Catalog
- Increase Efficiencies, Decrease Errors
- Integrate with Hospital ERP
- Convert Phone/Fax Orders to Online

Consolidation & Scale
- Critical Mass of Suppliers and Providers
- Reduce Redundancies in Online Markets
- Content Intelligence In-synch with Order
- Web, EDI Capabilities with Reporting
- Advanced Transaction Sets

Value Added Services
- Operational and Summary Reporting
- Sourceupdate, Product Cross Ref
- Intelligent Error Correction
- Requisitioning with Advanced Workflow
- Contract Price Validation and Eligibility
- Capital Procurement

Collaborative Commerce
- Electronic Bill Presentment
- Electronic Funds Transfer
- Contract Management & Analysis
- Decision Support Analysis
- VMI & Demand Planning
- Wireless Access for Services

EXHIBIT 17 Key Milestones in the Company's History

Source: Company records.

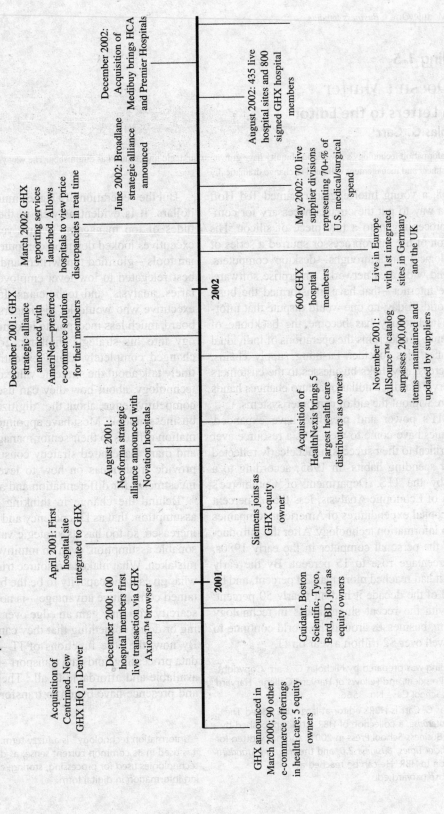

Acquisition of Centrimed. New GHX HQ in Denver

GHX announced in March 2000; 90 other e-commerce offerings in health care; 5 equity owners

December 2000: 100 hospital members first live transaction via GHX Axiom™ browser

Guidant, Boston Scientific, Tyco, Bard, BD, join as equity owners

2001

April 2001: First hospital site integrated to GHX

August 2001: Neoforma strategic alliance announced with Novation hospitals

Siemens joins as GHX equity owner

Acquisition of HealthNexis brings 5 largest health care distributors as owners

December 2001: GHX strategic alliance announced with AmeriNet—preferred e-commerce solution for their members

November 2001: AllSource™ catalog surpasses 200,000 items—maintained and updated by suppliers

2002

March 2002: GHX reporting services launched. Allows hospitals to view price discrepancies in real time

600 GHX hospital members

Live in Europe with 1st integrated sites in Germany and the UK

June 2002: Broadlane strategic alliance announced

May 2002: 70 live supplier divisions representing 70+% of U.S. medical/surgical spend

December 2002: Acquisition of Medibuy brings HCA and Premier Hospitals

August 2002: 435 live hospital sites and 800 signed GHX hospital members

Reading 1-5

IT Doesn't Matter

With Letters to the Editor

Nicholas G. Carr[1]

As information technology's power and ubiquity have grown, its strategic importance has diminished. The way you approach IT investment and management will need to change dramatically.

In 1968, a young Intel engineer named Ted Hoff found a way to put the circuits necessary for computer processing onto a tiny piece of silicon. His invention of the microprocessor spurred a series of technological breakthroughs—desktop computers, local and wide area networks, enterprise software, and the Internet—that have transformed the business world. Today, no one would dispute that information technology has become the backbone of commerce. It underpins the operations of individual companies, ties together far-flung supply chains, and, increasingly, links businesses to the customers they serve. Hardly a dollar or a euro changes hands anymore without the aid of computer systems.

As IT's power and presence have expanded, companies have come to view it as a resource ever more critical to their success, a fact clearly reflected in their spending habits. In 1965, according to a study by the U.S. Department of Commerce's Bureau of Economic Analysis, less than 5 percent of the capital expenditures of American companies went to information technology. After the introduction of the personal computer in the early 1980s, that percentage rose to 15 percent. By the early 1990s, it had reached more than 30 percent, and by the end of the decade it had hit nearly 50 percent. Even with the recent sluggishness in technology spending, businesses around the world continue to spend well over $2 trillion a year on IT.

[1] Nicholas G. Carr is HBR's editor-at-large. He edited *The Digital Enterprise,* a collection of HBR articles published by Harvard Business School Press in 2001, and has written for the *Financial Times, Business 2.0,* and the *Industry Standard* in addition to HBR. He can be reached at ncarr@hbsp.harvard.edu.

But the veneration of IT goes much deeper than dollars. It is evident as well in the shifting attitudes of top managers. Twenty years ago, most executives looked down on computers as proletarian tools—glorified typewriters and calculators—best relegated to low-level employees like secretaries, analysts, and technicians. It was the rare executive who would let his fingers touch a keyboard, much less incorporate information technology into his strategic thinking. Today, that has changed completely. Chief executives now routinely talk about the strategic value of information technology, about how they can use IT to gain a competitive edge, about the "digitization" of their business models. Most have appointed chief information officers to their senior management teams, and many have hired strategy consulting firms to provide fresh ideas on how to leverage their IT investments for differentiation and advantage.

Behind the change in thinking lies a simple assumption: that as IT's potency and ubiquity have increased, so too has its strategic value. It's a reasonable assumption, even an intuitive one. But it's mistaken. What makes a resource truly strategic—what gives it the capacity to be the basis for a sustained competitive advantage—is not ubiquity but scarcity. You only gain an edge over rivals by having or doing something that they can't have or do. By now, the core functions of IT—data storage, data processing, and data transport—have become available and affordable to all.[2] Their very power and presence have begun to transform them from

[2] "Information technology" is a fuzzy term. In this article, it is used in its common current sense, as denoting the technologies used for processing, storing, and transporting information in digital form.

potentially strategic resources into commodity factors of production. They are becoming costs of doing business that must be paid by all but provide distinction to none.

IT is best seen as the latest in a series of broadly adopted technologies that have reshaped industry over the past two centuries—from the steam engine and the railroad to the telegraph and the telephone to the electric generator and the internal combustion engine. For a brief period, as they were being built into the infrastructure of commerce, all these technologies opened opportunities for forward-looking companies to gain real advantages. But as their availability increased and their cost decreased—as they became ubiquitous—they became commodity inputs. From a strategic standpoint, they became invisible; they no longer mattered. That is exactly what is happening to information technology today, and the implications for corporate IT management are profound.

Vanishing Advantage

Many commentators have drawn parallels between the expansion of IT, particularly the Internet, and the rollouts of earlier technologies. Most of the comparisons, though, have focused on either the investment pattern associated with the technologies—the boom-to-bust cycle—or the technologies' roles in reshaping the operations of entire industries or even economies. Little has been said about the way the technologies influence, or fail to influence, competition at the firm level. Yet it is here that history offers some of its most important lessons to managers.

A distinction needs to be made between proprietary technologies and what might be called infrastructural technologies. Proprietary technologies can be owned, actually or effectively, by a single company. A pharmaceutical firm, for example, may hold a patent on a particular compound that serves as the basis for a family of drugs. An industrial manufacturer may discover an innovative way to employ a process technology that competitors find hard to replicate. A company that produces consumer goods may acquire exclusive rights to a new packaging material that gives its product a longer shelf life than competing brands. As long as they remain protected, proprietary technologies can be the foundations for long-term strategic advantages, enabling companies to reap higher profits than their rivals.

Infrastructural technologies, in contrast, offer far more value when shared than when used in isolation. Imagine yourself in the early nineteenth century, and suppose that one manufacturing company held the rights to all the technology required to create a railroad. If it wanted to, that company could just build proprietary lines between its suppliers, its factories, and its distributors and run its own locomotives and railcars on the tracks. And it might well operate more efficiently as a result. But, for the broader economy, the value produced by such an arrangement would be trivial compared with the value that would be produced by building an open rail network connecting many companies and many buyers. The characteristics and economics of infrastructural technologies, whether railroads or telegraph lines or power generators, make it inevitable that they will be broadly shared—that they will become part of the general business infrastructure.

In the earliest phases of its buildout, however, an infrastructural technology can take the form of a proprietary technology. As long as access to the technology is restricted—through physical limitations, intellectual property rights, high costs, or a lack of standards—a company can use it to gain advantages over rivals. Consider the period between the construction of the first electric power stations, around 1880, and the wiring of the electric grid early in the twentieth century. Electricity remained a scarce resource during this time, and those manufacturers able to tap into it—by, for example, building their plants near generating stations—often gained an important edge. It was no coincidence that the largest U.S. manufacturer of nuts and bolts at the turn of the century, Plumb, Burdict, and Barnard, located its factory near Niagara Falls in New York, the site of one of the earliest large-scale hydroelectric power plants.

Companies can also steal a march on their competitors by having superior insight into the use of a new technology. The introduction of electric power again provides a good example. Until the end of the nineteenth century, most manufacturers relied on water pressure or steam to operate their machinery. Power in those days came from a single, fixed source—a waterwheel at the side of a mill, for instance—and required an elaborate system of pulleys and gears to distribute it to individual workstations throughout the plant. When electric generators first became available, many manufacturers simply adopted them as a replacement single-point source, using them to power the existing system of pulleys and gears. Smart manufacturers, however, saw that one of the great advantages of electric power is that it is easily distributable—that it can be brought directly to workstations. By wiring their plants and installing electric motors in their machines, they were able to dispense with the cumbersome, inflexible, and costly gearing systems, gaining an important efficiency advantage over their slower-moving competitors.

In addition to enabling new, more efficient operating methods, infrastructural technologies often lead to broader market changes. Here, too, a company that sees what's coming can gain a step on myopic rivals. In the mid-1800s, when America started to lay down rail lines in earnest, it was already possible to transport goods over long distances—hundreds of steamships plied the country's rivers. Businessmen probably assumed that rail transport would essentially follow the steamship model, with some incremental enhancements. In fact, the greater speed, capacity, and reach of the railroads fundamentally changed the structure of American industry. It suddenly became economical to ship finished products, rather than just raw materials and industrial components, over great distances, and the mass consumer market came into being. Companies that were quick to recognize the broader opportunity rushed to build large-scale, mass-production factories. The resulting economies of scale allowed them to crush the small, local plants that until then had dominated manufacturing.

The trap that executives often fall into, however, is assuming that opportunities for advantage will be available indefinitely. In actuality, the window for gaining advantage from an infrastructural technology is open only briefly. When the technology's commercial potential begins to be broadly appreciated, huge amounts of cash are inevitably invested in it, and its buildout proceeds with extreme speed. Railroad tracks, telegraph wires, power lines—all were laid or strung in a frenzy of activity (a frenzy so intense in the case of rail lines that it cost hundreds of laborers their lives). In the 30 years between 1846 and 1876, reports Eric Hobsbawm in *The Age of Capital,* the world's total rail trackage increased from 17,424 kilometers to 309,641 kilometers. During this same period, total steamship tonnage also exploded, from 139,973 to 3,293,072 tons. The telegraph system spread even more swiftly. In Continental Europe, there were just 2,000 miles of telegraph wires in 1849; 20 years later, there were 110,000. The pattern continued with electrical power. The number of central stations operated by utilities grew from 468 in 1889 to 4,364 in 1917, and the average capacity of each increased more than tenfold. (For a discussion of the dangers of overinvestment, see "Too Much of a Good Thing.")

By the end of the buildout phase, the opportunities for individual advantage are largely gone. The rush to invest leads to more competition, greater capacity, and falling prices, making the technology broadly accessible and affordable. At the same time, the buildout forces users to adopt universal technical standards, rendering proprietary systems obsolete. Even the way the technology is used begins to become standardized, as best practices come to be widely understood and emulated. Often, in fact, the best practices end up being built into the infrastructure itself; after electrification, for example, all new factories were constructed with many well-distributed power outlets. Both the technology and its modes of use become, in effect, commoditized. The only meaningful advantage most companies can hope to gain from an infrastructural technology after its buildout is a cost advantage—and even that tends to be very hard to sustain.

That's not to say that infrastructural technologies don't continue to influence competition. They do, but their influence is felt at the macroeconomic level, not at the level of the individual company. If a particular country, for instance, lags in installing the technology—whether it's a national rail network, a power grid, or a communication infrastructure—its domestic industries will suffer heavily. Similarly, if an industry lags in harnessing the power of the technology, it will be vulnerable to displacement. As always, a company's fate is tied to broader forces affecting its region and its industry. The point is, however, that the technology's potential for differentiating one company from the pack—its strategic potential—inexorably declines as it becomes accessible and affordable to all.

The Commoditization of IT

Although more complex and malleable than its predecessors, IT has all the hallmarks of an infrastructural technology. In fact, its mix of characteristics guarantees particularly rapid commoditization. IT is, first of all, a transport mechanism—it carries digital information just as railroads carry goods and power grids carry electricity. And like any transport mechanism, it is far more valuable when shared than when used in isolation. The history of IT in business has been a history of increased interconnectivity and interoperability, from mainframe time-sharing to minicomputer-based local area networks to broader Ethernet networks and on to the Internet. Each stage in that progression has involved greater standardization of the technology and, at least recently, greater homogenization of its functionality. For most business applications today, the benefits of customization would be overwhelmed by the costs of isolation.

IT is also highly replicable. Indeed, it is hard to imagine a more perfect commodity than a byte of data—endlessly and perfectly reproducible at virtually no cost. The near-infinite scalability of many IT functions, when combined with technical standardization, dooms most proprietary applications to economic obsolescence. Why write your own application for word processing or e-mail or, for that matter, supply-chain management when you can buy a ready-made, state-of-the-art application

for a fraction of the cost? But it's not just the software that is replicable. Because most business activities and processes have come to be embedded in software, they become replicable, too. When companies buy a generic application, they buy a generic process as well. Both the cost savings and the interoperability benefits make the sacrifice of distinctiveness unavoidable.

The arrival of the Internet has accelerated the commoditization of IT by providing a perfect delivery channel for generic applications. More and more, companies will fulfill their IT requirements simply by purchasing fee-based "Web services" from third parties—similar to the way they currently buy electric power or telecommunications services. Most of the major business-technology vendors, from Microsoft to IBM, are trying to position themselves as IT utilities, companies that will control the provision of a diverse range of business applications over what is now called, tellingly, "the grid." Again, the upshot is ever greater homogenization of IT capabilities, as more companies replace customized applications with generic ones. (For more on the challenges facing IT companies, see "What about the Vendors?")

Finally, and for all the reasons already discussed, IT is subject to rapid price deflation. When Gordon Moore made his famously prescient assertion that the density of circuits on a computer chip would double every two years, he was making a prediction about the coming explosion in processing power. But he was also making a prediction about the coming free fall in the price of computer functionality. The cost of processing power has dropped relentlessly, from $480 per million instructions per second (MIPS) in 1978 to $50 per MIPS in 1985 to $4 per MIPS in 1995, a trend that continues unabated. Similar declines have occurred in the cost of data storage and transmission. The rapidly increasing affordability of IT functionality has not only democratized the computer revolution, it has destroyed one of the most important potential barriers to competitors. Even the most cutting-edge IT capabilities quickly become available to all.

Too Much of a Good Thing

As many experts have pointed out, the overinvestment in information technology in the 1990s echoes the overinvestment in railroads in the 1860s. In both cases, companies and individuals, dazzled by the seemingly unlimited commercial possibilities of the technologies, threw large quantities of money away on half-baked businesses and products. Even worse, the flood of capital led to enormous overcapacity, devastating entire industries.

We can only hope that the analogy ends there. The mid-nineteenth-century boom in railroads (and the closely related technologies of the steam engine and the telegraph) helped produce not only widespread industrial overcapacity but a surge in productivity. The combination set the stage for two solid decades of deflation. Although worldwide economic production continued to grow strongly between the mid-1870s and the mid-1890s, prices collapsed—in England, the dominant economic power of the time, price levels dropped 40 percent. In turn, business profits evaporated. Companies watched the value of their products erode while they were in the very process of making them. As the first worldwide depression took hold, economic malaise covered much of the globe. "Optimism about a future of indefinite progress gave way to uncertainty and a sense of agony," wrote historian D. S. Landes.

It's a very different world today, of course, and it would be dangerous to assume that history will repeat itself. But with companies struggling to boost profits and the entire world economy flirting with deflation, it would also be dangerous to assume it can't.

It's no surprise, given these characteristics, that IT's evolution has closely mirrored that of earlier infrastructural technologies. Its buildout has been every bit as breathtaking as that of the railroads (albeit with considerably fewer fatalities). Consider some statistics. During the last quarter of the twentieth century, the computational power of a microprocessor increased by a factor of 66,000. In the dozen years from 1989 to 2001, the number of host computers connected to the Internet grew from 80,000 to more than 125 million. Over the last ten years, the number of sites on the World Wide Web has grown from zero to nearly 40 million. And since the 1980s, more than 280 million miles of fiber-optic cable have been installed—enough, as *BusinessWeek* recently noted, to "circle the earth 11,320 times." (See the exhibit "The Sprint to Commoditization.")

As with earlier infrastructural technologies, IT provided forward-looking companies many opportunities for competitive advantage early in its buildout, when it could still be "owned" like a proprietary technology. A classic example is American Hospital Supply. A leading distributor of medical supplies, AHS introduced in 1976 an innovative system called Analytic Systems Automated Purchasing, or ASAP, that enabled hospitals to order goods electronically. Developed in-house, the innovative system used proprietary software running on a mainframe computer, and hospital purchasing agents accessed it through terminals at their sites. Because more efficient ordering enabled hospitals to reduce their inventories—and thus their costs—customers were quick to embrace the system. And because it was proprietary to AHS, it effectively locked out competitors. For several years, in fact, AHS was the only distributor offering electronic ordering, a competitive advantage that led to years of superior financial results. From 1978 to 1983, AHS's sales and profits rose at annual rates of 13 percent and 18 percent, respectively—well above industry averages.

AHS gained a true competitive advantage by capitalizing on characteristics of infrastructural technologies that are common in the early stages of their buildouts, in particular their high cost and lack of standardization. Within a decade, however, those barriers to competition were crumbling. The arrival of personal computers and packaged software, together with the emergence of networking standards, was rendering proprietary communication systems unattractive to their users and

What about the Vendors?

Just a few months ago, at the 2003 World Economic Forum in Davos, Switzerland, Bill Joy, the chief scientist and cofounder of Sun Microsystems, posed what for him must have been a painful question: "What if the reality is that people have already bought most of the stuff they want to own?" The people he was talking about are, of course, businesspeople, and the stuff is information technology. With the end of the great buildout of the commercial IT infrastructure apparently at hand, Joy's question is one that all IT vendors should be asking themselves. There is good reason to believe that companies' existing IT capabilities are largely sufficient for their needs and, hence, that the recent and widespread sluggishness in IT demand is as much a structural as a cyclical phenomenon.

Even if that's true, the picture may not be as bleak as it seems for vendors, at least those with the foresight and skill to adapt to the new environment. The importance of infrastructural technologies to the day-to-day operations of business means that they continue to absorb large amounts of corporate cash long after they have become commodities—indefinitely, in many cases. Virtually all companies today continue to spend heavily on electricity and phone service, for example, and many manufacturers continue to spend a lot on rail transport. Moreover, the standardized nature of infrastructural technologies often leads to the establishment of lucrative monopolies and oligopolies.

Many technology vendors are already repositioning themselves and their products in response to the changes in the market. Microsoft's push to turn its Office software suite from a packaged good into an annual subscription service is a tacit acknowledgment that companies are losing their need—and their appetite—for constant upgrades. Dell has succeeded by exploiting the commoditization of the PC market and is now extending that strategy to servers, storage, and even services. (Michael Dell's essential genius has always been his unsentimental trust in the commoditization of information technology.) And many of the major suppliers of corporate IT, including Microsoft, IBM, Sun, and Oracle, are battling to position themselves as dominant suppliers of "Web services"—to turn themselves, in effect, into utilities. This war for scale, combined with the continuing transformation of IT into a commodity, will lead to the further consolidation of many sectors of the IT industry. The winners will do very well; the losers will be gone.

uneconomical to their owners. Indeed, in an ironic, if predictable, twist, the closed nature and outdated technology of AHS's system turned it from an asset to a liability. By the dawn of the 1990s, after AHS had merged with Baxter Travenol to form Baxter International, the company's senior executives had come to view ASAP as "a millstone around their necks," according to a Harvard Business School case study.

Myriad other companies have gained important advantages through the innovative deployment of IT. Some, like American Airlines with its SABRE reservation system, Federal Express with its package-tracking system, and Mobil Oil with its automated Speedpass payment system, used IT to gain particular operating or marketing advantages—to leapfrog the competition in one process or activity. Others, like Reuters with its 1970s financial information network or, more recently, eBay with its Internet auctions, had superior insight into the way IT would fundamentally change an industry and were able to stake out commanding positions. In a few cases, the dominance companies gained through IT innovation conferred additional advantages, such as scale economies and brand recognition, that have proved more durable than the original technological edge. Wal-Mart and Dell Computer are renowned examples of firms that have been able to turn temporary technological advantages into enduring positioning advantages.

But the opportunities for gaining IT-based advantages are already dwindling. Best practices are now quickly built into software or otherwise replicated. And as for IT-spurred industry transformations, most of the ones that are going to happen have likely already happened or are in the process of happening. Industries and markets will continue to evolve, of course, and some will undergo fundamental changes—the future of the music business, for example, continues to be in doubt. But history shows that the power of an infrastructural technology to transform industries always diminishes as its buildout nears completion.

While no one can say precisely when the buildout of an infrastructural technology has concluded, there are many signs that the IT buildout is much closer to its end than its beginning. First, IT's power is outstripping most of the business needs it fulfills. Second, the price of essential IT functionality has dropped to the point where it is more or less affordable to all. Third, the capacity of the universal distribution network (the Internet) has caught up with demand—indeed, we already have considerably more fiber-optic capacity than we need. Fourth, IT vendors are rushing to position themselves as commodity suppliers or even as utilities. Finally, and most definitively, the investment bubble has burst, which historically has been a clear indication that an infrastructural technology is reaching the end of its buildout. A few companies may still be able to wrest advantages from highly specialized applications that don't offer strong economic incentives for replication, but those firms will be the exceptions that prove the rule.

At the close of the 1990s, when Internet hype was at full boil, technologists offered grand visions of an emerging "digital future." It may well be that, in terms of business strategy at least, the future has already arrived.

From Offense to Defense

So what should companies do? From a practical standpoint, the most important lesson to be learned from earlier infrastructural technologies may be this: When a resource becomes essential to competition but inconsequential to strategy, the risks it creates become more important than the advantages it provides. Think of electricity. Today, no company builds its business strategy around its electricity usage, but even a brief lapse in supply can be devastating (as some California businesses discovered during the energy crisis of 2000). The operational risks associated with IT are many—technical glitches, obsolescence, service outages, unreliable vendors or partners, security breaches, even terrorism—and some have become magnified as companies have moved from tightly controlled, proprietary systems to open, shared ones. Today, an IT disruption can paralyze a company's ability to make its products, deliver its services, and connect with its customers, not to mention foul its reputation. Yet few companies have done a thorough job of identifying and tempering their vulnerabilities. Worrying about what might go wrong may not be as glamorous a job as speculating about the future, but it is a more essential job right now. (See "New Rules for IT Management.")

In the long run, though, the greatest IT risk facing most companies is more prosaic than a catastrophe. It is, simply, overspending. IT may be a commodity, and its costs may fall rapidly enough to ensure that any new capabilities are quickly shared, but the very fact that it is entwined with so many business functions means that it will continue to consume a large portion of corporate spending. For most companies, just staying in business will require big outlays for IT. What's important—and this holds true for any commodity input—is to be able to separate essential investments from ones that are discretionary, unnecessary, or even counterproductive.

At a high level, stronger cost management requires more rigor in evaluating expected returns from systems investments, more creativity in exploring simpler and cheaper alternatives, and a greater openness to outsourcing and other partnerships. But most companies can also reap significant savings by simply cutting out waste. Personal computers are a good example. Every year, businesses purchase more than 100 million PCs, most of which replace older models. Yet the vast majority of workers who use PCs rely on only a few simple applications—word processing, spreadsheets, e-mail, and Web browsing. These applications have been technologically mature for years; they require only a fraction of the computing power provided by today's microprocessors. Nevertheless, companies continue to roll out across-the-board hardware and software upgrades.

The Sprint to Commoditization

One of the most salient characteristics of infrastructural technologies is the rapidity of their installation. Spurred by massive investment, capacity soon skyrockets, leading to falling prices and, quickly, commoditization.

Sources: railways: Eric Hobsbawm, *The Age of Capital* (Vintage, 1996); electric power: Richard B. Duboff, *Electric Power in Manufacturing, 1889–1958* (Arno, 1979); Internet hosts: Robert H. Zakon, *Hobbes' Internet Timeline* (www.zakon.org/robert/internet/timeline/).

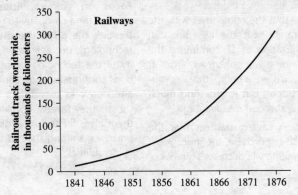

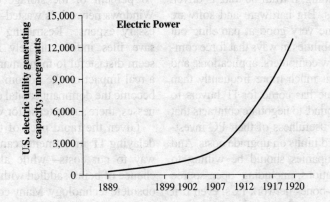

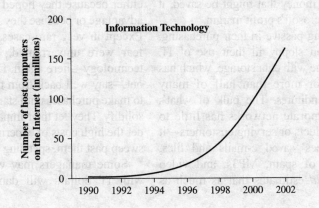

New Rules for IT Management

With the opportunities for gaining strategic advantage from information technology rapidly disappearing, many companies will want to take a hard look at how they invest in IT and manage their systems. As a starting point, here are three guidelines for the future:

Spend less. Studies show that the companies with the biggest IT investments rarely post the best financial results. As the commoditization of IT continues, the penalties for wasteful spending will only grow larger. It is getting much harder to achieve a competitive advantage through an IT investment, but it is getting much easier to put your business at a cost disadvantage.

Follow, don't lead. Moore's Law guarantees that the longer you wait to make an IT purchase, the more you'll get for your money. And waiting will decrease your risk of buying something technologically flawed or doomed to rapid obsolescence. In some cases, being on the cutting edge makes sense. But those cases are becoming rarer and rarer as IT capabilities become more homogenized.

Focus on vulnerabilities, not opportunities. It's unusual for a company to gain a competitive advantage through the distinctive use of a mature infrastructural technology, but even a brief disruption in the availability of the technology can be devastating. As corporations continue to cede control over their IT applications and networks to vendors and other third parties, the threats they face will proliferate. They need to prepare themselves for technical glitches, outages, and security breaches, shifting their attention from opportunities to vulnerabilities.

Much of that spending, if truth be told, is driven by vendors' strategies. Big hardware and software suppliers have become very good at parceling out new features and capabilities in ways that force companies into buying new computers, applications, and networking equipment much more frequently than they need to. The time has come for IT buyers to throw their weight around, to negotiate contracts that ensure the long-term usefulness of their PC investments and impose hard limits on upgrade costs. And if vendors balk, companies should be willing to explore cheaper solutions, including open-source applications and bare-bones network PCs, even if it means sacrificing features. If a company needs evidence of the kind of money that might be saved, it need only look at Microsoft's profit margin.

In addition to being passive in their purchasing, companies have been sloppy in their use of IT. That's particularly true with data storage, which has come to account for more than half of many companies' IT expenditures. The bulk of what's being stored on corporate networks has little to do with making products or serving customers—it consists of employees' saved e-mails and files, including terabytes of spam, MP3s, and video clips. *Computerworld* estimates that as much as 70 percent of the storage capacity of a typical Windows network is wasted—an enormous unnecessary expense. Restricting employees' ability to save files indiscriminately and indefinitely may seem distasteful to many managers, but it can have a real impact on the bottom line. Now that IT has become the dominant capital expense for most businesses, there's no excuse for waste and sloppiness.

Given the rapid pace of technology's advance, delaying IT investments can be another powerful way to cut costs—while also reducing a firm's chance of being saddled with buggy or soon-to-be-obsolete technology. Many companies, particularly during the 1990s, rushed their IT investments either because they hoped to capture a first-mover advantage or because they feared being left behind. Except in very rare cases, both the hope and the fear were unwarranted. The smartest users of technology—here again, Dell and Wal-Mart stand out—stay well back from the cutting edge, waiting to make purchases until standards and best practices solidify. They let their impatient competitors shoulder the high costs of experimentation, and then they sweep past them, spending less and getting more.

Some managers may worry that being stingy with IT dollars will damage their competitive positions. But studies of corporate IT spending consistently show that greater expenditures rarely translate into superior financial results. In fact, the opposite is usually true. In 2002, the consulting firm Alinean compared the IT expenditures and the financial results of 7,500 large U.S. companies and discovered that the top performers tended to be among the most tightfisted. The 25 companies that delivered the highest economic returns, for example, spent on average just 0.8 percent of their revenues on IT, while the typical company spent 3.7 percent. A recent study by Forrester Research showed, similarly, that the most lavish spenders on IT rarely post the best results. Even Oracle's Larry Ellison, one of the great technology salesmen, admitted in a recent interview that "most compa-

nies spend too much [on IT] and get very little in return." As the opportunities for IT-based advantage continue to narrow, the penalties for overspending will only grow.

IT management should, frankly, become boring. The key to success, for the vast majority of companies, is no longer to seek advantage aggressively but to manage costs and risks meticulously. If, like many executives, you've begun to take a more defensive posture toward IT in the last two years, spending more frugally and thinking more pragmatically, you're already on the right course. The challenge will be to maintain that discipline when the business cycle strengthens and the chorus of hype about IT's strategic value rises anew.

Letters to the Editor

Does IT Matter? An HBR Debate

Every magazine has an ideal, or an idealized, reader. For *Harvard Business Review,* he or she is an executive of uncommon intelligence and curiosity: the brightest CEO you know or can imagine, perhaps. We like to pretend that our ideal reader has chartered us to prepare a briefing every month. On the agenda, we've been told, should be three kinds of items.

First, our reader says, bring me important new ideas, research, or insights: "Boss, here's something you should know."

Second, bring me important eternal truths, rediscovered and refreshed: "Boss, here's something you shouldn't forget."

Third, bring me into the picture about important issues and arguments: "Boss, here's something you will want to know about."

New ideas, truths, and disputes: When we do our job well, HBR is a forum where you get some of each, and all of it is important. Nicholas G. Carr's "IT Doesn't Matter," published in the May 2003 issue, falls into the third category. It takes one side of an argument that's undeniably urgent and important to business leaders.

In 2000, nearly half of U.S. corporate capital spending went to information technology. Then the spending collapsed and the NASDAQ with it, and in every boardroom—and in every technology company—people began to wonder: What happened? What was that spending about? What's changed? What has not? And what do we do now? What is our technology strategy, and how does it affect our corporate strategy?

Forcefully, Carr argues that investments in IT, while profoundly important, are less and less likely to deliver a competitive edge to an individual company. "No one would dispute that information technology has become the backbone of commerce," Carr says. "The point is, however, that the technology's potential for differentiating one company from the pack—its strategic potential—inexorably diminishes as it becomes accessible and affordable to all."

Unsurprisingly, "IT Doesn't Matter" has generated an enormous amount of controversy. Our ideal reader wants that give-and-take, argument and counterargument, the better to understand the issues. Always in such cases, people are more likely to write to us when they disagree with an article's point of view than when they agree with it. Always in such cases, a few people mistake the argument. (In this instance, the most common misperception is that the article says that IT is dead and that it will not continue to be a source of dramatic, even transformational change. It doesn't say that. Instead, it says the odds are that the benefits of such changes will inure to whole industries rather than any one competitor. Instead of seeking advantage through technology, Carr argues, companies should manage IT defensively—watching costs and avoiding risks.)

And always in such cases, some very smart, thoughtful people present urgent, cogent, and forceful challenges to the article's conclusions.

We have received so many thoughtful letters that we have decided to publish them here, together with Carr's reply. That decision reflects—among other things—one way in which the ubiquity of IT has created new opportunities for us and for all publishers to interact with readers. It also reflects HBR's continuing commitment to offer readers a forum full of thoughtful voices, bringing you what's newly learned, what's fiercely argued, and what truly matters.

Thomas A. Stewart
Editor

Letter from John Seely Brown and John Hagel III

John Seely Brown, *Former Chief Scientist, Xerox, Palo Alto, California*
John Hagel III, *Management Consultant and Author, Burlingame, California*

Nicholas Carr's article "IT Doesn't Matter" (May 2003) is an important, perhaps even seminal, piece. It effectively captures the zeitgeist among senior managers of large enterprises and gives eloquent voice to the backlash that has swept through management suites regarding IT's business value.

As Carr's article says, businesses have overestimated the strategic value of IT. They have significantly overspent on technology in the

quest for business value. They need to manage large portions of their IT infrastructures more rigorously to reduce capital investment requirements and operating costs. As companies become more dependent on IT platforms for their day-to-day operations, they must focus on potential vulnerabilities and more aggressively manage for reliability and security. But such ideas are not inconsistent with the view that IT remains a profound catalyst for the creation of strategic differentiation.

In capturing today's management mood so effectively, Carr provides a valuable service. And yet his article is potentially dangerous, for it appears to endorse the notion that businesses should manage IT as a commodity input because the opportunities for strategic differentiation with IT have become so scarce. By giving voice to this perspective and making it so compelling, Carr is likely to perpetuate a misguided view.

The choice of article title is even more unfortunate. It may grab readers' attention, but it is misleading: Carr is not claiming that IT does not matter; rather, his main assertion is that IT is diminishing as a source of strategic differentiation. Unfortunately, given today's business climate, many readers will remember the article's title and forget its nuance.

The lesson to be learned from the past several decades is that IT by itself rarely, if ever, confers strategic differentiation. Yet, IT is inherently strategic because of its indirect effects—it creates possibilities and options that did not exist before. Companies that see, and act on, these possibilities before others do will continue to differentiate themselves in the marketplace and reap economic rewards. IT may become ubiquitous, but the insight required to harness its potential will not be so evenly distributed. Therein lies the opportunity for significant strategic advantage.

The experiences of the past several decades suggest three broad lessons regarding IT:

Extracting value from IT requires innovations in business practices. Companies that mechanically insert IT into their businesses without changing their practices for exploiting the new capabilities will only destroy IT's economic value. Unfortunately, all too many companies do this. For that reason, the research findings by Alinean and Forrester—that IT spending rarely correlates with superior financial results—are not surprising.

In October 2001, the McKinsey Global Institute published a study on "U.S. Productivity Growth, 1995–2000." That study was the first disciplined attempt to look at the correlation between IT investments and productivity by industry sector. The results were revealing. The study found a significant positive correlation between IT investments and productivity in only six out of 59 industries. The other 53 sectors, accounting for 70 percent of the economy, in aggregate saw negligible productivity improvements as a result of their IT investments.

Why only six industries? In each of these sectors, one or more companies introduced significant innovations in business practices to leverage their IT capabilities. This set into motion competitive pressures that forced other companies in the sector to implement comparable business practices. The classic example was retailing, where Wal-Mart innovated continuously around new generations of IT. Even as competitors adopted Wal-Mart's practices, the retailing giant focused on the next wave of innovations, preserving a significant productivity advantage (on the order of 40 percent) relative to competitors.

Significant opportunities for innovation continue to occur because advances in IT create possibilities not previously economically available. With few exceptions, companies have tended to think too narrowly about the possibilities. In particular, many companies have become locked into the view that IT can reduce transaction costs but then think of transaction costs as encompassing only the transfer of bits and data from one place to another. Viewed more broadly, transaction costs encompass such challenging business issues as the creation of meaning, the building of trust, and the development and dissemination of knowledge. These dimensions of transaction costs often represent significant bottlenecks to performance improvements and competitive advantage. Companies like Cisco in their e-learning initiatives are just beginning to explore the innovations in business practices required to exploit IT's potential for addressing such business challenges.

Companies also think too narrowly about IT's possibilities when they focus so heavily on business practices within the enterprise. In fact, many opportunities for business-practice innovations extend beyond the walls of the enterprise to include relationships with other companies. Rather than think in narrow transactional terms, as evidenced by the first wave of business-to-business marketplaces, executives would be far better advised to think in terms of opportunities to build long-term relationships with companies possessing complementary assets and capabilities. Companies like Li & Fung, with its orchestration model based on a loosely coupled approach to process management spanning thousands of companies, suggest opportunities for redefining relationships among companies and, in the process, creating significant differentiation.

In short, many executives have started to view IT as a commodity because they have not thought aggressively enough about how IT can bring about new business practices. The differentiation is not in IT itself but in the new practices it enables. IT does indeed matter. Although IT may be ubiquitous and increasingly less expensive, the insight and ability required for it to create economic value are in very short supply. It is far different from commodities like wheat and aluminum, where the processing operations are well understood and the economic advantage lies in being able to source the commodity at lower cost.

IT's economic impact comes from incremental innovations rather than "big bang" initiatives. In highlighting the significant opportunities for new business practices enabled by IT, we do not want to be misinterpreted as advocating big bang efforts to transform companies overnight. If we've learned one thing from the 1990s, it's that big bang, IT-driven initiatives rarely produce expected returns; they are complicated and expensive, take a long time to implement, and are fraught with risk. Rather than create economic value, more often than not they destroy it.

The companies most successful in harnessing IT's power typically proceed in waves of relatively short-term (often 6 to 12 months) operating initiatives designed to test and refine specific innovations in business practices. Changing business practices creates unintended consequences. By "chunking up" innovations in business practices and tying these initiatives to explicit operating performance metrics, management can create tighter feedback loops and accelerate the learning process. If done right, these innovations can also reduce the financial risks by generating near-term returns that can help fund subsequent waves of operating initiatives. Politically, this kind of incremental approach, with its relentless focus on tangible near-term returns, also helps deepen organizational support for new business practices while neutralizing potential opposition.

The strategic impact of IT investments comes from the cumulative effect of sustained initiatives to innovate business practices in the near term. If IT's economic value comes from very tactical near-term initiatives to innovate business practices, aren't we in fact conceding that IT has lost its power to provide strategic differentiation? Aren't we just saying that IT can provide tactical advantage that will be quickly copied by competitors? Far from it. The strategic differentiation emerges over time, based less on the specific innovations in business practices at any point in time and much more on the ability to continually innovate around IT's evolving capabilities.

To understand this point, it is essential to differentiate the characteristics of IT as an infrastructure technology relative to the variety of other infrastructure technologies cited by Carr—steam engines, railroads, electricity, and telephones. In each of those prior areas, the underlying technology burst forth in one relatively concentrated innovation. While the technology's performance continued to improve after it was introduced, the rate of improvement was far more modest and reached a point of diminishing returns much sooner than we have seen in the decades since the introduction of

digital technology. Thus, the ability to continually innovate business practices around these technologies also reached a period of diminishing returns. Another result was that these prior generations of technology produced a dominant design or architecture relatively quickly—for example, the standardization of railway gauges or alternating-current specifications. The emergence of these dominant designs or architectures catalyzed the various industry shakeouts and helped to further standardize the use of these technologies.

IT thus far has followed a very different path. Improvements in processing power, storage capacity, and bandwidth have continued at a rapid and sustained pace. Indeed, these performance improvements have had a multiplicative effect, coming together, for example, to form entirely new ways of storing, distributing, and accessing data. Not only are smart things getting smarter, but this technology is also being used to make dumb things smarter through such extensions as MEMS, RFID, and telematics. IT is also extending its reach to biological organisms, redefining the ways we diagnose, treat, and even design life forms.

This sustained pace and expanding range of digital technology innovation continues to precipitate fundamental new opportunities for thinking about how we organize such technology. We are now on the cusp of a shift to distributed service architectures that will unleash entirely new capabilities at least as significant as the shift from proprietary and centralized mainframe architectures to more distributed client-server architectures. Far from settling down into a dominant design or architecture, IT has crashed through several generations of architectures and continues to generate new ones. In fact, the emerging service-oriented architectures enable a kind of radical incrementalism that transcends what one might expect from simple incrementalism. Coupled with a strategy focused on both short-term wins and long-term goals, this new incrementalism is a source of competitive advantage.

The underlying technology components may be widely and cheaply available, but the skills required to organize them into high-value architectures are still in very short supply, and a new generation of skills must be developed with each new generation of architecture. These new architectures amplify the possibilities enabled by the performance improvements in the underlying technology components.

The gap between IT's potential and business's realization of that potential has not narrowed. Instead, it has steadily widened over the past several decades. This gap creates enormous instability in the business world. Wherever there is so much potential for instability, there is also fertile ground for new strategies.

To further amplify the effect of these performance improvements in terms of real business-practice innovation and to convert tactical advantage into strategic advantage, something else is required. Companies need to align themselves around a long-term view of the challenges and opportunities brought about by IT. Senior managers need a shared but high-level view of the kinds of markets they are likely to be operating in and the kinds of companies they will need to become if they are to continue creating economic value. This long-term view helps to focus and prioritize near-term innovations in business practices, thereby helping to build a sustainable strategic advantage across multiple waves of initiatives. It is exactly this kind of long-term view that guides Dell and Wal-Mart in their ongoing use of IT to create strategic advantage.

Without this view, even the most aggressive near-term incremental initiatives run the risk of becoming dispersed over too many fronts. The continuing performance improvements of IT create far more possibilities than any company can or should pursue. The temptation in this kind of environment is to launch too many initiatives. The result is that few, if any, of the near-term initiatives produce the expected results. Without focusing on the long-term, companies will have difficulty building momentum across multiple waves of operating initiatives. Each new wave responds to the events of the moment rather than driving toward a common destination. The focus remains entirely on near-term initiatives rather than on

building a more sustained capability to innovate and leverage IT's new capabilities. Short-term tactical advantage remains just that—tactical and transitory. In such a world, it is easy to see why management could come to believe that IT does not produce significant strategic differentiation.

Paradoxically, technology vendors themselves are somewhat responsible for the widespread belief that IT doesn't produce significant strategic differentiation. For too long, they have built their businesses around big bang, IT-centric selling propositions. Rather than help companies understand that IT is only a tool, technology vendors have tended to present it as a panacea. "Buy this technology and all your problems will be solved." It is a seductive proposition. Rather than focusing on the enormous challenge of innovating in business practices and creating the discipline required to generate economic value from these innovations, vendors have convinced many companies that signing a purchase order would deliver the required value. They even managed to convince companies, for a while, that they needed to buy a lot of the technology because the only way to stay competitive was through massive IT implementations. When the anticipated results didn't materialize, the backlash began to gather force in executive suites. Executives swing from one extreme to the other. If IT doesn't solve all their business problems, then it must not matter, at least in terms of strategic value. We still need it to run our business, but let's buy as little as we can and squeeze the vendors as much as we can.

It has never been true that IT matters in isolation. It only matters in the context of a concerted effort to innovate based on new possibilities and opportunities created by the technology. Then it matters—and will continue to—a lot.

That's a far more difficult message for IT vendors to communicate to customers. It's an even more difficult message for the vendors to execute against. It means changing their economic model, selling model, organizational model, and product strategies in fundamental and very painful ways. Yet, the alternative for technology vendors is to cope with the growing belief that IT really doesn't matter, at least in terms of its potential for strategic differentiation. In the end, that will be a far more painful world for them to confront. It will also be a tragedy for businesses that continue to miss the opportunities IT creates.

John Seely Brown
and John Hagel III

Letter from F. Warren McFarlan and Richard L. Nolan

F. Warren McFarlan, *Albert H. Gordon Professor of Business Administration, Harvard Business School, Boston*
Richard L. Nolan, *William Barclay Harding Professor of Business Administration, Harvard Business School, Boston*

In no other area is it more important to have a sense of what you *don't* know than it is in IT management. The most dangerous advice to CEOs has come from people who either had no idea of what they did not know, or from those who pretended to know what they didn't. Couple not knowing that you don't know with fuzzy logic, and you have the makings of Nicholas Carr's article.

Carr's examples of railroads and electric power played out over 80 years (not 40, as he suggests), turning society, business organizations, and lifestyles inside out. The deeper societal impacts came during the second 40 years, as society's insights on how to use the technology changed. It is worth noting that although these technologies mutated significantly (for trains, it meant moving from 15 miles an hour to 80 miles an hour), the mutation was on a totally different and much smaller scale than IT's.

The cost performance of IT technologies over the first 40 years changed by roughly 10 to the seventh, and for the foreseeable future will continue to evolve at the same rate. That is in sharp contrast to a train, which after 80 years moved six times faster than it had in the earlier period. This is impressive, but not nearly as dramatic as a computer produced in 2000, which runs 10 million times faster than a 1960s' computer.

Carr's graph on information technology stands as a subject lesson for Darrell Huff's well-known book *How to Lie with Statistics.* Carr's chart would look very different if he had tracked the number of MIPS or CPU cycles on the network from 1990 to 2002. Even using a log scale on the vertical axis would be barely enough to tilt a vertical straight line enough to create something resembling the curves of the other two schematics in Carr's article. With this explosion of cost-effectiveness has come the ability to do things truly differently. American Hospital Supply's distribution software and American Airlines' SABRE reservation system are examples of victories in past technologies. The firms were the first in their industries to see technology's transforming potential, they had the courage to invest in its performance, and they used it to gain a significant competitive edge. It is naive to assume that other sharply discontinuous technologies will not offer similar transformation opportunities in the future.

In our view, the most important thing that the CEO and senior management should understand about IT is its associated economics. Driven by Moore's Law, those evolving economics have enabled every industry's transaction costs to decrease continually, resulting in new economics for the firm and creating the feasibility of products and services not possible in the past. The economics of financial transactions have continually dropped from dollars to cents. New entrants have joined many industries and have focused on taking strategic advantage of IT's associated economics. Company boundaries have become permeable, organic, and global in scope through IT networks and the Internet.

As the pace of doing business increases, the CEO and senior management team must be aware of how IT can change rules and assumptions about competition. The economics of conducting business will likewise continue to improve—providing opportunities for businesses to expand the customer value proposition by providing more intangible information-based services. For example, the automobile value proposition continues to expand with technology that continuously senses road conditions and applies the appropriate wheel traction and suspension system pressures.

CEOs and senior management must understand that historical constraints of every kind continue to be knocked off IT because it is a "universal information-processing machine." Before e-mail and the Internet, the cost of communications was seen as limiting IT's wider use. Packet switching was invented as a way to digitize voice, data, and video in a matter that enabled digital computers (and its associated economics) to communicate, and the cost of communication sharply and suddenly dropped. Similar situations have transpired with the advent of digitized photography, use of radio frequencies for various handheld IT appliances, and the development of such products as elevators that call in to the service center or to a computer that automatically dispatches collective software or people when a part or system is about to fail. Often, only the senior management team's imagination limits new IT-based opportunities.

Our research suggests the following:

New technologies will continue to give companies the chance to differentiate themselves by service, product feature, and cost structure for some time to come. The first mover takes a risk and gains a temporary advantage (longer if there are follow-on possibilities). The fast follower is up against less risk but also has to recover lost ground. Charles Schwab versus Merrill Lynch and Walgreens versus CVS are examples of this playing out over the past decade. Our advice to the CEO is to look at IT use through several different lenses. One lens should be focused on improving cost savings and efficiencies. Another should be focused on the incremental improvement of organizational structure, products, and services. Still another should be focused on the creation of strategic advantage through extending competitive scope, partnerships (customers and other parties), the changing of the rules of competition, and the provision of new IT-based services to extend the customer value proposition.

Unless nurtured and evolved, IT-enabled competitive applications, like many competitive advantages, don't endure. Even historic strategic systems like American Hospital Supply's (after a decade of financial malnourishment) may wind up turning into a strategic liability. Others, however, like American Airlines' SABRE have shown extraordinary robustness and have permitted the survival of otherwise doomed organizations.

Evaluating these opportunities as well as thinking through their implications and timing, is vitally important, nonboring work. The new technologies will allow new things to be transformed in nonlinear ways. Radio-frequency identification devices for grocery stores, smart cards, and automated ordering systems for hospital physicians are all examples of new process targets that technologies will soon address. In the more distant future we will see the improved creation of drugs and treatments through the ability to rapidly and more deeply analyze huge databases. Understanding the potential and then deciding when the time is right to seize these transformative applications will be neither routine nor boring for the CEO or CIO.

Grid computing, standardization of components, and open systems, far from stifling differentiation, provide a stable platform to build on and offer new ways of differentiating, either by cost structure, product, or service. Just as literacy stimulated innovation, so do open systems and grids. Outsourcing the commodity infrastructure is a great way to control costs, build competence, and free up resources, which can be used to combine data bits in creative ways to add value. Relatively bulletproof operational reliability will be a key part of the price of success. Back-office or server farms, help desks, and network operations will be outsourced to specialists to attain this reliability (at rock-bottom costs). Packages like SAP further help remove commodity maintenance activities and allow firms to better analyze customer information and provide service at the sharp end. The package of skills needed inside an organization is changing very fast for competition in the information age.

The jobs of the CTO and CIO are and will be of unparalleled importance in the decades ahead. Max Hopper of American Airlines and Paul Strassmann of Kraft and NASA are not the last of a dying breed of dinosaurs, but prototypes of the leadership skills needed for survival.

If you take 1955 (with the IBM 701) as the start date and use 80 years as a technology cycle, 2035 may not be far off the mark for playing much of this out. Even then, the special recombinant nature of this technology makes us uncomfortable calling an end date. We wish Carr were right, because everyone's golf handicap could then improve. Unfortunately, the evidence is all to the contrary.

F. Warren McFarlan
and Richard L. Nolan

Letter from Jason Hittleman

Jason Hittleman, *IT Director, RKA Petroleum Companies, Romulus, Michigan*

I largely agree with Nicholas Carr's suggestions on how companies should respond to the unbearable reality that IT is becoming more of a commodity. But why does Carr suggest that IT management should become boring? Are leadership tasks such as managing risk and reining in costs any less engaging or challenging than seeking competitive advantage is?

Competitive advantage should never be the sole objective of IT. Rather, managing costs and assessing risk must become standard objectives as well. By focusing on systems and processes, more so than on just technologies, and by coupling the suggestions outlined in the article with an approach that embraces the mission of the company, IT management can remain challenging and rewarding.

IT will always matter—it will just matter in different ways now. IT must continue to support the business—not just through the logical application of technologies but also through the logical application of common sense.

Jason Hittleman

Letter from Paul A. Strassmann

Paul A. Strassmann, *Executive Advisor, NASA; Former CIO of General Foods, Kraft, Xerox, the Department of Defense, and NASA*

Nicholas Carr pronounces information technology strategically irrelevant to businesses and recommends adoption of the following policies: Cut IT budgets; do not invest in information technology innovations; invest only after others have succeeded (follow, do not lead); delay IT investments because prices are dropping and everything will be less expensive later; refocus from seeking opportunities to managing vulnerabilities and risks; disregard innovative offerings because vendors are seeking added revenues and are therefore suspect; and delay innovation as the preferred way for cutting IT costs. These recommendations are a departure from policies that have been pursued for the past 50 years. Therefore, each of the assertions Carr makes to support them warrants a commentary.

Assertion: IT has lost its strategic value. Carr argues that IT is no longer strategic because it has ceased to be a scarce good, and he contends that profit margins on IT-related innovations will consequently disappear. He does not support this argument with research findings (except for a reference to my own research and a misunderstood example from the Alinean Corporation). He bases his conclusions entirely on his reasoning, by analogy, that IT must follow the patterns that arose as businesses adopted steam engines, railroads, telephones, electric generators, and internal combustion motors. But any proof that rests entirely on analogies is flawed. This technique was used to uphold medieval dogma, and it delayed the advancement of science by centuries.

Carr's logic is defective because his examples deal exclusively with capital-intensive goods. Capital investments in machinery do indeed exhibit diminishing returns as markets saturate and the difference between marginal costs and marginal revenues disappears, but information goods are not subject to such effects. The marginal cost of information goods—especially of software, which now accounts for the dominant share of information technology costs—does not rise with increased scale. It drops asymptotically toward zero. Therefore, any firm that can steadily reduce marginal costs by deploying IT can make information technology investments enormously profitable and can generate a rising strategic value.

Assertion: IT is a commodity that does not offer a competitive distinction and therefore

does not provide a competitive advantage. It is true that Microsoft desktops running on Intel processors have become widespread, but they account for less than 12 percent of IT budgets, and that number is declining. Most IT products are diverse—they certainly are not commodities. And while many business processes do rely on standardized desktops, are those processes therefore doomed to uniformity? In other words, does partial standardization wipe out opportunities for gaining competitive advantage? The evidence does not support such a conclusion.

Competitive advantage is not the result of personal computers. It is the result of effective management by skilled and highly motivated people. Since 1982 I have shown (in numerous publications) that firms using identical information technologies and spending comparable amounts on IT display an enormous variability in profitability. My research, now confirmed by other investigators, has demonstrated that profitability and IT spending are unrelated, even if identical technologies are used.

Assertion: Because IT is an infrastructural technology that is easily acquired and copied, it cannot offer a competitive advantage. Easy availability of information technology makes it increasingly valuable. E-mail, fax, and cell phones gain in utility as they become more widely used, because they can be acquired on attractive terms. I have spent 40 years of my career implementing information technologies; for the first 30 years, that was a great pain. The technology was expensive, faulty, insecure, hard to manage, and unstable. I finally see the advent of an era in which low-cost ownership of information technologies is possible. This will be accomplished through services in which the vendors assume most of the risks of failure while increasing ease of use for billions of people.

Carr's advice to back off from information technologies just as they emerge from a long gestation period is mistimed and abortive. Information technology must be easily acquired and made available to everyone so that the global community can increase the standard of living through easier communications and lower-cost business transactions. Widespread availability creates new business opportunities.

Assertion: The influence of IT will henceforth be macroeconomic and not a means for competitive differentiation. The proposition that IT benefits will flow to consumers and not to firms is a contradiction. Sustainable profits materialize when benefits accrue to customers. There are as yet enormous gains in value to be delivered in health, education, entertainment, business services, and especially government. Extending the benefits of the global division of labor and the inclusion of billions of new consumers into the global marketplace will generate trillions of dollars of new revenues. Enabling the global marketplace to function effectively will require enormous new IT investments by individual firms. Surely there will be millions of enterprises that will be able to take advantage of such opportunities. The lower entry costs for using the power of information technologies will make that feasible. Carr completely disregards the explosive growth of small businesses, a development made possible by the Internet. Information technology is a killer of bureaucracies and a reducer of overhead expenses; those qualities increase its microeconomic viability. Asserting that benefits will accrue only to the economy at large and not to individual firms is a prescription for opting out of the information-based competitive races in the years to come.

Assertion: IT is primarily a transport technology, and because it is open to everyone, it offers no advantage. This proposition is a misunderstanding of what IT is all about. Message transport is *not* the primary reason why organizations deploy IT. Information technology adds value mainly by improving the management of information intelligence and collaboration among individuals, groups, and organizations. The transport function is essential, but IT's importance as a conduit is only tertiary. The value is in the message itself, not in the means of conveyance!

Information technologies now provide the primary means for extending the value of a firm's knowledge capital. They help companies manage the exploding accumulation of scientific, research, customer, engineering, property, and intellectual assets. Computers are the repositories of intelligence about customers, suppliers, and products; those repositories constitute the most valuable knowledge assets for any firm that realizes returns greater than its cost of financial capital. It is noteworthy that information technology is now recognized as the means for waging information warfare—a term that I apply not only to the military but also to commercial confrontations.

I have shown in published articles how and why firms' knowledge capital is now worth more than the assets reported on conventional financial statements. I have shown how people become enormously empowered when aided by information technologies because these tools magnify their ability to perform complex tasks. By trivializing information technologies as electronic messengers, Carr would prevent organizations from understanding how to deploy IT in such a way that it can be the weapon of choice in competitive contests.

Assertion: IT functions will be homogenized, and proprietary applications are therefore doomed. Citing the proliferation of off-the-shelf, standard applications, such as Microsoft Office, Carr predicts that information practices will march inexorably toward homogeneity. In such an environment of sameness, he says, no companies will be able to realize competitive gains.

The use of a standard software package does not doom an organization to homogeneity that destroys value. I suspect that Carr used the same software to write his essay that I did to write this critique, yet we have arrived at opposite conclusions! I consider the standardization of communication protocols, Web services, database languages, and applications to be a value-enhancing development, not a value detractor. I am particularly in favor of open systems that will make systems integration—now an enormous, resource-sapping burden—easy and financially attractive. Standards spare IT executives from unceasing difficulties in assuring the interoperability of routine business processes. With standards in place, the IT staff can finally

concentrate on what is indeed value enhancing for the enterprise, such as applications that reflect the firm's distinctive characteristics, and allow it to share information easily with customers and suppliers. Applications that were completely custom-designed in the past—and that Carr praises—inhibited the economic contributions of IT.

Assertion: Corporations will adopt generic applications; business processes will therefore be uniform and without competitive advantage. This assertion can be contradicted by anyone who has had experience with one-code-fits-all "enterprise" software suites that claim to deliver answers to most business-systems problems. Even the most tightly controlled generic application suite (SAP's enterprise resource planning application) can deliver completely different results for look-alike firms.

For routine business processes, generic applications can be useful in reducing the total cost of ownership of computer systems. But such applications have also been known to destroy firms that have attempted to squeeze unique company processes into generic molds. Carr's prediction that generic applications will take over is not supported by firms' rising reluctance to install comprehensive enterprise solutions. In fact, by insisting on data and protocol inter-operability, firms are seeking greater freedom to combine applications from a growing diversity of software offerings.

Assertion: Existing IT capabilities are largely sufficient for corporate needs. It is hubris to assert that we have already attained the pinnacle of what is ultimately achievable. The history of that assertion is a history of failures. The Chinese burned their fleet when they thought nothing further could be gained from overseas trade. The leaders of the Soviet Union retained their bankrupt central planning system because they considered it perfect for managing the economy.

Corporations are confronting increased uncertainty about markets, competition, resources, employee attitudes, and the impact of legislation. The corporate environment requires more complex coordination than ever before, and there is less time for taking corrective measures. As a result, there is a need for more and better information technologies. Carr's view that the time has come to arrest further IT developments and take a static posture is a prescription for inaction as challenges keep rising.

Assertion: Widespread adoption of best-practices software makes IT-based advantages disappear for everyone. The dissemination of information about best business practices is indeed gaining, and competitors are therefore getting smarter and faster. But Carr's view—that wins cannot be sustainable if everyone has access to the same means for engaging in contests—disregards the dynamics of competition. The proliferation of knowledge about how to design ever faster sailing boats has jacked up the cost of participating and increased the difficulty of winning, but it has not discouraged races. The dissemination of business best practices means survival today requires speed and innovation—and greater adoption of information technologies. The arrival of a new information-based best practice is usually seen by the more aggressive leaders as a signal to commence yet another round of more expensive competition with more, not less, IT.

Assertion: IT is arriving at the end of its growth cycle and is reaching saturation. After 50 years of cyclical growth, there is not a shred of evidence that IT developments have reached a plateau, as did innovations in industrial-age machinery. Physical mechanics impose limits on the size and performance of locomotives, turbines, airplanes, refrigerators, and trucks; there are no such confinements to information technologies, as far as we can tell. Software can endow computing devices with unrestricted variability in features and functions. The capability of a software-enriched global network has no boundaries. The current cyclical correction to the excesses of the past decade is a crucible for generating more and better innovation.

Assertion: IT risks now exceed advantages, requiring shifts in executive attention. The need to pay more attention to IT risks is indisputable, but I do not agree that the risks exceed the advantages. Carr advises executives to adopt a reclusive posture—to withdraw from the search for new opportunities. He recommends pursuing cost reduc-

tions through cutting off IT instead of searching for opportunities in the steady stream of new ideas.

I favor cost cutting, especially for any bloated computing capacity that was acquired in a frenzy of hype without an enterprise architecture or alignment with a strategic plan. And I share Carr's concerns about information security, network reliability, and systems corruption. But cutting off innovative investments is not the way to address those problems. The cure for most of the so-called "legacy" systems is radical innovation, such as shifting the accountability for systems performance to vendors, who will then have to face up to the responsibility of delivering reliable and robust applications. I have examined such options. An examination of a large collection of applications shows that the most financially attractive way of dealing with existing risks is to replace the systems. Instead of feeding the increasingly costly IT infrastructure and throwing money at rising software maintenance costs, companies should be ready to engage in yet another IT investment cycle to replace old systems.

Carr's assertions and recommendations could inhibit the most innovative and value-creating means available for increasing the economic benefits to enterprises and customers. Information technologies are too important to be pronounced irrelevant.

Paul A. Strassmann

Letter from Marianne Broadbent, Mark McDonald, and Richard Hunter

Marianne Broadbent, *Group Vice President and Gartner Fellow, Global Head of Research, Executive Programs, Gartner*
Mark McDonald, *Vice President and Research Director, Executive Programs, Gartner*
Richard Hunter, *Vice President and Gartner Fellow, Executive Programs, Gartner*

Nicholas Carr's well-written article takes the view that IT is now like other infrastructures and that, on average, the companies that are the biggest investors in IT are not the most successful in terms of business performance. He contends that firms should now focus on carefully managing costs and risks and not get carried away with IT's strategic role.

Carr is correct that hardware and network connectivity are commodity businesses and that some IT infrastructure services have evolved into commodity services. But the article misses a big part of the story. IT does matter, but not because of hardware or even standard commercial software. It is because the intelligent and innovative application of information solves business problems and creates customer value at high speed, low cost, and the right scale. To put it simply, it's not about the box; it's about what's inside the box.

Carr is right that the simple possession of infrastructure technology was for a time a source of competitive advantage. In the 1970s, the Dallas Cowboys' Tex Schram used a computer to manage information on NFL draft choices, assess the strengths of other football teams, and perform additional tasks that increased the Cowboys' ability to use information competitively. But the advantage disappeared when other teams began using computers. The source of competitive advantage shifted from simply having a computer to knowing how to use it.

Carr's examples are of companies looking for competitive advantage from the intrinsic performance characteristics of the hardware. In the case of American Hospital Supply, the characteristic was connectivity; at American Airlines, it was management of large amounts of complex data. In high tech, whenever you rely on hardware capability as a competitive technology, it's only a matter of time before others catch up.

The differentiation is about information, business processes, and applications. Sustainable advantage comes from consistently delivering greater value to customers. This comes from the "information" in information technology—that is, it comes from better understanding the customer, applying that understanding to your products, services, and processes, and integrating these to deliver on an improved value proposition.

That's what Wal-Mart and Dell have done. They have continuously used information better and with greater alignment to their value proposition. It's true that these companies have also continuously reinvested in new hardware and software platforms. But the sheer scale of their investment in infrastructure isn't the most important factor. Why have competitors been unable to copy Wal-Mart's and Dell's successes? The answer lies in large part in Wal-Mart's and Dell's ability to integrate IT into business processes—their "benefit conversion" ability.

It has been known for many years that the biggest investors in IT don't get the most value from the technologies. It is a key message in the Weill and Broadbent book *Leveraging the New Infrastructure: How Market Leaders Capitalize on Information Technology* (Harvard Business School Press, 1998) and in much subsequent work. What makes the difference is a set of benefit conversion factors that influence how well investments in IT-enabled business initiatives are turned into real business value. These factors include clear decision rights, accountability for IT-related decisions, integrated business and technology planning and execution, and the existence and reinforcement of strong collaborative behaviors. Many of these are not about IT as such but about effective executive processes, effective accountabilities, and business focus.

The major messages we have been giving CIOs over the past two years have been that they should manage costs and risks aggressively and work with business colleagues to design IT governance thoughtfully. Beyond that, as in any business area, executives must understand the need for risk-managed innovation.

Innovation through electronically enabled services, processes, and products has only just begun. As in the past, the benefits will go to firms where the business focus is clear and disciplined and where there is well-informed and integrated decision making across the organization. The danger is that by scanting the fantastic potential for innovation that lies ahead in IT, Carr will lead executives to focus only on controlling IT costs. That is a necessary discipline, but it is not the route to real business advantage.

Marianne Broadbent,
Mark McDonald,
and Richard Hunter

Letter from Bruce Skaistis

Bruce Skaistis, *President, eGlobal CIO, Tulsa, Oklahoma*

In "IT Doesn't Matter," Nicholas Carr is essentially issuing a warning: Organizations need to get realistic about what IT can and cannot do for them. In spite of all the hype, wireless systems and other exciting new computer technologies aren't going to create lasting strategic advantages.

I also think Carr is trying to help us learn from the mistakes we made during the late 1990s, when companies were making huge investments in e-business initiatives in an attempt to achieve competitive and strategic advantages. Many of those investments never produced significant benefits—many of the initiatives were never completed. With the benefit of hindsight, Carr is telling us most of those gigantic efforts were never going to deliver real strategic advantage, even if they had been successful.

IT does matter, and organizations should do the following to make sure their IT efforts and resources continue to matter:

Aim your IT efforts and resources at helping the business achieve its strategic objectives. Use IT to optimize and streamline critical business processes; speed up access to accurate information about operations, customers, and competitors; and integrate systems with customers and suppliers. Establish an active, effective IT management or governance structure, so leaders company-wide can participate in establishing technology priorities, allocating resources, and monitoring performance.

Focus on using IT to respond quickly to changing conditions and requirements. Everything in business today has to be done faster than ever, and everything is subject to immediate change. Therefore, IT decisions have to be made more quickly. Put critical IT initiatives at the top of the pri-

ority list. And slot them on a fast track; they need to be completed in the shortest time possible and updated frequently. (After all, your competitors are probably just a few steps behind.)

Focus on optimizing the cost effectiveness and performance of IT resources. Despite the fact that IT investments are typically among the largest a company makes, IT resources haven't always been under the same pressure as other functional areas to improve overall corporate performance and reduce costs. Now that some of the IT mystique has been eliminated, corporate IT has to play by the same rules as everyone else. That means refocusing the entire company on the importance of IT performance and cost effectiveness; creating new IT management structures to monitor performance and cost effectiveness; consolidating resources; and streamlining processes.

Focus on minimizing IT risks. Carr rightfully concludes that minimizing IT risks is a critical issue for all companies. Almost every day there is a new story about a major company or government agency having their networks hacked or their Web sites attacked. Every company should have some of its most talented people worrying about how to manage its IT efforts and outsourcing relationships; protect its networks, systems, and information; and mitigate other IT risks.

In a very straightforward way, Carr has put a stake in the heart of the misdirected thinking about IT that flourished in the free-spending 1990s. It's time for enterprises to be realistic about IT's role in their future. IT can produce significant strategic and competitive benefits for an organization—but only when it is used effectively.

Bruce Skaistis

Letter from Vladimir Zwass

Vladimir Zwass, *Distinguished Professor of Computer Science and MIS, Fairleigh Dickinson University, Teaneck, New Jersey, zwass@fdu.edu*

Two of the other articles in your May 2003 issue best refute Nicholas Carr's claim that "IT Doesn't Matter." As Gary Loveman describes in "Diamonds in the Data Mine," Harrah's Entertainment "has outplayed its competition" by basing its deep service orientation on how valuable its different kinds of customers are. The firm determines this value by mining the multifaceted and voluminous transactional information in its database. This is a textbook example of the strategic deployment of information technology to gain competitive advantage. Daniel Corsten and Nirmalya Kumar report in their Forethought article, "Profits in the Pie of the Beholder," that the suppliers that comprehensively adopt the IT-based "efficient consumer response" practices in their relationships with Sainsbury's Supermarkets attain higher levels of economic performance than do their peers. This is an excellent example of the successful use of interorganizational systems for competitive advantage.

The hardware and software components of information technology do indeed provide the infrastructure for data storage, communication, and processing. This basic aspect of IT is certainly being commoditized. However, as these and other examples show, information systems can be embedded in a company's organizational and interorganizational processes and combined inextricably with other capabilities and assets to produce superior performance. Dell's pull-based order processing and Wal-Mart's supplier-relationship management come to mind. The implementation of these IT-based systems does not come cheaply and requires continual retargeting, yet it underlies the success of many firms.

Vladimir Zwass

Letter from Mark S. Lewis

Mark S. Lewis, *Executive Vice President of New Ventures, Chief Technology Officer, EMC Corporation, Hopkinton, Massachusetts*

I agree with Nicholas Carr that the competitive edge gained by companies through IT in the past was not due to the fact that they had IT and others did not. It was due to *how* they used it, to the innovative business processes and models they created around new information technologies. Now, Carr tells us, best practices are being built into the infrastructure itself. He writes off any further strategic differentiation by arguing that IT is like other "infrastructure technologies" that lost their competitive potential once they became "accessible and affordable to all."

Carr's historical analogies to other infrastructure technologies are not convincing. Information technology has infinite and constantly expanding functionality, while Carr's other technologies—steam engines, railroads, electricity, telephones—have narrow functionality.

Electricity, for example, is simply a source of energy; it hasn't changed much since we found a way to harness it. And it can, and probably will, be replaced by another source of energy. Unlike electricity, IT is very different from what it was 30 or even 10 years ago. The technologies used for processing, storing, and transporting information continue to expand. Also growing is the demand for IT, with more businesses and types of organizations, more processes and activities, and more and more consumers at home and on the go in need of its productivity-enhancing functions. Should we believe Carr, who says that the build-out is over, or should we listen to Alan Greenspan, who argues that "there are still significant opportunities for firms to upgrade the quality of their technology and with it the level of productivity"? Or perhaps we should listen to genomics expert Craig Venter, who says that at least a decade or two will go by before computing can catch up with the current needs of biological investigation. Or maybe we should observe the millions of businesses and people around the world who are currently without affordable access to IT.

The key difference between IT and Carr's other "infrastructure technologies" is that the latter perform functions that lie outside human capabilities. By contrast, much of IT mirrors and amplifies the brain's key information-handling activities: processing, storage, and transmission. In addition, IT is a tool that automates and facilitates activities that otherwise would be done manually. Strategic advantage comes from how we apply IT, the unique and differentiating ways in which we marry information technologies with our intellectual capital: our business models, our organizational cultures, our creativity.

IT never mattered. What matters are the people who invent information technologies and who deploy and use them. Like any other human endeavor, IT has its share of failures, foibles, and fads. Computer scientist Michael Dertouzos reminded us that "IT acts like a magnifying lens, amplifying management's strengths but also its weaknesses." Carr's advice to avoid "waste and sloppiness" applies to any investment or purchase we make. A few years of over-investment followed by a few years of under-investment due to general economic and psychological conditions cannot change the nature of information technologies nor the industry built around them.

In my job, I talk with a lot of business executives and IT managers around the world. These conversations paint a very different future from the one Carr predicts. Rather than "ceding control" to a few large IT utilities guaranteed to use their monopoly status to raise profits and squash innovation, the executives I've spoken with are demanding more choice, more flexibility, and more advanced IT. They, unlike Carr, do not confuse the way they buy IT—increasingly moving toward a consumption-based model—with a lack of strategic importance.

In the next generation of IT, there can be no compromises. The use of IT is analogous to innovations in transportation, not power utilities. Common standards like roads and airports exist, but the cars we choose to drive and our methods of travel are based on individual preference. IT utilities will exist, but businesses will derive unique benefits from how they leverage specific technologies.

The greatest improvements in IT economics have come when customers were able to take control from "full-solution" providers and utilize the most cost-effective technology applicable for their needs. There is no going back. In the foreseeable future, customers will require the simplicity and affordability of complete IT solutions but will still want to be creative and use their brains to do more with IT and, yes, gain competitive advantage. I just think of walking into our living room and telling my kids that we now have a "TV utility" and the only channel we get is C-SPAN. I don't think they would consider this a step forward.

Mark S. Lewis

Letter from Tom Pisello

Tom Pisello, *CEO and Founder, Alinean Corporation, Orlando, Florida*

How a company manages its information technology—aligning investments with core business goals—is more strategic now than ever. Nicholas Carr's article "IT Doesn't Matter" draws attention to the very heart of the question CIOs and CFOs struggle with most: "What's most important when it comes to IT investments?" With dollars being scrutinized, the question merits closer examination.

In specific market segments and over the long term, it is true that companies spending frugally on IT are demonstrating superior overall results. But dig deeper and you'll find that there is no consistent correlation between IT spending levels and financial performance; two companies investing the same amounts in identical technologies will yield vastly different results.

What does this mean? What a company invests in, and how well it is applied to improve business practices, counts far more than how much is spent.

On the flip side, the worst-performing companies—those delivering the lowest return on shareholder investment—are equally penurious in their IT investment. Our research indicates that this laggardly group spends well below the industry average of 3.7 percent of revenue on IT (as do the top performers).

Examination of industry averages reveals certain best practices of companies deriving strategic impact from IT investments; one of these is the ability to quickly adapt plans to shifting market conditions. Best-performing companies have been able to scale back spending in this slow economy. When and if a shift occurs back toward favoring innovation, these same companies are likely to be adept at scaling back up.

Unfortunately, commoditization of technologies does not translate into making the best IT implementations easily replicable. That's because every organization has unique needs and priorities. However, one trend in particular holds great promise: Cheap, standards-based hardware and software are the single biggest driver of innovation, precisely because the heavy lifting can now be focused on activities that deliver much more value. (From databases, for instance, has sprung the promise of truly individualized customer contact; from the rudiments of factory planning come supply chains that can shift production within days of changes in customer demand or of geopolitical turmoil.)

Information technology is expected to manage companies' most vital and valuable intellectual assets and is the only tool companies have to turn this knowledge into the kind of competitive weapon that redefines industries—and its leaders. For this very reason, IT will continue to play an important role in our personal lives and in the companies that employ us. Those who recognize the importance of good management, not spending levels, will ultimately reap the rewards.

Tom Pisello

Letter from Roy L. Pike

Roy L. Pike, *Vice President of Information Technology and CIO, Millennium Chemicals, Hunt Valley, Maryland*

Everyone will agree with Nicholas Carr that the storage, transmission, and processing of digital information has become a utility service. We outsourced our global enterprise software data center in 1998. The problem is that since most executives think of IT in much broader terms, many readers may be misled unless they read the definition of IT he provides in the footnote.

In its broadest context, information technology is all about productivity. And nothing can be more strategic right now for manufacturing and service industries than improving productivity. During the 1980s and 1990s, IT gave rise to huge improvements in productivity by changing the

way individuals work—providing direct access to information and eliminating hordes of information gatherers and intermediaries who added no value to their businesses.

What Carr misses completely is that, after having improved the productivity of individual workers, IT still has the potential to improve productivity dramatically, this time by changing the way businesses work together. The new strategic task for IT is all about creating integrated business relationships in which suppliers, producers, and customers act as if they were in one company, sharing information on inventories, production, demand forecasts, lead times, and maybe costs and pricing. For decades, the solution to supply chain inefficiencies was inventory. Today, inventory is the problem. The savings in material inventories and streamlined delivery that IT can deliver will dwarf the efficiencies that have already been achieved.

Linking intercompany business processes is not using IT as a utility. A few standards have emerged in some industries, but there are practically no inter-industry standards. By linking business processes, IT is and will remain of strategic importance for the next ten years.

Roy L. Pike

Letter from Vijay Gurbaxani

Vijay Gurbaxani, *Faculty Chair, Professor of Information Systems, Director of the Center for Research on IT and Organizations, Graduate School of Management, University of California, Irvine*

Nicholas Carr's article makes many of the same points that Max Hopper made in HBR in 1990. In "Rattling SABRE—New Ways to Compete on Information" (May–June), he also argued that computing was becoming a utility. So these arguments aren't new. Nevertheless, while many of Carr's arguments are sound, the situation is subtler than he would like us to believe.

The scarce resource never was technology, as Carr assumes; it was always the set of managerial capabilities needed to create value with that technology. These capabilities involve more than just managing the technology itself. They also encompass the ability to understand how investments in organizational capital complement and magnify the payoffs from technology and the ability to produce relevant information from the systems through sophisticated decision-making techniques. Recent research has demonstrated that companies spend five or ten times as much on management practices that accompany technology introductions as they do on the technology itself. What's more, as technology evolves and becomes increasingly complex, these management skills become ever scarcer.

Most companies struggle to implement a sophisticated information-based strategy. One has only to read two other articles in the May 2003 HBR—Gary Loveman's insightful "Diamonds in the Data Mine," which describes how Harrah's mined its customer information to dramatically improve its performance, and Eric Bonabeau's "Don't Trust Your Gut," which demonstrates the value of sophisticated decision-support tools—to understand why so much of what companies can do with information technology will never be found in a standard software package and why some companies will pull it off while others won't.

Carr argues that companies don't need to develop their own technology management capabilities: They can just buy computing services that embody best practices. But that assumes, first of all, that such utilities exist. Check out the current utility-computing models of the technology service providers—they are a long way from being utilities. And when they are developed, the economics of software dictates that such shared systems must focus on a common denominator so they can be widely used. These common systems will not fit a company's processes out of the box; the firm will either need to customize the systems or change its business processes to accommodate the software. Neither approach is straightforward or always desirable. And as anyone who uses software knows, software is far from ideal.

What's more, even if companies share infrastructure and common application systems, they will not necessarily end up with identical systems or use them in similar ways. Executives will face a multitude of choices as to how they want to structure their databases and applications, what data they will collect, what information will flow out of their systems, and how they will manage it.

Still, I agree with Carr that the move to a common infrastructure is inevitable, though it will take a lot longer than he implies. Wal-Mart refuses to join industry exchanges because it believes its supply chain practices are unparalleled. And look how long it has been taking General Motors, DaimlerChrysler, and Ford to build their business-to-business exchange, Covisint, to provide the shared infrastructure and systems that will facilitate trade in the automobile industry. After investing billions of dollars, the exchange has gained only limited traction; the technological challenges and organizational changes needed are massive.

But the fundamental point is this: The move to a common infrastructure does not reduce the opportunities for competitive advantage; it increases them. Using these shared platforms, all firms will have the opportunity to build customized applications that exploit complex technological capabilities to give rise to new business strategies. When much of our investment in technology goes into shared infrastructure, the investments that we make in customization will be much more valuable.

Vijay Gurbaxani

Letter from Steven Alter

Steven Alter, *Professor of Information Systems, University of San Francisco School of Business and Management, San Francisco, alter@usfca.edu*

The argument in "IT Doesn't Matter" goes roughly like this: Kidneys don't matter. Kidneys are basically a commodity. Just about everyone has kidneys. People with one kidney often lead full lives with no problems. There is no evidence that CEOs with superior kidneys are more successful than CEOs with average kidneys. In fact, CEOs who spend more on their kidneys often don't do as well.

The title "IT Doesn't Matter" conveys a fallacy. An accurate but less catchy title would have been "IT Is Not the Headline." In my executive MBA courses on information systems, I use a similarly mistitled HBR case study to demonstrate why IT is essential but is not the headline. The 1997 case "The IT System That Couldn't Deliver" concerns management lapses in developing a new laptop-based tool for life insurance salespeople. The students read the case study before class and e-mail me a brief statement identifying "the system" and describing what it produces and how well it operates. Their answers are typically all over the map. As the discussion unfolds, it becomes clear that "the system" is neither the software itself nor the information system being created. Rather, it is a work system of selling insurance that has not been improved as hoped. The students usually realize that the mistakes in the case might not have happened if the CEO, CFO, and CIO had understood that the headline was the new work system, not the information system.

Still, while IT is not the headline, it certainly matters (just like kidneys) because the work systems cannot operate without IT.

Steven Alter

Letter from Cathy Hyatt

Cathy Hyatt, *IT Consultant, San Francisco*

If Nicholas Carr's article were correct, every CEO would get the same answer to the question "What is the cheapest IT solution?" Just as with electricity, companies' needs would vary only in quantity, not quality. However, those of us who have spent our careers in IT know that the answer to this question is always, "It depends."

And what it depends on, more than anything else, is the company's strategy. Typically, competitive strategy leans toward one of two forms: Being the low-cost provider of a commodity product or service, or being a value-added provider of a differentiated product or service. Because of the variety and complexity of IT, there is a vast number of "correct" IT solutions and investment strategies for either of these approaches—but the set of

solutions that works for one will not be the same as the set that works for the other. This, I think, makes IT management, which includes the selection, maintenance, and deployment of new and ongoing IT capability, a key strategic issue.

Carr says the main problem with IT management is overspending. If only those IT managers would get together and put pressure on their vendors, he says, this could be controlled. But he misses an important point related to the strategic use of IT. Let's say a business wants a particular new IT capability that would dramatically boost its differentiation or cost advantage. If the new product or service is incompatible with the outdated hardware and software that IT management has frugally kept in service past its vendor-supported life cycle, the firm will lose out on a key strategic advantage. Those of us who have experienced this problem know that a company's hardware and software can be intricately intertwined; sometimes a single piece of outdated software can derail the deployment of important new functionality with real strategic value.

Finally, Carr's analogy comparing the ubiquity of IT with that of electricity is only effective up to a point. The complexity and variety of IT, its evolving standards in many important areas, and its incredible innovation argue against his premise that its ubiquity eliminates its strategic value. IT's history of innovation undermines his assertion that technology-related business transformations are complete. The fact that IT spending does not correlate with financial success may be related to this, as effective business-process changes are frequently made after the initial deployment of technology. An example might be a business where CRM software delivers real advantage over a competitor that, although equally able to purchase the same package, is unable to successfully deploy or use it.

To improve the business results gained from IT, corporate leaders must continue to increase its alignment with strategy. To do this, most will need to gain a greater understanding of IT, better integrate IT leadership into their strategic planning processes, and insist on greater and greater strategic and leadership capability from their IT professionals. Getting IT "right" is a difficult problem that many executives face, and while some will appreciate the silver bullet Carr offers, most, I expect, will find his naïveté discouraging.

Cathy Hyatt

Letter from Chris Schlueter Langdon

Chris Schlueter Langdon, *Assistant Professor of Information and Operations Management, Marshall School of Business, University of Southern California, Los Angeles*

I am an information systems strategy professor, so it would be expected that I would disagree with Nicholas Carr's provocative assertion that IT doesn't matter. Indeed, I do. While I agree with much of Carr's excellent—but incomplete—analysis, I disagree with his conclusion.

Certain areas in IT have become commoditized and continue to be commoditized. Just like the phone system: A business user does not have to be a network engineer to use it; the phone is a plug-and-play utility available to anyone. The same is basically true for office-productivity software and computer networks—although many would argue that it is still much easier to plug in a new phone or fax machine than it is to hook up a PC to the Internet at home or to share a printer.

The analogy with the phone system breaks down at the point where Carr's analysis stops. Information systems, and software applications in particular, differ in versatility and adaptability. To exaggerate somewhat—but only a little—anything is possible with software, if not today, then tomorrow.

Increasingly, value added is being shifted from mechanical systems and their operations into software. For instance, much of the value added in the phone system is being provided by voice-over-IP software. The history of modern production is intimately tied to the automation of business processes. First, companies used steam engines, then conveyor belts, and today we use information systems, and especially software, to automate business activities. We might call it "softwarization." Companies in many industries now use ERP and CRM software to automate back-office and customer-related activities. And this softwarization is not a one-step affair, like flipping a switch, but an ongoing process. Value added is constantly being shifted into or embedded in software, with mature areas obviously becoming commoditized. Examples include computerized antilock brakes, credit cards and calling cards, airline ticketing, and yield-management systems.

Why would this process stop? Why would there suddenly be only mature areas? Are there not enough business activities left to be automated? Would it be too difficult or expensive to automate the remaining ones? The very commoditization of mature infrastructure technology reduces unit cost, which in turn frees up funding for continued softwarization without necessarily increasing total IT budgets.

Two trends ensure that the sky is the limit for softwarization. Carr mentioned the popular one—Moore's Law, which establishes that hardware will become more powerful and cheaper over time. Even more important are advances in how increased processing power can be used—which leads us into the world of systems and software architecture design, with its fast-growing jungle of acronyms and ideas. One key advance in this field has been the recent breakthrough of object-oriented programming. The concept and some tools, such as the Smalltalk programming language, have been around for decades, but only very recently has the concept been turned into commercially viable implementations.

The bottom line is that powerful hardware combined with more flexible software will continue to fuel a process in which value added is increasingly achieved with information systems. While mature areas do indeed get commoditized and probably outsourced, new softwarization should receive more, not less, of top management's attention. Why? As Michael Porter argues, "[Business] activities are the basic unit of competitive advantage." As these activities get automated using software, top management's attention should shift to information systems architecture design.

Chris Schlueter Langdon

Reply from Nicholas G. Carr

First and most important, let me thank these correspondents (and the many others I've heard from) for taking the time to so clearly and thoroughly express their points of view. Whatever the broader merits of my article, it has at least succeeded in setting off an important and long overdue debate about the role of information technology in business. That debate can only be constructive.

Let me quickly restate the gist of my argument, which at times gets lost in the responses. As IT's core functions—data processing, storage, and transmission—have become cheaper, more standardized, and more easily replicable, their ability to serve as the basis for competitive advantage has steadily eroded. Given this continuing and indeed inexorable trend, companies would be wise to manage IT as a commodity input, seeking to achieve competitively necessary levels of IT capability at the lowest possible cost and risk.

I find nothing in these letters to contradict that argument. As many of the writers point out, the way companies organize processes and use information plays a critical role in their ability to distinguish themselves from competitors. That's always been true and always will be true. But that does not mean that the information systems involved in managing processes and information are the source of the distinctiveness. It is better, I would argue, to start with the assumption that the technology is generic—that its functionality can be easily and quickly copied—and that the more tightly an advantage is tied to the technology, the more transient it will be. I would certainly be wary of following Paul Strassmann's recommendation that executives "be ready to engage in yet another IT investment cycle," as if spending more money on IT is itself a strategy. Many companies have taken that approach in the past, and most have come to regret it.

At the same time, I would disagree with Mark Lewis's suggestion that "IT never mattered." In the past, proprietary computer systems could indeed be the basis of long-lasting advantages, as the story of American Hospital Supply in my article shows. Dismissing the former strategic relevance of IT makes it too easy to ignore how IT's role in business has changed. And that can lead to strategic miscalculations. As Warren McFarlan and Richard Nolan point out, the value of being a first mover hinges on the speed with which fast followers catch up. As IT's power and presence have grown, fast followers have been able to catch up—or spring ahead—ever more quickly. Given the high cost of being an early investor in new IT functionality, a first mover strategy becomes harder to justify. Just because we continue to see new innovations in IT does not mean that it pays to be a pioneer.

Finally, I want to say that Jason Hittleman is right to chide me for suggesting that rigorous cost control and risk management are "boring." I used the term as a contrast to what John Seely Brown and John Hagel call "big bang" thinking in IT management—the "IT changes everything" school of thought that distorted so many business decisions during the 1990s. It was, however, an unfortunate word choice, and I apologize to the many dedicated IT professionals whose hard and valuable work is leading to a more efficient and pragmatic use of information systems—and to a more realistic understanding of those systems' limitations.

Nicholas G. Carr

Managing Infrastructure and Operations

Module 2

Robert D. Austin

In recent years, changes in computing infrastructure have led to fundamental changes in how businesses operate. As a result, today's managers must deal with new challenges and threats. Fortunately, ever-improving technologies offer a growing number of problem-solving options. Entirely new businesses and industries have emerged to help operational managers realize greater efficiencies and capabilities.

The chapters and cases in this module provide a basis for discussing how changing infrastructure affects business, how management priorities must shift, and how the risks that affect day-to-day operations can be reduced. The focus of the module is on frontline operational issues. Without management frameworks that deliver operational results, the best-laid plans, the greatest ideas, and the shrewdest strategies cannot create value. The four cases and one reading at the end of this module are intended to help readers understand how to finish the job of value creation by tackling the last step: execution.

CareGroup

This case examines the causes and consequences of a three-day network outage at Beth Israel Deaconess Medical Center, widely known as a leader in the use of IT in the health care industry. The company's experiences demonstrate how vital IT has become in modern organizations. The case offers opportunities to discuss the role of redundancy in a network, the challenges that arise from infrastructure complexity, and the importance of strong IT leadership.

The iPremier Company: Denial of Service Attack (A)

"The iPremier Company" depicts a crisis in progress. A luxury goods retailer with high-income customers finds itself under attack from an unknown hacker. The case describes the events as they unfold and demonstrates conclusively how decisions involved in securing IT infrastructures are, despite their technical complexity, necessarily in the mainstream of general management.

Ford Motor Company: Supply Chain Strategy and The Power of Virtual Integration: An Interview with Dell Computer's Michael Dell

In this case and its associated reading, a century-old U.S. manufacturer considers whether it should model its operations on those of an acclaimed young company. In the process, it must confront complex questions about how IT should support business operations. The case provides an opportunity to explore how Dell leverages information technologies to great advantage and how Ford's legacies (systems, organizations, and relationships) limit its opportunities.

Postgirot Bank and Provment AB: Managing the Cost of IT Operations

This case describes an organization's efforts to understand patterns of usage and costs within its IT infrastructure and to make decisions about platform consolidation. Analyzing Postgirot's models of server cost and use prompts a discussion of how to evaluate IT investments, how to deploy IT infrastructure to maximum advantage, and, more generally, how to track and manage IT assets.

CHAPTER 5

Understanding Internetworking Infrastructure[1]

Seventy-five percent of all IT dollars go to infrastructure. Isn't it time you learned what it is?[2]

Information technology (IT) infrastructure[3] lies at the heart of most companies' operating capabilities. Changes in IT lead therefore to fundamental changes in how businesses operate. Because many companies depend on these technologies, no longer is IT simply nice to have; no longer is IT just value-adding. It has become vital.

Recent advances have led to major changes in how IT services are delivered. For some time now, low-cost computing power has driven a shift toward more distributed processing. *Internetworking technologies,* which provide a low-cost way to connect virtually everyone on the same network, present new possibilities for addressing business computing needs. The operational mechanisms at the heart of many businesses continue to evolve. New technologies add to, improve, and interconnect older systems to yield infrastructures with complex operational characteristics.

Infrastructure evolution brings with it many benefits. IT services few envisioned several years ago have become commonplace. Older services can be delivered in new, more customer-responsive ways, and the cost structures underlying new service delivery methods are superior to those of older methods. New business models enabled by the new service possibilities have emerged. Industries restructure to realize greater efficiencies and capabilities as part of a long-term trend that will continue and accelerate regardless of occasional technology market slumps.

[1] This chapter is adapted from Professor Robert D. Austin's *Managing Information Technology Infrastructure* course module, Harvard Business School Publishing No. 603-104.

[2] From an IBM advertisement that ran in major newspapers in the fall of 2001.

[3] In this and the following chapters, we use the word *infrastructure* to refer to the entire layered fabric of hardware, software, systems, and media that collectively deliver IT services.

Along with benefits, however, come challenges. In this chapter and the next two, we address the challenges associated with changing infrastructure. Our focus is on front-line issues of execution. Grand visions are of little use unless they can be translated into reality. New business models and systems cannot succeed unless they can be relied on to operate at key moments. New technologies provide less value if they cannot interoperate effectively with the older technologies still present in most companies. Most seriously, IT infrastructure greatly determines a company's differentiating capabilities; effective infrastructure enhances capabilities, while ineffective infrastructure destroys them. In today's environment, a seemingly minor IT decision made two or three years ago by a low-level technical employee can turn out to be the decisive factor in defining a winning strategy, closing a sale or deal, or surviving a competitive challenge.

The constraints of past IT infrastructure decisions can be severe, for example, when a company deploys a technology that proves to be a loser in the marketplace; such a company can be left with poor (or no) vendor support, inferior business capabilities, and costly-to-maintain infrastructure that cannot easily be shut down or replaced. Infrastructure decisions are difficult because they arise in a dimly illuminated realm halfway between business and technology. In this realm, technology issues are tightly interwoven with business issues, and it is unclear who should be making the decisions. Often general managers are tempted to "leave it to the techies," but this is often a mistake. Technological aspects of decisions may seem alien to nontechnical managers, but technologists may see business issues in similar terms. The deepest challenges of infrastructure management, then, are in understanding and assigning responsibility for making these not just technical, not just business decisions, in bridging the gap between the business and technology domains. Only when we are successful in this will we see clearly how evolving technologies affect business, how management priorities should evolve, and how we can reduce the risks that affect day-to-day operations.

FIGURE 5.1

A Graphical Representation of Moore's Law

Source: Adapted by Mark Seager from *Microprocessor Report* 9(6), May 1995, and Aad Offerman, "ChipList 9.9.5," July 1998, http://einstein.et.tudelft.nl/~offerman/chiplist.html. See http://www.physics.udel.edu/wwwusers/watson/scen103/intel.html, April 20, 2000, George Watson, University of Delaware, 1998.

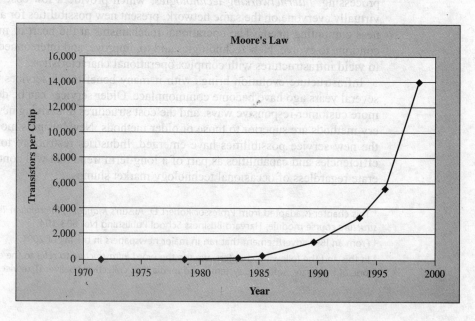

The Drivers of Change: Better Chips, Bigger Pipes

In 1965, Gordon Moore, who would later cofound Intel, noted that the performance of memory chips doubled every 18 to 24 months, whereas their size and cost remained roughly constant. He predicted that the trend would continue and that its impact on the world would be profound. Nearly four decades later, most people are familiar with changes wrought by Moore's "Law." The computing power in a twenty-first-century desktop, laptop, or even handheld computing device far exceeds that of machines the size of large rooms at the time of Moore's observation (see Figure 5.1). Equally significant is the low cost of modern devices. Once scarce, expensive, and therefore centrally controlled computing power is now abundant, inexpensive, and widely distributed in everything from general-purpose computers to toaster ovens.

Centralized computing architecture prevailed during the 1960s and 1970s (see Figure 5.2). Specialized data processing staffs presided over large mainframe computers accessed via awkward punch card, Teletype, and terminal machines. Dealings between humans and computers were not very interactive; programs ran infrequently, in batches, often only once each day. Access devices were "dumb"; they had little inherent capability but served merely as murky windows into complex mainframes. Mainframes provided all computational and storage capabilities. The occasional need to share information between mainframes led to the development of networks. These early networks were simple because they only had to handle traffic between a few large mainframe computers.

The impacts of Moore's Law disrupted the mainframe paradigm. An advertisement for the Intel 4004 in the fall 1971 issue of *Electronic News* exaggerated when it announced "a new era in integrated electronics," a "computer on a chip."[4] But the new era was not long in coming. The immediate successors of the programmable 4004 were the basis for the first general-purpose desktop computing machines capable of real business functionality: Personal computers (PCs). When the IBM PC appeared in late 1981, few realized how radically it would change business computing.

With the emergence of PCs, computing that had resided in centralized data processing enclaves spread throughout the organization and into the eager hands of business users. Financial analysts embraced spreadsheets. Marketers designed and analyzed their own databases. Engineers adopted computerized drawing packages and programmed their own PCs for more specialized purposes. For a growing number of computing tasks, reliance on the data processing staff became a distant memory.

As newly empowered computer users sought to share work, new communications infrastructures emerged. Local area networks (LANs) allowed businesspeople to share spreadsheets, word processing, and other documents, and to use common printers to obtain hard copies of their work. PCs and LANs became more sophisticated as users' computing needs expanded and as underlying technologies that were fundamentally different from earlier mainframe technologies advanced. The client-server movement was the culmination of this model: Higher-powered but still distributed computers (servers) combined with more elaborate networks and desktop PCs

---

[4] Paul Frieberger and Michael Swaine, *Fire in the Valley: The Making of the Personal Computer* (New York: McGraw-Hill, 2000), p. 20.

FIGURE 5.2 **The Evolution of Corporate IT Infrastructure**

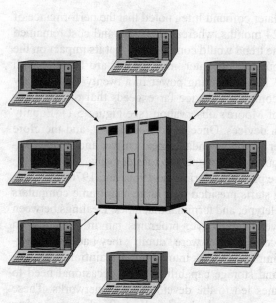

Mainframe-Based Centralized Computing (Pre-1980)

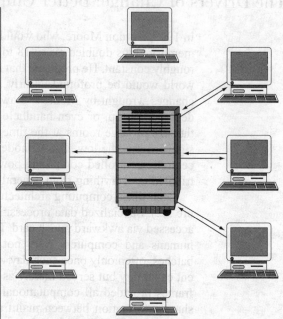

PC-Based Distributed Computing (1980s)

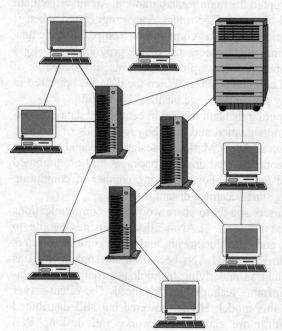

Client-Server Computing (Late 1980s, Early 1990s)

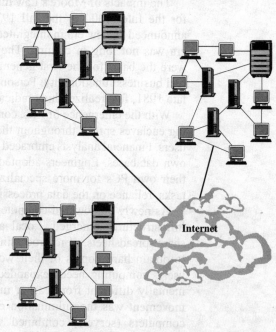

Internetwork-Based Computing (Mid-1990s to Present)

FIGURE 5.3
A Graphical
Illustration of
Metcalfe's Law

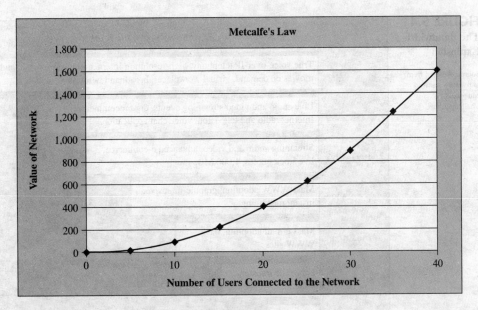

(clients) to provide IT services (i.e., payroll, order management, sales support, and beyond) formerly delivered by mainframe.

In the early 1990s, the rise to prominence of the commercial Internet, the Web, and underlying protocols (rules for how data would be moved across networks) led to new stages of evolution.[5] Transmission control protocol and Internet protocol, together known as TCP/IP, provided a robust standard for routing messages between LANs and created the potential to connect all computers on an ever-larger wide area network (WAN). Internetworking technologies were the legacy of U.S. Department of Defense (DOD) research (conducted in the 1960s against the backdrop of the Cold War) to develop communication networks without critical communication lines or nodes that could be targeted by an enemy. Because of their publicly funded origins, TCP/IP and other Internet protocols and technologies were *open* standards, not owned by any person or company. Computers, therefore, could be connected at low cost and with minimal central orchestration. Self-service hookup facilitated rapid growth in the worldwide Internet.

At first, the Internet was useful primarily for exchanging e-mail and large data files, but the Web, with its graphical user interfaces, made Internet communication valuable to those who were not computer specialists. Just as PCs had made computing accessible to a wide variety of nontechnical users, the Web made network resources (such as distant databases) and capabilities (such as over-the-Net collaboration) accessible. The number of connected computers shot upward, and the value of the network increased according to Metcalfe's Law: "The usefulness of a network increases with the square of the number of users connected to the network" (see Figure 5.3).[6]

---

[5] The Internet was not new in the 1990s. It had been in use by the military and by researchers since the 1960s. But commercial uses of these technologies accelerated dramatically in the 1990s.

[6] Metcalfe's Law is commonly attributed to Robert Metcalfe, one of the inventors of the Ethernet standard and the founder of 3Com Corporation.

FIGURE 5.4
The Bandwidth Explosion

Source: Adapted from http://www.stanford.edu/~yzarolia/Challenges.htm.

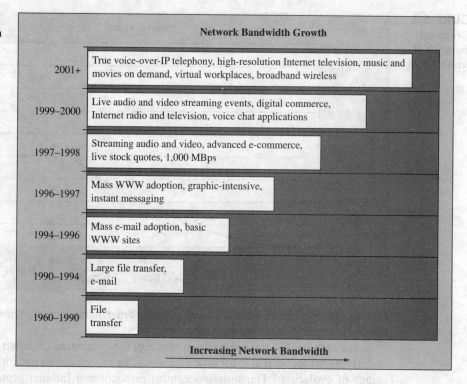

As the number of users grew, commercial potential mounted and network capacity expanded. Network capacity followed a curve steeper than the one that applied to chips (see Figure 5.4). The combination of powerful chips and large communication "pipes," both at low cost, fueled a process that would lead to qualitatively different computing infrastructures.

These related exponential trends—reduction in the cost of computing power and reduction in the cost of exchanging information between computers—have been fundamental drivers of changes in the business landscape that we continue to experience and try to understand. Because changes have been rapid, many businesses own a mix of technologies from different computing eras. Some companies still rely heavily on mainframes; as recently as 1997, for example, Ford Motor Company had over 300 million lines of COBOL software running vital company functions on mainframe computers, and it is likely that some of that remains in use today.[7] At the same time, companies have moved boldly to seize the benefits of newer technologies. Mainframes have been redefined and reborn as enterprise servers. The constant intermingling of old and new technologies adds to the complexity of infrastructure management problems. Understanding how shifting technology might combine with "legacy" systems to change business capabilities is a prerequisite for understanding how to manage IT infrastructures.

[7] For more details on this, see Robert D. Austin and Mark Cotteleer, "Ford Motor Company: Maximizing the Business Value of Web Technologies," Harvard Business School Case No. 198-006.

The Basic Components of Internetworking Infrastructures

For our purposes, IT infrastructures can be divided into three categories: network, processing systems, and facilities. *Network* refers to the technologies (hardware and software) that permit exchange of information between processing units and organizations. As network capacity increases, the network takes on greater importance as a component of IT infrastructure. *Processing systems* encompass the hardware and software that together provide an organization's ability to handle business transactions. They are newly interesting in the age of internetworking because they are being redesigned to better capitalize on the advantages offered by internetworking technologies. *Facilities,* the physical systems that house and protect computing and network devices, are the least glamorous infrastructure components. But they too are growing in importance as demand increases for high levels of availability, reliability, and security and as greater network capacity makes new facilities models possible.

Each of these infrastructure components generates opportunities and issues managers must understand and be able to address. Table 5.1 lists some of the supporting core technologies and identifies some of the key management issues that arise for each component. A major theme underlying the evolution of these components is that *internetworking creates many more degrees of freedom in how components can be arranged and managed.* Having more degrees of freedom creates possibilities for cost reduction, new capabilities, and new business models but also poses challenges in understanding the implications of possible infrastructure designs and management actions.

TABLE 5.1 **Fundamental Components of Internetworking Infrastructure**

	Core Technologies	Key Management Issues
Network	Fiber optics, cable systems, DSL, satellite, wireless, internetworking hardware (routers, switches, firewalls), content delivery software, identity and policy management, Net monitoring	• How to select technologies and standards • How to select partners • How to manage partner relationships • How to assure reliability • How to maintain security
Processing Systems	Transaction software (enterprise systems offered by companies such as SAP and Oracle or more targeted solutions, sometimes homegrown), servers, server appliances, client devices (PCs, handhelds)	• What to keep internal and what to outsource • How to deploy, grow, and modify • Enterprise system or best-of-breed hybrid • Relationships with legacies • How to manage incidents • How to recover after a "disaster"
Facilities	Corporate data centers, collocation data centers, managed services data centers, data closets	• Internal or external management • Choosing a facilities model suited to one's company • How to assure reliability • How to maintain security

The Technological Elements of Networks

Networks can be decomposed into technological elements; these are the key components that managers must understand, arrange, and maintain. Although the underlying technologies that constitute these elements vary, anyone involved in managing networks will need to make decisions about the design, management, and improvement of the following.

Local Area Networks

Local area networks (LANs), as the name implies, provide a way for computers that are physically close together to communicate (see Figure 5.5). LAN technologies define the physical features of solutions to local communication problems and needs (e.g., should we use coaxial or unshielded twisted pair cabling? should we go wireless?) and also the protocols—the rules—for "conversations" between computers (e.g., which wireless Ethernet standard should we choose?). Choices between different technologies and standards involve trade-offs, often in terms of cost versus capabilities but sometimes also, as in the case of wireless technologies, in terms of convenience versus data capacity or even information security.

Hubs, Switches, Wireless Access Points, and Network Adapters

Hubs, switches, "WAPs," and network adapters allow computers to be connected in LANs. Hubs and switches serve as central junctions into which cables from the computers on a LAN are connected. Wireless access points connect wireless devices into

FIGURE 5.5
A Simple LAN

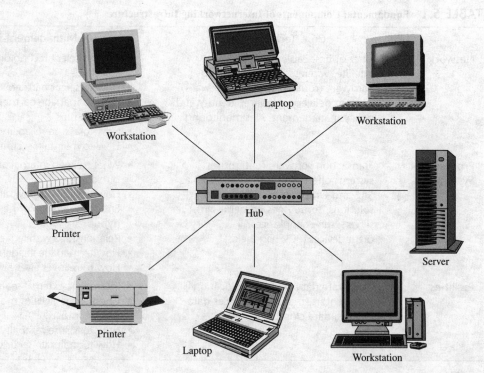

How LAN Protocols Work

The problem of computers "conversing" on a LAN is much like the problem of students conversing in a classroom. In a classroom, the air in the room (the "ether") readily supports students in speaking to each other. But if two people speak at the same time, they cannot be sure of communication. To avoid such problems in the classroom we employ protocols—rules—that govern our interactions. One possible set of rules might require that students speak in turn. To keep track of whose turn it is, we might pass a small object (a "token") in a pattern (maybe a "ring") around the room. Whoever has the token at the moment has speaking rights; everyone else must listen. These rules are very much like those used by computers as they speak onto the captive ether of LAN network cables, or into the actual ether of a wireless LAN, by using the Token Ring protocol. The popular Ethernet protocol is a little different. With Ethernet, computers speak out whenever they (1) have something to say, and (2) hear silence on the network for a moment. If two or more computers speak at the same time, the computers notice this—they detect the "collision"—and stop talking. Each waits a random amount of time and tries again. The Ethernet protocol works well as long as the amount of time it takes a computer to say something is small compared to the time available.

hubs and switches. Hubs are simple connection devices, but switches vary in complexity and capability from very simple to very large and sophisticated. Sophisticated switches connect LANs and larger networks to each other. Network adapters that are physically fitted into the computers on a LAN translate the computer's communications into a language that can be broadcast over the LAN and understood by listening computers. Network adapters also listen for communications from other computers and translate them into terms that can be understood by the connected computers (see the accompanying feature).

Wide Area Networks

Wide area networks (WANs), as the name implies, provide a way for computers physically distant from each other to communicate (see Figure 5.6). WANs are networks of networks, and enable LANs to connect and communicate. WAN technologies define the physical features of solutions and the standards for conducting conversations between computers and communication devices over long distances (e.g., should we use gigabit Ethernet or Asynchronous Transfer Mode to transmit large volumes of data over long distances?). A WAN inside the boundaries of a company's physical premises is sometimes called an *intranet*. A WAN that extends outward from a company's physical premises to business partners is sometimes called an *extranet*. Choices between different technologies and standards in building internetworks, whether they are intranets or extranets, involve trade-offs of cost versus data capacity, reliability, and security.

Routers

Routers are the devices that enable internetworking, the means by which messages are relayed across large distances. A router listens in on LAN conversations and recognizes messages intended for computers that are not on that LAN. The listening

FIGURE 5.6
An Example of a WAN

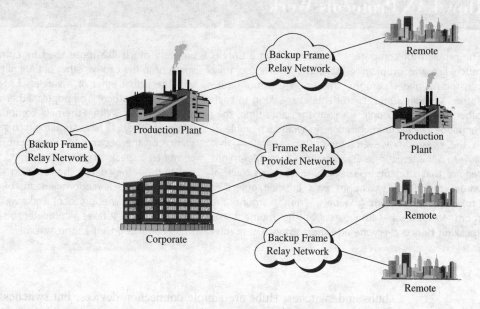

router relays those messages to other routers. Each router has some notion of the approximate direction of the message's destination across the larger network. As a message makes its way through a series of between-router "hops," it gradually arrives at routers that know more details about the location of the destination computer. Eventually a message finds a router that knows the destination machine's LAN and can complete the delivery of a message. Like switches, routers come in simple and sophisticated varieties. They are the glue with which networks are connected to each other and provide many degrees of freedom in network design (see the accompanying feature).

Firewalls and Other Security Systems and Devices

As we discuss in the next chapter, managers of computing infrastructure have reason to worry about the security and confidentiality of the information that traverses networks. A variety of network systems and devices addresses these worries. Firewalls act as security sentries at the boundaries of an organization's internal network to protect it from intrusion from the outside. Because firewalls are imperfect, network managers employ intrusion detection systems (IDSs) composed of a variety of software tools such as network monitoring software and hardware devices such as sensors and probes. Other network security devices help users open secure virtual "tunnels" across public and private networks to create virtual private networks (VPNs). The complexity of the configurations of security systems and devices increases with the changing nature and escalating magnitude of security threats.

Caching, Content Acceleration, and Other Specialized Network Devices

As the commercial uses of internetworks proliferate, so do devices aimed at accomplishing specialized network functions. Some devices help accelerate the delivery of

Imagine a complex highway system on which millions of cars are always moving. There are groups of cars that belong to the same travel party and are heading to the same place. But individual drivers know only the address where they are heading. They have no maps and no sense of direction. Members of groups make no attempt to stay together. At junctures along the highway network there are routing stations where cars stop, show their destination addresses, and are told, "Try going that way." A single routing station may send cars heading for the same destination in different directions. Eventually, though, a car arrives at its destination. It waits for other members of the travel party to arrive, and then they all do something useful together. This is an overly simple but fairly accurate analogy for how messages traverse internetworks.

information across the network, sometimes by "caching" (e.g. storing) information in a location close to the destination machine. This approach is used for information that does not change often. Other specialized devices help assure the efficient transmission of time-dependent information such as the sound and image data that accompany internetwork-based video delivery or video teleconferencing. As infrastructure evolves, there will be continuing growth in specialized network systems and devices for metering and management of messages and transactions to assure timely and error-free quality of services (QoS), facilitate information-based transactions, and accomplish a variety of other functions.

The Technological Elements of Processing Systems

Processing systems can be decomposed into technological elements managers must understand, arrange, and maintain. Although there is tremendous variety in the underlying hardware and software that constitute these elements, anyone involved in managing a company's processing systems will need to make decisions about the design, management, and improvement of the following.

Client Devices and Systems

Until quite recently, it was safe to think of client devices as PCs; in the last few years, however, variety in client devices has exploded to include handheld devices, cell phones, and even automotive components. Client systems are the software that runs on these devices to perform business functions, manage interactions with other computers, and handle certain low-level client machine operations (such as storing saved information). As the name implies, clients are often on the receiving end of IT services delivered from elsewhere in the network. Business users experience internetworking infrastructure primarily through client devices and systems. Unlike the terminals of the mainframe era, modern clients are not dumb; often they are capable of performing significant business functions even when separated from a network. Mobile users often use clients in both network-connected and unconnected modes; client software must manage intermittently connected devices and systems in a way that provides business advantage to users.

Server Devices and Systems

Servers occupy a role in internetworking infrastructure roughly equivalent to that of mainframe computers in an earlier era. Although based on microcomputer technology, servers handle the heavy processing required for high-volume business transactions and permit sharing of information across a large number of computer users. Servers are the source of many of the IT services that clients receive from across the network. Server systems consist of software to carry out mainline business functions (such as order or inventory management), manage transactions from other computers (such as those that update inventory information), and handle low-level machine operations (such as storing saved information). In essence, clients perform front-end processing (interaction with users) while servers perform back-end processing (heavy computation or interaction with other back-end computers). Servers are often physically located in data centers and managed by central staffs, as their mainframe ancestors were. Servers and their systems are increasingly designed as specialized appliances targeted at specific functions: database servers, Web servers, and application servers, for example (see Figure 5.7). Software systems that run on distributed, specialized

FIGURE 5.7
Servers in a Typical E-Commerce Configuration

Source: Robert D. Austin, Larry Leibrock, and Alan Murray, "The iPremier Company: Denial of Service Attack (A)," Harvard Business School Case No. 9-601-114.

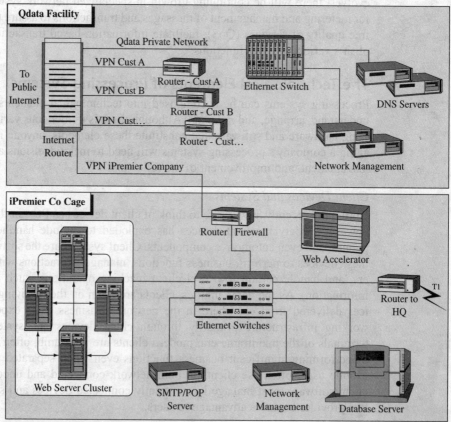

Diagram simplified for illustration purpose

architectures must be designed very differently from those of mainframe systems in which all processing happens on the same machine.

Mainframe Devices and Systems

Mainframe computers remain very much a part of modern IT infrastructure. In many companies, mainframes still do the vast majority of business-critical transaction processing. Some of these mainframes are modern, high-performance machines, the equivalent of very powerful servers that interoperate well with internetworks. Others are relics of an earlier era that are still performing vital business functions. As computing infrastructures become more interconnected, legacy mainframe systems pose complications. The open protocols of the internetworking world are not the native language of older mainframe computers. Mainframe manufacturers have developed systems that enable interaction between legacy mainframes and internetworks. These advanced systems allow users to access information on mainframes via new technologies, such as Web browsers. But interfaces between legacy mainframes and internetworks cannot always overcome the problems associated with the interaction of such different technologies. For example, some mainframe systems still process jobs in batches. Native internetworking systems and more modern mainframe systems, in contrast, usually are designed to operate in real time, to process new orders at the time they occur. Overcoming fundamental operational incompatibilities often eventually necessitates the replacement of a legacy system, but this takes time and money. Where mainframes remain in more modern renditions, their mission has changed so that they function effectively as real-time transaction processors.

Middleware

Middleware is the hodgepodge of enabling utilities, message handling and queuing systems, protocols, standards, software tool kits, and other systems that help clients, servers, mainframes, and their systems coordinate activities in time and across networks. Middleware, which often runs on servers, could be considered a category of server system, but it is important enough in orchestrating the activities of internetworking infrastructure to deserve separate mention. Many managers know little and understand less about middleware; it is a classic example of difficult-to-manage infrastructure. Few people know enough about both the technology and the business needs to make intelligent decisions in this area. And yet increasingly sophisticated middleware is the key to many new approaches to IT service delivery, such as those sometimes called *utility* or *on demand* or *grid* computing. The middleware domain is also where important "Web services" technologies usually operate. Middleware plays an increasing role in improving the flexibility capacity utilization, efficiency, and effectiveness of modern IT infrastructure.

Infrastructure Management Systems

A company must have systems for managing its computing infrastructure. These systems monitor the performance of systems, devices, and networks. They include systems that support the help desks when users are having trouble with computers or networks, and the systems that deliver new software to computers throughout an organization. The quality of infrastructure management systems influences how

Open Source Software

Many companies use "open source software" (OSS) systems, such as the Linux operating system or the Apache Web Server, as vital components of their IT infrastructure. OSS is neither purchased nor homegrown; rather, it is freely available from a worldwide community of volunteers who have worked together via the Internet to develop a product of common interest. You might think that software developed by informally organized volunteers could not perform well enough to become parts of a corporate IT infrastructure. But OSS (notably Linux and Apache, but there are other examples) performs *very* well. Often it outperforms commercially developed counterparts on important measures (e.g., reliability, security, speed). Experts attribute the excellent performance of OSS to the extreme transparency of the methods used to develop it; whereas commercial firms usually keep secret the inner workings of their software, OSS developers make their "code" available for anyone to see. When so many experts—potentially thousands of software developers—can "look under the hood" to see how a system works, most problems get noticed and fixed quickly.

When companies use open source, they pay no license fees. Although significant monetary savings may result from this fact, operating OSS does incur costs. Some commercial software vendors, especially those whose products compete with OSS, have argued that OSS is *more* expensive to operate than commercial software (e.g., support workers may need to be retrained). Critics of OSS also point to concerns about who "stands behind" software developed by an amorphous community of volunteers (when something goes wrong, who do you call?), and to the difficulty in assuring that no components within an OSS system are owned by a commercial firm (if proprietary software has found its way, perhaps inadvertently, into OSS, that could generate legal difficulties for companies using the software). OSS enthusiasts counter the first complaint by noting that many large, reputable firms, such as IBM and Novell, will now provide support for OSS (thus, "standing behind it"), and that OSS development practices are transparent enough to assure that proprietary software will not "contaminate" OSS to any consequential degree.

efficiently a company obtains value from its computing assets. Without strong systems management, expensive internetworks may become tied in knots; for example, too many transactions may flow to one computer while another is underused.

Business Applications

Computer users interact with the business applications layer of infrastructure constantly and directly. Most companies house an immense variety of installed business applications. Many applications are custom built by the IT staffs in the companies that use them. Others are off-the-shelf packages ranging from small client applications, such as a spreadsheet program, up to huge packages that cost tens of millions of dollars and take years to install, such as enterprise resource planning (ERP) systems. As the name suggests, business applications deliver actual business functionality. In a real sense, it is the job of the rest of an internetworking infrastructure to make possible the delivery of business functionality by this top layer.

The Technological Elements of Facilities

Facilities also can be decomposed into technological elements. Once a backwater left to real estate managers, facilities management has become an important aspect of infrastructure management, primarily due to the demands for always on, 24-hour, 7-days-a-week (24×7) operations. Consequently, anyone involved in managing a

FIGURE 5.8
A Modern Data Center

Source: Allegiance Telecom.

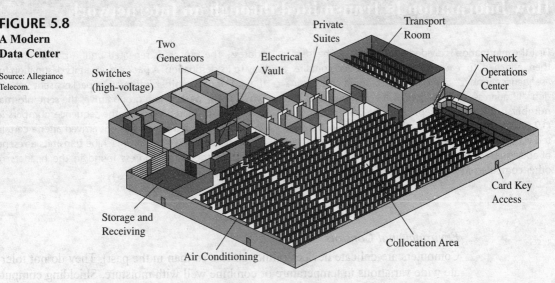

Two Generators

Switches (high-voltage)

Private Suites

Electrical Vault

Transport Room

Network Operations Center

Card Key Access

Storage and Receiving

Air Conditioning

Collocation Area

company's processing systems eventually will face decisions about the design, management, and improvement of the following.

Buildings and Physical Spaces

The physical characteristics of the buildings and rooms that house computing infrastructure strongly influence how well devices and systems function and how efficiently and effectively they can be managed (see Figure 5.8). The size of a facility, its physical features, how readily it lends itself to reconfiguration, and how well it protects its contents from external disruptions are important factors to consider in managing physical structures.

Network Conduits and Connections

The way in which systems within a facility are connected to wider networks also influences IT infrastructure performance. Among the factors managers must consider are the amount of redundancy in physical network connections, the number and selection of partners who will provide "backbone" connectivity to external networks, and the capacity of the data lines leased from service providers. All these factors involve trade-offs in terms of cost, performance, availability, and security. At stake in trade-off decisions are relationships with customers, suppliers, and other business partners.

Power

Computers do not run without power, and many businesses do not run without computers. Assuring that firms will have power when they need it is, then, a major concern for infrastructure managers. Decisions in this area involve trade-offs between cost and redundancy. Systems can obtain power from multiple power grids, uninterruptible power supplies (UPSs), backup generators, and even privately owned power plants. Determining which measures are worth their cost is a management decision.

First the information is divided into packets. A "header" is then attached to each packet; the header contains a "sequence number" and the packet's origin and destination "IP addresses." IP addresses are composed of four numbers, 0 to 255, separated by decimal points (19.67.89.134, for example). Packets are then transmitted via a router—a specialized computer that keeps track of addresses—across an available communication line to other computers in the rough direction of the destination address. The process is repeated until a packet finds its way to its destination. A packet waits at its destination for the arrival of the other information packets sent with it. When all the packets in a group arrive, the sent information is reconstructed by using the sequence numbers in packet headers. If a packet has not arrived after a certain period of time, the receiving machine transmits a resend request to the origin address found in the headers of other packets in the group.

Environmental Controls

Computers are delicate devices (although less so than in the past). They do not tolerate wide variations in temperature or combine well with moisture. Shielding computers from environmental hazards is another effort that can be pursued more or less thoroughly and at varying cost. As with power, how much should be paid for additional degrees of protection is a management decision.

Security

Computer devices and systems also must be protected from malicious attacks, both physical and network-based. Physical security requires facilities and methods that control access to machines, such as security guards, cages, and locks. Network security— a field of growing complexity—has numerous facilities implications. The threat from hacker attacks and intrusions is a growing problem. As with other facilities elements, security involves trade-offs, in this case between cost and level of protection.

Operational Characteristics of Internetworks[8]

Taken together, internetworking technologies have operational characteristics that distinguish them from other information technologies. In many ways, these characteristics determine the challenges of managing infrastructures based on internetworking technologies. Important operational characteristics of internetworking technologies that make them different from the technologies of previous eras in terms of how they perform and should be managed include the following (see the accompanying feature).

Internetworking Technologies Are Based on Open Standards

We have already mentioned this, but it bears repeating because of its importance. TCP/IP is the primary common language of internetworking technologies. TCP/IP standards define how computers send and receive data packets. Because the standards

[8] This section is based on Thomas Rodd and Robert D. Austin, "The Worldwide Web and Internet Technology: Technical Note," Harvard Business School Case No. 198-020.

were developed using public funds, they are public, not owned by anyone; they are open, not proprietary. The fact that TCP/IP can be freely used by anyone makes internetworks less dependent on solutions developed and marketed by private companies. Decreased reliance on proprietary technologies has generated huge economic benefits for purchasers of new technology by making systems from different vendors more interoperable and thus increasing competition. Prices are lower and performance better than they might have been if these technologies had remained proprietary. Insistence on open standards and solutions has become part of the ethos of the internetworking community of administrators and developers. This ethos has led to development of other important open standards, such as hypertext transport protocol (HTTP), used to deliver Web content.

Internetworking Technologies Operate Asynchronously

Information sent over an internetwork does not employ dedicated, bidirectional connections between sender and receiver, as for example, a telephone call. Instead, packets of information with accompanying address information are sent toward a destination, sometimes without any prior coordination between the sender and the receiver. Network services that exchange information quickly, such as the Web, require the sender and the receiver to be connected to the internetwork at the same time. But such communication is still asynchronous in that no dedicated link is established. For other services, such as e-mail, the receiver's computer need not even be switched on at the time the message is sent. As with postal mail, an e-mail recipient has a mailbox where mail can accumulate until it is accessed. Unlike regular mail though, e-mail messages can be sent around the globe almost instantaneously.

Internetwork Communications Have Inherent Latency

The computers that make up internetworks are connected by links of varying capacity (see Table 5.2). As packets carry information along different paths toward a common destination, some packets flow quickly through wide links while others move more slowly through narrow links. Packets that together constitute a single message do not arrive at the destination in the same moment. Thus, there is variable wait time between the sending of a message and the arrival at the destination of the last packet in a message.

TABLE 5.2 **Measuring Network Bandwidth**

Term	Definition
Bandwidth	Maximum rate at which information can be transmitted along a communication link
Bit	Smallest unit of information handled by computers
Bits per second (bps)	Bandwidth measurement unit

Information Measure	Bit Equivalent	Information Transfer Speed
1 kilobit (Kb)	1 thousand bits	1,000 bits/second
1 megabit (Mb)	1 million bits	1,000,000 bits/second
1 gigabit (Gb)	1 billion bits	1,000,000,000 bits/second

Because traffic volume is somewhat unpredictable, wait time—often called *latency*—can be difficult to predict. Managers can take actions to make it likely that latency will be within certain tolerances. At the very least, they can assure that network capacity between two points is great enough to avoid unacceptable wait times. New routing technologies provide more options; some make it possible to move high-priority packets to the top of the queues that form at narrow network links. But some degree of latency, and hence unpredictability, is inherent in internetworking technologies and must be taken into account in the design and management of internetworking systems.

Internetworking Technologies Are Naturally Decentralized

Largely due to their Defense Department heritage, which dictated that computer networks contain no single points of failure, internetworks have no central traffic control point. Computers connected to the network do not need to be defined to a central control authority, as is the case with some networking technologies. There is, in fact, no central authority that oversees or governs the development or administration of the public Internet except the ones that assign TCP/IP addresses. As a result, individuals and organizations are responsible for managing and maintaining their own facilities in a way that does not hinder the operation of the network as a whole.

Internetworking Technologies Are Scalable

Because communication is intelligently routed along multiple paths, adding to an internetwork is as simple as connecting to another machine. An internetwork as a whole is not affected significantly when a path is removed (packets simply get routed a different way). Additional paths can be added in parallel with overworked paths. Furthermore, internetworking technologies allow relatively easy reorganization of subnetworks; if a network segment has become overloaded, the network can be split up into more manageable subnetworks. In general, these new technologies allow more flexible expansion than do most other network technologies.

The Rise of Internetworking: Business Implications

Dr. Eric Schmidt, Google's chief executive officer (CEO), has observed that high-capacity networks enable a computer to interact just as well with another physically distant computer as with one that is only inches away. Given enough bandwidth, the physical location of computers ceases to matter much. Operationally, the communication pathways inside a computer become indistinguishable from the pathways that connect computers. The network itself becomes part of a larger processor composed of the network and all of its connected computers. To paraphrase a Sun Microsystems slogan: The network *becomes* a computer.

For business computer users who do not have access to this level of network bandwidth, Schmidt's observation remains theoretical (see Table 5.3). Nevertheless, the idea of an increasingly connected network, both inside and beyond the boundaries of organizations, in which the physical location of processors matters less and less is of great practical importance. Improved connections between machines, departments, companies, and customers mean *quicker realization of economic value* when parties interact; internetworking infrastructure is the means by which value is created and

TABLE 5.3   **Communication Technology, Bandwidths, and User Groups**

Communication Technology	Bandwidth*	User Groups
Telephone modem	33.6–56 kbps	Individuals and small businesses
Integrated services digital network (ISDN)	128 kbps	Individuals and small businesses
Cable modem	128 kbps–3 mbps	Individuals and small businesses
Digital subscriber line (DSL)	128 kbps–1.5 mbps	Individuals and small businesses
Ethernet LAN	10–100 mbps	Most businesses and organizations
Leased lines (T1, T3)	1.544–45 mbps	Government, universities, medium-size and large businesses
Asynchronous transfer mode (ATM)/Gigabit Ethernet	155 mbps–25.6 gbps	Government, universities, and large corporations

*We have listed the typical bandwidth performance. Some of the technologies are theoretically capable of higher bandwidths. Additionally, some technologies perform at different speeds upstream and downstream.

captured in real time. Transactions are initiated and consummated quickly. Activities that once were sequential occur simultaneously. Because the physical location of processing is less important, new possibilities for outsourcing, partnerships, and industry restructuring emerge. Along with these beneficial outcomes come drawbacks: Rising complexity, unpredictable interactions, and new types of threats to businesses and consumers. As a result, executives must understand the business implications of these powerful and pervasive networks.

The Emergence of Real-Time Infrastructures

In the mainframe era, scarcity of processing capacity required that business transactions be accumulated and processed in batches. A telephone calling card account might, for example, be updated by a batch run once each day. A stranded traveler who needed to reactivate a mistakenly deactivated card might have to wait for the once-a-day batch run for the card to be reactivated. As processing and communication capacity became more abundant, however, batch processing became less necessary. Delays between initiating a transaction and completing its processing have been greatly reduced. With real-time internetworking infrastructures, customers are serviced and economic value is realized immediately rather than over hours, days, or weeks. The potential benefits of real-time infrastructures are discussed below.

Better Data, Better Decisions

In most large organizations, people in different locations need access to the same data. Until recently, organizations had to keep copies of the same data in many places. But keeping the data synchronized was difficult and frequently did not happen. Discrepancies between copies of data led to errors, inefficiencies, and poor decision making. Abundant communication capacity has not eliminated the need for multiple copies, but it has reduced it. In addition, it has made it much easier to keep copies synchronized. For the first time, it is becoming possible to run a large business based on a set of financial and operational numbers that are consistent throughout an enterprise.

Improved Process Visibility

Older IT systems based on proprietary technologies often communicated poorly with each other. Consequently, viewing the progress of orders or other transactions across system boundaries was difficult. People in a company's sales organization could not access data in manufacturing, for example, to obtain information about the status of an order. New technologies based on open standards and compatible back-office transaction systems let users instantaneously view transactions with each step in procurement and fulfillment processes, beyond specific system boundaries, and even beyond the boundaries of a company into partners' systems.

Improved Process Efficiency

Many efficiency improvements result directly from enhanced process visibility. In manufacturing, workers who can see what supplies and orders are coming their way tend to hold less buffer stock ("just-in-case" inventory) to guard against uncertainty. Holding less buffer stock reduces working capital, shortens cycle times, and improves return on investment (ROI). A manager in charge of supplying plastic cases for portable radios, for example, can notice that orange radios are not selling well and quickly reduce orange in the color mix.

From Make-and-Sell to Sense-and-Respond [9]

Real-time infrastructures are a prerequisite for achieving highly responsive operations, those based on "sense-and-respond" principles rather than make-to-sell principles. The fundamental insight here is that if operating infrastructures can come close enough to real time, value-adding activities can be performed in response to *actual* customer demand rather than *forecasted* customer demand. Sense-and-respond organizations avoid losses caused by demand-forecasting errors. The most celebrated example is Dell Computer Corporation's make-to-order manufacturing process, which makes computers only in response to actual customer orders. But many other companies in both manufacturing and service industries are seeking ways to move to sense-and-respond models, including some with very complex products, such as automobiles.

In many companies, especially older ones, moving to real-time systems involves reengineering transaction systems to take advantage of greater processing and network capacities. Some companies have renewed transaction infrastructures by implementing large enterprise systems made, for example, by SAP or Oracle. Others have designed best-of-breed transaction infrastructures by connecting what they consider

---

[9] See Richard L. Nolan and Steven P. Bradley, *Sense and Respond: Capturing Value in the Network Era* (Boston: Harvard Business School Press, 1998).

the best products from a variety of vendors. Whichever approach a company takes, the objective is to remove elements from the transaction infrastructure that do not operate in real time, thereby realizing almost immediate economic value from transactions.

A company that succeeds in reengineering transaction and communication systems to operate more or less in real time has ascended to a new and important stage of evolution. When a company achieves real-time IT operations, it not only creates value more quickly, it also creates options for fully leveraging a shared public infrastructure, the Internet, for that company's private gain. But there are drawbacks in how real-time infrastructures operate. The same characteristics that allow immediate value creation also allow crisis acceleration. The connections to public networks that create leverage also increase exposure to external threats. While the drawbacks do not outweigh the benefits, they must be understood and managed.

Broader Exposure to Operational Threats

On October 19, 1987, the Dow Jones Industrial Average plummeted more than 500 points in the twentieth century's single largest percentage decrease. The 22.6 percent plunge was almost double the 12.9 percent drop in 1929 that foreshadowed the Great Depression. Unlike 1929, the market in 1987 quickly recovered, posting major gains in the two days after the crash and regaining its precrash level by September 1989. Nevertheless, the suddenness of these events prompted a search for explanations.

Many singled out the role of computerized program trading by large institutional investors as a primary cause of the 1987 crash. In program trading, computers initiate transactions automatically, without human intervention, when certain triggering conditions appear in the markets. No one anticipated that automatic trades could lead to a chain reaction of more automatic trades. Automatic trades themselves created market conditions that set off more automatic trades, which created conditions that set off more automatic trades, and so on, in a rapid-fire progression that was both unexpected and difficult to understand while it was in progress.

This example reveals a dark side of real-time computing that extends to internetworking infrastructures. As batch-processing delays are eliminated and more transactions move from initiation to completion without intervention by human operators, the potential grows for computerized chain reactions that produce unanticipated effects. Favorable effects such as value creation happen more immediately, but so do unfavorable effects. Malfunctions and errors propagate faster and have potentially broader impacts. Diagnosis and remediation of problems that result from fast-moving, complex interactions present major challenges to organizational and, indeed, human cognitive capabilities. Just figuring out what is going on during or in the immediate aftermath of an incident is often difficult.

IT infrastructures of the twenty-first century therefore must be less prone to malfunctions and errors that might trigger a chain reaction and more tolerant of them when they occur. Real-time operations demand 24×7 availability. Because some unintended effects will occur despite the best intentions and plans, responsible managers need to think in advance and in detail about how they will respond to incidents. Effective "disaster recovery" requires anticipating that incidents will occur despite the fact that one cannot anticipate their exact nature and practicing organizational responses. The range of incidents that require detailed response plans also includes those of a more sinister sort: Malicious attacks. Infrastructure managers must anticipate and protect systems from the many exploits creative individuals—hackers—use.

Technologies of the past were designed to deny access to systems unless someone intervened to authorize access. Internetworking systems are different. Because they evolved in an arena not oriented toward commerce but intended to support communities of researchers, internetworking technologies allow access unless someone intervenes to disallow it. Security measures to support commercial relationships, therefore, must be retrofitted onto the base technologies. Moreover, the universality of Internet connections—the fact that every computer is connected to every other computer—makes every computer a potential attack target and a potential base from which to launch attacks.

The average computer is connected to the Internet for only a few minutes before it is "port scanned," or probed for vulnerability to intrusion or attack. Many attempted incursions are the electronic equivalent of kids playing a prank. But recent evidence shows that more serious criminals have begun to explore the possibilities presented by the Internet. The threat is real, even from pranksters. Damaging attacks are alarmingly simple to initiate.

In February 2000, the business community received a wake-up call concerning its vulnerability to electronic attack (see Table 5.4). Total damages from a series of high-profile, centrally orchestrated "denial of service" attacks were estimated to be in excess of $100 million; the estimated costs incurred in more recent attacks reached into billions of dollars. As the Internet and the Web have risen to commercial prominence, computer security problems have progressed from being tactical nuisances that could be left to technicians into strategic infrastructure problems that require the involvement of business executives at the highest levels.

New Models of Service Delivery

In the early days of electric power generation, companies owned and managed their own power plants. Later, as standardization and technological advances made it possible to deliver power reliably via a more centralized model, companies began to purchase electric power from external providers. A similar shift is under way in the IT industry.

In today's companies, as increasingly reliable networks make the physical location of computers less important, services traditionally provided by internal IT departments can be acquired externally, across internetworks, from service providers. Fundamental economic forces such as scarcity of IT specialists and desire to reduce costs are driving this shift. The shift, which parallels the maturation of other industries, reveals a common pattern: Standardization and technology advances permit specialization by individual firms in value chains, resulting in economies of scale and higher service levels.

The transition under way is analogous to the move from telephone answering machines to voice mail. Telephone answering machines were purchased by companies and attached to individual telephones. When they broke, it was the company's job to fix or replace the machines. Messages were stored on magnetic tape inside the machine. In contrast, companies acquire voice mail from service providers for a monthly fee. The hardware that supports the service is owned by the provider and

TABLE 5.4   **Wake-Up Call: Denial of Service Attacks in February 2000***

Date	Target Company	Results of Attack
February 7	Yahoo!	• Overwhelming spike in traffic that lasted 3 hours. • Network availability dropped from 98% to 0%. • Attack originated from 50 different locations and was timed to occur during middle of business day. • Stock was down 3.2% for a week in which NASDAQ rose almost 3%.
February 8	Buy.com	• Attack occurred within an hour of the company's initial public offering (IPO). • Stock was down at week's end more than 20% from IPO price.
	eBay	• Stock was down 7.3% for a week in which NASDAQ rose almost 3%.
	CNN.com	• Service disrupted.
February 9	E*TRADE	• Attacked during peak trading hours. • Stock was down 7.6% for a week in which NASDAQ rose almost 3%.
	ZDNet	• Service disrupted.
February 18	Federal Bureau of Investigation (FBI)	• Service disrupted.
February 24	National Discount Brokers Group (NDB)	• Attacked during peak trading hours. • Operators accidentally crashed site as they attempted to defend against the attack.

*Overall performance of the Internet degraded by as much as 25% during the peak of the attacks as computers resent messages repeatedly and automatically, trying to recover interrupted transactions.

Source: Adapted from NetworkWorldFusion, www.nfusion.com, compiled by LeGrand Elebash.

physically resides in a central location unknown to most voice mail users. When voice mail breaks, the service provider is responsible for fixing it. Fixing it is easier and less expensive because the infrastructure that delivers the service is centralized and easily accessible. The potentially sensitive contents of voice mail messages no longer reside on the end user's desk; instead, the service provider is entrusted with their care and security.

The move to over-the-Net service delivery has been gradual and is far from complete. As supporting infrastructure matures, however, the economic advantages become more compelling. Even if actual software functionality is not acquired externally, external infrastructure management may still make sense. For example, a company may rent space in a vendor-owned IT hosting facility rather than incur the capital expenses required to build a data center, even as it retains internal management of the software.

As IT service models proliferate, service delivery depends on a growing number of service providers and other partners. One implication is that the reliability of vital services is only as good as the weakest link in the service provider chain.

Selecting strong partners and managing relationships are vital to reliable service delivery.

New service models that offer new capabilities and cost reduction cannot realize their full potential without being integrated into the rest of a company's IT infrastructure. Ideally, over-the-Net services would exchange data seamlessly, in real time, with a company's installed base of systems. Unfortunately, this is not easily accomplished. The questions involved in deciding how new services should interact with existing IT and organizational systems leads to the subject of managing legacies.

Managing Legacies

Few companies are so new that they have no artifacts left over from earlier eras that must coexist with new technologies. Legacy *systems* present one set of challenges. They are often based on outdated, obsolete, and proprietary technologies. Yet they are vital to the business as it operates from day to day. Fitting new infrastructure into complex legacy infrastructure, or vice versa, presents formidable challenges and uncertain outcomes.

But systems are not the only legacies companies must manage. Even more significant are legacy *processes, organizations,* and *cultures.* Changing the IT infrastructure has unavoidable effects on nontechnical elements of a company's operations. New technologies change how people work and interact. Managers must decide how much they want the company's culture to drive the design of its infrastructure or vice versa. In some companies, managers go to great lengths to make sure the IT infrastructure does not constrain culture or process. In others, managers use IT systems as "sledgehammers" to bring about organizational change. Both approaches can work, but the issues and decisions involved are complex.

The Future of Internetworking Infrastructure

The basic technology that supports moving data packets around an internetwork has existed in something like its present form since the late 1960s. The technologies we use to access internetworks—PCs, e-mail packages, and Web browsers, for example—have been appearing and maturing over the last 20 or so years. Although internetworking infrastructure continues to evolve significantly in both of these areas, there is a third area in which internetworking technologies are evolving even more rapidly.

The smooth functioning of markets and other kinds of business interactions presumes prerequisites that internetworking infrastructure still does not perfectly fulfill. We have mentioned some of these already. Markets do not tolerate the uncertainties of unreliable or unavailable infrastructure. Customers of a financial services firm, for example, will not tolerate loss of access to stock market trading. Similarly, business transactions cannot flourish when infrastructure is not highly secure. As we have seen, internetworks already are reasonably good at reliability, availability, and security, and they are getting better. But there are other, more subtle aspects of business support for which these technologies are not yet mature.

Ultimately, internetworking technologies must support all or nearly all the elements of business transactions that can occur in face-to-face transactions. If you are video-conferencing, for example, you need to be able to purchase guaranteed network bandwidth sufficient to make the conference approximate a productive face-to-face work experience; this is not yet possible everywhere. Consider another example: In business, you need to be sure the party you are interacting with is who he says he is, so he cannot later say, "That was not me you contracted with." This "nonrepudiation" requirement still presents difficulties in some internetworks. In general, the elements of infrastructure that support financial transactions are works in process; they constitute the above-mentioned third area in which infrastructure is evolving most rapidly. How we transport information within internetworks and how we access network resources are well defined, if continually changing, at this point in history. How companies will in the long run engage each other in real-time transactions, negotiate the terms of transactions, establish business linkages, and settle accounts depends on standards and technologies not yet fully developed.

Summary Internetworking infrastructures include the totality of existing client and server systems, new externally provided services, and older legacy systems. They interact with living organizations and have distinctive characteristics that are coming into clear view in the twenty-first century. They offer many more degrees of freedom in designing organizations and contain larger numbers of smaller components that interact in complex ways. Some of the components exist outside a firm's boundaries and thus are not fully under the control of company managers. The overall effect on a company's business is that there is *more inherent uncertainty in the operational environment.* This is at least partially offset by *more incremental options for managing that uncertainty.* Our ability to predict how a planned system will perform is limited, but options for experimenting to improve our understanding of emerging infrastructures are becoming more numerous and less expensive. Not surprisingly, our management frameworks are evolving in a way that reflects the uncertain and incremental nature of emerging infrastructure.

In this chapter we have described the technologies, functions, and components of internetworking infrastructure and how they are changing. We have explained how the changes generate new benefits, challenges, and threats. Approximately 75 percent of most companies' IT dollars go to infrastructure investments. If you are like many companies, that 75 percent approaches half of all your capital expenditures. Executives can use the following questions to assess the implications of the emergence of new technologies and infrastructures for their companies' operational capabilities:

1. What does the public infrastructure of the Internet mean to our business operations? Are we leveraging this infrastructure to maximum advantage? How dependent are we still on proprietary technologies?

2. How close do our company operations come to running in real time? What value creation opportunities can still be obtained by moving more in the direction of real-time value capture?

3. Has our company taken appropriate advantage of the many degrees of architectural and operational freedom offered by internetworking technologies? Have we thought through the inherent complexities and risks in those additional degrees of freedom?

4. Are we exploring new service delivery models aggressively enough?

5. Have we reexamined our management frameworks in light of the new and more adaptive capabilities that internetworking technologies offer? Most important, do senior business managers play an active and informed role in infrastructure design and planning decisions?

CHAPTER 6

Assuring Reliable and Secure IT Services[1]

The emergence of Web-based commerce has accelerated the expansion of a worldwide network capable of transmitting information reliably and securely across vast distances. The inherent reliability of modern internetworks is a legacy of U.S. Department of Defense research in the 1960s that led to technologies robust enough to withstand a military attack. The key to this inherent reliability is *redundancy:* The exceptionally large number of potential paths a message can take between any two points in a network. Because internetworking technologies automatically route messages around network problems, transmissions are highly likely to be successful.

Unfortunately, some components of a firm's infrastructure are *not* inherently reliable. The reliability of processing systems, for example, depends on how they are designed and managed. As with internetworks, the key to reliable systems is redundancy; however, reliability through redundancy comes at a price. It means buying extra equipment (computers, switches, software, electric generators, etc.) to guard against failures. Every increment of additional redundancy makes outages less likely, but every increment increases expenses as well.

How much reliability to buy is a management decision highly contingent on numerous, mostly business, factors. How costly is a 15-minute failure of the order management system? How costly is a 3-hour failure or a 12-hour failure? How likely are these failures? How about the e-mail system and the human resources system? Answers to these questions differ across businesses. Some costs of failures are intangible and hard to quantify. It may be possible to estimate the direct revenues your company will lose if your Web-based retail site goes down for two hours, but it is much harder to gauge how many customers frustrated by the outage will never return. In addition, it is difficult to estimate the probabilities of such events.

---

[1] This chapter is adapted from Professor Robert D. Austin's *Managing Information Technology Infrastructure* course module, Harvard Business School Publishing No. 603-104.

Redundant systems are more complex than nonredundant systems, and this complexity must be managed. Businesses need policies that determine how to integrate redundant elements into a company's overall infrastructure: How backup systems and equipment will be brought online, how problems will be diagnosed and triaged, and who will be responsible for responding to incidents. Since the efficacy and efficiency of incident response improve with practice, the frequency and form of rehearsals are also management decisions. Charles Perrow suggests in _Normal Accidents: Living with High Risk Technologies_ that failures are inevitable in "tightly coupled" complex systems. Typical precautions, Perrow writes, such as adding redundancy, help create new categories of accidents by adding complexity.[2] Thus, our efforts to make infrastructure designs more robust also make operational management more difficult.

Managers also must guard against malicious threats to computing infrastructure. Malicious threats, which are similar to accidental failures in their potential cost and unintended ripple effect, are designed specifically to damage a company's business. Attacks, intrusions, viruses, and worms have no legitimate uses when perpetrated against others' systems. Their designers, often extremely creative, are motivated by a desire to cause mayhem.

Instigators of malicious threats, called _hackers_,[3] range from pranksters to organized criminals and even international terrorists. Securing systems against malicious threats is an arms race, a high-stakes contest requiring constantly improving defenses against increasingly sophisticated weaponry. Some businesses have particular reason to fear being targeted. But even the most unobtrusive firms cannot count on low profiles ("security through obscurity") as a defense. Increasingly, attacks are automated and systematic, carried out by wrecking routines turned loose on the Internet to probe for vulnerabilities and inflict damage randomly.

In an age of real-time systems, global operations, and customers who expect always-on performance, reliability and security have taken on new importance. Technologies to assure 24×7 operations[4] get better all the time, but every increment of capability comes with additional infrastructure complexity and additional management challenges. Add new malicious threats to the mix and we see that twenty-first-century infrastructure managers have their hands full. Making the wrong decision in designing or maintaining infrastructure or in responding to incidents can severely harm a business.

---

[2] Charles Perrow, _Normal Accidents: Living with High Risk Technologies_ (Princeton, NJ: Princeton University Press, 1999).

[3] The term _hacker_ is controversial. Although the word is now used to describe a computer expert with malicious intent, it originally had no negative connotations. UNIX programming enthusiasts, beginning in the 1960s, called particularly excellent programmers hackers. Some have tried to preserve the positive interpretation by proposing the word _cracker_ to describe malicious hackers. In the popular perception, however, this battle seems largely lost; to most people, _hacker_ implies malicious intent, so that is how we use it in this book. We extend our apologies to purists on this point.

[4] That is, operations that run 24 hours per day, 7 days per week.

Availability Math

The reliability of computing infrastructure is often discussed in terms of the *availability* of a specific information technology (IT) service or system. A system that is 98 percent available is on average running and ready to be used 98 percent of the time. It is down, or not available for use, 2 percent of the time. In a day, 98 percent availability translates into just under one-half hour of downtime, which might be fine for some systems and businesses.

A business's tolerance for outages varies by system and situation. Downtime that occurs in large chunks, say, a two-hour outage every four days, might be more of a problem than the same total amount of downtime occurring in increments that never exceed three minutes in a single outage. Whether outages occur at predictable times matters too. A half-hour outage that always happens at 3:00 A.M. may not be a problem. Some systems require planned outages; for example, a system might need to be shut down each night to have all its data files copied to a backup tape. But planned outages are increasingly rare in the world of real-time infrastructures; and unplanned outages are not usually well behaved.

In modern contexts, a 98 percent availability rating for a system usually means that its probability of being up and running at any given time is 98 percent—period. A strong underlying presumption is that planned outages will be minimized, if not eliminated. Moreover, for real-time infrastructure 98 percent is not nearly good enough. In fact, the availability of today's IT infrastructure is often expressed in terms of a number of "nines." "Five nines" means 99.999 percent availability, which equates to less than a second of downtime in a 24-hour day, or no more than a minute in three months, on average. Not surprisingly, keeping systems available at such a high level requires much redundancy and highly sophisticated operations management.

We can better appreciate how difficult it is to achieve very high levels of reliability if we consider how rates of availability for components combine into overall system or service availability. Most IT services are not delivered by a single component but by a number of components working together. For example, a service that sends transactions from one server to another via a corporate internetwork might require two or more routers, one or more switches, and both servers—all up and running at the same time. Each of these devices has its own individual availability. Thus, overall *service* availability is generally lower than the availability of individual components. Many managers do not appreciate how rapidly service availability decreases as components are added in series. Let's consider how this works.

The Availability of Components in Series

Suppose you have five components connected in *series* that together deliver an IT service (see Figure 6.1). Assume that each component has an availability of 98 percent, which means, as we have noted, a half hour per day of downtime for each component on average. Computation of service availability is straightforward.

For the service to be up and running, all five components must be up and running. At any given time, the probability that a component is up and running is .98 (that's what 98 percent availability means), and so the probability that Component 1 *and*

FIGURE 6.1

Five Components in Series (Each 98 percent Available)

| Component 1 98% availability | Component 2 98% availability | Component 3 98% availability | Component 4 98% availability | Component 5 98% availability |

$.98 \times .98 \times .98 \times .98 \times .98 =$ service availability of 90%

Component 2 *and* Component 3 *and* Component 4 *and* Component 5 are all up and running is

$$.98 \times .98 \times .98 \times .98 \times .98 = .9$$

The overall service availability is 90 percent, which means the service is unavailable 10 percent of the time, or almost two and a half hours a day. If we take into account the fact that most services rely on many more than five devices operating in series, we can see that service availability degrades quite severely as we add components in a chain.

Figure 6.2 shows how service availability falls as we add components, assuming that individual components are 98 percent available. Notice that by the time we get to 15 devices in series—which is not hard to imagine in a modern IT infrastructure—downtime exceeds 25 percent. Reversing this logic leads to an important conclusion: If we need overall service availability of 99.999 percent (five nines) and service provision relies on 10 components, the availability of the individual components must average 99.9999 percent. For each of the 10 individual components, that equates to

FIGURE 6.2

Combining Components in Series Decreases Overall Availability

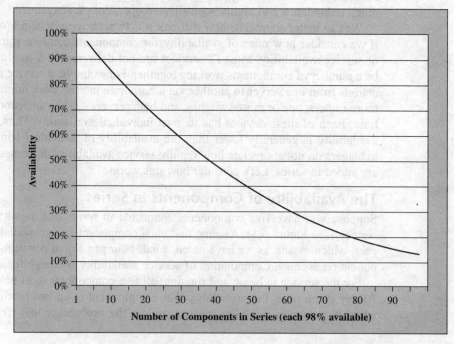

about 30 seconds of downtime per year. Thirty seconds is not enough time to restart most servers. If only one server needs rebooting in a year, that blows a five nines availability rating. Unfortunately, many popular server operating systems need to be rebooted more often than once a year. How, then, can we achieve five nines of availability? The answer to this question: Redundancy.

The Effect of Redundancy on Availability

Suppose you have five components connected in *parallel* involved in the provision of an IT service (see Figure 6.3). The components are identical, and any one of them can perform the functions needed to support the service. As in the earlier example, each individual component has an availability of 98 percent and each component experiences outages randomly. The computation for the overall availability of these parallel components is also straightforward.

Because any of the individual components can support the service, all five must fail at the same time to render this combination of components a failure. At any given time, the probability that a component is down is .02 (98 percent availability means 2 percent downtime), and so the probability that Component 1 *and* Component 2 *and* Component 3 *and* Component 4 *and* Component 5 will all fail at the same time is

$$.02 \times .02 \times .02 \times .02 \times .02 = .0000000032$$

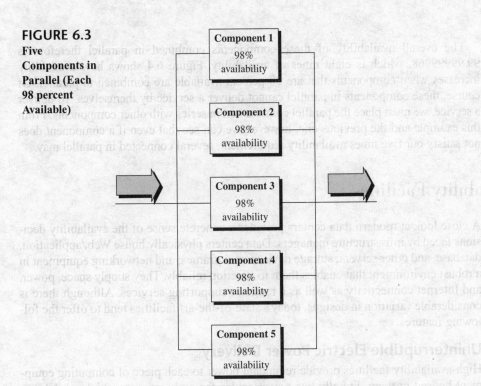

FIGURE 6.3

Five Components in Parallel (Each 98 percent Available)

Component 1
98% availability

Component 2
98% availability

Component 3
98% availability

Component 4
98% availability

Component 5
98% availability

.02 × .02 × .02 × .02 × .02 = .0000000032
Probability of Failure

FIGURE 6.4
Redundancy
Increases
Overall
Availability

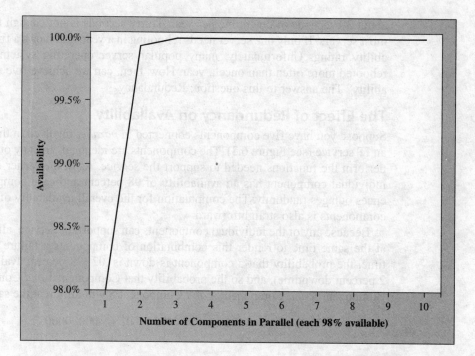

The overall availability of these components combined in parallel therefore is 99.99999968, which is eight nines of availability. Figure 6.4 shows how availability increases when components that are 98 percent available are combined in parallel. Of course, these components in parallel cannot deliver a service by themselves. To deliver a service, we must place the parallel combination in series with other components. From this example and the previous one, however, we can see that even if a component does not satisfy our five nines availability requirement, several connected in parallel may.

High-Availability Facilities

A close look at modern data centers provides a concrete sense of the availability decisions faced by infrastructure managers. Data centers physically house Web, application, database, and other servers; storage devices; mainframes; and networking equipment in a robust environment that enables them to function reliably. They supply space, power, and Internet connectivity as well as a range of supporting services. Although there is considerable variation in designs, today's state-of-the-art facilities tend to offer the following features.

Uninterruptible Electric Power Delivery

High-availability facilities provide redundant power to each piece of computing equipment housed in them, literally two power cables for each computer (high-availability computing equipment accepts two power inputs). Power distribution inside the facility is fully redundant and includes uninterruptible power supplies (UPSs) to maintain power even if power delivery to the facility is interrupted. Connections to outside sources of power are also redundant; usually facilities access two utility power grids. Diesel generators stand by for backup power generation; on-site fuel tanks contain fuel for a day or more of operation. Facilities managers have a plan for high-priority access to additional fuel in case of a long-lasting primary power outage (e.g., delivery by helicopter). High-end data centers may obtain primary power from on-site power plants, with first-level backup from local utility power grids and second-level backup from diesel generators; UPSs may employ batteryless, flywheel-based technologies.

Physical Security

Security guards posted in bulletproof enclaves protect points of entry and patrol the facility regularly. Closed-circuit television monitors critical infrastructure and provides immediate visibility into any area of the facility from a constantly attended security desk. Access to internal areas requires photo ID and presence on a prearranged list. Entry is through a buffer zone that can be locked down. Guards open and inspect the items (e.g., boxes, equipment) people bring into the facility. The building that houses the data center is dedicated to that use, not shared with other businesses. In some high-end facilities, the building is "hardened" against external explosions, earthquakes, and other disasters. Advanced entry systems force everyone through multiple, single-person (hostageproof) buffers with integrated metal and explosive detection. Biometric scanning technologies such as retinal scanners, palm readers, and voice recognition systems control access to zones within data centers. Motion sensors supplement video monitoring, and perimeter fencing surrounds the facility.

Climate Control and Fire Suppression

Facilities contain redundant heating, ventilating, and air-conditioning (HVAC) equipment capable of maintaining temperatures in ranges suitable for computing and network equipment. Mobile cooling units alleviate hot spots. Integrated fire suppression systems include smoke detection, alarming, and gas-based (i.e., no equipment-damaging water) fire suppression.

Network Connectivity

External connections to Internet backbone providers[5] are redundant, involve at least two backbone providers, and enter the building through separate points. The company that owns the data center has agreements with backbone providers that permit significant percentages, say, 50 percent, of network traffic to travel from origin to destination across the backbone company's private network, avoiding often-congested public Internet junctions. A 24×7 network operations center (NOC) is staffed with network engineers who monitor the connectivity infrastructure of the facility; a redundant NOC on another site is capable of delivering services of equal quality as those provided by the primary NOC. High-end facilities have agreements with three or more backbone providers that allow even more traffic, up to 90 percent, to stay on private networks.

---

[5] Backbone providers own the very large data transmission lines through which large quantities of data are moved long distances.

TABLE 6.1
Data Center
Uptime Levels

Uptime Level	Availability
Level 1	99 to 99.9 percent
Level 2	99.9 to 99.99 percent
Level 3	99.99 to 99.999 percent
Level 4	99.999 to 99.9999 percent

Help Desk and Incident Response Procedures

Customers can contact facility staff for assistance at any time during the day or night. The facility has procedures for responding to unplanned incidents. Automated problem-tracking systems are integrated with similar systems at service delivery partner sites, so complex problems involving interactions between services can be tracked down and quickly solved.

N + 1 and N + N Redundancy

Most modern data centers try to maintain at least an "N + 1" level of redundancy of mission-critical components. N + 1 means that for each type of critical component there should be at least one unit standing by. For example, if a facility needs four diesel generators to meet power demands in a primary power outage, N + 1 redundancy requires five such generators, four to operate and one to stand by. N + 1 redundancy provides a higher level of availability if the underlying number of components, the N in the N + 1, is small (you can verify this for yourself by using probability calculations such as those that we demonstrated earlier).

Some companies aspire to higher levels of infrastructure redundancy. "N + N" redundancy requires twice as many mission-critical components as are necessary to run a facility at any one time. For example, a facility that needs four diesel generators to meet its power demands needs eight generators to achieve N + N redundancy. Where N + 1 facilities are able to commit to service levels in the 99.9 percent availability range, N + N facilities can ensure availability levels at the 99.999 percent (five nines) level. Facilities are sometimes categorized according to the "level" of uptime they support (see Table 6.1). Level 1 data centers, which employ N + 1 redundancy, are available 99 to 99.9 percent of the time. Level 2 and Level 3 centers feature more redundancy. Level 4 data centers, the highest level of availability in current common usage, have N + N or better redundancy and achieve uptime in the range of 99.999 to 99.9999 percent. Downtime at a Level 4 facility, literally seconds per year, is unnoticeable by most users.

Not surprisingly, high levels of availability are costly. Increasing the availability of *a single Web site* from 99 percent to 99.999 percent would require additional spending of millions of dollars.[6] A 99.999 percent availability data center costs three or four times more than one capable of 99 to 99.9 percent availability.[7]

---

[6] Randy K. Souza with Harley Manning, Hollie Goldman, and Joyce Tong, "The Best of Retail Site Design," Forrester Research white paper, October 2000.

[7] Jeff Camp, April Henry, Jamie Gomez Surado, and Kristen Olsavsky, Morgan Stanley Dean Witter Research Report, November 2000.

FIGURE 6.5
A
Representative
E-Commerce
Infrastructure

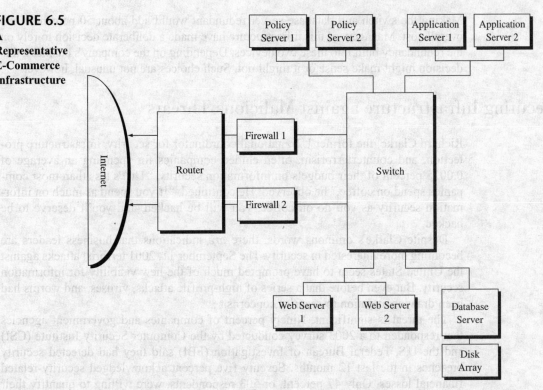

Management decisions about the design of IT infrastructures always involve trade-offs between availability and the expense of additional components. Figure 6.5 depicts an e-commerce infrastructure used by a real company for delivering a basic Web-based IT service. Notice that many infrastructure elements are redundant: The firewall devices, the Web servers, the application servers, and the policy servers. Notice, though, that the switch and the database server are not redundant. Why?

Although you cannot tell from the diagram, both the switch and the database servers have built-in redundancy. Both have redundant power supplies. In addition, the switch has redundant modules. The database server is shown connected to an array of disks that is set up in a 'RAID' (redundant array of inexpensive disks) configuration to write data to at least two separate disks at the same time.[8] Nevertheless, there are single points of failure in these two components. Thus, the question remains: Why would managers leave these two obviously central components without redundancy when they have made all the other components redundant?

The reason boils down to one word: Money. The two nonredundant components represent approximately half the cost of this several-hundred-thousand-dollar setup.

---

[8] Notice that there are usually many options for adding redundancy, some more expensive than others. For most high-availability equipment, redundancy is a matter of degree and can be purchased incrementally. Note also that redundancy does not necessarily mean purchasing another instance of exactly the same technology platform; cheaper platforms are sometimes used as temporary backups for expensive system components.

Making the switch and database server redundant would add about 50 percent to the overall cost. Managers of this infrastructure have made a deliberate decision to rely on the redundancy built into these two devices. Depending on the company's business, this decision might make sense or it might not. Such choices are not unusual, however.

Securing Infrastructure against Malicious Threats

Richard Clarke, the former U.S. national coordinator for security, infrastructure protection, and counterterrorism, often chided companies for spending an average of 0.0025 percent of their budgets on information security. "That's less than most companies spend on coffee," he observed. He continued: "If you spend as much on information security as you do on coffee, you will be hacked, and you'll deserve to be hacked."[9]

Despite Clarke's ominous words, there *are* indications that business leaders are becoming more interested in security. The September 11, 2001 terrorist attacks against the United States seem to have prompted much of the new visibility for information security. But even before that a series of high-profile attacks, viruses, and worms had been drawing attention to security concerns.

The threat is significant. Ninety percent of companies and government agencies that responded to a 2003 survey conducted by the Computer Security Institute (CSI) and the U.S. Federal Bureau of Investigation (FBI) said they had detected security breaches in the last 12 months. Seventy-five percent acknowledged security-related financial losses. Only 47 percent, or 503 respondents, were willing to quantify their losses, but those totaled about $201 million. The cost of attacks intended to take down computing infrastructure components increased by 250 percent during the year.[10]

Who are the attackers? Some are thrill seekers with too much time on their hands, people who like the challenge of defeating defenses or getting in where they are not supposed to be. Even if they intend no damage, they are unknown elements interacting with the complexity of IT infrastructure in unpredictable ways, which can precipitate accidents. Other attackers have taken a specific dislike to a company and intend to do it harm. Attackers of this kind are a significant problem because every defense has cracks and persistent attackers eventually find one. Another sinister type of attacker attempts to steal a company's proprietary data, such as information a company is storing in confidence for others (e.g., credit card numbers). Industrial espionage and terrorism are a concern, especially for high-profile corporations.

All attackers represent serious threats. Even a thrill seeker who gains access but does no damage can harm a company's reputation if word of the breach gets out. And even apparently harmless breaches must be investigated to determine that nothing more serious has occurred. Many hackers who penetrate a company's defenses set up routes through which they can return, opening doors that they hope company managers

---

[9] *InformationWeek Daily*, February 20, 2002, http://update.informationweek.com.

[10] "2003 CSI/FBI Crime and Security Survey," *Computer Security Issues & Trends*, VII, no. 1, Spring 2003. Note that these estimates probably underrepresent the problem to a large degree. There are many reasons why firms fail to disclose or underreport losses from security incidents. Financial losses reported in 2003 were, encouragingly, down for the first time in recent years.

will not notice. Many also share information with each other about how to break in to certain companies or open doors they left behind after their own break-ins. A thrill seeker who intends no real harm may pass information to people with malevolent aims.

Responsible managers must build defenses to secure a company's information-related assets—its data, infrastructure components, and reputation—against this escalating threat. When it comes to securing IT infrastructure, one size does not fit all, and so defenses must be customized to a company's situation, business, infrastructure technologies, and objectives. Sound approaches to securing IT infrastructure begin with a detailed understanding of the threats.

Classification of Threats

Hackers are always inventing new ways to make mayhem. There are many kinds of attacks, and there are subtle variations on each kind. Some threats are common, only too real in actual experience, while others are hypothetical, theoretically possible but never yet observed. Despite the variety, threats can be divided (very roughly) into categories: External attacks, intrusions, and viruses and worms.

External Attacks

External attacks are actions against computing infrastructure that harm it or degrade its services without actually gaining access to it. The most common external attacks are "denial of service" (DoS) attacks, which disable infrastructure devices (usually Web servers) by flooding them with an overwhelming number of messages. Attackers send data packets far more rapidly than the target machine can handle them. Each packet begins what appears to be an authentic "conversation" with the victim computer. The victim responds as it usually does to the beginning of a conversation, but the attacker abruptly terminates the conversation. The resources of the Web site are consumed by beginning a very large number of bogus conversations. Figure 6.6 compares how a

FIGURE 6.6
Normal and DoS Handshakes

Source: Robert D. Austin, "The iPremier Company, (A), (B), and (C): Denial of Service Attack," Harvard Business School Teaching Note No. 602-033.

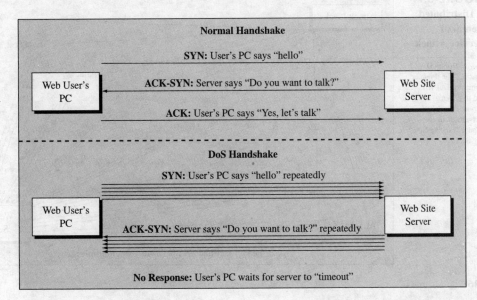

A normal "conversation" between a Web user's computer and a Web site begins with a three-part exchange of greetings commonly referred to as a "three-way handshake." The Web user's computer says "Hello" (actually "Synchronize" or "SYN") to the Web site. The Web site replies, "Do you want to start talking?" ("Synchronize Acknowledged" or "SYN-ACK") back to the Web user's machine. Finally, the Web user's computer responds, "Yes, let's start talking" ("Acknowledged" or "ACK"). At this point, the two ordinarily consider communications to be established and move to the next step of interaction, which is usually more content-based (for example,

sending a page image to the Web user's computer from the Web site).

In a common form of DoS attack called a SYN flood, the attacker sends swarms of SYN packets (that say, in effect, "Hello" to the Web site). The Web site responds with SYN-ACKs ("Do you want to start talking?"), but the attacker never completes the handshake by sending the final ACK. The contacted site will devote a certain amount of its resources to waiting for the final ACK before giving up on it. This use of resources, multiplied thousands of times in a few seconds, is what the attacker is counting on to paralyze the Web site.

normal and DoS conversation proceed between network-connected computers (also see the accompanying feature).

If attacks always came from a single location on the Internet, defeating them would be easy. Network monitoring software can automatically read the origin IP address from incoming packets, recognize that the flood is coming from a single address, and filter out flood traffic before it reaches its target. Attackers counter this defense, however, by sending packets that originate from multiple locations on the Internet or that appear to originate from multiple locations (see Figure 6.7). *Distributed* denial of

FIGURE 6.7
A Distributed Denial of Service Attack

Source: Robert D. Austin, "The iPremier Company, (A), (B), and (C): Denial of Service Attack." Harvard Business School Teaching Note No. 602-033.

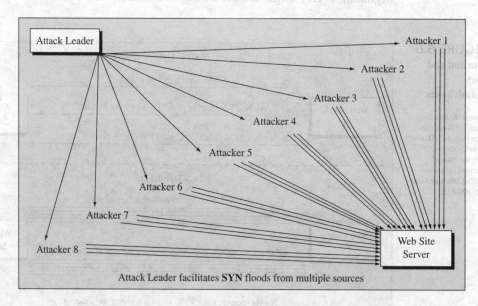

Attack Leader facilitates **SYN** floods from multiple sources

FIGURE 6.8
"Spoofing"

Source: Robert D.
Austin, "The iPremier
Company, (A), (B),
and (C): Denial of
Service Attack."
Harvard Business
School Teaching Note
No. 602-033.

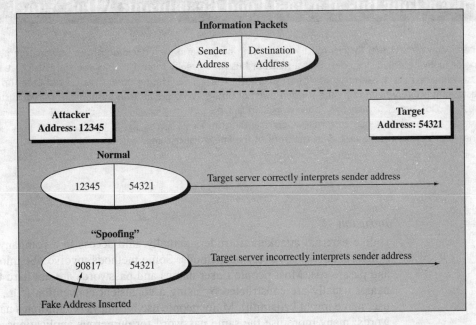

service (DDoS) attacks are carried out by automated routines secretly deposited on Internet-connected computers whose owners have not secured them against intrusion (a large percentage of DSL and cable modem–connected PCs fall into this unsecured category). Once implanted on the computers of unsuspecting users, these routines launch packets at targeted Web sites for a predefined duration or during a predetermined interval. Because the flood comes from many different addresses, network-monitoring software cannot easily recognize the flood as an attack. Clever attackers can simulate a distributed attack by inserting false origin information into packets to mislead filtering software at a target site (providing packets with false origin addresses is called "spoofing"; see Figure 6.8).

Unfortunately, DoS attacks are extremely easy to execute. Attack routines are available for download from sources on the Internet. Using the routines is almost as easy as sending e-mail. Attackers need not be programming experts; many, in fact, are "script kiddies," relatively unsophisticated computer users who run routines that others have written. Although DDoS and spoofing attacks are more difficult, they require no great technical skill. Computer users who do not secure their computers against mischievous use provide unintended assistance to attackers.

DoS attacks are very difficult to defend against. Most defensive methods rely on monitoring that can detect recognizable attack patterns, but it is relatively simple for attackers to vary their patterns of attack. Patterns of attack can be very similar to legitimate e-commerce traffic. A slow-motion DoS attack—recently observed attacks of this kind have been called "degradation of service" attacks—looks almost exactly like real e-commerce traffic. Although these attacks do not cause outages, they do affect infrastructure performance, waste company resources, and reduce customer satisfaction (see the accompanying feature).

Like a Tour Bus at a Fast Food Restaurant: A DoS Attack Analogy

Have you ever stopped for fast food while driving on a major highway only to discover that a full tour bus has just unloaded its passengers at the restaurant? The restaurant is overwhelmed by the sudden burst of business. A DoS attack is like this, only worse. In a DoS attack, it is as if tour bus customers were standing in line, interacting with the cashier at the front of the line, and then deciding not to buy anything. Customers who really intend to buy food are stuck at the back of the line. The restaurant wastes resources on fake customers who are indistinguishable from real customers.*

* We first heard this analogy from Dr. Larry Liebrock, a free-lance computer forensics expert.

Intrusion

Unlike external attackers, intruders actually gain access to a company's internal IT infrastructure by a variety of methods. Some methods involve obtaining user names and passwords. Most people's user names and passwords are not hard to guess; user names usually are constructed by using a consistent convention (e.g., John Smith's user name might be jsmith). Many people use birthdays or children's names for passwords; many more use the same password for numerous applications, which means an intruder can gain access to many systems with the same password. Few people change passwords frequently, and it is not uncommon to find passwords taped to computer monitors or sent out in the trash to dumpsters behind high-tech buildings. The term *social engineering* describes low-tech but highly effective techniques for getting people to freely divulge privileged information. Many people will reveal a password to an official-sounding telephone caller who pretends to be a company network engineer.

There are also high-tech ways to get inside a company's defenses. Hackers who gain physical access to a network can acquire passwords by eavesdropping on network conversations by using "sniffer" software; because network traffic often traverses many local area networks (LANs), a sniffer need not be attached to the LAN where traffic originates to get a password. Or intruders can exploit vulnerabilities left in software when it was developed to gain access to systems *without* first obtaining passwords. In some cases, software development mistakes allow hackers to trick a company's computer into executing their own code or to cause a failure that leaves them in control of the computer. Such vulnerabilities in software are common. New vulnerabilities in widely deployed software systems are discovered daily, sometimes by good guys, who notify vendors so that they can fix the problem, and sometimes by bad guys, who take advantage of the opening. Computers are "port scanned"—probed for vulnerability to intrusion—within a few minutes of connecting to the Internet. Hackers use automated routines that systematically scan IP addresses and then report back to their masters which addresses contain exploitable vulnerabilities.

Once inside, intruders have the same rights of access and control over systems and resources as legitimate users. Thus empowered, they can steal information, erase or alter data, or deface Web sites (internal and external). Or they can use a location inside a company to pose as a representative of the company. Such an imposter could, for example, send a message canceling an important meeting or send scandalous information (e.g., racist or pornographic) that appeared to originate from official sources inside the company. Intruders also can leave behind routines that use the company's computers as a base for attacks against other companies. Or they can deposit time bombs, seemingly innocuous bits of code scheduled to explode unexpectedly into catastrophic action at a future date.

One of the most difficult problems arising from intrusion is figuring out what exactly intruders might have done while they were inside company defenses. It can take companies a long time to discover trespassing on their systems or networks. Hackers generally try to cover their tracks. They may make subtle changes in a system, opening obscure doors, adding a small file to a disk drive, or slightly altering some data. Finding out what intruders have done, or whether they have done anything, can be very costly for victim companies, yet it must be done. A company that does not know exactly how its systems have been compromised may have difficulty deciding what to tell customers, business partners, and others about the security of data entrusted to the company. There is a very high public relations penalty for not knowing something consequential about your infrastructure that you should have known or, perhaps worse, for issuing assurances about the security of your systems that turn out to be spectacularly inaccurate.

Viruses and Worms

Viruses and worms are malicious software programs that replicate, spreading themselves to other computers. The damage they do may be minor, such as defacing a Web site, or severe, such as erasing the contents of a computer's disk drive. Although people disagree about the exact definitions of viruses and worms, they often are distinguished by their degree of automation and ability to replicate across networks. Simply put, viruses require assistance (often inadvertent) from users to replicate and propagate (e.g., opening a file attached to an e-mail message or even opening a Web page), whereas worms replicate and move across networks automatically.

What is perhaps most alarming about viruses and worms is that they increasingly incorporate and automate other kinds of attacks. The Code Red Worm, for example, (see the accompanying feature) moved across networks, automatically invaded systems with certain vulnerabilities, deposited a program to launch a DoS attack against another computer, and replicated itself across the Internet at an exponential rate. Although Code Red did little damage to infected systems (it defaced their Web sites), it is significant for the possibilities it suggests. Human hackers can attack companies at human speeds only, but self-propagating, automated attackers can potentially wreak havoc much faster and against arbitrary targets.

Defensive Measures

Defense against hackers is difficult. The threats are varied, sophisticated, and ever-evolving, and security is a matter of degree rather than absolutes. There is no master list against which a company can compare its defenses and, after checking off everything, declare its infrastructure secure. There are defensive measures that are effective in

From Code Red to Sasser and Beyond

On Friday the 13th in July of 2001, system administrators around the world began to notice that their Web sites had been defaced with a message: "Welcome to http://www.worm.com! Hacked by Chinese!" Investigation revealed that this message was the work of a worm named "Code Red." It was not immediately obvious what other damage the worm might do.

Over the next several days, experts learned that the worm infected only Microsoft's popular Internet Information Server (IIS) through a point of weakness accidentally left in the software. The worm spread by randomly scanning computers for vulnerability and then migrating to vulnerable machines. It spread to 15,000 computers by July 18, and an estimated 350,000 by July 31. Systems were only vulnerable if their administrators had failed to apply a "patch" that had been available from Microsoft for three weeks.

Code Red was programmed to launch a DoS attack on July 20th from every machine it had infected against the U.S. White House Web site. The White House changed its IP address in time to dodge the attack. The worm became dormant again on the 28th. A second version of the worm, dubbed "Code Red II" appeared in August but lacked the DoS attack feature. It installed "back doors" in systems it infected—openings that intruders could return to later.

Like Code Red, the "Sasser" worm, which appeared on the 1st of May in 2004, only infected machines running certain operating systems (Windows 2000 or Windows XP), and then only if users had not installed a patch made available earlier. But unlike Code Red, Sasser caused infected computers to shut down, and it spread more rapidly: According to some estimates, over a million PCs were infected by May 4. In Sydney, Australia, the worm shut down a train system and stranded 300,000 travelers; in the United Kingdom, it forced Coast Guard operations to revert to paper charts rather than digital maps; in Taiwan and Hong Kong it disrupted operations at government offices and hospitals.

As the world struggled to recover from Sasser, authors of the "Netsky" virus sent out a new variant (the 30th in a series) with a note claiming that it was a cure for Sasser. Desperate users trying to rid their systems of Sasser fell for this trap, installing the Netsky virus, which then attempted to disable antivirus software and steal e-mail addresses.

combination, elements of fortification that companies can erect around vital networks, computers, and systems. Like the fortifications of ancient castles, they must be able to repel hostile forces while admitting friendly parties. Elements of information security often marshaled for this task include security policies, firewalls, authentication, encryption, patching and change management, and intrusion detection and network monitoring.

Security Policies

To defend computing resources against inappropriate use, a company must first specify what is meant by "inappropriate." Good security policies specify not only what people should avoid doing because it is dangerous but also what people should do to be safe. A good policy also explains company decisions not to offer certain services or features because the security risks more than outweigh the benefits.

Security policies address questions such as the following:

- What kinds of passwords are users allowed to create for use on company systems, and how often should users change passwords?
- Who is allowed to have accounts on company systems?

- What security features must be activated on a computer before it can connect to a company network?
- What services are allowed to operate inside a company's network?
- What are users allowed to download?
- How is the security policy enforced?

Because a security policy cannot anticipate everything users might want to do or any situations that might arise, it is a living document. It must be accessible to the people who are expected to comply with it and not be written in overly technical language. And it must be reasonable from the standpoint of a user; a policy people perceive as unreasonable usually is ignored or subverted.

Firewalls

A firewall is a collection of hardware and software designed to prevent unauthorized access to a company's internal computer resources. Computer users outside a company's physical premises often have a legitimate need to access the company's computers. An employee who is traveling, for example, may need to access a system he or she often uses at work. A primary function of a firewall, then, is to facilitate legitimate interactions between computers inside and outside the company while preventing illegitimate interactions.

Firewalls usually are located at points of maximum leverage within a network, typically at the point of connection between a company's internal network and the external public network. Some work by filtering packets coming from outside the company before passing them along to computers inside the company's production facilities. They discard packets that do not comply with security policies, exhibit attack patterns, or appear harmful for other reasons. Others use a sentry computer that relays information between internal and external computers without allowing external packets direct entry.

Firewalls are also useful in other ways. They enforce aspects of a security policy by not allowing certain kinds of communication to traverse the internal network. They have a limited ability to filter out viruses as they enter company networks. Because they are located at the boundary of company systems, firewalls are excellent points at which to collect data about the traffic moving between inside and outside networks. Sometimes they are used between segments of an internal network to divide it into regions so that an intruder who penetrates one part will not be able to access the rest. Firewalls also conceal internal network configurations from external prying and thus serve as a sort of electronic camouflage that makes breaking in harder.

Firewalls do not provide perfect protection. Every design has weaknesses, some of which are not known at any point in time. They provide no defense against malicious insiders or against activity that does not traverse the firewall (such as traffic that enters a network via an unauthorized dial-up modem behind the firewall). It is best to think of a firewall as part of an overall strategy of defense. Although it reduces risks, it does not eliminate them.[11]

---

[11] Elizabeth D. Zwicky, Simon Cooper, and D. Brent Chapman, *Building Internet Firewalls*, 2nd ed. (Sebastapol, CA: O' Reilly, 2000), is an excellent reference on firewalls and their capabilities.

Digital Certificates

Digital certificates are analogous to the official physical documents people use to establish their identity in face-to-face business interactions. When someone writes a check at a retail store, the store may ask for proof of identity. To provide proof, people often offer a driver's license. Businesses trust a driver's license because they trust the issuing authority (the state agency that regulates motor vehicle use) to verify identity by using a rigorous procedure and because driver's licenses are difficult to forge. A digital certificate is much like the driver's license, a signed document that a trusted third-party organization stands behind that provides evidence of identity. Digital certificates are in fact much harder to forge than physical documents, although it is possible to trick people into issuing real certificates in error. Also, digital certificates are "bearer instruments," rather like driver's licenses with no photo on them; it is possible that the person presenting a certificate is not the person the certificate represents her or him to be.

Authentication

Authentication describes the variety of techniques and software used to control who accesses elements of computing infrastructure. Authentication can occur at many points. *Host* authentication controls access to specific computers (hosts); *network* authentication controls access to regions of a network. Host authentication and network authentication are used in combination. When used with sophisticated and well-managed directory technologies, which keep track of identities and access rights, access can be very granular, allowing many layers of access control throughout the infrastructure.

Strong authentication implies that passwords expire regularly and that forms of passwords are restricted to make them harder to guess. For example, a company might require that passwords be changed weekly and be composed of a combination of at least eight alpha and numeric characters. What minimally constitutes strong authentication is a matter of debate, but simple user name and password authentication does not meet the test. Strong authentication requires user name/password plus one other factor, such as certificate authentication (see the accompanying feature) or biometric verification of identity (e.g., iris scanning).

Encryption

Encryption renders the contents of electronic transmissions unreadable by anyone who might intercept them. Modern encryption technologies provide a high degree of protection against the vast majority of potential attackers. Legitimate recipients can decrypt transmission contents by using a piece of data called a "key" (see the accompanying feature). The recipient typically possesses the key for decryption as a result of a previous interaction. Like passwords, keys must be kept secret and protected from social engineering, physical theft, insecure transmission, and a variety of other techniques hostile forces use to obtain them. Encryption does little good if the key that decrypts is available to attackers. Nevertheless, modern encryption techniques provide excellent concealment of the contents of messages if the key is secret regardless of what else hackers might know about the encryption algorithm itself. By setting up

Public-Private Key Encryption and Digital Signatures

Public-private key encryption uses a mathematical algorithm with an interesting characteristic: If one unique key is used to transform a plain text message into encrypted form, a different unique key must be used to decrypt the message back into plain text at its destination. Typically, one key is made public and the other is kept private. A message can be sent confidentially if it is encrypted using the public key; then only a person possessing the private key can decrypt the message. A message can be "signed" by using the same process in reverse; if the public key can successfully decrypt the message, only the person in possession of the private key could have encrypted it; hence, it must have come from the person known to possess the private key.

encryption at both ends of a connection across public networks, a company can in effect extend its secure private network (such network extensions are called virtual private networks; see the accompanying feature).

Encryption does not conceal everything about a network transmission. Hackers still can gain useful information from the pattern of transmission, the lengths of messages, or their origin or destination addresses. Encryption does not prevent attackers from intercepting and changing the data in a transmission. The attackers may not know what they are changing, but subtle changes can still wreak havoc, especially if the intended recipient is a computer that expects data to arrive in a particular format.[12]

Patching and Change Management

A surprising number of attacks exploit weaknesses in systems for which "patches" (fixes) already exist at the time of the attack. Successful attacks of this kind sometimes represent administrative failures, but there are also a large number of contributing factors, such as shortage of IT staff to apply fixes to existing systems, or legitimate concerns about the unintended negative consequences of a system patch. Keeping track of the variety of systems in a company's infrastructure, their security weaknesses, the available patches, and whether patches have been applied is nontrivial. Consequently, attacks against known and presumably patched weaknesses often are successful.

Knowing exactly what software is running and whether it is patched is important for another reason: After an attack, this knowledge is essential to discerning whether attackers have changed anything within a company's infrastructure. Detecting a change in a file size or finding a file that should not be there would be an obvious sign of intruder activity. Best practice calls for keeping detailed records of all files that are *supposed* to be on production computers, including file sizes or even file "fingerprints."[13] Sadly, many companies fall short of this practice, sometimes for what seem like good business reasons. For example, managers hurrying to fix a customer-impacting problem may be tempted to shortcut formal change management procedures. The result is a gap in formal knowledge about what files and programs ought to be present on company systems.

---

[12] Jalal Feghi, Jalil Feghi, and Peter Williams, *Digital Certificates: Applied Internet Security* (Reading, MA: Addison-Wesley, 1999), is an excellent reference on the subject of encryption and digital certificates.

[13] There are technologies available to capture images of disk drives that act as a sort of fingerprinting.

Virtual Private Networks

Virtual private networks (VPNs) use encryption to create a connection across public networks that extend a company's private network. Traffic between two points—for example, a remote user and a computer inside a company's network—is encrypted at one end of the transmission, encapsulated inside new packets, and sent on to a destination where the packets are unencapsulated and decrypted. VPNs allow a secure private network to be extended securely across a public network to arbitrary points. There is a dark side to this, however. If an attacker can gain access to a remote VPN node, a company's network can be attacked as if from the inside. Thus, although VPNs extend security usefully, they also add to the complexity of the security management task.

Intrusion Detection and Network Monitoring

Intrusion detection and network monitoring together help network administrators recognize when their infrastructure is or has been under attack. Network monitoring automatically filters out external attack traffic at the boundary of company networks. Sophisticated intrusion detection systems include combinations of hardware probes and software diagnostic systems. They log activity throughout company networks and highlight patterns of suspicious activity for further investigation. Along with formal change management, which provides a baseline description of company system configurations, the information logged by intrusion detection systems can help companies reconstruct exactly what an intruder did.

A Security Management Framework

Securing a company's infrastructure involves design decisions, operating policy and procedure development, and steely execution. Information security is an evolving field with an evolving state of the art. Nevertheless, the following principles of security management have ongoing relevance.

Make Deliberate Security Decisions

This may seem obvious, but too many companies rely on a combination of blissful ignorance and security through obscurity. These are not reasonable approaches for companies seeking to connect to and leverage the public Internet. Ignorance is neither a strategy nor an excuse. General managers must educate themselves on security-related subjects and take responsibility for decisions in this area.

Consider Security a Moving Target

The forces of digital darkness are constantly searching for new ways to attack. Companies must maintain a solid defense, attack their own systems (do a safety check), and hire outside firms to audit their defenses for vulnerability to new threats on a regular basis. Indeed, companies must stay plugged in to sources of information about threats, such as the Computer Emergency Response Team (CERT) (www.cert.org). Information security is not something a company can do once and then forget about.

Practice Disciplined Change Management

The fix that needs to be rushed into production may be important, but if shortcutting formal procedures makes reconstructing the facts of a subsequent attack impossible, the costs of informality ultimately may be far greater. Companies need to know what they have running at all times and need a disciplined process for migrating infrastructure changes through testing and into production use. Not following such procedures represents reckless behavior for which general managers are ultimately responsible. Conversely, failure to promptly install available patches to counter known threats also risks unnecessary incidents. Best practice requires the prompt installation of patches while remaining within change management procedures.

Educate Users

Make sure users understand the dangers inherent in certain activities, such as sharing passwords and connecting behind-the-firewall dial-up modems to their desktop computers. Help them understand the reasons for security measures that may inconvenience them in some situations. Enlist them as allies in maintaining security.

Deploy Multilevel Technical Measures, as Many as You Can Afford

Use security at the host and network levels. Acquire defensive technologies as they develop. No company can afford an infinite amount of security, but managers need to be sure they have thought through the consequences of a breach of security. Managers must prioritize security measures appropriately.

Risk Management of Availability and Security

Companies cannot afford to address every threat to the availability and security of IT infrastructure with equal aggressiveness. Even if they could, doing so would not make business sense. Instead, risks must be characterized and addressed in proportion to their likelihood and potential consequences. Management actions to mitigate risks must be prioritized with an eye to their costs and potential benefits.

Figure 6.9 suggests a way of thinking about potential failures in terms of their probabilities and consequences. Incidents in the upper right corner are both likely and costly; mitigating these risks is obviously important. Risks in the other quadrants must be prioritized. One method of prioritizing involves computing the *expected loss* associated with incidents in these quadrants by multiplying the probability of an incident and its cost if it occurs. Incidents with higher expected losses get higher priorities. Needless to say, incidents in the upper left and lower right quadrants receive higher priorities than do the low-probability, low-cost incidents in the lower left quadrant.

For most companies, however, the logic of risk management is more complicated. Managers' attitudes toward risk may be too complex to be summarized by simple probabilities and costs. For example, managers may dread high-cost incidents so much that they prefer to address high-cost incidents first even if those incidents are very unlikely to occur and their associated expected loss (probability × cost) is small. Or managers may fear specific events for reasons that go beyond cost. A further complication arises from the difficulty of estimating costs and probabilities in some situations. The intangible costs of some incidents are exceedingly difficult to predict, and estimating probabilities often is no easier.

In addition, not all risks can be countered with well-defined management actions. Most companies choose between courses of action that vary in cost and address

FIGURE 6.9
Managing Infrastructure Risks: Consequences and Probabilities

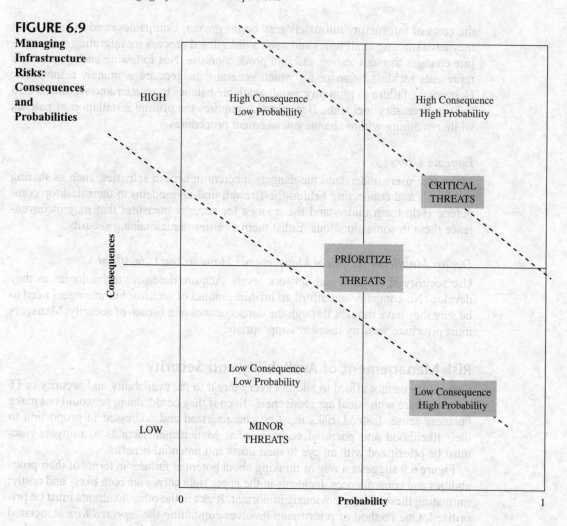

risks to varying degrees. Sometimes none of the possible actions address some serious risks. Sometimes addressing a serious risk is prohibitively expensive. Thus, after assigning priorities to risks, most companies perform an additional assessment step to decide which actions to take. This step takes into account not only the expected losses from incidents but also the costs of actions to reduce or eliminate risks.

New capabilities that come with new technologies generate another wrinkle in risk management thinking. Although new capabilities provide benefits, they often require taking on new risks to availability or security. Thus, managers also engage in risk management as they decide which new services to offer. A new service to support the business—for example, a collaborative videoconferencing technology—increases the complexity of infrastructure, which generates challenges for both availability and security. There is almost always a trade-off between performance or richness of features of a technology and infrastructure robustness. For example, running software with high levels of "logging" so that the details of activity are meticulously recorded will help a company detect intrusions more quickly. But logging degrades system performance, perhaps to a point where users complain or additional hardware must be purchased.

Consider the infrastructure configuration example introduced earlier: An e-commerce company that purchased some redundant components but left single points of failure in its infrastructure (Figure 6.5). Should this company buy another $65,000 switch? We could estimate the relevant costs and probabilities, and we could compute the expected loss from the failure of the current single switch. A second switch dramatically reduces the probability of a loss of switching, which in turn reduces the expected cost due to a loss of switching. If the improvement in expected loss from buying the second switch exceeds the $65,000 that the extra switch would cost, the company ought to buy it—in theory. In reality, however, other factors may intervene. The company may not have an extra $65,000, managers may not believe the cost and probability estimates, or there may be more urgent places to spend that $65,000. Whatever managers decide, deliberately thinking through the logic of risk management improves a company's chances of realizing business objectives.

Incident Management and Disaster Recovery

No matter how available and secure they make a company's infrastructure, managers can expect incidents. Infrastructure incidents present a rare business challenge: A need to solve problems under the pressure of a ticking clock. Though they are rare, the stakes are often high when real-time incidents occur. Managers' actions in a crisis can make a huge difference to the well-being of a company. We consider incident management in terms of actions that need to be taken before, during, and after an incident.

Managing Incidents before They Occur

The range of options available to managers in the middle of a crisis is largely determined by decisions made before the crisis. Precrisis practices that make incidents more manageable include the following:

Sound infrastructure design. If infrastructure has been designed with an eye to recoverability and tolerance for failures, the losses associated with an incident are more likely to be contained.

Disciplined execution of operating procedures. Change management procedures make the diagnosis of problems more effective by maintaining a baseline of knowledge about infrastructure configurations. Data backup procedures preserve data in case the data are lost. Scheduled infrastructure health audits uncover lurking problems or vulnerabilities.

Careful documentation. If procedures and configurations are carefully documented, crisis managers need not guess about crucial details. Reliable documentation saves time and increases certainty in dealing with a crisis.

Established crisis management procedures. Procedures for managing incidents guide the diagnosis of problems, help managers avoid decision-making traps, and specify who should be involved in problem-solving activities. Managing in a crisis is difficult enough without having to make up every response as you go. Crisis management always involves creativity, but familiar and useful procedures serve as bases from which managers can innovate under fire effectively.

Rehearsing incident response. Rehearsing responses to incidents makes decision makers more confident and effective during real crises. Even if the way an incident unfolds is different from the way it was practiced, practice makes the situation more familiar and better prepares managers to improvise solutions.

These preparations may seem basic, but a large number of companies do not make them. There is a tendency for other urgent business concerns, such as growing revenues, profits, product functionality, or the customer base, to take priority over hypothetical problems nobody wants to think about. In most companies, staff members who execute responses to incidents have no training in that area and are not necessarily trained in the nature of threats. Nevertheless, managers clearly bear responsibility when they do not foresee exposure to availability and security incidents. Good managers find the time to plan for high-cost events.

Managing during an Incident

When faced with a real-time crisis, human decision makers have numerous psychological obstacles to surmount in addition to the usually very serious technical difficulties inherent in the crisis. These obstacles include the following:

- Emotional responses, including confusion, denial, fear, and panic
- Wishful thinking and groupthink
- Political maneuvering, diving for cover, and ducking responsibility
- Leaping to conclusions and blindness to evidence that contradicts current beliefs

Awareness of psychological traps helps decision makers avoid them when situations turn dire.

Another difficulty managers face in crises is "public relations inhibition." Sometimes managers are reluctant to admit the seriousness of a problem because they do not want to take actions that communicate to others (customers, the public) that a serious incident has occurred. For example, the managers of an e-commerce company might not want to shut down their online retail site to confound a hacker until they have definitive proof of an intrusion. A shutdown would have to be explained to the press and might alarm customers. Obviously, the stakes of such a decision are very high.

Managing after an Incident

After an incident, infrastructure managers often need to rebuild parts of the infrastructure. Sometimes erasing and rebuilding everything from scratch is the only way to be sure the infrastructure is restored to its preincident state. If configurations and procedures have been carefully documented in advance, recovery can happen swiftly. But if records of how systems should be put together are not exact, rebuilding can run into hiccups: Problems that must be solved under the time pressure of getting the business back online. Rebuilding processes may have to be reinvented "on the fly." Furthermore, if there have been change management lapses—for example, if changes made to systems have not been documented—a rebuild can result in lost functionality (a problem solved earlier by an informal change in production may reappear).

To avoid future incidents of the same type, managers need to understand what happened. Figuring out exactly what caused an incident is sometimes difficult, but it must be done. Typically, a company owes business partners information about the nature of a failure so that those partners can determine the consequences that might flow to them as a result. There is no one best way to explain or disclose an incident to partners, customers, or the press and public. In formulating actions after an incident, however, it is essential to communicate the seriousness with which a company protects the information entrusted to it. A possible intrusion need not be a public relations disaster if subsequent steps to secure infrastructure are framed as "taking no chances."

Summary

The challenges of keeping real-time infrastructures always operational are formidable and evolving. Nevertheless, in this chapter we have outlined management actions and frameworks that will, if applied with discipline and effort, improve the chances of success. The economic consequences of ignoring or failing to take effective action in these areas may be dire indeed (see the accompanying feature).

We have demonstrated how the arithmetic of availability calls for increasing sophistication in infrastructure design and how redundancy, the primary means of increasing robustness, also adds operational complexity and management challenges. We have outlined a series of new and serious malicious threats to IT infrastructure and proposed frameworks for reducing the threats and for managing incidents when they occur. Executives can use the following questions to assess their own preparedness for these twenty-first-century challenges:

1. How available do our systems need to be? Are our infrastructure investments in availability aligned with requirements?

2. Are we taking security threats seriously enough? How secure is our current infrastructure? How do we assess information security on an ongoing basis? Have IT staff members received adequate training? How do we compare with information security best-in-class organizations?

3. Do we have a solid security policy in place? Were business managers as well as IT managers involved in creating it? Do users know about it and understand it? Do they accept it? How is the policy enforced?

4. Do we have plans for responding to infrastructure incidents? Do we practice them on a regular basis? Are staff members trained in incident response? What are our plans and policies for communicating information about incidents to external parties such as customers, partners, the press, and the public?

5. Do we practice risk management in availability and security decisions? Is our approach to dealing with hypothetical problems deliberate, structured, and well reasoned? Have the company's general managers embraced responsibility for availability and security?

A Dark Scenario for 2009

There are over two billion Internet-enabled devices in the United States now in 2009, each with its own Internet protocol, or IP, address. Worldwide the number of devices is six billion . . . Elevators, appliances, cars, trucks, manufacturing machinery, photocopiers, and traffic lights all have IP addresses. All are connected in some way to the single global network of networks loosely known as the Internet . . .

In the private sector, IT security and reliability spending accounts for almost one in every three dollars spent on information systems. Despite that expenditure, there are chronic security problems and system outages.

The routing tables for the six billion IP addresses are immense and unmanageable. Packets of messages routinely are lost in transmission, especially messages sent to large numbers of addressees. The result is that messages are frequently retransmitted, slowing already overburdened routers.

In addition to slowdowns and failures caused by the size of the system, malicious activity frequently confuses or corrupts the servers and routers that maintain IP addresses and pathway information, resulting in parts of the Internet (and on seven occasions by 2009, all of it) not working for days. During those "down days," clean copies of the address tables were distributed around the country on special military flights that were allowed to fly using visual flight rules (since the new air traffic system shuts down when the Internet does) . . .

Most of the attention to malicious activity in 2009 is . . . focused on Affinity Worms . . . [which enter] an Internet-enabled device using a vulnerability in an operating system and then branch out in a "chain letter" fashion . . . A major brokerage house was attacked in 2004 by an Affinity Worm that entered the wireless connection of the CEO's home security alarm system (from a laptop in a car two blocks away) and then wormed its way to the CEO's home PC and then through the virtual private network to the brokerage house's trading records, which it hopelessly scrambled. The market closed for three days that time . . . the power grid collapses of 2005 were the result of an Affinity Worm that

infected devices throughout the power grid (probably through wireless connections) and then had the devices simultaneously launch message traffic every second to flood the key routers supporting the grid. This technique was originally called a Distributed Denial of Service attack when it first surfaced in February, 2000. In the 2005 attack, the network operators had a choice of blocking traffic from their own devices (thereby collapsing the grid) or letting the flood of messages, or tsunami as it is now known, crash the routers. They chose the latter, which collapsed the grid.

After the success of that attack, a similar technique collapsed the key routers in the Tier 1 backbone providers in 2006 during the international crisis. No one could ever prove the attack was connected to the crisis because the IP addresses of the attackers were spoofed and anonymous accounts were used. Whoever did the attack, it did halt the rail and air traffic systems, causing the U.S. military buildup to slow. A diplomatic solution was quickly found, although not one favorable to U.S. interests.

How much had all of this cost the United States? The Federal Reserve Bank published an econometric analysis toward the end of 2009 that attempted to estimate the effects on GDP growth over the last seven years caused by the cyber attacks on the markets, the power grids, and the telecommunications systems. The report concluded that in the absence of those attacks and their cascading effects on the economy, growth could have averaged between 2.1% and 2.8%, instead of the seven-year average of 0.3%. Two days later the Fedwire was hit with a Data Base Scrambler attack that corrupted data on the Fed's main transaction data base and its two geographically separated backups. The resulting Bank Holiday caused the seven-year average to be readjusted to 0.28% growth in GDP.*

* Excerpt from Richard Clarke's "Straight Line Scenario: 2009." Presented by Howard A. Schmidt, vice chair, President's Critical Infrastructure Protection Board at the 2002 Internet2 Conference on May 8, 2002, in Arlington, VA. Reprinted by permission.

CHAPTER 7

Managing Diverse IT Infrastructures[1]

Before the emergence of the commercial Internet in the 1990s,[2] companies accomplished much that they now achieve through public internetworks entirely on their own by using proprietary technologies installed and managed inside each firm. For several reasons, this approach was expensive and unsatisfactory:

- To reach business partners and customers, every company had to develop its own communication infrastructure, a process that led to massive duplication in infrastructure investment. Often the multiplicity of technologies confused and confounded the partners and customers businesses wanted to reach.

- The technologies did not interoperate well. Many companies maintained complex software programs that had no purpose except to serve as a bridge between otherwise incompatible systems.

- Reliance on proprietary technologies meant that companies were locked in to specific vendor technologies. Once locked in, firms had little bargaining power and were at the mercy of the margin-maximizing inclinations of their technology providers.

Companies that installed hardware and software from many vendors suffered performance and reliability difficulties. IT managers, seemingly trapped in a losing game, were perennially blamed by business managers for delivering expensive systems that performed poorly or, worse, never worked at all.

The emergence of an accessible public Internet based on open standards has changed the way companies build IT capabilities. Corporate systems now gain leverage from

---

[1] This chapter is adapted from Professor Robert D. Austin's *Managing Information Technology Infrastructure* course module, Harvard Business School Publishing No. 603-104.

[2] The Internet itself arose much earlier, of course, but the *commercial* Internet really took off only with the introduction of Web browsers in the early 1990s. Some companies were using the Internet productively in the 1980s, but not very many.

their connections to public infrastructure. The new approaches compare favorably with previous approaches in numerous ways. Today, for example,

- Companies can share a communication infrastructure common to all business partners and customers. Customers and business partners can interact via common interfaces (usually Web browsers). This seamless interaction dramatically reduces complexity and confusion.
- Because of the open Transmission Control Protocol/Internet Protocol (TCP/IP) standard, communication technologies interoperate well. Software that bridges systems is simple, standardized, and inexpensive. In some cases it can be acquired for free.
- Companies are much less locked in to specific vendor technologies, a fact that creates more competition among vendors. More competition leads to lower prices and better-performing technology.

Companies can combine technologies from numerous vendors and expect them to interconnect seamlessly. Although the job of the information technology (IT) manager remains formidable, it is not the losing game it once was.

Reliable and secure connections to public networks provide new options for delivering IT services. Services historically provided by IT departments now can be acquired from service providers. This is outsourcing, but of a kind different from large-scale outsourcing programs (those still very important programs are discussed in Chapter 9). As communication technologies improve and become more compatible and modular, firms can obtain smaller increments of service from outside vendors, with shorter lead times and contract durations. "Web services" take incremental service ideas to a logical conclusion, depicting a world in which functions as narrow as, say, currency conversion will routinely be obtained externally for prices negotiated whenever a conversion is needed.

Although the standards and infrastructure necessary to bring this vision to reality are still works in progress, major IT vendors such as IBM and Microsoft profess a commitment to it. The underlying trend toward external acquisition of increasingly incremental services appears irresistible. Infrastructure that lends itself to incremental improvement enjoys favorable management attributes; for example, investment and implementation risks are easier to manage when improvements involve a series of many small steps rather than a few large "all-or-nothing" steps. Incremental improvement also facilitates experimentation and learning.[3]

Incremental service delivery also makes new business models possible, and those models act as catalysts for restructuring in service delivery industries. More and more, IT services are delivered by collections of service partners, each of which must perform well to deliver the service reliably and securely. Working with service providers means that IT managers must be especially careful in selecting and managing relationships with these business partners. Managing service provider relationships means sharing information—"virtually integrating," if you will—which requires surmounting technical communication challenges as well as challenges of incentive design.

---

[3] David Upton has written extensively on the benefits of incremental improvement strategies, especially the need to design operational infrastructures so that they can be incrementally improved. See, for example, *Designing, Managing, and Improving Operations* (Upper Saddle River, NJ: Prentice-Hall, 1998).

Service-level contracts provide a foundation for aligning incentives between parties collaborating in service delivery, but successful relationship management goes beyond contract administration.

When evolving service models connect to corporate systems, diverse IT infrastructure is the result. In many companies, legacy systems still perform vital functions and must be supported. In most companies, there is an accelerating trend toward heterogeneity in supported client devices. Increasingly, cell phones and personal digital assistants (PDAs), not personal computers (PCs), are the tools people use to interact with IT systems to conduct business. The variety of service delivery models and technologies creates complexity, which, as we have seen, generates management challenges. Not surprisingly, new ways of thinking are needed to manage diverse, distributed, and complex information and technology assets.

New Service Models

Since the emergence of PCs and client-server computing, end-user software has been designed to execute on PCs or on servers housed locally. Saved documents and other forms of data usually remain on a PC's hard drive or on storage devices connected to a nearby server or mainframe. In this scenario, there is close physical correspondence between the places where people use software and the location of the machines that deliver services. One can point to a nearby computer and say, for example, "that server runs our e-mail system."

With the advent of reliable, high-capacity networks, however, local software execution and data storage is no longer the only alternative or the best alternative from a business standpoint. Increasingly, software is designed to operate in geographically distant facilities that belong to service providers who deliver similar services to many customers. Even when software execution remains inside a company, it may happen in far away places. Servers and storage are shared among applications and users, so that it becomes much more difficult to associate a particular machine with particular IT services. Such service delivery scenarios offer efficiency and flexibility advantages. But they also pose management challenges.

In some scenarios, the end-user's company owns little of the infrastructure involved in service delivery and instead pays a monthly fee for a service bundle, which includes technical support services. When something goes wrong, business users call another company rather than their internal IT department to request resolution of the problem. Even when software applications are not managed externally, components of the infrastructure that delivers IT services may be outsourced. A company might, for example, rent space in a vendor-owned hosting facility rather than build its own data center. Or it might employ a specialized outside firm to monitor its intrusion detection systems and guard against sophisticated new security threats. The benefits of this kind of "incremental outsourcing" include the following:

Managing the shortage of specialized IT workers. Incremental outsourcing helps individual firms overcome the shortage of specialized skills by reducing the need for internal staff a firm must hire. This benefit is especially important to small and medium-size businesses that have difficulty attracting and retaining top IT talent.

Reduced time to market. Network-based service delivery models help companies develop new capabilities quickly. For example, existing companies can use externally hosted retailing packages to sell over the Web without having to purchase equipment or develop software.

The shift to 24×7 operations. Consumers expect company Web sites and supporting systems to be always available. Real-time operations require computers that are always on. But in many enterprises, facilities and equipment are not designed for high levels of availability. High availability requires large investments in redundant infrastructure. Because vendors are able to spread investments across many customers, they can achieve economies of scale that justify large investments. Vendors often can invest in levels of availability and security that individual firms cannot afford.

Favorable cash flow profiles. Traditionally, IT investments required large up-front cash outlays that only yielded deferred and often uncertain benefits (because of high project failure rates). Subscription-based IT services have a different cash flow profile. Firms pay a monthly fee to acquire services equivalent to those provided by internal systems in the past. With limited up-front purchases, payback flows in more quickly. This benefit is particularly important to small and medium-size companies that cannot afford the large up-front investments associated with some IT services. Figure 7.1 compares the cash flow profile of a traditional IT investment with that of a subscription-based service delivered through a prebuilt external infrastructure.

Cost reduction in IT service chains. Centralized service delivery can reduce support costs in many ways. With business functionality delivered from servers, upgrades to new versions of the software are done centrally, eliminating the need for support personnel to upgrade individual client computers. This service delivery approach also reduces the risk (and costs) of software piracy, because the software is never physically distributed. In addition, there is no inventory of physical media (e.g., CD-ROMs) for distributors and systems administrators to manage because services are distributed in real time to users. Vendors realize savings from economies of scale in using staff, which may be passed along to customers in the form of reduced prices.

Making applications globally accessible. When IT services are delivered over the Net, the geographic location of a computer is unimportant. Services are available at any computer with a Web browser for any user who has the authority to access the service. Traveling employees can access the same virtual workspace regardless of where they are in the world. Because the IT infrastructure is geography-neutral, much of the cost of moving a worker from one location to another is eliminated. This advantage combines with the continuing evolution in client devices (cell phones and PDAs, for example) to create new value opportunities.

Over-the-Net delivery models that permit realization of these advantages may take different forms. Many companies now manage certain corporate functions, such as human resource benefits administration, by procuring over-the-Net services from a vendor with benefits expertise; many employees manage investment of their retirement plan contributions using a Web browser to access a Web site owned and operated by a financial services company. Salesforce.com provides sales force automation to

FIGURE 7.1
Purchase versus Subscribe Cash Flows

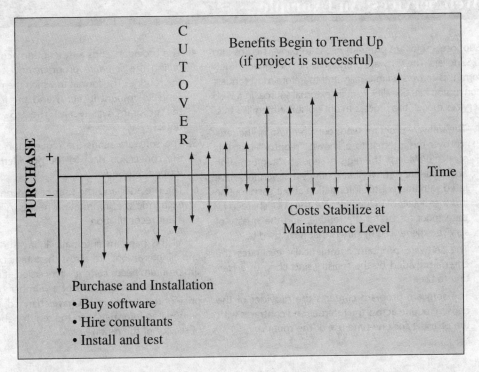

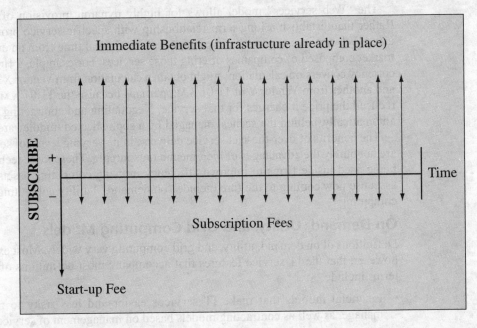

many companies via the "application service provider (ASP) model, which entails renting software functionality from a vendor for a monthly fee and accessing the functionality via a Web browser; data is stored securely in a central location managed by the ASP.

Web Services: An Example

Suppose a software program needs to convert euros into U.S. dollars. The software program is not designed to perform this conversion internally and therefore must request conversion functionality from an external source. In a Web services model, the process might go something like this:

1. The software program sends out a request for the service over the Internet to a known "registry" that lists service providers. The registry sends back information about currency conversion routines that vendors have listed with the registry. Information about each routine includes details of its functionality, the price charged by the vendor for use of the routine, and the quality of service experienced by others that have used it.

2. The software program automatically evaluates the criteria provided by the registry and chooses a routine to use.

3. The software program contacts the provider of the chosen routine across the Internet and contracts with the provider for one-time use of the routine.

4. The provider sends a description across the Internet telling the software program how to interact with the routine: The format in which the program should send its amount in euros and the format in which the program will receive the U.S. dollar amount back.

5. The software sends the request for conversion and the conversion data to the provider; the provider's routine responds.

6. The provider and the user of the conversion service exchange the information necessary to assure payment reconciliation.

All this happens automatically as the program runs, and all interactions are across the Internet. The next time this program needs currency conversion, it might choose a different provider for any of a number of reasons. The price of the service might have changed, or there might be updated information in the registry about the quality of service of the routine.

The "Web services" model allows for highly dynamic provision of IT services. Rather than establish a long-term relationship with specific service providers, firms using Web services negotiate and procure services in real time from an ever-changing market composed of companies offering those services. For example, a firm in need of currency conversion calculations might obtain a calculation from Vendor X at 11:00 A.M. and another from Vendor Y at 11:01 A.M., perhaps because the 11:01 A.M. vendor had reduced the price it charges for that service. Negotiating and contracting would occur automatically, behind the scenes, managed by a sophisticated middleware layer.

The benefits of over-the-Net service delivery, in its varying levels of sophistication, are not purely the advantages of incremental outsourcing. These same technologies are being used inside firms to improve efficiency in using computing assets. Models of asset use now coming to the fore include "on demand," "utility computing," and "grid computing."

On Demand, Utility, and Grid Computing Models

Definitions of on demand, utility, and grid computing vary widely. Most experts agree, however, that the IT service features that accompany most definitions of all of these terms include:

- Financial models that make IT services easier and less risky to procure and manage, as well as contracting models based on management of service levels.
- Restructuring and reengineering of existing applications to make them easier to manage and use.

- Enhancements to infrastructure to improve interoperability and efficiency in use of computing assets.

There is tremendous diversity in the possible and actual configurations of IT infrastructure to support these models, which creates great potential for cost savings and new capabilities, but which also creates additional infrastructure complexity.

In simplest form, financial models that underlie on demand, utility, or grid models can seem mundane, as when an IT vendor makes equipment available to a customer via favorable leasing arrangements, rather than traditional purchases. Taken to a more sophisticated extreme, financial models may allow customers to contract for a variable amount of computer power or storage capacity (or both), to be provided by a vendor for a fee that varies in proportion to the amount of power or capacity used. Such contracts may also include pricing that allows handling of surges in the load systems must bear. A customer firm that has to pay for surge capacity only when it is required, instead of maintaining it all the time even though it is usually not needed, can realize substantial savings from this kind of financial arrangement. In general, such financial arrangements allow cost savings or reduction in financial risk by adjusting the cash flow profiles involved in procuring services (as was illustrated in Figure 7.1).

Financial arrangements do not always correspond to characteristics of physical implementation—a company might obtain equipment via a lease labeled "on demand," for example, even when the use of the equipment is quite conventional—but the advantages of the financial arrangements can often be magnified by rearrangement of existing applications. Sometimes this means centralizing and commonizing applications, so that they can be managed in a central data center and accessed from anywhere. Other times it means large-scale reengineering of business processes, and rewriting or replacing with off-the-shelf packages large chunks of a company's applications portfolio. Still other times, restructuring applications might mean replacing existing applications with ASPs or Web services. In all cases, the idea is to better align application functionality with more efficient modes of management and use.

At the infrastructure level, on demand, utility, and grid computing refer to steps companies might take to make access to IT services more like access to traditional utilities, such as electricity and telephone. If, for example, server capacity or disk storage capacity can be managed as a fluid resource and easily reallocated to handle surges or to create efficiencies from sharing of equipment, then significant savings can be realized. The critical enablers of this approach to managing IT resources reside deep below the "floorboards" of IT infrastructure, in middleware layers that most business users never see. Middleware in support of these modes must address issues such as:

- *Provisioning,* providing access to new services or additional capacity in an automated and "on-the-fly" manner.
- *Resource virtualization,* which allows server or storage capacity to be accessed and referenced independent of its physical characteristics and location, which in turn allows power or capacity to be tapped in variable increments independent of how much capacity a particular server or disk array might have to offer.
- *Change management,* which permits centralized changes to infrastructure, to reduce the cost of making changes and to exert additional levels of control over processes critical to maintaining high availability.

FIGURE 7.2(a)   An "On Demand" Computing Environment

Source: Adapted from work by Arjun Chopra and Meghna Rao, Harvard Business School MBAs from the class of 2004.

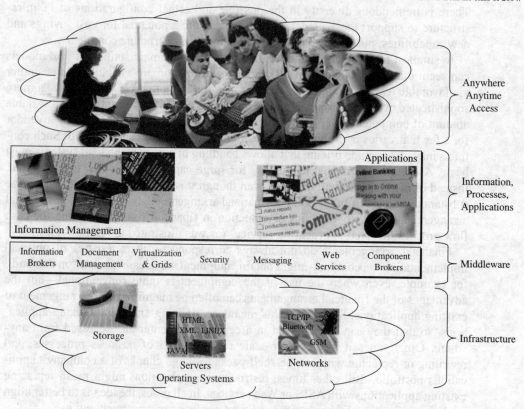

- *Performance monitoring and analytics,* which allow constant evaluation of the performance of computing infrastructure, both in terms of functionality and financial return, and suggests ongoing adjustments to improve the performance or return on investment in computing assets.

Figure 7.2 depicts an on demand computing environment that includes applications residing on an enabling middleware layer that provides virtualized and performance managed access to storage, server, and network resources.

Managing Risk through Incremental Outsourcing

As IT service chains proliferate and mature, companies often face the question of which services to outsource. Figure 7.3 outlines the steps many companies consider in making this decision. IT services that are unique to a company and provide it with significant advantages over competitors tend not to be outsourced, at least not to vendors that are trying to sell similar services to all of their customers. Such services are so

FIGURE 7.2(b)
An "On Demand" Computing Environment (continued)

IBM—Computing Portfolio	
Server Farms	BladeCenter on Intel (Win/Linux/Netware); xSeries on Intel (Linux/Win/Netware); Midrange iSeries (OS400/Linux); pSeries on IBM power4+ processors (AIX/Linux); zSeries MainFrames (z/OS/Linux); 32/64 bit Servers on AMD Opteron (Linux)
Storage Farms	IBM TotalStorageDisks/Tapes/SAN/NAS H/W
Network Resources	Use of third-party products (e.g., Cisco, Juniper)
Server Virtualization/App Provisioning	Purchased ThinkDynamics (5/03=$undisclosed) Tivoli Configuration/Provisioning Mgr
Storage Mgmt	IBM TotalStorage SAN F/S & SAN Vol Controller Tivoli Storage Manager
Network Mgmt	Tivoli NetView for network provisioning
Systems Mgmt	Tivoli Suite for Managing Multiple Platforms: Access Mgr, Systems Discovery, Provisioning, Monitoring, Reporting
Higher Level Web Services Apps	WebSphere ebusiness products, Rational (12/02 = $2bn) dev tools, Lotus collaboration products, DB2 database

core to a company's business that an internal capability to manage and extend them must be maintained. The exception to this rule arises when companies find themselves unable to develop a vital capability internally and must therefore rely on outsourcing to acquire the capability.

Many IT services do not provide competitive advantage. These services are essential in running a modern business, but there may be no reason one company's service must be different from that of its competitors. A company probably needs, for example, e-mail and word processing software, but the success or failure of a company usually has little to do with the features of these products. For these commodity-like services, the priorities are reliability and low cost (or a more favorable cash flow profile).

The logic of incremental outsourcing decisions parallels the logic of outsourcing large segments of the IT function, which we discuss fully in Chapter 9. But there are

FIGURE 7.3
Internal versus External Service Delivery

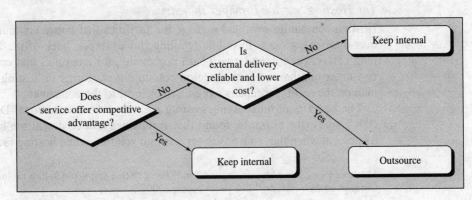

also differences. With incremental outsourcing, the economic stakes are not as high and the potential consequences of mismanagement are not as far-reaching. When a firm outsources only its travel expense reporting, for example, as opposed to its entire IT organization, risk is contained. Mistakes are more reversible and less painful. Also, because mistakes cost less, more experimentation is feasible. Trying something does not mean managers must suffer its effects for the duration of a long-term contract.

However, incremental outsourcing decisions cannot be taken lightly. A decision to outsource hosting or network management can have serious across-the-company implications if there are service problems. Furthermore, many individually correct incremental decisions can add up to a significant negative overall impact. Incremental decisions made in isolation must not add up to an incoherent or inconsistent business strategy.

Incremental outsourcing, however, offers new and attractive choices to managers seeking to improve IT infrastructure. In the past, managers often felt they faced two equally unpleasant choices: (1) do nothing and risk slipping behind competitors, or (2) wholesale replacement of major components of computing infrastructure, which risks huge cost overruns and potential business disruptions as consequences of an implementation failure. Decisions to replace legacy networks with TCP/IP-based networks have run this second risk, as have decisions about whether to implement enterprise systems. With the TCP/IP networks installed today, however, managers have intermediate options that lie between all-or-nothing choices. The importance of these options cannot be overemphasized. For perhaps the first time in the history of IT, it is possible to imagine incremental improvement paths, ways of getting from A to B and then to C and capturing significant economic benefits without putting the entire future of the firm at stake each time.

An Incremental Outsourcing Example: Hosting

Outsource hosting of a company's systems involves deciding where they should be located physically. Although on the surface this may seem like an all-or-nothing choice, a company can, in fact, precisely determine which management functions it turns over to a vendor when moving computers to a vendor's site. Some basic support functions, such as electrical power, are necessarily ceded, but beyond those, managers can choose the size of the increment of outsourcing. By doing so, managers exercise control over the risks that executing the outsourcing initiative entails. In this chapter, we consider hosting as an illustration of the incremental nature of modern service delivery options even in cases when, at first glance, outsourcing seems to present all-or-nothing options.

The Hosting Service Provider Industry

Hosting companies own and manage the facilities that house computers that provide over-the-Net services. In online retailing, for example, back-office functions (shopping cart, checkout, and credit card processing, for example) that enable Web-based consumer purchases often reside on computing platforms in hosting facilities rather than on the selling company's premises or local to the consumer.

The benefits of outsourcing hosting are many. An International Data Corporation (IDC) study, for example, found that companies reduce downtime by an average of 87 percent when they move Web servers into vendor-owned hosting facilities.[4] Morgan

---

[4] Melanie Posey, Beryl Muscarella, and Randy Perry, "Achieving Rapid Return on Investment in Outsourced Web Hosting," IDC white paper, 2000.

TABLE 7.1   Levels of Service from Hosting Providers

Level of Service	Description of Service
Business operating services	Administering and operating an application
Application support services	Support for software above the operating system level; application support; application performance monitoring and tuning; design of applications for scalability, reliability, security
Platform services	Support for hardware, operating system; reboot services; data backup and disaster recovery services; URL monitoring
Network services	Connectivity within the facility and externally to the public internet and to private peering networks; monitoring of network traffic at the transport layer; service-level assurances at the packet loss and network availability layers; network security
Real estate services (lowest level)	Suitable floor space and physical facilities; maintenance of the space and facilities

Stanley Dean Witter estimates that outsourcing hosting and data center management can reduce costs by as much as 80 to 90 percent.[5]

Service Levels in Hosting[6]

Table 7.1 shows the layers of services a hosting provider can offer. The base service level—real estate services—is similar to the business of leasing office space. Although this level of outsourcing provides robust facilities, it leaves the management and ownership of networks, computers, and software applications to the customer. All that has changed is the physical location of the computers delivering IT services. The same development and maintenance staff members care for the computers, and the customer continues to own all application computing equipment.

In addition to space and utilities, most hosting providers can manage networks, physical computing equipment, application performance, and even applications. As we move up the levels of service in Table 7.1, the outsourcing increment—the dollars the customer spends and the percentage of effort outsourced—grows larger.

Hosting models can be roughly categorized along service level lines, as follows:

Colocation hosting. Colocation hosting companies provide no-frills access to a facility and its infrastructure. Customers rent floor space, connectivity, and power. Everything beyond these basics is provided à la carte and not necessarily by the hosting provider. Customer space is usually enclosed inside floor-to-ceiling cages, and the customer owns and retains responsibility for all the servers and equipment

---

[5] Jeff Camp, April Henry, Jaime Gomezjurado, and Kristen Olsavsky, "The Internet Hosting Report," Morgan Stanley Dean Witter, November 2000.

[6] Some of the material in this section is adapted from Robert D. Austin, "Web and IT Hosting Facilities: Technology Note," Harvard Business School Publishing Note No. 601-134.

inside the cages. Often the hosting company knows little about the equipment or business operations inside customers' cages. This model requires customers to have (or acquire from a third party) the expertise to design, maintain, and operate the equipment inside the cages. This model, which supports a wide range of architectural possibilities, generally offers high availability.

Shared hosting. In shared hosting, servers are owned and operated by the hosting provider and customers purchase space on servers. Multiple customers share a single physical server. Some providers use sophisticated clustering technologies to achieve highly secure and reliable performance. Although some customers are wary of the degree of sharing implicit in this model, because of its perceived negative implications for security and reliability, this approach is becoming more prevalent as companies move to on demand, utility, and grid computing.

Dedicated hosting. As with shared hosting, in dedicated hosting, servers are owned and operated by the hosting provider. Unlike a shared model, however, customers do not share servers; the servers are "dedicated" to individual customers. Other infrastructure components that provide network, storage, and some other services are shared across customers. Usually, dedicated hosting providers offer a complete managed services package that includes everything needed to run the customer's systems at the required level of security and availability. Dedicated servers support high levels of security and availability, but forego some of the efficiencies promised by new service models.

Outsourcing data center infrastructure management is not an all-or-nothing choice. Connectivity service providers—to take another example—offer increasingly incremental service levels with much more attractive risk and expense management profiles for customers. Do you want one megabit per second (mbps) of connectivity to the Internet backbone? Ten mbps? How about one mbps "burstable"[7] to ten mbps? Gigabit Ethernet? The options in service provision are multiplying, and infrastructure managers now often can purchase exactly the service increments they want.

Managing Relationships with Service Providers

When companies acquire IT services externally, they find themselves engaged in relationships with a growing number of service providers. As the operations of service providers and their customers become intertwined, the customer firm comes to rely on the provider's capabilities as a basis for its own capabilities. Consequently, as with all outsourcing of important business functions, whether supplying just-in-time parts to a manufacturing assembly line or managing computing platforms, healthy relationships with vendors are critical to how well a company performs its primary business mission. Mistakes by vendors can be costly. Services are only as good as the weakest link in the service provider chain. Choosing reliable service providers and managing strong vendor relationships therefore are critical skills for an IT manager.

[7] Burstable bandwidth options allow customers to use extra bandwidth if they need it for short periods in return for a higher per megabit price.

Selecting Service Partners

The most critical step in assembling an IT service chain is the selection of providers. Providers differ greatly in the service increments they offer, how they charge for services, the guarantees they *can* make, and the guarantees they are *willing* to make. No expertise in relationship management can overcome choosing an unreliable service provider. Infrastructure managers therefore must take tremendous care in selecting business partners that perform vital service chain functions.

The most common process for selecting service providers involves writing a "request for proposal" (RFP) and submitting it to a set of apparently qualified vendors. An RFP asks prospective providers for information relevant to their service capabilities across a spectrum that includes financial, technical, and operational information. Responses become a primary basis for deciding between vendors. Companies, however, rarely rely entirely on RFP responses but instead gather additional information from industry analysts, from other companies that have used providers' services, and from visits to service provider sites. Many companies employ elaborate scoring mechanisms for combining information gathered from all sources into comparable bases. But selection always comes down to the judgment of management.

There is no single format for RFPs, nor are there universally agreed on categories of information or sources that should be consulted in selecting providers. RFPs, however, typically request information in the following categories:

Descriptive information. How it describes its business reveals much about a service provider's priorities and likely future direction. Descriptive information is equally relevant in evaluating the prospective provider's capacity to provide services (e.g., is it big enough to meet your demands?).

Financial information. A service provider's financial strength is a critical factor in evaluating the continuity of service and service quality a vendor is likely to provide. Providers that struggle financially may have trouble maintaining service quality or may require financial assistance that reduces or eliminates the economic benefits of acquiring a service externally. Worse, they may fail and shut down, leaving the customer firm to navigate the provider's bankruptcy.

Proposed plan for meeting service requirements. How the provider offers to meet the requirements laid out in the RFP indicates whether it truly understands the requirements. The plan for meeting the requirements can be evaluated on its merits and compared with proposed plans from other vendors. Partner firms that will be involved in the vendor's plan should be identified so that the customer firm can be assured of the qualifications of all the parties involved in service provision.

Mitigation of critical risks. A good RFP asks specific questions about potential service risks. Availability and security are two areas where it pays for customers to be sure they understand a service provider's approach.

Service guarantees. A service provider's guarantees (the levels of performance it is willing to back with penalty clauses in a contract) are important signals of the real level of confidence vendor managers have in their services. Often there is a substantial gap between what the performance service providers claim is their norm and what they are willing to guarantee. If the gap is too wide, services may

TABLE 7.2 **Summary Grid for Comparing Hosting Providers**

Source: Adapted from Robert D. Austin, "Selecting a Hosting Provider," Harvard Business School Exercise No. 601-171. Although based on real cases, these data are fictitious and do not pertain to any real hosting provider.

Comparison Dimension	Provider 1	Provider 2	Provider 3
Company description	Regional hosting and broadband (backbone, DSL) service provider	National hosting services provider	Regional telco, backbone and broadband service provider
Employees	1,600	3,300	28,000
Financial profile	Declined to provide (private company)	After-tax loss $180 million on sales of $600 million; strong cash position; new facilities building offered as explanation for lack of profitability	After-tax profit of $1.1 billion on sales of $13 billion (most not from hosting business)
Number of data centers managed/ total square feet	3 data centers/ 160,000 sq. ft.	28 data centers/ 1.6 million sq. ft.	5 (2 operational)/ 220,000 sq. ft. (45,000 operational)
Space offered (RFP specified space for six racks of equipment)	3 8'×8' cages (192 sq. ft.), partitions removed to provide contiguous space	3 8'×7' cages (168 sq. ft.), partitions removed to provide contiguous space	280 sq. ft. enclosed room
Physical security	Fully meets requirement	Fully meets requirement	Some concerns (see notes from site visit)
Power	Fully meets requirement	Fully meets requirement	Connected to only one power grid; two promised within 6 weeks
Connectivity	Fully meets requirement	Fully meets requirement	Not redundant to backbone; promised redundancy in 6 weeks
Service-level guarantees	Fully meets requirement	Fully meets requirement	Partially meets requirement
One-time setup cost, space	$6,500	$7,800	$10,800
Monthly space rental	3 × $6,500	3 × $6,800	$9,800
One-time setup cost, connectivity	$1,200	$1,500	$1,600
Variable connectivity cost	$1,200 per month plus $525 per month for each mbps above 10	$1,500 per month plus $589 per month for each mbps above 10	$900 per month plus $412 per month for each mbps above 10

not be as robust as advertised. Service guarantees are essential to aligning incentives between service providers so that overall, the service chain performs well.

Pricing. Pricing usually includes one-time and variable components and may be structured in other ways as well. Although pricing is important for most companies, usually it is not the most important factor in deciding between vendors.

Table 7.2 shows a summary of information about three hosting providers that might be gathered from an RFP and other sources.[8] A close look at the information demonstrates that often choices between vendors are nontrivial. Providers that are strong in one area may be weak in another, and often no clear choice emerges.

For example, in Table 7.2 the fact that Provider 1 seems unwilling to supply financial information is probably a red flag that signals further investigation. Even if Provider 1's funding sources are gold-plated, customers need specific assurance that a service provider has a viable business model and will be a strong partner well into the future. Similarly, infrastructure managers might reasonably be worried about Provider 2's lack of profitability. Provider 2 relates the losses to its expansion plans, but prospective customers might wonder if the company can transition as easily to profit-making as its managers suggest. In this scenario, Provider 3 looks like the solid choice because it is large and profitable and its fees are lower.

Unfortunately, there are reasons to worry about Provider 3. Most of the company's revenues come from business other than hosting services. This situation may translate into a lack of focus on the hosting business. Furthermore, Provider 3 seems to have some serious operational problems. Table 7.3 shows a discouraging report from a team that visited Provider 3's data center. In light of the report, one wonders whether Provider 3's lower prices are a miscalculation and perhaps evidence of the company's inexperience in hosting services. If so, the low prices eventually may become a problem for Provider 3's customers as well, especially if low profitability in the hosting business causes that provider's managers to further reduce their attention to hosting. Worse yet, if Provider 3 discovers it is losing money on hosting, it may seek to reduce costs in ways that affect service levels or even discontinue its hosting business.

We have stumbled here onto a general truth of outsourcing that we will return to in Chapter 9: *An outsourcing deal that is too one-sided, too favorable to one party at the expense of the other, usually ends up as a bad deal for both sides.* As they realize the deal is a loser, managers of a disadvantaged vendor almost always divert resources away from the relationship. This realization brings us to the next subject: managing relationships with providers once they are in place.

Relationship Management

Relationships with service provider partners require ongoing attention. Processes must be in place so that partners can share information and problems in the service chain can be solved quickly even when they result from complex interactions of infrastructure components owned by different players. Problem-tracking and customer relationship systems, for example, must be able to exchange problem-tracking information as

---

[8] This example is taken from Robert D. Austin, "Selecting a Hosting Provider," Harvard Business School Exercise No. 601-171.

TABLE 7.3 Sample Facility Visit Report for Hosting Provider 3

Source: Robert D. Austin, "Selecting a Hosting Provider," Harvard Business School Exercise No. 601-171. Information in this report is fictitious and not intended to pertain to a real hosting provider.

Initial walk around exterior: Renovated warehouse building (conventional brick, not hardened) shared with a delivery service. Urban setting amid a complex of warehouses. City workers doing roadwork near the facility, with heavy-duty digging (potentially fiber cable slicing) equipment. Data center on third floor. First floor and basement include a garage used by the delivery service. Panel trucks come and go on the lower levels on the north side. Second floor includes offices and appears to be empty. Never spoke to anyone who could tell us definitively how the second floor would be built out or if even that was the plan.
CCTV cameras visible around the perimeter of the facility. Diesel generators enclosed in 12-foot-high chain link, HVAC on roof. West side of building composed of a series of loading doors.
On day of visit, three loading doors were open. We succeeded in climbing up onto the loading dock and walking right into a power infrastructure room where many UPSs were housed. Waited there, expecting CCTV or alarm to summon security; no one ever showed up. (Staff later explained this lapse by saying that the door was open to facilitate construction and renovation and that the guard who was posted there had been reprimanded.)

Entering facility: First-level security is building security. Guard appeared not to realize that there was a data center in the building. Ushered us up to the third floor, where we encountered an unoccupied security desk behind a sliding glass partition. One CCTV console visible at desk. It would have been easy to climb through the opening to the security desk and let ourselves into the facility. Biometric palm reader visible but dust-covered at door. Security guard who had walked us up called someone on radio, and someone came to let us in. Person who let us in came from somewhere outside the data facility, then let us in by leaning through the opening and hitting the buzzer, which was in reach. We stood inside the door while he made out visitor badges for us. He did ask to see picture IDs, but security was kind of a farce by this point and everyone was a little embarrassed (including us for them). The room we were standing in while he prepared badges approximated a man trap in that there was another door about 20 feet away that opened into the data center proper. Unfortunately, that door was propped open.

Cages: No cages. Everyone gets an enclosed room with keypad access. No raised floor; power comes in from above, as do comms. Bolt-in racks and shelves provided. Walls of rooms do not extend to roof, so possible to climb over walls or to toss something into enclosed room.

Verification of redundancy, security, etc.: Redundant power and connectivity not yet in place, although promised within six weeks. Network hardware for facility was exposed in an open area anyone walking to his or her own enclosed space would need to pass. No on-site NOC, although they expressed willingness to provide specific network monitoring on site on a contract basis; noted too that network operations were monitored from a regional NOC. Guy giving tour kept apologizing for the construction.

Concerns: This facility is not fully built yet, although some customers are operational. Provider promises to have it in shape in time consistent with our project, but fact is that we cannot compare this facility on an equal basis with the others. Facility being under construction did not explain all the lapses we saw.

Overall assessment: These guys don't appear to have the hosting business figured out yet. Maybe it's just that they are in a construction phase. But there was little that we saw that offered warm feelings during our tour.

TABLE 7.4 An SLA Offered by a Hosting Provider

- Downtime—defined as sustained packet loss in excess of 50 percent for 15 consecutive minutes due to the failure of the hosting provider to provide services for that period (does not include scheduled maintenance time).
- Excess latency—defined as transmission latency in excess of 120 milliseconds round-trip time between any two points within the hosting provider's U.S. network.
- Excess packet loss—defined as packet loss in excess of 1 percent between any two points in the hosting provider's network.
- Each downtime period entitles customer to receive a credit equal to one day's recurring connectivity charge.
- Hosting provider guarantees two-hour response time in diagnosing problems within hosting provider and customer network.
- If problem is not within hosting provider and customer network, hosting provider will determine source within an additional two hours.
- Customer will be advised of reason for problem within one hour of hosting provider's discovery of the reason for the problem.
- If problem is within control of hosting provider, remedy for problem is guaranteed in two hours from diagnosis of the problem.
- Inability to deliver diagnosis or remedies within the times stated above entitles customer to an additional service credit for each two-hour period of delay.
- Customer can collect credits for no more than seven days' charges in a calendar month.
- Customer must request credits in writing within seven days of the event for which credits are compensation.
- Credits are granted at the sole discretion of the hosting provider.

well as, sometimes, customer account information. Procedures and technical interfaces between partner systems must be properly designed and maintained.

More significant than problems with information-sharing systems, though, are the many incentive problems that attend service relationships. The most formidable obstacles are sometimes not technical but "political." When avoiding responsibility for a problem intrudes into the process of solving it, service collaboration becomes less effective. The key to effective relationships is aligned incentives among partners.

A service-level agreement (SLA) aligns incentives in relationships with service providers. SLAs describe the specific conditions by which the service provider is held liable for a service interruption and the penalties that the service provider will incur as a result. Table 7.4 illustrates the kinds of contractual terms one finds in an SLA. In keeping with our earlier examples, this SLA is for a hosting provider. Notice that failure is specifically defined, penalties apply only when the service provider is responsible for the service interruption, and penalties are prespecified and limited. Why a service provider insists on careful definitions is clear: To limit its liability for problems not under its control. But the specific nature of the agreement complicates service quality assurance. What matters to the client company is any failure, regardless of which service provider causes it.

Managers of customer firms must therefore manage SLAs with many service providers. SLAs must interlock so that penalty payments flow through the service chain in a way that provides appropriate incentives. Suppose, for example, a company offering over-the-Net software functionality agrees to an SLA that requires it to pay a penalty if the system is not available for a period longer than 10 minutes. Suppose also that the actual cause of a failure is a different vendor, say, an Internet service provider (ISP). In that case an SLA in place between the software company and an ISP should specify that the ISP will reimburse the software company for the penalty it owes to the client company. Although the SLA arrangement between the software company and the ISP might seem a matter best left to those two entities, it is to the customer company's advantage to ensure that incentives are aligned. Disputes between partners in a service chain can have dire implications for the users of a service.

The conventional wisdom in defining SLAs calls for designing them with "teeth," so that service providers feel pain when failures occur. In practice, however, it is difficult to determine appropriate penalty levels. SLAs provide service providers with both incentives and a way to credibly express their intention to deliver reliable service, and so it is important that they be in place. But setting penalties too low has little impact. Setting them too high is detrimental to a provider's willingness (and, if penalties are high enough, ability) to be a strong partner. Thus it is a mistake to consider SLAs the only means by which partners are managed. The most successful relationships emphasize shared objectives and helping all the partners earn a reasonable return.

Since many outsourced services involve entrusting data to service providers, contractual relationships need to contain provisions about a customer firm's rights to control its own data. The concern here is not that a vendor might try to claim ownership of customer data but that the vendor might try to lock the customer into a relationship by making it inconvenient to switch vendors. The interests of service providers and their customers are poorly aligned when it comes to the degree of entanglement in their relationship. Managers who take insufficient care in avoiding unnecessary entanglements will find themselves at the mercy of service providers, forfeiting a principal benefit of incremental outsourcing: The ability to alter and improve IT infrastructure in small steps in an ongoing manner.

Managing Legacies

Not too long ago, tax accountants at a major U.S. company discovered they were not taking full advantage of a benefit they could claim under the U.S. tax code. The tax law details of this story are unimportant, but the benefit was worth a substantial amount of money to the company, if the accountants could claim it. But to claim the tax benefit, the company needed to process receivables in a very specific way. The tax accounting managers therefore convened a large meeting of all the people in the company who might have something to say about a change in how receivables were processed.

The meeting was nearly two-thirds finished when a young, junior employee seated near the back of the room interrupted the smooth flow of the meeting to the mild irritation of the senior manager from tax accounting.

"Excuse me," the young man said. Everyone knew he was from the IT department. "Can you help me . . . do I understand . . . ?" the young man stuttered as the room's attention turned entirely to him. "What you are proposing? Is it . . . ?" He then summarized his understanding of the proposal.

"Yes," the senior tax accounting manager answered. "That is the proposal, although we are working it through in detail with everyone here to make sure no one sees any issues with the change."

The young man smiled. "I've got news for you," he said. All those in the room braced themselves, expecting an explanation in incomprehensible IT terms of why the change could never be made within the company's IT infrastructure, at least not at a reasonable cost. What he said surprised everyone:

"We've been processing our receivables that way for the last 20 years. That's the way the system does it. That's how the program logic works."

The meeting was quickly adjourned as the tax accountants returned to their offices to see if they could figure out a way to apply for the benefit retroactively.

This story illustrates two very serious points. First and most obvious, company operations often are constrained by the way legacy systems process information. Old computer code often disturbingly manifests what have been called "core rigidities," the ossified remains of what were once capabilities.[9] Second, business managers often do not even know how their company performs certain vital business functions because the details are buried in how legacy systems operate. In this story, the managers' discovery about their company's operations was a happy one; more often, though, such discoveries are less welcome.

The difficulties that arise from legacy systems can be roughly categorized as follows:

Technology problems. Sometimes the constraints embedded in legacy systems result from inherent incompatibilities in older technologies. As we have seen, proprietary technologies that predate the internetworking era were not designed to converse easily with technologies from other vendors. This kind of problem must be worked around in modern internetworking infrastructures.

Residual process complexity. Some difficulties with legacy systems arise because the systems address problems that no longer exist. One example is the substantial amount of batch processing some companies still perform. Legacy systems were designed to operate in batch mode because processing power needed to be rationed and because the bandwidth available at that time did not allow computers to operate in real time. Now computing power and bandwidth are relatively abundant, but many batch systems have not been redesigned or replaced because of other priorities.

Local adaptation. Many legacy systems were developed for very focused business purposes within functional hierarchies. When such systems were designed, their architects had little inkling of the enterprise systems and real-time architectures of the then-distant future. Instead, systems were intended to solve a particularly narrow business problem. Not surprisingly, a system designed in the 1970s does not facilitate global uniform parts management in the twenty-first century, although it still may do its narrowly defined job very well.

Nonstandard data definitions. Throughout most companies, business units and divisions have used different conventions for important data elements. For example, the parts division might use a 15-character part number whereas the product development organization uses a 13-character part number. This may seem like a small difference (only two characters), but the legacy system implications are far-reaching. Differences in fundamental data definitions are built into a company's IT infrastructure in many specific places. They are difficult to change not only because they

---

[9] For a deeper discussion of core rigidities, see Dorothy A. Leonard, *Wellsprings of Knowledge: Building and Sustaining the Sources of Innovation* (Boston: Harvard Business School Press, 1998, paperback edition).

TABLE 7.5 **Key Questions in Managing Legacies**

Legacy systems	• How will new infrastructure exchange data with legacy systems?
	• Will new infrastructure obtain needed real-time interaction with legacy systems?
	• What work-arounds are necessary? Are they sustainable?
	• What is long-term strategy for renewing legacy systems?
Legacy organizations and cultures	• How will new infrastructure affect ways of working and communicating? Are anticipated changes acceptable?
	• Should technology drive organizational and cultural change?
	• Should organization and culture be protected from technology effects?
	• What are organizational expectations about common processes in different parts of the organization?
	• What are criteria for deciding whether systems or process will change when the two are not compatible?

touch so many elements of the IT infrastructure but because making definitions common requires an expensive and difficult to achieve companywide consensus.

Because of the tremendous variety in legacy systems across companies, it is not possible to develop a prescriptive approach to dealing with legacy issues. Tactics for solving legacy problems must fit individual companies and their specific situations. However, there are questions managers should think through carefully before they contemplate growing infrastructure by adding new systems or services on top of existing systems.

Table 7.5 lists questions managers might ask about legacy systems that will have to interact with a new system or service. The first issue is whether legacy systems can, in any modified or enhanced form, perform consistently with real-time infrastructure objectives. If the answer is no, replacement may be the only option. Often, though, the answer is not definitively negative. Questions then focus on "work-arounds," contrivances needed to facilitate interaction between new and old infrastructure elements: Whether they are sustainable and whether they represent reasonable cost/functionality trade-offs.

Many businesses have succeeded in adding interfaces to legacy systems that enable them to work with internetworking systems. This interfacing approach sometimes is called enterprise application integration (EAI). EAI practitioners recommend "non-invasive" interfaces that minimize changes to the internal operations of legacy systems. Even EAI enthusiasts, however, acknowledge limits to how well legacy systems can perform as components of real-time infrastructure. Sooner or later, getting work-arounds to operate satisfactorily becomes more difficult and more expensive than just replacing old systems. Infrastructure managers always must ask whether the complexity of work-arounds is unreasonable.

When installing new infrastructure or acquiring new services, infrastructure managers also run up against organizational rather than technical legacies. Changing IT infrastructure unavoidably affects nontechnical elements of a company's operations, especially how people work and interact. A complex interrelationship exists between core rigidities that manifest themselves in ossified legacy systems and a firm's social systems and processes. Sometimes the rigidity of workers' attachment to how a system works is more of an obstacle to change than any technology factor. Moreover, changes in how systems work almost always force changes in how people work to a greater or lesser degree. The degree to which systems force cultural and process changes is a key management decision. The second half of Table 7.5 suggests questions that managers should ask as they confront organizational legacies that interact with system legacies.

Managing IT Infrastructure Assets

In the mainframe era, keeping track of the assets that made up a company's IT infrastructure was relatively easy. The majority consisted of a small number of large mainframe machines in the corporate data center. A company's investment in IT had a tangible presence. Senior business managers could point to it, even rap their knuckles against it if they wished. Because a company's infrastructure was centralized and because services were deployed from mainframe assets, companies found it relatively easy to track how systems were being used and estimate how much value they were providing.

After the emergence of PCs, clients and servers, the Web, portable devices, and distributed network infrastructure, a company's investments in IT became much more diffuse. Computing assets were scattered in a large number of small machines located in different buildings. Some (i.e., laptops) moved around with their users and left the company's premises on a regular basis. Some new service delivery models cause assets (e.g., servers) to migrate back to the corporate data center, which might seem to herald a return to centralized management models. Other model variations, such as outsourced hosting, make it clear, though, that complexity of infrastructure and distribution of IT assets are here to stay. As service delivery models proliferate and improve, the variety of IT asset configurations will increase.

The variety of asset configurations in modern IT infrastructures makes certain business questions hard to answer: How are IT investments deployed across business lines or units? How are IT assets being used? Are they being used efficiently? Are they deployed to maximum business advantage? How can we adjust their deployment to create more value? Although never easy to answer, these questions were at least reasonable when assets were centralized. IT management frameworks over the past decade have focused on reclaiming management control over IT assets.

One approach to this problem has been called total cost of ownership (TCO) analysis. IT services are analyzed in terms of the costs and benefits associated with service delivery to each client device. For example, the total cost of delivering office productivity services to a PC desktop within an enterprise might be expressed as "$250 per client per month." Arriving at this number requires a detailed study to determine the total monthly costs associated with the delivery of each service available on that client, including costs shared with other clients and costs not necessarily accounted for as line items in budgets or accounting systems. Once monthly costs are computed, they must be allocated on a per client basis. Totaling costs without missing any that are material is difficult, as is allocating costs to clients in a way that preserves the management usefulness of the information.

Completing the analysis on the benefit side of the equation is also difficult but essential if IT assets are to be used efficiently. Many who attempt TCO analyses settle for usage information—what services are used and with what frequency—on the benefit side of the equation rather than attempting to estimate the actual benefits to each user. Usage information on a per client, per month basis can be helpful compared with cost of service delivery on a per client, per month basis. Usage information also may be useful when computed on the basis of other platform types. For example, usage information on a per server basis might be useful in server-to-server comparisons, in planning for growth in server capacity, or in discovering opportunities for consolidating underused servers into a smaller number nearer their capacities.

Cost and benefit analysis for IT assets and platforms provides a basis for evaluating a company's current IT services against new service alternatives. Outsourcing vendors often are asked to bid on a per platform basis. These prices can be compared to study results to evaluate a company's options and identify incremental opportunities for service delivery improvement. Where a firm's costs of delivering an IT service are out of line with the price at which it can be acquired externally, outsourcing becomes comparatively appealing.

Summary

This chapter has explored the increasingly diverse nature of the infrastructure used to deliver IT services in twenty-first-century companies. We have described how more available and secure network connections are creating more service delivery options and how new options have led to the creation and restructuring of the service provider industry. Today, companies acquire services externally from chains of service providers and integrate those external services into their internal legacy infrastructures. The shift toward incremental outsourcing and multiple, collaborating service delivery partners dictates a shift in management emphasis. The following questions should help a company assess the opportunities and the risks:

1. What services within our IT infrastructure are candidates for incremental outsourcing? Are there opportunities to convert large up-front IT investments into spread-over-time subscription services?

2. Are our service delivery partners technically and financially capable enough to support our evolving IT service needs? Do we have well-defined processes for partner selection to ensure that we will continue to have highly capable partners?

3. Do we have detailed service-level agreements in place with our service providers? Have we made sure that the SLAs in our service delivery chains interlock and that incentives are aligned up and down the chain? Do we have systems in place for virtually integrating with service delivery partners? Have we specified contract terms with service providers that preserve our options for incrementally improving our infrastructure?

4. What are our short-term and long-term strategies for dealing with legacy system issues? What systems should we replace, and when should we replace them?

Case 2-1

CareGroup

"The good news," reported John Halamka, the CareGroup CIO, as he opened his November 21, 2002 presentation to the board of directors, "is that health care did not suffer." Over the next 20 minutes, Halamka recounted a remarkable tale that explained why CareGroup IT systems had completely collapsed for three-and-a-half days the previous week, the steps staff members and vendors had taken to recover, and how the hospital had reverted to paper-based systems, many of which had not been used for a decade or more. Though his story contained challenges and travails, in the end the paper-based systems and recovery efforts had worked well. Care to some patients had been delayed, but not a single adverse event related to the outage had been reported. Even so, there were numerous lessons learned and some line items to be added to the IT budget; Halamka now outlined these for the board.

CareGroup

CareGroup was a team of health care professionals dedicated to providing the best quality care to patients in a highly personalized manner. CareGroup and its members offered a broad spectrum of health services to residents of eastern Massachusetts, in a variety of settings, ranging from world-renowned academic health centers and outstanding community hospitals, to physician offices and community health centers. CareGroup hospital members included Beth Israel Deaconess Medical Center in Boston, Mount Auburn Hospital in Cambridge, New England Baptist Hospital in Boston, Deaconess-Glover Hospital in Needham,

This case was prepared by Professors F. Warren McFarlan and Robert D. Austin. Copyright © 2003 President and Fellows of Harvard College. Harvard Business School Case No. 303-097.

and Deaconess-Nashoba Hospital in Ayer. With more than 13,000 employees and 2,000 medical staff, CareGroup offered community-based primary care and a wide range of specialty services close to where individuals live or worked.

CareGroup had been formed in a three-way merger on October 1, 1996. The Beth Israel Hospital, the Deaconess Hospital, and the Mount Auburn Hospital came together on that day. The Beth Israel and Deaconess hospitals, which were physically adjacent, merged into a single hospital; every department was merged and headed by one individual (i.e., the two surgical units were merged and a head of surgery appointed). The Mount Auburn Hospital, located in Cambridge, reported into CareGroup management as a separate entity, as did four other hospitals, which had formerly been a part of the Pathway Network, assembled over the previous decade by the Deaconess Hospital. (See Exhibit 1 for the organization chart of CareGroup, and Exhibit 2 for descriptions of the different hospitals.)

This merger produced a hospital group with $1.6 billion revenue, the second-largest group of hospitals in eastern Massachusetts. The merger was driven by the intense competitive environment, which existed in the mid-1995 period. On December 13, 1994, the Massachusetts medical community was stunned to discover that the two largest and most prestigious hospitals in Boston, Massachusetts, General Hospital and the Brigham and Women's Hospital, had agreed to merge in a holding-company structure called "Partners." The perceived pressure that this large organization was going to be able to put on the HMOs (which stood between individual patients and employees and the hospitals and doctors) led many hospitals to conclude they had subcritical mass in terms of their number of "covered lives"; in this new world, you would need a critical mass to get survival

**EXHIBIT 1
CareGroup
Organization
Chart,
January 1,
2003**

Source: CareGroup
internal documents.

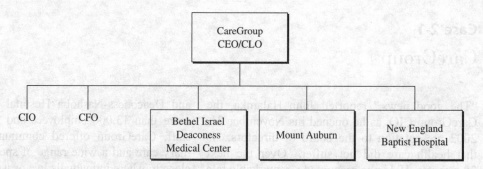

By December 31, 2002, Deaconess-Waltham Hospital and Deaconess-Nashoba Hospital were no longer part of CareGroup, and Nashoba-Glover Hospital reported into the Beth Israel Deaconess Medical Center.

prices from the HMOs (the more covered lives you had, the more the HMOs needed you). The hospitals felt they needed bulked-up negotiating power to push back against the HMOs, who themselves were under great financial pressure from companies in the region like FleetBank and Raytheon, who were trying to drive down their medical costs. Specifically, the factors that brought CareGroup together were:

- The contracting power needed by the hospitals against the HMOs.

- The possibility of developing integrated services across the hospitals that could improve quality of care and drive down costs.

- The need for a strong balance sheet in a complex price war, in which there were more than 40 percent excess hospital beds in the region; because of this excess supply, some hospitals were closing their doors.

Over the next seven years, under the leadership of two CEOs, CareGroup sought to deal with these issues. A brief summary of progress would include the following observations:

It was a time of extraordinary financial pressure for CareGroup. First, the Mount Auburn Hospital, which had been profitable for over 15 years, suddenly produced a $10 million loss and had to re-engineer its operations. Just as it recovered, Beth Israel Deaconess began losing significant amounts of money. Not until mid-2002, under the leadership of a new CEO, Paul Levy, did they begin to recover. At about that same time, the Baptist Hospital

suddenly incurred a $20 million loss, which led to the appointment of new management there. By early 2003, these problems were largely behind CareGroup. Each hospital in the group was headed by a different CEO than at the time of the merger, and financial stability issues were fading into the past.

Operational coordination across the hospitals had turned out to be extremely difficult because of their history of independence. Financial synergy in terms of lower debt costs, however, had been a strong feature. Similarly, joint contracting with the HMOs had been very successful.

An unexpected glittering success was the development of an integrated technology system, which linked the entire group together. The system was widely touted nationally; it was considered not only to be the best in health care, but also one of the very best in any industry.

In 2003, CareGroup senior management consisted of a CEO/chief legal officer, a CFO, and a CIO. In the past several years, one of the subsidiary hospitals, Waltham Hospital, had run into difficulty and the CareGroup board had begun the process of closing it down. This led to a real estate specialist stepping in and, in return for a third of the hospital's land, providing Waltham with additional funding that allowed it to emerge as a stand-alone organization with strong community support.

On December 31, 2002, Deaconess-Nashoba Hospital was spun off to Essent, a for-profit organization that committed significant funds to a massive renovation of the hospital over the next

EXHIBIT 2 Major CareGroup Medical Facilities

Source: CareGroup internal documents.

Beth Israel Deaconess Medical Center

Beth Israel Deaconess Medical Center is a Harvard-affiliated, research-intensive teaching hospital located in Boston's Longwood Medical Area. Serving as the principal academic and clinical resource of CareGroup, Beth Israel Deaconess Medical Center is home to several nationally recognized clinical centers of specialized expertise, including solid-organ transplantation; diabetes/vascular surgery; obstetrics; cardiology and cardiac surgery; gastroenterology; trauma; cancer (with a particular interest in breast cancer); and AIDS. Complementary, state-of-the-art inpatient and outpatient facilities, in addition to two regional outpatient centers, primary care offices in more than 30 communities, and transitional and palliative care units, enhance the broad array of clinical services available.

Mount Auburn Hospital

Mount Auburn Hospital in Cambridge is an acute care, Harvard-affiliated community teaching hospital, serving the health care needs of residents in Arlington, Belmont, Cambridge, Lexington, Medford, Somerville, Watertown, and Waltham. The hospital offers comprehensive inpatient and outpatient medical, surgical, obstetrical, and psychiatric services and is a leading provider of advanced, specialized care in cardiology, cardiac surgery, oncology, orthopedics, neurology, and vascular surgery. In addition, Mount Auburn Hospital offers an extensive network of satellite primary care practices in seven communities, as well as a broad range of community-based programs including Mount Auburn Home Care; outpatient specialty services; and occupational health. The hospital's Prevention and Recovery Center is a provider of education, intervention, and support programs for public health issues such as substance abuse and violence. The Mount Auburn Center for Problem Gambling is the first such outpatient clinic in the state.

New England Baptist Hospital

Established in 1893, New England Baptist Hospital is a 150-bed adult medical/surgical hospital, located in the Mission Hill neighborhood of Boston, with specialty services in musculoskeletal care, sports medicine, occupational medicine, and cardiology.

New England Baptist Hospital ranks among the nation's foremost providers of hip and knee replacement surgery. To solidify its commitment to musculoskeletal care, the hospital in 1995 formed the New England Baptist Bone & Joint Institute. The Institute is the region's leading resource for a full range of prevention and education, diagnostic, treatment and rehabilitation services in orthopedics and rheumatology, joint replacement, spine care, foot and ankle care, hand surgery, occupational medicine, and sports medicine. The hospital has a 40-bed skilled nursing unit, specializing in rehabilitative care for the orthopedic patient, in addition to postsurgical medical patients. NEBH is the sports medicine hospital of the Boston Celtics.

Deaconess-Glover Hospital

Deaconess-Glover Hospital is a 41-bed community hospital serving the primary and secondary healthcare needs of Needham residents and the surrounding communities of Dedham, Dover, Medfield, and Westwood. Founded more than 80 years ago as a municipal hospital, Deaconess-Glover provides a wide range of inpatient and outpatient services, including a full-service, 24-hour emergency department; state-of-the-art cardiac testing and treatment capabilities; diabetes care through the Joslin Center at Deaconess-Glover; and advanced diagnostic radiology. The hospital also houses clinical laboratory facilities and a new Occupational Health center for work-injury prevention, treatment, and rehabilitation. The medical staff comprises highly qualified primary-care physicians and specialists with advanced training in 30 medical and surgical disciplines, including arthritis and rheumatology; dermatology; endocrinology; gastroenterology; obstetrics and gynecology; oncology; orthopedics; pulmonary medicine; and urology, as well as plastic, thoracic, and vascular surgery.

(continued)

EXHIBIT 2   Major CareGroup Medical Facilities (continued)

Deaconess-Nashoba Hospital (spun off December 31, 2002)

Deaconess-Nashoba Hospital is a 41-bed community hospital serving 11 communities in north central Massachusetts. Located in Ayer, the hospital boasts a highly qualified medical staff with 122 active and associate member physicians offering community-based primary care and a wide range of specialty services. Founded in 1964, Deaconess-Nashoba is known for many clinical strengths, including emergency medicine; cardiology; gastroenterology; oncology; orthopedics; and surgery. The hospital also offers a diverse array of outpatient services in its Ambulatory Care Center, including a Joslin Diabetes Center. Other hospital facilities include a 123-bed nursing and rehabilitation center and a medical office building. The hospital also offers an onsite Occupational Health Center, which focuses on prevention of work-related injuries and illnesses, rehabilitation, and management of return-to-work issues.

two years (which CareGroup's capital structure did not permit). Finally, Deaconess-Glover Hospital was reorganized as a part of the Beth Israel Deaconess Medical Center because of its strong referral pattern there. All three of these hospitals continued to get all their IT support through CareGroup's IT organization, which had become a de facto outsourcing vendor for the hospitals that were no longer part of CareGroup.

On November 1, 1998, John Halamka became CIO of CareGroup as it was systematically working through a $41 million project to deal with the Y2K problem. At the time, the IT organization had 380 staff members and annual expenditures in excess of $50 million. Halamka brought an extraordinary background to the task. An undergraduate at Stanford University, majoring in computers and economics, he had founded a software company in his dorm room at age 18. After Stanford, he enrolled simultaneously at UCSF Medical School and Berkeley Engineering School, where he completed a combined mechanical/electrical/engineering and medical school program. At residency time, he sold his software company, which had by then grown to 35 people, and became an emergency medicine specialist in Los Angeles. In his spare time, he authored several books on computing subjects and wrote a hypertext system to coordinate all clinical information in the county hospital in Los Angeles. In 1996, he moved to Harvard to practice emergency

medicine at the Beth Israel Deaconess Medical Center and undertook postdoctoral work at the Massachusetts Institute of Technology in medical infomatics. He also headed a group of 50 data analysts and Web specialists, developing Web applications for CareGroup.

Halamka, in 2000, assumed the additional role of CIO of the Harvard Medical School. (Mt. Auburn and Beth Israel Deaconess were both Harvard teaching hospitals.) In talking about his background, Halamka observed:

> The reason why I've been successful is because I know all the technologies, I program in 12 languages, and I've written books on Unix system administration. I'm a doctor, so I understand the clinical domain and the technical requirements. But as I tell people, my own blind spot—I've wired a telephone closet, I've built 100 servers, hundreds of desktops, but never built anything beyond a home network. It's just the reality. But, I have now.

CareGroup IT

The IT organization that Halamka took over in October of 1998 was a decentralized, nonstandardized operation. Each of the hospitals ran their own homegrown legacy systems that predated the merger. At the Beth Israel Deaconess Medical Center, computer operations were complicated by having to run a mish-mash of the systems from each of the merged hospitals. In addition to internal IT staff, CareGroup employed an additional

78 consultants. Deaconess-Nashoba had an antiquated lab system with hand-typed results (IBM Selectric), no e-mail, and few PCs. Deaconess-Glover had a pathology system hosted at Neponset Valley with no electronic outputs and financials hosted by a third-party vendor that would fail during each thunderstorm. Deaconess-Waltham had a 10-year-old homegrown system with nonintegrated lab and radiology systems. NEBH had $500,000 per year outside consultants, a problematic lab system, a self-developed payroll system, a failed OR system installation, and a limited network incapable of remote access. Mount Auburn Hospital, the most sophisticated of the nonmedical center hospitals, was running on its own homegrown system built around the Meditech package.

By 2002, all of these hospitals had been brought together on a common system with the Meditech software at the center. All had state-of-the-art e-mail, networking, PCs, and clinical/financial information systems at costs similar or reduced from those at the time Halamka took over. For example, NEBH's IT budget dropped $135,000 in fiscal year 2002, and it was expected to drop another $400,000 in fiscal year 2003. By 2003, CareGroup believed it had the most advanced network in health care, the most advanced e-mail system in health care, the most advanced voice/wireless system in health care, the most advanced data center in health care, and the most advanced Web infrastructure in health care. It served 3,000 physicians, processed 40 terabytes of data per day, and handled 900,000 patient records dating back to 1977, all supported by a staff of 200.

All applications were Web-enabled. In late 2002, the case author, using Halamka's password, was able to access all of his own personal health records, X-rays, and records of office visits for the past decade on a PC five miles away from the hospital where he had received those services (he was delighted to find that they were accurate). The IT organization ran a complete "lights-out" data center with three back-up generators, and had not suffered a data center power outage in three years. In the first quarter 2003, the final IBM mainframe was scheduled to be decommissioned, and the network would be exclusively built around clustered Unix/Linux servers. Storage was 100 percent EMC (with no local server based storage). Paired CPUs for development, testing, and production assured that new software performed well by the time it was in use.

HP was the primary supplier of the Unix boxes and Compaq (now HP) was the primary supplier of Wintel boxes; Dell supplied machines for Linux clusters. Following a McKinsey Study at Harvard, IBM came in with a bid that undercut Dell prices for PCs by 50 percent. As a result, over a five-year period, all desktops (including at CareGroup, because it included Harvard teaching hospitals) were being replaced by IBM PCs. The data center housed tape backup systems that did incremental backups on the 40 terabytes of daily data, transferring them onto 3 gigabyte tapes. Every night those tapes were taken to an Iron Mountain storage facility that had once been a missile silo. PeopleSoft software handled HR, payroll, accounts payable, and general ledger. Physicians were provided free e-mail accounts and they had begun experimenting with wireless messaging devices such as Blackberry text pagers. As of the first quarter of 2003, all networks became IP based; Novell IPX would be replaced by year-end 2002, and AppleTalk would be gone by the end of the following quarter.

Also in 2002, there were two events that were not considered major when they happened, but that took on significance in retrospect. First, at Halamka's request, Cisco conducted a study of the CareGroup overall network in the summer, delivering their final report, complete with detailed recommendations for modernizing the network, in October; the results of the study were being analyzed in November, but nothing in it suggested imminent peril. Second, CareGroup's networking guru, who had long provided the last word on anything to do with the overall network, left his position in CareGroup IT to pursue another opportunity; although a replacement was being sought, no immediate impacts were apparent as a result of his departure.

CareGroup had cut capital budget expenditures by 90 percent in the three years prior to 2003

EXHIBIT 3
CareGroup IT Operating and Capital Expenses, FY98–FY01

Source: CareGroup internal documents.

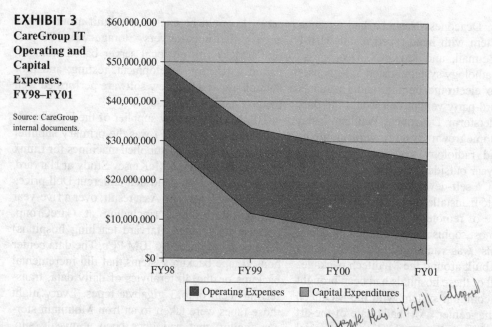

(see Exhibit 3). The Meditech installations in the various hospitals were done without consultants in half the usual time, at 20 percent of the cost. (Exhibit 4 shows the IT operating costs for the various hospitals, Exhibit 5 shows CareGroup's operating expenses vis-à-vis, Partners and Gartner

standards.) In September 2001, the CareGroup IT organization was ranked number 1 in America by *InformationWeek,* and it remained in the *InformationWeek* top 100 companies for the last three years. By November 2002, CareGroup's IT systems and services were widely viewed as critical to building clinical loyalty and were believed to provide the best knowledge management service in the United States. All of this was exhilarating and exciting, BUT . . .

EXHIBIT 4 **Benchmark Comparisons, FY01**

Source: CareGroup internal documents.

IT Operating Expenses as a Percentage of Organization Revenues	
CareGroup	1.9%
Partners	2.3%
Gartner benchmarks for 1B IDNs*	2.7%
Range for 2nd/3rd quintiles—1.9%–2.9%	

IT as a Percentage of Total Hospital Capital Expenditures	
CareGroup	10.0%
Partners	25.0%
Gartner benchmarks for 1B IDNs	21.0%
Range for 2nd/3rd quintiles—10%–26%	

*IDN = Integrated Delivery Network.

EXHIBIT 5 **Community Hospital IT Budgets (% of revenues)**

Source: CareGroup internal documents.

	FY01	FY02
Mt. Auburn	0.7%	.8%
NEBH	1.6	1.5
Waltham	1.8	1.9
Nashoba	1.2	1.3
Glover	1.0	1.1
All CareGroup, including BIDMC/PSN	1.9	1.9*

* Adjusted for PSN and capital reallocations in FY02.

November 13, 2002

In the days leading up to November 13, 2002, a researcher on the CareGroup network had begun experimenting with a knowledge management application based on file sharing, a sort of "Napster for health care." The software was designed to locate and copy information across the network automatically. No sooner had this researcher set up the software in its original configuration than he received a call from his wife telling him she was in labor. He departed hurriedly for a three-week paternity leave. The new software was left running in a basic mode, not yet tested or tuned for the environment in which it was operating. The new application began to explore the surrounding network, seeking out and copying data in larger and larger volumes from other computers. By afternoon Wednesday, November 13, the rogue software program was moving terabytes of data across the network.

The Network Collapse

These huge data transfers quickly monopolized the services of a centrally located network switch. No other data could get through this switch, neither was it able to respond to queries from other network components asking if it was still functioning. Other network components concluded, reasonably enough, that something had happened to the monopolized switch, that it had ceased to function as a reliable part of the network. Other network components then began to compute alternative paths for data flow through the network, paths that did not traverse the troubled switch.

Fortunately, the network was physically redundant throughout (see Exhibit 6); there *were* alternative paths along which data could flow. Network components had a built-in ability to recompute data paths in the event of failures. Theoretically, any computer on the CareGroup network could still communicate with any other computer, even though a major switch was no longer available.

Unfortunately, the evolved complexity of the overall network—the way individual smaller networks had been added one at a time, none of them

resulting in issues when they were added—had created a hidden problem that kicked in with a vengeance now that the network had lost the services of a major switch. As network components tried to calculate new paths along which data would flow, as they decided which redundant network components would now act as primaries and which would act as backups, they became confused. As the many smaller networks had been "glued" together over time, the network had gradually crept "out of spec"; algorithms for computing alternative data paths could no longer operate correctly.

Redundant components intended to operate in tandem, one as primary and the other as backup, began to operate at cross purposes, both becoming primary. They began to duplicate each other's functionality. Each relayed the other's messages; one switch would relay a single message to the other, then that switch would relay the same message back to the first, which would then relay it to the second again. All messages on the network began repeating in this way, reproducing rapidly in an endless loop until the network was totally disabled. (See Exhibit 7 for a more detailed account of this problem, and Exhibit 8 for a graphic of network traffic levels during the outage.)

None of these details of what was happening were apparent to users, operators, or managers of CareGroup's IT systems and network. All anyone could see on that November afternoon was that every software application that required network communication had stopped working, suddenly and without warning.

At Beth Israel Deaconess Medical Center, key areas and systems were affected: Clinical units, e-mail, admitting office functions, operating room functions, clinical laboratories, radiology, ambulatory services, pharmacy, medical records, fiscal/payroll systems, and emergency department functions. Physicians prescribing drugs for their patients had grown accustomed to computer assistance in identifying drug interactions; when a doctor placed a drug order for a patient, the system, which remembered perfectly which other drugs the patient was taking, flagged possible interactions,

EXHIBIT 6   **The Existing Network at the Time of the Outage (Loss of the East Campus Switch Labeled ly030 was the Trigger for the Event)**

Source: "CareGroup Network Outage," presentation by John D. Halamka, MD, November 25, 2002.

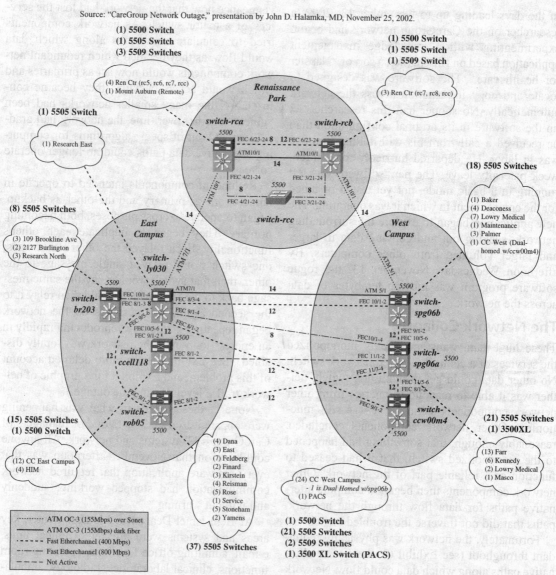

and even popped up recent FDA advisories. For years, X-rays had been digitized, and computer tools for viewing them provided many options for enhanced views that were widely used. The emergency room had come to rely on immediate access to patient medical history, often available and extremely valuable if a patient was incapacitated.

But with the network down, none of this worked. Doctors had to check drug interactions for themselves; radiology residents who had never actually touched an X-ray in "primitive" photographic film form got a crash course in diagnosis the old-fashioned way. Medical histories had to come entirely from patients. All across the

EXHIBIT 7   Simplified Description of the Problem that Caused the Network Outage

Source: Based on interviews with John Halamka and CareGroup documents, including
http://home.caregroup.org/templatesnew/departments/BID/network_outage.

The Ethernet Protocol

Computers on a small network communicate using rules much like those people abide by in a meeting of a small number of people. When a computer has something to say, it blurts it out. The computer or computers to whom the message is directed hear and attend to the message. This works well as long as two computers don't "talk" at the same time. When two computers *do* talk at the same time, a *collision* occurs. When there is a collision, the "speaking" computers must stop, wait a random amount of time, and then try again. This method works well, either with computers on a network or with people in a meeting, as long as there aren't too many computers/people involved in the network/meeting.

Bridges and Switches

As you add more people to a meeting, you may eventually determine that it has become too large. You might then break up a meeting into two submeetings. The two groups could set up in different rooms, and you might appoint a person to communicate between the rooms when things people say in one room are relevant to the work of the other. This same principle applies to networks. When too many computers join a single network and collisions become too common, networks are often divided into two separate segments, connected to each other by computer—a bridge or switch—that relays messages from one segment to another, when the message sender and receiver are on two different segments. If more computers are connected to these network segments, you may have to subdivide again. Or, you may need to connect another small network to yours; a bridge or switch can also be used for this purpose. Small networks connected together by bridges and switches in this way form a network topology experts often call "flat."

Redundant Bridges and Switches

To make sure messages can move reliably between network segments connected by bridges or switches, it is common to install them in a redundant configuration. That is, rather than install one bridge between two network segments, you install two. If one stops functioning, the other is there to pick up the work. When both are functioning, the two must keep track of which one is there to act as primary—to do all the bridging work—and which is there just to backup the primary—to step in if something happens to the primary. When this works correctly, the backup stands by, always listening to make sure the primary is operating, stepping in to act as a primary only if the primary goes silent.

Spanning Tree Protocol (STP) and STP Loops

When a network is first turned on, it needs a way to figure out which redundant components will act as primaries and which will be backups. *Spanning Tree Protocol* is the way networks composed of bridges and switches make these decisions. Once the roles, primary and backup, are established, they stay that way until something happens in the network that requires a change in roles for one or more of the components. For example, if a primary component fails somewhere in the network, Spanning Tree Protocol will once again kick in to decide roles for network components. Components communicate to decide their roles using special network messages. These messages have within them counters that keep track of how many "hops" they've made—how many network segments they've traversed. In Spanning Tree Protocol, if this counter exceeds seven (7), the special network message is dropped (ignored). What this means, in effect, is this: When the number of network segments connected together by bridges or switches exceeds seven (7), the network can have trouble resolving primary and backup roles properly. Rather than primary and backup pairs, you may end up with two redundant components operating as primary.

(continued)

EXHIBIT 7 · **Simplified Description of the Problem that Caused the Network Outage (continued)**

What happens when redundant components both operate as primary? They relay every message they hear to each other. A single message gets relayed by both components, to both components; each one then faithfully relays the same message again, as if it were new. A single message multiplies into many, reproducing in an endless, exponential loop, until all network capacity is consumed. When the switch in the CareGroup network was overwhelmed by the software package left running by a researcher, this is exactly what happened to the CareGroup network.

Getting the Network "In Spec"

The CareGroup network was "out of spec" because it contained numerous instances of more than seven (7) network segments connected by bridges or switches. To fix this flat topology network, it needed to be made less flat. Rather than connecting segments with bridges and switches, *routers* were substituted in some cases. Routers permit more intelligent transfer of messages across networks. By using routers to break up the evolved complexity of the many bridge and switch connected network segments, the network topology was made less flat and became immune to Spanning Tree Protocol loops. The intelligence in routers arises from their ability to make use of addressing information in the TCP/IP packets that encapsulate transmitted information in a modern, internetwork. Before routers will work, therefore, a network must be able to run TCP/IP. This is one reason the CareGroup network drifted out of spec. At the time that some smaller networks were added to the overall network, those smaller networks were based on proprietary technologies rather than TCP/IP. The messages that traversed those proprietary networks were therefore not "routable." Getting the network "in spec," so that routers could be used in place of bridges/switches, thus required getting rid of old proprietary networking technologies that were not routable.

EXHIBIT 8 · **Core Router CPU Use during the Outage (11/11/02 to 11/15/02)**

Source: "CareGroup Network Outage," presentation by John D. Halamka, MD, November 25, 2002.

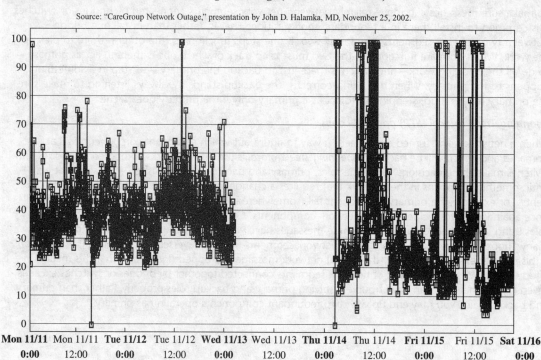

community of caregivers, myriad problems appeared. Telephones replaced e-mail. Paper forms were hauled out of closets and dusted off; old-timers began to explain to younger staff how the paper systems worked. "We became a hospital of the 1970s in an instant," explained Halamka.

The community hospitals used the Meditech package for all clinical operations and did not depend on access to the central CareGroup data center or Beth Israel Deaconess networks to retrieve clinical information. Thus, these hospitals were largely unaffected by the outage, other than by e-mail across the system. (Meditech has an internal messaging system that kept communications going inside a hospital.)

The CareGroup IT staff set themselves urgently to diagnosing the problem at Beth Israel Deaconess and trying to restore functionality. It was a formidable challenge. The primary symptom of the problem was that "nothing worked"; though extremely impressive in its effects, this fact conveyed little detailed information about *why* that might be. The network seemed like a strong candidate as the problem source since it was a common element in all that was not working, but it was not the only possible problem source. Even assuming that the network was the problem, there were a vast number of possible reasons for that. People began frantically forming ideas about what was wrong, and suggesting changes based on their ideas. Halamka, who had begun personally overseeing recovery efforts almost as soon as the incident had commenced, described what was happening:

> One person would say, "Oh, I know what the problem is. It's the wide area network connection out to Mount Auburn—we should shut off Mount Auburn." And somebody else would say, "Well, I don't know, I'm worried about the configuration of this network component." Everyone wanted to go and make a change. And the problem is that as soon as you make one change, then diagnosis of the problem gets harder.

Using tactical measures such as restarting network equipment, the IT group was able to restore services by 4:00 A.M. on Thursday, November 14, about 12 hours after the incident had begun. But as users began resuming business as usual, the network again misbehaved. Throughout the day on

Thursday, systems bounced up and down. Sometimes they were usable; sometimes they were not. Thursday evening, the IT staff once again believed that systems were restored. But by early morning on Friday, November 15, it was evident that network instability remained; failures were continuing to occur.

Calling in Cisco

At 4:00 P.M. on Thursday, about 24 hours after the first difficulties with the network, Halamka called Cisco and asked for urgent assistance. With his Cisco networking equipment under maintenance contract and a riveting story to tell, he had no trouble getting the attention of Cisco's advanced support engineering group. Cisco support engineers took the story to John Chambers, the Cisco CEO, who approved escalating the incident to "CAP status"; this set the company's customer support SWAT team in motion.

Within hours, Cisco had dispatched a Boeing 747 from Santa Clara, California, loaded with network equipment and support engineers. At the same time, an expert team from North Carolina, consisting of staff from Cisco and Callisma (a Cisco consulting partner), boarded commercial airline flights headed for Boston. The team and equipment were adequate to build an entire redundant core network to get CareGroup systems up and running again, should that prove necessary. In the late hours of Thursday night, as Halamka drove to the airport to meet the Cisco engineers, he realized just how tired he was; by then he had been awake for 36 consecutive hours. He knew that other members of his team were also tired, and badly needed the strong support he hoped he would get from Cisco.

When the Cisco team arrived at CareGroup, they took charge, immediately instituting their "CAP process." Halamka explained:

> Cisco has learned over the years that too many cooks in the kitchen do not ever heal a network. So the CAP process basically says, "We will freeze all changes." Cisco owns the problem and will put its entire business resources at your disposal until you become stable again. But you delegate *all* authority to solve this problem to Cisco. You don't do anything on your own.

Throughout the night, Cisco worked rapidly, carefully mapping the existing network. About 1:00 A.M. on Friday morning, they had zeroed in on at least part of the problem and decided to install a large, modern switch (a Cisco 6509) in place of an existing network component. They spent all night reconstructing a major part of the network. "In one night," recounted Halamka, "they did a month of work."

While implementing the CAP process, Cisco kept an average of about 10 people on site at Beth Israel Deaconess. But that was only the tip of the support iceberg. On-site engineers worked continuously with teams throughout the world. Halamka explained:

> They follow the sun. North Carolina to Japan to Amsterdam. We literally had worldwide teams handing off to each other. They had about 10 folks here, at least 3 engineers 24×7, from Thursday at about 6:00 until Tuesday. And their network reconstruction isolated that part of the CareGroup network. And we said, "Oh great, this is wonderful, we've got it now." We went into Friday and Saturday thinking "things are looking really pretty good." Until we discovered that there were two other parts of the network that had the same kind of problems.

The Decision to Remain on Backup Procedures

With each of the network failures, the medical center had enacted established backup procedures. When systems were believed restored, the medical center would attempt to revert to standard procedures. But by morning of November 15, it was obvious that the frequent switching between backup and standard processes carried more potential risk to patient care than remaining on backup processes for a more prolonged period. Halamka therefore recommended, and it was quickly agreed by CareGroup senior management, that the hospital remain on backup procedures until it was clear that the network was fully and definitively restored. Halamka described the rationale for this decision:

> The challenge for me, from a leadership standpoint, was that you want to believe you're one configuration change away from getting everybody back up to where they should be. So you've got the CEO, the COO saying, "OK,

where are we?" "Oh, we're almost there," you think. My people tell me we're almost there. Cisco tells me we're almost there.
>
> And so you had the organization, which is entirely electronic, saying, "OK, we'll go to downtime, we'll do paper—oh, I hear the network is back up, let's go to electronic." Just as the network is oscillating, they're oscillating their workflows. What I ended up telling [CEO] Paul Levy and [COO] Michael Epstein is, "I will believe what Cisco says and I will tell you when the network will be back up. When we have 24-hour functionality at full load, the network itself will be telling us it's back up. So in the meantime, let's move the entire organization to paper and keep them on paper, so that the engineers have the opportunity to make changes, and the organization isn't suffering this error likelihood of going between two work flows."

On November 15, Beth Israel Deaconess Medical Center activated an internal command center to coordinate a prolonged period on backup procedures. Access to the network was blocked so that intermittent use of computer systems would not occur. The Massachusetts Department of Public Health was notified upon activation of the command center. The command center was manned at all times by senior administrators, and key contacts were established with each clinical and administrative department. Experience during the period of intermittent outages revealed that clinical laboratories faced the greatest disruption in workflow in relation to the outage, and so these areas received particular attention and support.

Specific processes that were followed beginning on November 15 and throughout the outage included:

- Establishment of the command center as the central point for all communication.

- Establishment of morning and afternoon briefing sessions each day as part of a regular schedule. At each meeting, clinicians and staff were reminded that patient safety was of paramount importance, and special mechanisms for reporting patient safety concerns were established.

- Establishment of a system of "runners" available to retrieve specimens, tests, equipment, documentation, or supplies at any time.

- Paper documentation of all activity that was previously recorded electronically, using systems established as part of backup procedures.
- Call-back of all urgent lab results to the responsible clinician.
- Establishment of staggered lab draws so as to even out the demand on the clinical laboratories.
- Implementation of manual process for orders and pharmacy dispensing.
- Implementation of manual census lists by admitting office, updated every few hours.
- Establishment of a contingency plan for the outsourcing of all ambulatory laboratory volume (this never became necessary).
- Creation of hotlines for requesting/reporting lab results, patient care concerns, and need for any other forms of support.

The planning CareGroup had done to prepare for Y2K had made Halamka reasonably confident that the medical center could operate entirely paper-based. But things had changed since Y2K. No one knew where paper forms were. Medical staff wandered the halls, saying, "I know we have those paper forms somewhere. Where are they?" In one instance, forms were retrieved from the recycling center, literally pulled out of recycling bins. Additional personnel were called in to move forms around. Data that would normally have been sent along a wire had to be sent over "sneakernet" instead. Halamka described the teamwork and resourcefulness that allowed the medical center to quickly adapt to paper operations:

All day Friday we worked to optimize the backup processes. So we're on computerized order entry to the pharmacy entirely—how is it that we go back to handwritten orders and dose checking and drug-drug checking and drug-allergy checking? So you have [CEO] Paul Levy running Xerox copies of lab results that runners would then pick up and take to the Intensive Care Unit (ICU). The director of pharmacy manually reviewed every paper order for drug-drug interactions and drug-allergy interactions. It was amazing what people were able to do. The teamwork and problem solving spirit was just awesome.

It turned out that we actually could run the entire hospital on paper just fine. You just can't go back and forth because you take all of your paper orders and then you key them into the computer, and then the computer takes over—oh, but now the network is down again, you have to rewrite them all on paper. So you at least duplicate, if not triplicate, your work by oscillating back and forth.

The decision to function predominantly on a paper-based information system also helped the IT group in their efforts to diagnose the problem. Network tests could be conducted and problems isolated without concern for disruption of routine clinical activity.

In the end, services to patients and the Boston community were minimally interrupted. For approximately four hours on November 14, when it was not yet clear that patient throughput could be maintained, the emergency department announced to Boston Emergency Medical Services that it was closed. Also, the medical center was on ambulance diversion for a total of 13.5 hours from November 13–15. This amount of time on diversion would not be highly unusual for any hospital in the city of Boston. Otherwise ambulatory clinic activity, operating room activity, patient transfer, and patient walk-in activity continued according to standard policy and procedure during the outage.

After full restoration of computer systems, the directors of all clinical services were contacted to reinforce the importance of reporting any adverse clinical events related to the network outage. Twelve events were reported in response to this solicitation. The records relating to each of these was reviewed; they revealed that care had been delayed in some instances, but in no instance was there evidence of adverse outcome relating to the network outage. Incident reports and patient complaints were also reviewed for unexpected outcomes related to the network outage; no other events were documented.

Solving the Problem(s)

Subsequent mapping by the Cisco support team eventually discovered other places where the network had "evolved" until it was out of spec—until the algorithms for recalculating data paths across the network could not function correctly. Across the CareGroup wide area network, mapping revealed problems from changes to the network that had been casually made by users. Halamka offered an example:

> Some researchers ran out of ports on one of the switches. So what did they do? They daisy-chained a switch to a switch. Imagine that you have to run your barbecue to your hot tub to your Christmas lights, and you've got five extension cords without a breaker. You're going to blow! And so we discovered that was another source of the looping problem. Cardiology had also made some changes to the network that caused problems.

CareGroup IT and the Cisco SWAT team spent Saturday fixing all of the looping issues in the overall network. At the end of that task, they were disappointed to discover that there was still a problem somewhere in the network, which they tracked down to an old model router. The old router had a problem in its "firmware," the software that was permanently written into the microchips within the device. There was no way to upgrade the old router, so it was replaced.

The computer network was restored on November 18, but processes were transitioned back to computer-based formats gradually and in staggered fashion. Paper-based systems were retired only after information systems in each area had functioned continuously and without incident for at least 24 hours.

Following restoration of computer systems, all paper-based information was transferred to the appropriate electronic format within approximately 48 hours. The very large majority of documentation was easily located, but approximately 300 clinical test requests could not be reliably paired with a specimen or clinical result. For each of these cases, the ordering physician was contacted, and patients needing to be retested were informed that fees would be waived and parking/transportation costs reimbursed by the hospital.

Lessons Learned

For everyone who had been affected by the network outage, one lesson was deeply felt, as Halamka explained: "People realized, many for the first time, just how dependent they are on the technology. It had become so much a part of the culture. You didn't even think about it. We had begun to think about it like we think about the telephone. You pick up your phone and hear a dial tone. It's just there." Halamka also cited 10 more specific lessons that he, his staff, and the CareGroup management team had extracted from the experience:

Lesson #1: *Don't hesitate to bring in the experts to make sure your network is configured properly.* Since the network incident, Halamka had signed a $300,000 per year agreement for support from Cisco's Advanced Engineering services. As part of this deal, Cisco would make any changes to the CareGroup network that were considered significant. Cisco's ongoing review would assure that the network would stay "in spec." Two Cisco engineers would remain on-site at Beth Israel Deaconess permanently.

Lesson #2: *Don't let any one individual in your IT group become the sole point of failure.* In retrospect, Halamka realized that the CareGroup IT department had relied too heavily on a single employee to maintain the network. Because the IT staff relied exclusively on one expert, there was no one to offer a second opinion about the network's configuration, or to notice any precursors to the problem (if there had been any). "It's better to excise an excellent employee who may be brilliant and seems indispensable, if he or she is recalcitrant and not willing to open up, to work and share with others," suggested Halamka.

Lesson #3: *Keep your working knowledge current.* Not only had CareGroup depended too much on one networking expert, they had also allowed his knowledge to become out-of-date. After the fact, Cisco's support engineers summarized the problem at CareGroup this way: "The network at CareGroup was state-of-the-art for the early 1990s. In the late 1990s it had evolved into a fragile state, and the group's networking staff, which hadn't kept up on networking technologies, didn't see problems coming."

Lesson #4: *Beware of users armed with just enough knowledge to be dangerous*. A user experimenting with a new software package had triggered the outage. Although users, and especially researchers, would always engage in some experimentation with local IT resources, it was important that the IT group remain vigilant, noting changes and supervising user experiments as appropriate.

Lesson #5: *Institute rigorous network change control*. After the network outage, CareGroup established a formal procedure for making changes to the network. A Network Change Control Board was created with multidisciplinary membership, to review and approve all network infrastructure changes. The group classified changes into three categories: minimal, moderate, or substantial impact. Substantial changes required review by Cisco's Advanced Engineering team. Changes to the network were only made between 2 A.M and 5 A.M on weekends, and testing and incident recovery plans had to be in evidence before changes were allowed to go forward.

Lesson #6: *Adapt to externalities*. The CareGroup network had evolved into its "out of spec" condition as a result of mergers, reorganizations, and other external activities and events. The November network outage led IT staff to examine more carefully all events in the outside environment for possible impacts on existing IT functionality.

Lesson #7: *There are limits to customer-centric responsiveness*. The CareGroup IT staff could not take an "anything the customer wants" approach, but rather needed to balance customer-centricity with the risks to the network and IT systems posed by requests to support new technologies. Halamka offered an example of the IT group's new perspective on customer responsiveness in the aftermath of the outage:

The Department of Surgery has decided that minimally invasive surgery is a top priority. They've hired a guy to come help them with that, who is planning to use video over IP. He's going to need gigabit speed networks to show endoscopy to the world. He'll be here in February. Is that a problem? In the past, the idea was "Of course we will support video over IP by February." Now it's a "Nope, we'll bring in Cisco to look at the impact on the total environment." We'll place much more severe restrictions on what protocols and services anyone can run, what load you can put on the network, where you run it, and changes that we have to make.

A formal change control process would achieve little if processes were short-circuited every time there was an "urgent" business need.

Lesson #8: *Have backup procedures in which you can have confidence*. CareGroup was able to run the hospital on paper systems because of Y2K preparedness. With Y2K past, however, there remained an ongoing need to make sure backup procedures worked. Backup procedures needed to be effective enough to operate for a prolonged period. In the event of a serious outage, it would not be productive to move back and forth between computer and paper processes, so the paper system would need to be robust.

Lesson #9: *Component redundancy isn't enough; you need alternative access methods*. During the outage, some important systems could have continued to operate, albeit more slowly, if they could have been emergency-connected to dial-up modems. Telephone lines could have become a rudimentary backup network that would have preserved a significant amount of system functionality. After the outage, CareGroup acquired additional analog telephone capacity and added modem capabilities to 50 PCs throughout the medical center.[1]

Lesson #10: *Lifecycle manage your network components*. Routers, switches, and other network components need to be replaced every four years. During the CareGroup outage, a component more than four years old had

---

[1] For security reasons, these modems are only accessible from inside the CareGroup internal telephone network, and only in the event of an emergency.

EXHIBIT 9 **Changes Made or Planned in Response to Network Outage**

Source: Summarized from "CareGroup Network Outage," presentation by John D. Halamka, MD, November 25, 2002.

Specific improvements already put in place include:

- Redesign and rebuilding of the radiology computer network, the research campus network, and clinical campus network.
- Placement of 40 dial-up computers in strategic areas of the hospital.
- Addition of clinical system dial-up capability to 21-physician order entry desktops on patient care floors.
- Implementation of a redundant core network that can be plugged in to replace the existing core network.

The following improvements are either completed or will be completed within the next few weeks:

- Selective upgrade of noncore network hardware to increase the redundancy and stability of our network.
- Scheduling of downtime on weekends 2:00–5:00 A.M. to make network changes.
- Implementation of a strict change control process with all engineering changes overseen by Cisco.

The following improvements will be completed within one year:

- Reconfiguration of the core network.
- Introduction of redundancy in all hardware and links.
- Implement the most modern hardware and topologies.
- Implementation of network management software improvements.
- Schedule appropriate downtimes with emphasis on network stability.

caused a serious problem because of a flaw in its firmware; it was unable to function properly in a modern network. Replacing network components needs to be budgeted. The upgrades required after the CareGroup outage amounted to a multimillion-dollar one-time expense and an ongoing requirement for upgrades every year.

There were many other lessons as well, important though perhaps not as deserving of headlines (Exhibit 9 lists actions taken in the aftermath of the outage). The entire incident had been a tremendous opportunity to learn, and Halamka was convinced that sharing information about what had happened, and talking about it with others would ultimately strengthen CareGroup and its capabilities. The incident had also provided tutorials in both positive and negative aspects of human psychology. Halamka

had been tremendously impressed by how the organization—doctors, nurses, researchers, IT staff, and many others—had pulled together to perform extremely well in the crisis. But he also had renewed respect for the damaging human tendency to respond to a problem by just "doing something," by making impulsive changes to the IT infrastructure; if Halamka and his colleagues had not overcome that urge, diagnosis and recovery from the problem would have been much more difficult.

The outage also reminded Halamka that computer operations in a large organization have tens of thousands of "moving parts" and that his job was to manage the process of getting all of those moving parts to work in harmony. "They call me the 'chief information officer'," noted Halamka, "but I'm really the 'chief *integration* officer'; I make everything talk to everything else."

Case 2-2

The iPremier Company: Denial of Service Attack (A)

January 12, 2003, 4:31 A.M.

Somewhere a telephone was chirping. Bob Turley, CIO of the iPremier Company, turned beneath the bed sheets, wishing the sound would go away. It didn't. Lifting his head, he tried to make sense of his surroundings. Where was he?

The Westin in Times Square. New York City. That's right. He was there to meet with Wall Street analysts. He'd gotten in late. By the time his head had hit the pillow it was nearly 1:30 A.M. Now the digital display on the nearby clock made no sense. Who would be calling at this hour? Why would the hotel operator put a call through?

He reached for the phone at bedside and placed it against his ear. Dial tone. Huh? The chirping was coming from his cell phone. Hanging up the hotel phone, he staggered out of bed. No sooner had his feet met the floor than his pager went off. Almost simultaneously, the hotel phone erupted, as if protesting being placed back in its cradle. Fumbling in his briefcase, he located the cell phone and hit "answer" on the tiny keypad.

"This is Bob Turley."

"Mr. Turley?" There was panic in the voice at the other end of the line. "I'm sorry to wake you, Joanne told me to call you."

The pager was still sounding. He found it in his briefcase and silenced it. The hotel phone stopped ringing as suddenly as it had started.

"Who is this?"

"It's Leon. Leon Ledbetter. I'm in Ops. We met last week. I'm new. I mean I was new, last month."

"Why are you calling me at 4:30 in the morning, Leon?"

"I'm really sorry about that Mr. Turley, Joanne said—."

"No, I mean what's wrong? Why are you calling?"

"It's our Web site, sir. It's completely locked up. I've tried accessing it from three different computers and nothing's happening. Our customers can't access it either; the help desk is getting support calls."

"What's causing it?"

"Joanne thinks—if we could only—well, someone might have hacked us. Someone else might be controlling our site. Support has been getting these e-mails—We thought it was just the Web server, but I can't access anything over there. Joanne is on her way to the colo.[1] She said to call you. These weird e-mails, they're coming in about one per second."

"What do the e-mails say?"

"They say 'ha.'"

"Ha?"

"Yes, sir. Each one of them has one word in the subject line, 'ha.' It's like 'ha, ha, ha, ha.' Coming from an anonymous source. That's why we're thinking—."

"When you say they might have hacked us—could they be stealing customer information? Credit cards?"

"Well, I guess no firewall[2]—Joanne says—actually we're using a firewall service we purchase from the colo, so—."

This case was prepared by Professor Robert D. Austin; Dr. Larry Leibrock, Chief Technology Officer, McCombs School fo Business, University of Texas at Austin; and Alan Murray, Chief Scientist, Novell Service Provider Network. Copyright © 2001 President and Fellows of Harvard College. Harvard Business School Case No. 601-114.

[1] *Colo* is short for "colocation facility," where Internet companies often house their vital computing hardware. Colocation facilities are sometimes called "Internet data Centers" or simply "hosting facilities." They provide floor space, redundant power supplies, high-speed connectivity to the Internet, and a variety of other services to their customers.

[2] A *firewall* is a combination hardware/software platform that is designed to protect a local network and the computers that reside on it against unauthorized access.

"Can you call someone at the colo? We pay them for monitoring 24×7, don't we?"

"Joanne is calling them. I'm pretty sure. Is there anything you want me to do?"

"Does Joanne have her cell?"

"Yes sir, she's on her way to the colo. I just talked to her."

"Call me back if anything else happens."

"Yes sir."

Turley stood up, realizing only then that he had been sitting on the floor. His eyes were bleary but adrenaline was now cranking in his bloodstream. Steadying himself against a chair, he felt a vague wave of nausea. This was no way to wake up.

He made his way to the bathroom and splashed water on his face. This trip to New York was a great assignment for someone who had been with the company such a short time. It demonstrated the great confidence CEO Jack Samuelson had in him as the new CIO. For a moment Turley savored a memory of the meeting in which Samuelson had told him he would be the one to go to New York. As that memory passed another emerged, this one from an earlier session with the CEO. Samuelson was worried that the company might eventually suffer from "a deficit in operating procedures." "Make it one of your top priorities," he had said. "We need to run things professionally. I've hired you to take us to the next level."

Looking himself over in the mirror, seeing his hair tousled and his face wet, Turley lodged a protest with no one in particular: "But I've barely been here three months."

The iPremier Company

Founded in 1994 by two students at Swarthmore College, the iPremier Company had evolved into one of the few success stories of Web-based commerce. From its humble beginnings, it had risen to become one of the top two retail businesses selling luxury, rare, and vintage goods on the Web. It was also one of the few profitable entities in the so-called new economy. Based in Seattle, Washington, the firm had grown at a rapid rate and held its own against incursions into its

space from a number of well-funded challengers. For the fiscal year 2001, profits were $2.1 million on sales of $32 million. Sales had grown at more than a 50 percent annual rate for more than three years, and profits had begun to trend favorably.

Immediately following its IPO in late 1998, the company's stock price had nearly tripled. It had continued up from there amid the euphoria of the 1999 markets, eventually tripling again. A follow-on offering had left the company in a strong cash position. During the NASDAQ bloodbath of 2000, the stock had fallen dramatically, but it had eventually stabilized and even climbed again, although not to pre-2000 levels. In the treacherous business-to-consumer (B2C) segment, the iPremier Company was one of a very few survivors.

Most of the company's products were priced between fifty and a few hundred dollars, but there were a small number of items priced in the thousands of dollars. Customers paid for items online using their credit cards. The company had flexible return policies, intended to allow customers to thoroughly examine products before deciding whether to keep them. The iPremier Company's customer base was high-end, so much so that credit limits on charge cards were rarely an issue, even for the highest-priced products.

Management and Culture

The management team at the iPremier Company was a mix of talented young people who had been with the company for some time and more experienced managers who were gradually being hired as the firm grew. Recruitment had focused on well-educated technical and business professionals with reputations for high performance. Getting hired into a senior management position required excelling in an intense series of three-on-one interviews. The CEO interviewed every prospective manager at the director level and above. The reward, for those who made the grade, was base compensation above the average of managers at similar firms, and variable compensation that could be a significant multiple of the base. All employees had options based on the company stock price, and managers received particularly lucrative incentives. When the share price had fallen off in 2000, senior management had gone to the company's board of directors twice to reorganize the option plans and maintain strong employee incentives. All employees were subject to quarterly performance reviews that were tied directly to their compensation. Unsuccessful managers did not last long.

Most managers at the iPremier Company described the environment as intense. The company formally stated its governing values in terms of "discipline, professionalism, commitment to delivering results, and partnership for achieving profits." Unlike many Internet companies, the iPremier Company had emphasized a balanced approach to growth and profitability, although growth had tended to rule the day. Throughout the company, there was a strong orientation toward doing "whatever it takes" to get projects done on schedule, especially when it came to system features that would benefit customers. The software development team was proud of its record of consistently launching new features and programs a few months ahead of major competitor MarketTop. Value statements aside, it was well-understood by senior managers that their compensation and future prospects with the company depended primarily on executing to plan. Managers pursued "the numbers" with almost obsessive zeal.

Technical Architecture

The company had historically tended to outsource management of its technical architecture and had a long-standing relationship with Qdata, a company that hosted most of the iPremier Company's computer equipment and provided connectivity to the Internet. Qdata was an early entrant into the Internet hosting and colocation business, but it had lost any prospect of market leadership. The facility was close to the corporate offices of the iPremier Company, but some felt there was little else to recommend it. Qdata was a steady provider of basic floor space, power, connectivity, environmental control, and physical security, and it offered some higher-level "management services," such as monitoring of Web sites for customers at its network operations center (NOC) and some Internet security services (such as the firewall service used by the iPremier Company). But Qdata had not been quick to invest in advanced technology and had experienced difficulty in retaining staff.

The iPremier Company had a long-standing initiative aimed at eventually moving its computing to another facility, but several factors had conspired to keep this from happening. First, and most significant, the iPremier Company had been very busy growing; hence the move to a better facility had never quite made it to the top of the priority list. Second, the cost of more modern facilities was considerably higher—two-to-three times as expensive on a per-square-foot basis. iPremier Company computers occupied a good deal of space, so a move to another facility would have increased costs significantly enough to affect the slender but increasing profit trend the company was eager to maintain. Third, there was a perception—not necessarily supported by fact, according to the operations staff—that a move might risk service interruption to customers. The operations staff maintained that with appropriate modernization of the computing infrastructure, growth could be accomplished by adding installations in other facilities, rather than by expanding floor space in the existing facility. The work of planning how this might be carried out had never been done, though. Finally, one of the founders of the iPremier Company felt a personal commitment to the owners of Qdata because the latter company had been willing to renegotiate their contract at a particularly difficult time in iPremier's early days.

Exhibit 1 provides a diagram of the iPremier Company's technical architecture.

4:39 A.M.

Turley situated himself at the desk in his hotel room and began paging through the digital phonebook on his cell phone. Before he could find the number for Joanne Ripley—his technical operations team leader—the phone began to chirp. The incoming call was from Ripley. Turley tapped the answer key.

"Hello, Joanne. How are you this morning?"

EXHIBIT 1   The iPremier Company's Technical Architecture

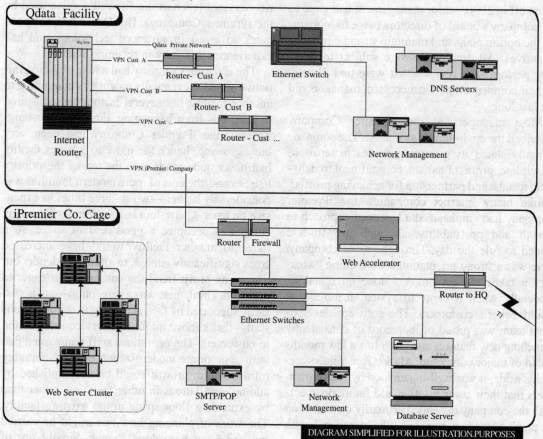

Qdata Facility

Big Iron

To Public Internet

Internet Router

Qdata Private Network

VPN Cust A — Router- Cust A

VPN Cust B — Router- Cust B

VPN Cust ... — Router - Cust ...

VPN iPremier Company

Ethernet Switch

DNS Servers

Network Management

iPremier Co. Cage

Router   Firewall

Web Accelerator

Router to HQ

Web Server Cluster

Ethernet Switches

SMTP/POP Server

Network Management

Database Server

T1

DIAGRAM SIMPLIFIED FOR ILLUSTRATION.PURPOSES

A cautious laugh came from the other end of the circuit. "About the same as you, I'm guessing. I assume Leon reached you."

"He did, but he doesn't know anything. What's going on?"

"I don't know much either, yet. I'm in the car, on my way to the colo."

"You can't do anything from home?"

"Well—no. Leon can't access any of the boxes behind the firewall via the T1 line at the office,[3] so

something is screwy with our connectivity to the colo. Sounds like a problem outside the perimeter of our architecture. I called Qdata, but they assure me that there is no problem with connectivity into or out of the building. They're looking into it further, but their night shift is on duty. I don't know where they get those bozos. I haven't talked to anyone yet who knows what he's doing."

"How long till you get there?"

"I'm driving fast and running red lights. I ought to be there in five minutes."

"How long after that until we are back up and running?"

"Depends on what's wrong. I'll try restarting the Web server as soon as I get there, but if someone has hacked us, or if there's some kind of attack

---

[3] The hosting facility where the production computer equipment was housed was connected to the iPremier Company's offices via a leased "T1" line. This line would ordinarily permit people at the office to connect to production computers without traversing the public Internet.

going on, that might not do it. Did Leon tell you about the e-mails?"

"The 'ha, ha' e-mails? Yeah. Makes it sound like something deliberate."

"I'd have to agree with that."

"Can we track the e-mails?"

"Not soon enough. They're coming through an anonymizer that's probably in Europe or Asia. If we're lucky, we'll find out sometime in the next 18 months who sent them. Then we'll discover they're originating from some DSL-connected PC in Podunk, Idaho, and that the Joe Schmo who owns it has no idea that it's been compromised by hackers."

"Any chance they're stealing credit cards?"

There was a long pause at the other end of the phone.

"There's really no way of knowing without more info."

"Can we pull the plug? Disconnect the communications lines?"

"We can. But if we start pulling cables out of the wall it may take us a while to put things back together. Right now most of our customers are asleep. Whoops." There was a pause while Ripley negotiated a traffic obstacle. "Sorry. Anyway, let me restart the Web server and see what happens. Maybe we can get out of this without too much customer impact."

Turley thought about it for a moment. "Okay. But if you see something that makes you think credit cards are being stolen, I want to know that as soon as possible. We may have to take drastic actions."

"Understood. I'll call you back as soon as I know anything."

"Good. One more thing: Who else knows this is going on?"

"I haven't called anyone else. Leon might have. I'll call him and call you right back."

"Thanks."

Turley flipped his cell closed then picked up the hotel phone. After a series of transfers, he found someone who would bring coffee to his room, despite the odd hour. Never before had he so desperately wanted coffee.

Just as he replaced the hotel phone his cell rang again. He looked at the display to see who was calling.

"Damn." It was Warren Spangler, VP of business development. Turley remembered vaguely that Leon Ledbetter had come into the organization via a recommendation by Spangler. They were old high school buddies or something. Ledbetter had almost certainly called Spangler.

"Hi, Warren," said Turley, flipping the phone open.

"Hi, Bob. I hear we've got some kind of incident going on. What's the story?"

"Something's definitely going on, but we're not sure what yet. We're trying to minimize customer impact. Fortunately for us it's the middle of the night."

"Wow. So is it just a technical problem or is somebody actually doing it to us?"

Turley was eager to call the chief technology officer (CTO), so he didn't really have time to continue this discussion. But he didn't want to be abrupt. He was still getting to know his colleagues.

"We don't know. Look, I've got to—."

"Leon said something about e-mails—."

"Yes, there are suspicious e-mails coming in so it could be someone doing it."

"Oh, man. I bet the stock takes a hit tomorrow. Just when I was going to exercise some options. Shouldn't we call the police?"

"Sure, why don't you see what you can do there, that'd be a big help. Look, I've got to—."

"Seattle police? Do we know where the e-mails are coming from? Maybe we should call the FBI? No. Wait. If we call the police, the press might hear about this from them. Whoa. Then our stock would really take a hit."

"I've really got to go, Warren."

"Sure thing. I'll start thinking about PR. And I'll work with Leon on this end. We got you covered here, bro. Keep the faith."

"Will do, Warren. Thanks."

Turley ended that call and began searching through his cell phone's memory to find the number for Tim Mandel, the company's CTO. He and

Mandel had already cemented a great working relationship. Turley wanted his opinion. Just as Turley was about to initiate the call, though, another call came in from Ripley.

Turley flipped the phone open and said: "Leon called Spanger, I know. Anything else?"

"That's it for now. Bye."

Turley dialed Mandel. At first the call switched over to voice mail, but he retried immediately. This time Mandel answered sleepily. It took five full minutes to wake Mandel and tell him what was happening.

"So what do you think, should we just pull the plug?" Turley asked.

"I wouldn't. You might lose some logging data that would help us figure out what happened. Whatever we do, we want to preserve evidence of what has happened or else we may never know exactly."

"I'm not sure that's the most important thing to me right now, knowing exactly what is happening."

"I suggest you change your mind about that. If you don't know what happened this time, it can happen again. Worse than that, if you don't know what happened you won't know what, if anything, you need to disclose publicly."

Turley thought about that for a moment. What if they halted the attack but he could not be sure of the danger, if any, to customer information? What would the company need to say publicly? It was too much to sort out on the fly. Mandel was saying something else.

"Come to think of it, Bob, preserving the logs is irrelevant because I'm pretty sure detailed logging is not enabled. Detailed logging takes up a lot of disk space on the server. To run at higher logging levels we would have to add significantly to our storage arrays, and I've never been able to convince the finance guys that the expenditure was necessary. Plus detailed logging adds a performance penalty of about 20 percent and nobody's been game for that."

"So we aren't going to have evidence of what happened anyway."

"There'll be some, but not as much as we'll want."

Another call was coming in.

"Hold on, Tim." Turley kicked the phone over to the waiting call. It was Peter Stewart, the company's legal counsel. What was he doing awake?

"This is Turley."

"Hey, Bob, it's Pete. Pull the plug, Bob. Shut off the power, pull the comm lines out of their sockets, everything. We can't risk having credit cards stolen."

"Spangler call you?"

"Huh? No, Jack. Samuelson. He called me three minutes ago, said hackers had control of our Web site. Told me in no uncertain terms to call you and 'provide a legal perspective.' That's just what he said: 'Provide a legal perspective.'"

So the CEO was awake. The result, no doubt, of Spangler's "helping" from that end. Stewart continued to speak legalese at him for what seemed like an eternity. By this time, Turley was incapable of paying attention to him.

"Thanks for your thoughts, Pete. I've got to go, I've got Tim on the other line."

"Okay. For the record, though, I say pull the plug. I'll let Jack know you and I spoke."

"Thanks, Pete."

Turley switched back over to the call with Mandel.

"Spangler's got bloody everybody awake, including Jack. I recommend you get dressed and head into the office, my friend."

"Is Joanne on this?"

"Yes, she's at the colo by now." Turley's phone rang "Got a call coming in from her now."

He switched the phone.

"What's up Joanne?"

"Well I'm at Qdata," she said in an angry voice, "and they won't let me into the NOC. There's no one here who knows anything about the network monitoring software and that's what I need to use to see the traffic coming into our site. The Qdata guy who can do it is vacationing in Aruba. I tried rebooting the Web server, but we've still got a problem. My current theory is an attack directed at our firewall, but to be sure I've got to see the packets coming in, and the firewall is their equipment.

You got an escalation contact to get these dudes off their butts?"

"I'm in New York, Joanne. I've got zip for Qdata contact information with me. But let me see what I can do."

"Okay. I'll keep working it from this end. The security guard doesn't look too fierce. I think I could take him."

"Do what you can."

Turley hung up. He noticed that Mandel had disconnected also. For a moment Turley just sat back in the chair, not sure what to do next. There was a knock at the door. Coffee. Good news, for a change.

5:27 A.M.

He had just taken his first sip of hot coffee when he got the call he'd been dreading. It was from Jack Samuelson, the CEO.

"Hi Jack."

"Bob. Exciting morning?"

"More than I like it."

"Are we working a plan?"

"Yes, sir. Not everything is going according to plan, but we are working a plan."

"Is there anything I can do?"

"Actually, Jack, there is. Call someone senior at Qdata and tell them we need their full and immediate support. They're giving Joanne the runaround about access to their NOC."

"I'll do that right now, Bob."

"Thanks, Jack."

"Bob, the stock is probably going to be impacted and we'll have to put a solid PR face on this, but that's not your concern right now. You focus on getting us back up and running. Understand?"

"I do."

The call ended. It had gone better than Turley had feared. He avoided the temptation to analyze Samuelson's every word for clues to his innermost thoughts. Instead, he dialed Joanne.

"Hi, Bob," she said, sounding mildly cheerful. "They let me in. I'm sitting in front of the console

right now. It looks like a SYN flood[4] from multiple sites directed at the router[5] that runs our firewall service. It's not a proper firewall, Bob; we need to work on something better."

"Fine, but what can we do right now?"

"Well, looks like the attack is coming from about 30 sites. A classic distributed denial of service (DoS) attack. If the guys here will let me, I'm going to start shutting down traffic from those IP addresses."[6]

"Samuelson is waking up the senior guys at Qdata. If the night shift gives you any trouble, tell them it's going to be raining executives really soon."

"Samuelson, huh? So everybody's up for our little party. Okay, I'm going to try shutting off traffic from the attacking IP addresses. I'll have to set the phone down for a minute."

There was a pause of a couple of minutes. Turley heard some muffled conversation in the background, then several exclamations. Ripley came back on the line.

"Damn it, Bob, they're spawning zombies. It's 'Dawn of the Dead' out there."

"You're going to have to translate that one for me, Ripley."

"Every time we shut down traffic from an IP address, the zombie we've shut off automatically triggers attacks from two other sites. I'll try it a

---

[4] Each "conversation" with a Web server begins with a sequence of "handshake" interactions. The initiating computer first sends a "SYNCHRONIZE" or "SYN." The contacted Web server responds with a "SYNCHRONIZE-ACKNOWLEDGE" or "SYN-ACK." The initiating computer then completes the handshake with an "ACKNOWLEDGE" or "ACK." A "SYN flood" is an attack on a Web server intended to make it think a very large number of "conversations" are being initiated in rapid succession. Because each interaction looks like real traffic to the Web site, the Web server expends resources dealing with each one. By flooding the site, an attacker can effectively paralyze the Web server by trying to start too many conversations with it.

[5] As the name suggests, a *router* is a hardware platform that routes traffic across internal networks and the Internet.

[6] An *IP address* corresponds to a particular machine located somewhere on the Internet.

few more times, but right now it looks like that's just going to make things worse."

"If it's a denial of service attack, they haven't hacked us, right? It means it's an attack, not an intrusion. They haven't gained entry to our system. So the credit cards and other customer data are safe. Can we say that?"

"That'd be my first take on it, yeah. There's nothing that makes a DoS attack and an intrusion mutually exclusive, of course. But, yeah, the script kiddy[7] hackers who usually launch these kinds of attacks aren't sophisticated enough to get inside our firewall." She paused for a moment as if reconsidering what she had just said. "On the other hand, targeting the firewall strikes me as a fairly sophisticated attack."

It was not the straight answer he had hoped for, but it would have to do for the time being. "I'll let you get back to it. Call me with an update when there is something to tell."

Turley hung up and thought about whether to call Samuelson and what to tell him. He could say that it was a DoS attack. He could say that it therefore probably didn't put customer information at risk. But Turley wanted to think before he went on record with that position. He'd talk to Tim, see what he thought.

---

[7] *Script kiddies* are relatively unsophisticated hackers who use automated routines—"scripts"—written by other more sophisticated hackers. These scripts are generally available to anyone willing to spend a little time searching for them on the Internet.

For a moment, everything was quiet. He put the cell phone down on the desk and poured another cup of coffee. Pacing across the room, he picked up the TV remote and hit the "ON" button. A movie appeared, an old Hitchcock film. An airplane was straffing Cary Grant. He muted the sound then walked to the window and pulled the curtain aside. There was a red glow in the sky to the east.

His cell phone rang. He went to it and picked it up. It was Ripley.

"It stopped," she said excitedly. "The attack is over."

"What did you do?"

"Nothing. It just stopped. The attack just stopped at 5:46 A.M."

"So—what do we do now?"

"The Web site is running. A customer who visits our site now wouldn't know anything had ever been wrong. We can resume business as usual."

"Business as usual?"

"Actually, I'd recommend that we give everything a proper going over after an attack like this. We really ought to do a thorough audit. I've been thinking about how they targeted the firewall, and I don't think it sounds like script kiddies."

"Sit down when you get a chance and write me an e-mail that summarizes what you think we should do. Tell me how whatever you recommend will impact on customers, if at all. I've got to figure out what to tell Samuelson."

Case 2-3

Ford Motor Company: Supply Chain Strategy

Teri Takai, the director of supply chain systems, had set aside this time on her calendar to contemplate recommendations to senior executives. The question they'd asked was widely agreed to be extremely important to Ford's future: How should the company use emerging information technologies (e.g., Internet technologies) and ideas from new high-tech industries to change the way it interacted with suppliers? Members of her team had different views on the subject.

Some argued that Ford needed to radically redesign its supply chain and other activities or risk being left behind. This group favored "virtual integration," modeling the Ford supply chain on that of companies, such as Dell,[1] which had aggressively used technology to reduce working capital and exposure to inventory obsolescence. Proponents of this approach argued that although the auto business was very complex both for historical reasons and because of the inherent complexity of the automotive product, there was no reason such models could not provide a conceptual blueprint for what Ford should attempt.

Another group was more cautious, believing that the differences between the auto business and computer manufacturing were important and substantive. Some noted, for example, that relative to Dell, the Ford supplier network had many more layers and many more companies and that Ford's purchasing organization historically had played a more prominent and independent role than had

The case was prepared by Professor Robert D. Austin. Copyright © 1999 President and Fellows of Harvard College. Harvard Business School Case No. 699-198.

[1] Information on Dell included in this case was obtained by Ford from public sources, including the 1997 Dell annual report, the Dell Web site (www.dell.com), and Joan Magretta, "The Power of Virtual Integration: An Interview with Dell Computer's Michael Dell," *Harvard Business Review,* March–April 1998 (reprint 98208). This article is included in this book.

Dell's. These differences and others posed complications when examined closely, and it was difficult to determine the appropriate and feasible scope for redesign of the process.

As she read through the documents provided by her team, she thought about the chief executive officer's recent companywide emphasis on shareholder value and customer responsiveness. It was widely acknowledged that Dell had delivered on those dimensions, but would the same methods deliver results for Ford?

Company and Industry Background

Based in Dearborn, Michigan, the Ford Motor Company was the second-largest industrial corporation in the world, with revenues of more than $144 billion and about 370,000 employees. Operations spanned 200 countries. Although Ford obtained significant revenues and profits from its financial services subsidiaries, the company's core business had remained the design and manufacture of automobiles for sale on the consumer market. Since Henry Ford had incorporated in 1903, the company had produced over 260 million vehicles.

The auto industry had grown much more competitive over the last two decades. Since the 1970s, the Big Three U.S. automakers—General Motors (GM), Ford, and Chrysler—had seen their home markets encroached upon by the expansion of foreign-based auto manufacturers such as Toyota and Honda. The industry was also facing increasing overcapacity (estimated at 20 million vehicles) as developing and industrialized nations, recognizing the wealth and job-producing effects of automobile manufacturing, encouraged development and expansion of their own export-oriented auto industries.

Although manufacturers varied in their degree of market presence in different geographic regions, the battle for advantage in the industry was fast becoming global. Faced with the need to continue to improve quality and reduce cycle times while dramatically lowering the costs of developing and building cars, Ford and the other large automakers were looking for ways to take advantage of their size and global presence. One element of the effort to achieve advantage in size and scale was a movement toward industry consolidation. In the summer of 1998, Chrysler merged with Daimler-Benz to form a more global automaker. In early 1999, Ford announced that it would acquire Sweden's Volvo.

In 1995, Ford had embarked on an ambitious restructuring plan called Ford 2000, which included merging its North American, European, and international automotive operations into a single global organization. Ford 2000 called for dramatic cost reductions to be obtained by reengineering and globalizing corporate organizations and processes. Product development activities were consolidated into five vehicle centers (VCs), each responsible for the development of vehicles in a particular consumer market segment (one VC was in Europe). By making processes and products globally common, Ford intended to eliminate organizational and process redundancies and realize huge economies of scale in manufacturing and purchasing. Major reengineering projects were initiated around major company processes such as order to delivery (OTD) and Ford production system (FPS), with goals such as reducing OTD time from more than 60 days to less than 15.

Ford's new global approach required that technology be employed to overcome the constraints usually imposed by geography on information flow. Teams on different continents needed to be able to work together as if they were in the same building. Furthermore, in virtually every reengineering project, information technology (IT) had emerged as a critical enabler. The link between reengineering success and the company's IT groups was made explicit in the Ford 2000 restructuring: IT was placed within the process reengineering organization. In the supply chain area, there was general agreement that IT also could be deployed to dramatically enhance material flows and reduce inventories, substituting information for inventory, as the expression went.

As Ford 2000 unfolded, the Internet revolution unfolded in parallel, creating new possibilities for reengineering processes within and between enterprises. Ford launched a public Internet site in mid-1995; by mid-1997 the number of visits to the site had reached more than 1 million per day. A companywide *intra*net was launched in mid-1996, and by January 1997 Ford had in place a business-to-business (B2B) capability through which the intranet could be extended in a secure manner beyond company boundaries into an *extra*net potentially connecting Ford with its suppliers. Ford teamed with Chrysler and General Motors to work on the Automotive Network Exchange (ANX), which aimed to create consistency in technology standards and processes in the supplier network so that suppliers, already pressed to lower costs, would not have to manage different means of interaction with each automaker.

On January 1, 1999, Jac Nasser took over the CEO job from Alex Trotman. Nasser had been Trotman's second in command throughout the Ford 2000 rollout and had a long-standing reputation as a tough-minded cost cutter. Even before taking the helm, he had begun to focus Ford senior management on shareholder value. In the period 1995–1999, Ford had seen companies with fewer physical assets and much lower revenues and profits achieve market capitalization well in excess of Ford's. Corporate staff members began to study models such as Cisco and Dell to try to understand whether Ford could produce shareholder value in the ways these newer companies had.

As the end of 1998 approached, Ford had amassed profits of $6.9 billion, employees enjoyed record profit sharing, and return on sales (3.9 percent in 1997) was trending solidly upward. The company was the world leader in trucks. It had taken over the U.S. industry lead in profit per vehicle ($1,770) from Chrysler, and it was the most improved automaker on the 1997 J. D. Power

Initial Quality Study (in fourth place overall, behind Honda, Toyota, and Nissan).

Ford's Supply Chain and Customer Responsiveness Initiatives

Ford had a number of initiatives under way that were aimed at positioning the company favorably for success in integrating with the extended enterprise that also included suppliers and customers. In addition, there were historical factors that would have to be taken into account in any virtual integration strategy.

Ford's Supply Base

The existing supply base was, in many respects, a product of history. As the company had grown over the years, so had the supply base, to the point where in the late 1980s there were several thousand suppliers of production material in a complex network of business relationships. Suppliers were picked primarily on the basis of cost, and little regard was given to overall supply chain costs, including the complexity of dealing with such a large network of suppliers.

Beginning in the early 1990s, Ford had begun to try actively to decrease the number of suppliers the company dealt with directly. Rather than fostering strong price competition among suppliers for individual components, there was a shift toward longer-term relationships with a subset of very capable suppliers who would provide entire vehicle subsystems. These "Tier 1" suppliers would manage relationships with a larger base of suppliers of components of subsystems—Tier 2 and below suppliers. Ford made its expertise available to assist suppliers in improving their operations through a range of techniques, including just-in-time (JIT) inventory, total quality management (TQM), and statistical process control (SPC). In exchange for the closer relationships and long-term commitments, Ford expected yearly price reductions from suppliers. While first tier suppliers had fairly well developed IT capabilities

(many interacted with Ford via electronic data interchange links), they were not able to invest in new technologies at the rate Ford itself could. Also, IT maturity (understanding and modernity of technology) decreased rapidly in lower tiers of the supply chain. As more cautious members of Takai's staff had often observed, this supply base was different in its nature and complexity from Dell's supply base.

Another major difference between Dell and Ford was organizational. At Dell, purchasing activities reported into the product development organization. At Ford, purchasing was organizationally independent of product development and had been—historically and up to the present—a powerful force within the company. Because of the sheer volume of materials and services Ford purchased, a very slim reduction in purchasing cost could result in very significant savings. Consequently, purchasing was involved closely in nearly every product decision. Engineers were counseled to avoid discussing prices in interactions with suppliers, as price negotiation was the sole province of purchasing agents. How this might work in a more virtually integrated system was unclear.

Ford Production System

The Ford 2000 initiative produced five major, corporationwide reengineering projects. One was Ford production system. Modeled roughly on the Toyota production system, FPS involved a multi-year project that drew on internal and external expertise worldwide. FPS was an integrated system aimed at making Ford manufacturing operations leaner, more responsive, and more efficient. It focused on key attributes of the production process, aspiring to level production and move to a more pull-based system, with synchronized production, continuous flow, and stability throughout the process. One important part of FPS was synchronous material flow (SMF), which Ford defined as "a process or system that produces a continuous flow of material and products driven by a fixed, sequenced, and leveled vehicle schedule, utilizing flexibility and lean manufacturing concepts." One key to SMF was in-line vehicle sequencing (ILVS), a system that used vehicle in-process storage devices (such as banks and ASRSs[2]) and computer software to assure that vehicles were assembled in order sequence. By assuring assembly in order sequence, Ford could tell suppliers exactly when and where certain components would be needed days in advance, and buffer stocks thus could be reduced dramatically. If such sequenced assembly could be kept level and if it was well-forecasted, the benefits would be felt throughout the supply chain. The vision was of trucks constantly in motion throughout their lives, in continuous circuits between suppliers and Ford, stopping only to refuel or change drivers, feeding a process that worked like a finely tuned and smoothly running precision instrument.

Order to Delivery

Another key process Ford reengineering initiative was order to delivery. The purpose of the OTD project was to reduce to 15 days the time from a customer's order to delivery of the finished product—a significant reduction from the present performance of 45 to 65 days. Ford took a holistic approach to the reengineering. Pilot studies in 1997 and 1998 identified bottlenecks throughout Ford's supply chain, including its marketing, material planning, vehicle production, and transportation processes. Ford's approach to implementing an improved OTD process relied on several elements: (1) ongoing forecasting of customer demand from dealers—before OTD Ford had never officially involved dealers in forecasting demand, (2) a minimum of 15 days of vehicles

in each assembly plant's order bank to increase manufacturing stability—gaps in the order bank are filled with "suggested" dealer orders based on historical buying patterns, (3) regional "mixing centers" that optimize schedules and deliveries of finished vehicles via rail transportation, and (4) a robust order amendment process to allow vehicles to be amended for minor color and trim variations without the need to submit new orders. The OTD vision was to create a lean, flexible, and predictable process that harmonized the efforts of all of Ford's components to enable it to provide consumers with the right products in the right place at the right time. Ford believed that success in achieving this vision would provide better quality, higher customer satisfaction, improved customer selection, better plant productivity, stability for its supply base, and lower dealer and company costs.

Ford Retail Network

On July 1, 1998, Ford launched the first of its Ford retail network (FRN) ventures in Tulsa, Oklahoma, under the newly formed Ford Investment Enterprises Company (FIECo). Ford Investment Enterprises was formed to take advantage of the changing face of retail vehicle distribution systems in North America. FIECo had two primary goals: (1) to be a test bed for best practices in retail distribution and drive those practices throughout the dealer network, and (2) to create an alternative distribution channel to compete with new, publicly owned retail chains. Ownership in the FRN varied from market to market; in some Ford would be the majority owner, and in others Ford would be the minority owner. In Rochester, New York, Ford was partnering with Republic, another large, publicly owned corporation. One of the principles of the FRN was to buy all the Ford dealers in a local market so that the dealers were in competition with the "real" competition (i.e., GM, Toyota, Honda) rather than with each other. The overriding goal was to give consumers the highest level of treatment and create an experience they would want to come back to again and again. Showrooms would have a consistent look on the

---

[2] A bank is a storage area into which partially assembled vehicles can be directed for the purpose of removing them in a different order from the order in which they entered (i.e., resequencing). An ASRS (automated storage and retrieval system) is essentially a multilevel bank (vehicles are literally stored on top of each other). Whereas an ordinary bank provides some resequencing flexibility, an ASRS provides the ability to access any vehicle in the bank at any time. As might be imagined, to hold a large number of vehicles and allow them to be accessed randomly, an ASRS must be very large (roughly the size of a several-story building).

outside, with customized interiors for the different Ford brands: Ford, Mercury, Lincoln, and Jaguar. The number of showrooms would be consolidated to focus resources on creating a superior selling experience, while the number of service outlets would increase to be closer to customer population centers. Ford expected personnel and advertising cost savings as well as inventory efficiencies due to economies of scale and greater use of the Internet. Ford also believed that the FRN would provide an opportunity to increase business not just in new and used vehicles but also in parts and service, body shop operations, and Ford Credit.

Dell's Integrated Supply Chain

See "The Power of Virtual Integration: An Interview with Dell Computer's Michael Dell," *Harvard Business Review,* March–April 1998, pp. 72–84, which is included in this book.

The Decision

Takai perused the neatly prepared documents that had been provided by her staff. There was a broad-based comparison between Dell and Ford on many important dimensions (see Exhibit 1). Virtual

EXHIBIT 1
Dell and Ford Compared

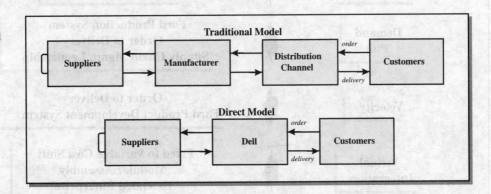

Comparative Metrics

Source: Dell 1998 financial report, Ford 1997 annual report, *Wall Street Journal Interactive.*

	Dell	Ford	
		Automotive	**Financial Services**
Employees	16,100	363,892	
Assets ($millions)	4,300	85,100	194,000
Revenue ($millions)	12,300	122,900	30,700
Net income ($millions)	944	4,700	2,200
Return on sales	7.7%	3.8%	7.2%
Cash ($millions)	320	14,500	2,200
Manufacturing facilities	3 (Texas, Ireland, Malaysia)	180 (in North and South America, Europe, Asia, Australia)	
Market capitalization ($millions)	58,469	66,886	
Price-earnings ratio	60	10*	
5-year average revenue growth	55% per year	6% per year	
5-year average stock price growth	133% per year	33.4% per year	

*Excludes earning from associates spin-off.

(*continued*)

EXHIBIT 1 Dell and Ford Compared (continued)

Enterprise Model Comparison

A high-level comparison of the Dell and Ford Motor enterprise models is shown below. Besides the lack of a dealer distribution channel, other key differences are Dell's ownership of assembly plants only—all component/subassembly manufacturing is done by its supply base—and the more integrated nature of Dell's sales, R&D, and manufacturing operations. All the operating principles that underlie Dell's success have counterparts in Ford's breakthrough objectives and key business plan initiatives.

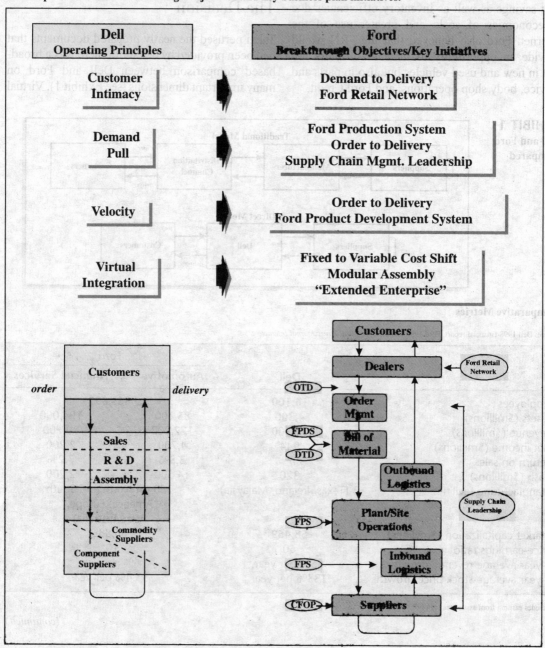

EXHIBIT 1   Dell and Ford Compared (continued)

Dell Processes	Ford
Suppliers own inventory until it is used in production	
Suppliers maintain nearby ship points; delivery time 15 minutes to 1 hour	√
External logistics supplier used to manage inbound supply chain	√
Customers frequently steered to PCs with high availability to balance supply and demand	√
Demand forecasting is critical—changes are shared immediately within Dell and with supply base	
Demand pull throughout value chain—"information for inventory" substitution	
Focused on strategic partnerships: suppliers down from 200 to 47	√
Complexity is low: 50 components, 8–10 key, 100 permutations	

integration would require changes in fundamental operations; some of the changes, framed as a shift from "push" to "pull" processes, were identified in another document (Exhibit 2). Whatever she decided, she would have to do it soon. Meetings were already scheduled with the vice president of quality and process leadership, and from there the recommendations would move upward, eventually reaching the CEO.

EXHIBIT 2   Moving from Push to Pull

	Process	Push	Pull
Design	Design strategy	Please everyone	Mainstream customer wants
	Vehicle combinations	More is better	Minimal
Marketing	Pricing strategy	Budget-driven	Market-driven
	Vehicle purchase incentives	Higher	Lower
Manufacturing and supply	Capacity planning	Multiple material/capacity constraints, driven by program budget	Market-driven (no constraints, FPV/CPV* + 10% for vehicle, + 15% for components
	Schedule and build stability	Maximize production; make whatever you can build	Schedule from customer-driven order bank, build to schedule
Dealer network	Dealer ordering	Orders based on allocations and capacity constraints	Orders based on customer demand
	Order to delivery times	Longer (60 + days)	Shorter (15 days or less)
	Inventory	High with low turnover	Low with rapid turnover
	Dealership model	Independent dealerships, negotiations with company	Company-controlled dealerships (Ford Retail Network)

*FPV, or financial planning volume, is the volume of components expected to be required by the supply base when assembling the business case for a particular vehicle model. CPV, or capacity planning volume, is the volume of components that will be expected that is communicated to suppliers. Typically these numbers are the same, but the recommendation of Takai's staff is that these numbers should include some contingency (+10 percent, +15 percent) to allow suppliers to tool up for the possibility of "hot options," to avoid shortages.

Reading 2-4

The Power of Virtual Integration: An Interview with Dell Computer's Michael Dell

How do you create a $12 billion company in just 13 years?

Michael Dell began in 1984 with a simple business insight: He could bypass the dealer channel through which personal computers were then being sold. Instead, he would sell directly to customers and build products to order. In one swoop, Dell eliminated the reseller's markup and the costs and risks associated with carrying large inventories of finished goods. The formula became known as the direct business model, and it gave Dell Computer Corporation a substantial cost advantage.

The direct model turned out to have other benefits that even Michael Dell couldn't have anticipated when he founded his company. "You actually get to have a relationship with the customer," he explains. "And that creates valuable information, which, in turn, allows us to leverage our relationships with both suppliers and customers. Couple that information with technology, and you have the infrastructure to revolutionize the fundamental business models of major global companies."

In this interview with HBR editor-at-large Joan Magretta, Michael Dell describes how his company is using technology and information to blur the traditional boundaries in the value chain among suppliers, manufacturers, and end users. In so doing, Dell Computer is evolving in a direction that Michael Dell calls *virtual integration*. The individual pieces of the strategy—customer focus, supplier partnerships, mass customization, just-in-time manufacturing—may all be familiar. But Michael Dell's insight into how to combine them is highly innovative: Technology is enabling coordination across company boundaries to achieve new levels of efficiency and productivity, as well

This reading was conducted by Joan Magretta. Copyright © 1998 President and Fellows of Harvard College. *Harvard Business Review* No. 98208.

as extraordinary returns to investors. Virtual integration harnesses the economic benefits of two very different business models. It offers the advantages of a tightly coordinated supply chain that have traditionally come through vertical integration. At the same time, it benefits from the focus and specialization that drive virtual corporations. Virtual integration, as Michael Dell envisions it, has the potential to achieve both coordination and focus. If it delivers on that promise, it may well become a new organizational model for the information age.

How has Dell pioneered a new business model within the computer industry?

If you look back to the industry's inception, the founding companies essentially had to create all the components themselves. They had to manufacture disk drives and memory chips and application software; all the various pieces of the industry had to be vertically integrated within one firm.

So the companies that were the stars ten years ago, the Digital Equipments of this world, had to build massive structures to produce everything a computer needed. They had no choice but to become expert in a wide array of components, some of which had nothing to do with creating value for the customer.

As the industry grew, more specialized companies developed to produce specific components. That opened up the opportunity to create a business that was far more focused and efficient. As a small start-up, Dell couldn't afford to create every piece of the value chain. But more to the point, why should we want to? We concluded we'd be better off leveraging the investments others have made and focusing on delivering solutions and systems to customers.

Consider a component like a graphics chip. Five or ten years ago, a whole bunch of companies in the personal computer industry were trying to create their own graphics chips. Now, if you've got a race with 20 players that are all vying to produce the fastest graphics chip in the world, do you want to be the 21st horse, or do you want to evaluate the field of 20 and pick the best one?

It's a pretty simple strategy, but at the time it went against the dominant, "engineering-centric" view of the industry. The IBMs and Compaqs and HPs subscribed to a "we-have-to-develop-everything" view of the world. If you weren't doing component assembly, you weren't a real computer company. It was like a rite of passage. You somehow proved your manhood by placing small semiconductor chips on printed circuit boards.

And Dell Computer came along and said, "Now wait a second. If I understand this correctly, the companies that do nothing but put chips on motherboards don't actually earn tremendous profit doing it. If we want to earn higher returns, shouldn't we be more selective and put our capital into activities where we can add value for our customers, not just into activities that need to get done?" I'm not saying those activities are unimportant. They need to get done very, very well. But they're not sources of value that Dell is going to create.

When the company started, I don't think we knew how far the direct model could take us. It has provided a consistent underlying strategy for Dell despite a lot of change in our industry. Along the way, we have learned a lot, and the model has evolved. Most important, the direct model has allowed us to leverage our relationships with both suppliers and customers to such an extent that I believe it's fair to think of our companies as being virtually integrated. That allows us to focus on where we add value and to build a much larger firm much more quickly. I don't think we could have created a $12 billion business in 13 years if we had tried to be vertically integrated.

Why can you grow so much faster without all those physical assets?

There are fewer things to manage, fewer things to go wrong. You don't have the drag effect of taking 50,000 people with you. Suppose we have two

suppliers building monitors for us, and one of them loses its edge. It's a lot easier for us to get more capacity from the remaining supplier than to set up a new manufacturing plant ourselves. If we had to build our own factories for every single component of the system, growing at 57 percent per year just would not be possible. I would spend 500 percent of my time interviewing prospective vice presidents because the company would have not 15,000 employees but 80,000.

Indirectly, we employ something like that many people today. There are, for example, 10,000 service technicians in the field who service our products, but only a small number of them work for us. They're contracted with other firms. But ask the customer, "Who was that person who just fixed your computer?" The vast majority think that person works for us, which is just great. That's part of virtual integration.

Aren't you just outsourcing your after-sales service? Is what you're describing fundamentally different from outsourcing?

Outsourcing, at least in the IT world, is almost always a way to get rid of a problem a company hasn't been able to solve itself. The classic case is the company with 2,000 people in the IT department. Nobody knows what they do, and nobody knows why they do it. The solution—outsource IT to a service provider, and hopefully they'll fix it. But if you look at what happens five years later, it's not necessarily a pretty picture.

That's not what we're doing at all. We focus on how we can coordinate our activities to create the most value for customers.

With our service providers, we're working to set quality measures and, more important, to build data linkages that let us see in real time how we're doing—when parts are dispatched, for instance, or how long it takes to respond to a request for service. We look at our business and see, for example, that over the next 10 years we are going to be making lots of notebook computers. Dell might need 20 million flat-panel displays, and some years there will be more demand than supply. Other years, there will be more supply than demand. A few companies are currently making multibillion-dollar investments in the manufacture of these displays.

So we cook up a little deal where the supplier agrees to meet 25 percent of our volume requirements for displays, and because of the long-term commitment we make to them, we'll get our displays year in and year out, even when there's more demand than supply. The supplier effectively becomes our partner. They assign their engineers to our design team, and we start to treat them as if they were part of the company. For example, when we launch a new product, their engineers are stationed right in our plants. If a customer calls in with a problem, we'll stop shipping product while they fix design flaws in real time.

Figuring out how many partners we need has been a process of trial and error. You learn when you operate on the cutting edge of technology that things don't always work as planned. The rule we follow is to have as few partners as possible. And they will last as long as they maintain their leadership in technology and quality. This isn't like the automobile business, where you find a tire supplier that you will probably stick with forever. Where the technology is fairly stable—in monitors, for example—we expect our partnerships to last a long time. Others will be more volatile. But regardless of how long these relationships last, virtual integration means you're basically stitching together a business with partners that are treated as if they're inside the company. You're sharing information in a real-time fashion.

We tell our suppliers exactly what our daily production requirements are. So it's not, "Well, every two weeks deliver 5,000 to this warehouse, and we'll put them on the shelf, and then we'll take them off the shelf." It's, "Tomorrow morning we need 8,562, and deliver them to door number seven by 7 A.M."

You would deal with an internal supplier that way, and you can do so because you share information and plans very freely. Why doesn't the same sharing of information take place across company boundaries? Buyers are often so busy trying to protect themselves that the seller can't really add a lot of value. Government purchasing is the extreme case, with its overly structured procurement system. Protecting the buyer usually ends up disabling the seller—and both lose.

The technology available today really boosts the value of information sharing. We can share design databases and methodologies with supplier-partners in ways that just weren't possible 5 to 10 years ago. This speeds time to market—often dramatically—and creates a lot of value that can be shared between buyer and supplier. So technology enhances the economic incentives to collaborate.

What are the challenges involved in establishing these collaborations?

The key challenge—and the biggest change from business as usual—is changing the focus from how much inventory there is to how fast it's moving. All computer chips carry a four-digit date code. For example, "97–23" means it was built in the twenty-third week of 1997. You can take the cover off any computer and find out how old its parts are, how long it took to make its way through the system. In our industry, if you can get people to think about how fast inventory is moving, then you create real value. Why? Because if I've got 11 days of inventory and my competitor has 80, and Intel comes out with a new 450-megahertz chip, that means I'm going to get to market 69 days sooner.

I think about it this way: Assets collect risks around them in one form or another. Inventory is one risk, and accounts receivable is another risk. In our case—with 70 percent of our sales going to large corporate customers—accounts receivable isn't hard to manage because companies like Goldman Sachs and Microsoft and Oracle tend to be able to pay their bills. But in the computer industry, inventory can actually be a pretty massive risk because if the cost of materials goes down 50 percent a year and you have two or three months of inventory versus 11 days, you've got a big cost disadvantage. And you're vulnerable to product transitions, when you can get stuck with obsolete inventory.

Inventory velocity is one of a handful of key performance measures we watch very closely. It focuses us on working with our suppliers to keep reducing inventory and increasing speed. With a supplier like Sony, which makes very good, reliable monitors, we figure there's no need for us to have any inventory at all. We are confident in putting the Dell name on them, and they work fine. We don't even take these monitors out of the box to test them because we've gotten them to under 1,000 defects per million. So what's the point in having a monitor put on a truck to Austin, Texas, and then taken off the truck and sent on a little tour around the warehouse, only to be put back on another truck? That's just a big waste of time and money, unless we get our jollies from touching monitors, which we don't.

So we went to Sony and said, "Hey, we're going to buy two or three million of these monitors this year. Why don't we just pick them up every day as we need them?" At first, it's a little confusing to the suppliers because you're saying, "Now listen carefully. If you will help us get your product from the end of your line to our customer faster, we won't have any in our warehouse." And the suppliers look at you like you're crazy and not making any sense. They're used to delivering in larger quantities, so at first they think this means you're going to buy less from them. And then the lightbulb goes on, and they realize we'll be buying more because we'll be taking it faster.

So now you have Sony producing a level supply of monitors for you. What happens next?

We tell Airborne Express or UPS to come to Austin and pick up 10,000 computers a day and go over to the Sony factory in Mexico and pick up the corresponding number of monitors. Then while we're all sleeping, they match up the computers and the monitors and deliver them to the customer.

Of course, this requires sophisticated data exchange. Most people are familiar with the way a company like Black & Decker uses information links with the thousands of retailers that sell its products. When a customer in Omaha buys a drill from his local hardware store, the system immediately tells Black & Decker to send another unit of that particular drill to that particular store. So their

system has to replenish supply, unit by unit, to thousands of outlets. From the supplier's point of view, Dell is dramatically simpler. Our orders are typically for thousands of units, and they need to go to only one of three manufacturing centers: Austin, Ireland, and Malaysia. It's almost ideal from a supplier standpoint because we have real-time information on what the demand is, and all the supplier has to do is get the product to us.

And because we build to our customers' order, typically, with just five or six days of lead time, suppliers don't have to worry about sell-through. We only maintain a few days—in some cases a few hours—of raw materials on hand. We communicate inventory levels and replenishment needs regularly—with some vendors, hourly.

The typical case in our industry is the factory building 10,000 units a day, day in and day out. First the machines stack up in the warehouse, and then they stack up in the channel. And all of a sudden, the guy at the end of the chain hollers, "Whoa, hey, we've got too many of these. Everybody stop!" And the order to stop flows back through the chain until it reaches every component supplier. It's literally stop and start, because if you have a 90-day lag between the point of demand and the point of supply, you're going to have a lot of inefficiency in the process. And the more inventory and time you have, the more variability, and the more problems.

In our industry, there's a lot of what I call bad hygiene. Companies stuff the channel to get rid of old inventory and to meet short-term financial objectives. We think our approach is better. We substitute information for inventory and ship only when we have real demand from real end customers.

How does the direct model benefit your suppliers?

We can go to Sony and say, "We're going to be pulling monitors from you in a very consistent, predictable way because the distance between the demand and the source of supply is totally shrunk." The longer that distance, the more intermediary channels you add, the less likely it is you will have good information about demand—so you will end up with more variability, more inventory, higher costs, and more risk.

Another factor that helps keep our demand for computers level is the mix of customers we serve. We don't have any customer that represents more than 1 percent to 2 percent of our revenues. One week Exxon is buying, the next week Shell is buying, the next week Ford is buying. But all companies don't decide in unison, "Well, this week we're going to buy, next week we're not."

You mention your customer mix. Does the direct model imply a particular customer strategy?

If you'd asked me that question 12 years ago, I would have said that we didn't differentiate much between our largest and our smallest customer. Today we do. Our customer strategy is one area where our model has evolved. We've become good at developing what we call "scalable" businesses—that is, those in which we can grow revenues faster than expenses. We really look closely at financial measures like gross margins by customer segment—and we focus on segments we can serve profitably as we achieve scale. People are sometimes surprised to learn that 90 percent of our sales go to institutions—business or government—and 70 percent to very large customers that buy at least $1 million in PCs per year.

When you're trying to target profitable segments, averages obscure a lot, and aggregate financial statements are pretty meaningless. Our approach to segmentation is to take really big numbers and "de-average" them. Until you look inside and understand what's going on by business, by customer, by geography, you don't know anything. This is a lesson we learned the hard way. We incorrectly entered the retail business in 1989, thinking that our direct business wouldn't grow enough, and went into computer superstores and warehouse clubs. But when we really started to understand the segment's profitability, we realized we'd made a mistake, and so we exited.

For years, we didn't actively pursue the consumer market because we couldn't reach our profit objectives. So we let our competitors introduce machines with rock-bottom prices and zero margins. We figured they could be the ones to teach consumers about PCs while we focused our efforts on more profitable segments. And then, because we're direct and can see who is buying what, we noticed something interesting. The industry's average selling price to consumers was going down, but ours was going up. Consumers who were now buying their second or third machines—who wanted the most powerful machines and needed less hand holding—were coming to us. And without focusing on it in a significant way, we had a billion-dollar consumer business that was profitable. So we decided in 1997 that it was time to dedicate a group to serving that segment.

So, over time, you cut the market into finer and finer segments?

Yes, for a lot of reasons. One is to identify unique opportunities and economics. The other is purely a managerial issue: You can't possibly manage something well if it's too big. Segmentation gives us better attention and focus [see Exhibit 1].

Each segment has its own issues. In education, for instance, how do you get tech support to a classroom when the teacher doesn't have a telephone? You need a totally different approach. Segmenting lets you tailor your programs to the customers' needs. If you just lump diverse customers together, you can be sure that some of them will come last on some manager's list, and he may never get around to solving their problems. That's why we make serving one segment the manager's only job.

Do you get other benefits from segmenting your customers?

Segmentation gets us closer to them. It allows us to understand their needs in a really deep way. This closeness gives us access to information that's absolutely critical to our strategy. It helps us forecast what they're going to need and when. And good forecasts are the key to keeping our costs down.

We turn our inventory over 30 times per year. If you look at the complexity and the diversity of our

EXHIBIT 1 Fast-Cycle Segmentation

Dell's rapid growth in recent years has been accompanied by even finer cuts at customer segmentation. This is an important element of Dell's virtual integration with customers. The finer the segmentation, the better able Dell is to forecast what its customers are going to need and when. Dell then coordinates the flow of that strategic information all the way back to its suppliers, effectively substituting information for inventory.

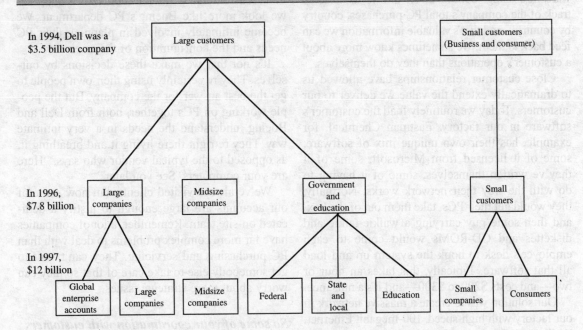

In 1994, Dell was a $3.5 billion company

In 1996, $7.8 billion

In 1997, $12 billion

product line, there's no way we could do that unless we had credible information about what the customer is actually buying. It's a key part of why rivals have had great difficulty competing with Dell. It's not just that we sell direct, it's also our ability to forecast demand—it's both the design of the product and the way the information from the customer flows all the way through manufacturing to our suppliers. If you don't have that tight linkage—the kind of coordination of information that used to be possible only in vertically integrated companies—then trying to manage to 11 days of inventory would be insane. We simply couldn't do it without customers who work with us as partners.

Could you describe how you forecast demand?

We see forecasting as a critical sales skill. We teach our sales-account managers to lead customers through a discussion of their future PC needs.

We'll walk a customer through every department of his company, asking him to designate which needs are certain and which are contingent. And when they're contingent on some event, the salesperson will know what that event is so he can follow up. We can do this with our large accounts, which make up the bulk of our business. With smaller customers, we have real-time information about what they're buying from our direct telephone salespeople. And we can also steer them in real time, on the phone, toward configurations that are available, so this is another way we can fine-tune the balance between supply and demand.

Is that what you mean by virtual integration with your customers?

It's part of it. There are so many information links between us and our customers. For example, we can help large global customers manage their total purchase of PCs by selling them a standard product. Then when the guy whose computer isn't working calls in from Singapore, the IT people don't have to spend the first 30 minutes just figuring out what configuration of hardware and software he's using. Selling direct allows us to keep track of the company's total PC purchases, country by country—and that's valuable information we can feed back to them. We sometimes know more about a customer's operations than they do themselves.

Close customer relationships have allowed us to dramatically extend the value we deliver to our customers. Today we routinely load the customer's software in our factory. Eastman Chemical, for example, has their own unique mix of software, some of it licensed from Microsoft, some of it they've written themselves, some of it having to do with the way their network works. Normally, they would get their PCs, take them out of the box, and then some guy carrying a walkie-talkie and diskettes and CD-ROMs would come to each employee's desk to hook the system up and load all that software. Typically, this takes an hour or two—and costs $200 to $300—and it's a nuisance.

Our solution was to create a massive network in our factory with high-speed, 100-megabit Ethernet. We'll load Eastman Chemical's software onto a huge Dell server. Then when a machine comes down the assembly line and says, "I'm an Eastman Chemical analyst workstation, configuration number 14," all of a sudden a few hundred megabytes of data come rushing through the network and onto the workstation's hard disk, just as part of the progressive build through our factory. If the customer wants, we can put an asset tag with the company's logo on the machine, and we can keep an electronic register of the customer's assets. That's a lot easier than the customer sending some guy around on a thankless mission, placing asset tags on computers when he can find them.

What happens to the money our customer is saving? They get to keep most of it. We could say, "Well, it costs you $300 to do it, so we'll charge you $250." But instead we charge $15 or $20, and we make our product and our service much more valuable. It also means we're not going to be just

your PC vendor anymore. We're going to be your IT department for PCs.

Boeing, for example, has 100,000 Dell PCs, and we have 30 people that live at Boeing, and if you look at the things we're doing for them or for other customers, we don't look like a supplier, we look more like Boeing's PC department. We become intimately involved in planning their PC needs and the configuration of their network.

It's not that we make these decisions by ourselves. They're certainly using their own people to get the best answer for the company. But the people working on PCs together, both from Dell and Boeing, understand the needs in a very intimate way. They're right there living it and breathing it, as opposed to the typical vendor who says, "Here are your computers. See you later."

We've always visited clients, but now some of our accounts are large enough to justify a dedicated on-site team. Remember, a lot of companies have far more complex problems to deal with than PC purchasing and servicing. They can't wait to get somebody else to take care of that so they can worry about more strategic issues.

So some of your coordination with customers is made possible through technology, but there's still a good measure of old-fashioned, face-to-face human contact?

Yes, that's right. The idea is to use technology to free people up to solve more complicated problems. For example, a customer like MCI can access our internal support tools online in the same way our own technical-support teams do, saving time and money on both sides. They simply go to www.dell.com, enter some information about their system, and they have immediate access to the same information that we use at Dell to help customers. These tools are used by internal help-desk groups at large companies as well as by individuals.

We've developed customized intranet sites called Premier Pages for well over 200 of our largest global customers. These exist securely within the customers' firewalls, and they give them direct access to purchasing and technical information about the specific configurations they buy from us. One of our customers, for example, allows its 50,000 employees to view and select products online. They use the Premier Page as an interactive catalog of all the configurations the company authorizes; employees can then price and order the PC they want. They are happy to have some choice, and Dell and the customer are both happy to eliminate the paperwork and sales time normally associated with corporate purchasing. That frees our salespeople to play a more consultative role.

We also have developed tools to help customers set up their own customized versions of dell.com. There are about 7,000 of these to date.

How else do you stay close to your customers?

In a direct business like ours, you have, by definition, a relationship with customers. But beyond the mechanisms we have for sales and support, we have set up a number of forums to ensure the free flow of information with the customer on a constant basis. Our Platinum Councils, for example, are regional meetings—in Asia-Pacific, Japan, the United States, and Europe—of our largest customers. They meet every six to nine months; in the larger regions, there's one for the information executives—the CIO types—and then there's one for the technical types.

In these meetings, our senior technologists share their views on where the technology is heading and lay out road maps of product plans over the next two years. There are also breakout sessions and working groups in which our engineering teams focus on specific product areas and talk about how to solve problems that may not necessarily have anything to do with the commercial relationship with Dell. For example, Is leasing better than buying? or How do you manage the transition to Windows NT? or How do you manage a field force of notebook computers?

People in businesses as dissimilar as Unilever and ICI can learn from each other because, amazingly, they have very similar problems when it comes to PCs. And we send not only our top technologists and engineers but also the real engineers, the people who usually don't get out to talk to customers because they're too busy developing products. All of our senior executives from around the company participate, spending time with the customer, listening to how we're doing. The ratio is about one Dell person to one customer. At our last session, we had about 100 customers.

The councils are another way we're able to play more of an advisory role, trying to help our customers understand what the flow of new technology really means, how it will translate into specific products. We try to help the customer anticipate what's happening and be ready. And that helps us, as well, with our own demand forecasting. So we're helping each other in important ways. We hire a lot of people from other companies in the industry, and they tell us that these meetings are unique.

Do you spend a significant amount of your time at these meetings?

I spend three days at each of them. They're great events. In the normal course of our business, I have lots of opportunity to talk to customers one on one, but there is something much more powerful about this kind of forum. Customers tend to speak more openly when they're with their peers and they know we're there and we're listening.

At every Platinum Council, we review what they told us last time and what we did about it. We keep an ongoing record of the issues. Let me give you a concrete example: A few years ago, the engineers responsible for our desktops were operating on the theory that customers really wanted performance from these products—the faster the better. But what the customers actually said at the Platinum Councils was, "Yeah, performance, that's okay. But what I really want is a stable product that doesn't change. Because if I'm trying to run a bank or an airline, I don't care if it's 2 percent faster or 3 percent slower. What really matters is stability." So our engineers thought one thing, the customers thought another thing. It took the direct feedback from the Platinum Councils to spotlight this failure to communicate. We responded by building product with intergenerational consistency over many years. The same feedback has helped shape the creation of our brands. For both our desktop and notebook businesses, we created different brands designed to deliver greater stability to corporate customers, as opposed to the fast technology changes that consumers demand.

As I think back to some of those council meetings, things that would seem fairly small at the time have often turned out three or four years later to become the basis for billions of dollars of revenue—notebooks with longer-life batteries, for example, or loading customers' software for them in our plants.

As your customer strategy has evolved, has the Dell brand changed as well?

A big piece of our brand is being the most efficient and effective way for customers to buy Intel or Microsoft technologies. But beyond that, we're evolving into a technology selector, or navigator. We often talk to customers about "relevant technology." Intel and Microsoft tend to launch into a massive variety of things, some of which are speculative and aimed at exploring new technologies. We think it's our job to help our customers sort out the technology relevant to today's needs from the bleeding edge.

How does that strategy affect your own R&D function? What role does R&D play in your company?

At Dell, we believe the customer is in control, and our job is to take all the technology that's out there and apply it in a useful way to meet the customer's needs. We're not trying to invent new architecture ourselves, but we'll spend a quarter of a billion dollars this year and employ some 1,500 people to improve the whole user experience—that means delivering the latest relevant technology, making it easy to use, and keeping costs down. And in addition to selecting appropriate technology, our R&D group focuses on process and quality improvements in manufacturing.

Before industry standards came into play, the proprietary computing environment bred a kind of technical arrogance that, fortunately, won't fly anymore. Once standards were established, the customer started to define what was going to be

successful, and it didn't matter what you invented or how good it was or how fast it was. Increasingly, what matters is what the customers want and whether it works with all their other stuff.

That means we have to stay on top of our customers' needs, and we have to monitor and understand the innovations in the material science world—everything from semiconductors to polymers to liquid crystal displays. You need to track anything having to do with the flow of electrons, and you need to keep asking how these marvelous developments might be useful to customers. The customer doesn't come to you and say, "Boy, I really like lithium ion batteries. I can't wait to get my hands on some lithium ion." The customer says, "I want a notebook computer that lasts the whole day. I don't want it to run out when I'm on the plane."

I was about to leave a meeting at Sony in Tokyo in January of 1993 when someone ran up to me and said, "Oh, Mr. Dell, please wait one minute. I'm from Sony's power technology company. We have a new power-system technology we want to explain to you." And I remember thinking, Is this guy going to try to sell me a power plant? He starts showing me chart after chart about the performance of lithium ion batteries. This is wonderful, I tell him. And if it's true, we're going to put this in every notebook computer we make.

We then sent a team over to check it out, and a year and a half later we were the first computer company to have a notebook that lasted five and a half, six hours. We tested it with American Airlines, handing out the notebooks to passengers at the start of flights from New York to Los Angeles. By the end, the notebooks were still running.

How are the challenges of leadership in a virtually integrated organization different from those you would encounter running a corporation with more traditional boundaries?

The whole idea behind virtual integration is that it lets you meet customers' needs faster and more efficiently than any other model [see Exhibit 2].

EXHIBIT 2   **The Evolution of a Faster Business Model**

The dominant model in the personal computer industry—a value chain with
arm's-length transactions from one layer to the next:

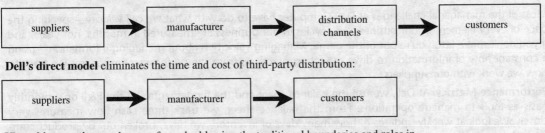

| suppliers | → | manufacturer | → | distribution channels | → | customers |

Dell's direct model eliminates the time and cost of third-party distribution:

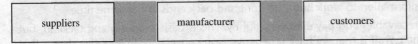

| suppliers | → | manufacturer | → | customers |

Virtual integration works even faster by blurring the traditional boundaries and roles in
the value chain:

| suppliers | manufacturer | customers |

With vertical integration, you can be an efficient producer—as long as the world isn't changing very much. But virtual integration lets you be efficient and responsive to change at the same time—at least, that's what we're trying to do. We think about Internet commerce as a logical extension of our direct model—and within our first year, we reached a run rate of $2 million a day. It's now about $3 million a day, and during the peak of the Christmas buying season we saw several $6 million days. I'm only half joking when I say that the only thing better than the Internet would be mental telepathy. Because what we're all about is shrinking the time and the resources it takes to meet customers' needs. And we're trying to do that in a world where those needs are changing.

To lead in that kind of environment, you have to be on the lookout for shifts in value, and if the customer decides, "Hey, I don't care about that anymore, now I care about this," we may have to develop new capabilities rather quickly. One of the biggest challenges we face today is finding managers who can sense and respond to rapid shifts, people who can process new information very quickly and make decisions in real time. It's a problem for the computer industry as a whole—and not just for Dell—that the industry's growth has outpaced its ability to create managers. We tell

prospective hires, "If you want an environment that is never going to change, don't come here. This is not the place for you." •

Our goal is to be one or two steps ahead of the change, and, in fact, to be creating or shaping it, to some extent. That's why we spend so much time with our customers. It's why I personally spend about 40 percent of my time with customers. Often it's a lead customer that says, "Hey, can you put an asset tag on my PC?" And the first reaction is, "Gee, we've never done that before, but why not? Let's give it a try." And then you do it for one customer, then for ten, then for a hundred, and eventually it becomes a standard offering. Putting asset tags on computers isn't by itself a major value shift, but what happens is that we get a series of seemingly small innovations that over time add up to a huge improvement. That's not a bad description of the way we get into businesses. We don't come at it the other way around, with a consulting study that says, "That's an attractive business. Let's go." Nor do we sit around and say, "What do we suppose our customers would like? If we were customers, what would we be thinking?"

So looking for value shifts is probably the most important dimension of leadership. Then there's the question of managing such a tightly coordinated value chain—and there it's all about execution.

EXHIBIT 3

Using Information to Speed Execution
by Kevin Rollins

Most of the managerial challenges at Dell Computer have to do with what we call *velocity*—speeding the pace of every element of our business. Life cycles in our business are measured in months, not years, and if you don't move fast, you're out of the game. Managing velocity is about managing information—using a constant flow of information to drive operating practices, from the performance measures we track to how we work with our suppliers.

Performance Metrics. At Dell, we use the balance sheet and the fundamentals of the P&L on a monthly basis as tools to manage operations. From the balance sheet, we track three cash flow measures very closely. We look at weekly updates of how many days of inventory we have, broken out by product component. We can then work closely with our suppliers so we end up with the right inventory. When it's not quite right, we can use our direct-sales model to steer customers toward comparable products that we do have. So we use inventory information to work both the front and back ends at the same time.

We also track and manage receivables and payables very tightly. This is basic blocking and tackling, but we give it a high priority. The payoff is that we have a negative cash-conversion cycle of five days—that is, we get paid before we have to pay our suppliers. Since our competitors usually have to support their resellers by offering them credit, the direct model gives us an inherent cost advantage. And the more we can shorten our cash-collection cycle, the greater our advantage.

The real-time performance measures in the P&L that we regard as the best indicators of the company's health are our margins, our average selling price, and the overhead associated with selling. We split the P&L into these core elements by customer segment, by product, and by country. These metrics can alert us instantly to problems, for example, with the mix of products being sold in any particular country.

Working with Suppliers. The greatest challenge in working with suppliers is getting them in sync with the fast pace we have to maintain. The key to making it work is information. The right information flows allow us to work with our partners in ways that enhance speed, either directly by improving logistics or indirectly by improving quality.

Take our service strategy, for example. Customers pay us for service and support, and we contract with third-party maintainers (TPMs) to make the service calls. Customers call us when they have problems, and that initial call will trigger two electronic dispatches—one to ship the needed parts directly from Dell to the customers' sites and one to dispatch the TPMs to the customers. Our role as information broker facilitates the TPMs' work by making sure the necessary parts will be on-site when they arrive.

If you look at Dell's P&L structure, I think you'd be hard-pressed to find companies that deliver the kind of value added we do with such a small markup. My theory is that if we can continue to keep our markup as low as it is today, we're going to be able to capture most of the opportunities available to us. But that means we cannot get complacent about our growth and get careless about execution.

Sometimes I'm taken aback when I talk to people who've been in the company for six months or a year and who talk about "the model" as if it were an all-powerful being that will take care of everything. It's scary because I know that nothing is ever 100 percent constant, and the last thing we should do is assume that we're always going to be doing well. But for now, it's working. The direct system really delivers value to the customer all the way from distribution back through manufacturing and design. If you tried to divide Dell up into a manufacturer and a channel, you'd destroy the company's unique value. It's something completely new that nobody in our industry has ever done before [see Exhibit 3].

Case 2-5

Postgirot Bank and Provment AB: Managing the Cost of IT Operations

In August 2001, Roland Löwling, information technology (IT) operations manager of Postgirot Bank in Stockholm, Sweden, was gazing over the steely gray waters of the Baltic, considering some 70 NT[1] servers recently brought under his management. The last six months had been focused on an information-gathering and rationalization project for the bank's 68 Unix[2] servers using Provment AB's[3] IM-System,[4] long established as a utilization assessment tool in OS/390 mainframe environments. Roland had been eager to expand its use to the recently centralized Unix systems and was pleased, though a bit surprised, with the results. Now the question was whether he should further extend his use of IM-System to include the NT servers. Would the anticipated cost savings and availability of improved management control "numbers" make Postgirot Bank more appealing to potential acquirers? Additionally, the bank had not yet settled on an appropriate management reporting structure to get the most out of the information provided by the new efforts.

Roland had a meeting scheduled with Provment's founder, Torsten Wenell, to inform him of his decision as soon as both returned from vacation.

This case was prepared by Research Associate Nancy Bartlett under the supervision of Professor F. Warren McFarlan. Copyright © 2002 President and Fellows of Harvard College. Harvard Business School Case No. 302-061.

[1] Microsoft Windows NT (a registered trademark owned by Microsoft Corporation).

[2] Unix is an operating system developed by AT&T's Bell Laboratories.

[3] AB is an abbreviation for Aktie Bolag, meaning "limited liability (stock) corporation." Provment AB is a consulting service and software company based in Stockholm, Sweden.

[4] IM-System is Provment AB's proprietary IT information management tool.

Provment AB

Over several years Torsten Wenell had organized a group to pursue his vision of managing IT productivity "by the numbers." These Stockholm-based individuals had general experience in IT operations. Torsten's background included data center management, followed by a key role in developing an international financial accounting and reporting software application for IBM and then consulting with organizations that managed IT resources. In 1997, he formed the company now called Provment AB and developed its IT measurement tool: Interactive Management for IT operations (IM-System).

Provment's IM-System focused on a methodology that allowed organizations "to create and distribute data needed for rational IT productivity decisions." As Torsten saw it, a key differentiator of IM-System from other analysis tools was that IM-System transferred IT usage information, and thus cost and productivity measurement, from the exclusive purview of IT into the hands of the company. He believed that IT *and* non-IT management at all levels needed to collaborate more closely to manage IT production resources effectively. Accordingly, he developed IM-System to collect and communicate cost-related utilization information throughout the organization and to facilitate discussion. IM-System provided understandable productivity information in paper-based and Web-based reports, with a focus and level of detail that correlated with the reader's role. As Torsten noted:

> An IT management and control system is successful only if complex technical information can be evaluated and consolidated, as well as standardized and simplified, so that both technicians and managers can understand and use the system to make sound decisions. The alternative—educating the technicians regarding the company's business so that the technicians make the proper business

EXHIBIT 1
IT Information Paths

Source: Provment AB.

Managing the Operation of IT

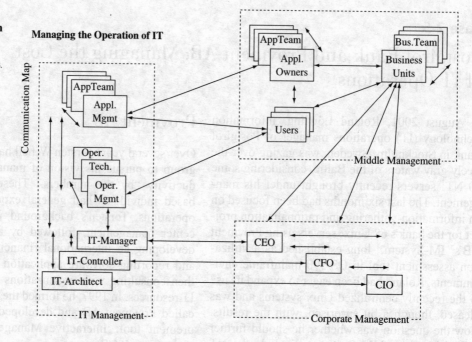

decisions—would at best be very time consuming and difficult. And I don't know of a discipline or school that trains IT operations efficiency specialists (see Exhibit 1).

Postgirot Bank

Background

In 1919, to meet the Swedish community's need for effective payment transfers, a task force was appointed that subsequently proposed the establishment of a "postal check"[5] system, following examples already established in Europe. World War I had been followed by a period of economic depression, unemployment, and reduced tax revenue. A cost reduction committee established in 1923 had calculated that a postal giro[6] system (previously the

[5] Postal checks are payment authorization documents written by individuals, companies, or other organizations for transferring funds. The documents themselves are not physically "cleared" for return to the sender.

[6] Bank giro as well as postal giro systems were common and widely used in Europe. The first such system, for credit transfers between banks, was developed in 1619 by the Giro Bank of Hamburg, Germany.

postal check system) would reduce the government's need to handle cash and correspondingly save money. In 1924, a proposal was introduced into the Swedish parliament to create Postgirot Bank as part of the Postal Savings Bank. The proposal became law in 1925, and Postgirot Bank was founded to process payments. The idea of cashless payments through the giro system was quickly accepted, and over 5,000 accounts were opened during its first year of operation. On March 1, 1994, the Swedish Postal Service became a public company with an independent board of directors, new management accountability and flexibility, and possible access to capital markets. This was seen as a culminating step for its wholly owned subsidiary, Postgirot Bank, as it evolved into providing full banking services. Postgirot Bank's charter was to:

Provide payment transfer and other financial services, to meet customer needs, now and in the future.

Nearly all Swedish companies, nonprofits, and private persons have had a business relationship with Postgirot Bank either directly or through an affiliate bank. Customers included 425,000 companies and nonprofits and 915,000 private individuals. By May 2000, there were 155,000 accounts using online services. The bank proudly claims it is unique in its ability (and willingness) to let transactions "meet." That is, transactions can be processed through an account if the starting balance plus incoming transactions cover the withdrawals for the same day (as opposed to "bouncing" withdrawals and/or charging fees based on a prior date's "available balance"). More than 4.9 trillion Swedish crowns (SEK)[7] changed hands in 400 million transactions during 1999.

In 2000 Postgirot Bank had 3,000 employees. Operating earnings were 668 million SEK, and return on net worth was 21.1 percent (compared to 9.0 percent in 1999). Earnings had improved over those of previous years due to higher net interest rates combined with reduced IT development costs. (See Exhibit 2 for Postgirot Bank's organizational structure.)

Postgirot Bank's Future

Since late 1997, the banking sector had been forced to consolidate due to increasing competition as well as Swedish banks' relatively small size from a European perspective. By 1999, there had already been numerous mergers within financial services, and the Swedish government, the owner of the Postal Service, decided that Postgirot Bank should be sold. A proposal was made to form a jointly owned subsidiary, owned by a consortium of four Swedish banks (Handelsbanken, SEB, Nordbanken, and Föreningssparbanken), with each to hold 25 percent of Postgirot Bank. However, in February 2001, the Swedish Competition Office ruled against this transaction, which would have resulted in a merger of the four banks' "Bankgirot" and Postgirot Bank's competing payment services. Despite this setback, the government's ambition to sell its bank remained active if an acceptable

purchaser could be found. Negotiations with several parties continued, with the possibility that Postgirot Bank could be sold to an overseas financial institution.

Postgirot Bank IT

Swedish banks were leaders in the adoption of IT, with all major Swedish banks offering Internet services. A 1999 IBM and Interbrand survey found that three of the top four banks featuring transactions via the Internet were Swedish.[8] To be a strong competitor, Postgirot Bank had successfully made information processing a primary aspect of its business.

Postgirot Bank had been processing electronic payment transfers for 25 years. The bank's vision was to operate a completely paperless system (i.e., without microfilm/fiche), and by 2000, it was well on its way to achieving that goal. Imaging technology had advanced to the point where nearly all post-data-entry processing was paperless and users were supported with Internet and other electronic access services.[9] In June 2001, 14,000 accounts accessed statement information via the Web, setting a growth rate record for a new Postgirot Bank service. (See Exhibit 3 for details on Postgirot Bank operations.)

In the late 1990s, Postgirot Bank managed its technology needs within a traditional line organization. Projects were run within a departmental structure in which the organization viewed itself as a series of "decentralized and goal-oriented units." Operating responsibilities were expected to be clearly defined to facilitate high productivity levels. All systems (OS/390, Unix, and NT) processed transactions, images, and data archives with "the extensive discipline and total security

---

[8] The Economist Intelligence Unit, *Country Profile 2001: Sweden.*

[9] In 2000, Sweden was one of the most advanced countries worldwide in terms of its telecommunications and Internet infrastructure and usage. According to a 1999 IDC survey, nearly 73 percent of all Swedes had access to a mobile phone, while almost half of all Swedes age 16 to 84 had access to the Internet at home.

---

[7] In June 2001, 1 U.S. dollar (US$) was equivalent to 10.85 Swedish crowns (SEK).

EXHIBIT 2
Postgirot Bank's Organizational Structure

Source: Postgirot Bank.

Postgirot Bank operated as four business units:

- *Corporations* was responsible for relationships with other banks, larger businesses, and international business, as well as county, regional, and national governments.
- *Private and Small Business* was responsible for Postgirot Bank's relationship with private individuals, small businesses, nonprofit organizations, and the bank's branch offices.
- *Postgirot Bank Direct* was a telephone-based customer service established in 1999.
- *Finance* was responsible for short- and long-term investments as well as for foreign currency.

POSTGIROT BANK AB

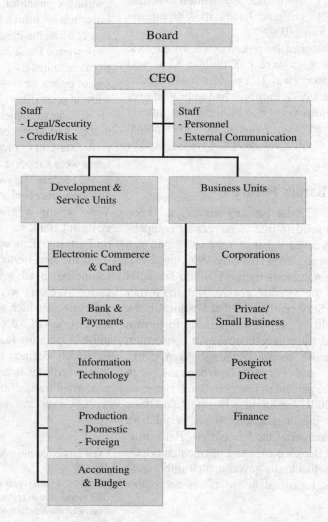

- Board
- CEO
- Staff
  - Legal/Security
  - Credit/Risk
- Staff
  - Personnel
  - External Communication
- Development & Service Units
  - Electronic Commerce & Card
  - Bank & Payments
  - Information Technology
  - Production
    - Domestic
    - Foreign
  - Accounting & Budget
- Business Units
  - Corporations
  - Private/ Small Business
  - Postgirot Direct
  - Finance

EXHIBIT 3   Postgirot Bank Operations

Source: Postgirot Bank.

Banking Operations

- The bank has been processing electronic payment transfers for 25 years.
- An average of 35 million payment transactions per month move some 25 billion SEK per day.
- All payment transactions were completed within 24 hours, including confirmation to the customer.
- Transactions were allowed to "meet"; that is, transactions were processed through an account if starting balance plus incoming transactions covered withdrawals for the same day.
- At the end of June 2001, "ePostgirot" (Internet banking) had approximately 155,000 accounts, of which 120,000 were for private individuals.

Paperless System

- Immediately upon receipt, payment vouchers were scanned. Each voucher's numeric value was automatically read (OCR and ICR), and every image was stored electronically for direct access by the bank and by its customers.
- Images collected for each account and payment were presented (printed or electronically accessed) with statements. This provided the customer with a full audit trail as well as access to any notations on the voucher.
- Electronic transfers (mostly to companies) reduced the need to print and deliver statements for manual processing.
- Image processing and storage were very reliable and had been approved by the Swedish Bank Inspection (Sweden's bank regulator) as the sole vehicle for archiving payment vouchers.
- Electronic archiving was fully implemented, with customer service and Postgirot Bank's accounting relying fully on stored images. Printed paper production was outsourced and decreased as customers used electronic statements.
- Customer Web access was introduced in October 2000.
- Account accessing statement information via the Web reached 14,000 accounts in June 2001. This set a new record of growth for any new Postgirot Bank service.
- By June 2001, 60 percent of payment vouchers (payment instructions drawn against the customer's account) were paper, while 40 percent were electronic.
- Core systems processed the monthly and year-end peak volumes that were up to four times higher than daily averages.
- Plans were in place to extend archiving to cover the legal requirement of 10-year record retention; this was expected to dramatically increase storage requirements. Customers will be able to access even the oldest records (transaction details and images) in a maximum of 15 to 20 seconds.

Pages Archived

Document Type	Pages per Year (millions)
Account statements	2
Payment voucher images	258
Internal accounting	440
Total	700

required for such a large organization." The bank's IT charter was to:

> Provide effective IT solutions that support Postgirot Bank's services in conformity with a negotiated service level. This requires focus on delivering IT services on time, within budget, and with the content that client organizations require now and in the future.

The IT organization's major responsibility was to provide IT production, development, and/or acquisition as well as maintenance of information systems. At the end of 2000, its 400 employees (740 million SEK budget in 2000) became focused on an additional task: Preparing for the changes a sale of Postgirot Bank would bring. The organizational structure was being streamlined with the thought that a potential purchaser could economically integrate the unit into its own IT resources.

Special attention had been paid to managing IT services, as Postgirot Bank line operating units assigned "system owners" to each major application. The system owners consisted of a high-level business-side manager[10] and a technically focused IT manager. These system owners managed daily and long-term operational and design/development tasks. The business-side manager chaired regularly scheduled meetings of development, systems support, operations, and user department staff. This network of individuals dealt with all issues to assure that an application or group of applications effectively supported business objectives in the short term and the long term. Postgirot Bank felt that this model provided a formalized, goal-oriented system for the planning and delivery of IT services.

IT-Operations

IT-Operations was a unit of the bank's IT organization (see Exhibit 4). Its major task was the development and support of production platforms

and their accompanying system and application programs for Postgirot Bank and a few external customers. Production commitments were defined by service-level agreements (SLAs) negotiated between IT and its user department partners. IT-Operations' charter was to:

> Provide cost-effective, high-quality IT services in support of Postgirot Bank's business.

IT-Operations combined its technical expertise with sophisticated technology to successfully meet the bank customers' evolving needs. The center supported 35 million payment transactions per month, moving on average 25 billion SEK per day. Core systems processed predictable monthly and year-end activity peaks that were up to four times higher than daily average volumes. All payment transactions were completed in 24 hours, including confirmation to the customer (excluding mail delivery time for customers who were not getting confirmations electronically). (See Exhibit 5 for IT-Operations systems infrastructure.)

As with the other IT units, IT-Operations' 158 employees (275 million SEK budget in 2000) became focused on preparing for a potential acquisition of the bank. Service cost projections and evaluations were under review so that an accurate picture of the department's costs, performance, and reliability could be shown to a new owner. Everyone was aware that a move to outsourcing was always a possibility after a sale, and so there was strong motivation to demonstrate IT-Operations' cost-effective and high-quality service performance.

In 1995, Postgirot Bank had decided to centralize its Unix server operations to provide more professional, reliable, and cost-effective service. This was physically realized in the winter of 1998 as the Bank's IT-Operations center was moved to an underground granite chamber so secure that it could withstand a direct hit from an atomic bomb. Then, in 1999, ownership and management of hardware and software of Unix servers was transferred to IT-Operations to address long-standing concerns about system management and utilization. Numerous servers had been added over the years as a result of inherent business growth and

---

[10] In cases of applications or services that supported two or more business functions (e.g., a database) a single business-side owner was still assigned. That owner would consult other business units but was alone in being ultimately responsible for final decisions, since it was believed that "sharing of decision making" led to poorer results in the long run.

EXHIBIT 4
Postgirot Bank
IT
Organization
Chart

Source: Postgirot
Bank.

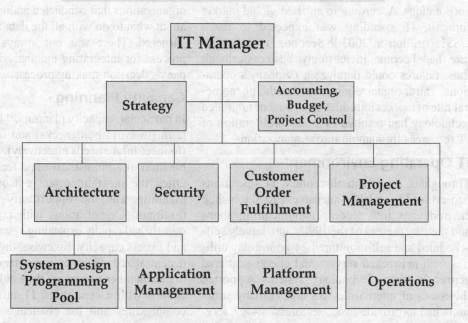

Postgirot Bank – IT Services

because of the previously decentralized IT structure. Historically, business units would have a server installed to meet their individual needs. Once these independent servers were brought together in the centralization process and evaluated, it became apparent that many servers were significantly underutilized. This prompted Roland to seek a system to objectively measure and evaluate his Unix IT resources.

The Need for an IT Measurement System

Three trends that were converging at the end of 2000 drove the need for many organizations to gain access to information regarding their IT operations' efficiency and cost. First, there was the overall size and increasing growth rate of IT budgets. By 1998,

EXHIBIT 5 **IT-Operations Systems Infrastructure**

Source: Postgirot Bank.

Unix Environment

- 68 installed Unix servers, mostly SUN and HP machines of various sizes.
- Storage capacity was 2.4 terabytes.

OS/390 Environment

- One Hitachi P68 (640 MIPS) and one IBM R65 (301 MIPS).
- Storage capacity was 15 terabytes, supplemented by two Powderhorn Robot archives for 5,500 (Timberline-9840) cassettes.
- The OS/390 mainframes hosted internal and external accounting systems. The chart of accounts was closely integrated with much of the bank's IT processing and structures reporting.

companies and consumers were spending US$1.0 trillion a year on IT, almost 80 percent of it from corporations. According to an IBM global market forecast, IT spending was expected to reach US$1.7 trillion in 2003.[11] Second, IT infrastructure had become increasingly business-critical; thus, failures could paralyze a company's operations. Third, organizations saw that the phenomenal rate of market introduction of new or upgraded technology had resulted in a vast proliferation of IT resources throughout most organizations.

IT Operating Environment

Throughout the twentieth century, IT operations had evolved from labor-intensive, batch, job-shop environments into process-manufacturing shops and then, by the end of the 1990s, into largely self-scheduled and self-monitored 24-hour-a-day utilities with networked servers and clients scattered across the firm. Technology systems supported thousands of internal devices and in many situations had to provide fast, "seamless" 24×7 service[12] to customers and suppliers around the globe. IT organizations needed to devote resources to both ongoing operations (running networks, scheduling equipment usage, etc.) and new application development. There was no such thing as a standard IT operations management control system or an ideal measurement of performance. IT management faced the challenge of balancing quality of service, response time of online systems, the ability to handle unexpected jobs and costs easily, installation and upgrades of hardware and software, and the ability to meet schedules on batch systems that varied from one organization to another.[13]

Meeting these challenges within the continuously evolving IT environment required a high level of skill. The monitoring processes that existed were complex and time-consuming, and organizations that conducted audits were uncertain about what to do with all the data and information garnered. There was not always an established process for integrating the analysis into the company's decision-making process.

Capacity Planning

In particular, capacity planning,[14] both in the short term (to avoid bottlenecks) and in the long term (to meet future needs effectively), required a combination of administrative and technical thinking. Often the most important outcome of capacity planning was the opportunity to consolidate machines. Organizations with rapid growth frequently had rapidly expanding systems departments and excess capacity. Likewise, organizations with decentralized IT operations tended to have a higher number of servers than did similar organizations with a centralized IT infrastructure. The complexities and the challenge of both understanding a system's capacity and utilization patterns and formulating a realistic consolidation plan (i.e., a rationalization plan) added up to a task that few organizations were inclined to undertake.

Roland and Torsten agreed that capacity planning needed to take into consideration a number of factors, including the following:

- Determination of how much excess capacity to build into the systems.
- Understanding of the size and frequency of usage peaks.
- Identification of potential bottlenecks.
- Consideration of the diversity and proliferation of hardware and software applications across the organization.
- Assessment of the skill level of the technical staff and its ability to conduct the analysis.
- Design of appropriate infrastructure backup (e.g., redundant applications).

---

[11] Standard & Poor's Industry Surveys, *Computers: Hardware,* May 10, 2001.

[12] Service available twenty-four hours a day, seven days a week.

[13] Lynda M. Applegate, F. Warren McFarlan, and James L. McKenney, *Corporate Information Systems Management: The Challenges of Managing in an Information Age,* 5th ed. (Boston: Irwin/McGraw-Hill, 1999), pp. 222–223.

[14] Capacity planning is the process of determining the economically suitable size and number of computer systems in an installation.

TABLE 1   **Machine Comparison Based on RU**

Source: Provment AB.

Model/Platform	CPU	Internal Memory	Disk Space	RU Capacity
Sun Enterprise 420R	4 × UltraSPARC-II 450 MHz	2 GB	20 GB	129
Sun Ultra 5	1 × UltraSPARC 33 MHz	64 MB	8 GB	24

See the Technical Appendix, Part A, for a discussion of Torsten's view of capacity planning theory.

Postgirot Bank's issues were similar to those of many organizations: IT-Operations had to balance bank-mandated functions and new implementations; increasingly, the bank was operating in the complex and technology-dependent Internet environment, and its IT-Operations infrastructure had grown significantly over the years. By 2000, there was a deepened need, as with any other "factory" or production facility, to gain control and proactively manage resources and costs.

Simultaneously, Torsten had concluded that there were significant "inadequacies within existing analytical tools," especially given the challenges of capacity planning and the growing size and complexity of IT operations. As a result he saw the need for a new, comprehensive, and usable IT measurement methodology.

Provment's Resource Unit

A key aspect of Provment's IM-System was that it related IT capacity and utilization to actual cost numbers. In implementing his theory, Torsten was faced with the challenge of finding a measurement unit that would support uniform and understandable analyses across various system configurations. Taking into consideration the strengths and weaknesses of standard measurement units, Provment developed a comprehensive measurement unit: The resource unit (RU). A set of complex calculations balanced four dimensions traditionally used for measuring a server: Central processing unit (CPU) performance, internal memory, input/output (I/O) capacity, and disk storage

capacity. RU values were calculated by a software program (collector agent) that resided on each production server (see Table 1).

Since the RU had a "standard" value, it made it possible to compare the capacity, utilization rates, and cost of computing across servers, operating systems, or applications. (See the Technical Appendix, Part B, for further details.)

IM-System within the Bank's Unix Environment

For some time, Postgirot Bank had been using IM-System to manage its OS/390 mainframe resources. By the end of 2000, the latest version of the program supported AS/400, Unix, and NT/Win2000 platforms and included expanded reporting functionality. Torsten proposed that Roland use this latest version within his Unix environment.

Postgirot Bank's Unix Systems

The bank's Unix shop was typical of formerly decentralized IT operations which had experienced uncontrolled growth. (See Exhibit 6 for an inventory of Unix hardware.) In 2000, the bank had 68 Unix servers in two locations.[15] There was no formalized management and control structure but instead a culture of "speed and efficiency" within which the Unix operation had evolved over time. The young Unix staff (compared with the bank's older, more experienced OS/390 staff, who would

---

[15] There were 48 servers in Stockholm and 20 at a bank-owned data center in Alingsås, a four-hour drive southwest of Stockholm.

EXHIBIT 6
Inventory of Unix Hardware, March 2001

Source: Postgirot Bank.

Purchase Year	Number of Machines	Purchase Cost (SEK)	Book Value (SEK)
1997	3	3,000,000	600,000
1998	4	1,400,000	500,000
1999	16	7,400,000	4,200,000
2000	37	13,500,000	11,100,000
January–March 2001	8	4,900,000	4,700,000
Total	68	30,200,000	21,100,000

hardly have accepted the brisk pace and less orderly work situation of the Unix group) was a team of "fast-on-their-feet" professionals who installed hardware and software at a breathtaking pace. The problems this style generated were met with fast and effective solutions, but development of orderly resource control and planning had been neglected even as the need for control had increased with each additional machine or application. While Roland saw the need to bring this inherited Unix operation back under control (in line with his mainframe shop), there was little or no support for deferring new installations while he introduced a nonessential system.

From Torsten's perspective, this lack of control was often found in installations that subscribed to the popular idea that "small" computers were "cheap":

> There are many Unix and NT shops [compared with OS/390] where most purchasing decisions involve money amounts typically authorized far down in the organization, without careful review by top management and without the formalities of capital budgeting. While individual purchases may have less financial impact than OS/390 did historically, their accumulated cost and impact on the business can often be greater.

Preliminary estimates showed that the average total cost for a single Postgirot Bank Unix machine was 240,000 SEK per year. While the bank did not know precisely what the percentage CPU utilization of its Unix servers was, it was believed to be quite low. Traditionally, IT-Operations built in a "safety margin" when designing and managing infrastructure. This ensured that it could meet the daily and long-term IT needs of

the company. Over time, safety margins could be narrowed. (As IT departments gained experience in running their operations and clarified the IT requirements to support the company's business operations, they were better able to estimate IT needs.)

In conducting its own preliminary utilization review, IT-Operations managers felt that with a narrowing of the safety margin and the results of the centralization of operations, they could eliminate 10 Unix servers. While this preliminary calculation was relatively simple to conduct, managers understood that the implementation of such a consolidation was highly complex, requiring the "merging" of various applications and processes onto single machines. In addition to eliminating machines, they expected to cut labor costs through reduced hiring coupled with natural attrition. These reductions translated into a one-time estimated savings of 2.4 million SEK, or about 1 percent of the total IT-Operations budget (see Exhibit 7).

EXHIBIT 7 **Annual IT Operating Costs, December 2000 (SEK thousands)**

Source: Postgirot Bank.

	Total Annual Costs	OS/390 Costs
Hardware	46,000	24,092
System programs	101,400	66,028
Staff	94,900	38,171
Office costs	1,800	1,420
Other	31,000	10,548
Total	275,100	140,259

While Roland was excited about the possible cost savings, he saw a project that required Postgirot Bank IT staff to install the system. Also, while Torsten's concept sounded straightforward, he believed special skills, as well as particular experience and personalities, were essential to its success. A decision was hard to make until the day Torsten asked Roland a "heart-to-heart question" over lunch: Why, in the face of big savings and improved control, was it taking him (like several other Swedish customers) so long to reach a decision? Roland's answer came quickly and was simple: Neither he nor other managers could think of putting a "housekeeping" effort ahead of their daily service delivery obligations, and pulling staff off the implementation of new applications simply would not be accepted.

This was not the first time Torsten had heard this comment from a prospective client. The challenge Roland and other IT managers faced was accepting and managing short-term diminished efficiency in order to "take the time" to install a system which could potentially increase the unit's long-term effectiveness. As Roland explained to Torsten:

> We just can't do it ourselves within a reasonable time frame. We are obligated to use core skills and our best people for bank-mandated tasks. It makes good sense to buy a service like Provment's management system, and it wouldn't be cost-effective to build skills internally for such a specialized task. I'd like you to lift us over this threshold.

This conversation highlighted the challenge Torsten faced in positioning his product in the marketplace. He had developed software to fulfill a need for data center management information because there was no other way to get the information. In the process, however, he had shifted to a business model of selling a software package. Although the package was easy to install, the system required special skills and substantial effort to implement. Additionally, Provment was at the early stage of product introduction, and thus the benefits had not been widely proved in the Unix or NT marketplace. With this new insight, Provment revisited its business plan and shifted its strategy to providing a turnkey service, taking on the role of installing the system at customer sites. It also shifted its focus to gaining a number of successful reference customers to help build market acceptance.

Roland's Unix Decision

In addressing Roland's concerns, Torsten and Roland sketched steps for moving ahead and expanding IM-System to the Unix servers. The same day, Roland outlined what he saw as essential requirements for the success of a Unix resource management system project:

- System security should not be compromised.
- System access should be controlled.
- The system should not disrupt current operations.
- IT-Operations staff should be burdened as little as possible.
- The tool should be in operation quickly.
- The installation project should include a study and a plan for immediate consolidation.

This preliminary list was not a formal document. However, given Roland and Torsten's long consulting relationship and the Swedish business culture, this was a "handshake" agreement that initiated the next negotiating steps. Meeting with Roland over the subsequent few weeks, Torsten responded to the issues as follows:

System security. IM-System was set up as an internal system designed to work entirely within an organization's intranet. IM-System "collector agents" were installed on all servers and mainframes running in an IT operation, and they continually checked that the data collected were reasonable and in the correct format. The collector agent would deactivate itself immediately if variations or serious exceptions were discovered. Secure file transfer protocol (FTP) moved files from the collector agents to IM-System's central server. All data transfers were simple files, not programs or program modules, so that no program could be installed remotely. A customer ID on each agent prevented data from being transferred to a computer other than the customer's own central server.

System access. Access to IM-System was controlled by a system administrator who added or removed authorizations for individual users. Each user ID was associated with an access profile which determined the objects and parts of the system a user was allowed to access. The profile also determined the language used for information presentation. (See Exhibit 8 for IM-System installation requirements.)

Operations disruption. Provment assured Postgirot Bank that the Unix server "collector agents" had never caused crashes but in the worst case could easily be deactivated. The agents consumed less than 0.5 percent of the CPU, negligible internal memory, and only modest disk space. Data transmitted over the network would be negligible.

Staffing resources. To extend the management system with minimal effort from Roland's side, it was agreed that Provment staff would handle the bulk of the hands-on implementation and that the equivalent of only two weeks of one IT-Operations staff person's time would be needed.

Time frame. The installation would be completed in 60 days. (Two additional months would be required to accumulate enough data to begin useful decision-making analysis.)

Cost and consolidation plan. Costs for installation and the first year of operation (at a discounted "internal" cost) would equate to the approximate cost of four Unix servers. (Thus, if

---

EXHIBIT 8   **IM-System Installation Requirements**

Source: Provment AB.

Central IM-Server

- A PC with a Linux-compatible CPU.
- Disk requirements: Data and statistical files 400 to 20,000 Kb per day and per agent machine, depending on agent machine size. Minimum consumption is approximately 15 Kb (reduced functionality) per day. Detailed system operational data are saved from a minimum of 34 days (approximately 13 to 680 Mb total per agent machine) to a maximum of 99 days ($\approx$ 40 to 2,000 Mb total per agent machine).

Unix and NT Servers Running IM-System Agents

- Disk requirements: Data and statistical files 400 to 20,000 Kb per day depending on agent machine size. Minimum consumption is approximately 15 Kb (reduced functionality) per day. A medium-size Unix machine is estimated to need approximately 15 Mb of storage for the Provment statistical data (process data are stored for only 5 days on the agent machine).

Memory Requirements (Virtual Memory)

- 12 to 200 Kb depending on Unix operating system and version.
- Approximately 3,000 Kb, depending on NT version.

Miscellaneous Requirements

- At midnight every day cleanup, data consolidation, and data transfer are initialized. These processes require 10 to 200 Kb of virtual memory, depending on Unix system.
- The impact of file transfers on the Provment Web server and the network is minimized by randomly spreading transfers over a 1½-hour time frame.
- Agent collector processes consume less than 1 CPU minute per continuous month of operation, and CPU consumption is always less than 0.5%.

Postgirot Bank was able to eliminate four Unix servers, the system would "pay for itself.")

Torsten submitted a more formal proposal to Postgirot Bank at the end of January 2001.

In addition to installing the system, Provment staff played an internal marketing role. They worked with the bank's IT-Operations and business staff to educate them on the benefits the system would bring to IT-Operations, the business units, and the bank overall. Torsten and his team felt several skills were needed for the task at hand:

> The skills we needed included (1) technical skills; Provment's team would convince operating staff that the new system would not disrupt ongoing operations as well as provide assistance in working with their "customers"; (2) economic skills to help accounting and business analysts focus on the right numbers and convince technicians of the validity of results produced by the RU approach; and (3) management skills to help IT managers realize the potential from better communication with business unit managers as well as to assist senior managers in regaining a place in the most essential aspects of high-level IT decision making.

Unix Project Results

In early 2001, the appropriate IM-System programs were installed by IT-Operations on each Unix machine to identify and collect operational data. Information contained in Postgirot Bank's accounting system was also extracted and collected on the central server and made accessible to interested parties via the corporate intranet. A summary of the bank's data was transferred monthly to Provment to be merged and compared with similar information collected from other organizations.[16] Consolidated benchmarking data (i.e., summaries of anonymous data from similar

---

[16] Data needed to be accumulated for two to three months before reports could be meaningful. As with OS/390 and AS/400, data were to be collected and grouped according to industry and type of installation to disguise the source of the data and then returned as industry comparison values to subscriber companies. This would soon facilitate ongoing benchmarking against comparable companies.

organizations) would be available at Provment for automatic collection by the 12th of each month. Thus, Postgirot Bank's central server itself would contain the necessary data that could be presented in relevant reports for all levels of bank management that would allow Postgirot Bank to compare itself to others.

By June 2001, IM-System was running on all 48 Unix servers at Postgirot Bank's Stockholm center. Immediately, Roland was pleased with the implementation of Provment's IM-System within his Unix environment. While everyone had anticipated that the recently inherited servers would be underutilized, many managers in the bank were surprised at some of the details. The first series of reports showed that average actual load across the 48 Unix servers was less than 10 percent during the prime shift and that theoretically (with appropriate safety margins) 40 servers could be decommissioned (see Exhibit 9). Torsten summarized:

> While a reduction of, say, 15 to 20 machines was thought more likely, it was clear that the initial cost justification for installing IM-System (i.e., 4 machines) was within easy reach. This will leave ample opportunity for continued usage growth without adding machines or for further consolidations and associated cost savings.

The consolidation of machines was expected to net Postgirot Bank 5 million SEK by the end of 2001 and 14 million SEK annually (over 5 percent of Roland's budget) thereafter. It was essential that managers and technicians "accept" these numbers. To do this, they needed either a rudimentary understanding of the concepts described in the Technical Appendix or, more often, faith in the technicians who told them, "These values are correct and thus useful for analysis." Correspondingly, technicians needed assurance from managers that these were the numbers they should produce for decision making—the numbers managers would understand.

Additionally, analysis of the new data showed that each Unix server had an average annual operating cost of 850,000 SEK. This was more than triple the previous December's high-end cost estimate of 240,000 SEK (see Table 2).

EXHIBIT 9 **Postgirot Resource Comparisons, Using RU**

Source: Provment AB.

Unix Servers by Machine Size

RU Capacity Range	Number of Servers within RU Range	Monthly Server Cost (SEK)	Server Cost (% Total)	Total Installed RUs	Total Utilized RUs	Percent RU Utilization	Cost per Installed RU (SEK)	Cost per Utilized RU (SEK)
0–49	28	1,759,000	62	571	32	6	3,081	54,969
50–99	11	829,000	29	584	30	5	1,420	27,633
100–149	4	265,000	9	517	95	18	513	2,789
Total / Average	**43**	**2,853,000**	**100%**	**1,672**	**157**	**9%**	**1,706**	**18,172**

Note: The total cost for servers with less than 50-RU capacity is more than six times greater than the total cost for servers with more than 100-RU capacity. Because the small servers are less heavily utilized, their effective cost is about 20 times as great.

Unix Servers by Operating System / Version

Operating System (Dialect)	Monthly Server Cost (SEK)	Server Cost (% Total)	Total Installed RUs	Total Utilized RUs	Percent RU Utilization	Cost per Installed RU (SEK)	Cost per Utilized RU (SEK)
Operating system A	10,000	0	33	0	0	303	NA
Operating system B	1,238,000	43	565	68	12	2,191	18,206
Operating system C	805,000	28	246	9	4	3,272	89,444
Total / Average	**2,853,000**	**100%**	**1,672**	**157**	**9%**	**1,706**	**18,172**

Note: This example shows operating system C's server costs (cost/installed RU) to be almost 1.5 times as great as those for operating system B. Because operating system C servers are less heavily utilized, their effective cost is almost 5 times as great.

Unix Servers by Usage Group

Usage Group	Monthly Server Cost (SEK)	Server Cost (% Total)	Total Installed RUs	Total Utilized RUs	Percent RU Utilization	Cost per Installed RU (SEK)	Cost per Utilized RU (SEK)
Alpha	156,000	5	126	5	4	1,238	32,000
Bravo	353,000	12	358	20	6	986	17,650
Caesar	598,000	21	468	113	24	1,278	5,292
Delta	219,000	8	98	4	4	2,235	54,750
Total / Average	**2,853,000**	**100%**	**1,672**	**157**	**9%**	**1,706**	**18,172**

Note: The heavily used "Caesar" application is by far the least costly to operate. That is, if applications "Bravo" and "Delta" were comparably effective, their costs could be reduced by factors of 3 and 10, respectively.

Throughout the bank, key user groups received comprehensive reports generated by IM-System corresponding to each manager's role and level of influence on operations and strategy. The reports provided graphical and numerical representation of cost and volume data for machines/applications and were starting to be used as a basis for discussion among IT and financial managers to spot trends, highlight areas of concern, and identify resource needs.

TABLE 2 **Annual Costs for Operating Postgirot Bank's 68 Unix Servers (Estimated in June 2001)**

Source: Postgirot Bank.

Item	Cost (SEK thousands)	Percent of Total Budget
Hardware	15,600	27
System programs	15,100	26
Staff	22,500	39
Office costs	2,300	4
Other	2,300	4
Total	**57,800**	**100%**

A scorecard report highlighted measurement values for each group, showing efficiency and cost data. Consolidated total information was also distributed. (See Exhibit 10 for a sample scorecard report.) Since there was broad distribution of this data across all levels and units within Postgirot Bank, the new process allowed management to participate in decision making in a way that had not previously been possible. Roland felt a foundation was being laid for more productive engagement of unit managers (his customers) and top management which he hoped would support a more productive dialog for managing costs and delivering value.

EXHIBIT 10
Scorecard Report

Source: Provment AB.

The scorecard gives a management level summary of the most pertinent key values. (See Technical Appendix, Part B, for further discussion of the RU values.) This single sheet provides a focused summary of how IT operations are functioning.

```
ScoreCard
Period 01-01 -- 01-06
Preliminary financial values - month 06

                        01-06         LAST MONTH AVERAGE
                                      3        6        9       12

Cost/ RU/CPW            1706         1706     1706
        Trend                        0%       0%       0%       0%

Cost/ RU/CPW used       18172        21113    23775
        Trend                        -15%     -34%     0%       0%


CPU used "peak"         40%          37%      36%      0%       0%
        Trend                        8%       11%      0%       0%

CPU used "average"      9%           8%       7%       0%       0%
        Trend                        13%      25%      0%       0%

Disk used "average"     47%          44%      40%      0%       0%
        Trend                        6%       18%      0%       0%


Inst. RU/CPW:S          1672         1672     1672
        Trend                        0%       0%       0%       0%

Used RU/CPW:s           157          135      120
        Trend                        16%      31%      0%       0%

Cost               2853000     2853000  2853000
        Trend                        0%       0%       0%       0%
```

Note: Cost per RU used has decreased over time because usage level has increased. In addition, CPU used has a "peak" (average across machines) of 40%. It could be concluded that this peak implies that the substantial excess capacity (CPU used average 9%) is justified for production reserve. However, it is quite common for such peaks to be correctly reported but misleading for an analyst or decision maker. The peaks might, for example, be due to heavy backup or database-load batch jobs run at night or at other noncritical hours.

Expanding the System

Even in the short time Provment's IM-System had been running, it confirmed Roland's and Torsten's expectation that the Unix operation had excess capacity and that its growth rate could be harnessed and managed. Thus Roland had to decide if and/or when he should implement IM-System for his NT/Win2000 servers. As a result of the centralization process, all 70 production NT servers (the number as of June 15, 2001) were coming into his IT-Operations, and he would be responsible for rationalizing costs and operations. NT growth had been rapid, and so he expected the same sparse server loads and excess number of machines as had been experienced in the Unix environment. Operating costs were perhaps as high and certainly more complex than for Unix; however, this was based on an educated guess rather than actual measurement. Until 2001, costs for NT operations were spread across many departments (one manager used the term *fragmented*) and were neither uniformly classified nor carefully followed. Thus it was not realistically possible for Roland to obtain complete or accurate cost data until he had full management of the systems.

In addition to the issue of expanding the measurement program, Roland saw another major decision: How to integrate the measurement results into Postgirot Bank's management infrastructure (e.g., ongoing IT operations, budgeting, strategic planning) and into the organization's way of thinking. In January 2001, he had quietly informed top managers and key customers (i.e., business unit managers) of his hopes to use the results from IM-System to further involve them in evaluating IT costs relative to business value. While many of the managers were interested in a process that could save them money, Roland had to convince them that an investment of their time was critical in ensuring the program's success.

There was discussion within Postgirot Bank of establishing an internal organization to integrate new IM-System information into corporatewide management processes. Postgirot Bank had begun thinking about the manager and the appropriate reporting relationship for this new unit. Possibilities included the IT-Operations manager (Roland), the IT manager, the controller, the chief financial officer (CFO), or one of the business unit managers. Regardless of the reporting structure, there was a major effort ahead to further sell the concept across the organization and to realize the full potential of a new IT measurement tool.

Technical Appendix, Part A

Capacity Planning and Baseline Theory

This white paper material was derived from an interview with Torsten Wenell, founder of Provment AB.

Vast numbers of computers have been installed due to increasing use of client-server and Web-based applications. As more new systems are installed and as older systems mature and become increasingly essential to the operation of a business, the need increases for planning and control. This leads to a greater need for practical tools to help managers improve utilization of IT production resources.

It is not unusual to find situations where the number of installed machines has gotten out of control and large financial gains can be achieved through a consolidation effort. The number and to some degree the size of machines can be key cost drivers, and so it is important to understand what determines the number of machines. In Unix and NT shops, the number of computers is largely determined by the number of user applications, not least because people seem to agree it is easiest and safest to run (or develop or test) a single application on one machine. But when cost and rationalized operation are considered, filling up machines starts to make sense. Because there can be technical reasons against running different applications on the same machine, an awareness of potential problems with cohabitation of applications is central to any hardware consolidation effort.

Yet with the press of meeting daily obligations, most IT operations seem never to have enough time to stop and think clearly about machine utilization levels, let alone take concrete steps toward rationalizing and balancing machine capacity. It is almost as if organizations collectively believed it is easier to spend extra dollars on comfortable safety margins to meet future growth. But also the complexities and challenge of understanding load and utilization patterns, as well as formulating a realistic consolidation (rationalization) plan, make it too easy to put the task off to another day, quarter, or year. Another reason to put off this inherently difficult task is the need to predict the impact consolidation would have on operations. Typically, such an assessment is conducted by using simulation, but these techniques can be very complex and it can take months to collect the necessary information. Managing the growth of server installations requires capacity planning that extends beyond daily and monthly monitoring. Provment's IM-System was designed to address these issues by making a consolidation proposal more practical.

Baseline Theory

A *single measure* is needed to weigh and integrate the relevant utilization of operating components into a simple, usable unit for analysis, discussion, and decision making. Such a measure must describe both average and peak usage levels. Provment developed its baseline theory to do this. A baseline is the capacity level which, on a machine-by-machine basis, will give an acceptable number of peaks while optimizing machine

size and subsequent costs. Thus, baseline theory is a tool managers use to determine which application should be processed at peak times and what safety margins are needed to meet quality and service-level requirements.

Baseline takes into account that peak times occur differently for various applications, customers/users, and equipment. (For example, an OS/390 CPU is partitioned into multiple logical sections in which every section can utilize available machine capacity for other applications. Thus, total peak usage can continually exceed more than 100 percent of designed maximum capacity.) To obtain correct machine dimensions for any operating system, it is essential that:

- Utilization of every component (CPU, internal memory, etc.) be balanced in such a way that desired performance is achieved without bottlenecks that impact other components.
- Components needed for peaks be considered.
- Components needed for servicing longer time periods be considered.

Figure A1 shows a sample overview screen generated by applying baseline theory to consolidate servers. The chart depicts a family of machines ranked by machine size (RU capacity) and usage level. From this overview, a user can drill down to analyze internal processes (e.g., programs, operating system components).

The need for quick response times can require fast components even when modest capacity is sufficient, or alternatively, a requirement to process large transaction volumes can demand large capacity even if the speed of individual components is not as important. For this reason, you might find a situation where a fast processor with limited capacity might better meet service requirements than a number of slower processors with greater total capacity (or vice versa).

Consolidation Process

There are many reasons to keep applications running on separate machines. For example, budgeting issues, special reliability or utilization

FIGURE A1   Server Consolidation Overview Screen

Source: Provment AB.

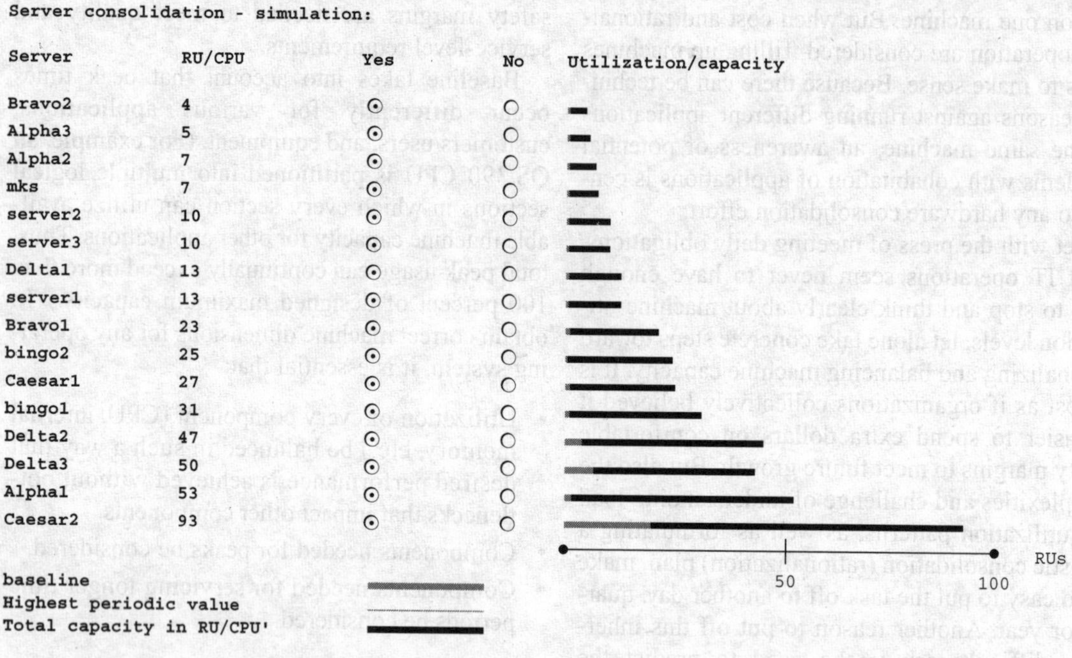

```
Server consolidation - simulation:
```

Server	RU/CPU	Yes	No	Utilization/capacity
Bravo2	4	⊙	○	
Alpha3	5	⊙	○	
Alpha2	7	⊙	○	
mks	7	⊙	○	
server2	10	⊙	○	
server3	10	⊙	○	
Delta1	13	⊙	○	
server1	13	⊙	○	
Bravo1	23	⊙	○	
bingo2	25	⊙	○	
Caesar1	27	⊙	○	
bingo1	31	⊙	○	
Delta2	47	⊙	○	
Delta3	50	⊙	○	
Alpha1	53	⊙	○	
Caesar2	93	⊙	○	

```
baseline
Highest periodic value
Total capacity in RU/CPU'
```

RUs   50   100

requirements (system must be 100 percent available or an application must not disturb other users with crashes or heavy load), or firewall structure and other security limitations should be taken into account. In addition, the application software may require a certain version of an operating system (application "Caesar" won't run on "server xxx" because the software is not yet upgraded to accommodate the more recent operating system version).[17] But in many situations a consolidation of servers is practical and sound.

From the Overview screen, clicking on the Server Consolidation-Simulation button produces a consolidation proposal (as shown in Figure A2).

This chart depicts the capacity of the machines to be eliminated and the capacity and projected load, allowing for peaks, on the (simulated) consolidated machine. IM-System generates a scenario like this for each operating system version or dialect. The algorithm starts with the smallest machines and collects them onto larger servers as long as (projected) capacity is available. Machines marked with "No" are bypassed.

The simplicity of this presentation (and cleaner underlying processes) can help an IT manager understand and participate. The manager is then in a position to add his or her point of view about tactics and strategy and to pave the way for consideration by top management. Because the consolidation proposal is a straightforward single page, it can be useful in keeping top management (or the customer in a purchased-service situation) apprised of progress during the consolidation effort. From here, a study by technical staff must be made to confirm the detailed feasibility of each consolidation proposal. (For example, does the

[17] In fact, analysis shows this logic is surprisingly expensive because it leads to proliferation of operating system versions within a data center and heavy associated maintenance cost. It is much more effective to have at most two versions of the operating system (the old outgoing and the new incoming) than to focus resources on making the applications conform to the coming operating system versions.

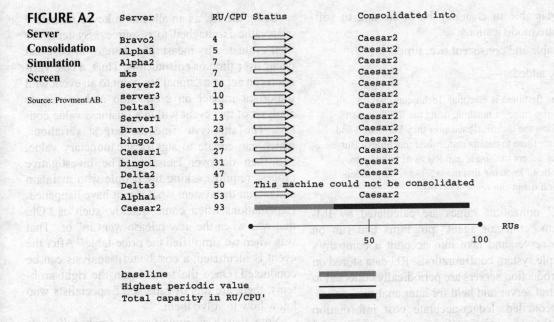

FIGURE A2
Server Consolidation Simulation Screen

Source: Provment AB.

Server	RU/CPU	Status	Consolidated into
Bravo2	4	⇒	Caesar2
Alpha3	5	⇒	Caesar2
Alpha2	7	⇒	Caesar2
mks	7	⇒	Caesar2
server2	10	⇒	Caesar2
server3	10	⇒	Caesar2
Delta1	13	⇒	Caesar2
Server1	13	⇒	Caesar2
Bravo1	23	⇒	Caesar2
bingo2	25	⇒	Caesar2
Caesar1	27	⇒	Caesar2
bingo1	31	⇒	Caesar2
Delta2	47	⇒	Caesar2
Delta3	50	This machine could not be consolidated	
Alpha1	53	⇒	Caesar2
Caesar2	93		Caesar2

RUs

50   100

baseline
Highest periodic value
Total capacity in RU/CPU'

target machine really have enough memory, hard disk, CPUs? Can the applications really coexist?) Once there has been acceptance of an undertaking to reduce the number of servers in an IT shop, a consolidation proposal can be the seed needed to get the process moving. From this beginning, the creative powers of the management/technical specialist team can move forward with a task that in many organizations doesn't ever really get off the ground.

Technical Appendix, Part B

Using RU to Identify and Track Cost Drivers

This white paper material was derived from an interview with Torsten Wenell, founder of Provment AB.

The Resource Unit

Provment has developed a comprehensive measurement unit–the resource unit, or RU–by balancing strengths and weaknesses of standard measurement units (CPU size, internal memory, I/O capacity,[18] and disk storage capacity). The four

hardware dimensions are weighted according to their economic impact to produce a single measurement unit.

Torsten noted that a single unit of measurement had to be:

- Acceptable and useful to both technicians and managers.
- Applicable across various system configurations.
- Easy to interpret using tables and graphs.

[18] I/O capacity is a complex empirical value that is dependent on several factors, including disk transfer speed, bus speed, and operating system.

- Adaptable to changing hardware and to software modifications.
- Stable and consistent over time.

He added:

The first item is essential. Technicians would hardly "tune" a machine using the RU (to tune they follow the technical measures they know well and relate them to details inside their machines). But they accept the single unit RU as a "valid approximation," knowing that managers say they understand it and can relate it to costs.

RU utilization values are calculated by IM-System "collector agent" programs that run on every server and take into account a company's multiple system configurations. RU data stored on the production servers are periodically collected to a central server and held for later analysis.

Reconciled, ledger-accurate cost information from the accounting system resides on the central server as well, where tools are used to present tables and charts showing RU and cost values and any variations that occur. Graphics facilitate the process in that they highlight trends and areas of concern, provide consistent interpretation of data across the organization, and thus enable analysis and discussion. The same formats can be used for varied comparisons such as installed or utilized capacity, total costs, costs per machine type, cost per site (or data center), cost per application, and cost per customer or customer group.

Cost Drivers

Collecting capacity and usage information and relating it to costs are essential, but the key is to focus on the most important factors; that is, the idea is to identify the most important "cost drivers." IT costs traditionally have been driven by factors such as number of computers, users, or transactions. In a "normal" or expected production situation, conventional wisdom says costs should vary in direct proportion to one or more of these factors or "cost drivers," but it isn't usually that simple. Torsten proposes linking RU to cost.

Using the RU as an allocation key, a monetary cost value is attached to resources. Systems are then evaluated by measuring changes in cost that occur over time or episodically. Thus, a cost variation can act as a "signal" to point to an event with important impact on production and to initiate analysis of this event within a business value context. The aim is to find the largest variations, which can equate to significant monetary value, and then discover causality. The investigative process requires asking the people who maintain and/or run the system what might have happened. Explanations often come quickly, such as "Oh, that was when the new release went in" or "That was when we simplified the price-table." After the event is identified, a cost/benefit analysis can be conducted. Once the focus is on the right problems, there are lots of capable IT specialists who know how to solve them.

Note that it is important to track *full* costs which emphasize the long-term economic picture, compared to looking at *marginal* or *variable* costs, which would tend to increase complexity and lead to a less productive discussion of assumptions. But experience has also shown that underlying assumptions are not usually the focus of analysis or questioning. Indeed, the first decimal place of cost-linked RU values usually conveys the important information, not the second, third, or later decimals.

A "signal system" that can be used to monitor cost has special benefit over time. The basic design of a software application and how it is used determine the long-term cost of computer systems, as do the numerous changes inevitably made during the useful life of a software application to meet business needs. Unfortunately, business units paying for IT services seldom have any way of coupling changes to their impact on long-term costs. That is, often no business evaluation of benefits versus cost is made, and incremental changes add up, sometimes resulting in increased operating costs which were never weighed against benefits. As IT costs become an increasingly large proportion of total business costs, it is crucial to hone methods for linking the impact of technical operations changes to costs. In situations where there is a service-charge relationship between the IT operation and a client department or customer, especially where that service charge is used in business decision making, the customer must be assured that cost reports are valid and are based on knowledge of detailed and reconciled cost information. In a long-term customer/supplier relationship, the surest way for the customer to get a lower price is to thoroughly understand the supplier's costs and to adjust requirements and purchases in a way that keeps the supplier's costs down. RU usage information and associated cost driver analysis can enhance that understanding.

To say it all another way, when managers and technicians are able to get a clear picture of cost drivers, they can focus on their most costly problems. (Technicians are equipped with training and excellent tools to study resource-use issues when asked, and they can come up with some very profitable suggestions if they are studying the most costly problems.) A team or task force can focus on identifying application changes that significantly reduce costs while not negatively impacting the business value derived from the application. In Torsten's experience, examples of 10 to 50 percent savings in production costs are not unusual.

Leadership Issues

F. Warren McFarlan

Although leadership of the IT function has changed dramatically in the past two decades, some core issues have persisted. How should IT staff be organized to support business activities? Which IT functions should be performed inside the firm and which should be performed outside? How should we manage IT projects, especially megaprojects that have increased in size beyond anything in our past experience? We have inherited these questions from the past, but the responses have changed.

The chapters and cases in this module provide a basis for discussing these issues in their twenty-first-century form. We adopt a contingency approach intended to identify the factors that differ between organizations, business situations, and projects and to make recommendations appropriate to specific markets, firms, and projects. The overall result of our analysis is a portfolio framework that allows questions and recommendations to be formulated into policies consistent with a company's overall strategic direction. The cases at the end of this module are intended to help readers understand the relationship between business strategy and key organizational and project decisions.

Cathay Pacific: Doing More with Less

Cathay Pacific is a Hong Kong–based airline that, in 1995, moved two-thirds of its IT activities to Sydney, Australia, and then outsourced them to IBM. The case explores the reasons for these moves and permits a discussion of the situation that Cathay Pacific finds itself in, in 2004. The case allows a very rich discussion of contemporary global outsourcing issues.

Royal Caribbean Cruise Lines (RCCL)

The number 2 cruise company in the world, RCCL is a deeply information-enabled organization with a complex series of investment alternatives ahead of it. The case talks about IT planning from the time a new management team came in during the late 1990s through the convulsive period following 9/11 and its aftermath. The case permits a rich discussion of how to best align IT initiatives against corporate priorities in a resource-constrained world.

Rakuten

A 1995 start up, Rakuten is the number 2 portal in Japan. The company, which began as an online shopping mall, has achieved explosive growth and profitability. The key question is: How should executives prioritize investments considering the many opportunities and important cultural constraints in a world where portfolio uses and culture are deeper than that of the United States? This case raises the very special dimensions of IT strategy in a global economy.

Telecomunicacoes de Sao Paulo SA (Telesp)

Telesp was formed in 1998 as a result of privatization of the Brazilian telecommunications industry. Until 2002, the Brazilian government's universal access laws had dictated company strategy as Telesp spent all of its resources laying new lines and meeting service quality standards. In early 2002, the company had met the requirements for providing "universal access" and was free to compete by entering new markets, launching new services, and developing new channels. How should the company target its growth? More importantly, how should the new CEO approach the tough task of redesigning the organization and culture of this "line-laying machine"?

Outsourcing IT: The Global Landscape in 2004

Offshoring of IT has been an explosive issue in the past several years. This note focuses on the extraordinary growth of this activity primarily in India. It is, however, today expanding with great speed to the Philippines, China, and others. This note explores the reasons for this growth and identifies the new global players in this arena.

CHAPTER 8

Organizing and Leading the IT Function

The management structures needed to introduce new technologies into a company are quite different from those needed to maintain older, established technologies. A guiding principle is to encourage the information technology (IT) staff and business users to innovate with newer technologies while simultaneously focusing on control and efficiency of the existing systems. In the early twenty-first century, as we shift into the world of internetworking, technology innovation is probably the more important of these concerns. In this chapter, we discuss the range of alternatives in assigning responsibility and roles to business users, the IT staff, IT suppliers, and general managers in conducting IT activities and formulating IT policy.

Organizational Issues in the Control of IT Activities

Two sets of tensions guide policies for developing, deploying, and managing IT systems. The first set is between innovation and control. The emphasis a firm should place on aggressive innovation depends on a broad assessment of the potential strategic impact of IT on a firm and on management's willingness to take risks. If IT can greatly help a firm achieve its strategic objectives and managers are not too risk-averse, a significantly greater investment in innovation is called for than is the case if IT is considered merely helpful or if managers want to avoid all unnecessary risks. In today's IT environment, the benefits promised by real-time internetworking systems have shifted the emphasis toward more innovation.

As a company selects priorities and enlists resources to pursue its objectives, a second set of tensions may develop between the IT staff and business users. Users often are inclined to focus on short-term need fulfillment, solving today's problems right now, frequently at the expense of long-term IT architectural concerns, maintenance needs, or orderly deployment. The IT department, in contrast, tends to be preoccupied with standardization of solutions, mastery of technology, maintenance difficulties, and orderly deployment at the cost of a slow response, or no response, to legitimate business needs. Balancing the tension between the two groups is difficult and must take

TABLE 8.1 Possible Implications of Excessive IT and User Dominance

IT Dominance	User Dominance
Too much emphasis on database and system maintenance	Too much emphasis on problem focus
All new systems must fit data structure of existing system	IT feels out of control
	Explosive growth in number of new systems and supporting staff
All requests for service require system study with benefit identification	Multiple suppliers deliver services; frequent change in supplier of specific service
Standardization dominates with few exceptions	Lack of standardization and control over data and systems; not enough emphasis on robust infrastructure
IT designs/constructs everything	
Benefits of user control over development are discussed but never implemented	Hard evidence of benefits nonexistent
	Soft evidence of benefits not organized
Study always shows construction costs less than outside purchase	Few measurements/objectives for new system
Headcount of distributed minis and development staff growing surreptitiously	Technical advice of IT not sought; if received, considered irrelevant
IT specializing in technical frontiers, not user-oriented markets	User buying design, construction, maintenance, and operations services from outside
IT spending 80% on maintenance and 20% on development	User building networks to own unique needs, not to corporate need
IT thinks it is in control of everything	Some users growing rapidly in experience and use, while others feel nothing is relevant because they do not understand
Users express unhappiness	
Portfolio of development opportunities firmly under IT control	No coordinated effort between users for technology transfer or learning from experience
No strong user group exists	Growth in duplication of technical staffs
General management is not involved but concerned	Dramatically rising communications costs because of redundancy
	Duplication of effort and input everywhere because different data, hardware, and communications will not allow seamless movement

into account many factors, including corporate culture, IT's potential strategic impacts, and the urgency of short-term problems.

Table 8.1 illustrates the consequences when either the IT staff or business users inappropriately dominate IT resource allocation and project priorities. Very different application portfolios and operating problems emerge in the two circumstances. Because it is difficult to anticipate the implications of the introduction of new technology, neither the IT perspective nor the user perspective is more correct. Decisions about the proper balance between innovation and stability and the degree of IT or user control of priorities and resources are highly contingent on the business situation. In particular, when rapid innovation is required, managers must be sure that rigid policies do not interfere with experimentation and learning. As the following four examples demonstrate, there is no perfect prescription for successful IT innovation.

1. From Centralized, IT-Driven Innovation to Decentralized, User-Driven Innovation

Over a four-year period in the early 1990s, a major textile company invested heavily in new systems for electronic commerce and order management. By executing a few very large, centrally managed projects, the company's IT department assured adherence to companywide standards for software, computing platforms, and communications. The new systems were considered a success by all involved. In 1998, however, management moved systems development activity from the central IT department to the divisions, a change that involved some 80 people. The goal was to align the development of new applications more quickly and effectively with the needs of senior divisional management. With IT standardization problems largely solved, the company was able to install a new organizational structure that enabled the divisions to innovate more rapidly around individual agendas. The results since the reorganization suggest that it has been extremely effective. In addition, IT standards have not yet been eroded, and the company's intranet and extranet activities have been a great success.

2. User-Driven Innovation over IT Department Protests

The number one priority in a large machine-tool manufacturer's engineering department was implementing computer-aided design (CAD). Early success led the company to expand the CAD system scope significantly: Engineers modified the digital output from the system so that department personnel could feed it directly to computer-driven machine tools. To maximize the speed of deployment, engineers deliberately kept the project separate from concurrent work by the IT department on a related bill of material system. Although the CAD project was a major success, integration into the bill of material system remained an outstanding requirement.

Because it was short-staffed, the IT department delayed the integration with the bill of material system. Emboldened by their success with the CAD system, the engineers proceeded with the integration on their own over the objections of IT management. IT managers feared that the engineers would not adhere to standards and, consequently, major operational problems would result. Nevertheless, because of the project's potential to immediately affect the company's product development life cycle, the engineering department received full support from senior management.

The enthusiastic engineers made the project work: The project slashed new product development time by half. The IT department remained decidedly unenthusiastic throughout the project. Although some integration issues remained after completion, the project was judged a great success.

3. From Decentralized, User-Driven Innovation to Centralized IT Management

A division of a large consumer products company made a substantial investment in desktop services with modest up-front cost justification. Even though it had only cursory direction and training, the IT department encouraged managers and administrative support personnel to "use" desktop systems. In the first year a number of uncoordinated projects emerged within the user community, including several sales force support applications and a number of spreadsheet applications. Users gained confidence and pursued new programs with enthusiasm.

Six months later the IT department was asked to develop a program to support these "experienced" users and bring some commonality and order to their disparate activities. By then, business user applications were so fragmented that an IT manager estimated that it would take roughly two years to deploy an effective support program. Two years seemed like a long time to company managers. They asked themselves whether they should have developed the support program in advance and deployed desktop services with more centralized IT control in place.

The consensus answer to that question was no. Both IT and business management felt that an IT-driven desktop services project would have been viewed as an IT initiative and therefore would not have been embraced enthusiastically by business users. The two years it would take to gain management control of distributed user initiatives was a price the company was willing to pay for the zeal with which users had embraced the new technology. This decentralized approach stood in marked contrast with the company's traditionally centralized approach to managing its mature data processing technologies.

4. From Decentralized, User-Driven Innovation to Unexpected Centralized Innovation

A large South African retail chain installed a point-of-sale (POS) inventory tracking system in each of its 50-plus stores. The company's retail division initially funded the project for a narrow business purpose: To assist store managers in controlling inventory. POS information was to be used inside individual stores exclusively in order to accumulate daily sales totals and trigger reorders. The project was successful, and stores quickly achieved significant inventory savings.

Later, senior business managers asked the IT department to link store POS systems with central systems at corporate headquarters. The proposed links would feed data to new corporate software designed to measure product performance across stores and help manage warehouse stock levels throughout the retail chain. Because the communication protocols used by POS systems were incompatible with the protocols in use by IT at headquarters, implementing the project was expensive. Managers asked themselves whether the expensive incompatibility between POS systems and corporate systems was evidence of a deficiency in their planning process.

The consensus answer to that question was no. A planning process that explored all possible future uses of POS data would have taken too long and delayed inventory savings in individual stores. Furthermore, planning stage estimates of the benefits of linking POS and corporate systems would have been highly speculative (if they could have been identified at all). The excess time necessary to link corporate systems might have weakened the cost/benefit case to the point where the project might have been cancelled. The success of the first system set a baseline for future systems. The firm has since used the POS-to-corporate network to implement a customer loyalty card and gain a detailed understanding of the individual buying habits of its key customers.

Implications and Conclusions

These examples powerfully illustrate the impossibility of foreseeing the full impact of new technology and the consequent difficulty of specifying a single best way to allocate control over priorities and resource allocation in systems development and deployment. Too much focus on prescriptive policies, centralized control, or rapid proof of favorable results in the early stages of the adoption of new technology can prevent important learning that may lead to even more useful applications. Neither IT professionals nor business users have outstanding records in anticipating how new technologies will affect organizations. A general manager's role, therefore, is to facilitate the assimilation of new technology by continuously monitoring tensions and shifting emphases as appropriate between centralized and decentralized IT and user control-driven innovation.

In the balance of this chapter, we discuss three aspects of the organizational issues in more detail. First, we address the key drivers in business users' desire to gain control over IT development, deployment, and management activities. Second, we analyze the need for centralized coordination of systems deployment and the pitfalls of uncontrolled proliferation of user-developed systems. Third, we identify and discuss core policies that IT management, user management, and general management must implement to balance tensions and produce favorable results. As we shall see, the general manager's role is particularly critical in creating an environment that facilitates technological change and organizational adaptation to that change.

Drivers toward User Dominance

A number of critical drivers encourage users to exercise control over internal systems development resources and sometimes to engage external IT resources (consultants or systems integrators) to address business needs. These drivers can be grouped into the following five categories.

Pent-Up User Demand

IT departments and suppliers often do not have the staff and budget needed to handle the volume of IT activities and projects. There are a number of causes for this disparity. Existing systems, for example, require sustained maintenance to accommodate changing regulatory and business requirements. As the number of automated systems in a firm increases and as systems age, the total volume of change requests increases. Ongoing customization of existing systems increases system complexity, makes enhancements more difficult, and increases maintenance costs. In addition, systems need to be adapted to major changes in IT architecture, such as the transition to enterprise and internetworking systems.[1]

Bringing about these conversions, which are increasingly urgent as we move to real-time infrastructures, has been very expensive. They strain IT staff resources and at the

---

[1] This problem began to emerge in the 1970s, when systems design philosophy shifted from incorporating data into programs to separating data from the processes that use the data.

same time effectively starve other departments of resources. It also is common for IT departments to expend significant resources to maintain and enhance existing systems but keep only a few resources available for developing and deploying new systems. To make matters worse, the most challenging, high-status, and high-paying IT jobs in the industry tend to be with computer vendors and software houses. The most talented members of a company's in-house IT staff are tempted to move to more glamorous jobs. Consequently, sometimes it is easier for IT departments to secure budget money than to find qualified staff. Delays caused by these factors have led to frustration and a strong desire by users to take matters into their own hands. As we shall see, the same factors act as drivers toward outsourcing.

The Need for Staff Flexibility

When an IT department and its vendors appear unresponsive to users' demands, the users see developing systems themselves as a nonconfrontational way to get work done. By deploying their own staff in IT roles or engaging services from outside integration or application service companies, business users significantly speed the process of meeting their requirements for IT functionality. There are benefits from closely linking both physical and operational IT resources and end users. Basing IT staff in the business user's department helps educate users to IT's value-adding potential. It reduces communication problems between developers/deployers and users. It makes employee promotions that involve rotating IT staff to other (non-IT) jobs within the department easier, thus enhancing user-IT coordination, and it facilitates moving end users to IT positions.

Growth in the IT Services Industry

Thousands of commercial off-the-shelf software packages are now available for specific IT applications. These packages range from simple accounts payable products to complete enterprise systems products. As we have seen, over-the-Net applications and other outsourcing options are proliferating as well. To frustrated business users with urgent short-term business needs, these options appear beguiling. These systems are marketed by hardware and software vendors to business managers, and their functional features are emphasized; vendor sales representatives soft-pedal incompatibilities with the firm's existing infrastructure and software upgrade or maintenance problems. Frequently, a proposed point solution to a short-term business problem appears more cost-effective than having the work done or purchased by a central IT department. Often vendors quote a simple up-front price. Such projects seem to hold out the promise of freedom from red tape. Vendors argue, with some justification, that they are able to bring people into the project who are more skilled in current technologies than are those in the IT department.

Users' Desire to Control Their Own Destiny

The idea of regaining control over a part of their business operations, particularly if IT has become mission-critical, greatly appeals to business users. Control in this context has at least two dimensions.

First, users can exercise direct control over systems development priorities. By using either their own staff or software and services companies they select, users hope to obtain a system with vastly improved features in less time than it would take to navigate the priority-setting process in the corporate IT department. Additionally, development and deployment errors made by a user-managed group are sometimes easier to excuse than those made by a distant, centralized group. As a result, project difficulties may be more openly discussed, which can facilitate experimentation and learning during development.

Second, as business conditions change, business users often wish to control systems maintenance priorities. At the time of installation, users may not have weighed the importance of ongoing systems maintenance sufficiently. When they discover how relentlessly business changes drive system change requests, users become less willing to place their maintenance request in the queue with those of other business groups. If managers are being evaluated by how well their business units perform, the desire to have more complete control over change priorities is not altogether unreasonable.

Fit with the Organization

As companies become more global and their operations become more geographically dispersed, users sometimes feel compelled to control systems development and deployment. Their local concerns increasingly diverge from corporate IT initiatives. Similarly, when divisions adopt highly specialized business models that differ from those of other divisions, choices made by corporate IT staffs seem less consistent with the needs of the division. For example, a division of a pharmaceuticals firm focused on cost leadership in commodity products (such as IV fluid bags or other hospital supplies) will take a different approach to IT than will a division with a more traditional research and development (R&D)-intensive, high-margin business model. If corporate IT is driven by high-margin assumptions, inherent priorities may be poorly suited to a more cost-conscious division. Decentralized IT activities may then gain appeal. Decentralized development, deployment, and management avoid the high levels of coordination effort required to keep centralized IT departments attuned to local needs. Finally, if a company decides to divest a unit, the process will be easier if IT activities are not completely integrated with the rest of the company.

Together, these five drivers represent a powerful argument for a strong user role in systems development and suggest when that role might be dominant. Although benefits sometimes can be achieved, as the earlier examples demonstrated, when business users control development, deployment, and management of IT resources, there also may be a downside. As one might expect, the downside of a decentralized IT structure alternative supports the argument for centralized control of IT projects and resources, to which we now turn our discussion.

Drivers toward a Centralized IT Structure

A number of pressures encourage firms to consolidate IT development resources into a more centralized unit. These pressures can be grouped into the following categories.

Staff Professionalism

Maintaining a central IT department enhances an organization's ability to recruit and retain specialized technical personnel by providing more obvious career paths for talented IT employees. In addition, it is easier to keep centralized staff up to date on the latest technologies and develop the necessary skill sets. Moreover, an IT department serves as the focus of deliberate efforts to maintain certain areas of technical competence or expertise. The employees of a centralized IT group have fewer concerns, therefore, about losing pace with the advance of technology or getting lost in the organization when it comes to career development. The inability of some firms to manage the personal development of the IT staff is a key driver for outsourcing IT activities.

Standard Setting and Ensuring System Maintainability

Many organizations experience periodic swings of the centralize/decentralize pendulum because over time the benefits of change often give way to new problems. As we have seen, standardized computing infrastructure pays dividends by reducing the complexity and cost of maintaining a firm's IT capabilities. When IT resources are centrally concentrated, developing and enforcing standards in infrastructure and in IT management practice are easier. Indeed, if IT resources are not centralized but report directly to business user organizations, setting companywide standards almost always takes a backseat to short-term business concerns. Inefficiency in maintaining the IT infrastructure is the cumulative long-term effect of consistently sacrificing standards in favor of short-term concerns. Ironically, inefficiency is a major reason why IT resources are sometimes not available to address short-term business needs. Conversely, centralized IT management activities can increase efficiency dramatically. For example, a study at a manufacturing firm showed that centralizing control of its $16 million investment in networked personal computers yielded maintenance cost savings of 40 percent.

In 1988, a large chemical company faced deteriorating relationships between its central IT department and key business user constituencies. When the situation grew chronic, company managers responded by redistributing 80 percent of IT development staff to four divisions, changing both reporting responsibilities and physical locations. Although the change stimulated new ideas and better relationships with users, by 1993 the need for standards to control the costs associated with proliferating user-driven systems development became so intense that the company instituted significantly tighter standards and management practices. In 1997, company managers outsourced the crash development of intranets and extranets. The basic decentralized structure, however, was still in place in 2003.

Central staff expertise is particularly important for reviewing user-designed systems before they go live. Lacking practical systems design experience, users often ignore data management and security policies, corporate standards, and costing practices that incorporate the full cost of running an application. The managers at a large financial firm learned this lesson the hard way when they discovered that all the user employees who had developed an essential system had left the company without creating any documentation or operating instructions. Even worse, the system had not been subjected to any version control, and the source code was nowhere to be found. All that remained were machine-readable object programs. The system ran, but no one knew exactly what it was doing, and the managers could not change the system.

Envisioning Possibilities and Determining Feasibility

Not surprisingly, most business users are not adept at envisioning the possibilities inherent in new technologies or expert in judging the feasibility of technical applications. Users often focus on obtaining a specific service to address an immediate need without recognizing the fact that successful first applications tend to generate unanticipated second applications (and then third applications, etc.). Their limited experience with IT makes it difficult for business users to see the full implications of the application of a technology; an example is planning that fails to account for possible growth or future expansion of applications. This problem caused some users to see the Web at first as merely a better way to manage documentation. Inability to envision what a system may someday become and to make choices consistent with those possibilities can make future expansion expensive or even infeasible.

User-driven feasibility studies may contain major technical mistakes. Typical consequences include a system that does not handle growing processing requirements or is not cost effective in operation. Users are often inclined to acquire products with attractive visible features from unstable vendors. Indeed, users may be unable to see the technological drawbacks of an IT product that may predispose its vendor to fail. Accurate assessment of vendor stability is critical because many systems eventually insinuate themselves into the heart of a company's operations. In many cases, extracting unsupported systems from a company's infrastructure is expensive and exceedingly difficult, as is converting applications to new systems and platforms. A single experience with a failed vendor can be a painful learning process.

Corporate Data Management

As we have seen in earlier chapters, the internetworking capabilities of today's corporations make it possible to synchronize databases across an enterprise. A modern data management strategy requires central coordination of physically distributed databases so that users, regardless of their physical location, can access data files as needed. A central IT staff provides a focal point for conceptualizing and developing the architecture of these systems.

The need for data sharing varies widely with the nature of a company's activities. A conglomerate usually has much less need for data sharing across the firm than does a functionally organized, one-product company. Most firms, however, need companywide, fully interoperable e-mail, videoconferencing, video streaming, and financial systems, to name only a few. All these applications employ database components. Increasingly, enterprisewide interoperability and data exchange are a part of new IT projects. Only a central IT department can cost effectively develop and distribute such systems to users or coordinate distributed development projects in a way that assures interoperability.

Whenever the subject of decentralized development within individual business units is broached, a competent IT manager's first concern is that the company may lose its ability to manage and control data flows between disparate applications. The narrow perspective of development driven by the short-term problems of a particular business unit may produce data definitions, structures, and systems that lock up data in a nonstandardized format and in inaccessible locations so that they cannot be used enterprisewide. Modern data management and communication standards make it easier to avoid such outcomes. In fact, effective data management policies and standards make it possible for a company to achieve the best of both organizational worlds: Responsive decentralized development and products that interoperate through centralized data management hubs. Databases constructed to be consistent with corporate data standards can exchange data periodically or, in some cases, continuously with physically distant databases, keeping the company's data in sync.

In recent years, finding ways to keep data secure has been a growing concern. Security issues are best addressed through centralized control. And security standards are more easily achieved with centrally organized electronic files. In a world of increasingly clever hackers, a company needs to be sure its data are secure and certainly needs to know where all data stores are located. Indeed, some data are so sensitive that they are best kept off the network entirely.

Cost Estimation and Analysis

Because it has practical experience in a broad range of systems efforts, a centralized IT group usually has a better chance of producing realistic systems development and deployment estimates than do decentralized user-based groups. This is not always the case; estimation is often difficult and poorly done even in the best conditions. Inexperienced estimators tend to be too optimistic. Additionally, during the project changes, they take insufficient account of possible complications that add overhead time and cost to the project.

Users seldom understand the true costs of operating the existing services. In many companies, complicated charge-back schemes for allocating the centralized costs of IT services and facilities back to business user departments add to the confusion about costs. Many charge-back methods are historical remnants of frameworks convenient for cost accountants. Often they present measurements of computer resource use that are unfathomable to the business user; for example, each month an unintelligible bill arrives with an unpredictable amount due. In management control environments, where the business user is responsible for variance from budgets, the unpredictability of the true costs causes frustration. In comparison, a locally developed system exhibits understandable and predictable costs. Because corporate charge-back systems are designed to allocate all centralized costs and because overhead allocation methods are often problematical, charges often appear unfairly distributed and sometimes very high to business users. Disproportionately high allocations provide some business users with strong but corporately suboptimal incentives for local development.

In the short run, much of a company's IT cost is fixed, but it appears to the individual user, because of the charge-back system, as if it were a variable cost that could be reduced. This representation, especially for overhead allocation, is not accurate and sometimes encourages individual user cost reductions that actually generate cost increases for the company as a whole. Cost analysis and management, using an activity-based computing utility framework, is the only way to assure that local decision making is consistent with overall company objectives. This kind of cost management is best mounted from within a centralized IT group oriented toward corporate rather than local objectives.

Long-term perspectives and methodical deployment of architectural ideals characterize pressures toward centralized IT control. The benefits of central control are long-term cost avoidance and technological risk reduction. The downside of this approach, however, is lack of short-term responsiveness to local business issues and problems. In this age of internetworking, stand-alone systems and business units tend to become part of a centralized network. Thus, the tensions involved in managing IT development and deployment are fully in play. Policies for managing the trade-offs between the obvious short-term benefits and the long-term risks are necessary but delicate to administer.

Coordination and Location of IT Policy

The tension between IT staff and business users can be managed by establishing clear policies that specify the user domain, the IT domain, and senior management's role. Senior management must play a significant role in ensuring that these policies are developed and evolve appropriately over time. Both IT staff and users must understand the implications of their roles and the conflicts that may arise as they work together.

IT Responsibilities

The following tasks constitute the central core of IT responsibilities—the minimum for managing the long-term IT needs of an organization.

1. Develop and manage the long-term architectural plan and ensure that new projects fit within the plan. Periodically review and revise the plan and be sure IT stakeholders agree about the objectives and details of the plan. In today's world of enterprise systems and real-time internetworking, stakeholder agreement and backing are critical.

2. Develop a process to establish, maintain, and evolve company standards in the following areas:

   - Telecommunication protocols and platforms

   - Client devices and client software configurations

   - Server devices, middleware, and database management systems

   - Programming and configuration languages

   - Documentation procedures and formats

   - Data definitions, especially for data elements used throughout the company

   - Storage redundancy, backup, and disaster recovery procedures

   - Information security policy and incident response procedures

   This process and the resulting standards must accommodate innovation by business users, experimentation that can lead to important learning, and real differences in the business requirements of particular business units.

3. Establish procedures that consider outsourcing options when new IT projects are proposed. Ensure that outsourced or user-executed projects adhere closely to

corporate standards, are consistent with overall corporate objectives, and take into account interfaces to corporate systems.

4. Maintain an inventory of installed and planned systems and services. To the degree possible, periodically reexamine the total benefits and costs of operating and maintaining these systems and services for consistency with business objectives.

5. Identify career paths for IT staff. Include lateral transfers within and between IT units, upward movement within the IT organization, and outward movement from IT to other functional units. When IT activities are decentralized, this task takes on special importance because career paths for IT personnel may not seem obvious.

6. Establish internal marketing efforts that help business users understand the challenges of IT support and the hidden costs of maintaining IT systems. Encourage business units to modernize when their systems become expensive to run because of age. Also encourage business units that are pushing too fast into leading-edge technologies to slow down or at least take account of their full exposure to risks and costs.

7. Incorporate, as a standard part of the request for proposal (RFP) process when acquiring new hardware or software, a detailed checklist that includes questions about compatibility with existing architecture and standards. For example:

   • Is the proposed new hardware or software technology consistent with corporate standards? If not, where are the points of departure? Do they have serious consequences?

   • Will the new technology support future growth and does it support information exchange within the company's evolving real-time infrastructure?

   • Is the new technology maintainable over the long term?

8. Identify and maintain relationships with preferred systems suppliers. In entering a relationship with a vendor, be sure that the client company's standards enforcement efforts have a basis in the contract with the vendor and that vendor pricing and planning take into account the need to comply with standards.

9. Establish education programs for business users that introduce the benefits and pitfalls of new technologies. Define users' roles in ensuring the successful introduction of new technology in their departments.

10. Set up a process for ongoing review of legacy systems to determine when they should be redesigned and/or replaced.

The tasks for which IT is responsible are particularly important for systems that will become deeply embedded in a company's day-to-day operations. For less operationally critical systems, IT managers can afford more flexibility with respect to standards and responsibilities, although the increasingly integrated nature of infrastructure imposes additional demands even on systems traditionally considered less mission-critical.

If a company's situation warrants it, these core responsibilities can be expanded significantly to impose much tighter and more formal controls. As we have seen, though, because of the uncertain implications of new technology and the resulting difficulty in fully foreseeing impacts, users must apply standards and responsibilities intelligently. A company (or a division or smaller organizational group) might reasonably choose to depart from standards as it tries a new technology. Because standards and responsibilities are not ends in themselves, they should be reviewed frequently. The tendency in IT is to weigh long-term issues more heavily than short-term business needs. Often this is reasonable, but in some cases, if short-term needs are not addressed adequately, there may not be long-term benefits. IT managers therefore must remain flexible as they carry out their duties.

User Responsibilities

To identify IT opportunities, implement new IT services, and understand the uses, costs, and impacts of IT on an organization, business users should take on the following responsibilities:

1. Seek to understand the scope of all IT activities supporting business users. As much as possible, figure out the IT charge-back system and pressure the IT department to establish an activity-based overhead allocation system that users can understand and use in decision making.

2. Develop realistic estimates of the amount of user personnel investment required for new projects both during development/deployment and in ongoing operation and use. Business users have a tendency to underestimate or even ignore new project costs of this type.

3. Ensure comprehensive user input for all IT projects that support vital aspects of the unit's operations. Take a strong interest in how the service will operate, how it will be introduced, and the level of user training required for both staff and managers.

4. Ensure that the nature of staffing interfaces is consistent with a new technology's strategic relevance to a business unit. If a new technology project is very important, the staffing interface must be close, customized, and based on personal relationships. If the new project is not strategically important, staffing interfaces can be more arm's-length and standardized.

5. Periodically audit system reliability standards, communications services performance, and security procedures.

6. Participate in developing and maintaining IT plans that set new technology priorities, schedule the transfer of IT among groups, and evaluate projects in light of the company's overall strategy.[2]

These responsibilities represent the minimum advisable level of user involvement in a company's IT activities. Depending on a firm's geography, corporate management style, degree of reliance on IT capabilities, stage of IT evolution, mix of technologies, and a variety of other factors, more extensive levels of user involvement may be appropriate. In general, more user involvement is preferable to less. Many companies have come to associate the assignment of full-time user staff to IT projects with expectations of project success.

General Management Support and Policy Overview

In most companies there is a cluster of IT policy and directional activities that require a senior management perspective. In the past, these activities were carried out within a central IT organization. Today, because IT has become so critical a part of strategy

[2] For further discussion of this topic, see Cathleen Benko and F. W. McFarlan, *Connecting the Dots* (Boston: HBS Press, 2003).

and day-to-day operational capabilities for so many companies, these activities are carried out at a higher level, in the context of a broader business discussion. In many companies, then, long-range IT planning activities are separated from day-to-day operational activities. Increasingly, the long-range discussions involve senior general managers supported by talented technology specialists.

A chemical company, for example, reorganized in 1990 to establish a 500-person systems and operations department reporting directly to the head of administrative services. This department oversees the company's implementation and operational IT work on a month-to-month, year-to-year basis. At the same time, a 25- to 30-person IT policy group, which reports directly to the head of research, works on overall IT policy and long-range IT strategy for the firm. Similarly, a major conglomerate whose development staff and hardware are distributed in business units still maintains a small but important policy-oriented group at the headquarters level. Even firms that outsource most or all of their IT development and operations need such a policy group to facilitate senior management involvement in vital IT strategy issues.

The key responsibilities of a corporate IT policy group include the following:

1. Ensure an appropriate balance between IT and business users to prevent one group's perspective from dominating. Transfer personnel, reorganize, or create new organizational bodies to keep tensions in balance. For example, an executive steering committee might provide more user input and thus might rectify a situation where the balance had tipped too far toward IT control.

2. Make sure the company has a comprehensive corporate IT strategy. Base the strategy on an overview of technology trends, assessment of the company's current IT capabilities, and the potential of IT initiatives to support overall corporate goals. Such a strategy is particularly important in companies with decentralized IT resources.

3. Manage the inventory of hardware and software systems and services and assure that a corporate orientation extends to purchasing relationships and contracts. In most companies, a corporate group is the appropriate place to identify and manage standard policies for relationships with vendors.

4. Establish standards for acquisition, development, and IT systems operation. Ensure that the standards are applied appropriately. With standards adherence, corporate policy groups sometimes play a combined role as consultant and auditor. Hence, a corporate policy group needs to have a technically competent and interpersonally sensitive staff.

5. Facilitate the transfer of technology from one unit to another. Successful corporate policy groups will develop a knack for spotting synergistic technology and system opportunities. The tools the policy group can use to facilitate technology transfer include staff visits across business units, periodic corporate conferences on IT themes, and other communication means, such as newsletters and streamed audio or video programs.

6. Actively encourage technical experimentation. A limited program of research is a very appropriate part of the IT function. An important role of the corporate policy group is to ensure that research and scanning for new technology opportunities do

for each organization the direction in which the correct answer lies—for now, anyway. Executives can answer the following questions to assess whether they are adequately addressing issues of leadership and organization of IT activities:

1. What is the appropriate balance of emphasis between innovation and control in your organization? Do your IT budgets and organizational structures fit well with that balance?

2. To what degree is the success of your company's business driven by factors local to geographies or business units? Conversely, to what extent is success driven by common factors across geographies and business units? Does the degree of centralization/decentralization of your IT activities fit well with the nature of your business?

3. Have the IT staff or business user perspectives become too dominant in the organization? Is senior management engaged in maintaining an appropriate balance of power between these two perspectives?

4. Are there standards and processes in place to assure efficient data interchange between different business units regardless of the degree of centralization or decentralization of IT resources now or in the future?

5. Does your company have a central IT policy group? Is it successful in enlisting senior managers in IT policy discussions?

CHAPTER 9

Managing IT Outsourcing[1]

Increasingly, companies are outsourcing all or significant parts of their management of information technology (IT). The reasons include concern for cost and quality, lagging IT performance, supplier pressure, access to special technical and application skills, and other financial factors. From a relatively unusual entrepreneurial activity in the past, IT outsourcing has become a fact of life across the global corporate landscape. Xerox, United Technologies, Commonwealth Bank (Australia), Procter & Gamble, and the United Kingdom's National Health Service are just a few of the large deals struck since the early 1990s. Like marriages, however, outsourcing arrangements are much easier to enter than to sustain or dissolve. The special economic technology issues surrounding outsourcing agreements necessarily make them more complex and fluid than an ordinary contract. For outsourcing to be successful, both parties must make a sustained effort to work together. Indeed, in the long term the management of a strategic alliance is *the* dominant challenge of effective IT outsourcing.

In this chapter we identify the characteristics of situations where outsourcing major portions of a firm's IT activities or infrastructure makes sense and discuss how to structure and manage the resulting alliance. Moreover, we provide a concrete framework to help senior managers think about IT outsourcing. Although many aspects of the framework are relevant to incremental outsourcing, as was discussed in Chapter 7, we concentrate here on programs that involve major, long-term alliances between customer and vendor firms. Major outsourcing programs typically involve larger investments, higher stakes, and greater overall management complexity than does incremental outsourcing. Usually they are born of strategic rather than operational motivations, and their impacts on outsourcing customers are much broader. However, the two approaches are complementary and often are used together. Ultimately, the distinction between major programs and incremental outsourcing may blur, but in today's business settings, the unique challenges posed by strategic alliance-based programs consitute a subject deserving of its own discussion.

[1] This chapter is adapted from F. Warren McFarlan and Richard L. Nolan, "How to Manage an IT Outsourcing Alliance," *Sloan Management Review* 36, no. 2 (Winter 1995).

Why Outsourcing Alliances Are So Difficult

Many major outsourcing contracts are structured to expand over long periods of time. However, these agreements exist in a world of fast-moving technical and business change. Eight to ten years is the normal length of a contract in an environment in which computer chip performance is improving by 20 to 30 percent per year. The standard contract length addresses the customer's difficulties in switching vendors as well as economic issues. But a deal that made sense at the beginning of the contract may not make economic sense three years later and may require adjustments to function effectively.

The timing of benefits to the customer and the vendor exacerbates the situation. Benefits in the first year are clear to the customer, who often receives a one-time capital payment in exchange for assets that are being transferred to the vendor. Having been paid and having shifted problems and issues to the vendor, the customer firm may feel relieved. Moreover, the tangible payments in the first year occur in an environment where the outputs most closely resemble those anticipated in the contract. In each subsequent year, however, the contract payment stream becomes less and less tied to the initial set of planned outputs (as the world changes) and thus more subject to negotiation and possible misunderstanding between the customer and the vendor.

From the outsourcing vendor's perspective, the situation is the reverse. The first year may require a heavy capital payment followed by the extraordinary costs of taking on responsibility for the customer's IT operations and executing agreed-upon cost reduction and quality control initiatives. All this is completed in anticipation of a back-loaded profit flow. At precisely the time the vendor is finally moving into its planned profit stream, the customer, perhaps feeling the need for new services, is chafing under the monthly charges and anxious to move to new IT architectures. If the customer is not experienced in partnering activities, profound tensions may develop in the relationship.

A further complication is the fact that only a few outsourcing vendors have the critical mass and access to capital markets to undertake large data center outsourcing contracts. Electronic Data Systems (EDS), Computer Sciences Corporation (CSC), Perot Systems, and IBM are the main U.S. competitors. A much larger group of firms, such as Lockheed Martin, Cap Gemini, and other application service providers (ASPs), specialize in certain niches in the outsourcing market. Rapidly growing players in India such as Tata Consulting Service, Wipro, and Infosys (all over $1 billion in sales in 2003) have made dramatic inroads in global outsourcing markets (see "Outsourcing IT: The Global Landscape in 2004," Case 3-5).

If an outsourcing relationship is not working, a company's options for resolving the situation include insourcing or offshoring. A common situation is typified by a major international packaging company that was forced on short notice to transfer its relationship to another outsourcing vendor when the original arrangement no longer fit the strategy of that outsourcing vendor.

Finally, the evolution of technologies often changes the strategic relevance of IT to a firm. From the customer's viewpoint, assigning a commodity service to an outsider is very attractive if the price is right. But delegating a firm's service differentiator is another matter (this, however, is increasingly being done, as will be described later).

Outsourcing in Retrospect

Outsourcing IT has been used by organizations for a long time. In the mid-1960s, for example, computer services bureaus ran a variety of programs whose applications focused heavily on the financial and operations support areas (general ledger, payroll, inventory control, and so on). The programs were both customized and general-purpose, and the individual firm had to accommodate its operations to the standard options in the package. Service bureau customers were mostly small and medium-size firms, although some large firms used them for specialized needs or highly confidential items such as executive payroll.

ADP is a good example of a provider in the outsourcing industry. In 1949, ADP began as a small punch card payroll company. By 2005, it had grown into an over $8.5 billion organization that specialized in large-volume, standard transaction-type activities such as payroll and handling proxy solicitations (almost 100 percent of the industry). Other categories include software contracting companies such as Accenture in the private sector and CSC in the public sector. These firms developed large turnkey applications for organizations that required either a large or a specialized staff, either of which the organization deemed inconvenient, imprudent, or impossible to retain. EDS, in the state and local government sector, provided full outsourcing for organizations whose cultures and salary scales made it impossible to attract people with the necessary skills in a competitive job market.

Despite these examples, before 1990 the general trend was in-house development of IT. At that time, the major drivers for outsourcing were primarily:

- Cost-effective access to specialized or occasionally needed computing power or systems development skills.
- Avoidance of building in-house IT skills, primarily an issue for small and very low-technology organizations.
- Access to special functional capabilities. Outsourcing during this period was important but in retrospect largely peripheral to the main IT activities that took place in midsize and large organizations.

In 1990, Kodak's decision to outsource IT was the seminal event that legitimized the idea of allowing a vendor to provide major components of IT services. Kodak's chief information officer (CIO), who had been a general manager rather than a computer professional, took an aggressive position in outsourcing mainframes, telecommunications, and personal computer (PC) maintenance and service. Until then, outsourcing for midsize to large companies had been mostly a sideshow, and outsourcing generally was reserved for small and medium-size companies with problematic, grossly mismanaged informations systems (IS) departments.

Outsourcing in the Twenty-First Century

As we enter the twenty-first century, it has become abundantly clear that IT outsourcing is not a transitory management fad. IT outsourcing, a harbinger of traditional IT department transformation, provides a glimpse at the emerging organizational structures of the networked economy. By 1995, more than half of midsize to large firms had outsourced or were considering outsourcing significant IT activities. And this phenomenon is not limited to the United States. Novartis (Switzerland), British Aerospace (the United Kingdom), and the AMP Insurance Company (Australia), for example, have all outsourced substantial parts of their IT activities.[2]

Two factors affect the growth of IT outsourcing: Acceptance of strategic alliances and changes in the technological environment.

Acceptance of Strategic Alliances

The value of strategic alliances is widely recognized, and interrelated forces motivate their creation. On one level, finding a strong partner to complement an area of weakness gives an organization an island of stability in a turbulent world. Alliances allow a company to simplify its management agenda safely and gain access to higher-quality resources. On another level, alliances allow a firm to leverage a key part of its value chain by bringing in a strong partner that complements its skills. Such a partner may create an opportunity to innovate synergistically, with the two companies working together so that the whole becomes greater than the sum of the parts. Also, early and successful experiences with alliances increase a firm's confidence in undertaking new alliances in other parts of the value chain as a profitable way to do business. The early experience provides insight into ways to increase the likelihood of a successful alliance.

For an alliance to be successful and endure for the long term, both firms must believe they are winners because they benefit from the synergistic potential of the relationship and the opportunity to specialize. As we suggested in Chapter 7, a vendor that concludes that a deal has become a loser will, reasonably enough, divert resources to other, more promising opportunities. The mutually beneficial economics of a successful alliance therefore must outlast the careers of the participants who put the deal together.

IT's Changing Environment

As we have observed throughout this book, today's firms are not limiting IT only to internal transaction processing systems. Instead, they are integrating internal systems with those of their customers and suppliers and, in the process, changing their organizational structure to compete efficiently in the global marketplace. As we also have seen, this integration places extraordinary pressures on firms trying to keep the old services running while developing the interconnections and services demanded by the new environment. Thus, outsourcing has become a viable way for firms to access appropriate skills and speed the transition reliably and cost effectively.

In fact, as shown in Table 9.1, the development of most of the code that companies now use is already outsourced. A distinct minority of the code in operating systems, e-mail systems, word processing packages, and spreadsheet software actually has been developed within the firm (with a much smaller percentage expected in the future). This trend, which occurred for obvious reasons of economies of scale and scarcity of competent staff, will continue. Currently, Computer Associates, Oracle, SAP, IBM, Microsoft, and a few enterprise software vendors are the de facto software providers to most companies. The internal IT organization is already a selector and integrator of code rather than a developer.

[2] Ibid.

TABLE 9.1 **IT Markets**

Location	Physical Aspects	Information
Internal	*Automating:* Computerizing physical and clerical processes Data Processing (DP) era (1960–1980) • Dominant use of mainframes and minicomputers • Operational-level systems automated primarily with COBOL • Process controls automated primarily with machine language • Standard packages for payroll and general ledger • Applications portfolio consists of millions of lines of code, with 50% typically purchased from outside	*Informating:* Leveraging knowledge workers with computers Networking era (1990–?) • User tasks leveraged through direct use of microcomputers enabled by graphical user interfaces (GUI) and purchased software such as word processing, spreadsheet, graphics, and computer-aided design and manufacturing • Local area networks (LANs)—user-oriented software for e-mail, database sharing, file transfer, and groupware for work teams • Microcomputer software consists of millions of lines of code, almost 100% purchased from other companies
External	*Embedding:* Integrating computers into products and services. Micro era (1980–1995) • Specialized code embedded in products and services to enhance function • Microcomputers in physical products such as automobiles and "smart cards" in services • Thousands of lines of code developed by both specialized internal programmers and outside contract programmers	*Networking:* "The Information Highway" Network era (1990–?) • Wide area networks (WANs) networking workers, suppliers, and customers • Internet for commercial use • Millions of lines of code, almost 100% purchased from and maintained by outside software firms

In addition, many organizations see outsourcing as a means to transform legacy applications so that they interact effectively as part of real-time internetworking infrastructure. Companies look to vendors for low-cost maintenance of the old systems to ensure that they operate reliably as well as for access to the new skills that permit their transformation to the new model. Some companies outsource the operation of old systems and use internal staff to develop new IT capabilities; others do the opposite. This shift toward outsourcing as a major source of new capabilities is as significant today as the move from tabulating equipment was 40 years ago.

What Drives Outsourcing?

Despite the mix of factors that suggests outsourcing varies widely from one company to another, a series of themes in the aggregate explains most of the pressures to outsource.

General Managers' Concerns about Costs and Quality

The same questions about IT costs and responsiveness come up repeatedly when managers consider outsourcing: Can we get our existing services for a reduced price at acceptable quality standards? Can we get new systems developed faster? An outsourcing vendor can save money for a customer in several ways:

- Tighter overhead cost control of fringe benefits. On balance, outsourcing vendors run much leaner overhead structures than do many of their customers.

- More aggressive use of low-cost labor pools by using geography creatively. Frequently, the outsourcing vendor moves data centers and gives portions of the development activity to low-cost areas such as India and Northern Ireland (modern telecommunications make this possible).

- Tough world-class standards applied to the company's existing staff, all of whom have to requalify for appointment at the time of outsourcing. Maintaining high standards keeps employees from losing their skills in leading-edge IT practices.

- More effective bulk purchasing and leasing arrangements for all aspects of the hardware/software configuration through discounts and better use of capacity.

- Better management of excess hardware capacity. By combining many firms' work in the same operations center, an outsourcing vendor actually can use less hardware. One small firm's online operations (a $27 million, 10-year contract) were transferred to a larger data center at no extra cost to the outsourcing vendor. Capacity was simply better used.

- Better control over software licenses through both negotiation and realistic examination.

- More aggressive management of service and response time to meet, but not wildly exceed, corporate standards. Tighter control over inventories.

- Hustle. Outsourcing vendors are professionals. Outsourcing is their only business, and their success is measured by satisfied customers who recommend them to others, bottom-line profitability, and stock market performance.

- The ability to run with a leaner management structure because of increased competence and critical-mass volumes of work.

- The ability to access higher levels of IT staff skills, IT application skills (such as SAP and Oracle), or special customer industry skills.

- Creative and more realistic structuring of leases.

While the cumulative impact of these savings can be significant, there are a few caveats. Unless several knowledgeable bidders closely analyze an existing operation before proposing an alliance, the true picture will not be revealed. An IT efficiency study funded by the IT department and performed by a consulting company hoping to get future business is self-serving and inadequate. Equally important is assessing whether the outsourcing vendor can mobilize its staff rapidly for quick-response development jobs when a customer needs to get products and services to market much faster.

Breakdown in IT Performance

Failure to meet service standards forces general management to find other ways to achieve reliability. As we reflect on the last 30 years of computer growth in most companies, it is not unusual to find a company in which cumulative IT management neglect eventually culminated in an out-of-control situation. For example, Massachusetts Blue Cross and Blue Shield's decision to outsource to EDS was triggered by the failure of three major systems development projects (and losses in the tens of millions of dollars). It saw outsourcing as a way to fix a broken department. Similarly, a midsize bank's interest in outsourcing came after a one-day total collapse of its automated teller machine (ATM) network. Faulty software patches, which had been designed internally, caused the failure.

An additional driving factor toward outsourcing is the need for companies to rapidly retool backward IT structures in order to remain competitive. In one firm, general managers thought the internal IT culture was both frozen and backward; it needed to leap forward in performance. The general managers, who lacked both the time and the inclination to undertake the task personally, found outsourcing a good choice for making a rapid transition.

Intense Vendor Pressures

Kodak's decision to outsource its data center and telecommunications to IBM, DEC, and Businessland in 1990 was, as we have noted, a flash point. Suddenly many general managers saw outsourcing as a highly viable, if often misunderstood, alternative. At the same time, IBM was looking for new value-added services to reach its customer base and compensate for declining hardware margins and sales. It moved aggressively into the field with an expanded and highly energetic sales force. EDS, the largest independent firm in the field, used its General Motors operations center to demonstrate its expertise. CSC, which was strong in the federal sector, built a bridge to the commercial sector with its General Dynamics contract. The visibility of these and other arrangements, combined with the vendors' aggressive sales forces, enabled vendors to approach general managers with compelling reasons to outsource. Today numerous large and small vendors serve the industry.

Simplified General Management Agenda

A firm under intense cost or competitive pressures which does not see IT as its core competence may find outsourcing a way to delegate time-consuming, messy problems. The firm then can focus its energy on other competitive differentiators. If managers perceive the outsourcing vendor as competent and are able to transfer a noncore function to reliable hands, they will not hesitate to choose outsourcing. These IT activities must perform reasonably well, but the firm's long-term competitive differentiation does not come from these activities.

Financial Factors

Several financial issues make outsourcing appealing. One is the opportunity to liquidate the firm's intangible IT asset and thus strengthen the balance sheet and avoid a future stream of sporadic capital investments. An important part of many arrangements has been the significant up-front capital paid by the outsourcing vendor to the customer for both the real value of the hardware/software assets and the intangible value of its IT systems. General Dynamics, for example, received $200 million for its IT asset.

Outsourcing can turn a largely fixed-cost business into one with variable costs. This change is particularly important for firms whose activities vary widely in volume from year to year or which face significant downsizing. The outsourcing vendor can make the change much less painful to a downsizing firm. It can broker the slack more effectively and potentially provide greater employment stability for the company's IT employees (who are there because of the outsourcing vendor's ability to handle multiple operations). In fact, staff members transferred to a vendor as part of an outsourcing deal often view the deal positively for some of the same financial reasons. They see themselves leaving a cost-constrained environment with limited potential for promotion and entering a growth environment where IT (their core competence) is the firm's only business.

A third-party relationship also brings an entirely different set of dynamics to a firm's view of IT expenditures. The company is now dealing with a hard-dollar expenditure that all users must take seriously (it is no longer soft-dollar allocation). There is a sense of discipline and tough-mindedness that even an arm's-length, fully charged-back internal IT department has trouble achieving. Further, firms that do not see IT as a high-leverage function may perceive outside professionals as adding special value.

For a firm considering divestiture or outright sale of one or more of its divisions, outsourcing liquidates and gets value for an asset unlikely to be recognized in the divestiture. It gives the acquirer fewer problems to deal with in assimilating the firm. Also, the outsourcing contract may provide a very nice dowry, particularly if the firm is small in relation to the acquirer. With little or no additional expense, the firm can phase out the contract neatly and add the IT transaction volume to the firm's internal IT activities.

Corporate Culture

Sometimes a company's values make it hard for managers to take certain actions that make business sense. Consider, for example, a firm with several internal data centers and an obvious and compelling case for consolidating them. The internal IT department simply lacked the clout to pull off a centralized strategy in what was a highly decentralized firm built up over the years by acquisitions. The firm saw the decentralized culture as a major strength, not subject to reconsideration. Outsourcing, driven by very senior management, provided the fulcrum for overcoming this impasse, since it was not directly associated with any division or corporate staff.

Eliminating an Internal Irritant

No matter how competent and adaptive a firm's IT management and staff are (and usually they are very good), tension often exists between the end users of the resources and the IT staff. The different language IT professionals use, lack of career paths for IT staff across the organization, perceived high IT costs, perceived unresponsiveness to urgent requests, and perceived technical obsolescence frequently exacerbate this tension. In this context the notion of a remote, efficient, experienced outsourcing vendor is particularly compelling even though the internal perceptions are not necessarily realistic.

Other Factors

A variety of other drivers for outsourcing appear in specific situations. At one midsize high-tech firm, for example, outsourcing provided access to skills the company needed to run a series of critical applications. The firm's managers felt that outsourcing had substantially reduced their corporate risk while providing needed access to specialized knowledge. In another example, a large firm received a level of commitment and energy that it felt would not have been forthcoming from an in-house unit. Still another firm obtained an infrastructure modernization "adrenaline boost" from outsourcing that netted a two-thirds improvement in time to market.

When to Outsource

When do the benefits of outsourcing outweigh the risks? Five factors tip the scale one way or the other.

Position on the Strategic Grid

As shown in Figure 9.1, for companies in the support quadrant, the outsourcing presumption is yes, particularly for large firms. For companies in the factory quadrant, the presumption is yes unless they are huge and are perceived as exceptionally well managed. For firms in the turnaround quadrant, the presumption is mixed; it may represent an unnecessary, unacceptable delegation of competitiveness, although conversely, it may be the only way to acquire those skills. For companies in the strategic quadrant, the presumption also is mixed. Not facing a crisis of IT competence, some companies in the strategic quadrant find it hard to justify outsourcing; others find it indispensable for gaining access to otherwise unavailable skills. Also, having a sub-critical mass in potentially core differentiating skills for the firm is an important driver that has moved companies to outsourcing.

FIGURE 9.1
Strategic Grid for Information Resource Management

IT Impact on Core Operations — **High** / **Low**

Factory—uninterrupted service-oriented information resource management *Outsourcing presumption:* Yes, unless company is huge and well managed Reasons to consider outsourcing: • Possibilities of economies of scale for small and midsize firms • Higher-quality service and backup • Management focus facilitated • Fiber-optic and extended channel technologies facilitate international IT solutions	*Strategic information resource management* *Outsourcing presumption:* Mixed Reasons to consider outsourcing: • Rescue an out-of-control internal IT unit • Tap source of cash • Facilitate cost flexibility • Facilitate management of divestiture • Provide access to technology applications and staffing skills otherwise not available
Support-oriented information resource management *Outsourcing presumption:* Yes Reasons to consider outsourcing: • Access to higher IT professionalism • Possibility of laying off is of low priority and problematic • Access to current IT technologies • Risk of inappropriate IT architecture reduced	*Turnaround information resource management* *Outsourcing presumption:* Mixed Reasons to consider outsourcing: • Internal IT unit not capable in required technologies • Internal IT unit not capable in required project management skills • Access to technology applications and staffing otherwise not available

Low — *IT Impact on Core Strategy* — **High**

For larger multidivisional firms, this analysis suggests that various divisions and clusters of application systems can be treated differently. For example, an international oil company outsourced its operationally troubled Brazilian subsidiary's IT activities but kept in-house the IT activities of a subsidiary in another country. Similarly, because of the dynamic nature of the grid, firms under profit pressures after a period of sustained strategic innovation (in either the turnaround or the strategic quadrant) are good candidates for outsourcing as a means to clean up their shop and procedures. This was true for one large high-technology organization that saved over $100 million per year by outsourcing.

Development Portfolio

The higher the percentage of IT resources working on maintenance or high-structured projects is, the more the portfolio is a candidate for outsourcing. By high-structured projects we mean those in which the end outputs are clearly defined; there is little opportunity to redefine them and little or no organizational change involved in implementing them. Outsourcing vendors with access to high-quality cheap labor pools (in, for example, Russia, China, India, or Ireland) and good project management skills consistently outperform, on both cost and quality, local units that are caught in a high-cost geographic area but still have the contacts, skills, and confidence to manage extended relationships. The growth of global fiber-optic networks has made conventional thinking on where work should be placed obsolete. For example, Citibank, based in New York, does much of its processing work in South Dakota. Further, literally hundreds of thousands of programmers are working in India on software development for U.S. and European firms (see "Outsourcing IT: The Global Landscape in 2004," Case 3-5).

High-technology, highly structured work (e.g., building a vehicle-tracking system) is also a strong candidate for outsourcing because this type of work requires staff with specialized, leading-edge technical skills. These skills are widely available in Ireland, India, and the Philippines. China is growing very fast in this arena.

Conversely, large, low-structured projects pose difficult coordination problems for outsourcing. In low-structured projects the end outputs and processes are susceptible to significant evolution as the project unfolds. Design is iterative because users discover what they really want by trial and error. Design work requires that key elements of the design infrastructure be physically closer to consumers. It can, of course, be outsourced, but that requires more coordination to be effective than do the projects described above. One firm outsourced significant design work to a very standards-oriented outsourcing vendor as a way of bringing discipline to an undisciplined organization.

Organizational Learning

A firm's organizational learning ability influences whether it can manage an outsourcing arrangement effectively. Many firms' development portfolios include a large number of projects aimed at process reengineering and organizational transformation. Process reengineering seeks to install very different procedures for handling transactions and doing the firm's work. Organizational transformation tries to redesign where decisions in the firm are made and what controls are used. The success of both types of projects depends on having the internal staff radically change the way it works. It often involves significant downsizing as well.

Responsibility for development work is the hardest to outsource. In gauging the responsibility for success, a firm with substantial experience in restructuring will have less difficulty drawing a dividing line between the outsourcing vendor and the customer. Firms that have not yet worked on these projects will find that outsourcing significantly complicates an already difficult task.

A Firm's Position in the Market

The world of real-time infrastructure is so different from the large COBOL systems and stand-alone PCs of the 1980s and earlier that it is often prohibitively challenging for a firm to modernize by itself. Firms that are far behind their peers often do not have the IT leadership, staff skills, or architecture to upgrade quickly to state-of-the-art technology. The outsourcing vendor, in contrast, cannot afford to keep old systems running but must go forward with contemporary practice and technology. For a firm whose IT capabilities have become obsolete, it is not worth dwelling on how the firm got where it is but vital to determine how it can extricate itself.

Current IT Organization

The more IT activities are already segregated in organizational and accounting terms, the easier it is to negotiate an enduring outsourcing contract. A stand-alone IT unit has already developed the fundamental integrating and control mechanisms necessary for an outsourcing contract. Where such mechanisms do not exist, developing an enduring contract is much more complex because the firm must establish both the framework for resolving issues and the specific technical approaches.

Structuring the Alliance

Successful outsourcing begins by carefully crafting the structure of an outsourcing arrangement. The right structure is not a guarantee of success, but the wrong structure will make the governance process almost impossible. Several factors are vital to a successful alliance.

Contract Flexibility

Most outsourcing deals change over time, often radically. Kodak, for example, repeatedly altered its outsourcing contracts because both business circumstances and technologies changed. Evolving technology, changing economic conditions, and new service options make change inevitable. Outsourcing contracts therefore must be written to allow for evolution. Because contracts often need adjustments, the noncontractual aspects of the relationship are extremely important. If there is mutual interest in the relationship and if there are shared approaches to problem solving, the alliance is more likely to be successful. If this is not the case, trouble may arise.

No matter how much detail and thought go into drafting a contract, it will not provide total protection if things go wrong. Indeed, the process of drafting the contract, which often takes six to eight months, is likely to be more important than the contract itself. During the process each side gains insights into the other's values. When the process is successful, it is a basis for personal relationships that go beyond the written contract.

Standards and Control

Companies are understandably concerned about the prospect of handing control over an important part of a firm's operations to a third party (such as an outsourcing vendor), particularly if IT innovation is vital to the firm's success or if the firm is very dependent on IT for smooth operations. The outsourcing agreement must address these concerns.

Control is, in part, a state of mind. Most organizations are accustomed to lacking direct control over certain segments of the business. Vendors already control many vital aspects of a firm's day-to-day operations. For example, third parties normally provide electricity and telephone services, and the interruption of those services can cripple an organization in a short time. Providing sustained internal backup for these services is often impractical or impossible. As we have seen in some cases, vendors are better able to provide highly reliable services than are their customers.

Putting innovation and responsibility for new services and products in the hands of a third party is correctly seen as more risky and high-stakes than outsourcing operations. Concerns about outsourcing responsibility for new services and products are more easily resolved for firms in the factory and support quadrants of the strategy grid, where innovation is much less important, than they are for firms in the turn-around and strategic quadrants. Whatever a firm's grid location, however, it must carefully develop detailed performance standards for systems response time, availability of service, responsiveness to systems requests, and so on. These standards must be explicitly written into the contract.

Areas to Outsource

A company can outsource many aspects of IT activities. Broken Hill, for example, outsourced all of its IT activities. Kodak kept systems development but outsourced data center operations, communications, and PC acquisition, each to a different vendor. As we noted earlier, significant portions of firms' IT activities have been outsourced for years. What is at stake here is a discontinuous shift to move additional portions of a firm's IT activities outside the firm. Between the current situation and total outsourcing lie a variety of scenarios. When assessing incremental outsourcing, managers should ask the following questions:

- Can the portion of IT proposed for outsourcing be separated easily from the rest of the firm, or will the complexities of disentangling systems absorb most of the savings?
- Do the activities proposed for outsourcing require particular specialized competencies that we do not possess or lack the time to build?
- How central are the activities to be outsourced to the strategy of our firm? Are they more or less significant to the firm's value chain than the other IT activities?

In outsourcing smaller portions of IT activities, it is important to take into account coordination costs. Companies whose outsourcing approaches over time became fragmented experience enormous coordination costs as they attempt to manage relationships with a large number of vendors.

Cost Savings

Some CIOs believe that the firm's IT activities are so well managed or so unique that there is no way to achieve savings through outsourcing or for the vendor to profit. Skepticism about such beliefs is often warranted, however. The IT department often has a vested interest in status quo organizational arrangements and may resist outsourcing at every turn. Thus, carrying out an objective assessment of the benefits of outsourcing can be very difficult. At one company, an internally initiated study done by a consultant retained by the IT department showed that the firm's IT operations were 40 percent more efficient than the average in its industry. The results from a subsequent study refuted that claim.

If properly engaged by a firm's senior managers, however, outsourcing consultants can make a real contribution to efforts to evaluate cost savings as well as in negotiating a contract with an outsourcing vendor. Customer firms outsource infrequently, in some cases only once. Outsourcing vendors are more practiced at negotiating outsourcing deals. Without outside assistance, a customer firm can be overmatched in an unbalanced negotiating process.

Supplier Stability and Quality

During the typical 10-year term of an outsourcing contract, technologies will evolve. A supplier that pays insufficient attention to ongoing modernization and retraining will become a liability as a strategic partner. The stability of the outsourcing vendor's financial structure is also critical. Vendor cash crunches, Subchapter 11, and worse situations are nightmares for customers. Once a firm outsources, it is very hard to bring the applications back to the company. Key aspects of the firm's technical and managerial competence will have evaporated since the outsourcing deal was consummated. Although it is difficult to move quickly from one outsourcing vendor to another (usually the only practical alternative), if it considers the possibility in advance, a firm can mitigate the risks.

Problems are intensified if the way a firm uses technology becomes incompatible with the outsourcing vendor's skill base. For example, a firm in the factory quadrant that selects an operationally strong outsourcing vendor may be in trouble if it suddenly moves toward the strategic quadrant and its partner (the outsourcing vendor) lacks the necessary project management and innovation skills to operate there.

The firm and the outsourcing vendor must manage any potential conflict of interest carefully so that it does not ruin the relationship. The outsourcing vendor makes money by lengthening leases, driving down operational costs, and charging premium prices for new value-added services. The outsourcing customer has little interest in harvesting old technology benefits; old technology is usually one reason the firm outsourced in the first place. The mechanisms for managing potential tensions must be written into the contract. Both firms must make a profit. The more the customer moves to the strategic quadrant, however, the more challenging it is to design a good fit with an outsourcing vendor.

Management Fit

Putting together a 10-year, flexible evolving relationship requires more than just technical skill and contract wizardry. A shared approach to problem solving, similar values, and good personal chemistry among key staff people are critical determinants of long-term success. Outsourcing vendors have very different management cultures and styles. It is often worthwhile for a customer firm to give up something in price to engage an outsourcing partner that will work well over the long term. The information gained in a tortuous six- to eight-month process of putting an alliance together is crucial for identifying the likelihood of a successful partnership. Personal chemistry is a necessity, but it is an insufficient condition for success. Corporate culture fit is the most important factor. Years after the people key to establishing the initial relationship have moved to other assignments, the outsourcing relationship will remain in place.

Conversion Problems

The period of time during an outsourcing study and conversion is one of great stress for a company's IT staff. Uncertainties about career paths and job security contribute to the potential for problems. The sooner plans and processes for dealing with staff career issues, outplacement processes, and separation pay are addressed, the more effective the results will be. Fear of the unknown is almost invariably worse than any reality.

Managing the Alliance

The ongoing management of an alliance is the single most important aspect of the success of outsourcing. There are four critical areas that require close attention.

The CIO Function

The customer firm must retain a strong, active CIO function. The heart of the CIO's job is planning—ensuring that IT resources are at the right level and are appropriately distributed. This role has always been distinctly separate from the active line management of networks, data centers, and systems development, although this has not always been recognized. Line activities can be outsourced, but sustained internal CIO responsibility for the following critical areas must be maintained even in a company that has fully outsourced its IT function.

- *Partnership/contract management.* An informed CIO who monitors performance against the contract and plans for and deals with issues that arise helps an outsourcing alliance adapt to change. The outsourcing experiences of Kodak and J. P. Morgan/Chase provide clear evidence of the need for this ongoing role.

- *Architecture planning.* A CIO's staff must visualize and coordinate a long-term approach to networks, hardware and software standards, and database architectures. The firm can delegate execution of these areas but not its assessment of what it needs to support the firm in the long term. A staff roughly 5 percent the size of the outsourced IT organization is the norm, although in practice the percentage may vary in either direction. In general, organizations should err on the side of too much coordinating staff.

- *Emerging technologies.* A company must develop a clear grasp of emerging technologies and their potential applications. To understand new technology, managers must attend vendor briefings and peer group seminars and visit firms that currently are using the new technology. Assessing technology alternatives cannot be delegated to a third party. At one large pharmaceutical organization, the CIO's staff was vindicated when it became clear that it had first spotted business process redesign as an emerging area, funded appropriate pilot projects (which were skillfully transferred to line management), and finally repositioned the firm's entire IT effort. Users and an outside systems integrator executed the project, with the CIO playing the crucial initiator role. An outsourcing vendor has an incentive to suggest new ideas that lead to additional work. Delegating responsibility for IT-enabled innovation in strategic and turnaround firms is risky because this is such an important part of the firm's value chain.

- *Continuous learning.* A firm should create an internal IT learning environment to bring users up to speed so that they are comfortable in a climate of continuous change. An aerospace firm felt this was so important that, when outsourcing, it kept the internal learning environment in-house.

Performance Measurement

Realistic measurement of outsourcing success is generally difficult, and so companies must develop performance standards, measure results, and then interpret them continuously. Individual firms bring entirely different motivations and expectations to the table. In addition, many of the most important measures of success are intangible and play out over a long period of time. Concrete, immediate cost savings, for example, may be measurable, at least in the short run, but simplification of the general management agenda is impossible to assess.

The most celebrated cases of outsourcing have evolved in interesting ways. Whereas Kodak's major vendor remains intact, another vendor has gone through several organizational transformations triggered by financial distress. In its first 18 months of outsourcing General Dynamics spun off three divisions along with their contracts. EDS and General Motors (GM) took years to work out an acceptable agreement; ultimately, EDS was spun out as a separate company, and its share of GM's internal IT work has been shrinking. Recently Sears transferred its outsourcing of infrastructure from IBM to CSC, and now with its acquisition by Kmart, back in house.

A major power company postponed an outsourcing study for a year. Its general managers believed their internal IT staff and processes were so bloated that while outsourcing IT would clearly produce major savings, they would still be leaving money on the table. Consequently, they reduced their IT staff from 450 to 250 and reduced the total IT expenditure level by 30 percent. With the "easy" things done, they then entertained several outsourcing proposals to examine more closely what additional savings and changes in their method of operation would be appropriate and then proceeded to outsource.

Mix and Coordination of Tasks

As we noted earlier, the larger the percentage of a firm's systems development portfolio devoted to maintaining legacy systems, the lower the risk of outsourcing the portfolio. The question becomes: Can we get these tasks done significantly faster and less expensively? The bigger the percentage of large, low-structured projects in the systems development portfolio is, the more difficult it becomes to execute a prudent outsourcing arrangement because the necessary coordination work to be done is much more intense. Large systems development projects using advanced technology play directly to outsourcing vendors' strengths. Conversely, issues relating to structure (and thus close, sustained give-and-take by users) require so much extra coordination that many outsourcing benefits tend to evaporate.

If not carefully managed, both the contract and the different geographic locations of the outsourcing vendor's development staff may inhibit discussion and lead to additional costs. Managing the dialogue across two organizations with very different financial structures and motivations is both challenging and, at the core, critical to the alliance's success. Concerns in this area led J. P. Morgan and Dupont not to outsource significant portions of their development activity.

Customer-Vendor Interface

The importance of the sensitive interface between the customer and the outsourcing vendor cannot be overestimated. First, outsourcing cannot imply delegation of final responsibility to the outsourcing vendor. The reality is that oversight cannot be entrusted to someone outside the firm, and as we have mentioned, a CIO and the supporting staff need to manage the agreement and relationships. Additionally, the interfaces between the customer and the outsourcing vendor are very complex and usually must occur at multiple levels. At the most senior levels there must be links to deal with major issues of policy and relationship restructuring, whereas at lower levels there must be mechanisms for identifying and handling more operational and tactical issues. For firms in the strategic quadrant, these policy discussions occur at the CEO level and involve the board of directors.

Both the customer and the outsourcing vendor need regular full-time relationship managers and coordinating groups lower in the organization to deal with narrow operational issues and potential difficulties. These integrators are crucial for managing different economic motivations and friction. The smaller the firm is in relationship to the outsourcing vendor's total business, the more important it is that these arrangements be specified in advance before they get lost among other priorities.

During the last 10 years an entirely different way of gaining IT support for outsourcing has emerged. While outsourcing is not for everyone, a number of very large and sophisticated organizations have made the transition successfully, and the practice is growing rapidly. What determines success or failure is managing the relationship less as a contract and more as a strategic alliance.

Summary

In this chapter we described a framework for managing large outsourcing programs. The framework identifies the characteristics of situations in which outsourcing makes sense and the issues involved in structuring and managing outsourcing alliances. Many aspects of the framework are relevant to the earlier discussion of incremental outsourcing, but the unique challenges posed by strategic alliance-based programs require special attention. Executives can use the following questions to assess whether they are seizing the opportunities provided by outsourcing and managing the associated risks:

1. Have you assessed the case for outsourcing some or all of your company's IT activities? If past studies indicated that outsourcing did not make sense, how confident are you of the objectivity of those studies?

2. If you are engaged in outsourcing relationships, have you built the need to change the relationship over time into the contract? Do you have specific mechanisms in place to indicate when an adjustment to the contract might be called for?

3. Do your outsourcing arrangements provide profits for both parties to the agreement?

4. Have you retained an internal CIO function to perform the IT planning and contract monitoring functions that cannot be delegated? Have you adequately funded and staffed this internal group?

5. Do you have practices in place to nurture and maintain the health of the outsourcing relationship?

10

A Portfolio Approach to Managing IT Projects

A division of a major chemical company halts its SAP installation and takes a major write-off. Although the company had successfully implemented SAP before, this time an inexperienced project manager misjudges the amount of change that must be managed during the project. The company starts over with an experienced project manager and a change management consultant. Losses are in the millions.

A major credit card company underestimates processing requirements by more than tenfold as it moves its online credit card processing to a new service provider and discovers this only as the system "goes live." It crashes. One and one-half million accounts are at risk. Service levels plunge. The chief information officer (CIO) and one of his direct reports lose their jobs.

A manufacturing company consolidates activities from more than 50 plants, field offices, and order entry points into a national service center. Only after consolidation is well under way does the company realize that wait time to confirm orders averages 25 seconds. In the estimation of firm managers, any wait longer than 2 seconds makes the system unusable.

Two major insurance companies attempt to install the same software package to solve an identical problem with their field sales forces. In one company, the new technology generates a 46 percent increase in sales from one year to the next. In the other, all the money is wasted; $600 million is written off with no benefit.

These examples are disturbingly recent. Most date from the end of the 1990s, some from the years since 2000. Despite 40 years of accumulated experience in managing information technology (IT) projects, big disasters on major IT projects still occur. Why? Research over the last 10 years suggest three deficiencies that involve general and IT management could be responsible: (1) failure to assess (or acknowledge) the implementation risk of a project at the time it is funded, (2) failure to consider the aggregate implementation risk of a portfolio of projects, and (3) failure to recognize that different projects require different managerial approaches. In this chapter we examine the sources of implementation risk and suggest strategies for managing it.

Sources of Implementation Risk

Risk is a necessary part of a project experience. And it is not inherently bad. Rather, it is an essential characteristic of projects that promise benefits. The idea of taking on higher risk for a higher return is basic to business thinking. All beneficial business activities undertake risk, and project management is no different.

Project feasibility studies typically provide estimates of financial benefits, qualitative benefits, implementation costs, target milestone and completion dates, and staffing levels. Developers of estimates often provide voluminous supporting documentation. Only rarely, however, do they deal frankly with the risks of slippage in time or cost overruns, or the possibility of outright failure. This need not be true. Discernible characteristics of projects can be translated into indicators of project risk that are every bit as tangible as project cost or duration.

Three important project dimensions influence *inherent* implementation risk:

Project size. The larger the project in terms of budget, staffing levels, duration, and number of departments affected, the greater the risk. Multimillion-dollar projects carry more risk than do $50,000 efforts and tend to affect the company more if the risk is realized. Project size is relative. A $1 million project in a department whose average undertaking costs $2 million to $3 million usually has lower implicit risk than does a $250,000 project in a department whose projects have never cost more than $50,000.

Experience with the technology. Project risk increases when the project team and organization are unfamiliar with the hardware, software, or other project technologies. New technology projects are intrinsically more risky than are projects that use familiar technologies. A project posing a slight risk for a large, leading-edge IT group may be highly risky for a smaller, less technically advanced group. By hiring consultants with expertise in those technologies, a company can potentially reduce the risk associated with unfamiliar technologies, but hiring experts is not a cure-all.

Requirements volatility. For some projects the nature of the task fully and clearly defines project outputs. From the project's beginning throughout its duration, outputs remain fixed. Inherent stable requirements make these projects easier to manage. Other projects do not have such convenient characteristics. Requirements for these projects are volatile, difficult to determine, and they tend to evolve throughout the project.

An insurance company's project to create a notebook computer version of an agent's rate book provides an example of a project with low requirements volatility. At the beginning of the project, planners reached an agreement on the product lines to be included, the layout of each page screen, the process of generating each number, and the type of client illustration that would be possible. Throughout the life of the project these decisions were never altered. Consequently, the team organized itself to reach a stable, fixed output rather than to cope with a potentially mobile target. The key risk, effectively managed, was training the agents to operate in new ways.

FIGURE 10.1
Effect of Adding Risk Factors (Large Size, High Technology, High Requirements Volatility) on Project Risk

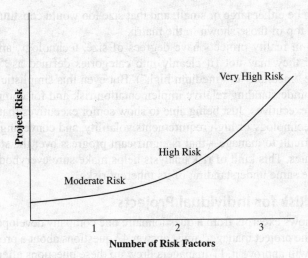

Project Categories and Degree of Risk

Figure 10.1 shows how the project characteristics just identified influence project risk. If we consider *large* project size, *high* technology, and *high* requirements volatility to be risk factors, then each factor that we add increases the project risk. Moreover, as risk factors accumulate, the risk increases at an even greater pace. In other words, a project with two risk factors—say large size and high requirements volatility—is more than twice as risky as a project with just one of those factors.

Figure 10.2 provides examples of projects that fit into high-risk categories because of high technology or high requirements volatility. We omit project size from this matrix for simplicity (and because project size is a more intuitive concept than technology or requirements volatility). But it should be clear that a project in any of these

FIGURE 10.2
Project Examples by Implementation Risk Categories

	High Requirements Volatility	Low Requirements Volatility
Low Technology*	Spreadsheet support for budgeting	Year 2000 compliance work
High Technology*	Online graphic support for advertising copy	Artificial intelligence (AI)–driven bond trading

*As we have noted, high or low technology must be judged relative to a company's past experiences. What is high tech for one company may be low tech for another (and vice versa).

categories can be either large or small, and that size too would constitute an additional risk factor on top of those shown in the matrix.

Of course, in reality projects have degrees of size, technology, and requirements volatility, and they may not fit cleanly into categories defined as "high" or "low" (some may be "medium" or "medium high"). But even this simplistic view can be of great use for understanding relative implementation risk and for communicating that risk to senior executives. Just being able to show senior executives that a project leans toward high technology or high requirements volatility, and conveying that it is therefore more difficult to manage—that is significant progress over the state of affairs in many companies. This kind of risk analysis helps make sure everybody involved in a project has the same understanding of its inherent risks.

Assessing Risk for Individual Projects

Figure 10.3 shows excerpts from a questionnaire one company developed for assessing project risk. The project manager[1] must answer 42 questions about a project before senior managers will approve it. IT managers drew up these questions after analyzing past experiences with successful and unsuccessful projects. Although these questions may not be appropriate for all companies, they provide a starting point for thinking about implementation risk. Other companies have developed their own questionnaires. Such questionnaires take many forms, but all serve a common purpose: To translate project characteristics into indicators of project risk that can inform management decisions.

The questions not only highlight the sources of implementation risk but also suggest alternative routes to conceiving the project and managing it to reduce risk. If the initial aggregate risk score seems high, analyses of the answers can suggest ways of reducing the risk: By reducing project scope, using more familiar technology, or breaking the project into multiple phases. Awareness of risk can encourage better approaches to project management. Questions 5 and 6 in the "Risk Factor–Requirements Volatility" section of the questionnaire are good examples of questions that could trigger changes.

The higher the risk score, the greater the need for senior approval. In the company that developed this questionnaire, only the executive committee can approve projects with very high scores. This approach ensures that top managers are aware of significant hazards and are making appropriate trade-offs between risk and strategic benefits.

The questionnaire is readministered several times during the project to reveal changes in risks. Ideally, risk assessment scores decline throughout implementation as the number and size of the remaining tasks dwindle and familiarity with the technology increases.

When senior managers believe a project has low implementation risk but IT managers know it has high implementation risk, horror stories can result. The questionnaire helps prevent potential misunderstandings by encouraging a common understanding among senior management, IT managers, and business managers about a project's degree of risk.

---

[1] Actually, both the project leader and the key user answer these questions, and then they reconcile the differences in their answers. Of course, the questionnaire data are no better than the quality of thinking that goes into the answers.

Managing the "Dip" during Project Implementation[2]

In most IT projects, there arrives a time when substantial difficulties materialize, even if managers and IT staff have planned and executed well. In most cases, this happens at "cutover," when the new system goes live. Even some of the most successful implementations experience a feeling of everything going bad or everything suddenly being broken at cutover. When this occurs, business users and their managers can quickly lose confidence in the system and the IT staff. A crisis may ensue. How managers handle such a crisis is a major determinant of project success; thus, managing this "dip" in performance is an important part of managing project risk.

Figure 10.3 compares the expectations of business users about the performance impact of a new computer system with the way such impacts actually happen. Not surprisingly, business users and executives primarily think about new systems in terms of the improvement they will provide. Indeed, advocates of a new system may have engaged in a certain amount of "selling" of a project as they sought approval to go ahead with it. Frequently a project is sold on the basis of the picture at the top of Figure 10.4; people are surprised when it unfolds in a pattern more like the one depicted on the bottom in Figure 10.4.

Moreover, when a company arrives at that point in time corresponding to the downward slope of the dip, business managers see only the downward trend, which ends in disaster if it continues, not the eventual upturn. As we noted at the beginning of this chapter, concerns that the dip might be deep or that it might end in disaster are far from misplaced. Many projects do go bad or become disasters, often at cutover. Business users may even feel betrayed. They were promised improvement but instead the new system seems to have made their jobs harder. Nostalgia for the old system appears rapidly and the new system gets compared to an ideal version of the old system, its shortcomings forgotten amid cutover trauma.

When faced with cutover difficulties, project managers must find a way to focus, despite a possibly overwhelming torrent of problems and complaints. Problems must be tackled one at a time, in order of importance. IT managers must work hard to educate senior business managers about the inevitability of the dip and the likelihood of upturn, and also to enlist business managers in helping to set priorities for solving problems. Everything may seem like an emergency in such situations, but it is crucial to differentiate between degrees of urgency, between *bad* problems and *very bad* problems, so the latter can be handled first. Business managers can also help during a cutover crisis if they are willing to intervene to protect the project team from unconstructive complaints, which are not uncommon when people are very frustrated. For example, if a business user sends an e-mail "rant" to everyone in a department or company, his or her manager might provide assistance by reminding the user to provide feedback in a professional manner.

Ideally, IT managers will work to communicate the likelihood of a performance dip before it occurs. If business managers expect a dip, they may be less prone to panic when it actually happens. But no amount of expectations management can fully prepare

[2] Our HBS colleague Andrew McAfee has done important research on this phenomenon. See, for example, McAfee, Andrew. "The Impact of Enterprise Technology Adoption on Operational Performance: An Empirical Investigation," *Production and Operations Management Journal* 11, no. 1 (Spring 2002).

FIGURE 10.3   One Company's Project Implementation Risk Assessment Questionnaire (Excerpts from a Total of 42 Questions)

Risk Factor—Size			Weight
1. Total development work-hours for system*			5
100 to 3,000	Low	1	
3,000 to 15,000	Medium	2	
15,000 to 30,000	Medium	3	
More than 30,000	High	4	
2. Estimated project duration			4
12 months or less	Low	1	
13 months to 24 months	Medium	2	
More than 24 months	High	3	
3. Number of departments (other than IT) involved with system			4
One	Low	1	
Two	Medium	2	
Three or more	High	3	

Risk Factor—Requirements Volatility			Weight
1. If replacement system is proposed, what percentage of existing functions are being replaced			5
0–25%	High	3	
25–50%	Medium	2	
50–100%	Low	1	
2. What is the severity of business procedural changes caused by the proposed system?			5
Low		1	
Medium		2	
High		3	
3. How much change is needed in the user organization's structure to meet requirements of the new system?			5
None		0	
Minimal	Low	1	
Somewhat	Medium	2	
Major	High	3	
4. What is the general attitude of the user?			5
Poor, against IT solution	High	3	
Fair, sometimes reluctant	Medium	2	
Good, understands value of IT solution		0	
5. How committed is upper-level business management to the system?			5
Somewhat reluctant or unknown	High	3	
Adequate	Medium	2	
Extremely enthusiastic	Low	1	
6. Has a joint IT-business team been established?			5
No	High	3	
Part-time user representative appointed	Low	1	
Full-time user representative appointed		0	

FIGURE 10.3   One Company's Project Implementation Risk Assessment Questionnaire (Excerpts from a Total of 42 Questions) (continued)

Risk Factor—Technology			Weight
1. Which components of the hardware are new to the company?[†]			5
None		0	
Server	High	3	
Peripherals and/or storage system	High	3	
Client devices	High	3	
Networking or other	High	3	
2. Are major software components or packages new to IT project team?[†]			5
No		0	
Programming language	High	3	
Database or components	High	3	
Large off-the-shelf application	High	3	
Other (please specify)	High	3	
3. How knowledgeable is business in area of IT?			5
First exposure	High	3	
Previous exposure but limited knowledge	Medium	2	
High degree of capability	Low	1	
4. How knowledgeable is business representative in proposed application area?			5
Limited	High	3	
Understands concept but has no experience	Medium	2	
Has been involved in prior implementation efforts	Low	1	
5. How knowledgeable is IT team in proposed application area?			5
Limited	High	3	
Understands concept but has no experience	Medium	2	
Has been involved in prior implementation efforts	Low	1	

Note: Since the questions vary in importance, the company assigned weights to them subjectively. The numerical answer to a question is multiplied by the question's weight to calculate the question's contribution to the project's risk. The numbers are then added to produce a risk score for the project. Projects with risk scores within 10 points of each other are indistinguishable in their relative risk, but those separated by 100 points or more are very different in their implementation risk to even the casual observer.

*Time to develop includes system design, programming, testing, and installation.

†This question is scored by multiplying the sum of the numbers attached to the positive responses by the weight.

Source: This questionnaire is adapted from "Dallas Tire," Harvard Business School Case No. 180-006. Copyright © 1980 President and Fellows of Harvard College.

business users and their managers for the shock of sudden and severe difficulties that they may face at cutover. This point in a project often amounts to a moment of truth; managers can respond constructively or not. How well managers, both IT and business, perform during cutover crises is a factor that separates companies destined for success with major project implementation from those destined to descend into disaster.

Portfolio Risk

In addition to determining relative risk for single projects, a company should develop a profile of aggregate implementation risk for its portfolio of systems projects. Different portfolio risk profiles are appropriate to different companies and strategies.

For example, in an industry where IT is strategic (such as retailing or catalog sales), managers should be concerned if there are no high-risk projects in the project portfolio.

FIGURE 10.4

What People Expect and What Often Happens at System Cutover

Major improvement programs are usually "sold" within an organization with a picture (sometimes implicit) that looks something like this:

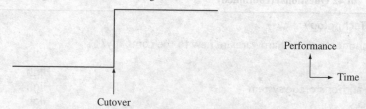

When these programs begin, they proceed in accord with a picture that looks more like this:

Such a cautious stance may open a product or service gap through which the competition may seize advantage. A portfolio loaded with high-risk projects, however, suggests that the company may be vulnerable to operational disruptions if projects are not completed as planned. Referring back to the strategic grid discussed in earlier chapters, for "support" companies, heavy investment in high-risk projects may not be appropriate; they should not be taking strategic gambles in the IT arena. Yet even these companies should have some technologically challenging ventures to ensure familiarity with leading-edge technology and maintain staff morale and interest.

These examples suggest that the aggregate implementation risk profiles of the portfolios of any two companies can legitimately differ. The risk profile should include projects executed by outside systems integrators as well as those of the internal systems development group. IT's aggregate impact on corporate strategy is an important determinant of the appropriate amount of implementation risk to undertake.

Figure 10.5 depicts a way of thinking about a portfolio of projects in terms of aggregate risk. Projects tend to cluster around the diagonal in this picture because, in business, high risk tends to be associated with the potential for high reward. But projects may be distributed differently along the diagonal; they could be spread out evenly, or they could be clumped at the upper left or lower right. How they should be distributed depends on the firm's business strategy. If a company includes "aggressive use of technology to maintain competitive advantage" in its strategy statements but has IT projects clumped at the bottom right in this picture, managers ought to contemplate whether this makes sense. If a company's managers do not expect new IT systems to contribute significantly to the firm's competitive strategy, projects clumped in the upper left corner should prompt a serious review.

In many companies, project portfolios drift out of alignment with business strategy. The most prominent reason: Projects are usually conceived and financially justified one at a time, not as a group. Formal financial criteria, such as return on investment, often favor derivative projects, which are similar to projects already completed and

FIGURE 10.5

Risk and Return Distribution for a Portfolio of Projects

Source: Adapted from Steven C. Wheelwright and Kim B. Clark, *Revolutionizing Product Development: Quantum Leaps in Speed, Efficiency and Quality* (New York: Free Press, 1992).

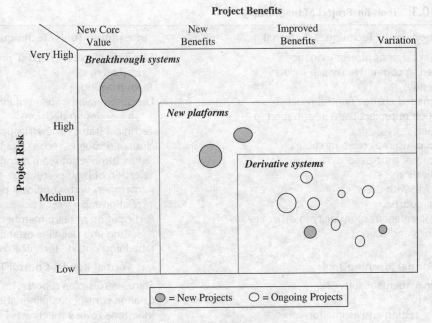

known to be valuable. Breakthrough projects do less well in formal project evaluation because their potential benefits are less certain and because they entail higher risk. In companies that rely heavily on formal approval processes, project portfolios may shift down and to the right over time. Periods of great technology enthusiasm, such as the late 1990s, produce the opposite problem: Project portfolios shift to the upper left, toward more risk than may be consistent with a company's business strategy.

Project Management: A Contingency Approach

Inexperienced project managers sometimes assume that there is a single right approach to project management. There are indeed general-purpose tools that can be used in managing IT implementation (we describe some later), but the contribution each makes to project planning and control depends on the project's characteristics. Further, the means of involving the user—through steering committees, representation on the team, or as a team leader—should also vary by project type: In short, there is no single correct approach to all projects.

Management Tools

Tools for managing projects are of four types:

External integration tools include organizational and other communication devices that link the project team's work to system users, current and prospective, at both managerial and lower levels.

Internal integration tools, which include various personnel controls and communication devices, ensure that a project team operates as an integrated unit.

TABLE 10.1 Tools for Project Management

Integration Tools/Techniques, External	Integration Tools/Techniques, Internal
Selection of user as project manager	Selection of experienced IT professional to lead team
User steering committee (which meets frequently)	Team meetings
User-managed change control process	Distribution within team of information on key design decisions
Distribution of project team information to key users	Technical status reviews/inspections
Selection of users as team members	Human resources techniques to maintain low turnover of team members
User approval process for system specifications	Selection of high percentage of team members with significant previous work relationships
Prototyping with users	Participation of team members in goal setting and deadline establishment
Progress reports	Obtaining outside technical assistance
User involvement/responsibility in other key decisions and actions	

Formal Planning Tools	Formal Results Control Tools
Project management software	Status-versus-plan reports
PERT, CPM	Change control disciplines and systems
Milestone setting and estimation tools	Milestone review meetings
Systems specifications processes	Analysis of deviations from plan
Project approval processes	
Postproject audit procedures	

Formal planning tools help structure the sequence of project tasks in advance and estimate the time, money, and technical resources the team will need to execute them.

Formal result controls help managers evaluate progress and spot potential discrepancies so that corrective action can be taken.

Table 10.1 provides many examples of tools in each of these categories. Integration tools primarily assist with the communications necessary to develop a common understanding of project objectives, characteristics, and potential outcomes. When successful, they make sure everyone is "on the same page," both business and IT staff (external integration) and within the project team (internal integration). Planning tools help translate what is known about a project into summary indicators that matter from a business standpoint: Costs, timelines, and definitions of expected outcomes; they are primarily aimed at making a project more understandable. Result controls help managers determine whether a project is on course; they are evaluative and sometimes help diagnose problems with how a project is going.

Influences on Tool Selection

Different project types call for the use of different management tools. Using the project categories in Figure 10.2, we describe the tools most suitable for each project type below.

Low Requirements Volatility/Low-Technology Projects

Projects with stable requirements that present familiar technical problems are the easiest projects to manage. Unfortunately, they are also the least common. When requirements are stable, significant change management issues are not present. Project leaders do not have to create extensive administrative processes just to maintain commitment to a design. External integration practices such as assigning IT systems analysts to user departments, mandating heavy representation of users on the design team, and requiring formal user approval of design specifications are unnecessary for this type of project. Other integrating actions, however, such as training users how to operate the system, remain important.

Since the system's concept and design are stable throughout the duration of this type of project and since the technology involved is familiar to the company, the project can be staffed with people with average skill levels. The project leader does not need extraordinary skills. This type of project provides opportunities to train the IT department's junior managers without exposure to high risk.

Formal planning tools (such as program evaluation and review technique [PERT] and critical path method [CPM]) are likely to work well on this type of project. They force the team to develop a thorough and detailed plan that exposes areas of "soft" thinking. Such projects are likely to meet the resulting milestone dates and adhere to the target budget. Results-control techniques for measuring progress against dates and budgets provide reliable data for spotting discrepancies and building a desirable tension within the design team in regard to working harder to avoid slippage.

A portfolio in which 90 percent of the projects are of this type should produce little unplanned excitement for senior and user managers. It also requires a much more limited set of skills for the IT organization than would be needed for portfolios with a different mix of project types.

Low Requirements Volatility/High-Technology Projects

Projects in this category are not easy to manage. Projects involving high technology call for significant elaboration on the practices outlined in most project management handbooks. Converting a mainframe system to run on client-server architecture is a good example of this type of project so long as the objective is replicating the same functions on the new platform. Another example is a firm's initial efforts at Web-enabling access to key content for internal use by company employees.

For this type of project to succeed, interaction between the project team and the business users is not crucial. The outputs are well defined by the nature of the undertaking so dealing with changes that users request is relatively unimportant. Interaction with users, however, is important in two respects: (1) to ensure agreement on business procedure changes necessary for project success, and (2) to deal with adjustments made necessary by unexpected shortcomings in the project's technology.

In this kind of project, it is common to discover during implementation that the selected technology is inadequate for the task; this may force a postponement while new technology is chosen or vital features of the system are modified to make the task fit the available technology. This was true of the firm described at the beginning of the chapter that consolidated activities from over 50 plants into a national call center.

For this type of project, technical complexity drives the characteristics of a successful manager. The manager should have a strong background in high-technology projects (preferably, but not necessarily, in an IT environment) and should be able to "connect" with the deep technologists the project will require. The ideal manager will foster an atmosphere of communication within the project that will help anticipate difficulties before technologists understand they have a problem. When managing large projects in this category, an effective project leader must establish and maintain teamwork, develop a record of all key design decisions, and call subproject meetings as needed.

Formal planning methods that identify tasks and set completion dates will have much less predictive value. The team will not understand key elements of the technology in advance. All too often, seemingly minor bugs will have major financial consequences.

At one company, an online banking system generated "garbage" (Os and Xs) across all the computer screens roughly once each hour. One keystroke erased the "ghost," but it remained a disconcerting aspect of a banking system. Four months and more than $200,000 were dedicated to eliminating the mysterious quirk. Solving the problem involved uncovering a complex interaction of hardware features, operating system functions, and application traffic patterns. Indeed, a vendor ultimately had to redesign several microprocessor chips to solve the problem once and for all. Formal results-control mechanisms have limits in monitoring the progress of such projects, and personnel controls become more important.

In summary, technical leadership and internal integration are the keys in this type of project; external integration plays a distinctly secondary role. Formal planning tools yield estimates that may contain major inaccuracies, and great danger results when neither IT managers nor high-level executives recognize this. Managers who do not acknowledge the inherent level of uncertainty may believe they have precise planning and close controls in place when in fact they have neither.

High Requirements Volatility/Low-Technology Projects

When high volatility/low-technology projects are well managed, they present low-risk profiles. Too often, though, such projects fail because of inadequate understanding and focus on business requirements. Indeed, the key to operating this kind of project lies in effective efforts to involve the users in design, development, and implementation.

Developing substantial user support for a system design and keeping the users committed to that design are critical. Such projects therefore benefit from the following:

1. A user as project leader or as the number two person on the team.
2. A user steering committee to evaluate the design periodically.
3. Breaking the project into a sequence of small, discrete subprojects.
4. Formal user review and approval on all key project specifications.
5. Distributing minutes of all key design meetings to the users.
6. Adhering, when possible, to all key subproject time schedules. Low turnover among users is important here; a consensus reached with a user manager's predecessor is of dubious value.

The SAP debacle described in the beginning of the chapter illustrates what can happen when a project in this category does not benefit from adequate user involvement. End-user requirements for the system were unclear from the beginning. The project manager and his staff paid little heed to communications with users or to change management. In the middle of the project people with limited technical backgrounds and no familiarity with the division's operations replaced key users. Although the technology was familiar to the company, a mismatch grew between the design of the system and the needs of the organization. Eventually the mismatch became impossible to ignore. At a cost of millions of dollars, the project was halted, restaffed, and restarted.

Once the design is finalized, the importance of user leadership increases. At some point after the design is finalized, users almost always come up with "great new ideas." Unless the alternatives they suggest are critical to the business (a judgment best made by a responsible user-oriented project manager), the change requests generated by great ideas must be addressed in a formal change-control process. Unless change control follows a disciplined process, users will make change after change. When this happens, a project evolves rapidly into a state of permanent deferral, its completion forever six months in the future.

If the project is well integrated with users, formal planning tools are very helpful in structuring tasks and removing the remaining uncertainties. Target completion dates can be quite firm as long as the system's target remains fixed. Similarly, the formal results controls afford clear insight into progress to date, flagging both advances and slippages (as long as the systems target remains fixed). Personnel controls also are vital here. If integration with user departments is weak, for example, excessive reliance on results controls will produce an entirely unwarranted feeling of confidence in the project team. By definition, however, the problems of technology management are usually less difficult in a low-technology project than in high-technology ventures, and a staff with a normal mixture of technical backgrounds should be adequate.

In almost every respect a high volatility/low-technology project differs from other types. The key to success is close, aggressive management of external integration, supplemented by formal planning and control tools. Leadership must flow from users rather than from technologists.

High Requirements Volatility/High-Technology Projects

Projects in this category have outputs not clearly defined at the project's start. Such projects are also technically complex. Managers therefore require technical expertise and an ability to communicate with users about business needs. The same intensive external integration needed for high volatility/low-technology projects is necessary here. Total user commitment to a particular set of design specifications is again critical. At the same time, strong technical leadership and internal project integration are vital. This effort requires highly experienced project leaders, and those leaders need wholehearted support from the users. Before undertaking such a project, managers should seriously explore whether the project can be divided in smaller parts or can employ less innovative technology. High volatility/high-technology projects are extremely difficult and should not be undertaken lightly.

Although formal planning and results-control tools are useful here, in the early stages they contribute little to reducing uncertainty or highlighting problems. Planning tools do allow the manager to structure the sequence of tasks. Unfortunately, new tasks crop up with regularity, and those that appear simple and small can suddenly become complex and protracted. Further, unsuspected interdependencies between tasks often become apparent. Time, cost, and the resulting technical performance are almost impossible to predict simultaneously. In NASA's Apollo moon project, for example, technical performance was key and cost and time were secondary. In the private sector, cost and timing usually cannot be considered secondary.

Relative Contribution of Management Tools

The usual corporate handbook on project management, with its single-minded prescriptive approach, fails to deal with the realities of the tasks facing today's managers, particularly those dealing with information technology. The right approach to managing a project flows from the specific characteristics of the project.

Additionally, the need to deal with the corporate culture within which both IT and the project team operate further complicates the project management problem. Formal project planning and results-control tools are much more likely to produce successful results in highly formal environments than they are in companies where the prevailing culture is more informal. Similarly, selecting and effectively using integrating mechanisms is very much a function of the corporate culture. Too many former IT managers have made the fatal assumption that they were in an ideal position to reform the corporate culture.

Emergence of Adaptive Project Management Methods[3]

The trend in the last decade has been toward projects with very volatile requirements that challenge traditional tools for project management and entail very high implementation risk. Business requirements for many enterprise systems are not well defined in advance and also involve new technologies. As investments, these systems have unattractive profiles. They require large investments, most of which must be spent up-front, to achieve uncertain (because of their inherently high implementation risk) benefits.

As we have noted, results-control tools and traditional planning methodologies do not work well in the presence of so much outcome uncertainty. Project managers who are expert in communicating with the user and in project technologies can help mediate the risks. Increasingly, however, outcome uncertainty and difficulty in determining system requirements are leading to evolution in the project management process.

An emerging response to these conditions is *adaptive methods:* Approaches to design, deployment, implementation, and investment that assume a need to gather information and to learn as one goes. To be used successfully, adaptive methods require that project staff be able to experiment during a project without incurring prohibitively high costs. Although evolving prototyping technologies allow low-cost project experimentation, adaptive methods are not yet universally applicable. To understand adaptive methods, consider the methodologies they are intended to replace.

Software Development Life Cycles

Traditionally, the activities necessary to design, implement, and operate information systems have been combined into a methodology that is sometimes called the system

---

[3] The materials on "adaptive methods" are based on work by Professor Austin. For a more thorough discussion of such approaches, see Robert D. Austin and Lee Devin, *Artful Making: What Managers Need to Know About How Artists Work* (Upper Saddle River, NJ: Financial Times, Prentice Hall, 2003).

development life cycle (SDLC).[4] SDLC represents IT projects in a sequence of phases. The names of the phases vary across SDLC examples, but most are more or less consistent with the following:

Analysis and design. The traditional process begins with a comprehensive analysis of requirements, followed by documentation of the desired capabilities of the system in a form that can be used by system developers to code and implement the system. Either a user request or a joint IT department/user proposal which includes a formal statement of costs and benefits often initiates the process. IT professionals typically manage the design process. Today, business users and technology specialists—often supported by vendors and/or consultants—determine the requirements for developing a new system or adapting a software package or in-place system.

Construction. Once requirements, costs, and benefits are defined and specifications are developed, the system can be assembled. Traditionally, construction was a highly specialized activity that combined high levels of technological skill with a large dose of art, experience, and logic. Today, system construction involves selecting appropriate computer equipment and then creating, buying, and adapting the computer programs needed to meet system requirements. The final step is to test the system both in the laboratory (often called alpha testing) and in the real-world user environment (often called beta testing). Intense coordination and control are required to assure that the project remains on track, within budget, and focused on user requirements. Even the best designs require numerous interdependent decisions that must be made in real time as the system is being constructed. Large, often dispersed project teams must coordinate closely to ensure that the system components will work together flawlessly. The decision to outsource portions of the project or the entire project markedly increases coordination and control costs because all technical decisions and tasks still must be managed, but this time across firm boundaries.

Implementation. Implementing a new IT system involves extensive coordination between the user and the technologist as the transition is made from the predominantly technical IT-driven task of construction to user-driven ongoing management of the completed system. Whether the system is bought or made, the implementation phase is very much a joint effort. Extensive testing, which may disrupt normal business operations, must be performed; training is required; and work procedures and communication patterns may be disrupted. Often achieving the benefits of the system is dependent on the ability of individuals and groups to learn to use information from the system to make better decisions and add value to the business. It is essential to shape the organization's operational and management structure, processes, and incentives to exploit the potential of an IT system. In this world of electronic commerce, the impact of the system often extends to

---

[4] It is worth noting that the list of responsibilities inherent in this methodology remains with the firm regardless of whether all or a portion of the system development process and IT operations/management is outsourced. The job of IT and business management is to ensure that those tasks are performed in the most effective and efficient manner regardless of where or by whom they are performed.

groups and individuals outside the organization, which further complicates implementation.

Operation and maintenance. To avoid ongoing problems, operation and maintenance are planned in advance, ideally during the early stages of requirements definition and design. Maintenance is complex, particularly for older systems. It requires highly competent professionals to perform the necessary changes safely and in a way that does not bring the system (and the firm) to a crashing halt.

Adaptive Methodologies

Adaptive and prototyping-intensive methodologies call for quickly building a rough preliminary version of the system without going through a lengthy or formal requirement definition or design phase. Interacting with an early prototype makes the system easier to visualize for both users and developers. Thus, adaptive approaches iterate quickly through the traditional phases of design, construction, implementation, and operation, improving the performance of the product each time. Instead of moving slowly and deliberately through development phases, adaptive projects try to loop through each phase every week or even every day. Early prototypes are typically crude, but they are an excellent basis for discussions about system requirements between developers and users throughout development.

Companies that have implemented large enterprise systems successfully, such as Cisco and Tektronix, have tended to restructure projects to formally incorporate the idea of in-progress learning and midcourse adjustment. Although adaptive projects are carried out in a variety of ways, they share five basic characteristics:

1. They are iterative. Design, construction, and implementation occur in small increments that result from each iteration so that outcomes and interactions can be tested as they appear.

2. They rely on fast cycles and require frequent delivery of value so that incremental implementation does not slow down a project. Long lead times and variable delivery timing are discouraged.

3. They emphasize early delivery to end users of functionality, however limited, so that feedback can be incorporated into learning and improvement cycles.

4. They require skilled project staff capable of learning and making midcourse adjustments in the middle of deployment.

5. They often resist return on investment (ROI) and other similar tools for investment decision making that implicitly assume predictability of outcomes, instead emphasizing "buying of information" about outcomes as a legitimate expenditure.[5]

Although Cisco's managers did not explicitly identify their project management approach as "adaptive," they explicitly emphasized "rapid, iterative prototyping" as

---

[5] Robert D. Austin and Richard L. Nolan have suggested in the paper "Manage ERP Initiatives as New Ventures, Not IT Projects" (Harvard Business School Working Paper 99–024) that very large IT projects have risk profiles that resemble those of new ventures more than those of traditional IT projects. Venture investors cope with risky venture profiles by using a variety of adaptive techniques that legitimize the notion of buying information about the new venture. Large IT projects must adopt a similar approach that recognizes the impossibility of knowing everything in advance and the importance of in-progress learning.

the basis for their approach. Tektronix divided its project into more than 20 "waves" that provided formal opportunities for deliberation, adjustment, and learning.

In recent years, adaptive methods have made significant inroads into the ways in which developers create systems and software. As more off-the-shelf system components and more over-the-Net IT services become available, many firms are doing less and less software development internally. But even installing vendor software requires systems development. "Extreme programming" (or XP)[6] and "adaptive software development"[7] are examples of popular adaptive development approaches. Open-source software development, a technique that has led to the development of widely used infrastructure components such as the Linux operating system and the Apache Web server, also has adaptive characteristics.[8]

Adaptive methods emphasize low-cost experimentation and rapid delivery of system prototypes. They deemphasize up-front planning intended to "get it right the first time." In essence, the adaptive approach is to create something that works roughly as quickly as possible, begin to experience unexpected effects as soon as possible, and then change and improve the system rapidly. Adaptive methods are designed to offset the inevitability of unexpected outcomes.

It is worth noting that formal results-oriented controls not only work badly for large, risky projects but also can lead to dysfunction and disaster. For example, holding tightly to early schedule and functionality promises can provide project managers with incentives to downplay or ignore complicating factors that come to light as a project unfolds. Within an adaptive framework, unexpected complications are learning inputs that prompt midcourse adjustments. In a traditional results-oriented framework, complications often are swept under the rug because they interfere with the achievement of preset project milestones and because implementation team members are reluctant to admit that they failed to anticipate the complications. This dysfunctional dynamic can be especially significant if a company has hired expert consultants to assist with implementation. Consultants hired as experts dread admitting that they did not foresee complications, and client company managers often assume that experts must have anticipated all the possible complications. In this situation, an unexpected complication can translate into systemic lack of communication between consultants, who do not want to admit what they did not anticipate, and client managers, who have unrealistic expectations about what the consultants should have foreseen.

Adaptive Methods and Change Management

Earlier in this chapter we noted the importance of exercising discipline when considering the system changes that users suggest once a design is finalized. Adaptive methods do not aspire to finalize a design in a discrete early phase of a project; instead, adaptive methods call for an acceptable design to emerge gradually during the development process. It would be a serious mistake, however, to conclude that change management is less important for adaptive projects.

[6] Kent Beck, *Extreme Programming Explained: Embrace Change* (Reading, MA: Addison-Wesley, 1999).

[7] James A. Highsmith III, *Adaptive Software Development: A Collaborative Approach to Managing Complex Systems* (New York: Dorset House, 1999).

[8] Eric S. Raymond, *Cathedral & the Bazaar: Musings on Linux & Open Source by an Accidental Revolutionary* (O'Reilly & Associates, 2001).

Adaptive projects achieve change management in part by intensely involving users in evaluating the outcome of each development iteration and deciding on the next enhancement to be introduced into the system. Users are forced to confront at every iteration trade-offs between delay in obtaining useful results and implementation of their "great ideas." When the development process is an active collaboration between users and the IT staff, a natural discipline evolves to control unreasonable user requests.

But change management becomes important for adaptive projects in a different sense as well. Adaptive methods are an emerging response to outcome uncertainty in systems development. Rigorous *change management* is the corresponding response to the same kind of uncertainty when one changes existing systems vital to a company's operations. The approaches are two halves of a management system for balancing IT systems agility with rigorous operational control.

The essence of sound change management is to strictly control the migration of system features from development, through testing, into production with a clear understanding of the benefits and the potential for unanticipated problems at each stage. Successful change managers introduce new system features into production infrastructure with high confidence in the changes. They know at all times exactly what is running in their production environment and are therefore better able to diagnose problems and respond to incidents quickly. Effective change management in fact makes adaptive development possible by insulating the production environment from adaptive experimentation. Adaptive methods make sense only when the experiments do not result in catastrophic consequences, and effective change management prevents that situation.

Process Consistency and Agility in Project Management[9]

In practice, project management always involves balancing a tension between process consistency and process agility. Project managers need to ensure a thorough and disciplined approach to make sure that no balls are dropped, all requirements are met adequately, and no important details go unnoticed. This usually is accomplished through formal specification of project steps, required documentation, and compliance mechanisms (such as reviews or progress reports). At the same time, however, companies need to retain an ability to change direction, in the middle of a project if necessary, when business conditions require it. The tension arises from the fact that the tools used to improve consistency—specifications, documentation, compliance mechanisms—often are perceived as encumbrances that work against project responsiveness and agility. A firm that is well practiced and expert in its established routines may have trouble changing them. A firm that has grown accustomed to using certain tools may continue to try to use them in business conditions in which they are less appropriate.

In the last decade, many companies have struggled with this issue, including many technology companies for which responsiveness to market and time to market were overriding concerns. For the most part, these companies resisted full-fledged adoption of traditional project methodologies because they perceived that adoption as too damaging to project agility. In place of traditional project management methodologies,

[9] The materials in this section are based on curriculum materials developed by Professor Robert Austin.

many companies have attempted to develop "light" methodologies that contain the essential elements of "heavy" methodologies but are not as cumbersome.

The companies that have been most successful in balancing discipline and agility have neither eschewed process formalization altogether nor let process formalization efforts overwhelm them. Rather, they have developed simple process management tools based on the idea that the best balance is one that includes the minimum formal specification critical to the success of a project. These simple tools fall into three categories:

Flow. People working on projects need to understand the relationships between their activities and those of others. That is, they need to understand the overall process "flow." Process tools in this category can be simple depictions of the process context that are intended to give decision makers at specific points in the process a sense of the overall business picture. Deep detail is not required or recommended. Simple schedules and flowcharts work well here.

Completeness. People working on projects need to be sure that everything is being done, that no ball is being dropped. This is where detail comes into the picture. Tools in this category can be simple lists to convey what needs to be done, when it needs to be done, by whom, and whether it is complete. Simple checklists work well here.

Visibility. People working on projects need to be able to review processes while they are being executed to get status information. Ideally anyone, whether from engineering, marketing, or elsewhere, can review the same "picture" and come away with the information he or she needs. Visibility is not easy to achieve. Computerized status-reporting systems can provide this kind of visibility, but some of the best solutions are simple wall charts that allow status to be tracked in a way that everyone (in one physical location, anyway) can see.

In some contexts, another category of tools must be added: Tools to ensure that project activities are auditable. This may be true of projects that will result in government systems or safety-related systems.

Managing the tension between consistency and agility is, for most companies, a general process issue that extends well beyond project management. Process frameworks from earlier times, when systems were proprietary and the common Internet platform was not available for commerce, significantly encumber many firms. As these companies work to make the transition to new ways of doing business, they face the difficult task of distilling processes down to essential elements to reclaim lost project and organizational agility.

Summary

The last decade has brought new challenges to IT project management and new insights into the management process. Our research in these areas leads us to three conclusions:

1. Firms will continue to experience major disappointments as they push into new application areas and technologies. Today, however, the dimensions of implementation risk can be identified in advance, and this information can be included in the decision process. If a firm implements only high-risk projects, sometimes it will fail.

2. A firm's IT projects in the aggregate represent a portfolio. Just as financial fund managers calculate and manage the risks within their portfolios, general management must make critical strategic decisions on the aggregate implementation risk profile of the IT portfolio.

3. Project management in the IT field is complex and multidimensional; different types of projects require different clusters of management tools.

As we have seen, progress in understanding how to manage projects continues. The emergence of adaptive methods is an interesting development, but we are still evaluating its ultimate applicability. Executives can use the following questions to assess whether they are managing the risks inherent in IT projects to maximize gain:

1. Have we established risk assessment procedures (such as the questionnaire in Figure 10.3) to evaluate the risk of individual projects? Is such a procedure a standard part of project approval and status reporting at the company?

2. Do our project planning, tracking, and control processes account adequately for differences in types of projects (high/low structure, high/low technology)? Are our management expectations about projects sufficiently contingent on inherent project risk factors?

3. Have we performed a risk analysis on our portfolio of application projects? If so, is the portfolio risk profile appropriate to the quadrant of the strategic grid in which we operate? Is it a good fit with our business objectives and strategies?

4. Are we exploring emerging project management methodologies to determine their applicability to our business?

Case 3-1

Cathay Pacific: Doing More with Less

From his office on the sixth floor of Cathay City—Cathay Pacific's state-of-the-art global headquarters at Hong Kong's new international airport—acting general manager of information management, Anthony Yeung, watched a Cathay 747-400 take off for a distant location. As he sipped his morning coffee, he glanced at the December 2002 issue of *CX World*, Cathay's internal newsletter. The cover story headline was a quotation—as well as a directive—from his boss, Cathay Pacific CEO David Turnbull: "Costs Must Come Down to Compete." As Yeung skimmed the article, the message from Turnbull was succinct, clear, and immediate: "Our product is great and our balance sheet is strong. 2002 has been a strange year. At the start we expected to break even at best. It has been a tough year for some airlines, but we have done remarkably well." Turnbull indicated that in order for Cathay Pacific to sustain its profitability, "we must lower our costs and deliver a premium product. The challenge to cut costs is never ending, and our task is to work together to get them down year by year."[1]

The message was crystal clear and echoed across the organization, particularly in the information technology division. Yeung sat back and reviewed the past 30 years of his career in the information management department at Cathay Pacific. During the past five years, Cathay had outsourced several key IT functions, and now with 65 percent of his operating budget outside the company, Yeung wondered what the next steps should be, what else should be outsourced, what should be retained in-house. Yeung wondered

whether the "Smartsourcing" relationship with Cathay's two strategic vendors had proceeded according to plan and how else he could "do more with less," the cost-cutting mandate from above.

Hong Kong Origins

Hong Kong-based Cathay Pacific Airways was founded in 1946 by American Roy C. Farrell and Australian Sydney H. de Kantzow. Initially, Cathay operated two DC-3 passenger flights to Manila, Bangkok, Singapore, and Shanghai. In 1948, one of Hong Kong's largest trading companies, Butterfield & Swire (later known as the Swire Group), acquired a 45 percent share in the company. Cathay Pacific was Hong Kong's *de facto* flagship carrier, and during the 1960s, business grew at an average rate of 20 percent a year with Cathay initiating its first route to Japan.

Along with complete conversion to an all-jet fleet during the 1970s, Cathay Pacific adopted what at the time was cutting-edge technology including flight simulators and a computerized reservation system developed in-house. The first Boeing 747 arrived in Hong Kong in mid-1979, and by the end of the year, Cathay opened routes to London and eventually Europe and North America. The airline industry expanded apace with rapid global economic growth during the 1980s: More business travelers, tourists, and cargo flew on Cathay than ever before and the carrier expanded its route map to include Amsterdam, Frankfurt, Vancouver, Rome, San Francisco, Paris, and Zurich. Deregulation of the airline industry during the 1980s created a highly competitive environment in which all major carriers were forced to cut costs and improve operational efficiency.

In the early 1990s, Cathay embarked on a corporate rebranding exercise, and a new "brushwing" logo similar to the Nike "swoosh" emerged. In part, thanks to Hong Kong's traditional roles as

This case was prepared by Professor F. Warren McFarlan and Senior Researcher Fred Young from the Asia-Pacific Research Center. Copyright © 2003 President and Fellows of Harvard College. Harvard Business School Case No. 303-106.

[1] "Costs Must Come Down to Compete," *CX World*, December 2002, Issue 81, p. 1.

EXHIBIT 1
Cathay Pacific Route Map

Source: Cathay Pacific Web site, http://www.cathaypacific.com/intl/plan/routes/0,,,00.html, 20, March 20, 2003.

✈ **Routes and Destinations**

We think that our fast-growing network of regional and worldwide destinations speaks for itself . . .

• 80 destinations worldwide
• Operates to 30 countries and territories

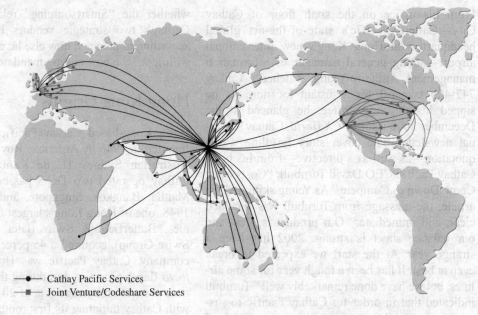

——●—— Cathay Pacific Services
——■—— Joint Venture/Codeshare Services

• Global network with **one**world partners with connections to 135 countries and over 570 destinations
• Connections to 18 destinations in China (through our associated airline, Dragonair)

regional travel hub and trade entrepôt, Cathay continued to expand. By the mid-1990s, Cathay had assembled a comparatively "young" fleet with acquisitions of new aircraft amounting to US$9 billion. Cathay's cargo division grew concurrently with rapid growth in passenger services, with cargo contributing nearly 30 percent of Cathay revenue in late 2002. To better the services offered by both regional and international competitors, Cathay upgraded its inflight services including cuisine and entertainment offerings as well as premium Marco Polo Club and its AsiaMiles Frequent Flyer services.

At the time that Hong Kong relocated its international airport from Kai Tak to Chep Lap Kok in 1998, Cathay simultaneously moved into its new US$628 million state-of-the-art global headquarters at Cathay City. The millennium and the network era brought Cathay online and offered passengers a variety of special services including trip scheduling, online booking, online check-in, and special services targeting frequent flyers and Marco Polo Club premium customers. By November 2002, Cathay employed 15,000 staff and flew around one million passengers every month in 77 wide-bodied aircraft to 62 international destinations. (Exhibit 1 illustrates Cathay Pacific's route map.)

The Cathay Pacific Group made a profit attributable to shareholders of US$511 million during 2002, a sixfold increase over US$84 million in 2001, and had a market capitalization of roughly US$4.9 billion in December 2002. (Exhibit 2 shows earnings from Cathay Pacific's

EXHIBIT 2 Earnings from Cathay Pacific Annual Report: Consolidated Balance Sheet/P&L Account

Source: Cathay Pacific Airways Limited Annual Report 2001 and 2002.

	2002	2001	2000	1999	1998	1997	1996	1995	1994	1993	1992
Consolidated profit and loss summary (HK$M)											
Passenger services	22,376	20,580	22,878	18,979	15,532	21,851	23,680	22,128	20,027	18,321	18,284
Cargo services	9,387	8,343	10,136	8,391	6,995	7,712	6,797	6,641	5,573	4,277	3,974
Catering and other services	1,327	1,513	1,509	1,332	1,123	1,014	1,037	941	800	738	585
Total turnover	33,090	30,436	34,523	28,702	26,610	30,577	31,514	29,710	26,400	23,336	22,843
Operating expenses	(28,340)	(29,604)	(29,234)	(25,891)	(27,281)	(28,537)	(27,738)	(25,956)	(23,258)	(20,767)	(19,230)
Operating profit/(loss)	4,750	832	5,289	2,811	(671)	2,040	3,776	3,754	3,142	2,569	3,613
Net finance charges	(743)	(571)	(367)	(918)	(311)	(335)	(384)	(597)	(557)	(280)	(319)
Profit on sale of investments	—	452	—	482	185	—	559	—	—	—	—
Share of profits on associated companies	324	188	279	108	172	306	363	379	381	316	233
Profit/(loss) before taxation	4,331	901	5,201	2,483	(625)	2,011	4,314	3,536	2,966	2,605	3,527
Taxation	(328)	(202)	(110)	(219)	104	(291)	(484)	(516)	(560)	(288)	(505)
Profit/(loss) after taxation	4,003	699	5,091	2,264	(521)	1,720	3,830	3,020	2,406	2,317	3,022
Minority interests	(20)	(42)	(86)	(84)	(35)	(40)	(17)	(57)	(33)	(32)	(22)
Profit/(loss) attributable to shareholders	3,983	657	5,005	2,180	(556)	1,680	3,813	2,963	2,373	2,285	3,000
Dividends		(1,915)	(1,585)	(339)	(694)	(1,817)	(1,455)	(1,217)	(1,203)	(1,203)	(1,203)
Retained (loss)/profit for the year		(1,258)	3,240	1,841	(1,250)	(137)	2,358	1,746	1,170	1,082	1,797
Consolidated balance sheet summary (HK$M)											
Fixed and intangible assets	52,114		48,959	48,541	47,985	41,787	38,138	28,930	24,226	22,249	20,072
Long-term receivables and investments		3,165	3,756	3,548	3,635	2,728	2,302	2,149	1,789	1,459	1,319
Borrowings		(24,024)	(20,838)	(24,783)	(27,198)	(23,122)	(26,043)	(21,722)	(22,036)	(21,182)	(19,920)
Liquid funds less bank overdrafts		9,746	10,952	11,567	12,240	14,327	20,178	13,926	14,975	14,383	13,755
Net borrowings		(14,278)	(9,886)	(13,216)	(14,958)	(8,795)	(5,865)	(7,796)	(7,061)	(6,799)	(6,165)

(continued)

EXHIBIT 2 Earnings from Cathay Pacific Annual Report: Consolidated Balance Sheet/P&L Account (continued)

	2002	2001	2000	1999	1998	1997	1996	1995	1994	1993	1992
Net current liabilities (excluding liquid funds and bank overdrafts)		(1,764)	(2,752)	(3,944)	(3,970)	(2,652)	(2,904)	(2,539)	(2,153)	(1,705)	(1,962)
Deferred taxation		(7,836)	(7,146)	(6,714)	(6,359)	(5,802)	(5,359)	(3,954)	(3,006)	(1,951)	(962)
Minority interests		(93)	(99)	(86)	(108)	(104)	(78)	(99)	(88)	(33)	(45)
Net assets	32,115	31,308	32,832	28,129	26,225	27,162	26,234	16,591	13,707	13,220	12,257
Financed by:											
Shareholders' funds		31,308	32,832	28,129	26,225	27,162	26,234	16,591	13,707	13,220	12,257
Per share											
Shareholders' funds (HK$)		9.40	9.80	8.31	7.75	8.02	7.63	5.79	4.78	4.61	4.28
EBITDA (HK$)		1.4	2.70	2.07	0.91	1.47	2.06	2.40	2.16	1.69	2.06
Earnings/(loss) (HK cents)		19.7	148.4	64.4	(16.4)	49.1	119.7	103.4	82.8	78.8	104.7
Dividend (HK cents)		17.5	65.0	30.0	10.0	29.0	43.0	48.0	42.0	42.0	42.0
Ratios											
Profit/(loss) margin %		2.2	14.5	7.6	(2.1)	5.5	12.1	10.0	9.0	9.8	13.1
Return of average shareholders' funds %		2.0	16.4	8.0	(2.1)	6.3	17.8	19.6	17.6	17.9	27.5
Dividend cover Times		1.1	2.3	2.1	(1.6)	1.7	2.1	2.2	2.0	1.9	2.5
Interest cover Times		1.5	14.4	3.1	(2.2)	6.1	9.8	6.3	5.6	9.2	11.3
Gross debt/equity ratio Times		0.77	0.63	0.88	1.04	0.85	0.99	1.31	1.61	1.60	1.63
Net debt/equity ratio Times		0.46	0.30	0.47	0.57	0.32	0.22	0.47	0.52	0.51	0.50

2001 Annual Report.) Turnover increased 8.7 percent to US$4.24 billion over 2001, a year that was marked by a precipitous slowdown in global travel following the September 11, 2001 terrorist attacks in the United States, reflecting a gradual recovery in market conditions. With more people traveling, earlier grounded capacity returned to the skies, restoring services temporarily suspended following 9/11. Cathay extended new services to its route schedule including a fifth daily flight to Tokyo and four additional flights to London.

Early System Development

While still predominantly a regional carrier, during the 1970s Cathay developed most of its systems in-house. Yeung, who started his career in IT in 1968 right after graduation, joined Cathay Pacific in 1970 as a programmer and wrote the first reservations system for Cathay called "CPARS," a program that was eventually sold to other airlines. Yeung and a team of systems developers were responsible for writing the code for Cathay's proprietary applications including accounting systems, engineering systems, personnel systems, and flight systems as well as a host of other internal applications. The department started with fewer than 30 systems developers in 1970, and by the late 1990s, had grown into a team of 200.

Cathay Pacific's Data Center coordinated fundamental airline IT functions such as reservation, ticketing, cargo handling, flight scheduling, passenger check-in, engineering requests, flight and ground crew roster scheduling, as well as processing of financial data. Recent years also saw the addition of airline planning systems, customer information systems (CIS), passenger revenue optimization systems, and human resource management systems (HRMS). Critical business functions like these were at the core of any world-class airline and required a robust, fail-safe IT infrastructure.

During the late 1980s, Cathay's Data Center was separated into three locations, one in Kowloon,

near the Kai Tak International Airport, and the other two across the harbor on Hong Kong Island in two separate facilities. Together Cathay's entire Data Center consisted of 10 to 12 mainframe boxes located in climate-controlled facilities to protect the computers from Hong Kong's ubiquitous humidity and dust particulates. Apart from mainframes, the Data Center ran applications and network systems 24 hours a day to provide uninterrupted information to the carrier's mission-critical operations.

In August 1991, a nearby explosion caused a fire at Cathay's Quarry Bay Data Center on Hong Kong Island, thereby interrupting critical business functions such as passenger reservations, departure control, engineering, flight, and crew operations for over 12 hours. (Quarry Bay was a densely populated residential neighborhood in Hong Kong located just across Victoria Harbor from Kai Tak, then Hong Kong's international airport.) When operations were interrupted and all Data Center applications systems were shut down, data had to be backed up with more than 100 data storage tapes physically transferred from Quarry Bay to Kowloon. Mission-critical systems such as crew scheduling, departure control, and reservation systems were finally brought back online following the costly half-day interruption. Meanwhile, the Quarry Bay Data Center took nearly two weeks to eventually restore and resume normal operations.

The fire provided a stark reminder to Cathay management that IT touched every element of the airline; therefore, a reliable facility with secure systems was imperative. With the existing Data Center spread out in three separate locations around Hong Kong and no further space left for expansion at any of them, IT Operations Management began to consider building a reliable, centralized, dedicated facility for the Data Center. An IM operations manager at the time even cautioned that Cathay would require a fourth or even fifth data center facility to meet the company's IT needs if the airline had continued to expand at its current pace.

Moving Mainframes Down Under

With Hong Kong then topping the charts as the most expensive international location for office real estate just behind Tokyo, the general manager of MIS and IT operations manager at the time assessed alternate locations for Cathay's Data Center. People's Republic of China, Singapore, Thailand, Philippines, Australia, and Canada were evaluated based on several key criteria including (1) stable economic and political climate with both a mature business environment and legal framework; (2) developed IT infrastructure with well-established computer fiber-optic networks and strong IT vendor presence; (3) competent IT skill base with ample and affordable human resources to fulfill the Data Center's staffing needs; (4) availability of inexpensive real estate in a location with reliable communication, transportation, and power supply infrastructure; and (5) proximity to Cathay's Hong Kong corporate headquarters, with a time zone close to that of Hong Kong.

For Cathay Pacific, Australia ultimately proved to be the most attractive option for several reasons. For one, the local New South Wales government offered Cathay an exemption from the 20+ percent tax on the import of its 10–12 mainframe boxes and other high tech equipment shipped from Hong Kong. The Australian government also guaranteed automatic free resident visas to all Cathay IM staff asked to relocate to Australia. Secondly, land was far cheaper in Sydney than Hong Kong and sites were available that were not located in expensive, overcrowded business or residential areas. Finally, IT labor costs were on a par with pay levels in Hong Kong, if not cheaper.

Apart from location-specific competitive advantages, on the whole, Australia had an extensive fiber-optic network infrastructure in place with a fast-growing cohort of IT professionals. Several large multinational IT vendors such as CSC, EDS, and IBM had established their presence in the Australian market. This ensured rapid support delivery located in a time zone only two to three hours' different from Hong Kong. Sydney was also only a nine-hour direct flight away from Hong Kong on an existing Cathay direct route. Finally, Australia was fast becoming an increasingly attractive emigration destination for Hong Kong residents planning to either study or work abroad, particularly with the 1997 British handover of Hong Kong to China on many people's minds, thereby ensuring that the Data Center would not be located in a hardship location undesirable to IM staff who were asked to consider relocation.

Located in Sydney's Baulkham Hills, Cathay opened its Data Center in September 1995 with around 25 employees sent from Hong Kong. Apart from the US$30 million data processing facility, Cathay originally had also planned to relocate its training facility to Australia but opted to remain in Hong Kong after more reasonably priced land was made available by the Hong Kong government in early 1996.

Outsourcing: The First Steps

In 1992, Cathay initiated a companywide strategic review exercise known internally as "Operation Better Shape." This initiative involved feasibility studies and stemmed from the realization that Cathay could not afford to operate in the same manner as it had before. In order to remain competitive, cost reductions had to take place across the entire organization, with no department or division excluded. According to one Hong Kong–based analyst: "The company is highly, perhaps too highly, vertically integrated. It does so many things in-house which it should have outsourced."[2] Outsourcing was identified as one critical strategic approach to cutting costs. With nonstrategic functions outsourced to contractors with their

---

[2] Yulanda Chung, "Cost Cutting, Restructuring, and Forays into the New Economy, That's How these Companies Overcame the Crisis," *AsiaWeek*, July 14, 2000.

own individual vertical specialization, it was hoped that a leaner Cathay could focus on its core aviation competencies. The companywide study pointed to the recent outsourcing of business processes such as:

- Building Maintenance
- Lift Maintenance
- Renovation
- Printing
- Transportation
- Medical Services

For the last two processes, Cathay formerly operated buses for its staff, a function outsourced to Cathay subsidiary HAS[3] in 1998. Cathay's clinic was also outsourced in 1998. Information technology outsourcing was thus introduced to Cathay in conjunction with other business process outsourcing initiatives. The key distinction was that in comparison to other more peripheral business units, IT had always been considered a strategic resource. Referring to the IM department's ability to fulfill demand for IT across the company, Yeung acknowledged, "At one point, even in the 1980s, we realized that we could not do it all ourselves, that it took too much time to develop applications, so we started to look at what packages were available." Cathay started purchasing software packages as early as the 1980s. However, according to Yeung, "the Cathay-developed systems, engineering, accounting, etc., all ran quite well and hence there was a resistance to touch these big systems."

During the late 1980s, Yeung's unit changed its name from "Systems Development and Support" to "Systems Delivery" to reflect its changing role: No longer would his team be responsible for writing code and developing applications, but rather delivering IT systems to Cathay business units.

(Exhibit 3 depicts the IM organizational structure in 1999.) The IM department realized that it could no longer afford to spend time and resources developing proprietary applications and instead opted for purchasing packages and deploying open-systems-based applications across the organization. By no longer building and operating their own systems, Cathay hoped that it could deliver systems at less cost, faster, and with reduced risks.

The decision to outsource Cathay's networks to SITA was made during the mid-1980s, when establishing global linkages was an important step of the airline's transition from regional to international carrier. For years, Cathay had purchased services from SITA, a Geneva-based nonprofit cooperative organization providing integrated telecommunications and IT solutions to the air transport industry around the world, with the goal of facilitating connections between carriers. SITA was an acronym for "Airline Telecommunications and Information Services" (from the French "Société internationale de télécommunications aéronautiques"). SITA products covered a range of application, desktop, network, and infrastructure services; systems integration; outsourcing; and consulting. In 2002, SITA had roughly 740 members and served 1,800 customers including airlines, airports, travel reservation systems, and airfreight companies. (See http://www.sita.int.)

Outsourcing was identified as a means to bridge the gap between the IM department and the business side. Fifteen-year Cathay veteran Jessica Cheung, manager of IT planning and architecture, pointed out that "It would take forever for IM to fulfill the requirements of the business side. We had to shift from building and operating to acquiring and managing."

1994–1995: Additional Steps

In mid-1994, a new general manager of IM was appointed with a mandate from then managing director David Turnbull to conduct a strategic review of Cathay's IT systems. The new GM had extensive experience with outsourcing from his

---

[3] Although HAS was 70% owned by Cathay Pacific and 30% by Dragonair, it not only served those two airlines but also all flights at Hong Kong International Airport.

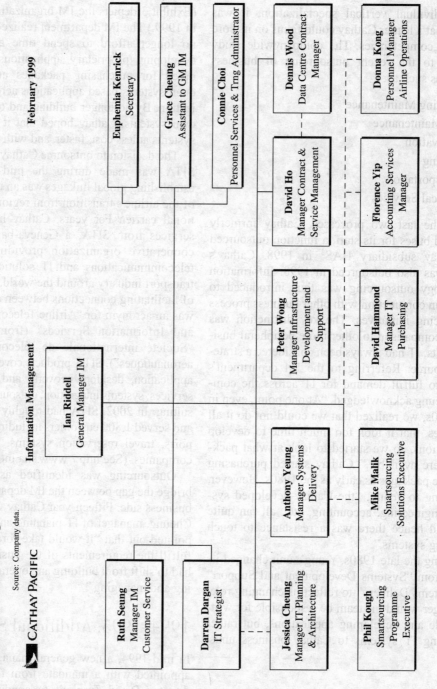

EXHIBIT 3 1999 IM Organization Chart

CATHAY PACIFIC

Source: Company data.

EXHIBIT 4
Cathay Pacific
Information
Technology
Strategy

Source: Company
data.

1. *Focus the use of information technologies on:*

    Providing information to Cathay Pacific managers and staff to enhance their effectiveness in serving customers and managing the business.

    Creating flexibility for the business by making location, time, and structure transparent.

    Supporting or enabling strategic business initiatives designed to capitalize on Cathay Pacific's geographical location in the "Heart of Asia."

    Aggressively pursuing strategic initiatives consistent with this focus, shifting a significant portion of the resources toward their attainment.

2. *Assume a position of being a quick follower with industry practices in the adaptation of information technology, taking selective leadership only for clear and compelling strategic benefits.*

3. *Provide information technology capabilities by:*

    Deploying (and consolidating) IT resources close to the activities they are supporting and gradually devolving their management to the business.

    Focusing a small core of IT resources on ensuring that computing across Cathay is performed efficiently and effectively.

    Strengthening IT managerial oversight across the company.

    Optimally utilizing external IT resources, known as Smartsourcing, for unique competencies and for mitigating investment requirements.

previous tenure at a regional carrier, during which time he established a joint venture between the airline and a local IT company. A three- to five-year business plan was established outlining the strategic components of Cathay's IT strategy, which is summarized in Exhibit 4.

Three operating principles of IM's new IT ideology were:

1. Assume the position of quick follower.
2. Acquire and manage rather than develop and operate.
3. Adopt a vendor strategy of fewer but more strategic suppliers, and to identify key strategic suppliers.

Rather than expend limited IM resources on developing proprietary applications, Cathay decided instead to monitor and follow industry practices in the adoption of new technology. Instead of teams of programmers spending years writing code for Cathay applications such as reservations, engineering, revenue accounting, and so on, the IM team shifted its focus to acquisitions of software packages and managing IT resources as strategic commodities. (Exhibits 5 and 6 illustrate major application systems at Cathay Pacific.)

Finally, the department elected to narrow its choice of IT vendors down to a carefully chosen strategic few, a precursor to finalizing strategic outsourcing alliances that Cathay was then in the process of evaluating.

1997–1998: Tough Times for Cathay

1997 and 1998 had been particularly difficult transitional years for the carrier. For one, Hong Kong's 1997 handover from British administration to PRC rule brought about a change of local government, significant for Cathay given that the Hong Kong government controlled all traffic rights. Within days of the handover, the free float of the Thai baht precipitated regional currency upheaval, leading to what would eventually become known as the "East Asian Economic Crisis." The region became mired in recession which affected the airline industry especially hard, particularly Cathay's lucrative short-haul routes such as Japan to Hong Kong. In early 1997, roughly 25 percent of the airline's gross earnings had come from the Japanese inbound market, but by 1998,

EXHIBIT 5
Major In-
house Cathay
Applications
Systems

Source: Company
data.

Major Applications

CUPAC departure control
SCS service control
CIS customer info

AirOps ops control
EAGLE flight plan
CAFES air-ground comm
BASIS safety information

QIKRES reservation keypad
CUPID pax info
COINS pax revenue optimisation

Ultramain M&E
TDOC tech doc

CUBIC cargo
Cargo Yield Mgt

FACTS crew control
ICRS crew rostering
Airline Planning
• **FAM**
• **APM**

PeopleCX human resources

FINeCX finance
CAPITAL revenue accounting

EXHIBIT 6
Cathay
e-Business
Applications

Source: Company
data.

e-Business Applications

tourist arrivals from Japan dropped off by 60 percent to 70 percent.

To make matters worse, during more prosperous times the airline had ordered 13 new aircraft, which it was contractually committed to purchase on schedule, not a transaction the airline would typically choose during a downturn. In order to cut costs, nearly 1,000 employees out of a global staff of 14,500 were made redundant in January 1998. Repackaging of pay and perks were announced for other Cathay employees and pilots threatened to strike. In tandem with the move of Hong Kong's international airport in 1998 from Kai Tak to Chep Lap Kok, Cathay relocated its entire operations to Cathay City, a US$628 million state-of-the-art facility, constituting yet another expense for the airline. Announcing a US$69 million deficit in 1998, Cathay's first annual loss in over 40 years, chairman Peter Sutch said, "1998 will stand out as one of the most difficult years in the history of Cathay Pacific."[4]

Apart from contingency cost-cutting measures such as layoffs and leasing or selling older aircraft, outsourcing nonstrategic business functions was believed to contribute to the airline's ability to post a $281 million profit the following year in 1999 despite continued decline in the air travel market.

Smartsourcing

Dubbed by senior management as "Smartsourcing," a decision was made to identify strategic suppliers that would be able to fulfill the company's burgeoning IT needs. Smartsourcing was implemented in 1997 during austere times when the company faced immense pressure to cut costs. Cathay had previously outsourced its network to SITA, and management felt that further outsourcing of IT functions

was an important way to move from fixed cost to variable cost. As Yeung noted, "Outsourcing was not new to Cathay, it was just in the process of becoming more explicit."

Smartsourcing took place on two fronts: Infrastructure and airline applications. Since no single supplier was able to fulfill both of these needs and there was no single "off-the-shelf" solution available to fit the airline's needs, a search was mounted for an optimal combination of suppliers combining the best of each vendor's solutions and technology. The condition was that each supplier had to have a proven track record for managing IT infrastructure, project management, airline-specific applications, service delivery, and customer service. The Cathay search yielded three distinct pairings including Lufthansa Systems, EDS, and AT&T as well as three or four smaller suppliers. Ultimately the decision was made to partner with IBM Global Services for infrastructure and SABRE Airline Solutions for applications.

Following extensive contract negotiations that lasted over a year, a tripartite relationship was established, which Yeung described as "we help them as well as them helping us." IBM was to bring best practice to the relationship; SABRE Airline Solutions would bring its application portfolio; and Cathay would bring to bear its international, particularly Asian, expertise. Cathay made it clear to the two vendors that they were not exclusive suppliers; however, internal IM mechanisms ensured that IBM and SABRE Airline Solutions received preferential consideration over other vendors. Purchasing IT services from vendors other than these two Smartsourcing partners required special approval from IM. If the services or solutions of an alternate vendor were requested, a special proposal had to be submitted and approved detailing why that particular vendor's services were deemed essential.

SABRE Airline Solutions was a provider of software applications and services for the airline industry. Its aviation industry-specific solutions included airline planning, revenue management, flight operations, reservations hosting, inventory

[4] Jenni McManus, "How Cathay Looked at the Face of Oblivion and Survived," *Independent Business Weekly*, November 3, 1999, p. 29.

management, and departure control. (See http://www.sabreairlinesolutions.com.) Through the Smartsourcing relationship, Cathay Pacific adopted a complete suite of SABRE Airline Solutions, code-named "AiraCX," covering the areas of airline planning, airline operations, revenue management, and crew schedule pattern management.

IBM Global Services was the one of the world's largest information technology services providers providing integrated service, hardware, and software solutions and was the fastest growing division of IBM with 150,000 staff based in 160 different countries. (See http://www.ibm.com/services.) Initially, IBM Global Services was to manage Cathay's IBM and Unisys mainframes, provide systems and asset management, in addition to standard technical and business recovery services. In 1994, IBM established its Global Travel and Transportation Industry Solutions Unit to target IT service business opportunities within the travel and transport industry that included airlines, hotels, and railways. (See http://www.ibm.com/travel.)

After over a year of negotiation, the Smartsourcing contract with IBM and SABRE Airline Solutions was signed in April 1997, retroactive to January 1, 1997. The agreement consisted of two parts, the Relationship and Framework Agreements. Signed by all three parties, the Relationship Agreement was not legally binding and covered the intent, goals, and guiding principles of the Smartsourcing contract. By contrast, the Framework Agreement was contractually binding and outlined the precise terms for doing business, skill levels, and a fee structure that was inflation adjusted and index linked.

Data Center Outsourcing

Not long after Cathay's migration of its Data Center to Australia, Yeung spent more than six months in Sydney negotiating a contract to outsource Cathay's Data Center to IBM. After the contract was signed on December 24, 1997 and announced, initially the IBM contract met with resistance from within the IM department. Even though in theory the move to an IT-focused organization such as IBM might have seemed appealing to technical staff, many operations people who had worked at Cathay for over 15 years did not want to leave, citing "deep-seated emotional and psychological ties to Cathay." In the wake of the Data Center outsourcing controversy, IM operations manager Esther Hui resigned. Of the 90 Cathay staff in place at the Sydney Data Center, 30 to 40 percent had recently moved to Sydney from Hong Kong. As a key condition of its contract with Cathay, IBM agreed to absorb all of the Cathay Data Center staff, which was not a problem for IBM whose business was then still growing.

But what proved most difficult to many IM staff members was their transition to another role. According to Anthony Yeung, "People know things, do things, but now they don't need to know the technology in depth, but rather just enough to ask questions. No longer was it necessary to write code and do it ourselves, now we only need to be skilled enough to manage the suppliers, to understand the value of IT to the business. This can make technical people feel uneasy and unfulfilled."

Contract Management

Cathay Pacific's outsourcing contract with IBM for the Data Center took effect on January 1, 1998 and was negotiated over a period of one year, with Cathay imposing three key conditions: First, IBM had to offer a fee structure that was 10 to 15 percent below in-house base cost. Furthermore, IBM had to provide "as good or better" services than existing in-house capability. Finally, in order for Cathay to agree to outsource its Data Center, all of its IT staff employed in the facility would have to be absorbed by IBM. A great deal of time went into negotiating the outsourcing contract, thereby obviating the need for subsequent amendments to the contract.

According to Peter Nuttall, Cathay consultant on IT project management, it was "essential to establish a solid legal contract with a supplier before entering into any outsourcing deal."[5] The contract, Nuttall indicated, "could be the key to success or failure" and therefore it was necessary to retain legal advisers and involve supplier managers, purchasing, finance, and technical staff as well as human resources in the negotiation process. Nuttall cautioned, "Try to anticipate in the contract anything that might happen," including contractual flexibility to eliminate services that were no longer required or that were not performed well.

Governance and Benchmarking

Benchmarking was one mechanism used to establish cost discipline in the contract. One concern was that vendors ran profit centers and might pressure Cathay to purchase more services than were actually necessary. As a way to ensure that the outsourcing charges were competitive on an ongoing basis, provisions were established in the contract to benchmark IBM charges against market prices for the same services.

According to Sydney-based Dennis Wood, manager of contracts and service management: "Periodic benchmarking was now already into the third study. Benchmarking has teeth—it is a powerful tool." Furthermore, based on his unit's examination of other local businesses, Wood felt confident that "in terms of IT, Cathay is miles ahead of other Asian organizations."

There were several governance processes built into the Data Center outsourcing and Smartsourcing contracts. Weekly operational meetings took place between Cathay and IBM as well as more formal monthly meetings that were presided over by Wood. For the Smartsourcing contract, IM's director chaired a quarterly review board with managers from the business side. Together with IBM and SABRE Airline Solutions management, the parties assessed the overall status of IT operations and projects on a regular basis. Finally, Cathay's CEO and executives of equal seniority from both

IBM and SABRE Airline Solutions chaired a high-level semiannual Management Review Board.

Vendor Relationship

Cathay Pacific and IBM did not share financial data with each other and, as a result of not sitting in a room and sharing spreadsheets, neither side was able to assess whether or not the other was getting a good deal. Several managers felt that Smartsourcing eliminated commercial tension and competition from the purchasing process and therefore expressed concern that expenditures could be excessive. Although the IM doctrine was to opt for "fewer and more strategic suppliers," one senior IM manager questioned at times why a Smartsourcing vendor was chosen even though the supplier's proposal was not necessarily the best on the table. Manager of purchasing for IT, David Hammond, felt that institutionalizing trust was no trivial feat given these differences and required nothing less than "establishing critical success factors, mutual objectives, trust in each other's competence, and mutual dependency."

To estimate cost, Cathay did not issue RFPs or elicit bids from other vendors. Instead, according to one manager, "Only after the decision to buy was already made did we ask the vendor for a price." Hammond felt that Cathay was not able to request pricing information from EDS since EDS already knew that Cathay would likely purchase from IBM anyway. On the other hand, since IBM was aware that Cathay had not approached other vendors, it therefore knew that Cathay lacked competitive supplier pricing information to benchmark against. Cognizant of these factors, Hammond considered how tension could be introduced to what was otherwise a "tensionless relationship," adding that "closed books were a recipe for distrust."

Cathay instead developed pricing parameters based on material collected from IT conferences as well as from research and advisory firm Gartner Inc. as a means of fixing costs with IBM. These internally developed "hurdles" represented a surrogate form of competitive pressure and it

[5] Benedict Rogers, "Outsourcing Gains Weight in Times of Economic Strife," *Hong Kong iMail*, November 10, 2001.

was hoped that these would ultimately instill cost discipline in the contract.

Culture Contrast

A key aspect of managing the vendor relationship was the role that culture played. Cathay was an Asian company and accustomed to operating in an environment where relationships, both business and personal, were perceived differently than in the United States. Moreover, in contrast to Cathay, where extreme seniority existed within the IM department and it was not unusual to have people in the same unit for well over ten years, IBM was an organization that rotated its personnel every two to three years.

Desktop Outsourcing

In the first significant outsourcing initiative pursued since Smartsourcing had been concluded, Cathay outsourced its desktop PC environment to IBM in 2001. Five years before, PC distribution depended on each staff member's level of security access and consequently, some had PCs while others did not. In contrast with 1997, by 2002 nearly every Cathay staff member operated their own individual desktop PC and each had access to identical applications and e-mail on a standard intranet interface called "IntraCX."

As part of its continuing effort to outsource nonstrategic IT resources, Cathay chose IBM to maintain and manage its desktop PC and workstation infrastructure and in February 2001 concluded a US$50 million contract lasting five years. A Cathay Pacific officer noted: "This arrangement is a natural next step in our relationship with IBM and puts in place a major component of support for our IT infrastructure. We have worked closely with IBM for the past four years, and their experience in IT outsourcing solutions will enable us to deliver superior levels of service and support to our customers and staff."[6]

According to Jessica Cheung, in this case, the arrangement to outsource "commodity" IT resources was straightforward: "If it is something we can afford, we should outsource, especially if it is not our core competency. The less strategic the component, the easier it is to outsource because generally the supply is more mature. Items like MIPs[7] are more of a commodity and we can always buy these. Cathay's business is not in desktop PC management; therefore, we should focus our efforts elsewhere and outsource this."

However, out of all three primary components of Cathay's information technology that had been outsourced—data center, network, and desktop infrastructure—Cheung felt that the latter had been the most difficult. For one, desktop outsourcing was comprised of two elements, hardware, which were Cathay assets, and software, which was licensed to Cathay, not IBM. Furthermore, desktop outsourcing was relatively new and had only started gaining acceptance within recent years. According to Cheung, there were too many changes in the dynamic desktop environment and it was difficult to manage these changes as well as manage the supplier.

Finally, in marked contrast with the previous Data Center contract under which IBM absorbed all of Cathay's displaced IT staff, desktop outsourcing led to redundancies, sending shudders throughout the IM department.

Information Management Department in 2002

Appointment of an Acting CIO

In 2001, Cathay's CIO left, and long-time systems delivery IT veteran Anthony Yeung picked up the mantle and began his tenure as acting general manager of IM. (Exhibit 7 depicts the organizational structure of Cathay's IM Department in December 2002.) The IT strategy that his predecessor had set in motion was still in place.

Unlike most carriers after the turn of the century, Cathay's investment in IT resources had focused on strategic exploitation of information

---

[6] "Cathay Pacific Signs Expanded Outsourcing Agreement with IBM," *M2 Presswire*, January 8, 2001.

[7] Millions of instructions per second, a unit used to give the rate at which a processor executes instructions.

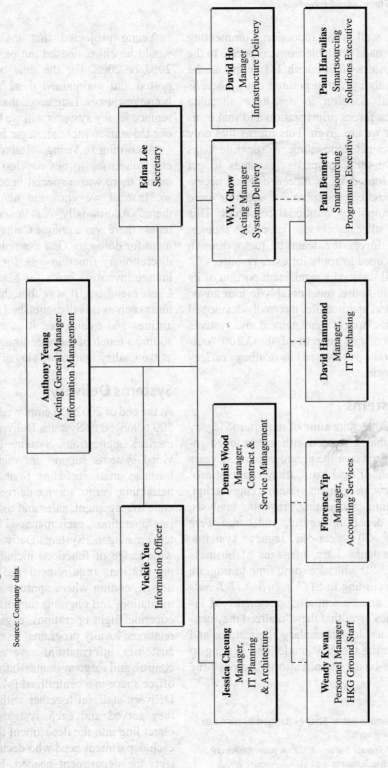

EXHIBIT 7 2002 MIS Organization Chart—Information Management

Source: Company data.

Anthony Yeung
Acting General Manager
Information Management

Edna Lee
Secretary

David Ho
Manager
Infrastructure Delivery

Paul Harvalias
Smartsourcing
Solutions Executive

W.Y. Chow
Acting Manager
Systems Delivery

Paul Bennett
Smartsourcing
Programme Executive

David Hammond
Manager,
IT Purchasing

Dennis Wood
Manager,
Contract &
Service Management

Florence Yip
Manager,
Accounting Services

Jessica Cheung
Manager,
IT Planning
& Architecture

Wendy Kwan
Personnel Manager
HKG Ground Staff

Vickie Yue
Information Officer

technology as well as cost reduction. Commenting on resources made available from corporate to the individual business units, with IM acting as the custodian, Anthony Yeung pointed out: "There is an intentional decision to *not* have adequate resources; this forces prioritization and makes us do with what we are given. This means that only essential tasks get done; some worthwhile tasks may not have the appropriate resources to get done, but if something is indeed deemed necessary, it is possible to submit a separate case requesting temporary additional resources. This ensures that all projects are carefully thought through and forces the team to jump through hoops if they need to apply for extra resources."

Cathay still retained a significant portion of its IT resources in-house, most notably in four areas: IT planning and architecture, internally developed legacy systems, project management and systems implementation, and support of the 3,200 "outport" workstations located in Cathay offices around the world.

Legacy Systems

By late 2002, the entire suite of mainframe legacy applications that had been either developed in-house or acquired over the previous 20 or 30 years still remained critical to Cathay's operations. Flight and crew assignment systems, engineering, HRMS, revenue accounting, revenue analysis, reservations, departure control, and cargo were still run by 20+-year-old legacy systems. According to Jenny Lam, manager of business improvement,[8] "It will take some time to migrate them out." According to SITA's *Airline IT Trends Survey 2002*, one "essential characteristic of IT-enabled airlines" was that they "realized they cannot afford to develop proprietary applications and [should] be using the ASP model and moving to open-systems-based applications across the organization."[9]

[8] In 1998, Operations Better Shape changed its name to "Business Improvement."

[9] "The Airline IT Trends Survey 2002: A Joint Research Project from Airline Business and SITA," August 2002.

Yeung projected that IM's legacy systems would be either phased out or fully converted by 2007 or 2008. For the time being, Cathay supported and maintained these systems using in-house resources. Lam noted that: "not until we can replace legacy systems will we be able to redeploy our IM staff to more strategic initiatives."

According to Yeung, "Today, there was a general consensus to not develop our own systems unless there was a special need for Cathay to do so. Instead we chose to acquire and manage them." Additionally, customization was avoided unless there was a unique Cathay-specific requirement for doing so. One example of a customized, discretionary function was, for example, printing lounge invitation cards for Marco Polo and First Class members. It was thought that special features such as this distinguished Cathay from other airlines and established it as a premium carrier, adding a touch of "service straight from the heart" as the Cathay marketing slogan promised.

Systems Delivery

At the end of 2002, IM employed 300 staff of which 200 belonged to Systems Delivery and handled the carrier's applications. Systems Delivery staff provided systems support for eight separate major business areas, including finance, e-business and marketing, cargo, service delivery, personnel, revenue management, sales and distribution, and airline operations, each managed by individual systems managers. Systems Delivery encompassed a wide range of functions including business case preparation, requirement definitions, systems design, coding where appropriate, system implementation, and ongoing support and maintenance covering flight operations, engineering, customer relations, loyalty programs, revenue management, customer information, reservations, departure control, and cargo systems. Rather than occupying office space in a centralized IM location, Systems Delivery staff sat together with the Cathay units they served and each systems manager had a direct line into the department they served. It was each department head who decided which IT projects the department needed, but ultimately IM decided specifically how to deploy these resources to deliver the projects.

IM's remaining 100 staff were engaged in IT planning and architecture work and acted as middlemen interfacing between the supplier and Cathay employees in managing Cathay's IT infrastructure as well as managing the vendor relationship. According to one manager, "If my machine doesn't work, I call the vendor. But if I want something new, then I talk to IM." Comprising the majority of its staff, Systems Delivery's 200 employees constituted the largest overhead for IM in terms of personnel resources.

Packages

As part of its strategy of replacing in-house legacy systems developed over 20+ years ago, IM procured a number of packages. While these packages had gained acceptance in the organization, IM avoided package customization unless it was deemed absolutely necessary. Examples of packages managed and deployed by Cathay's IM department included the following:

Walker Financial, a world-class financial software suite.

Ultramain, a software package that tracked and predicted maintenance requirements and costs for Cathay aircraft and components.

"PeopleCX," a PeopleSoft-developed online human resources management system for Cathay, launched in the second quarter of 2001 and aimed at "improving processing efficiency and creating a self-service culture within the company." (See www.peoplesoft.com.)

CXeBuy, an Oracle-based e-business centralized purchasing platform intended to simplify Cathay's procurement processes of everything from office supplies to machinery.

"AiraCX" from SABRE Airline Solutions, comprised of a suite of systems covering airline planning, airline operations, revenue management, and crew schedule pattern generation.

Outport Workstations

With 47 regional offices or "outports" located around the world, in 2001 Cathay contemplated outsourcing IT infrastructure for outports but ultimately decided to retain management of these IT resources in-house. At each of the 47 outports there were two to three office locations, a cargo office, a town office, and an airport office. Thirty-three crew hotels were also included as outports. Following a rigorous internal review process designed to evaluate whether or not outsourcing outports would improve their service levels as well as reduce costs, Cathay determined that neither was the case.

David Ho, manager of infrastructure delivery, noted that supporting 3,200 workstations was not at all straightforward and entirely different from supporting workstations in one centralized location as in Hong Kong. Coverage for all 47 outports around the world with its scattered offices presented formidable logistical challenges. Ho concluded that: "We did not feel comfortable with outsourcing these as we could not make the case for outsourcing look viable from a business standpoint."

VIP Support

In addition to the day-to-day support provided by IBM, IM provided personalized support to roughly 10 Cathay directors as well as their secretaries. These select few were supported by IM's infrastructure delivery unit to ensure that consistent and extraordinary quality of service was provided.

Web Hosting

Cathay established its purchasing department in 1996 before the advent of Smartsourcing. As manager of IT purchasing, Hammond had two primary responsibilities, overlooking the sourcing process and managing vendor relationships. In the past, while benchmarking may have indicated higher pricing from time to time, as a practice Cathay typically did not push the vendor excessively on pricing in order to maintain the relationship.

Working in parallel with purchasing, the business improvement department functioned as a review team, evaluating all outsourcing and purchasing deals. According to Jenny Lam, "Many staff within the IT department initially did not have a clear idea of what outsourcing meant, or what were the obligations of Cathay or the obligations of the vendors." In July 2001, in conjunction with airline purchasing and business improvement, IM conducted a review of the Smartsourcing arrangement, benchmarking it with industry best practice as well as with other world-class local and international companies.

One result of this review was that after nearly six years of designating IBM, SABRE Airline Solutions, and SITA as "preferred partners," in 2002, IM's purchasing unit began implementing best practice purchasing processes. Whereas before Smartsourcing partners were automatically considered before other vendors, as part of its new, more competitive sourcing model, IM purchasing could at its discretion issue standard RFIs (request for information) and RFPs (request for proposal). In such cases, only after careful consideration of RFIs and RFPs would purchases be approved and executed. However, the Smartsourcing partners still retained their "strategic partner" status, and solutions from them still received favorable consideration if it was demonstrated that they were competitive. The key difference was that Smartsourcing partners would have to prove themselves rather than being automatically considered for business.

IM's recently revamped purchasing process was reflected in the department's decision to outsource Cathay's Web hosting. Purchasing issued RFPs and, in August 2002, ultimately chose to outsource Web hosting to Hewlett-Packard, a company with which Cathay had no previous outsourcing agreement. After evaluating several Web hosting vendors, it was decided that Hewlett-Packard was the best choice in terms of its ability to introduce superior technology and best practice at the most cost-effective levels. Hewlett-Packard and Cathay Pacific concluded a "two-year-and-one" contract—in other words, a duration of two

years with an option to renew for an additional year. Assuming responsibility for the airline's Internet initiatives, Hewlett-Packard took over support of Cathay's e-business infrastructure in November 2002.

The Road Ahead

Already into his second cup of coffee, Yeung glanced at the day's newspaper that reported the bankruptcy of United Airlines, one of the airline industry's behemoths. The global airline industry faced a $9 billion loss in 2002[10] and Yeung wondered how Cathay would be able to expand in an increasingly competitive marketplace. Considering the pervasive presence of IT within the carrier, Yeung knew that IT could make a difference. Things had changed: In the past, boosting revenue and enhancing customer service were the main drivers of outsourcing; now equal or perhaps stronger emphasis was placed on improving staff productivity and cost-cutting. Instead of paying premiums for customer loyalty output such as printing lounge invitation cards for Marco Polo and First Class members, resources might have to be shifted to other innovative measures such as the development of a paperless office. Paperless, electronic tickets cost US$8 or $9 per ticket less to process than conventional paper tickets, and savings as high as $35 to $40 for tickets with multiple airline connecting flights.[11]

Wondering what other ways IM might trim expenses, Yeung turned to a recent survey of airlines which indicated that 59 percent of all airlines invested in IT primarily to cut costs and increase operating efficiency. In an accompanying article, Yeung's former boss, Ian Riddell, now COO at SITA, declared that: "This year the focus is on cost reduction yet achieving that presents a paradox; in order to get the pot of gold of substantial savings,

---

[10] International Air Transport Association Survey of 2002.

[11] Zach Coleman, "Asian Airlines Shift Focus of Spending on Technology," *The Asian Wall Street Journal*, August 24, 2001, p. M3.

investment is necessary."[12] But how should Cathay direct its IT expenditures and in what other ways could savings be achieved?

Since 1998, Cathay had turned things around. After reporting losses for the second half of 2001, during the first half of 2002 the airline posted a 6.3 percent increase in turnover with solid growth in both passenger and cargo traffic. Six new aircraft were on order, and Cathay announced it would hire 1,300 Hong Kong-based staff. Codeshares with oneworld alliance partners British Airways and American Airlines promised increased passenger traffic. Meanwhile, Cathay was voted Asia's best airline brand for a third consecutive year in *Reader's Digest* magazine's SuperBrands 2002 Survey and "Best Airline—Asia" by four million travelers polled by U.K.-based consulting firm Skytrax. In the IT field, Cathay was named Best Business-to-Consumer e-commerce Web site by VISA, Best E-Commerce Strategy by FinanceAsia, and Best Airline Web site by U.K.-based business travel company OAG.

But if things were going so well for Cathay, then why the renewed emphasis on cost-cutting? Looking down the runway, Yeung considered the potential competition that local equivalents of "no-frills" airlines such as Ryanair and easyJet, both growing at 40 percent, might introduce. While the general view was that these no-frills carriers might not present any real threat in the Asian market in the near future, it was widely believed that they would eventually appear. An analyst had noted that "the traditional full-service airline model requires significant modification, if not open-heart surgery . . . airline travel has been commoditized—especially in the short-haul markets where boarding an aircraft has become akin to taking a bus ride."[13] Moreover, "the historical model's failure is not a new phenomenon but has been obvious [. . .] in the returns generated by those carriers seeking to differentiate themselves

the greatest on the basis of quality."[14] Over the course of the past decade, Cathay Pacific's ROI had decreased by 12.6 percent, as was the case at regional competitor Singapore Airlines, where ROI declined by 16.2 percent.

Smartsourcing at the Midpoint

Yeung considered the multimillion deals with IBM and SABRE Airline Solutions and turned his attention to Smartsourcing. Yeung considered several issues: In retrospect, he wondered whether the contract with IBM and SABRE Airline Solutions had been as successful as was originally hoped when he negotiated the Data Center outsourcing contract six years ago. (See Exhibit 8 for a chronology of Cathay's IM department.) To what extent had the disparate corporate cultures of these companies resulted in a difficult marriage and what conflicts still needed resolution? Looking back over the past five years, what should Cathay have done differently? How, if at all, should the contracts be renegotiated and restructured? Had the Smartsourcing alliance been managed effectively? Were IT budget savings of 10 to 15 percent adequate to constitute success? And from the supplier's perspective, had the Smartsourcing relationship with Cathay been profitable? One month before, in November 2002, the Data Center in Australia had been sold to a third party, and now the facility that initially cost Cathay US$30 million to build—a nonstrategic asset—was no longer on the airline's books.

Five years after it initially leased the Baulkham Hills Data Center from Cathay in 1997, IBM served 50 to 60 clients there, including a number of major companies in Australia. Of the original Cathay IT staff who had migrated to IBM, 70 to 75 percent still worked at the Data Center. Roughly 10 percent had moved up the ranks at IBM, with only the remaining 10 percent gone. Clearly this facility had resulted in a highly successful strategic regional foothold for IBM along with a talented pool of Cathay employees.

---

[12] Daniel Michaels, "Airlines Face Complex Woes," *The Wall Street Journal*, September 16, 2002, p. B4.

[13] *Asian Airline Analyzer*, July 2002, *UBS Warburg*, p. 2.

[14] Ibid.

EXHIBIT 8   Cathay Pacific IT Evolution Chronology

Source: Company data.

1967–1968:	Cathay Pacific engages SITA in the provision of network services.
1991–1993:	Operation Better Shape identifies outsourcing as key cost-cutting measure.
mid-1994:	Ian Riddell joins as general manager, Information Management Division.
1995:	Australia Data Center initiates operation.
April 1997:	Smartsourcing contract with IBM and SABRE Airline Solutions signed; retroactive to January 1, 1997.
24 December 1997:	Data Center Outsourcing contract with IBM signed.
01 January 1998:	Data Center Outsourcing contract takes effect.
May 1998:	Cathay City Campus Network outsourced to SITA.
1999:	"Help Desk" and "Server Farm" operations outsourced to IBM.
2000:	Role of CIO created: GM-IM promoted to Director—IM.
February 2001:	HKG Desktop Infrastructure contract finalized, covered e-mail systems, Novell, support, PC maintenance, Help Desk.
2Q 2002:	PeopleCX launched, PeopleSoft system.
mid-2001:	Ian Riddell leaves Cathay; Anthony Yeung assumes role of acting GM, IM.
November 2002:	Sale of Cathay Pacific-owned Data Center in Australia.
01 January 2003:	Edward Nicol appointed as director of IM.
01 February 2003:	Anthony Yeung appointed as general manager of IM.

Furthermore, IBM had been able to parlay its success with Cathay into other lucrative contracts both in Hong Kong and Asia. In November 1998, IBM reached a $400 million outsourcing deal with Korean Air and in July 2001 signed a US$664 million, ten-year outsourcing agreement with Japan Airlines. First Pacific Bank became the first Hong Kong bank to outsource its Data Center to IBM in a US$15.4 million, seven-year contract and IBM subsequently secured several outsourcing contracts with prominent Hong Kong companies such as Dah Sing Bank and Hong Kong Monetary Authority. But had the relationship been as equally beneficial for Cathay Pacific? If not, what governance mechanisms were necessary to ensure that the contract was working to Cathay's favor?

China

In contrast to struggling airlines around the world, China's aviation industry was the fastest growing in the world and still possessed enormous growth potential. Given the size of its market and proximity to Hong Kong, the mainland loomed large in

Cathay's future. In 2002, the carrier applied to re-establish lucrative routes to destinations in China for the first time since 1990 when these routes were transferred and restricted by the Hong Kong government to Dragonair,[15] now a regional competitor. With PRC aviation market deregulation and Hong Kong seeking to establish itself as a key regional hub, Cathay applied to operate service to Shanghai, Beijing, and Xiamen, Dragonair's most profitable routes in China.

But China was not only significant in terms of destination traffic. For the first time since 1949, in December 2002 direct flights between Taiwan and China were being negotiated with chartered flights actually operating during the Chinese New Year in early 2003, jeopardizing Hong Kong's

[15] In 1986 the Hong Kong government implemented a "one-route, one airline" policy in order to eliminate competition between Hong Kong's two airlines. Cathay was forced to relinquish its right to fly to Shanghai and Beijing in favor of Dragonair, in which Cathay owned a 17.79% share.

traditional role of mandatory transit point between Taiwan and mainland China. It was estimated that Cathay derived anywhere from 10 to 15 percent of total profit from its Taiwan route. Also, with vastly improved IT infrastructure in China compared with seven years earlier when Cathay first launched its Data Center in Sydney as well as an affordable cohort of talented IT engineers in the PRC, what opportunities, if any, should Cathay be evaluating? Moreover, with Chinese carriers closely examining and even emulating Cathay's IT system, should Cathay consider offering IT services to up-and-coming Chinese airlines, and if so, should some partners be identified? With unprecedented restructuring of China's airlines taking place, major PRC carriers searched for foreign strategic partners. Cathay already had a close relationship with China Eastern that operated 142 aircraft and serviced 386 PRC routes, while two other carriers, China National Aviation Co. and China Southern, had comparable numbers of aircraft and operated 307 and 666 routes, respectively.[16]

What Next?

By December 2002, Cathay had already outsourced most of the noncompetitive, nonstrategic aspects of its IT resources but Yeung wondered to himself whether or not Cathay had gone as far as it could. Currently, roughly 65 percent of his IT budget was outside of the company, with nearly a third of that devoted to Cathay's network, a third to the data center, and another third to desktop outsourcing following the recent contract with IBM. Yeung contemplated what ought to be the long-term role of his Systems Delivery group, Yeung's bailiwick before assuming the role of acting GM of IM. Systems Delivery still employed 200 out of IM's 300 staff; Yeung wondered how this group would change and whether there was a more cost-effective model to deliver the same services that Systems Delivery currently provided. Yeung considered the decision to retain in-house

[16] Ben Dolven, "Dogfight Over China," *Far Eastern Economic Review*, February 6, 2003, p. 28.

support for Cathay's 3,200 outport workstations, and whether it would be eventually possible to resolve the contractual complexities of reaching a cost-effective agreement to outsource IT support for these locations. Moreover, Yeung also considered the desirability of not owning the desktop hardware and software and instead switching to a "utility" model of pay-per-use for these workstations. As outsourcing gained increased acceptance in Asia, competing regional carriers had also turned to external management of IT operations and, like Yeung, their own IT departments also examined ways of reducing IT budgets.

More drastically, Yeung contemplated the business case of going the way of Finnair or Air Canada—in other words, outsourcing Cathay's entire IT operation. To someone who had joined Cathay as a young programmer and wrote code for the airline's first reservation systems over 30 years ago, this would have been inconceivable back when he first started working at Cathay. But, even if it were to happen, before moving IT infrastructure entirely outside of the company, according to one senior manager, IM would have to "clean our own house first and evaluate the way we manage our vendors more carefully." In other words, despite mounting cost pressures, Cathay would have to consider ways of managing its strategic Smartsourcing alliance partners as well as the outsourcing process more carefully before further commitments were made and contracts signed. Nevertheless, Yeung mused, with outsourcing already in place, the issue was more one of pace and when, not if, further outsourcing should take place.

On January 1, 2003, Cathay Pacific appointed airline industry veteran Edward Nicol as director of IM, a position equivalent to that of CIO and reporting directly to Cathay's CEO, David Turnbull. Originally working for Cathay's parent company John Swire & Sons, Nicol started his career with Cathay Pacific in 1975. During his long tenure with Cathay, he served as country manager for a number of Asian and Middle East outports, then became general manager for sales and revenue management and then subsequently

GM of inflight services. In recent years, before returning as Cathay's new CIO, Nicol was appointed to run various aviation companies either wholly or partially owned by Cathay, acting in the capacity of either director or CEO.

One month following Nicol's appointment, on February 1, 2003, Anthony Yeung was appointed general manager of IM. Both appointments provided an indication of the importance that Cathay attached to IT as a strategic resource of the company. According to Yeung, if IM were a company unto itself, "Nicol's role would be CEO whereas my role would be that of COO." For 18 months Cathay had only an acting general manager but, within the space of a month, both a director and GM of IM were appointed. It remained to be seen what impact this organizational change would ultimately have on Cathay's future IT direction.

Case 3-2

Royal Caribbean Cruises Ltd.

In early July 2003, looking over the sparkling waters of the intercoastal waterway from his third-floor corner office, Tom Murphy, CIO of Royal Caribbean Cruises Ltd. (RCCL), was putting the final touches on his recommendations to the corporate planning committee chaired by Jack Williams, president and chief operating officer (COO), for his 2004 information technology (IT) plan. Whether to recommend a modest budget increase, a significant budget increase, or a return to the glory days before 9/11 was a key issue confronting him. How he could assure optimum alignment of IT spending with the direction of the company was another key issue.

Company Background

RCCL, incorporated in Liberia, was founded in 1969 by Edwin W. Stephan. Stephan's idea was to create cruise ships especially designed for pleasure cruises in the warm-water Caribbean. With the financial support of Norwegian shipping magnates IM Skaugen, Anders Wilhemsen, and Gotass-Larsen, Stephan established RCCL's first office in Miami (where it is still headquartered), with two buildings in the port of Miami and another 25 miles away in Miramar, Florida (IT). Additional locations were at Blue Lagoon, Florida (new-building[1] team), Hallendale[2] (IT shipboard software configuration center), and Wichita, Kansas (call center). RCCL's first ship, the 724-passenger

Song of Norway, was built in Finland and first sailed out of Miami in November 1970. Many other ships followed Song of Norway, with each new ship featuring increased size, capacity, accommodations, and shipboard amenities (today RCCL's largest ship carries 3,200 passengers).

In 1988, RCCL and Admiral Cruises merged, and A. Wilhemsen & Company became the full owner. Wilhemsen (24 percent) then set up a joint ownership agreement with the Ofer family (owner of one of the largest shipping companies in the world) and an entity of the Pritzker family (25 percent) (Hyatt Hotel chain's owner). That was the start of a heavy-growth decade. The company went public and traded on the New York Stock Exchange in 1993. In 1997, RCCL acquired Celebrity Cruises from the Greek Chandris Lines. By 2003, RCCL was the number two company in the industry (a distant number two behind Carnival Cruise Company), with $3.4 billion in revenue in 2002, $351 million net income, and 27,800 employees. (Exhibit 1 contains recent financial statements.) RCCL owned 25 ships and planned to add three new ships in the next year. (Exhibit 2 lists the ships for RCCL.) RCCL sailed mainly in the Caribbean but also across the globe toward destinations that included Alaska, Bermuda, Canada/New England, Europe (Mediterranean), Hawaii, Mexico, the Pacific Northwest, Panama, and transatlantic. It transported over 2.7 million passengers a year[3] (82 percent of its revenues came from the United States).

RCCL's Organization

RCCL ships operated through two brands: Royal Caribbean International and Celebrity Cruises. The cruise industry was divided into four major market segments. Segments included contemporary,

---

This case was prepared by Professor F. Warren McFarlan and Valerie Massoni (MBA '03). Copyright © 2003 President and Fellows of Harvard College. Harvard Business School Case No. 304-019.

[1] New building refers to new ships. Blue Lagoon is operational in nature. It has designers, architects, art people, and some marine experts who design and track progress on new ships.

[2] Hallendale is an IT configuration center where RCCL tests and assures the quality of all of the applications going into its existing ships. It also builds out and configures all equipment going to new ships.

[3] www.rclinvestor.com; http://www.corporate-ir.net/ireye/ir_site.zhtml?ticker=rcl&script=11919&item_id='rcl_000425 _ keystats.htm'.

EXHIBIT 1   Recent Financial Statements

Source: RCCL, http://globalbb.onesource.com/Sharedscripts/Reports/GetReport.asp?KeyID=L166301&Process=CP & One SourceRC= annincst.

Annual Income Statement (US$ million)

	December 31, 2002	December 31, 2001	December 31, 2000	December 31, 1999	December 31, 1998
Total sales	3,434.3	3,145.3	2,865.8	2,546.2	2,636.3
Total expenses	2,883.4	2,689.6	2,296.3	2,066.0	2,417.6
Pretax income	351.3	254.5	445.4	383.9	330.8
Income after taxes	351.3	254.5	445.4	383.9	330.8

Source: RCCL, http://globalbb.onesource.com/Sharedscripts/Reports/GetReport.asp?KeyID=L166301&Process=CP&OneSourceRC= annbal.

RCCL Annual Balance Sheet (US$ million)

	December 31, 2002	December 31, 2001	December 31, 2000	December 31, 1999	December 31, 1998
Assets					
Total Current Assets	447.7	886.1	310.7	194.4	286.3
Property, plant and equipment	10,828.2	9,830.4	7,766.6	6,652.1	5,681.3
Accumulated depreciation and amortization	−1,551.8	−1,225.0	−934.7	−793.9	−608.3
Property, plant and equipment, net	9,276.5	8,605.4	6,831.8	5,858.2	5,073.0
Goodwill/Intangibles	278.6	278.6	289.0	299.4	309.8
Other long-term assets	535.7	598.7	397.0	28.6	16.9
Total Assets	10,538.5	10,368.8	7,828.5	6,380.5	5,686.1
Liabilities					
Total Current Liabilities	1,169.9	1,112.6	912.4	905.3	890.2
Total Long-Term Debt	5,322.3	5,407.5	3,300.2	2,214.1	2,341.2
Total Liabilities	6,503.8	6,612.2	4,212.6	3,119.4	3,231.3
Total Shareholders' Equity	4,034.7	3,756.6	3,615.9	3,261.2	2,454.8
Total Liabilities and Shareholders' Equity	10,538.5	10,368.8	7,828.5	6,380.5	5,686.1

premium, luxury, and ultraluxury. RCCL chairman and CEO Richard Fain noted RCCL had a higher price in each market segment it competed in, but also offered a better quality and enhanced experience to its customers at each service point. Royal Caribbean International targeted the volume cruise vacation market in the contemporary and premium segments with 16 ships (two- to 16-day-long cruises, across-the-world itineraries, a variety of shipboard activities, amenities, services, and shore excursions) while Celebrity, with its nine ships, offered cruises to the high-end premium, luxury, and ultraluxury segments, targeting vacationers who wanted an enhanced experience (two- to 17-day cruises, gourmet dining, premium service, luxurious facilities, and modern vessels).

EXHIBIT 2   Fleet Data for Royal Caribbean International and Celebrity Cruises

Source: www.rclinvestor.com.

	Year in Service	Estimated Capacity	Gross Tons
ROYAL CARIBBEAN INTERNATIONAL			
Navigator of the Seas	2002	3,100	142,000
Brilliance of the Seas	2002	2,100	90,000
Adventure of the Seas	2001	3,100	142,000
Radiance of the Seas	2001	2,100	90,000
Explorer of the Seas	2000	3,100	142,000
Voyager of the Seas	1999	3,100	142,000
Vision of the Seas	1998	2,000	78,491
Enchantment of the Seas	1997	1,950	74,140
Rhapsody of the Seas	1997	2,000	78,491
Grandeur of the Seas	1996	1,950	74,140
Splendour of the Seas	1996	1,800	69,130
Legend of the Seas	1995	1,800	69,130
Majesty of the Seas	1992	2,350	73,941
Monarch of the Seas	1991	2,350	73,941
Nordic Empress	1990	1,600	48,563
Sovereign of the Seas	1988	2,250	73,192
CELEBRITY CRUISES			
Constellation	2002	2,000	91,000
Summit	2001	2,000	91,000
Infinity	2001	2,000	91,000
Millennium	2000	2,000	91,000
Mercury	1997	1,850	77,713
Galaxy	1996	1,850	77,713
Century	1995	1,750	70,606
Zenith	1992	1,350	47,255
Horizon	1990	1,350	46,811

Note: Brand berths rounded to nearest 100 in public documents.

Fleet Expansion Projects			
	Estimated Delivery	Estimated Capacity	Estimated Gross Tons
ROYAL CARIBBEAN INTERNATIONAL			
Navigator of the Seas	3Q 2003	2,100	90,000
Brilliance of the Seas	4Q 2003	3,100	142,000
Adventure of the Seas	2Q 2004	2,100	90,000

Celebrity Cruises attracted more demanding and experienced cruisers from the contemporary- and premium-cruise categories.

Fain noted, "It was important to keep the individual personality of each brand and avoid too much homogenization." Of course, there were some synergies across the two brands. Fain noted, for example, the Silverwhere program (a method for allocating optimal table-seating assignments) cost the same to develop whether it was used in

Source: Adapted from the cruise lines. U.S. top-three cruise-ship operators ranked by number of ships operating berths, reported as of April 28, 2003, with number of brand names, ships, and berths in 2006 forecast, http://globalbb.onesource.com/sharedscripts/text/getarticle.asp?process=CP&docid=TBA_01087575&KeyID=166301&SN="Royal%20Caribbean%20Cruises.

The Big Three

Company	Brands	Ships	Berths	Ships by 2006	Berths by 2006
Carnival Corp.	13	66	100,000	83	142,300
Royal Caribbean Cruises Ltd.	2	26	53,042	28	60,356
Star/NCL Group	3	18	27,609	21	N/A

one or 25 ships and thus was implemented in both brands' ships.

Industry Background

A Consolidated Industry

Three main players dominated the $15 billion worldwide cruise-line industry. Carnival Corporation, the world's largest cruise-ship company, was number one by far since its recent acquisition of P&O Princess in April 2003. It had 13 brands, 66 ships (17 additional ships on order), and 100,000 berths; carried 4.7 million passengers in 2002; and had 49 percent market share in North America. Prior to the P&O Princess acquisition, Carnival 2002 revenues were $4.4 billion with net income of $1.01 billion. P&O's 2002 revenues were $2.5 billion. P&O had originally worked a deal to merge with RCCL in November 2001. Subsequently, Carnival launched a counteroffer that ultimately won. It completed the $5.5 billion acquisition in April 2003. A key component of Carnival's strategy was tight cost controls. It reduced costs on ship design and construction by standardizing its fleets down to details as small as bedspreads and barstools. There were no rock-climbing walls or ice-skating rinks, common on ships of RCCL. "They're too expensive," said Bob Dickinson, Carnival's president.[4]

RCCL was number two in the industry with its two brands, 26 ships, and 2.7 million passengers a year. Together, Carnival and RCCL controlled over 80 percent of the cruise-line market. After RCCL came Norwegian Cruise Lines with three brands, 18 ships, and 28,000 berths.

New Development: Deployment of Ships to U.S. Ports

The heightened level of fear of flying after 9/11, a depressed economy, and the uncertain winter and spring 2003 environment due to the war in Iraq and SARS caused cruise companies to start relocating some of their ships to U.S. ports. As Brian Rice, senior vice president of revenue performance at RCCL, noted: "If Mohammed won't come to the mountain, let's take the mountain to Mohammed." In order to reduce barriers to buying RCCL's products, RCCL was now deploying ships out of New York, Boston, Baltimore, Jacksonville, and New Orleans, in addition to Miami.

Pricing: Promotion and High Discount

Two main factors forced cruise companies to cut their prices drastically in 2002 and 2003. First, 9/11 deeply impacted the global travel industry. To entice customers to travel, the lines were forced to "slash ticket prices from pre-September 11 levels. As a consequence, the average price of a cruise in 2003 is the same as it was in 1999, and analysts do not foresee price increases until 2005. As a result, prices are shockingly low compared to the recent past. For example, a seven-day Caribbean cruise in an ocean view room on the Carnival Victory sells for $1,500 a person, down from $2,100 just a year ago."[5]

---

[4] "Cruising for a Bruising?" *Fortune,* May 27, 2003.

[5] "Cruising for a Bruising?" *Fortune,* May 27, 2003.

EXHIBIT 3
Promotions
Pictures, Ads,
and Pop-ups
for Last-
minute Deals

Source: RCCL.

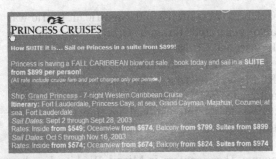

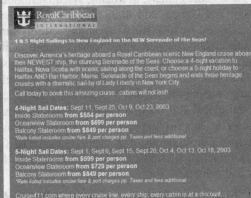

Additionally, the combination of heightened geopolitical uncertainties, a weakening economy, and increased capacity (created by new ships coming on line) put downward pressure on prices. As cruise lines offered more and more last-minute deals to fill their berths, they were also forced to compensate customers who previously purchased their cruise packages at a higher price.

Given the distribution channel structure and commercial conditions—an average 15 percent commission (varied based on status of travel agent) given to travel agents (travel agents were reluctant to adjust prices downward because it hurt their commission)—credits were given on board to the guests, rather than direct cash rebates. (Exhibit 3 shows typical advertisings for last-minute promotions.)

Distribution: Travel Agent is the Key Distribution Channel

The travel agent was the critical front-end distribution vehicle. Ninety-eight percent of bookings

were made through travel agents. Travel agents booked both online (50 percent) and through RCCL's call center (50 percent). Rice, noting the critical role of the travel agent community, said, "A cruise is a global experience and not a commodity, like an airline seat." He further noted, "A cruise must be sold as opposed to an air ticket, which is bought." Travel agents recommended specific cruise options, selected itineraries to fit customer needs, and finally did the detailed bookings of guests aboard. Booking online by a customer was still very limited, since most customers needed advice and preliminary reassurance and thus booked through agents. RCCL got only very limited bookings a day online directly from the customers, noted Mike Sutten, vice president, product sales systems. Web sites, however, were key for customers to get preliminary information on cruises—from pricing, itineraries, types of rooms, facilities, and amenities to the availability of shore excursions. On a normal day, the Royal brand's Web site got 50,000 to 60,000 hits and the

Celebrity Web site 10,000. Significant traffic was also generated through Orbitz, Expedia.com, Icruise, and Cruise 411.

In 1991, by introducing Cruise Match 2000, RCCL was the first to provide a real-time, fully automated reservation system with direct online access to its international inventory of 29,000 travel agents.

RCCL had five call centers to support travel agents. Those centers, in Miami, Wichita, London, Oslo, and Genoa, had 400, 500, 40, 10, and 10 employees, respectively. Despite a high staff turnover rate (60 percent), the Miami call center saw its 400 jobs as critical to being seen as a good member of the community. Wichita was the telemarketing capital of the country and had exceptional global skills. London created its own small center to support the special needs of its travel agents. Consequently, for many reasons RCCL was reluctant to consider global outsourcing for its call centers.

A "No-growth/Low-growth" Period

Williams, president and COO of RCI and Celebrity, described the company as heading into a "no-growth/low-growth" period and noted therefore that efficiency was key. He stressed that RCCL was dedicated to using better tools to increase its productivity and was focused on improving its activities with travel agency air/sea departments and with groups.

The industrywide supply of berths was increasing (9.8 percent in 2003 and 12 percent projected in 2004) much faster than the five-year demand trend of 7.8 percent.[6] The three main players kept up by ordering new ships, creating ever-increasing capacity. (Carnival Corp., RCCL, and NCL planned to add 17, 3, and 3 additional ships, respectively, by 2006.) The total number of onboard beds of the combined company of Carnival and P&O Princess would rise by 17.6 percent in 2003 and another 16 percent in 2004. That was seen as one reason why Carnival's once-soaring stock price

dropped from $34 in May 2002 to $20 in March 2003.[7] Demand would need to accelerate in 2003 and 2004 to keep up with the supply and the continued growth in capacity. A contrary view was posed by some experts who anticipated steady volume growth because of the strong value proposition of the cruise industry and the fact that cruising's penetration of the leisure travel category was at 5 percent (only 12 percent of North Americans had taken a cruise).[8]

Complicating life were risks: An uncertain geopolitical climate (war in Iraq, threatening in North Korea), terrorism, the earlier Norwalk virus and the recent terrifying SARS, as well as higher fuel prices. Additionally, customers tended to book much more at the last minute, a relatively new phenomenon that greatly increased post-9/11, thus creating uncertainty. In combination with more numerous shorter cruises, an increasing inventory, higher discounted last-minute deals, and better informed consumers thanks to the Internet, huge pressure was placed on yield management.

Corporate Strategy

RCCL's strategy was a three-legged one aimed at (1) enhancing the customer and travel trade experience, (2) reducing costs (management saw current pricing insufficient vis-à-vis Carnival to cover RCCL's extra costs), and (3) increasing revenues. The core proposition was that RCCL cruise customers paid a higher price and, in return, got a better cruising and vacation experience.

Enhancing the Guest Experience

RCCL was aggressively moving to enhance the guest experience. The Silverwhere program, for example, allocated dinner seating of RCCL guests on a cruise ship. The program fed in several criteria such as age, nationality, sex, language, group needs, and guest preferences and proposed a set of table groupings as sociable as possible for the

---

[6] "Americas/U.S. Travel & Leisure," analyst reports, Credit Suisse First Boston, January 15, 2003.

[7] "Cruising for a Bruising?" *Fortune*, May 27, 2003.

[8] "Americas/U.S. Travel & Leisure," analyst reports, Credit Suisse First Boston, January 15, 2003.

guests. Organizing table groupings on a cruise ship was a complex process: As many as 3,200 guests, guests traveling together but who made separate reservations and bookings at different places, guests coming from all around the world with different language abilities. This program linked all those criteria and proposed specific groupings, thus providing a better level of service to guests (more likelihood of compatible companions at a meal and a higher level of satisfaction) as well as vastly improving the ability to change a guest's dining situation quickly.

Another recent innovation had been the popular Internet cafes, which give Internet access on the ship to the cruise passengers so they could constantly be in touch with the outside world. A third example related to disembarkation. The disembarkation and embarkation processes could be very long and frustrating for passengers when clearing the ship at ports—to the extent that it could ruin their reaction to the entire vacation (i.e., first and last experiences on the vacation were often the most critical in terms of the total experience). RCCL's introduction of the debark card improved debarkation time by two hours. The debark card captured the information required by the Immigration and Naturalization Service and was printed the night before debarkation and delivered to each guest room.

Cost Reduction

CIO Murphy cited the shore-excursion booking system part of the Web site as a terrific success. Booking shore excursions used to be done manually after passengers got on the ship and was a labor-intensive process. Passengers did not get any confirmation for their excursion until they had almost reached a port (very frustrating in some cases as the passengers discovered at the last minute that there was not enough space and availability on an excursion). By introducing the shore-excursion program on the Web site, RCCL won on both sides. It both made RCCL customers happier and drove costs down. In addition, passengers who had their excursions booked and confirmed in advance spent more money on board, thus increasing revenues.

Supply chain was another area where savings were potentially significant, coming from effective use of leverage in the marketplace and operating efficiencies (supplier rationalization, standardization of product, effective forecasting, demand planning). As a first step, RCCL initiated a project under the Leapfrog umbrella to upgrade its core JD Edwards financial system (now 10 years old) to JDE's latest Web-enabled financial (implemented in summer 2002) and procurement (implemented and went live in August 2003) suite, OneWorld. Project implementation turned out to be quite difficult due to the interaction of various shipboard and shoreside systems and the inherent complexity of the actual cruise ship supply chain. A cruise ship as a *floating city* posed exceptionally complex supply chain issues as a result of several factors.

1. **Variety.** The supply chain could be split into two very different parts mirroring how the ship was organized: The hotel supply chain and the technical supply chain. The hotel supply chain contained 14,000 stock-keeping units (SKUs) and encompassed food and beverage, dry goods (restroom supplies, towels, utensils), and kitchen equipment. The technical supply chain had 3 million SKUs embracing all the goods—technical and mechanical parts—to operate the ship (tools, gaskets, oils, nuts, and bolts). It included desalination equipment, air conditioning systems, elevators, fuel to power the ship, and so on. The yearly procurement budget was split among food and beverage (25 percent), fuel (23 percent), technical/marine goods (11 percent), hotel goods (not food) (6 percent), IT (4 percent), and new build (outfitting new ships) (19 percent).

2. **Logistics.** From a logistics perspective, the ships were equivalent to factories, but they moved. Within the 8 to 12 hours a ship was in port, there was only limited time to store the vessel with everything it needed for the next 7 to 17 days. A miss, that is, failure to deliver goods at the designated time and place, was a huge problem and led either to guest dissatisfaction or ship maintenance issues or both. There

was virtually no room for error in the order and delivery cycle.

3. **Connectivity.** Satellite position issues were such that 100 percent (24×7) reliable connections from ship to shore were not always possible. Additionally, bandwidth issues constrained certain kinds of extranet linkages with key suppliers. Satellites facilitated communication to onshore purchasing agents and then on to vendors. Four to five times a day there was ship-to-shore synchronization. On the hotel side, nearly 100,000 purchase orders were directly transmitted annually from corporate to vendors. One-hundred-sixty-nine vendors represented 80 percent of supply chain spending. Among them, 55 vendors were EDI partners accounting for 31 percent of total supply chain spending. The remaining 20 percent was split between 2,327 vendors, out of which 55 were EDI partners (2.5 percent of the total budget).[9]

The backbone of the supply chain systems approach was JDE. It was the financial system and was critical for the accounting of inventory and cash management. However, the diverse nature of the ship environment required special information subsystems to fulfill specialized functions.

On the technical side, planned maintenance was critical for the ships' safety and legal requirements. This ranged from galley equipment to engines, electrical systems, valves, and even consumable items such as paint and chlorine. AMOS,[10] developed by Xantic Software Company, the information system specifically designed for ship maintenance, was fully implemented at RCCL, but there was significant work needed to standardize the parts database (the same item could have different numbers from one ship to another).

On the hotel side, food and beverage inventory management was critical. A recipe was equivalent

[9] Source: RCCL.

[10] AMOS is a software developed by Xantic Software Company. It is a niche product for the marine technical industry. It is the planned maintenance system on more than 70 percent of the world's shipping fleet, not just cruise ships. Source: RCCL.

to a bill of material and therefore any good enterprise resource planning (ERP) system (JDE was an example) should work. However, categorizing and moving food and beverage, interfacing to point-of-sale systems, and managing inventory consistently across multiple ship outlets required strong central control and standards. Menus, recipes, and item specifications were determined for the brand and then deployed all over the world 24 hours a day with absolute consistency. RCCL chose Crunchtime (developed by Crunchtime, a Boston-based software company established in 1995),[11] now the cruise industry standard for food and beverage management.

Jeff Danis, the new vice president of supply chain, noted that there was little overlap between the "stuff" one bought or the supplier base between the two sides of the house and, thus, little need to have one system for both sides of the house. The operating needs determined the critical components, and Danis's job was to link them seamlessly for shoreside supply chain management. This included not only the financial interfaces in JDE but also those for effective logistics management and EDI.

Danis chose to use these operating systems for purchasing functionality and to integrate to JDE using a "thin interface" mandate to achieve common enterprise needs. "The operating systems, Crunchtime and AMOS, were not designed specifically for integrated supply chain needs, but they work well enough to fulfill basic needs. Integrating selectively and with minimum data flows will provide the functions we need across the supply chain with the lowest risk," said Danis. The transparency provided by the combined supply chain projects would give RCCL greater control of shipboard inventory, (food) production control, usage and waste control, and supplier pricing leverage.

Increasing Revenue

The shore-excursion booking program not only increased RCCL's guests' satisfaction but also allowed RCCL to increase its on-board revenues.

[11] See www.crunchtime.com.

Murphy noted that these had amounted to $22 million and more than 300,000 bookings in the past 10 months. When excursions were booked and paid for in advance, guests tended to forget that when on the cruise and were willing to spend almost as much on board as before (even though less onboard money now went to excursions).

The successful implementation of Internet cafes as well as Web access to crew members in their cabins also created additional revenue (RCCL charged $0.50/minute for access for guests, but the crew only paid $0.10/minute for access).

Williams wondered whether in the future he could use actual demand from a cabin's minibar to stock it with more relevant items for specific passengers. For example, if the two minibottles of rum were consumed two days in a row, perhaps adding more rum the next day to the minibar and decreasing some unused item might improve consumption and thus revenue.

Finally, one of the great moves as to how technology had been used to improve service and generate revenues was RCCL's decision to replace diesel engines with gas engines, thus freeing up space for 55 more cabins as well as reducing noise (the savings partially offset by extra fuel costs).

RCCL recently had won an award for having the best travel Web site. Despite this, however, it was refreshing the site, making it an even more user-efficient one stop for everything, with features such as 360-degree filming of cabins. In addition, passengers with a sailing confirmation number could fill in embarkation forms online well in advance of the trip.

History of Innovation

RCCL had a reputation for innovation. With its high tech movie theaters, ice skating rinks, and rock climbing walls, RCCL was constantly at the edge. Its ships were the latest in luxury, holding more than $10 million of IT equipment and software to support the hotel (e.g., Web access in passenger cabins for the most recent ships, Web access in the crew cabins, and Internet cafes).

Jack Williams, President and COO

Williams had come from American Airlines six-and-a-half years ago. Since his arrival, RCCL had grown from eight ships to 25 ships, with its workforce doubling. "Under his leadership, the company both uses old tools differently and has moved to more modern-day tools": "There was no e-mail at RCCL six-and-a-half years ago. You cannot live without it today!" The top 30 people lived and died by their Blackberry. Prior to Williams, employees were grown either from within RCCL or the cruise industry. Now, as a result of his focus on external recruiting of the best, significant numbers of managers' early careers were outside the cruise industry. Examples included the new yield management leadership from American Airlines, head of dining on Royal from United Airlines, Danis from P&O Princess for supply chain management, and Murphy, the CIO, from Bristol Hotels & Resorts. All of this was part of the transition from a small to a medium-size company. Medium size because, despite its 27,800 employees, with 90 percent of employees on board, shoreside staff was only 3,000 people.

Central to the ongoing operations of RCCL was the planning committee, which included Fain (chairman and CEO), Williams (president and COO), Bonnie Biumi (senior vice president—corporate treasurer), Murphy (CIO), Adam Goldstein (executive vice president, RCI brand operations), and Luis Leon (EVP, chief financial officer). It met every Monday morning to review strategic issues, strategic plans, and operations. (Exhibit 4 shows the current RCCL organizational chart.)

IT at Royal Caribbean

Historically, IT, although physically at corporate headquarters, was organizationally a stand-alone, technically focused remote unit until 1997. The IT department was very poorly regarded by the rest of the company, encompassing a command and control culture, low innovation, and excessive cost focus. IT had neither vision nor strategy. "Businesses were

EXHIBIT 4 Organizational Chart

Source: RCCL.

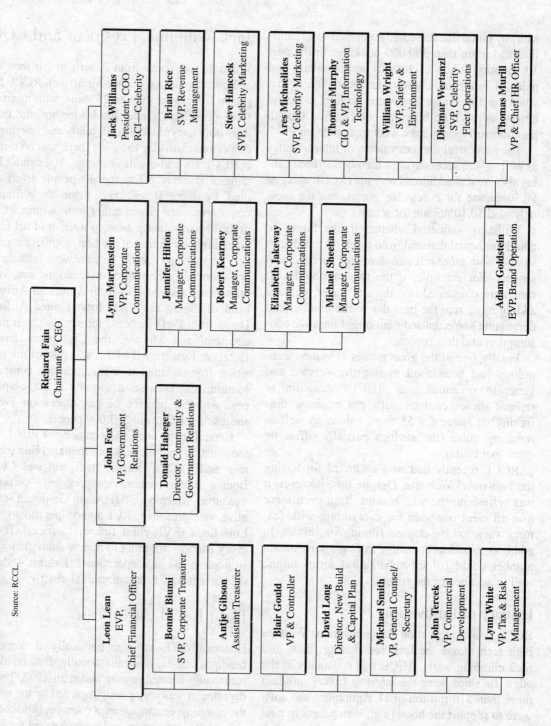

Richard Fain
Chairman & CEO

Jack Williams
President, COO
RCI–Celebrity

Lynn Martenstein
VP, Corporate
Communications

John Fox
VP, Government
Relations

Leon Lean
EVP,
Chief Financial Officer

Brian Rice
SVP, Revenue
Management

Steve Hancock
SVP, Celebrity Marketing

Ares Michaelides
SVP, Celebrity Marketing

Thomas Murphy
CIO & VP, Information
Technology

William Wright
SVP, Safety &
Environment

Dietmar Wertanzl
SVP, Celebrity
Fleet Operations

Thomas Murill
VP & Chief HR Officer

Jennifer Hilton
Manager, Corporate
Communications

Robert Kearney
Manager, Corporate
Communications

Elizabeth Jakeway
Manager, Corporate
Communications

Michael Sheehan
Manager, Corporate
Communications

Adam Goldstein
EVP, Brand Operation

Donald Habeger
Director, Community &
Government Relations

Bonnie Biumi
SVP, Corporate Treasurer

Antje Gibson
Assistant Treasurer

Blair Gould
VP & Controller

David Long
Director, New Build
& Capital Plan

Michael Smith
VP, General Counsel/
Secretary

John Tercek
VP, Commercial
Development

Lynn White
VP, Tax & Risk
Management

504

used to blaming everything on IT. It was an easy scapegoat." Organizationally, there was a VP of IT, who reported directly to the CFO and did not network into the organization. Self-contained and isolated, IT had developed its software by itself (packages were an anathema). Coming from American Airlines, where IT was a critical part of strategy, Williams had a sharply different vision. What he found at RCCL was a company with no e-mail and all data locked up in systems and inaccessible: The exact opposite of American Airlines. The challenge was two-sided: On the one hand was a technological challenge to change what IT was doing; on the other hand, it had to be integrated into the firm's real needs and managers. Over the past six years the IT team had grown with a substantial infusion of both human and technical skills to a point where now Williams viewed RCCL's IT leadership team as second to none. Moreover, Computerworld selected RCCL as one of the top workplaces for IT professionals in its 10th annual "Best Places to Work in IT" survey three out of the past four years.[12]

Tom Murphy

To deal with these two challenges, Williams brought in Murphy in April 1999 to report directly to him, giving Murphy a clear mission of transforming the business into a more powerful brand. Williams made sure that Murphy understood what he was getting into (i.e., "shake things up at a $2.9 billion Miami-based company and bring it into the digital world").[13] When Murphy came in, he faced several challenges. He first had to win over the IT team and have the people on his side. He changed most of the leadership in the first two years and engaged IBM's Business Services unit to work with both shoreside and ships' organizations on their system development and technology needs. He worked to transition the IT team to a customer-oriented one that emphasized a culture of openness and candor. He brought Mike Sutten in to get greater technology depth in the management team. Discovering there was little alignment between the company's direction and ongoing IT projects, he devoted considerable personal time to understanding the business strategy. He worked hard to gain the confidence of business IT users and develop solid relationships with them. He came to understand that RCCL's business strategy was all about growth, and it was not going to happen with either the existing infrastructure or IT organization.

Murphy's Background

Murphy was not a techie; he went to the University of Richmond and graduated with a B.A. in English and a minor in marketing. Murphy asserted he had a good grasp of IT but admitted it was not his first love. He was all about relationships and, in particular, 110 percent focused on customer service and satisfaction. Prior to RCCL, he worked mainly in IT and the hospitality industry. He started with Marriott Hotels as support manager, property management systems and quickly moved up to the position of director, property management systems and telecommunications. He then evolved to VP of information systems at Omni Hotels and Avis Rent-A-Car. Hired by Bristol Hotels & Resorts as VP and CIO, he came to RCCL as CIO in April 1999. Murphy considered that his human and interpersonal skills were key in his successful and fast-track career path. Moreover, he had practical expertise and understanding in implementing systems and managing installation teams. Murphy viewed himself, in his CIO position, as a business leader.[14]

Murphy's Team Background

In contrast, one of his earliest hires and a direct report, Sutten, VP of solutions development, had a strong technical background. Graduating in 1981 with degrees in engineering, Sutten worked for the intelligence community for ten years designing hardware and software, then for GE Labs for two years in charge of IT research. He joined Sybase,

---

[12] "Royal Caribbean Cruises Ltd. Selected as One of Best Places to Work in Information Technology," PRNewswire-FirstCall, www.rclinvestor.com, July 22, 2002.

[13] "Murphy's law," http://www.cioinsight.com/print_article/0,3668,a=22143,00.asp, January 1, 2002.

[14] "RCCL President Chose his CIO Carefully," http://www.informationweek.com/810/roya.htm.

a commercial software company, to be in charge of software development for replications servers for five years. Previous to RCCL, he worked with Koch Industry as CIO for three years, and then as CTO.

Similarly, Bernard Gay, VP, enterprise technology and operations, also a direct report, came with more than ten years of experience in design, implementation, and systems management for enterprise LAN/WAN and distributed computing networks. The enterprise technology department was charged with rearchitecting the technical infrastructure for the company's distributed computing environment, both ship and shore.

Paul Radziewski, manager, information technology finance and administration, project management office—also Murphy's direct report—joined RCCL in June 1998 as a senior financial analyst in the IT division, where he assumed the responsibility of developing, controlling, and reporting on IT's $40 million annual capital and operating plans and forecasts.

As a result of the company's rapid growth, fleet new-build programs, the Celebrity Cruises merger, Y2K compliance, new accounting regulations, and increased emphasis on customer and back-office strategic technological innovation and improvements, IT annual spending grew to $80 million and required a larger administrative organization to revamp processes and implement controls. In 2000, Radziewski was appointed manager of the newly formed IT finance and administration department, where emphasis was placed upon process improvement, administrative/project management software tools, audit controls, and ongoing management. During this period, centralization, process improvements, and controls were made to areas such as invoice processing, contract negotiation/management, telecommunication administration, human asset management, hardware/software asset management, project return on investment, project justification, project prioritization, and company strategic alignment. In 2003, Radziewski's responsibilities had expanded beyond managing the accounting and finance areas to overseeing the program management office and technology training.

Murphy's Strategy up to 9/11

Murphy initially worked to create a flexible and adaptive IT organization. He made it clear that his main goal was to service IT's customers 110 percent; customers in his view were the business units, not the guests (who went on cruises). IT's responsibility was to make sure that the business units had all the tools and the data necessary for them to exceed the ultimate guests' expectations.

From the trade perspective, RCCL for a long time had been seen as the leader and technological innovator, always one step ahead of the competition. Carnival and RCCL were in a ship-technology horse race. RCCL was also perceived as better in IT, but prior to 1997, that had not been a high priority to the corporation. IT had been just a means to an end. Thus, Murphy and Williams's idea that IT was to be leveraged as a competitive advantage was news to everyone.

From day one, Murphy was clear that change would come. Two VPs were fired, and several welcomed resignations occurred. Many managers displayed an "already tried before" attitude. The concept of customer service was foreign. Some were described as "rocks that blocked the flowers to blossom." Once the rock was removed, one could find this beautiful flower waiting to blossom. Perry Sandberg (AVP, product delivery system), a 10-year systems employee, was a typical flower: A can-do guy who loved the company, he took many innovative initiatives to increase customer service, and delivered. He moved from manager to director to AVP under Murphy and was responsible for all shipboard systems and research and development.

Murphy worked tirelessly to improve IT's reputation with its customers and to understand their needs better. At the same time, new tools such as NIKU, time management processes, and a program management office were installed to provide better controls over IT's efficiency and productivity.

Leapfrog Project

By 2000, Murphy had gotten his house in order. The IT department was reorganized and focused on the business, and the corporate strategic plan had been rewritten "with IT wrapped around the plan." The Leapfrog project was then conceived. It was designed to be a quantum leap forward in IT's support of the business. The significance of Leapfrog was such that Murphy was the first non-executive officer who had ever presented to the board of directors. However, to Fain, it was essential that Murphy present the $200 million project so the board could fully understand his enthusiasm as to why the project would transform the company. The project was approved.

Leapfrog's Three Main IT Projects

Leapfrog was really three strategic pillars—supply chain, employee systems, and customer. There were many individual application developments, rewrite projects, and package implementations under each of those categories.

The first pillar—supply chain—was the automation and simplification of the shoreside purchasing and procurement process through the upgrading of JD Edwards's ERP software to its newest version of its OneWorld package. It was intended to rationalize the purchasing process, reduce costs, leverage RCCL bargaining power with vendors to get better prices, and improve inventory planning.

The second project—employee systems—focused on tracking employees by upgrading the PeopleSoft Inc. human resource system. PeopleSoft Shoreside was the first of many employee systems under Leapfrog, including knowledge/document management, PeopleSoft Shipboard, and crew movement systems. This Web-enabled version would provide ships at sea real-time access through satellite connections as well as allow ships' officers access to licensing, training, and employees' backgrounds. Given the ambitious five-year plan to grow the headcount from 17,000 to 40,000 people, an automated and efficient HR management tool was critical.

Leapfrog's third pillar—customer—was the building of a $50 million Web-enabled reservation system (called NexGenRes) as well as many other initiatives based on the Web. Murphy compared the current reservation system to a bowl of spaghetti. Seven different reservation systems existed that did not talk to one another, thus preventing the providing of both useful detailed information and a common view of the customer to the sales and marketing departments. As Rice noted, business users needed a holistic view of customers and the ability to access the information through a single source.

By June 2001, RCCL still had different systems, which prevented it from seeing the whole picture of a customer's history; that is, it had a separate reservation system, a loyalty system, a shipboard system, and a revenue system. It was working hard to integrate them.

In parallel to Leapfrog, for the first time in the industry's history, RCCL launched four ships in 2001. This was a huge project for IT with Leapfrog going on, since a $10 million IT investment had to be installed on each of the four new ships. The investment included not only technology in the back of the house with 35 servers, three networks, thousands of components, property management, satellite connections, and point of sale, but also technology in front of RCCL's guests with services such as Internet cafes and interactive TVs. These were new first-time efforts for IT providing service to passengers on the ships.

By August, the IT team had grown to 450 people (including contract labor), and team morale was high. A huge agenda of work lay ahead of the department to make RCCL even more competitive, but there was momentum.

9/11

When the tragic 9/11 events occurred, Murphy was halfway through the Leapfrog project implementation. The impact of 9/11 on the company was immediate and devastating. Bookings immediately plunged, down 50 percent from the same week the year before,[15] and the company went into an urgent belt-tightening survival mode. A six-person "survive and thrive" committee reporting to Fain and Williams was established to review all alternatives. Murphy presented three options for the Leapfrog project to the committee. The first

[15] "Murphy's law," http://www.cioinsight.com/print_article/ 0,3668,a=22143,00.asp, January 1, 2002.

EXHIBIT 5
Leapfrog Project Before and After 9/11

Source: RCCL;
"Murphy's law,"
http://www.
cioinsight.com/
print_article/0,3668,a=
22143,00.asp,
January 1, 2002.

	Reservations	Supply Chain	Employee Management
Problem	Twelve different, incompatible, glitch-prone, legacy reservation systems could not reliably handle 45,000 calls per day and did not give marketing a common view of the customers before they boarded ship.	Spike in fleet size, from 23 ships to 29, threatened to stretch the supply chain to the breaking point.	A surge of 27,000 employees would overwhelm RCCL's unwired HR department.
Solution	Build a $50 million, Web-enabled reservation system, the company's first.	Design new in-house network to coordinate and leverage purchasing, fleet management, entertainment, food and maintenance schedules, and supplies.	Build Web-enabled, in-house HR network onshore and on board ships to coordinate and manage all employees.
Planned Payoff	Boost revenues and customer loyalty by letting agents book more customized vacations for clients.	Cut costs by millions of dollars annually, reduce duplicate purchasing, leverage buys for volume discounts.	Cut employee costs, reduce HR headcount, win volume discounts on health plans, track employee performance ratings and skill sets, and trade expertise across locations.
Status	On hold.	Scaled back from a $9 million project to $1.4 million for 2002.	Shoreside portion complete, shipside portion on hold indefinitely.

option was to slow down and cut 25 percent off some projects; the second one consisted of shelving some of them completely, reducing overall costs by 50 percent; while the third was to shelve the whole thing except for a small part of the supply chain ($1.4 million in 2002). To Murphy's surprise and shock, Fain decided to go for the third option. (Exhibit 5 shows the Leapfrog project before and after 9/11.)

In the next two weeks Murphy and his team cut 33 percent of their IT people and 90 percent of their contractors, leading to a 50 percent total staff cut. The annual IT budget dropped from $83 million in 2002 to an annualized level of $42 million by October. An overwhelming task was done in two weeks. People and systems were identified and decisions made on who and what to keep.

To fire people on short notice due to events outside their control was very painful, and to let go people with very specific application knowledge

was even more difficult. Often some of the most able were let go to ensure enough staff was on board to maintain the old legacy systems.

The timing was critical. By October 5, Murphy completed the layoffs. Murphy's fast action encouraged the rest of the company to hurry up. The process was done with such style that he received a number of e-mails from people who had to leave the company, thanking him for having been able to work with him and for RCCL. In the next two years, Murphy was able to bring back many of those people as the environment improved.

Back to Basics: October 5, 2001–November 2001

The second step—"back to basics"—aimed at focusing the IT staff on its new mission for 2002. The 2002 budget was focused on basic IT services and making core processes more efficient. Core activities included running the utilities of e-mail and network services. "Back to basics" positioned the staff to reconsider Leapfrog when better times came. Yet, Murphy felt so depressed with the lay-offs and Leapfrog's postponement that he considered resigning. Williams refused his resignation and reassured him that Leapfrog would resume at some point in the future.

Restart: November 2001 and On

Murphy started planning how Leapfrog's ideas could be implemented incrementally over the next three to four years. For example, the reservation system project, Jumpstart, would be number one. Murphy explained, "NexGenRes is one element of Jumpstart. RCCL's development approach [iterative, smaller cycles, pull-out/rewrite/plug back in, develop over a longer period of time] will get the company to the same place but over a longer period of time." Then, purchasing should be done. The HR tracking plan would be deferred indefinitely. The crisis of 9/11 and its aftermath helped the organization to be more focused and efficient. In a fast-changing and highly uncertain environment, Murphy learned to respond more quickly by breaking IT's goals into smaller projects and spreading them over a longer period of time to meet cash flow objectives. The idea of microstrategy allowed him to be more flexible and adaptive and to react faster to new environments. (Appendix A shows the top 20 projects RCCL was working on in mid-2003.)

IT Organization

The IT department headed by Murphy contained 282 people in June 2003 and was budgeted to increase to 341 people by the end of the year. (Appendix B is the IT organizational chart, and Appendix C is the department's recent expenditures and budget.) Since Murphy's arrival, there had been a 50 percent staff turnover in four years, and the revamped IT team had won significant awards in the past year.

An 18-month-old IT project prioritization committee was in place, meeting four times a year with the main objective to ensure projects' alignment with company goals. The members included Williams, Goldstein, Biumi, and Leon; Dan Hanrahan, SVP, RCI marketing and sales; Steve Hancock, SVP, Celebrity marketing; Craig Milan, president, Royal Celebrity Tours (land-based tour company); Gary Bruton, SVP, international; Dietmar Wertanzl, SVP, Celebrity brand operations; Harri Kulavarra, SVP, RCI fleet operations; Brian Rice, SVP, revenue operations; Tom Murrill, VP, human resources; and Bill Wright, SVP, safety and environment. Murphy, Sutten, and Radziewski from IT were also members.

IT Operations

Operations centers were located in Florida on the third floor of the Miami port location (on the waterfront) and in Miramar, with disaster recovery backup arrangements in Armonk, New York (IBM). These centers had to function 24×7. Miami was the primary data center, while Miramar was the newest, eventually to be redundant with Miami (see Appendix D).

RCCL also had a small integration lab in Hallendale (ship mock-up with satellite communications links), where it did all its testing of configurations of systems to be installed shipboard. Three and six people, respectively, worked in Hallendale to support existing shipboard software and develop new shipboard projects. Each ship had a data center that housed all of the servers. The number of servers per ship ranged from 20 in the smallest ship to 40 on board the newest ships. Several IT staff worked on each ship for maintenance and troubleshooting. They reported directly to the ships' management but had a dotted line to Murphy's organization.

On shore, RCCL had roughly 250 servers in Miami and an additional 45 in Wichita (as shown in Exhibit 9). The Miami data center had an AS400 plus a number of servers. IBM was the standard desktop platform, Compaq and HP the standard for Wintel servers, and Cisco the network supplier.

Bernard Gay noted they measured server-capacity utilization but were still developing standards. It was not, however, a major priority.

They were acquiring some of the newest system management tools. Gay was expending R&D efforts around tools such as VMWare to take advantage of items such as logical partitioning in the Wintel space. By partitioning a server logically by memory, processor, and disk, VMWare facilitated much fuller use of servers by opening the possibility of running multiple applications in parallel on a single server, thus enabling consolidation of servers. Sutten had also been pushing to better understand their Wintel space to see if performance could be enhanced by adding more Web servers in strategic locations. The tool they currently used for this analysis was Aleita. It pulled the system and performance log data from the Wintel environment to look at what CPU utilization and aggregate format would be like under different simulated traffic loads and configurations. They used it to aggregate information across a group of servers all serving the same application. They were transitioning to Mercury, with their agentless monitoring tools, to get this information in real time in terms of monitoring, alerting, and reporting.

Five-Year View

Murphy, in looking to the future, set as a five-year technology strategy for the fleet the development of fully redundant systems, where an authorized user could access data anytime anywhere. He saw driving costs for RCCL down as a result of consolidating and simplifying the systems, which had been developed separately for Celebrity and Royal Caribbean International. In this environment, they would move to a package environment using packages such as PeopleSoft's and JD Edwards' OneWorld as quickly as possible. Maintaining legacy systems and code was just not economically viable. At the same time, directory servers would be added and a major focus on security would take place as a result of the explosion of online systems. The new systems would be made to the extent possible self-healing and self-tuning. Finally, intense efforts would be made to consolidate servers as much as possible, to drive costs down and increase process efficiency. In short, Murphy saw his vision was "to create an infrastructure that is flexible to dynamic customer requirements, provide common core services, and focus on centralization [with ownership and shoreside], where it meets customer and business requirements." (Exhibit 9 shows the planned architecture evolution.)

The Challenge

However, the reality, in the short term, was more sobering. Murphy saw three options:

1. Do nothing beyond the current expenditure level.
2. Make an additional $8 million infrastructure investment in the next 12 months to untangle the seven reservation systems as a step to rapidly developing a single reservation system.
3. Introduce change even more quickly, with a much sharper increase in budget than planned and envisioned in option two.

In all three scenarios, ensuring projects were aligned to RCCL objectives while preserving innovation was key. It was an immense task in early July 2003. RCCL had 1,000 ongoing projects (800 maintenance and 200 new projects).

APPENDIX A Top 20 Projects List

Source: RCCL.

Project Description	Project Justification	Executive Sponsor	Tier*	Work Type	Actual Hours (as of 6/11/03)	Project ETCs (remaining time until completion)	TTL (total time in hours)
Operations enhancements of all servers and changes for data center operations	Cost	Tom Murphy	Tier 1	Project	13,180	22,467	35,647
First of several phases to consolidate all customer information databases (marketing: who bought what, who received a brochure, who did which cruises)	Revenue & enhancement	Tom Murphy	Tier 3	Capital Project	1,823	26,673	28,496
Three-part application that services the selling of shore excursions. Today shore excursions are sold to the public via Internet, via telephone (reservation center), and on the ships. Enhancements to this application	Revenue	Adam Goldstein	Tier 1	Capital Project	0	23,000	23,000
Reorganization and refreshing of Celebrity Web site (was refreshed two years ago)	Customer experience & revenue	Steve Hancock	Pending	Project	0	21,940	21,940
Reorganization of systems that oversee the supply chain to the ships (hotel side)	Cost	Adam Goldstein	Rollover	Capital Project	8,191	6,239	14,430
New application to organize and optimize guests' dinner seating on the ships. Completion in the remaining half of the fleet	Cost	Adam Goldstein	Rollover	Project	7,210	3,432	10,642
Extension of iKNOW project	Revenue & enhancement	Tom Murphy	Tier 3	Capital Project	254	10,291	10,545

(continued)

APPENDIX A Top 20 Projects List (continued)

Project Description	Project Justification	Executive Sponsor	Tier*	Work Type	Actual Hours (as of 6/11/03)	Project ETCs (remaining time until completion)	TTL (total time in hours)
Install AS400 technology mainframe technology. Effort to do business in a more modern environment	Cost	Tom Murphy	Tier 3	Capital Project	3,641	5,491	9,132
Property management system on the ships; movement of material from shore to ship and back (luggage, for example)	Cost	Adam Goldstein	Pending	Capital Project	586	7,387	7,973
Update throughout the company desktop PCs	Cost	Tom Murphy	Tier 1	Capital Project	348	6,908	7,256
Split of Celebrity and RCI sales force to allow the two sales forces to be organized independently	Revenue	Adam Goldstein	Pending	Capital Project	0	6,892	6,892
Install Lily pad software	Cost	Tom Murphy	Tier 3	Capital Project	1,856	4,719	6,575
Large effort to enhance and modernize whole system of applications and databases that support the sales to groups	Revenue	Brian Rice	Pending	Project	0	5,940	5,940
Beginning of an effort to make our systems more responsive to customers	Revenue	Brian Rice	Tier 1	Capital Project	0	5,800	5,800
Bring hardware on the ships up to a higher level. Each time there is a new ship, it comes with the leading-edge technology of that time. These systems are very diverse. Standardize as much as possible ships' architectures	Cost	Tom Murphy	Tier 1	Project	748	4,919	5,667

Description	Cost/Enhancement	Owner	Rollover	Project			
Beta test of systems designed to do better time- and record-keeping on the ship	Cost	Tom Murrill	Rollover	Project	267	5,309	5,576
Part of Lily pad software change	Cost	Tom Murphy	Tier 3	Capital Project	2,487	3,006	5,493
Similar to maps program. Another way of monitoring people time and assignment on the ships	Cost	Adam Goldstein	Tier 1	Capital Project	836	4,053	4,889
Migrate to new Microsoft functionality to make it more capable and efficient. Pure technical upgrade to the way the servers are configured	Cost & enhancement	Tom Murphy	Tier 3	Capital Project	840	3,363	4,203

*Tier definition:

Tier 1: Maintenance on core software; necessary/regulatory/new business function within current headcount

Tier 2: Additional priorities/not affordable without additional headcount beyond planned December 31 level

Tier 3: Jumpstart (the new reservation system, which replaces seven existing reservation systems)

Tier 4: Other pipeline projects (PeopleSoft)

Allocation of Development Activities at Present

	2003 Q1	2003 Q2	2003 Q3	2003 Q4
Fix and support existing applications	53.0%	40%	40%	40%
New projects	44.6%	60%	60%	60%
Enhancement to existing applications	2.0%			

(continued)

APPENDIX A Top 20 Projects List (continued)

Projects by Tier Ranking

Write-Ups Included	Project Name	Top 20 Projects List	Business Unit	Business Priority	Justification	Incremental Gross G&A	Incremental Capital Allocations	Incremental Net G&A
Tier 1								
Yes	Dining–expansion of dining preferences to accommodate flexible dining room seating	Siverwhere Dining Room project	Adam	1	Strategic	—	150,000	(150,000)
Yes	Cruise Pay IV	Project Phoenix group system enhancement	Bonnie	1	Business Expansion	—	200,000	(200,000)
Yes	Phoenix phase II		Bonnie	1	Strategic	626,000	698,000	(72,000)
No	Group renovations 2003		Brian	1	Guest Satisfaction	172,500	—	172,500
No	Custom air enhancements		Brian	2	Financial	—	20,000	(20,000)
Yes	Consumer response system		Brian	3	Guest Satisfaction	170,000	100,000	70,000
Yes	Work force mgmt		Brian	4	Financial	6,000	—	6,000
Yes	Comprehensive customer analytics		Brian	5	Financial	130,000	—	130,000
Yes	E-Docs phase II		Brian	10	Guest Satisfaction	—	75,000	(75,000)
Yes	Advocate		Brian	7	Financial	—	13,200	(13,200)
Yes	Sales outbound call center–phase II/III		Dan	2	Financial	270,000	200,000	70,000
Yes	CCI Fleet—Kronos 4.0 & TimeClocks		Dietmar	1	Strategic	197,000	239,000	(42,000)
Yes	ShoreX phase II—shipboard & activities	ShoreX phase II project	Dietmar	2	Financial	100,000	1,255,000	(1,155,000)
Yes	E-air ticket int'l		Gary	2	Financial	875	175,000	(174,125)
Yes	SeaPass phase 2—fleet visitor module & enhancements		Harri	1	Safety & Environment	103,000	178,000	(75,000)
Yes	Shoreside personal computing environment refresh	Shoreside Citrix environment & PC refresh	Murphy	1	Strategic	250,600	561,113	(310,513)

Project		Owner		Category			
Shipboard retro and 4690 POS retro	Yes	Murphy	3	Strategic	223,000	438,000	(215,000)
Marketing CIC	Yes	Steve	1	Strategic	37,500	100,000	(62,500)
Totals					**2,286,475**	**4,402,313**	**(2,115,838)**
Tier 2							
RCI POS automated F&B pilot	Yes	Adam	2	Strategic	33,500	31,500	2,000
Encore enhancements	Yes	Adam	6	Strategic	280,500	277,500	3,000
POS Revelation 2.8 + WTA + Udb	No	Adam	None	Strategic	120,500	—	120,500
Enterprise balance scorecard TGSRCI	Yes	Adam	3	Strategic	350,000	297,500	52,500
Cruise compass wizard/Fluent Seas	Yes	Adam	8	Financial	20,000	—	20,000
SQM reports and tools	Yes	Bill	1	Safety & Environment	20,000	—	20,000
Web payment enhancement (hotel, expense rpt.)	Yes	Bonnie	2	Business Expansion	156,000	156,000	—
Web name entry for groups	Yes	Brian	9	Guest Satisfaction/Financial	175,000	—	175,000
Enterprise imaging and document management	Yes	Brian	6	Guest Satisfaction	150,000	50,000	100,000
Best services routing	No	Brian	8	Guest Satisfaction	7,000	—	7,000
Web air/hotel tool for cruise only guest	Yes	Brian	11	Guest Satisfaction	3,000	—	3,000
Bag transfer/tracking and airline check in	Yes	Brian	13	Financial	62,100	60,000	2,100
RCT phase II	Yes	Craig	1	Business Expansion	155,250	150,000	5,250
RCI refresh	Yes	Dan	1	Strategic	1,740,000	20,000	1,720,000
Celebrity TTG/GUI embarkation	Yes	Dietmar	3	Strategic	109,000	109,000	—
CCI VingCard: upgrade Century-class (3 ships)	Yes	Dietmar	None	Guest Satisfaction	23,900	20,900	3,000

(continued)

APPENDIX A Top 20 Projects List (continued)

Projects by Tier Ranking

Write-Ups Included	Project Name	Top 20 Projects List	Business Unit	Business Priority	Justification	Incremental Gross G&A	Incremental Capital Allocations	Incremental Net G&A
Yes	CCI VingCard printing upgrades (7 ships)		Dietmar	4	Guest Satisfaction	63,300	56,300	7,000
No	Expedited debarkation card for INS		Harri	2	Guest Satisfaction	20,000	—	20,000
Yes	Royal emergency Plan enhancements		Harri	3	Safety & Environment	12,500		12,500
Yes	VingCard: Deploy release 3.1 to fleet beta in 2002—NV/Miami pier		Harri	4	Strategic	44,500	—	44,500
No	DE CAM relaunch		Murrill	1	Strategic	136,000	—	136,000
Yes	MTG insource		Steve	3	Financial	1,695,000	613,000	1,082,000
					Totals	**5,377,050**	**1,841,700**	**3,535,350**
Tier 3	Jumpstart PH II	Jumpstart program Plan	Tom	2	Strategic	3,431,963	2,919,000	512,963
					Totals	**3,431,963**	**2,919,000**	**512,963**
Tier 4	PeopleSoft		Murrill		Strategic	1,769,320	1,123,360	645,960
					Totals	**1,769,320**	**1,123,360**	**645,960**

APPENDIX B
IT Organizational Chart

Source: RCCL.

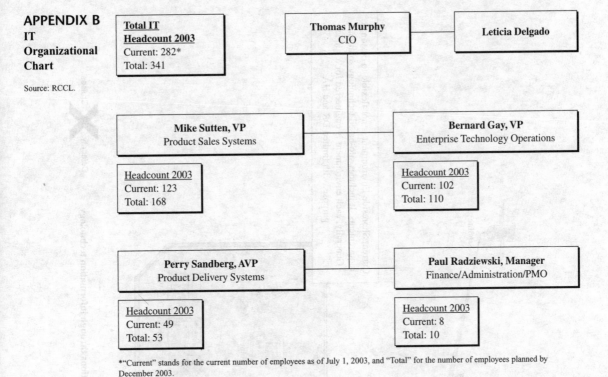

*"Current" stands for the current number of employees as of July 1, 2003, and "Total" for the number of employees planned by December 2003.

APPENDIX C   IT Budget (Total General and Administrative Expense)

Source: RCCL.

Year	1999	2000	2001	2002	2003 Forecast	2004 Forecast	2005 Forecast
IT budget by main departments							
Product sales—Application development	19,098	30,459	25,170	8,570	17,848	19,812	21,991
Product delivery—New build-shipboard	14,302	5,413	2,121	4,536	6,420	7,127	7,911
ETO	20,217	24,667	32,836	32,249	34,786	38,613	42,860
Finance and administration	Not a separate cost center prior to 2000	2,076	3,560	4,085	4,798	5,326	5,912
Total IT	53,618	62,616	63,690	49,441	63,855	70,879	78,676

APPENDIX D Current Data Center

Source: RCCL.

Current Shoreside Architecture

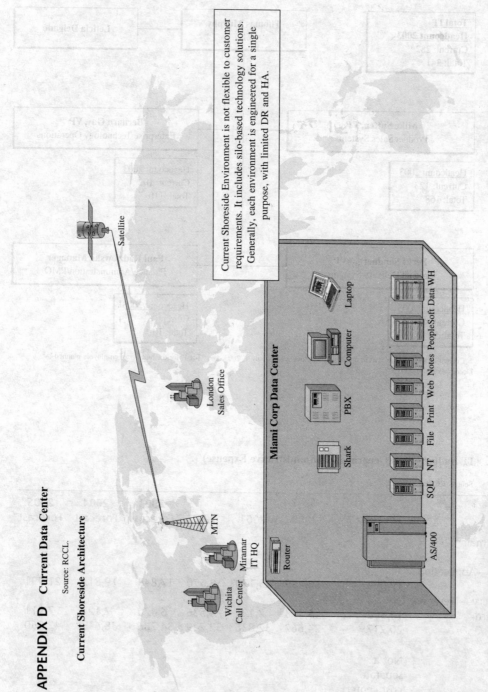

Current Shoreside Environment is not flexible to customer requirements. It includes silo-based technology solutions. Generally, each environment is engineered for a single purpose, with limited DR and HA.

Satellite

London Sales Office

Miramar IT HQ

MTN

Wichita Call Center

Router

AS/400

Shark SQL NT File Print Web Notes PeopleSoft Data WH

PBX

Computer

Laptop

Miami Corp Data Center

RoyalCaribbean
INTERNATIONAL

Celebrity Cruises'

Delivering great vacations through information technology

APPENDIX D Current Data Center (continued)

2004 Shoreside Architecture

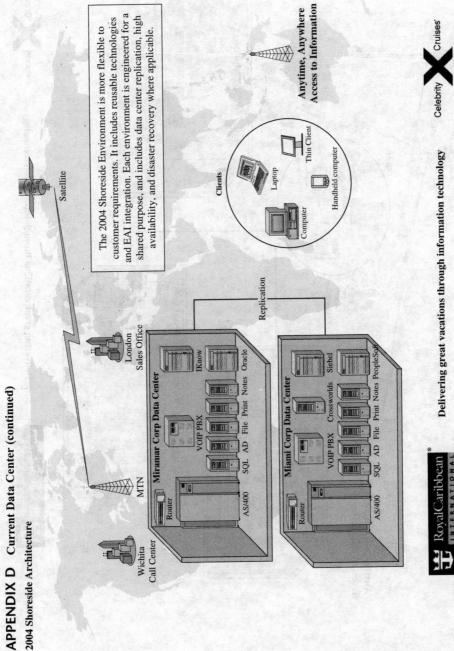

The 2004 Shoreside Environment is more flexible to customer requirements. It includes reusable technologies and EAI integration. Each environment is engineered for a shared purpose, and includes data center replication, high availability, and disaster recovery where applicable.

Anytime, Anywhere Access to Information

Satellite

Wichita Call Center

London Sales Office

MTN

Router

Miramar Corp Data Center

AS/400   SQL   AD   File   Print   Notes   Oracle

VOIP PBX

IKnow

Replication

Router

Miami Corp Data Center

AS/400   SQL   AD   File   Print   Notes   PeopleSoft

VOIP PBX

Crossworlds

Siebel

Clients

Computer

Laptop

Thin Client

Handheld computer

Celebrity Cruises

Delivering great vacations through information technology

Royal Caribbean
INTERNATIONAL

APPENDIX D Current Data Center (continued)

2006 Fleet & Shoreside Architecture

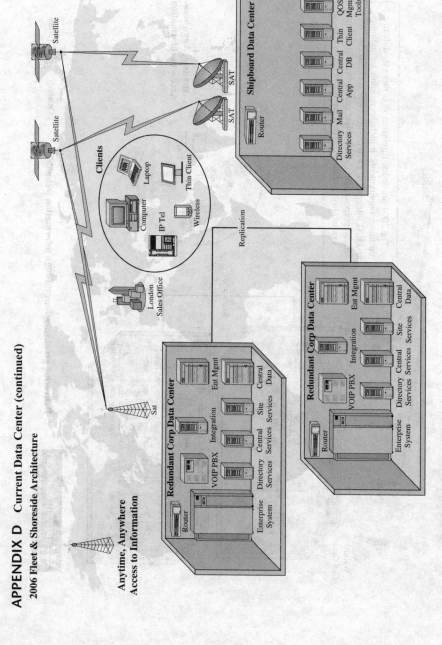

**Anytime, Anywhere
Access to Information**

Delivering great vacations through information technology

Celebrity Cruises®

RoyalCaribbean
INTERNATIONAL

Case 3-3

Rakuten

The basic concept is empowering small merchants. We will bring entrepreneurial opportunity to small companies.

Hiroshi Mikitani, president and CEO, Rakuten Inc.

Founded in 1997 by Hiroshi Mikitani (HBS MBA 1993), Rakuten Inc. quickly became Japan's leading e-commerce company. By July 2004, its shopping mall hosted around 16,200 merchants who offered a total of 8.4 million products[1] via virtual shops that they created with Rakuten's software platform (see Exhibit 1). The company was rated number two in terms of unique audience in Japan by NetRatings, trailing Yahoo! but ahead of MSN, Nifty, Sony, and Amazon (see Exhibit 2). *Nikkei's* survey on e-commerce ranked Rakuten first, ahead of Amazon and Yahoo! Shopping.[2]

Over the past several years, through organic growth, acquisitions, and joint ventures, Rakuten had added various services including portal, auction, greeting card, community, lottery, golf reservation, and business-to-business (B2B) services. Recent acquisitions enabled Rakuten to become a leading player in travel service and online securities brokering businesses as well. In 2003 the company generated overall revenues of 181 billion yen (¥)[3]

and operating profits of ¥48 billion (see Exhibits 3 and 4). Its share price went up more than four times during the past 12 months, making the company's market capitalization around ¥800 billion (see Exhibit 5). In 2002, *Fortune* magazine selected Mikitani as the world's sixth wealthiest businessman under 40.[4]

In July 2004, he contemplated the next move. Two weeks earlier, the company announced an investment in Ctrip.com, a leading consolidator[5] of hotel accommodations and airline tickets in China. Mikitani had an ambitious target for his company to generate ¥100 billion in pretax income; only 30 or so Japanese companies exceeded this hurdle. Could Rakuten keep growing its e-commerce business in the face of more aggressive competition from Yahoo! Japan and Amazon? Should the company expand internationally? Should it continue with its diversification toward the goal of becoming the number one Internet company in the world? If so, which businesses should Rakuten target next?

Early Years: Launching an Internet Shopping Mall

Returning to Japan in 1993 with MBA in hand, Mikitani was posted to the mergers and acquisitions department of the Industrial Bank of Japan

---

This case was prepared by Professor F. W. McFarlan and Valerie Massoni (MBA' 03). Copyright © 2004 President and Fellows of Harvard College. Harvard Business School Case No. 305-050.

[1] Company Web site, www.rakuten.co.jp, accessed July 30, 2004. These numbers include merchants and products at the shopping mall, Rakuten Ichiba (Marketplace), as well as other group companies. The number of merchants at Rakuten Ichiba as of June 30, 2004 was 8,777.

[2] *Nikkei Industrial Journal*, June 28, 2004. According to the survey conducted by *Nikkei's* affiliate research institute, Rakuten had the largest share with 33.8 percent, followed by Amazon (27.2 percent), Senshukai (25.0 percent), and Yahoo! Shopping (21.2 percent).

[3] As of July 23, 2004, the exchange rate was ¥109.65 = $1.

[4] "Young and Rich: 40 under 40," *Fortune*, September 16, 2002.

[5] As a consolidator, Ctrip had discount agreements with over 2,000 hotels and all leading airlines serving China. Ctrip served strictly as an agent and did not take inventory risk; its revenue was derived from commissions paid by hotels and airlines.

EXHIBIT 1   Growth of Merchants

Source: Company data.

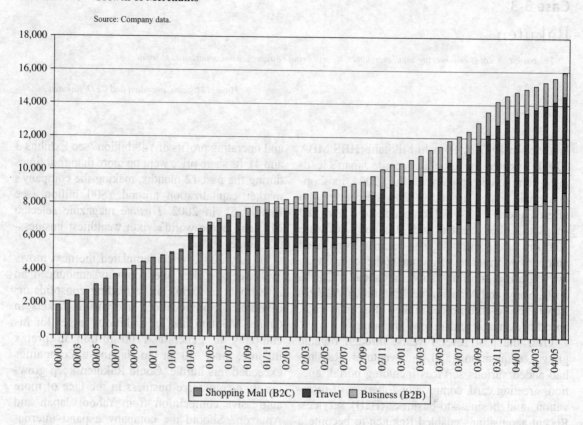

■ Shopping Mall (B2C)   ■ Travel   ■ Business (B2B)

EXHIBIT 2   Top 10 Web Properties in Japan (June 2004)

Source: Compiled from Net Ratings, www.Netratings.co.jp/US/monthly/properties.htm, accessed July 26, 2004.

Property	Unique Audience	Reach (%)	Time per Person
1. Yahoo!	28,230,000	83.64	3:13:10
2. Rakuten	20,609,000	61.06	0:51:48
3. MSN	19,036,000	56.40	0:32:27
4. Nifty	16,826,000	49.85	0:29:34
5. NEC	14,663,000	43.45	0:18:59
6. Microsoft	13,880,000	41.12	0:06:17
7. Global Media Online	13,275,000	39.33	0:25:58
8. Sony	12,548,000	37.18	0:16:09
9. NTT Communications	11,678,000	34.60	0:13:30
10. Amazon	10,037,000	29.74	0:11:56

Note: The reported Internet usage estimates are based on a sample of households that have access to the Internet and use the following platforms: Windows 95/98/NT, and MacOS 8 or higher. The Nielsen/NetRatings Internet universe is defined as all members (two years of age or older) of Japan households that currently have access to the Internet.

EXHIBIT 3   Rakuten's Comparative Position in Internet Services

Source: Company data.

Shopping	Travel	Online Brokerage	Golf Tee-time Reservation	Community
1. Rakuten	1. Rakuten	1. E*TRADE	1. Rakuten	1. Rakuten
2. Amazon	2. ISIZE	2. Matsui	2. GolfDigest Online	2. Y! Geocities
3. Yahoo! Shopping	3. yadojozu	3. Rakuten	3. e-golf	3. 2 Channel
4. Bidders	4. bestreserve	4. Kabu.com		4. teacup
5. Kakaku.com	5. yadoplaza	5. Monex		5. tok2.com

Rakuten Ichiba	Mytrip.net + Rakuten Travel	DLJdirectSFG	GORA + Golfport	Isweb + Rakuten Hiroba
Unique Audience	Estimated online hotel bookings	Dec. 2003, Domestic Stock Trading Volume	Unique Audience	Page Views

Portal	Greeting Card	Auction	Books	B2B Service
1. Yahoo!	1. Rakuten	1. Yahoo! Auction	1. Amazon	1. Rakuten
2. Rakuten	2. Yahoo! Greetings	2. Rakuten	2. Rakuten	2. B2B Japan
3. MSN	3. ISIZE eCard	3. Bidders	3. eS! Books	3. e-Anken
4. Goo	4.	4. WANTED	4. Shogakukan	4. Submit
5. Excite	5.	5. Guruguru	5. Kinokuniya	5. Oshigoto Auction

Infoseek	Ynot + Rakuten Greeting	Rakuten Flea Market	Rakuten Books	Rakuten Business
Unique Audience	Unique Audience	# of items posted	Unique Audience	# of requests per month

EXHIBIT 4A Financial Summary (millions of yen)

Source: Company data.

	Year Ended December 31,			
	2000	**2001**	**2002**	**2003**
Sales	3,225	6,781	9,895	18,082
Operating profit	1,047	1,800	2,550	4,750
Pretax profit	968	1,408	2,242	4,438
Net profit	(9,515)	(4,158)	(3,277)	(52,643)
Operating margin	32.5%	26.5%	25.8%	26.3%
Pretax profit margin	30.0%	20.8%	22.7%	24.5%
Cash and equivalents	31,940	21,359	19,672	25,791
Shareholders' equity	38,340	33,746	30,220	26,364
Total assets	40,255	36,387	34,055	188,016
Shareholders' equity/total assets	95.2%	92.7%	88.7%	14.0%
Number of shares outstanding	98,898	98,759	1,006,727	1,120,411
Net assets per share	387,676	341,703	30,093	188,016
Dividend per share	—	125	125	250

(IBJ), his employer since 1988.[6] There he got to know many of Japan's most entrepreneurial businesspeople and became enamored of opportunities that he did not see awaiting him at IBJ. In 1995, he resigned from the bank to set up his own consultancy. When mulling ideas for a start-up venture, he was aided by Shinnosuke Honjo, a Keio University graduate student who approached Mikitani in autumn 1996 to ask about IBJ. Impressed by Mikitani's conviction that his real opportunities lay outside Japan's traditional corporate world, Honjo dropped his IBJ plans and joined Mikitani's brainstorming. As Honjo recalled:

> We didn't have people, and we didn't have money, so we went with the Internet shopping mall. But we couldn't afford to hold inventory. Instead we tried to recruit as many shops as possible. In order to get attractive stores, we thought motivation was the key. If shops

were motivated, they would sell attractive goods. With attractive goods, people would visit the Web site. Some of them would buy products, and we could increase sales. More shops would join the mall. We could create a virtuous cycle.

> At the time, few merchants had the technical ability to build Internet shops; they had no choice but to outsource. But if they outsourced, their prices would rise to reflect increased costs, and customers would not buy from them. We saw our niche in helping shops overcome their barriers in skill and knowledge.

Soon thereafter, Mikitani considered acquiring a U.S. company that was building a software platform for online malls but did not proceed with the transaction. He believed that building the software in a local way, attuned to local characteristics, was critical to the success of Internet malls. Indeed, Rakuten derived its name from the free market that existed in sixteenth-century Japan and a Japanese word meaning optimism, while most other Japanese Internet ventures had English names, including words such as *net* and *cyber*.

After several false starts on software development, two engineers joined to work with Honjo.

---

[6] The Industrial Bank of Japan, which became part of Mizuho Financial Group in 2000, had long been a leading bank and one of Japan's most prestigious employers.

EXHIBIT 4B Quarterly Results by Segment (millions of yen)

Source: Company data.

	2002				2003				2004	
	1Q	2Q	3Q	4Q	1Q	2Q	3Q	4Q	1Q	Breakdown
Sales										
E-Commerce business group	1,507	1,833	2,015	2,233	2,370	2,926	3,016	3,670	4,225	43.2%
Portal business company	441	469	487	638	973	920	908	1,280	1,335	13.6%
Travel entertainment business company	—	—	—	—	—	—	—	1,497	1,375	14.0%
Rakuten Securities	—	—	—	—	—	—	—	—	3,093	31.6%
Other businesses	161	203	212	231	576	653	750	—	—	—
Internal elimination	(125)	(132)	(112)	(166)	(287)	(378)	(460)	(330)	(239)	−2.4%
Total	1,984	2,372	2,602	2,936	3,631	4,120	4,214	6,117	9,790	100.0%
Operating Profit										
E-Commerce business group	369	523	577	735	634	945	896	1,377	1,405	41.5%
Portal business company	42	34	47	36	21	53	92	125	322	9.5%
Travel entertainment business company	—	—	—	—	—	—	—	420	442	13.1%
Rakuten Securities	—	—	—	—	—	—	—	—	1,214	35.9%
Other businesses	29	47	63	47	36	58	84	—	—	—
Internal elimination	—	1	(1)	1	—	(1)	2	5	(2)	−0.1%
Total	440	605	687	819	691	1,056	1,075	1,929	3,382	100.0%
Operating Margin										
E-Commerce business group	24.5%	28.5%	28.6%	32.9%	26.8%	32.3%	29.7%	37.5%	33.3%	
Portal business company	9.5%	7.2%	9.7%	5.6%	2.2%	5.8%	10.1%	9.8%	24.1%	
Travel entertainment business company	—	—	—	—	—	—	—	28.1%	32.1%	
Rakuten Securities	—	—	—	—	—	—	—	—	39.2%	
Other businesses	18.0%	23.2%	29.7%	20.3%	6.3%	8.9%	11.2%	—	—	
Internal elimination	NA	NA	NA	NA	NA	NA	NA	NA	NA	
Total	22.2%	25.5%	26.4%	27.9%	19.0%	25.6%	25.5%	31.5%	34.5%	

EXHIBIT 5
Share Price Performance

Source: Thomson
Financial Datastream
International.

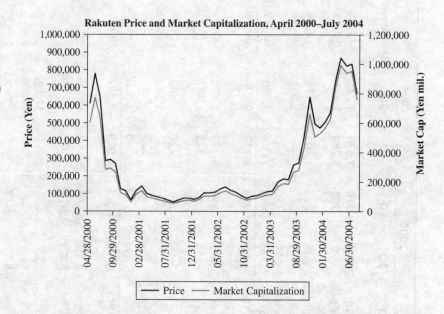

Rakuten Price and Market Capitalization, April 2000–July 2004

Kazuyoshi Masuda, the primary engineer, recalled the long hours (see Exhibit 6):

> Before I started working full time for Rakuten in March 1997, I would work at another job before going over to Rakuten to program until midnight every night. We were very motivated; we had a dream. So I worked and worked. Mikitani often suggested new ideas, and I would make them happen. We made a lot of changes. We were proud of our systems, so we kept on going. I guess you can call it "craftsmanship spirit." I got good at sleeping in my chair. In 1996, Mikitani wanted to start as soon as possible, preferably January 1997. We took a little more time and launched in May. In the beginning, Rakuten Ichiba had only 13 shops.

EXHIBIT 6
Summary Biographies of Selected Rakuten Managers

Source: Company
documents.

Hiroshi Mikitani Founder, president, and CEO. With Hitotsubashi undergraduate degree, joined IBJ in 1988. Graduated HBS in 1993 and posted to M&A Department in IBJ. Left IBJ in 1995 to found a consulting group and then Rakuten in 1996.

Yoshihisa Yamada Director and managing executive officer in charge of travel and entertainment company. Formerly CFO of Rakuten and deputy president of Infoseek. Graduated HBS in 1992. Left IBJ in 1999 to join Goldman Sachs. In 2000, left Goldman to join Rakuten.

Takashi Yoshida Director and managing executive officer in charge of system integration. Formerly worked at Recruit, a major human resources management and information service company. Joined Rakuten in 1999 and served as general manager, marketing, until 2002.

Atsushi Kunishige Managing executive officer in charge of finance business company. Received MBA from MIT Sloan School. Formerly worked at Sumitomo Mitsui Banking Corporation and DJL Direct SFG Securities, which was acquired by Rakuten in November 2003.

Ken Takayama Director, executive officer, operations and CFO. Left IBJ's M&A Department to join 25 other employees at Rakuten as CFO in November 1999. IBJ colleague of Mikitani's in 1988. Appointed head of human resources in 2002, when headcount reached 200.

Ryota Matsuzaki Executive officer and general manager, corporate planning. Formerly worked with Mikitani in M&A Department at IBJ. Received MBA from Cornell. Left IBJ in 2000 to join Rakuten.

Working with Merchants

The Rakuten Merchant Server

The result of the long hours was the Rakuten Merchant Server (RMS), a software platform that allowed even computer novices to create and edit their own virtual storefronts in accordance with their marketing and promotional preferences. RMS also allowed merchants to process transactions, evaluate Web site traffic, and communicate with customers.

RMS let merchants manage their shops independently of Rakuten. Takashi Yoshida, managing executive officer in charge of system integration, summed it up: "If you can use Microsoft Word, then it is easy. You can always see in real time what you have created and change the way it appears." Because merchants accessed their Web pages directly, those pages could be updated and customized with no input from Rakuten.[7] For individual assistance in creating and launching their virtual storefronts, merchants could consult Rakuten's Shop Open support team by phone. Once merchants had launched, e-commerce consultants (ECCs) were on call to help them attract additional customers and repeat business from existing customers. A call center staffed with temps assisted with more mundane problems like changing Web page font or color.[8] Merchant traffic information was available to both merchants and Rakuten ECCs, who used it to calculate total Rakuten traffic and to troubleshoot problems in individual shops.

An important early decision concerned distribution. Rakuten chose to distribute the RMS program to merchants through remote authoring, as an application service provider (ASP).[9] This allowed the company to revise the software easily and inexpensively and to respond immediately to merchant feedback, increasing customer satisfaction at minimal cost.

Rakuten invested a modest share of revenue in software and hardware from inception through 2000. Mikitani believed that software development cost and customer acquisition cost created a significant entry barrier for independent merchants. He explained, "Think about what [others] can build independently by setting up their own servers and introducing new services. If you are Amazon, it might make sense to do it yourself. If you are these small and medium merchants with attractive products, it does not. Even big companies can't independently build an online presence because their customer acquisition cost is so high." Rakuten overcame this problem by averaging the cost over many customers and reducing the cost per merchant.

Rakuten knew how frequently consumers bought from each of its merchants but did not share the Rakuten visitor list or convey the overall purchasing profiles of individual consumers to any of its merchants. Consequently, merchants could not cross-market to Rakuten customers who had purchased exclusively from their category rivals. Instead, the company disclosed to merchants the aggregate traffic and sales information for all merchants within relevant categories and the profile of the best-selling category merchant as reference, then urged each shop to do its best to increase sales independently. More generally, said an employee, "We put effort into increasing the total number of Rakuten customers, but we ask each shop to put their maximum effort in increasing their own revenues. We e-mail Rakuten magazines and send tailored messages to customers who visit the fashion section, for example."

In return for affiliation with Rakuten and the use of this all-purpose platform to list up to 1,000 separate items, merchants signed one-year contracts with Rakuten obligating them to pay a basic monthly fee of ¥50,000. Six months of the total was payable in advance. Yoshihisa Yamada (HBS

---

[7] This was not necessarily true of other online malls, whose merchants relied on the mall's IT staff to make even the most minor changes to their storefronts.

[8] There were more than 100 ECCs and call center staff members in 2004.

[9] An application service provider (ASP) allows its customers to access, over the Internet, software applications hosted on the ASP's remote servers.

MBA 1992), director and managing executive officer, recalled:

> When we started the business in 1997, other malls charged ¥200,000 or ¥300,000 per month, but we charged ¥50,000 per month. It was a fixed fee, due even if the merchants had no sales at all. We needed this fixed revenue to keep our operations running. Mikitani also made merchants pay half of the yearly total at the start of the contract period. This meant that Rakuten was never short of cash. Mikitani never had to borrow or seek venture capital. The company has been cash positive since the end of its first year.

Educating Merchants

In addition to technical support, the contracts gave Rakuten merchants access to Rakuten University. Originally comprising information that was offered free of charge as a way to educate Internet neophytes, Rakuten University later formalized a curriculum of nearly 20 half-day courses focusing on marketing and technical issues. About 20 to 30 classes were held each month in Tokyo and 15 to 20 classes in Osaka, and each class was attended by 15 to 30 merchants. There were also several e-learning courses. Each course cost ¥15,000.

Rakuten devoted a lot of resources to building a community of merchants. The company provided a merchant-only discussion boardroom devoted to discussion of promotional strategies. It also arranged a collaborative merchant "retreat." Drawn by the goal of increasing revenues tenfold in three months, a dozen merchants at a time would gather to discuss strategies with the aim of generating and sharing ideas on how to draw more traffic, increase the size of per customer purchases, and encourage repeat purchases.

The point was not to make the merchants Web-savvy as much as it was to give merchants tools to reach new customers. As Yamada related, "We told everyone to spend 80 percent of their time communicating with clients and 20 percent making the Web page. Don't spend time making Web pages with the latest technology. Instead, write e-mail or e-mail magazines and communicate with your clients. Our emphasis on that was very different from other shopping malls."

Rakuten began to give annual "The Shop of the Year" awards in 1999. The recipients of those awards were announced at Rakuten's New Year Conference; in 2004, around 1,500 merchants attended the conference and 41 different awards were given.

Building Traffic

In addition to mailings from merchants to their customers, Rakuten periodically distributed its own opt-out electronic magazine, *Rakuten Ichiba News*.[10] The newsletter grew out of a series of early e-mail messages written by Haruko Shimoyama, Mikitani's wife, to merchants and customers. Using the pen name Kamiya, Shimoyama would convey vignettes about day-to-day events at Rakuten, note attractive new products, and update Rakuten customers on the latest developments. As she remembered:

> At Hiroshi's request, I started to publish the e-mail magazine twice a week in 1998. It was a lot of work since I had to pick out attractive new products by going through the mall, consider what appeals to our customers, and then write the personalized e-mail magazine. But we found very quickly that it was extremely effective. After a product was featured in the e-mail magazine, we would immediately receive several orders for it. I tried to make our e-mail magazine very personal and not too pushy.

Over time, as Rakuten began to charge the merchants to advertise in *Rakuten Ichiba News*, it became a very strong revenue source for the company.

In 1999, the company initiated a greeting card service to build traffic to its Web site and enhance exposure to its potential customers.

Among the factors that helped Rakuten grow, said Yamada, was Mikitani's leadership and determination: "Once you start the business, you can't analyze and worry about it; you just have to do it, you just have to have the will. And his will is just unwavering. He has 100 percent confidence." Mikitani always believed that his business was going to work even though the early efforts to build online malls in the United States had failed. He set a goal of winning 100 customers for himself.

---

[10] In 2004, *Rakuten Ichiba News* was distributed to about 5 million subscribers.

Through hard work and pavement pounding, he signed up 100 customers by autumn 1997.

Nor did Rakuten managers minimize the impact of the publicity that Mikitani generated for the business. Said Yamada: "If you try to put the media coverage that he got even prior to the April 2000 IPO [initial public offering] into monetary terms, it was just huge. Mikitani was the only guy running a dot-com with his background: A prestigious college, hired by IBJ, and then an MBA from Harvard. There was nobody like him. And in 1995 nobody else would have quit IBJ to start his own company."

Consumer Experience

As Rakuten attracted more and more merchants, it became clear to Mikitani that "the biggest reason for Rakuten's success is the scope of the product line, and that is difficult to replicate. For example, we have 80,000 wines. I brought back a very rare wine from Napa Valley only to find it available on Rakuten."

Mikitani also noted consumers found online shopping cheaper: "It takes $2 to $4 to take the subway to Akihabara, Tokyo's famous electronics shopping district, and then you spend an hour deciding which model to buy. In total, it takes three or four hours to buy a PC. On the Internet, you just buy the PC and buy it cheaper. That gives us an opportunity as well, since the advantage of Rakuten is in being able to compare and contrast available products." In the early days, RMS did not provide "configurator" software tools that facilitated side-by-side comparison of products from different Rakuten merchants. Later Rakuten added a special feature that allowed shoppers to compare products such as PCs.

Because it was an online mall, consumers using Rakuten went from shop to shop viewing the offerings and making purchases. As each merchant was responsible for inventory control, shipping, and billing, a customer's purchases could not be packed and shipped in aggregate. A consumer buying three items from three merchants would pay for three separate transactions and receive three separate packages. RMS could cope with any payment alternative, including credit cards, cash on delivery, wire transfer through banks or post offices, and payment at convenience stores; each shop selected its own preferred alternatives.[11] In case of either payment fraud on the part of customers or a merchant's failure to deliver the expected goods, customers and merchants dealt directly with each other, although Rakuten often received initial complaints from customers and worked closely with merchants to solve those problems.

Merchants could not pay special fees to receive favorable placement on Rakuten's home page or its category pages, though they could place banner or other advertisements on such pages. Mikitani believed that Rakuten should empower small merchants and should not favor those with large promotional budgets. Therefore, placement within Rakuten Ichiba was random, although the same order was kept for a certain period so that shoppers could find items they had looked up a few days earlier. When the customer searched for the shops (rather than products), shops were listed in the order of the number of items offered. For auctions and group buys,[12] the items were placed in the order of time remaining before deadlines; for auctions and flea markets, the lowest-priced items were placed first.

Rakuten allowed shoppers to jump directly to the relevant pages within the marketplace from third-party search engines. For instance, if a customer searched for a particular item using Google, he or she might be linked directly to the page of the merchant selling the item and purchase it without realizing that he or she was shopping through

[11] While each merchant was responsible for selecting the payment and delivery alternatives for his or her own store and making arrangements with vendors, Rakuten negotiated favorable terms with leading credit card and logistics companies and provided introductions to merchants.

[12] "Group buys" are a special offer made to shoppers. When an item is offered as a "group buy" special, the final sales price is determined by how many people register to buy the product. For example, the higher the number of purchases registered, the lower the final price.

Rakuten. Customers were not obliged to register with Rakuten to make purchases at its site but were encouraged to do so, since it would save them the burden of inputing their address and other details every time. Also, only those who registered could earn "super points" (described below) entitling them to additional purchasing power at Rakuten. Even if a shopper did not register, RMS kept records of all customers who made purchases. As the customer information was jointly owned by each merchant and Rakuten, customers received opt-out mailings from merchants as well as Rakuten.

Rakuten put mechanisms in place to guarantee merchant quality and reliability. Mikitani said, "We screen the merchants. We check their Web sites. We have an evaluation process. We advise them to improve if need be." Yoshida elaborated:

> The client marketing division [five people] is charged with promoting Rakuten through the Web, radio, and on a paper basis. Its focus is increasingly turning to improving merchant quality. Our legal division can block merchants from opening their stores on Rakuten. For example, if a shop handles food, then it must receive certification to do so. If a shop sells branded goods, then it must prove that the products they sell are genuine.

Rakuten sent e-mails to its customers two weeks after their purchases asking about their shopping experience. The results of the survey were closely monitored by both merchants and Rakuten. If a merchant received a lot of negative feedback, Rakuten's marketing staff worked with the merchant to investigate the background and to improve the service.

Competition

While traditional retailers did not represent a significant threat to Rakuten, the competition from Internet players was fierce. The one formidable competitor was Yahoo! Japan, which through its market-leading search engine had the reach to bring significantly larger numbers of Japanese consumers to its Web site. (Exhibit 2 compares the reach of Japan's leading online groups.) Yahoo! Japan had become the country's dominant portal, with 28.2 million unique users, an 83.6 percent

reach, and a time per person of 3 hours and 13 minutes, which contrasted with 20.6 million unique users, a 61.1 percent reach, and a time per person of 52 minutes for Rakuten. The stock market accorded Yahoo! Japan a market capitalization exceeding ¥3 trillion, over four times that of Rakuten.

Yahoo! Japan generated most of its profits from auctions and advertising; shopping accounted for less than 10 percent of its revenue (see Exhibit 7A). For the moment, Rakuten was the dominant Internet shopping mall. The transaction volume of Yahoo! Shopping was a fraction of Rakuten's, but recently Yahoo! Japan had begun aggressive marketing to increase its number of merchants. As of June 2004, Yahoo! had 2,039 merchants, which grew by 25.6 percent in three months. Gross merchandise sales increased by 8.2 percent during the same period (see Exhibit 7B). In contrast to Rakuten, which worked with small merchants from the outset, Yahoo! Japan traditionally focused on large merchants. In 2003, however, Yahoo! began to go after smaller merchants and, in early 2004, lowered its fees 20 percent to 50 percent below Rakuten's. With more traffic for lower fees, Yahoo! Japan posed an attractive alternative for Rakuten merchants. Some merchants had shops at both Rakuten and Yahoo! (see Exhibit 8). The customer profile of both companies in terms of age, gender, education, and profession was identical.

Rakuten and Yahoo! Japan had other differences. Rakuten developed its unique business model through trial and error, while Yahoo! Japan relied heavily on the expertise of its American parent, transplanting business models that had proved successful in the United States. Yahoo! Japan, as a portal, had succeeded in expanding the use of the Internet in Japan and was credited for pioneering the Japanese Internet auction market. Since Yahoo! Japan focused on enhancing the reach of its portal, its Web site was designed to cater to all kinds of users, including narrowband users who used the Internet infrequently. In contrast, Rakuten's Web site targeted broadband users and included a lot of photos and appealing design features. Finally, the two companies had very different corporate cultures. Typical Rakuten employees were dressed in

EXHIBIT 7A Revenue Mix and Performance of Yahoo! Japan (millions of yen)

Source: Yahoo! Japan annual reports.

	2002				2003				2004	
	1Q	2Q	3Q	4Q	1Q	2Q	3Q	4Q	1Q	Breakdown
Sales										
Auction	1,262	2,686	3,355	3,757	4,349	4,851	5,795	5,841	6,085	43.2%
Yahoo! Broadband (DSL service)	1,974	2,346	2,815	2,726	2,588	3,118	3,306	3,746	3,809	13.6
Listing[a]	1,721	1,806	2,054	2,340	2,455	3,060	3,642	4,456	5,637	14.0
Shopping	1,060	1,178	1,377	1,418	1,463	1,537	1,683	1,904	1,994	31.6
Media[b]	684	712	906	1,289	1,350	1,426	1,576	2,058	2,053	—
Business Solutions[c]	50	66	98	236	248	268	268	309	351	-2.4
Shared Business[d]	1,722	2,102	2,315	2,625	3,108	3,284	3,809	4,262	4,564	
Total	8,476	10,899	12,923	14,394	15,564	17,549	20,081	22,580	24,495	100.0%
Operating Profit										
Auction	819	2,085	2,634	2,812	3,378	3,691	4,370	4,039	4,232	41.5%
Yahoo! BB	1,517	1,710	1,804	1,821	1,552	1,825	2,104	2,481	2,320	9.5
Listing[a]	982	894	1,141	1,366	1,649	2,162	2,659	3,325	4,304	13.1
Shopping	155	145	195	178	166	185	217	301	277	35.9
Media[b]	(29)	(48)	115	320	356	338	382	698	602	—
Business Solutions[c]	(3)	3	7	44	44	37	(10)	(15)	(23)	-0.1
Shared Business[d]	652	591	909	1,244	1,285	985	1,381	1,611	1,755	
Total	4,094	5,382	6,807	7,788	8,433	9,227	11,106	12,443	13,470	100.0%
Operating Margin										
Auction	64.9%	77.6%	78.5%	74.8%	77.7%	76.1%	75.4%	69.2%	69.6%	
Yahoo! BB	76.9	72.9	64.1	66.8	60.0	58.5	63.7	66.2	60.9	
Listing[a]	57.1	49.5	55.6	58.4	67.2	70.7	73.0	74.6	76.4	
Shopping	14.7	12.3	14.2	12.6	11.4	12.0	12.9	15.9	13.9	
Media[b]	-4.3	-6.8	12.7	24.9	26.4	23.8	24.3	33.9	29.3	
Business Solutions[c]	-6.9	4.8	7.6	18.9	18.0	14.1	-3.8	-5.1	-6.8	
Shared Business[d]	37.9	28.2	39.3	47.4	41.4	30.0	36.3	37.8	38.5	
Total	48.3%	49.4%	52.7%	54.1%	54.2%	52.6%	55.3%	55.1%	55.0%	

[a] Listing: Information listing services, regional information services, and directory search services, including sponsor site services.
[b] Media: Provides useful information, both free of charge and for fees.
[c] Business Solutions: Provides services to enterprises based on the technology and experience of Yahoo! Japan.
[d] Corporate and Elimination: Includes ad sales of Yahoo! Japan and premium member fees.

EXHIBIT 7B

Yahoo! Shopping Transaction Volume and Merchant Growth

Source: Yahoo! Japan annual reports.

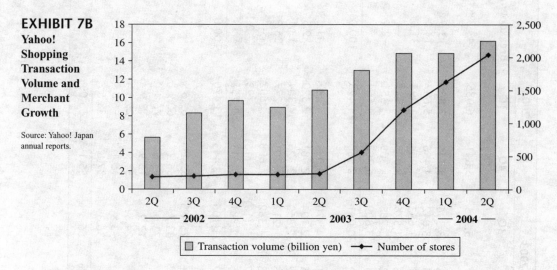

suits and adhered to strict rules; for instance, it was required that all materials should be locked in desks when employees left the office. In contrast, Yahoo! Japan was similar to many Internet ventures, with employees dressing casually and fewer formal rules.[13]

Amazon Japan was another potential competitor, even though its business model differed from

Rakuten's and Amazon's Japanese operations were still small. Amazon Japan's parent had substantial retail expertise and resources, including technological capabilities unmatched by domestic Japanese players. In 2000, Amazon had created a successful online mall in the United States, called "zShops," but as of late 2004 had not yet launched a mall in Japan. However, Amazon Japan was aggressively upgrading its infrastructure and expanding its product offerings. It did not charge for delivery for

[13] _Asahi Shimbun Weekly Aera,_ January 12, 2004.

EXHIBIT 8

Comparison of Rakuten, Amazon, and Yahoo! Japan

Source: NetRatings Press Release, May 31, 2004.

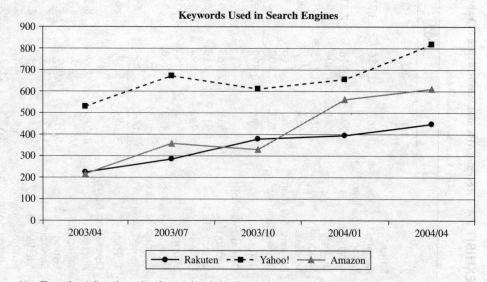

Note: The numbers indicate the number of users in households who used the respective keyword per month.

purchases of ¥1,500 or above. It was believed that the company turned profitable at the end of 2002 and was growing rapidly. The number of Internet users who entered "Amazon" into portal search engines increased almost threefold from April 2003 through April 2004. During the same period, those who entered Yahoo! increased by 35 percent and Rakuten by 102 percent (see Exhibit 8).

Building Momentum

Japan's excitement for Internet business reached a peak in early 2000. Many U.S. Internet companies rushed to the Japanese market, hoping to replicate their success at home, and Japanese entrepreneurs tried to start up their own ventures. Competition was intense. eBay entered the Japanese market in November 1999, four months after Yahoo! Japan had launched an auction business for Japanese customers. Lack of localization and a mistake in the choice of a local partner cost eBay dearly. Unable to close the gap, eBay Japan shut down in mid-2001. Other U.S. companies made similar mistakes. After less than a year in operation, Charles Schwab, the leading U.S. online stockbroker, was forced to withdraw from an Internet trading joint venture with Tokio Marine and Fire—Japan's biggest property insurance company.

At the time of its IPO in April 2000, Rakuten hosted 2,728 merchants, double the number it had six months earlier. By January 2001, the number hit 5,000 but leveled off thereafter (see Exhibit 1). The primary reason for the plateau was cancellations. Looking back, Rakuten managers felt that many merchants had joined out of enthusiasm for Internet shopping and Rakuten's IPO, hoping to prosper by joining the trend. After discovering that an online presence did not automatically confer riches, some did not renew their Rakuten contracts after the first year.

Acquisitions and New Initiatives

Rakuten used the IPO proceeds to augment its capabilities and enhance the customer base. In late 2000, the company acquired Infoseek Japan, an Internet portal, primarily to build access to a large new pool of users, including more male users.

Infoseek retained its own brand name, even though Rakuten managed its operations. On Infoseek's home page, the only association with the parent was its banner advertisement; conversely, there was no button or banner for Infoseek on Rakuten's home page. In December 2002, Rakuten acquired a 90 percent stake in another portal, Lycos Japan. To attract new customers, Mikitani also acquired two cable television channels, one a broadband portal that provided music, movies, and other content on demand and the other a home shopping channel. The company also partnered with several mobile providers to expand its mobile user base.

Rakuten's focus gradually shifted over time. As Mikitani described Rakuten's strategy in 2002, "We have not been active in auctions because our mall business is B2C [business to consumer]. But because we want to become the one-stop shop for everything, we must strengthen our C2C [consumer-to-consumer] segment as well. We will seriously push C2C—though B2C remains our main business—and see how they do. They are all branded Rakuten."

Within the mall, Rakuten also expanded its categories through joint ventures, acquisitions, and start-ups. The company expanded its original business model with some of these categories. Rather than hosting many small merchants, a Rakuten-affiliated company served as the sole retailer/service provider in certain categories. For example, Rakuten Books was launched in December 2000 in a joint venture with Nippon Shuppan Hanbai Inc., the largest book distributor in Japan. Rakuten Golf followed in April 2001 as a result of an acquisition of an online golf reservation company, while Rakuten Travel was a start-up launched in April 2001 targeting online hotel bookings. Rakuten Auto was another new business, launched in March 2002 to help online users find and purchase automobiles and spare parts.

Investors watched carefully to see whether Rakuten management made efficient use of the IPO proceeds. Although some analysts questioned Rakuten's acquisition strategy, management believed that the acquired properties expanded the reach of the group.

New Contract, New Fee Structure

In October 2001, Rakuten introduced a new contract, Rakuten Lite. The new contract differed from the standard contract in duration (three months vs. a year), monthly cost (¥39,800 vs. ¥50,000), and capacity (100 items vs. 1,000 items).[14] In September 2002, new merchants were almost evenly divided between Rakuten Lite and Rakuten Standard.

Another important change was to a transaction-based revenue model. Rakuten Lite introduced a systems fee of 3.5 to 5 percent of every shop transaction. In April 2002, Rakuten Standard also introduced a systems fee of 2 to 3 percent of each shop's monthly sales in excess of ¥1 million. At the same time, the maximum number of items that each merchant could list under the standard plan was raised from 1,000 to 1,500. Yamada preferred a transaction-based model to a fee-based model, even though low transaction volume for a shop reduced Rakuten's cash flow. According to him, "If you want to be profitable from year one, then you'd better have a fixed fee. Now that our growth in number of stores has slowed down to cruising speed but the transaction amount is still rising, we want to shift our revenue base from the number of stores to the transaction amount. We invest the incremental revenue in marketing and systems."

Merchant reaction to the new fee structure was in line with expectations. Of the 152 stores that left Rakuten during a grace period prior to the imposition of transaction fees on standard contract holders, only 30 to 40 merchants left principally because of the fees. In fact, only 16 of the 152 departing merchants had sales greater than the ¥1 million hurdle beyond which the fee was imposed. Of the 16, three merchants had monthly sales on Rakuten exceeding ¥10 million.[15] As a result of this change in fee structure, Rakuten was able to develop systems fees as a third source of revenue in addition to merchant fixed fees and advertising. By the end of 2002, systems fees

[14] By early 2004, the terms of Rakuten Standard and Rakuten Lite had been slightly revised, and Rakuten Premium Lite had also been introduced.

[15] Yoshiko Motoyama, "Rakuten," Morgan Stanley Japan, May 17, 2002, p. 4.

accounted for around 20 percent of the company's e-commerce revenue; by the middle of 2004, they grew to account for about 30 percent.

Winning Merchants

"We place our greatest efforts into acquiring new merchants," said Yoshida. "Everyone we hire outside engineering, even designers or HTML coding staff, first works in sales, so that everyone speaks a common language and understands the issues, questions, and problems that new clients face."

Nearly 50 staff members were dedicated to acquiring new merchants. They were organized by both category and geography. The process of signing up prospective merchants often started with prospects requesting information from Rakuten by registering their address and other details and receiving *The Handbook of Rakuten Service*. This 80-page booklet included case studies of merchants that substantially grew sales through e-commerce, a tariff schedule, a description of RMS, a discussion of payment and delivery alternatives, advertisement menus, information on Rakuten University, and application forms.

Every month the company arranged free, one-hour-long e-commerce (EC) seminars in major cities throughout the country, sometimes jointly with local chambers of commerce. Each seminar was attended by 40 to 80 prospects.

During 2002, the annual net increase in the number of merchants was 16.6 percent, with 3 to 6 percent of the merchants canceling their contracts each month. In the following year, growth in e-commerce led to a pickup in the number of new merchants by 23 percent, yielding a net increase of 1,424 stores. Since cancelations often resulted from poor sales performance, Rakuten began to work closely with shops that were struggling to increase sales. It reorganized the categories of products to better meet the needs of merchants and customers. For instance, a new category, "kids, baby, and maternity," was created within "fashion items." Such efforts improved the retention rate of merchants to 90 percent in the first quarter of 2004 from 85.5 percent a year before, with monthly churn declining to 2 to 4 percent.

Increasing Traffic

Rakuten tried many strategies to build traffic to its Web site. The most important element of its traffic-building strategy was working closely with merchants to encourage them to communicate frequently and effectively with their existing customers. Also, in 2004, Rakuten was distributing 30 e-mail magazines focusing on certain categories (such as fashion, wines, and IT products), best-selling items, auctions, group buys, coupons, and so forth. Those e-mail magazines featured products advertised by certain merchants as well as products selected by Rakuten. Opt-out e-mail magazines that focused on certain categories were distributed to all the customers who made purchases at any shop in those categories. In 2002, Rakuten had launched an offline magazine, *Rakuten Magazine,* jointly with a major Japanese publisher, but it was discontinued after 12 months.

In May 2003, Rakuten began affiliate programs, through which online partners directing traffic to Rakuten received a commission for any resulting sales (typically 1 percent). By mid-2004, thanks to an easy-to-understand interface, the number of affiliate sites reached 130,000, making Rakuten the largest affiliate service in Japan. Some affiliate sites posted monthly sales in excess of $20,000. The company also provided access to its shopping mall through 14 third-party portals including OCN, ODN, and AOL. By 2004, affiliate and original equipment manufacturer (OEM) programs contributed 20 to 30 percent of Rakuten's gross merchandise sales.

Search engines provided another means to drive traffic to Rakuten. The company's engineers used search engine optimization techniques to improve the odds that links to various Rakuten product categories would appear high in Internet search results. The company also invested in "paid search"—small text ads that appeared adjacent to Web search results—to promote certain categories but did not promote individual merchants or particular products. Some Rakuten merchants independently used paid search or bought banner ads linked to specific terms entered into portal search engines.

Comparing first-quarter 2003 with first-quarter 2004, the number of unique buyers grew from 1.12 million to 1.81 million and the number of transactions from 2.18 million to 3.73 million, while the average number of transactions per unique buyer and average basket price remained almost constant at around two times and ¥9,800, respectively.

Customer Retention: Super Points Program

In November 2002, Rakuten launched a program to reward loyal users, Rakuten Super Points, which allowed the shoppers to accumulate points in a manner similar to airline mileage programs. Users could earn points (typically valued at 1 percent of the purchase price) after they registered as members. Those points would expire if the users did not make another purchase within the next 12 months, thus creating incentive to visit the site periodically. The points also entitled them to free gifts and lotteries. According to Yamada, "The number of unique buyers, those who made a purchase at least once at Rakuten, jumped 16 percent from 860,000 in the third quarter to 1 million in the fourth quarter. This is the largest quarter-to-quarter increase we have ever experienced."

In April 2003, the loyalty program was expanded to all stores, allowing customers to earn points for any item available at Rakuten. Although Rakuten initially subsidized the cost of those points, it eventually convinced merchants to bear the cost of points as promotional expenses. In September 2003, Rakuten Points Club was launched, and customers who accumulated large points were entitled to gold and silver membership. In March 2004, Rakuten announced a marketing partnership with All Nippon Airways (ANA), Japan's second-largest airline and a member of the Star Alliance, enabling ANA customers to exchange their frequent-flier miles for Rakuten points and vice versa.

Growth Opportunities

The secular decline in telecommunication charges and the increasing penetration of Internet access in Japan augured well for continued growth. By December 2003, Japanese Internet connections increased to 77.3 million, exceeding 60 percent of the population, and the number of households with broadband access reached 48 percent of households with Internet connections, thanks to a sharp decline in ADSL prices resulting from intense competition led by Yahoo! Japan and its parent, Softbank. Japan had quickly become the cheapest high-speed Internet country; Mikitani noted, "In 2001 it was the most expensive. A year later it was the cheapest, cheaper than the United States or Korea: Only $17 to $18 a month."

By early 2004, 62 percent of the population and 94 percent of all households in Japan had a cell phone, of which 84 percent were Web-enabled. Rakuten began to offer its service through i-mode (NTT DoCoMo's mobile Internet service) in 2000. Late in 2002, the company began advertising that popular electronics products, such as plasma TVs, computers, and DVD recorders, were available through its merchants at prices 10 to 30 percent lower than those of the most competitive offline discount stores. Conceivably, consumers could comparison shop at the discount stores but actually purchase the product they chose with Rakuten using their cell phones. When Rakuten joined i-mode's official portal[16] in March 2004, its daily gross merchandise sales from mobile users went up by 40 percent and homepage views increased by 55 percent.

Historically, Rakuten generated 30 to 40 percent of its revenue from advertisements, although the ratio declined to less than 20 percent in the first quarter of 2004 as the company made large acquisitions during 2003. The advertisement revenue for the 12 months ending March 2004 was ¥6,568 million, a 58 percent increase over the previous 12 months. About 55 percent of the advertising revenue came from merchants and the balance from other companies. The merchants paid for advertisements in Rakuten's various e-mail magazines and for banner ads on the marketplace home and category pages, while other companies paid to advertise on Infoseek and other Rakuten properties, including its greeting cards.

Organization and Corporate Culture

Mikitani set the objective for Rakuten to become the number one global Internet company in August 1999, when its revenues were still just several million dollars. While he held such a grand vision, he also paid attention to details and execution issues. He always experimented before launching a new idea, saying, "First, try small. If it is going to work, then grow big. I like *kaizen*;[17] we need to move incrementally." Indeed, along with this vision, he developed "Five Concepts at Rakuten" that emphasized the importance of incremental improvements, professionalism, and experimentation (see Exhibit 9).

In March 2003, Rakuten was reorganized into seven business company units and ten executive officers were appointed. The company appointed three additional external directors to improve corporate governance, making the total number of external directors five. Those external directors consisted of experts in the Internet business as well as Honjo, a founding member who left Rakuten in 2002 to pursue his dream in education.

In October 2003, Rakuten relocated its office to a new complex in Roppongi, a more central location in Tokyo, and consolidated its nearly 800 staff members,[18] who were previously scattered around six buildings. Rakuten allowed all its employees access to a broad array of company information, including financials. Transaction volume was reported electronically to senior managers every hour. Basic operational statistics were issued weekly on paper. Every Monday at 8 A.M., all Rakuten employees gathered for companywide assemblies, where each of 60 managers spoke for one minute summarizing his or her team's activities during the past week and the action plan for the current week. In preparation for those assemblies, senior officers gathered one hour earlier to discuss the week's priorities and strategic initiatives.

All of the salespeople at Rakuten headquarters worked from grouped open-plan desks within

[16] NTT DoCoMo allowed only selected content providers to be shown on its i-mode official portal. As of March 2004, there were 4,144 sites on its official portal and 74,605 unofficial sites.

[17] *Kaizen* is a Japanese word meaning improvement that is widely used at manufacturing companies in Japan.

[18] The number of staff totaled 1,200 including part-time employees. The average age of Rakuten employees was 30 years old.

EXHIBIT 9
**Concepts of
Success by
Hiroshi
Mikitani**

Source: Company
data.

1. **Always Kaizen, Always Improvement**
   There are only two types of individuals; those who get things done and those who try on best efforts basis and make excuses to themselves. All individuals should have strong will to get things done.

2. **Professionalism**
   Rakuten is a business group consisting of professionals. You need to think 100 times more than others to compete, and need to grow through self-discipline.

3. **Hypothesize → Implement → Test → Incorporate into Routine**
   Concrete action plans are critical.

4. **Maximize Customer Satisfaction**
   Rakuten is a "service company." Do not be arrogant, but always be proud. Increase customer satisfaction.

5. **Speed!! Speed!! Speed!!**
   You need to do in one month what other companies do in one year. You will win or lose in the next two or three years.

sight of whiteboards that displayed current individual performance against specific sales targets. Approximately 30 new recruits joined annually, most coming from undergraduate colleges. The company hired 165 people as midcareer hires in 2003; engineers were hired through external agencies. As Ken Takayama, director and general manager, operations, pointed out:

> We put new hires in sales. That way, they can see Rakuten's strengths and weaknesses from an outsider's perspective. When recruiting our salespeople, we look for potential and self-motivation. Once they arrive, we throw them out in the street and make them get 300 name cards. The message is that "if you are shy, you can't do business. You can't recruit new customers." We throw parties on a quarterly basis, and we put efforts into motivating people, frequently through cash and awards for performance.

Perhaps uniquely for a Japanese company, Rakuten each year during performance reviews singled out a small percentage of the worst-performing staff by reducing their salaries. Many of these individuals were asked to leave, and others naturally assumed they would have a hard time progressing and left on their own.

Mikitani believed that his primary responsibility was to lead others:

> Sometimes I got really nervous because my sales force was not motivated. So at 3 A.M. one night I moved my desk in front of the sales team. Keeping employee energy level high is the real issue. If we have that, we will find a

way. But the company still needs my energy. If there is a specific project, I need to show how to do it, either by building a control system or by picking up several projects personally and showing the way to execute. I also communicate all important management issues on a daily basis. Communication is very important.

Around the time of its IPO, the company had established a stock option plan for its directors, officers, and employees. In addition, in mid-2004 Mikitani decided to give each employee one share out of his personal holdings to encourage a sense of ownership. Mikitani endorsed every share certificate with the name of each recipient, then handed it to each employee in person.

Building Additional Revenue Sources

Travel Services

Aiming at becoming a one-stop shop for all online services, Rakuten invested heavily in its travel business. The biggest player in this field was Mytrip.net, which had a 40 to 50 percent share in domestic online bookings. In September 2003, as Mytrip.net was preparing for an IPO, Rakuten stepped in and acquired it for ¥32.3 billion. Yamada, who took charge of the travel business following the acquisition, speculated, "Based on its projection of ¥100 billion bookings in 2004, Mytrip.net would rank number 10 in terms of gross bookings among all travel service companies in Japan." It was particularly strong in the business segment, accounting for 13 percent of the market. A majority of its revenue came from bookings of so-called *business hotels*—basic hotels typically used for business trips. Yamada continued, "As 80 percent of the company's bookings come from business travel, we see a significant opportunity to grow leisure travel. Online travel bookings account for only 5 percent of the market in Japan, while the ratio is over 10 percent in the U.S." He also planned to offer more packages, combining airline or train tickets with hotels. Mytrip.net's site was integrated with Rakuten Travel's site in September 2004.

In June 2004, Rakuten announced a ¥12 billion investment to acquire 21.6 percent of Ctrip.com International, Inc., a leading consolidator of hotel accommodations and airline tickets in China that traded on NASDAQ. It was estimated that Ctrip.com had about 2 million members and accounted for approximately 50 percent of the market that catered to so-called FIT, or frequent independent travelers. Rakuten and Ctrip entered into discussions to collaborate to take advantage of the traffic between China and Japan[19] and to compete against Expedia, Hotels.com, and Priceline in Europe and North America. Mikitani explained the logic behind this acquisition, saying, "We cannot build e-commerce business in China, since the logistics infrastructure is still poor. But with travel services, which does not require delivery of goods, there is an enormous opportunity with rapid economic growth."

Financial Services

In November 2003, Rakuten won a competitive bid to acquire DLJ*direct* SFG Securities, the third-largest Japanese online trading company, from Credit Suisse First Boston, which had decided to exit the retail business in 2002 and had been waiting for the Japanese stock market recovery. Rakuten paid ¥30.1 billion for the acquisition and

proceeded with an equity offering of ¥46.4 billion to finance the acquisition and to reduce leverage. DLJ*direct* SFG had been established in 1999 as a joint venture between CSFB*direct* Asia Holdings, Sumitomo Mitsui Banking Corporation (SMBC), and other Sumitomo group companies. Atsushi Kunishige, president, DLJ*direct* SFG, a 35-year veteran originally from SMBC, was optimistic about the prospects of the Japanese stock market and synergy with Rakuten:

> During the last three years, the stock market was so bad that only active traders kept trading. So in September 2002, our company shifted the focus on active traders or so-called day traders. In September 2003, the market sentiment changed and investors came back. Since January 2004, newcomers have joined the market. So this is the turning point of our strategy. We would like to broaden our focus to include average investors. Since February, we launched a point exchange program. Now customers can exchange DLJ points for Rakuten points.

In early July the company changed its name to Rakuten Securities and launched promotional services to attract new investors. Both Mikitani and Kunishige hoped to convince Rakuten shoppers to start online trading, even though competitors questioned the strategy, arguing that the customers of the two companies were quite different.

Mikitani also planned to develop a consumer finance business. Because of his background in banking, he was confident that he could build a successful financial business. By the middle of 2004, the company had reached an agreement with Sumitomo Mitsui Card Company, Limited, Japan's leading credit card company, to launch a Rakuten-branded credit card. The cardholders could earn Rakuten points when using those credit cards; Rakuten also planned to provide loans to those cardholders. Ryota Matsuzaki, general manager, corporate planning, pointed out other opportunities: "Recently Rakuten began to get in the middle of credit card companies and small merchants. Due to the large volume, we can obtain volume discounts in commissions from the credit card companies and pass on part of the discounts to small merchants. They find such arrangements attractive relative to what they can achieve independently."

---

[19] About 4.4 million Japanese visited greater China, while 1.6 million Chinese visited Japan in 2003.

Challenges

In January 2004, at the request of his hometown, Kobe, Mikitani acquired Vissel Kobe, a professional soccer team with financial problems, through his private company, Crimson Group. This news gave a big boost to Rakuten's name recognition. According to Mikitani, "When Rakuten announced acquisition of Mytrip.net, only a few dozen journalists from financial and economic circles showed up at the press conference. But the press conference on acquisition of Vissel Kobe was full of people from all kinds of media." After Mikitani took control of the team, he drafted strong players and implemented measures to attract more audience; he wanted to show that a sports team could be run like a business. He spent weekends in Kobe to manage the soccer team. The soccer players wore uniforms bearing the Rakuten logo, and the tickets to the games were sold through Rakuten Ticket.

While the acquisition of travel and financial service companies substantially increased Rakuten's sales and profits in the first quarter of 2004, its traditional e-commerce business also showed strong results. The gross merchandise sales grew by 79 percent year-on-year and the number of transactions by 84 percent. Matsuzaki said, "The tremendous growth was achieved by the combination of more new users and core users buying more." In spite of those impressive results, Mikitani felt that its e-commerce business was not growing fast enough and, in March, decided to come back as general manager of the e-commerce business company and become general manager of the portal and media company, in addition to his responsibility as CEO. At the same time, the corporate structure was streamlined by reducing the number of company units from seven to four (see Exhibit 10). Mikitani set his eyes on the long-term target of generating ¥100 billion in pretax income. He explained

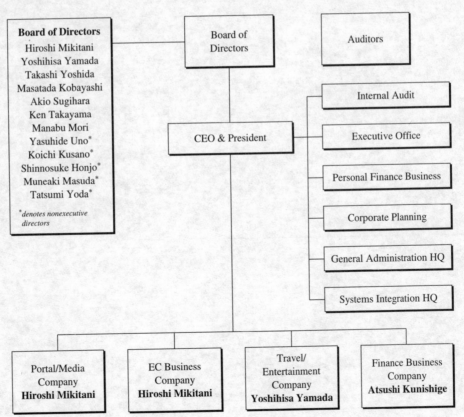

EXHIBIT 10
Corporate Structure (as of March 1, 2004)

Source: Company data.

Board of Directors
Hiroshi Mikitani
Yoshihisa Yamada
Takashi Yoshida
Masatada Kobayashi
Akio Sugihara
Ken Takayama
Manabu Mori
Yasuhide Uno*
Koichi Kusano*
Shinnosuke Honjo*
Muneaki Masuda*
Tatsumi Yoda*

*denotes nonexecutive directors

Board of Directors

Auditors

CEO & President

Internal Audit

Executive Office

Personal Finance Business

Corporate Planning

General Administration HQ

Systems Integration HQ

Portal/Media Company
Hiroshi Mikitani

EC Business Company
Hiroshi Mikitani

Travel/Entertainment Company
Yoshihisa Yamada

Finance Business Company
Atsushi Kunishige

his rationale for major acquisitions in 2003: "Acquisitions are not necessary if we are aiming for pretax profits of ¥20 to ¥30 billion. But in order to achieve ¥100 billion target . . . we need several businesses. I expect both Mytrip and DLJ to contribute ¥20 to ¥30 billion in profits. Our goal is to double the profits every year for the next three to four years for all lines of businesses. I believe ¥100 billion is a realistic target."[20]

Since Internet shopping had merely scratched the surface in Japan, Mikitani was confident that there was substantial upside in e-commerce. But he was also keen to expand and diversify Rakuten's domain to achieve the goal of becoming the world's leading Internet company. According to him:

[20] *Nikkei Business*, December 22, 2003, pp. 6–7.

I try to prioritize the next acquisition targets or business areas we should be involved in, but it is very difficult since there are so many opportunities. Recently I began to think that it is easier to think of businesses Rakuten should *not* get involved in. So, I have decided that I will not get involved in *connectivity, banking,* and *logistics.* I do not like banking because there are too many regulations, even though banking is close to consumer finance.

The opportunities appeared enormous. Which businesses should Rakuten expand in the next few years? Should the company allocate more resources to international opportunities? Could it continue to grow e-commerce business in the face of more aggressive competition from Yahoo! Japan and Amazon? If the current growth rate continued, could Mikitani continue his present style of hands-on management? Everything seemed to be going so well with the company: Was there any downside?

Case 3-4

Telecomunicacoes de São Paulo SA (Telesp)

"Telesp has been extremely successful over the past three years, reaching the goal of providing universal access in the São Paulo region ahead of the schedule set by Anatel, the Brazilian telecommunications regulatory agency. Our prowess as a telecom operator has provided the residents and businesses of São Paulo with state-of-the-art telecommunications infrastructure and services. We are now free to pursue other opportunities. But to be successful in the future, we must turn Telesp into a more entrepreneurial, customer-savvy company. Deciding which opportunities to pursue and then developing the organizational capabilities to execute our new strategy is our major challenge."

Manoel Amorim, CEO, Telesp, March 2002[1]

Brazil's telecommunications operators had marched to the tune of universal wireline services since 1998, when Anatel awarded Telesp, Telemar, and Brasil Telecom concession contracts to provide local and within-region long-distance services in nonoverlapping areas (see Exhibit 1). A fourth telecommunications operator, Embratel, provided interregional and international residential and business long-distance services while also providing business data communications services. The three regional telecom operators and Embratel were required to achieve the ambitious social goal of offering telecom services to all individuals requesting such services, regardless of income level or potential value as customers, within their respective regions by the end of 2003. Once a telecom operator had achieved the "universalization goals," it would be able to enter other regions and compete with incumbents from that region.

To meet these universalization targets, Telesp's chief executive officer, Manoel Amorim,

had overseen the final phase of a head-down, pell-mell rush to extend infrastructure in a country in which, in 1998, São Paulo residents waited up to 44 months and paid more than US$1,500 for telephone service in their areas. As a result of its efforts, Telesp was the first of the three regional telecom operators to meet Anatel's targets, having achieved the goal in late 2001—two years early.

At the beginning of 2002, Amorim faced a classic "prisoner's dilemma."[2] Previously the government's universalization requirements had dictated the company's strategy; now, Telesp could chart its own path. Many expected that Telesp would choose to muscle into the other two geographic regions in Brazil before the other regional incumbent operators or Embratel could enter its region. But Amorim and other Telesp senior executives believed that the decision was much more complex. Pursuing an expansion/"attack" strategy would enable the company to leverage its current capabilities to

This case was prepard by Professor Lynda M. Applegate and Research Associates Elizabeth L. Collins and Ricardo Reisen de Pinho prepared this case with assistance from Ana Fernandez (MBA 2002), Fernando Sigueira (MBA 2002), Guilherme Lago (MBA 2005), and Wilson Darosa (MBA 2005). Copyright © 2004 President and Fellows of Harvard College. Harvard Business School Case No. 804-149.

[1] Amorim joined Telesp in 2000 and was appointed chief executive in 2001 to lead the post-universalization strategy and the transformational changes required. He was previously the CEO of AOL Brazil and a general manager at Procter & Gamble Latin America.

[2] A non-zero-sum game called the *prisoner's dilemma* was first developed by Merrill Flood and Melvin Dresher in 1950 as part of a Rand Corporation investigation into game theory. According to the *Stanford Encyclopedia of Philosophy*, the dilemma faced by the prisoners in the game is that "whatever the other does, each is better off confessing than remaining silent. But the outcome obtained when both confess is worse for each of them than the outcome they would have obtained had both remained silent" (plato.stanford.edu/entries/prisoner-dilemma, accessed October 18, 2003).

EXHIBIT 1 Concession Regions (Fall 2001)

Source: Compiled by author from P. Budde, "Brazil, Key Statistics, Telecom Market and Regulatory Overview," www.securities.com, January 30, 2004; IBGE, http://www.sidra.ibge.gov.br, 2002; "Telefonica," Morgan Stanley Equity Research, June 25, 2001, p. 31; and Raphael Duailibi, "Brazilian 2002 Market Liberalization," *Convergent Communications Latin America*, 3, no. 1, January 2002; and Raphael Duailibi, "A Second Wave: The Brazil Internet User Forecast," *Brazil Market Strategies*, 2, no. 12, July 2001.

	Region I Telemar	Region II Brasil Telecom	Region III Telesp	Total Brazil
Number of states	16 states	9 states and the Federal District	1 state (São Paulo)	26 states and the Federal District
Area covered (000 km²)	5,582	2,739	249	8,570
Population density[a] (per km²)	16.0	14.0	142.9	
Population (millions)	89.5	38.3	35.5	163.3
Installed lines	20.6 million	10.6 million	14.4 million	
% = % of total Brazil installed lines	45.2%	23.2%	31.6%	45.6 million
% GDP[b]	39%	25%	36%	100%
GDP per capita	3,365	5,005	7,597	
Number of urban households (in thousands)	18,947	9,436	9,673	38,055
Socioeconomic status (SES) A	818	589	839	2,247
SES B	1,522	1,040	1,490	4,052
SES C	3,237	2,149	2,558	7,944
SES D/E	13,369	5,657	4,786	23,812
Number of companies (% = % of total Brazil)	1,483,000	1,227,000	1,177,000	3,887,000
Micro (less than 10 employees)	1,343,000 (37.9%)	1,136,000 (32.0%)	1,066,000 (30.1%)	3,545,000
Small (10–99 employees)	127,000 (40.6%)	84,000 (26.8%)	102,000 (32.6%)	313,000
Medium (100–499 employees)	10,400 (42.6%)	6,100 (25.0%)	7,900 (32.4%)	24,400
Large (500 or more employees)	2,100 (45.9%)	1,200 (24.8%)	2,400 (29.3%)	4,600
Percentage of Total Brazil	38.1%	31.6%	30.3%	100%

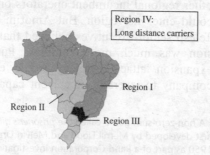

Region IV: Long distance carriers

Region I

Region II

Region III

SES A—more than 20 minimum wages

SES B—between 10 and 20 minimum wages

SES C—between 5 and 10 minimum wages

SES D/E—less than 5 minimum wages

[a] Population density is equal to the total population divided by total area. For example, for Region I (Telemar), 89,500,000/5,582,000 = 16 inhabitants by km². The unit of measure for SES is the number of urban households. In Region I (Telemar), there are 18,947,000 urban households. Of these, 818,000 urban households had a monthly income of more than 20% minimum wages (in December 2001, the minimum wage was R$180.00).
[b] Brazil GDP in 2002 = US$452.4 billion; US $1.00 = R$1.2087; GDP growth rate in 2002 = 1.5%.
Total telecommunications industry revenues (2002) = US$9.7 billion.
Total telecommunications investments (2002) = US$5.2 billion.

extend the footprint of its infrastructure and basic telecom services but would also consume significant resources and management attention at a time of increasing resource constraints and growing country and telecom market risk. Such a strategy would almost ensure that other regional incumbents would enter the lucrative São Paulo region. Given that Telemar was on target to meet its universalization targets in late 2002 and Brazil Telecom was not far behind, a better approach might be to focus attention on providing new value-added services (such as premium broadband services, integrated mobile/fixed wireline services, or expanded business services) to existing residential and business customers in its own area. In fact, Telesp had already begun to offer residential value-added services, having successfully launched in 1999 São Paulo's first asymmetric digital subscriber line (ADSL) broadband service,[3] called Speedy, and a wide range of digital voice services, such as call waiting, voice mail, and three-way party lines.

In addition, Telesp had to consider the threat from Embratel. Amorim explained:

> Embratel also has universalization targets that it needs to meet. Once these targets are met, Embratel will be free to compete with us directly by providing local voice and data services to our customers. The threat from Embratel is significant. The company has a well-recognized, high-quality brand and currently has market leadership for data services for business and government customers in São Paulo. They provide these important customers with a

data services infrastructure—including "last mile"[4] access—and a wide range of value-added data and communication services. In addition, Embratel is the only telecom operator in Brazil that already has a national infrastructure.

Finally, Telesp needed to decide whether to become an Internet service provider (ISP). Amorim knew that this strategic decision was as much a defensive move as it was an offensive move:

> The Internet was both a growth opportunity and a threat for Telesp. By becoming an ISP, Telesp would be able to offer a wide range of value-added services to its residential and business customers in São Paulo and in other regions without having to add significant new infrastructure. Brazil was considered to be one of the "ripest Internet markets" in Latin America,[5] and Telesp's primary shareholder, Telefonica Group,[6] could provide the resources that the company needed to build a differentiated ISP offering. More importantly, if Telesp were successful in becoming a major ISP for the region, it could stop the drain on its profits caused by an imbalance in interconnection fees that we are currently paying to ISPs that provide access to their servers using our competitors' networks.[7]

---

[3] Digital subscriber line (DSL) technology dramatically increases the speed and capacity of ordinary telephone lines. Asymmetric digital subscriber line (ADSL) provides fast download with slower upload. This is especially well suited to Internet traffic, where a user is downloading large files (Web pages, documents, video, etc.) but uploading much shorter text messages and commands. Symmetric (SDSL or HDSL) provides high-speed connections for both uploading and downloading (http://www.techweb.com/encyclopedia/defineterm?term=DSL). Definitions of technical terms used throughout the case are adapted from TechWeb (www.techweb.com).

[4] The connection between a customer and a telephone, cable, or cellular service provider (also called the local loop). The last mile for traditional residential telephone service—also known as plain old telephone service (POTS)—traditionally used copper-based telephone wire, which is the slowest and least reliable of physical networking alternatives (for example, coaxial cable, fiber-optic cable). Other wireless alternatives for last mile and long-distance networking include cellular and satellite. See J. Light, L. Applegate, D. Green, "The Last Mile of Broadband Access: Technical Note," HBS No. 800-076, for a more in-depth discussion of telecommunications technology and players.

[5] 2000 Jupiter Strategic Planning Services/MMLAT00-V01.

[6] At the time of the case, Telefonica Group, located in Spain, was one of the world's largest global telecommunications and multimedia companies and was committed to becoming the dominant player within all Spanish- and Portuguese-speaking areas of the world. See Appendix for a description of Telefonica Group.

[7] Due to an oddity in Anatel's structure of network interconnection fees, Internet traffic had created an imbalance in interconnection fees among telecom operators that, within the next few years, could drain a significant portion of Telesp's yearly EBITDA and net profits. The interconnection fee structure is explained in more detail later in the case.

While we were aggressively working with Anatel to revise its fee structure, we also had to consider whether to launch an ISP to protect ourselves if our efforts were to fail. If we did launch an ISP, we had to decide whether to go for maximum market share by offering free ISP services on our networks or whether to attempt to cover our costs by charging for ISP services—a move that might give us a lot less market share given the ready availability of free ISP services within São Paulo and Brazil. We could also pursue a more aggressive strategy and extend our ISP service—either free or paid—outside of our region and attempt to generate revenues from the interconnection fee imbalance from incumbents in other regions.

Amorim had strong cards in his hand as he pondered these strategic opportunities and threats. Telesp had a huge installed base—9 million households in late 2001, expected to grow to 13 million by the fall of 2002[8]—and a virtual monopoly for within-region residential and business voice services in the state of São Paulo. While only 20 percent of the Brazilian population lived in the state, São Paulo represented 40 percent of the country's gross domestic product (GDP), with approximately 52 percent of the country's corporations headquartered in the São Paulo region.[9] In addition, approximately 35 percent of all domestic long-distance telecommunications traffic in Brazil originated or terminated within the state.[10] Amorim and his predecessor had already done the hard work of transforming a state-owned company into a highly efficient line-laying machine with a 2001 productivity level that would have been the envy of any telecommunications company in the world. Yet significant threats loomed large on the horizon. How quickly would other telecom operators turn hungry eyes on the riches of São Paulo?

[8] Patrick Grenham, "Brazilian Telecom Overview," Salomon Smith Barney Equity Research: Latin America, September 27, 2001.

[9] "PASTE: Perspectives on the Expansion and Modernization of the Telecommunications Sector," National Telecommunications Agency, Brazilian Government, Anatel, 2000.

[10] Securities and Exchange Commission Form 20-F as of July 1998.

En route to the Telesp board meeting in early 2002, Amorim pondered which of the strategic opportunities to pursue. He also considered the organizational changes that would be necessary to move the company from the relentless pursuit of a single, well-understood goal to the much more complex and uncertain pursuit of new strategic opportunities. "Most Telesp employees were used to focused, short-term planning," said Amorim. "They knew how to install new lines to meet well-defined targets, but we needed to develop long-term strategic thinking in the organization and consider what we would do differently once the lines were in place." How could an organization with a strong heritage as a state-owned monopoly transform itself to become an aggressive, customer-focused competitor?

A Collect Call to the Private Sector

We got the jewel of the crown. No one can be big in Latin America without the fixed-line business in São Paulo.

Juan Villalonga, CEO, Telefonica Group[11]

By 1972, the Brazilian telecom system was on the verge of collapse. Customers had to wait more than six hours to complete calls between the main cities of the country and could often not get a dial tone for local calls. Over 900 different companies offered a patchwork of poorly integrated basic voice services. In that year the government interceded, creating a holding company (Telebras) that controlled 26 operating companies corresponding to the states in Brazil. In addition, Embratel was established as the domestic and international long-distance operator. This state-owned monopoly suffered from poor management, lack of competition, and underinvestment and, as a result, made few improvements over the next two-and-a-half decades.

[11] Consuelo Dieguez and Ronaldo Franca, "22 Bi No Bolso," *Veja*, August 5, 1998.

By 1997, 17 million Brazilians were on a two-year waiting list for phone lines; in the state of São Paulo alone, there was unmet demand for 7 million lines. Only 11 in 100 inhabitants had access to telephone lines at home, compared with 18 in Argentina and 68 in Sweden.[12] In addition, the 16 percent wealthiest Brazilians owned 81 percent of the phone lines, while the 57 percent lowest-income Brazilians controlled only 2 percent of the lines. Service quality was notoriously poor. During peak hours in the urban areas, almost 30 percent of calls were not completed.

The move toward a model that could better benefit the Brazilian consumer started in August 1995, when the National Congress amended the Constitution to permit private companies to purchase telecommunications concessions. Anatel was created in 1997 to oversee the changes and implement the privatization process.[13] The goal of providing universal access meeting good quality standards was almost as important as the goal to stimulate competition (see Exhibit 2 for more information on the regulatory framework and universalization requirements). The culmination of the process was an auction held in 1998 that returned telecommunications services in Brazil to private control.

The Telecom Gold Rush

On July 29, 1998, in the third-largest telecommunications privatization at the time,[14] the Brazilian government held a closed-envelope auction. This event attracted the global heavy hitters of the day such as Sprint and MCI Worldcom (U.S.), France Telecom, Spain's Telefonica Group (Telefonica), and Telecom Italia. Bidders for Telesp, led by

Telefonica, paid R$5.8 billion[15] or 64 percent over the minimum price Anatel had set (see Exhibit 3 for the auction results). This high price reflected the importance of the concession to Telefonica's strategy of geographic expansion centered on the integration of different types of services.[16] As Juan Villalonga, Telefonica's CEO at the time, explained to shareholders in the 1998 annual report:

> The acquisitions made in Brazil have placed Telefonica in the position of leading operator in the largest telecom market of the region. These investments are part of the company's strategy to maintain as its primary objective the creation of shareholder value. I would like to specifically endorse the company's commitment to leadership in the Spanish and Portuguese speaking market, a commitment that will guarantee growth for years to come.

Besides Telesp, Telefonica bought two of the eight regional cellular companies that the government also auctioned, Tele Sudeste Celular and Tele Leste Celular. Later on, it also guaranteed its participation in the São Paulo cellular company through a joint venture with Portugal Telecom (see Appendix for an overview of Telefonica Group).

Rules of the Game

Inspired by the experience of the U.S. "Baby Bells" in the early 1980s, Anatel spun off Telebras into eight cellular operators, three fixed-line

---

[12] Thais Costa, "Telefonica diz que ja cumpriu metas de 2002," *Gazeta Mercantil*, September 27, 2001, p. C-1.

[13] For more information on Anatel and the Brazilian telecommunications regulatory environment see www.anatel.gov.br.

[14] Third after NTT in Japan and British Telecom in the United Kingdom. Consuelo Dieguez and Ronaldo Franca, "22 Bi No Bolso," *Veja*, August 5, 1998.

[15] At the time of the case, the exchange rate was 2.36 (US$1 = R$2.36). During 2002 and 2003, the exchange rate ranged between 2.2730 (on April 11, 2002) and 3.9450 (on October 10, 2002). Source: U.S. Federal Reserve Board.

[16] By acquiring Telesp, Telefonica added 6 million lines to the 11.6 million it already owned in other Latin American telecommunication operators. As long as network expansion and service-quality restrictions were strictly met, the Telesp concession was valid until 2005 and was renewable for 20 years. Until 2003, Telesp's concession was only for the provision of fixed wireline local service, intraregional long distance, data transmission, and network services. Meeting Anatel's 2003 targets would free Telesp to provide national coverage with a complete service offering and a broad product spectrum.

EXHIBIT 2 Anatel and the Brazilian Regulatory Environment

Anatel, the Brazilian telecommunications regulatory agency, was created in October 1997 to replace the Ministry of Telecommunication as the principal telecommunications regulator. Anatel was administratively independent of the Brazilian government, a self-financed entity with its budget deriving from taxes levied on concessionaires and fees charged for licenses. Its directorate was nominated by the president and confirmed by the senate for a single, nonrenewable, five-year term. Anatel was responsible for proposing a complementary legal framework through the issuance of regulations not covered by the General Telecom Law (see Table A).

TABLE A Brazilian Telecommunications Legal Framework

Source: Author based on data from "Brazilian Fixed Line," BBVA Securities, January 26, 2001.

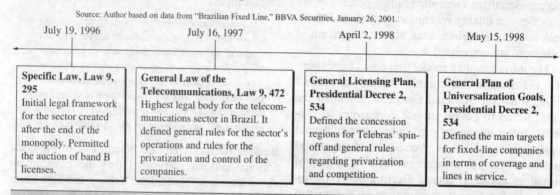

July 19, 1996	July 16, 1997	April 2, 1998	May 15, 1998
Specific Law, Law 9, 295 Initial legal framework for the sector created after the end of the monopoly. Permitted the auction of band B licenses.	**General Law of the Telecommunications, Law 9, 472** Highest legal body for the telecommunications sector in Brazil. It defined general rules for the sector's operations and rules for the privatization and control of the companies.	**General Licensing Plan, Presidential Decree 2, 534** Defined the concession regions for Telebras' spin-off and general rules regarding privatization and competition.	**General Plan of Universalization Goals, Presidential Decree 2, 534** Defined the main targets for fixed-line companies in terms of coverage and lines in service.

Anatel's goal was to facilitate the rapid expansion of the telecom infrastructure through promoting competition and ensuring universal access (see Table B for Telesp requirements), while supervising any anti-competitive practices and verifying that concessionaires complied with their contracts. The agency was also responsible for overseeing merger and acquisition activities to avoid the threat of a rapid consolidation and discourage short-term investments just after privatization.

TABLE B Telesp Requirements

Source: Adapted from Salomon Smith Barney equity research on Telesp, May 12, 1999, p. 32.

Telesp Network Expansion/Modernization Requirements	1999	2001	2003	2005
Minimum lines installed (in millions)	7.8	10.7	—	—
Maximum wait for line installation (in weeks)	—	4	2	—
Minimum public phones (in thousands)	217.5	271.3	—	—
Minimum public phones/1,000 residents	—	—	7.5	8.0
Minimum network digitization (in %)	75%	85%	95%	100%
Maximum distance to a public phone (in meters)	800	500	300	—
Telesp Quality of Services Requirements				
Dial tone within 3 seconds (in %)	98%	99%	99.5%	—
Call completion rate (% of calls attempted)	60%	65%	70%	—
Maximum monthly busy circuits (% of calls)	6%	5%	4%	—
Maximum monthly repair requests/100 lines	3.0	2.5	2.0	1.5
Residential repair response (% within 24 hours)	95%	96%	97%	98%
Nonresidential repair response (% within 8 hours)	95%	96%	97%	98%
Operator availability (% answer within 10 seconds)	92%	93%	94%	95%
Maximum billing inaccuracies/100 bills	0.4	0.3	0.2	—
Credit for billing inaccuracies issued within 1 billing cycle (in %)	95%	96%	97%	98%

EXHIBIT 3 Auction Results, July 29, 1998

Source: Adapted by author from Marcelo Andrade Pimenta, "O Comércio Eletrônico e a Privatização do Sistema Telebrás," http://www.informaticapublica.mg.gov.br/revista0102/ip0102pimenta.pdf; and from "Sinopse—Resumo dos Jornais," http://www.radiobras.gov.br/anteriores/1998/sinopses_3007.htm.

Company	Telesp	Telemar	Brasil Telecom	Embratel
Shareholders	Telefonica Group Portugal Telecom Iberdrola Bilbao Vizcaya	La Fonte GP Investimentos Andrade Gutierrez Pension Funds BNDESPar	Opportunity Pension Funds Telecom Italia	MCI
Main service	Local voice	Local voice	Local voice	Long distance
Coverage area	São Paulo state	North/East	South/West	National
Auction price ($R million)	5,783	3,434	2,070	2,650
Minimum price ($R million)	3,526	3,400	1,953	1,803
Premium paid	64%	1%	6%	47%
Mirror company	Vesper	Vesper	GVT	Intelig

regional operators (Telesp, Telemar, and Brasil Telecom), and one fixed-line long-distance carrier (Embratel). Of the three regional operators, Telemar received the largest area, covering 16 states, and Telesp received the smallest area, covering only the single state of São Paulo (refer back to Exhibit 1 for a map of the concession areas and key metrics). The division was roughly equal in terms of GDP, but, because of the urban concentration in São Paulo, Telesp's Region III was by far the most physically concentrated target. In some of Telemar's northeastern states, for example, the GDP per capita was less than $1,000, or 6.5 times lower than that in São Paulo.[17]

Each concession was auctioned through a process designed to attract the much-needed expertise and resources of global telecommunication companies that desired to extend their foot-

print within Brazil and Latin America. To retain the concessions, private operators had to abide by the "pillars of the program," defined by Anatel as quality, universalization, and competition. These goals often made social, not economic, sense, given the enormous disparities in the country, with 22 percent of the population below the poverty line. To compensate, the three regional operators would have a monopoly for 18 months. Then the government would grant concessions to one wireline competitor per region. These "mirror companies" were granted permission to operate in the same areas and provide the same type of services as the incumbents. Instead of incurring the added expense of building out a competitive fixed-line infrastructure, the mirror companies were permitted to either purchase fixed-line infrastructure services from incumbents or to use wireless technology, which allowed them to avoid fees while lowering the cost of deploying a competitive network infrastructure.

If an incumbent met its 2003 universalization target after January of 2001, it would be free to acquire the licenses to compete with other regional operators in other Brazilian regions as

[17] Adapted from the Brazilian Central Bank Web page (www.bacen.gov.br/), Brazilian Institute of Geography and Statistics (IBGE) Web page (www.ibge.gov.br/home/estatistica/populacao/censo2000/) (April 13, 2002), and IPEADATA Web page (http://www.ipeadata.gov.br/) (April 2002).

EXHIBIT 4 Unibanco Analyst Projections for Telesp Growth (2002–2010)

Source: Author based on data from "Telefonica/Telesp Fixa," Unibanco Research, March 4, 2002, p. 7.

Lines in Service, Installed, Used Capacity (thousands)												
	1999	2000	2001	2002	2003	2004	2005	2006	2007	2008	2009	2010
Installed Capacity	9,500	12,500	15,000	17,000	17,500	18,000	19,000	19,700	20,000	20,500	21,000	21,500
Used Capacity	11,500	8,000	10,500	13,000	15,000	15,000	16,500	17,000	18,500	20,000	22,000	25,000
LIS-Lines in Service	8,000	10,500	13,000	15,000	15,400	16,000	17,500	18,000	19,000	19,500	20,000	20,500
ARPU—(R$/month)		64.5	65.7	65.7	65.7	65.7	65.5	65.0	64.8	64.3	64.0	NA

Note: Statistics for 2002 on are estimates.

well as to offer long-distance services outside of its region. By 2003, whether regional targets were met or not, incumbents and mirror companies from any region could apply to compete in any region. In this way, Anatel planned to harness "market forces emerging with the introduction of competition."

Telesp: Meeting the Universalization Target

From 1999 to 2002, Telefonica Group invested approximately US$6.5 billion in Telesp to enable the company to quickly meet Anatel's targets. The company aggressively rolled out infrastructure and installed new lines. All cash flow generated was reinvested. As Amorim explained:

During this period, Anatel set our agenda. There was a huge waiting list of citizens wanting their first phone lines and much modernization to accomplish. We completed this work in an excellent manner. In fact, we received many visits from telecom operators around the world that were eager to figure out how we were able to install infrastructure at that rate, while also significantly reducing our costs. By 2002, Telesp was one of the most efficient, state-of-the-art telecommunications operators in the world, with more lines added per employee than operators in the United States and other developed countries in Europe and Asia.

Between 1998 and 2002, Telesp increased the number of lines from 6.4 million to 12.6 million,

decreased the waiting time for a new line from 44 months to 14 days, and dropped the cost of a line for its residential customers from US$1,500 to US$31. Digitalization rates increased from 70 percent in 1998 to over 98 percent in 2001. In fact, between 1998 and 2001, Telesp installed more lines than it had in the 20 years prior to privatization. The company's number of lines in service per employee was 1,198, compared with an average of 600 for the United States and 500 for European operators.[18] (See Exhibit 4 for analyst projections for Telesp's growth in installed and used capacity and average revenue per user—also called ARPU—for 2002 to 2010.)

Because of the speed with which the company laid lines, Amorim knew Telesp would soon face the same problem that Telefonica had faced in Spain—flat market demand for fixed lines due to market saturation and pressure from cellular phones. He also recognized that there was pent-up demand for advanced services in São Paulo's high-end markets. To respond to this demand, Telesp launched Speedy in late 2000, the first broadband Internet access option in São Paulo, and a wide range of other value-added services

[18] Authors' interview with Manoel Amorim, September 2003.

EXHIBIT 5 **Speedy Key Metrics (2000–2002)**

Source: Telesp internal reports.

	2000	2001	1Q2002
Lines in service (end of period) (in thousands)	40	198	215
Average monthly fee per line (R$)	65	50	60
Penetration on total Internet accounts (in %)	N/A	12%	17%

(see Exhibit 5 for key metrics for the rollout of Speedy). A Telesp manager recalled:

> Speedy was totally different from the traditional services Telesp provided. We needed to go into the customer's home, install our equipment, and configure their computer. This required that we develop new technical expertise and also new customer service and support expertise. All of a sudden we had customers calling to complain that they could not access Web site X or that Web page Y loaded too slowly. These customers were the early adopters and often knew more about broadband, ADSL, and the Internet than our traditional technical support and customer service employees. We quickly realized that we needed a dedicated support team and customer call center to handle these problems but that the dedicated unit needed to be able to access our traditional technical and customer support teams.

Not only did Speedy serve as an important prototype for developing a more customer-focused, integrated strategy and organization, but also it was viewed as critical to the strategy of Telefonica Group. As Cesar Alierta, Telefonica chairman and CEO, explained in a 2001 letter to shareholders, "Telefonica's strategy now and in the future will revolve around leading the digital revolution . . . Our endeavors to promote widespread use of ADSL will put Telefonica Spain in the forefront of Europe in broadband development and growth, proving it is capable of spearheading this movement in the international markets in which it operates."

Telesp's achievements gave the company high visibility and support within Telefonica Group. In early 2002, its companies in Brazil represented 20.9 percent of Telefonica Group's EBITDA and one-third of its lines in service.[19] In addition, Telefonica Group was the only telecom operator in Europe that obtained over 50 percent of its EBITDA outside its home country.[20] Between 1998 and 2002, Telesp represented Telefonica's major source of growth (see Exhibit 6 for Telesp financials).

Jockeying for Position in the Brazilian Telecommunications Industry

> Even allowing for the high level of operating investment in 2001, [Telesp's] cash flow was enough to pay for its net debt 1.2 times, [which placed Telefonica Group] in quite a different position from that of its incumbent European and American peers.
>
> *"Telefonica/Telesp Fixa," Unibanco Research,*
> *March 4, 2002*

As players in the Brazilian telecommunications industry prepared for increased competition, battle lines were drawn in the three primary industry sectors: Fixed line, cellular, and consumer Internet.[21] In addition, the fixed-line incumbents eyed one another's assets and partnerships as they tried to anticipate what each would do when Anatel's restrictions were lifted.

[19] Telefonica Annual Report, 2001, December 31, 2001, p. 14; Telesp 20-F, Securities and Exchange filing, December 31, 2000.

[20] Telefonica Annual Report, December 31, 2001, p. 8.

[21] On January 30, 2001, Telesp spun out its business data transmission services into a wholly owned subsidiary, Data Brasil.

Fixed-Line Sector

In 2002, fixed-line voice service accounted for 70 percent of industry revenues and was the only segment delivering superior results.[22] Collectively, the three regional telecom operators (in industry terminology these three players were called incumbent local exchange carriers, or ILECs)[23] achieved an unprecedented level of local service in Brazil, laying the infrastructure for Brazil to aggressively participate in the global network economy. In 2000, the teledensity rates in Brazil exceeded those of Argentina and Mexico, which had privatized their telecom sectors in the early 1990s. By 2001, the teledensity rate in Brazil had grown to 28 percent, and the 29 million additional fixed lines installed between 1997 and 2001 represented 1.5 times the total number of lines installed before the auction.

Because the three regional ILECs inherited all the existing networks and controlled the local connections to voice customers (last mile or local loop), competition was minimal in the local voice market, with each incumbent playing the role of the "800-pound gorilla" in its own region (see Exhibit 7 for the major fixed-line telecom operators in Brazil). The mirror companies, Vesper, GVT, and Intelig (long distance), pursued different strategies. While GVT did not focus on fighting for market share in basic residential voice services but pursued more focused high-margin customer segments (such as corporate and high-end residential) and value-added services (such as corporate data services and content services), the other two made less clear choices and faced severe financial problems. (Exhibit 8 contains forecasts of the expected growth in customer adoption of various market segments and telecommunication services.) The challenge was well expressed by Amorim: "There were instances in which we spent over US$1,000 to install a line to a new subscriber, who dropped the service a few days later. You can't make money in this business unless you retain customers and increase ARPU by selling new value-added services."[24]

The mirror companies faced huge obstacles. "They did not have a large customer base and didn't have a well-recognized, respected brand, and they had a limited portfolio of the services required by customers," Amorim continued. In addition, mirror companies were forced either to pay interconnection fees to the incumbents that owned the last mile to end customers or assume the risk of building their own infrastructures, often using less stable emerging technologies for which industry standards had not yet been defined and accepted (for example, fixed wireless).[25] (See Exhibit 9 for the interconnection fee structure in Brazil.)

Two-thirds of the regional ILECs' revenues came from services associated with local telephony. In contrast, the majority of Embratel's revenues came from data and long-distance voice services, the segments that many analysts thought would face the highest level of competition in 2002. Once universalization targets were met, regional ILECs would be free to offer long-distance voice and data services. Similarly, once Embratel reached its

---

[22] Interview with Leonel Jorge, Booz Allen & Hamilton, Brazilian office.

[23] Competitive local exchange carriers (CLECs) are companies (or other entities) that provide local telephone services that compete with (or replace) ILECS. In the United States, the Telecommunications Act of 1996 allowed competitors to enter local markets and provide voice and data services. See http://www.techweb.com/encyclopedia/defineterm?term=CLEC&x=24&y=3 for more information on the relationships among players in the telecommunications industry.

[24] Average revenue per user (ARPU) is a primary metric used by analysts to value telecommunications companies. It is also used by telecommunications companies to compare the value of different market segments or product offerings.

[25] Fixed wireless networks are point-to-point wireless networks that utilize antennae that are attached to a fixed object, such as a building. At the time of the case, most analysts felt that fixed wireless networks offered promise but lacked the technical sophistication and standards needed to become a widespread alternative. By late 2003, fixed wireless "mesh networks" were becoming more technologically feasible (see P. Mannion, "Wireless Networks Gain Traction," www.techweb.com, November 17, 2003), but a lack of standards for high-speed digital wireless network communications continued to delay adoption (see R. Baines, "Multilingual 3G Basestations Will Prevail," www.techweb.com, November 18, 2003).

targets (expected in late 2002 or early 2003), it would be able to enter local markets. (See Exhibit 10 for the incumbents' 2001 revenue composition.)

Cellular Sector

In contrast to the fixed-line business, the mobile market was very competitive in Brazil. In early 2002, most wireless carriers in Brazil offered second-generation (2G) networks, employing either code division multiple access (CDMA) or time division multiple access (TDMA) network communication technologies. In addition, global satellite (GSM) network providers were also entering the market.[26] Incumbent players held only 66 percent market share.[27] (Exhibit 11 shows the evolutionary path of wireless technologies, and Exhibit 12 provides an overview of the key wireless service providers in Brazil.) Mirror mobile companies focused heavily on providing prepaid mobile services, and this segment accounted for 68 percent of the 28.7 million mobile phones in 2001.[28] Mobile activation fees averaged $18, down from $136 in 1997,[29] but usage fees remained higher than the usage fees for fixed-line calls.[30] It was expected that once usage costs decreased and data transmission rates and service quality increased, wireless providers would become important competitors for providing Internet services.[31]

Internet Sector

By 2002, Brazil had become a very competitive market for Internet service providers, with more than 250 ISPs fighting for market share.[32] Contributing to the attractiveness of the Internet market was the highly urbanized and young population, with over 48 percent of the population under the age of 25.[33] However, mainly as a consequence of high levels of income inequality and low levels of education, only 20 percent of the population in Brazil, all members of the middle class or above, were expected to have sufficient financial resources and skills to become regular Internet users and repeat online shoppers.[34] (Exhibit 13 provides data on Internet penetration in Brazil and Latin America.) Low PC penetration was another daunting inhibitor to further residential Internet access growth, though several efforts were directed to increase PC availability such as government subsidization and private-sector financing.[35]

Universo On Line (UOL) was the market leader with a 31 percent share of the total paid subscriber base.[36] UOL's dominance was partly a result of its early start before the privatization of the telecom sector. In addition to global heavyweights such as America Online and Terra Networks, local multimedia and content players like Globo had

---

[26] The first generation (1G) of mobile wireless (cellular) communication networks was based on analog technology that was appropriate for communicating voice traffic but was too slow and unreliable for communicating data traffic. Beginning in the 1990s, 2G digital wireless networks that used data communication network communication standards were introduced—primarily CDMA or TDMA. In 2003, 3G networks were emerging, but different communication standards were being adopted in each region of the world.

[27] "Mobile Market Atlas Latin America," Pyramid Research, February 2002, pp. 11–12.

[28] "Prepaid users are 68 percent of 28.7 million mobiles," *Teletime News,* Edition 203, January 31, 2002.

[29] Ibid.

[30] A local call made from a cellular to a fixed-line phone in peak hour was R$0.51 per minute, whereas a call from a fixed-line to a fixed-line phone was R$0.09 every four minutes. Comparisons made between basic tariff rates of Telesp Celular and Telefonica in the city of São Paulo. Available from Telesp Celular Web page, http://www.lojatelespcelular.com.br/PrecosTarifas/tab_plan_bas.html *eMarketer* (May 4, 2002), and Telefonica Web page, http://www.telefonica.net.br/sp/fprecos.htm (April 30, 2002).

[31] N. Elkin, "The eLatin America Report," *eMarketer,* 2002, p. 30.

[32] Pyramid research estimates, adapted from N. Elkin "The eLatin America Report," *eMarketer,* 2002, p. 53.

[33] While this high percentage of people under age 25 was common in Latin America, this was not true in the United States and Europe, where only 30 percent and 35 percent of the population were 25 years and younger. N. Elkin, "The eLatin America Report," *eMarketer,* p. 22.

[34] N. Elkin, "The eLatin America Report," *eMarketer,* 2002, p. 26.

[35] "Guide to Latin America's ISP Markets, 2001," The Yankee Group, p. 17.

[36] Ibid.

launched ISPs, on their own or in partnership (see Exhibit 14).

Free ISPs were created with an appealing business concept: They did not charge customers, but they expected to generate revenues from interconnection fees paid by the ILECs and, secondarily, from e-commerce and advertising fees paid by corporations offering information, goods, and services on the Internet.[37] Very little infrastructure was required to launch a dial-up ISP,[38] since the service could piggy-back off the network infrastructure that supported traditional voice telephone services. As a result, when U.K. ISP FreeServe launched the free ISP model in 1998, the model caught on quickly around the world.

Within a short time of the launch of Brazil's first free dial-up ISP in 1999, numerous competing free ISPs had entered the market. By late 2000, free ISPs had captured 45 percent of total residential Internet accounts in Brazil.[39] Given the low barriers to entry, established ISPs created their own free ISP services that provided simple access with no value-added services or premium content. But, by 2002, many free ISPs had gone out of business, and others were struggling as advertising and e-commerce revenues declined significantly once the bottom fell out of the Internet markets in early 2000. As they attempted to start charging for services, customers who were once so easy to attract became very hard to upgrade to pay services. By early 2002, industry analysts believed that, given the market size and low purchasing power in Brazil, only a single dominant free ISP player would survive the shakeout.[40] In Brazil, this survivor would still depend on interconnection fees coming from association with the network of a local telecom competitor to the ILECs. The ability to upgrade selected customers to paying for value-added services was seen as the key to long-term survival.

While many analysts believed that Telesp was better positioned to capture growth opportunities than its current competitors, Amorim knew that decisions concerning which opportunities to pursue—and more importantly, which not to pursue—were only the first step in leveraging its position, resources, and capabilities.[41] Building the capabilities to execute the new strategy and to continue to innovate in the rapidly changing world was an ongoing challenge that occupied the majority of Amorim's attention as the company shifted to what it called "Phase 2" of its transformation.

Transforming Telesp: Phase 2

I need all employees to understand what the company's objectives are. I want them to be focused on serving our current customers better, providing them with new services. They need to be able to make decisions with the customers without depending so much on our existing hierarchy.

Manoel Amorim, CEO, Telesp

With the worldwide economic slowdown in 2002, foreign firms, first attracted by the privatization bonanza, were being forced to sell assets, while debt defaults loomed for the Latin America business

---

[37] After 2002, universalization restrictions were lifted, and it was expected that free ISPs would be permitted to move their services to competitive local exchange carriers' networks. As discussed in Exhibit 9, this would create an interconnection fee imbalance.

[38] Dial-up ISPs use the traditional voice telephone service network infrastructure. The traditional residential telephone infrastructure was developed for two-way, analog voice communication, and the last mile utilized "narrowband" communications technology with a maximum transmission speed of about 56 thousand bits (56K) per second of information. "Broadband" communication networks utilized coaxial cable, fiber-optic, and satellite networks and transmission protocols. In 2002, ADSL speeds were up to 12 million bits per second for download speed and about 1.5 million bits per second for upload speeds.

[39] "Latin America: Paid Dial-Up Internet Subscriber Accounts Update," The Yankee Group, February 2001 (UOL shut down its free division NetGratuita, and Terra Lycos' Terra Livre was relegated to a limited trial for branding purposes).

[40] Interview by the author with Noah Elkin, *eMarketer*, April 4, 2002.

[41] "Telefonica/Telesp Fixa," Unibanco Research, March 4, 2002; "Brazilian 2002 Market Liberalization," *Convergent Communications: Latin America*, 3, no.1, The Yankee Group, p. 6; "Telefonica/Telesp Fixa," Unibanco Research, March 4, 2002, p. 3.

units of multinational companies.[42] Market consolidation was expected to be a key trend, with a small number of integrated telecommunications service providers (or coalitions among different players) delivering one-stop telecommunications services in Brazil and, eventually, across Latin America. All the regional ILEC incumbents and Embratel were expected to compete aggressively to be one of the survivors.[43] Global telecommunications players were expected to increase their presence and efforts in Latin America once the industry recovered from the crippling downturn that threatened the survival of even the strongest players. As he surveyed the emerging competitive landscape in early 2002, Amorim began to build the capabilities that would be needed to transform Telesp from a "line-laying machine" to an aggressive and innovative strategic competitor.

Building Organizational Capabilities

Amorim was appointed CEO of Telesp in January 2001 with the charge to lead both the strategic and organizational transformation in Phase 2 of its privatization. Amorim knew that this transformation would require that all employees develop a different approach to how they worked and how they made decisions. They had to learn to view the world from a broader perspective, shifting their focus from internal goals and quality measures to external market and competitive dynamics. Clearly this could not happen overnight. Amorim needed to find ways to communicate his vision down into the organization. He also needed its help to refine his vision based on a deep understanding of real-time business operations and the benefits of newly launched offerings for customers. Developing a more customer-focused organization and a more interactive management process were important first steps in empowering employees to think creatively about the challenges and

opportunities that Telesp faced. Amorim explained the magnitude of the task:

> When I assumed the leadership role, Telesp was very hierarchical. All decisions were made at the top, and the company's primary goal was to meet the universalization targets. The decisions were very tactical in nature, since the government and our parents had defined a very clear set of marching orders that we all needed to follow. Flawless execution was the name of the game, and the path to flawless execution was well defined and didn't change. Everyone knew exactly what he or she needed to do to meet their individual commitments, and those individual commitments rolled up into a set of well-defined organizational commitments. Telesp was like a very disciplined, efficient "installation army."
>
> But as we prepared to launch Phase 2, both strategy and its execution were much less well defined. Financial targets were well defined, but the way to reach and sustain them was less clear. We needed to get information flowing—top down, bottom up, and middle out. We needed to listen to the voice of the customer and the employees who serve them. What do *they* value? What do we do now that they *don't* value? What is working and what is not working as we launch new product initiatives and enter new markets? This was key to enable us to develop the strategies and plans to achieve our financial targets. In addition, to be effective, everyone—including employees on the line— needed to know more about the market, our competitors, and our strategy. They needed a dynamic view of our goals, resources, and targets to keep pace with the dynamically changing business environment and strategy. In short, we needed to close the loop between strategy and action and provide feedback to ensure that we were responding and learning in real time.

Recognizing that strategy is a journey—not a destination—Amorim knew that it was important to get started by identifying ways to change behavior that would lead to the desired culture change without disrupting the efficient functioning of the organization. His goal in these early change initiatives was to empower employees and customers and get the information flowing.

Empowerment and Information Sharing

As a first step, in mid-2001, Amorim opened up lines of communication and developed a new 360-degree performance review and feedback process.

[42] "Defaults Seem Near for Latin Units of BellSouth and Verizon," *The New York Times,* March 29, 2002.

[43] "Brazilian 2002 Market Liberalization," *Convergent Communications Latin America,* The Yankee Group, 3, no. 1, p. 17.

Amorim started by changing the behavior at the top, getting out into the organization and talking with people:

> When I first took over, senior managers spent most of their time talking to each other and to other senior industry leaders. Employees in the organization and our customers rarely ever talked to the boss. So I started our culture change by getting out of my office and into the organization. I went into the field and talked with employees. Many had never seen the senior executives. I was surprised by how many brought cameras to get their pictures taken with me. I felt like Santa Claus. I went out to visit customers and talked with them. I also encouraged the other senior executives to begin doing the same thing and to encourage their direct reports to get into the field. As the information began flowing, we debated what we were learning. The process not only began to inform our strategy and goals, it also helped us develop a new set of performance metrics that emphasized external measures and targets and those internal drivers that linked to our success in meeting external targets.
>
> Armed with these new measures, I asked my direct reports to review my performance and to suggest ways that I could improve my leadership in both the short term and the long term. It was a big change; before, managers reviewed subordinates, but no one had ever asked them to provide a review for their boss. We then began to cascade a 360-degree performance review process down into the organization and develop a compensation and reward system that motivated the performance against our new targets. These changes in patterns of communication, performance metrics, and rewards began to change the culture of the organization without any formal change in structure or process reengineering initiative."

While many welcomed the change in culture, some employees did not readily embrace the more open, customer-focused metrics and performance review process. "It was hard for some to accept the changes," Amorim continued.

> We were a very successful organization that was doing extremely well at meeting the universalization goals better than our future competitors. We had spent years measuring success based on the number of lines that we laid. People had risen to the challenge of developing a state-of-the-art infrastructure, and people were very proud of what they had accomplished. I needed to help them understand that we should be proud of what we had accomplished but that we needed to shift our focus in the future.

Some groups were concerned about the shift to Phase 2 and what it would mean to their own personal well-being and performance. For example, some line employees and managers involved in network-expansion activities felt that demand for their job would drastically decrease, while other skills would be required in the organization. Middle managers who were used to a hierarchical management style felt that they would lose power once line employees became more empowered and information began to flow around them.

Dealing with Resistance while Creating an Entrepreneurial, Learning Organization

Amorim credited the "Race of the Champions" initiative as the most important program to help break down resistance and enable employees at all levels to internalize the new culture. The program was quite simple in design but powerful in its outcome. Employees at all levels were asked to volunteer ideas for ways to improve the value that Telesp offered to its customers or other stakeholders. Executives and middle managers helped the employees refine the ideas and develop performance metrics. The employees were then given the resources and support needed to implement the program, and all participating individuals and teams competed with others to win prizes. Amorim explained:

> We have held three competitions since the program was started in April 2001. Each one revolved around a specific theme. The first two competitions were designed to identify opportunities for cost saving, and the third was designed to improve quality and customer service. The current competition is designed around the theme of improving job satisfaction and morale. The Race of the Champions program has really captured the spirit of innovation, involvement, and engagement that we were trying to build. The first year, only about 10 percent of the employees and their managers were participating. That year the prize of $10,000 went to a team of line installers who proposed a substitute for a simple component we used in the process that saved the company a significant amount of money. We made a video of the competition and the comments of the employees and distributed it widely. Now we have almost everyone in the company involved. Last year, when the competition centered

around quality, we chose customers to participate on the jury that decided which team received the top prize.

To further institutionalize the information-sharing and learning processes and the important role of middle management, Amorim created a more interactive management process through which the top 50 executives in the company met monthly to discuss strategic developments, opportunities, risks, and performance. Within 10 days of the meeting, every employee in the company received a report back from his or her boss on the key information shared at the meeting, decisions made, and often a related assignment. Three weeks later, human resources conducted phone interviews with all employees asking them whether they had talked with their manager about the meeting and, if so, what they understood to be the key points. "We are doing this to ensure that we open up lines of communication," Amorim explained. "In a company like ours, fighting to change its hierarchical culture, you need to ensure that the messages get through and that managers get used to assuming the key communication role."

In addition to the programs discussed above, the company launched a comprehensive set of education programs that provided new skills around customer relationship management, performance measurement, and leadership.

As he opened up lines of communication and started learning more about the opportunities and challenges in the industry, Amorim recognized that he needed to create a dedicated team of people who would devote all of their attention to analyzing future opportunities and threats and providing direction for the company's strategy moving forward. Previously, strategic planning focused on auditing, legal, and control. After the reorganization, the strategic planning group was organized around new business development, product development, and long-term planning. A quality and customer service unit was also created (see Exhibit 15).

Identifying Opportunities

With limited capital available, Amorim and his management team had to be very selective about the opportunities they chose to pursue. They pondered a range of options. In every case, the root issues were the same. Basic voice services over fixed-line networks were increasingly becoming commodity businesses. While maintaining scale in these commodity businesses was needed to preserve margins that were already being squeezed by increased competition and consolidation, the increased penetration of mobile phones was expected to cannibalize fixed-line voice services and decrease scale. As their core business eroded, Telesp and other fixed-line operators needed to find new value-added, high-margin opportunities that would grow revenues while also defending base businesses required to stay in the game. In early January 2002, Amorim and his senior planning team considered the following options.

Expand Nationally vs. *Offer Value-added Services in São Paulo*

At the time of the initial auctions by Anatel, it was expected that Telesp and other regional ILECs would rush to meet universalization goals in their own region so that they could then enter other regions to build national voice and data networks. But, as Amorim and his team reviewed this option, they became concerned about the cost of building a competing infrastructure in another region. In addition, it was not clear how the firm would make money if it needed to buy infrastructure services from competitors. Clearly, the mirror companies had made few inroads in competing to provide basic local services, and it was expected that there would be little cooperation from regional incumbents if Telesp attempted to sell services using competing fixed-line infrastructure owned by competitors.

A more attractive opportunity would be to leverage infrastructure that Telesp or its parent, Telefonica Group, already owned. For example, Telefonica Group was a majority owner of Emergia, which, in turn, owned a cable network with more than 25,000 kilometers of undersea cables in Latin America and four points of presence in Brazil. This cable infrastructure provided high-speed digital communications services throughout Latin America. Finally, Telefonica Group's wireless infrastructure could also be leveraged. (Refer back to Exhibit 12 and Appendix.)

Amorim and his team also looked closely at providing interregional and international long-distance voice services nationwide. Until Telesp met its universalization target, it had been limited to offering long-distance services between cities in the state of São Paulo. Telesp could not complete or generate calls between São Paulo and Rio de Janeiro, for example, because the latter city was outside its region. But in 2002, Telesp was free to compete in any domestic market. While by law the other three incumbents were required to allow Telesp to leverage their infrastructure (for a fee), the cost of establishing a brand name outside of São Paulo and of paying interconnection fees needed to be considered. An alternative was to offer long-distance services only to its existing clients, to make Telesp a "one-stop shop." Amorim knew that Embratel posed a more serious competitive threat to Telesp than the other ILECs, as it already had an infrastructure to offer data and long distance in São Paulo and had already announced that it would offer voice service to São Paulo corporations as soon as it met its own universalization obligations.

Indeed, Amorim and his team knew that they must face the reality that the value to a competitor, including Embratel, of entering Telesp's market was much higher than the value that Telesp would gain by entering one of their markets. In addition, the smaller size, more urban location (half the population of the region—20 million people—lived within the city of São Paulo), higher standard of living, and more developed business infrastructure meant that the cost of entering the São Paulo market would be much lower for one of Telesp's competitors than it would be for Telesp to enter a competitor market. Given that Telesp already had a 98 percent market share in São Paulo, a well-recognized and established brand, and long-standing relationships with its customers, the team felt that it might make sense to devote resources and attention to improving customer loyalty and increasing ARPU within its current residential markets—especially at the high end. At the same time, it could increase customer loyalty and ARPU

by delivering high value-added voice and data services to business customers—especially those that had offices outside of São Paulo.

To begin to better understand the customers and the opportunities for value-added services, Amorim commissioned two studies. A field-study team from Harvard Business School was charged with looking at opportunities for improving loyalty and ARPU for residential customers. And, McKinsey consultants were hired to identify opportunities for business customers. The results of both studies would be available in 2002.

Preliminary results from the HBS field-study team outlined key priorities for residential customers (see Exhibit 16). Possible opportunities included video surveillance systems for home security, audio conferencing, voice portals, telephone bill payment, integrated communication and data services for SOHOs (small office/home office), and broadband services.

If Telesp chose to focus on its own customers, which customers should it target and with which service offerings? Cesar Alierta, Telefonica Group's chairman and CEO, emphasized broadband Internet services as a key source of organic growth:

> In terms of new lines of business, broadband will require very special attention as the natural evolution of the fixed-line telephony business. Internet is a global phenomenon that is here to stay; it enables new forms of leisure and ways of doing business, and broadband is a channel with huge potential for generating value. [This explains] Telefonica Group's solid commitment to this business.[44]

If it chose to expand its broadband offerings, Telesp could draw on the resources and capabilities it had developed through the launch of Speedy and the 90 percent share of the broadband market in São Paulo that Speedy had gained. It could also draw on the vast Spanish- and Portuguese-speaking content resources of its parent and its domestic and international broadband infrastructure.

Launch a Narrowband ISP

Another opportunity was to enter the narrowband segment of the Internet more aggressively by

[44] Ibid., p. 63.

offering ISP services. If Telesp decided to enter this market, it could develop its own ISP or partner with Terra Networks. If the latter option were pursued, Telesp would have to deal with Terra Networks' low market share in the São Paulo region. (Terra had built a strong presence in Brasil Telecom's region.) Would its parent, Telefonica Group, let Telesp acquire an ISP with strong presence in São Paulo? Potential conflicts with Terra would be a very delicate issue.

Telesp's good relationship with its customers, strong brand recognition, and efficient billing system would enable it to compete favorably with other ISPs. In addition, the subsidiary that offered its Speedy service would be a natural home for managing narrowband ISP services.

The launch of its own ISP would also help solve the increasing drain on profitability due to the high cost of interconnection fees paid to telecom providers hosting current market-leading ISPs. After months of attempting to change regulation, it appeared that Anatel would not address the problem within the short term.

And finally, if Telesp decided to launch its own ISP, should it be a paid or free ISP?

Develop Integrated Fixed-line/Wireless Voice Services

By 2001, most analysts foresaw the integration of fixed-line and cellular voice services in the near future. Experience had shown that a fixed-line operator could build an integrated mobile network for 20 percent less than pure-play cellular network service providers. Furthermore, an integrated operator could expect to save 30 to 35 percent in network-operating and provisioning costs.[45] Should Telesp partner with its parent to offer integrated cellular and fixed-line voice services in its own region and potentially within other regions?

Thriving in a Competitive Market

As Amorim put the finishing touches on his presentation to the Telesp board, he felt that there was much to be proud of and to celebrate. But, the future offered many potential paths—all offering tremendous opportunity but fraught with significant risk. Given the recent telecom sector crisis and the increasing country risk, the board had already warned that it would be looking to Telefonica Brazil for increasing EBITDA and cash contributions. Decisions made at the meeting would set the future direction of the company.

---

[45] "Putting Latin American Telcos in Perspective," Santander Central Hispanico, December 2001, p. 15.

EXHIBIT 6   Telesp Financials, Annual Income Statement (standardized, R millions)

Source: 2003 Multex.com Inc., published by OneSource Information Services, Inc., December 2003.

	12 Months Ending			
	31-Dec-2001	31-Dec-2000	31-Dec-1999	31-Dec-1998
Revenue	9,048.8	7,515.4	6,140.9	5,399.5
Total Revenue	9,048.8	7,515.4	6,140.9	5,399.5
Cost of Revenue, Total	5,788.2	5,118.2	4,375.3	3,302.0
Gross Profit	3,260.6	2,397.2	1,765.5	2,097.5
Selling/General/Administrative Expenses, Total	1,750.9	1,359.8	1,177.8	1,109.8
Interest Expense (Income), Net Operating	335.7	64.4	247.1	NA
Other Operating Expense	NA	NA	NA	−115.9
Other, Net	260.2	21.3	−147.0	NA
Other Operating Expenses, Total	260.2	21.3	−147.0	−115.9
Total Operating Expense	8,135.0	6,563.8	5,653.2	4,296.0
Operating Income	913.8	951.6	487.6	1,103.6
Interest/Investment Income, Non-Operating	NA	NA	NA	0.0
Interest Income (Expense), Net Non-Operating	NA	NA	NA	212.4
Other Non-Operating Income (Expense)	−46.0	29.9	−105.5	−44.0
Other, Net	−46.0	29.9	−105.5	−44.0
Income Before Tax	867.8	981.6	382.1	1,272.0
Income Tax—Total	−63.1	51.5	−360.3	230.3
Income After Tax	930.8	930.1	742.4	1,041.7
Minority Interest	0.0	−1.5	−205.3	−384.4
U.S. GAAP Adjustment	277.9	109.7	−691.8	148.1
Net Income Before Extra. Items	1,208.7	1,038.2	−154.8	805.4
Accounting Change	30.0	0.0	0.0	NA
Total Extraordinary Items	30.0	0.0	0.0	NA
Net Income	1,238.7	1,038.2	−154.8	805.4
Income Available to Common Excl. Extra. Items	1,208.7	1,038.2	−154.8	805.4
Income Available to Common Incl. Extra. Items	1,238.7	1,038.2	−154.8	805.4
Basic/Primary Weighted Average Shares	493.7	493.7	489.5	330.4
Basic/Primary EPS Excl. Extra. Items	2.45	2.10	−0.32	2.44
Basic/Primary EPS Incl. Extra. Items	2.51	2.10	−0.32	2.44
Dilution Adjustment	NA	NA	0.0	NA
Diluted Net Income	1,238.7	1,038.2	−154.8	805.4
Diluted Weighted Average Shares	493.67	493.67	489.49	330.40
Diluted EPS Excl. Extra. Items	2.45	2.10	−0.32	2.44
Diluted EPS Incl. Extra. Items	2.51	2.10	−0.32	2.44
Dividends per Share—Common Stock Primary Issue	1.83	1.53	0.61	1.49
Gross Dividends—Common Stock	901.3	696.5	300.5	483.2
Interest Expense, Supplemental	351.4	165.9	151.5	0.0
Depreciation, Supplemental	3,289.8	2,949.2	2,616.5	1,812.6
Normalized Income Before Tax	867.8	981.6	382.1	1,272.0
Effect of Special Items on Income Taxes (STEC)	0.0	NA	0.0	NA
Inc. Tax Ex. Impact of Sp. Items	−63.1	51.5	−360.3	230.3
Normalized Income After Tax	930.8	930.1	742.4	1,041.7
Normalized Inc. Avail to Com.	1,208.7	1,038.2	−154.8	805.4
Basic Normalized EPS	2.45	2.10	−0.32	2.44
Diluted Normalized EPS	2.45	2.10	−0.32	2.44

	31-Dec-2001	31-Dec-2000	31-Dec-1999	31-Dec-1998
Cash & Equivalents	206.3	97.0	68.5	1,076.1
Short Term Investments	NA	NA	17.3	NA
Cash and Short Term Investments	206.3	97.0	85.8	1,076.1
Trade Accounts Receivable, Net	1,781.4	1,618.5	1,226.7	949.1
Other Receivables	1,074.1	701.3	618.4	624.2
Total Receivables, Net	2,855.4	2,319.8	1,845.0	1,573.3
Total Inventory	454.6	215.5	23.2	NA
Prepaid Expenses	79.9	13.7	NA	NA
Other Current Assets	69.2	213.6	192.2	183.9
Other Current Assets, Total	69.2	213.6	192.2	183.9
Total Current Assets	3,665.5	2,859.6	2,146.2	2,833.4
Buildings	8,655.0	7,973.5	NA	6,489.0
Land/Improvements	345.5	330.9	NA	NA
Machinery/Equipment	36,024.6	31,863.0	NA	22,788.6
Construction in Progress	1,540.0	3,327.0	NA	2,608.7
Other Prop./Plant/Equip.	810.6	715.9	NA	2,256.5
Property/Plant/Equipment—Gross	47,375.7	44,210.3	NA	34,142.8
Accumulated Depreciation	−26,257.1	−23,900.6	NA	−17,446.6
Property/Plant/Equip., Net	21,118.6	20,309.7	13,380.3	16,696.2
LT Investments—Other	162.0	148.1	1,037.8	216.0
Long Term Investments	162.0	148.1	1,037.8	216.0
Deferred Charges	190.8	171.5	0.0	NA
Other Long Term Assets	1,324.1	1,116.7	1,292.3	542.4
Other Long Term Assets, Total	1,514.9	1,288.1	1,292.3	542.4
Total Assets	26,461.0	24,605.5	17,856.8	20,288.0
Accounts Payable	1,265.4	1,685.7	1,426.7	1,080.4
Current Port. LT Debt/Capital Leases	2,636.2	1,193.8	388.1	540.8
Dividends Payable	901.3	854.6	665.1	472.7
Income Taxes Payable	707.8	504.1	244.8	419.3
Other Current Liabilities	741.3	359.3	226.2	502.4
Other Current Liabilities, Total	2,350.4	1,717.9	1,136.0	1,394.3
Total Current Liabilities	6,252.0	4,597.4	2,950.8	3,015.5
Long Term Debt	1,367.8	704.6	684.1	586.9
Total Long Term Debt	1,367.8	704.6	684.1	586.9
Total Debt	4,004.0	1,898.4	1,072.2	1,127.7
Deferred Income Tax—LT Liability	1,152.6	1,560.4	62.8	593.1
Deferred Income Tax	1,152.6	1,560.4	62.8	593.1
Minority Interest	NA	NA	NA	4,909.1
Pension Benefits—Underfunded	144.2	0.0	NA	NA
Other Long Term Liabilities	445.6	223.5	196.5	113.7
Other Liabilities, Total	589.8	223.5	196.5	113.7
Total Liabilities	9,362.2	7,085.9	3,894.2	9,218.2
Common Stock	7,436.2	7,654.2	5,709.2	3,889.1
Common Stock	7,436.2	7,654.2	5,709.2	3,889.1
Additional Paid-In Capital	3,486.2	3,485.3	2,708.8	0.2
Retained Earnings (Accum. Deficit)	5,333.6	5,616.5	4,599.5	2,965.4
Other Equity, Total	842.8	763.6	945.0	4,215.0
Total Equity	17,098.8	17,519.6	13,962.6	11,069.8
Total Liabilities & Shareholders' Equity	26,461.0	24,605.5	17,856.8	20,288.0
Shares Outs.—Common Stock Primary Issue	493.7	493.7	489.5	323.5
Total Common Shares Outstanding	493.7	493.7	489.5	323.5
Treasury Shares—Common Primary Issue	0.7	0.7	NA	NA

EXHIBIT 6 Telesp Financials, Annual Cash Flow (standardized, R millions) (continued)

	12 Months Ending			
	31-Dec-2001	31-Dec-2000	31-Dec-1999	31-Dec-1998
Net Income/Starting Line	930.8	928.5	537.1	657.3
Depreciation/Depletion	3,289.8	2,949.2	2,616.5	1,812.6
Amortization	34.6	35.0	0.0	NA
Equity in Net Earnings/Loss	−4.5	4.3	5.6	46.8
Other Non-Cash Items	589.7	96.6	536.9	407.5
Non-Cash Items	652.1	53.4	606.4	425.0
Cash Taxes Paid	328.6	174.0	182.9	761.0
Cash Interest Paid	182.4	107.6	197.9	75.8
Accounts Receivable	−485.8	−335.3	−367.7	−393.2
Other Assets	−667.9	−210.8	−50.2	11.6
Accounts Payable	−367.7	254.1	215.4	682.5
Accrued Expenses	92.4	33.3	−96.5	−7.8
Taxes Payable	−322.7	238.7	−183.5	−551.2
Other Liabilities	207.3	−148.4	−256.3	−46.4
Other Operating Cash Flow	406.3	−170.0	−67.8	−35.7
Changes in Working Capital	−1,138.0	−338.4	−806.5	−340.3
Cash from Operating Activities	3,769.3	3,627.8	2,953.5	2,554.6
Purchase of Fixed Assets	−4,478.6	−4,217.8	−3,144.3	−3,098.3
Capital Expenditures	−4,478.6	−4,217.8	−3,144.3	−3,098.3
Sale of Fixed Assets	8.1	5.4	28.3	23.2
Sale/Maturity of Investment	0.2	172.1	0.0	NA
Investment, Net	0.0	−279.5	−184.0	−3.2
Other Investing Cash Flow	−55.5	−1.6	0.0	−38.6
Other Investing Cash Flow Items, Total	−47.2	−103.6	−155.7	−18.7
Cash from Investing Activities	−4,525.8	−4,321.3	−3,300.0	−3,117.0
Other Financing Cash Flow	−55.6	−19.7	216.8	778.6
Financing Cash Flow Items	−55.6	−19.7	216.8	778.6
Total Cash Dividends Paid	−809.4	−572.5	−564.7	−136.2
Sale/Issuance of Common	0.0	0.0	0.0	NA
Common Stock, Net	0.0	0.0	0.0	NA
Issuance (Retirement) of Stock, Net	0.0	0.0	0.0	NA
Long Term Debt Issued	3,057.7	1,894.8	374.1	0.6
Long Term Debt Reduction	−1,327.1	−587.3	−787.6	−35.2
Long Term Debt, Net	1,730.7	1,307.5	−413.5	−34.6
Issuance (Retirement) of Debt, Net	1,730.7	1,307.5	−413.5	−34.6
Cash from Financing Activities	865.7	715.3	−761.4	607.8
Net Change in Cash	109.3	21.8	−1,107.9	45.3
Net Cash—Beginning Balance	97.0	75.3	1,183.2	1,030.8
Net Cash—Ending Balance	206.3	97.0	75.3	1,076.1
Cash Taxes Paid, Supplemental	328.6	174.0	182.9	761.0

EXHIBIT 7   Major Fixed-Line Telecom Operators in Brazil

Source: Author from data drawn from "Brazilian 2002 Market Liberalization" and "Portugal Telecom: A Busy Year in the Brazilian Internet Industry," The Yankee Group; Anatel Web site, http://www.anatel.gov.br; and IBGE Web site, www.ibge.gov.br.

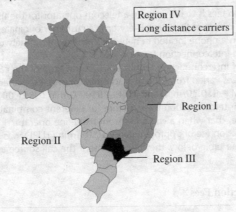

Region	Company	Control	Type	Market Share[a]	% of GDP[b]
I	Telemar	Financial investors	Incumbent	74%	41%
I	Vesper	Bell Canada, Qualcomm	Attacker	25%	
II	Brasil Telecom	Financial investors	Incumbent	91%	25%
II	GVT	Financial investors	Attacker	9%	
III	Telefonica (Telesp)	Telefonica Group	Incumbent	91%	34%
III	Vesper	Bell Canada, Qualcomm	Attacker	9%	
IV	Embratel	MCI Worldcom	Incumbent	93%	100%
IV	Intelig	National Grid, Sprint	Attacker	7%	

[a]Based on access points available as of January 2002, except for Region IV (based on sales estimate).
[b]GDP of the region served over total Brazilian GDP.

EXHIBIT 8   Brazil Telecommunications Subscriptions by Household (1999–2005)

Source: Adapted by authors from Patrick Grenham, Marc Estigarribia, and Randal Farr, "Latin America Telecommunications Services: Third Quarter 2001 Preview," Salomon Smith Barney Equity Research: Latin America, October 12, 2001.

	(% Number of Households)							
	1999	2000	2001	2002E	2003E	2004E	2005E	CAGR 1999–2005
Fixed lines in service	45.3	54.4	70.2	74.8	79	81	83.3	10.7
Mobile subscribers	27.3	42.5	52.7	63.1	72.4	81.2	89.3	21.8
Pay TV	5.2	7.4	10.1	13.6	17.7	22.7	28.1	32.5
Internet subscribers	13.1	16.6	21.7	26.8	36.9	48.5	63.1	30.0

EXHIBIT 9   Interconnection Fee Structure in Brazil

Source: Authors and company documents.

The objective of the interconnection fees is to remunerate a telecom operator for the use of its network by another operator in order to provide services to clients of the latter. Every time a customer originates a call from a phone in network 1 and this same call is terminated in a phone located in network 2, the owner of network 1 charges the customer for that call, and network 2 charges an interconnection fee to network 1.

There were three main types of interconnection fees in Brazil at the time of the case: local (TURL), cellular (TUM), and long distance (TUIU). These fees varied from operator to operator and also varied based on the time of day: on average, TURL ~ R$0.05/min, TUM ~ R$0.30/min, and TUIU ~ R$0.10/min (US$1.00 ~ R$2.30).

The table below describes the interconnection fee structure for different combinations of call source and destination. This table shows, for example, that when a customer from fixed-line operator 1 called a customer from fixed-line operator 2, a local interconnection fee of approximately R$0.05/min (TURL) was charged to fixed-line operator 1 (the source of the call). Note: In the table below, the rows represent the call source and the columns the call destination.

Overview of Interconnection Fees

Customer Operator Source	Customer Operator Destination							
	Local Calls				Long-Distance Calls*			
	Fixed-line 1	Fixed-line 2	Mobile 1	Mobile 2	Fixed-line 1	Fixed-line 2	Mobile 1	Mobile 2
Fixed-line 1	—	TURL	TUM	TUM	TUIU	TUIU TURL	TUIU TUM	TUIU TUM
Fixed-line 2	TURL	—	TUM	TUM	TUIU TURL	TUIU	TUIU TUM	TUIU TUM
Mobile 1	TURL	TURL	—	TUM	TUIU TURL	TUIU TURL	TUIU	TUIU TUM
Mobile 2	TURL	TURL	TUM	—	TUIU TURL	TUIU TURL	TUIU TUM	TUIU

*Assumes the use of an independent long-distance operator's network.

This interconnection fee structure would not result in major problems for the Brazilian incumbent telecom operators if it was applicable only to voice traffic. Statistically, voice traffic between two networks tends to be "balanced," that is, the number of calls terminated in one of the two networks tends to be approximately the same as the number of calls originated in that same network. As a result, between any two networks the interconnection payables and receivables tended to cancel each other with no major economic impact for any party.

The growth of Internet traffic, accelerated with the entry of free ISPs, changed the interconnection game dramatically as it created an arbitrage opportunity for CLECs. With very little investment, those new entrants could potentially focus their network offers to ISPs at costs below those offered by ILECs like Telesp. Since most residential and business customers were with the ILECs, the interconnection traffic between the ILEC and the CLEC would no longer be "balanced." (Note: Internet traffic is typically "unidirectional," i.e., ILEC's residential and business clients call the ISPs in the CLEC's network.) The CLEC could then share the interconnection revenues received from the ILECs with the ISP, making the offer hard to beat. To make matters worse, ISP calls were usually much longer in length than standard voice calls and usually occurred during off-peak times (late at night and on weekends). During these off-peak times, ILECS charged customers a flat-rate connection fee that did not cover the interconnection fees paid to the CLEC. Throughout the time that a customer was connected to an ISP, the incumbents continued to pay the full per-minute connection fees to the competitor, while it could only charge a low flat rate per call in off-peak periods to its clients. In early 2002, many industry experts predicted that the entry of new CLECs and the growth of free ISPs could represent a significant drain on the ILECs' profitability—as much as 10 percent of their EBITDA.

EXHIBIT 9   Interconnection Fee Structure in Brazil (continued)

Situation 1: Before the Internet, mostly voice traffic

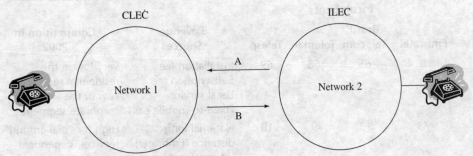

- Number of minutes from network 1 to network 2 (A) is balanced with the number of minutes from network 2 to network 1 (B).
- Interconnection fees related to B (network 2's revenues) approximately the same as interconnection fees related to A (network 2's costs).

Situation 2: CLECs focus on ISPs (with Internet growth)

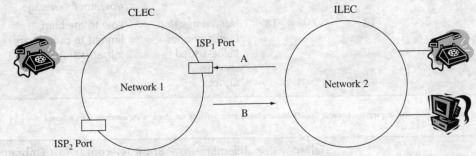

- Traffic is mostly from network 2 to network 1.
- Interconnection fees paid must be paid by network 2 to network 1.

EXHIBIT 10 Incumbents' 2001 Revenue Composition

Source: Adapted by authors from operators and Raphael Duailibi, "Brazilian 2002 Market Liberalization," *Convergent Communications Latin America,* 3, no. 1, The Yankee Group, January 2002.

	Incumbents				Revenue Sources	Competition in 2002
	Embratel	Brasil Telecom	Telemar	Telesp		
Local telephony	0	65	68	69	Installation fee Subscription fee Local service Fixed-to-mobile calls	Very low in the residential segment Low in the corporate segment
Voice long distance	73	13	9	10	National long distance (Embratel) International long distance (Embratel) Intraregional long distance (all)	High for "dial-around" services, dependent on promotions Medium for "dedicated" services, limited to contract length
Data/Internet	24	4	6	3	Corporate networks	Medium, limited to contract length and operators' coverage
Other	3	18	17	18	Interconnection Public phones Value-added services Other	Low to medium, limited to proprietary infrastructure

Source: Developed by the authors from company reports, available from OneSource Information Services, Inc., http://www.onesource.com, accessed January 17, 2002.

	Telesp	Telemar	Brasil Telecom	Embratel
Financial Performance				
Operational measures				
Revenues / lines in service (R$)	788	742	724	N/A
EBITDA margin (%)	53%	34%	43%	14%
Uncollectibles / net revenues (%)	3.4%	8.0%	5.3%	16.0%
Financial Measures				
EBT margin (%)	20%	2%	9%	−10%
CAPEX / sales (%)	49%	100%	56%	20%
Net debt / equity (%)	23%	70%	45%	58%
Net debt / EBITDA (%)	0.9x	2.5x	1.0x	3.0x

EXHIBIT 11   Evolutionary Path to 3G Wireless

Source: Adapted by authors from Computer Desktop Encyclopedia, Ó The Computer Language Co., Inc., 2002 (original diagram by Roger Peterson, Motorola).

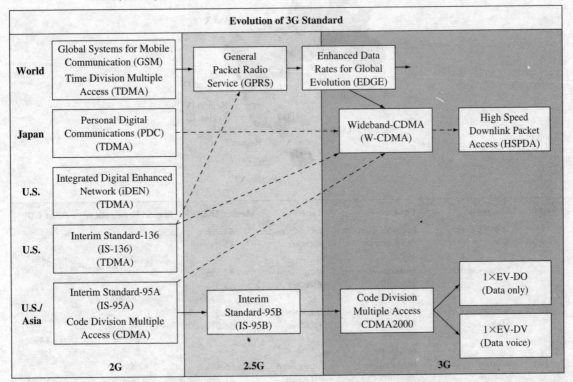

Time Division Multiple Access—A satellite and cellular phone technology that interleaves multiple digital signals onto a single high-speed channel.

Code Division Multiple Access—A method for transmitting simultaneous signals over a shared portion of the spectrum.

General Packet Radio Service—An enhancement to the GSM mobile communications system that supports data packets.

Enhanced Data rates for Global Evolution—An enhancement to the GSM and TDMA wireless communications systems that increases data throughput to 384 Kbps.

CDMA2000—A 3G wireless technology that offers twice the voice capacity and data speed (up to 307 Kbps) on a single 1.25 MHz (1X) carrier in new or existing spectrum.

Wideband-CDMA—A 3G technology that increases data transmission rates in GSM systems by using the CDMA air interface instead of TDMA.

Personal Digital Communications—A digital cellular phone system widely used in Japan. Based on TDMA, it transmits in the 810–826 MHz and 1477–1501 MHz bands.

Integrated Digital Enhanced Network—A wireless communications technology from Motorola that provides support for voice, data, short messages (SMS), and dispatch radio (two-way radio) in one phone.

Interim Standard-136—The second generation of the TDMA digital cellular system.

Interim Standard-95—The standards name for CDMA (code division multiple access) technology.

High Speed Downlink Packet Access—An enhancement to the W-CDMA 3G technology that increases the downlink speed by applying different modulation and coding techniques as well as multiple antennas.

1×EV—An evolution of CDMA2000 that provides higher speeds on a single 1.25 MHz channel. CDMA2000 1×EV-DO (data only) is Phase 1 and delivers data on a separate channel at rates up to 2.4 Mbps. Phase 2 is 1×EV-DV (data voice), which integrates voice and data on the same carrier.

EXHIBIT 12 Major Mobile Telecom Operators in Brazil

Source: Compiled by authors from Jeffrey Noble and Carlos Firetti, "Brazilian Fixed-line—Future shock? Brazil's big bang looms large," BBVA Securities, January 26, 2001; Alexandre Gartner, Laura Mello, and Leonardo Paranagua, "Brazilian Telecoms—The mists of Telecom," March 2002, available from Thomson Research, http://research.thomsonib.com; Instituto Brasileiro de Estatística e Geografia— IBGE, www.ibge.gov.br; and Anatel, www.anatel.gov.br.

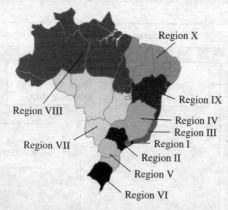

Region	Company	Control	Type	Market Share[a]	Region Penetration[b]	% of GDP[c]
I	Telesp Celular BCP	Portugal Telecom Bell Canada, Safra	Incumbent Attacker	64.7% 35.3%	27%	34%[d]
II	Telesp Celular Tess	Portugal Telecom Telecom Americas	Incumbent Attacker	63.5% 35.3%	16%	
III	**Telefonica Celular** ATL	**Telefonica Group** Telecom Americas	**Incumbent** Attacker	**62.0%** 38.0%	**277%**	**14%**
IV	Telemig Maxitel	Financial investors TIM	Incumbent Attacker	66.4% 27.2%	14.4%	10%
V	Tele Celular Sul Global Telecom	TIM Portugal Telecom	Incumbent Attacker	63.5% 35.0%	16.4%	10%
VI	**Telefonica Celular** Telet	**Telefonica Group** Telecom Americas	**Incumbent** Attacker	**70.0%** 28.7%	**23.3%**	**8%**
VII I	Tele Centro Oeste Celular Americel	Telecom suppliers Telecom Americas	Incumbent Attacker	77.4% 22.1%	19.5%	7%
VIII	Tele Norte Celular Norte Brasil Telecom	Financial investors Telecom suppliers	Incumbent Attacker	70.5% 29.5%	8.1%	5%
1X	**Telefonica Celular** Maxitel	**Telefonica Group** TIM	**Incumbent** Attacker	**63.0%** 37.0%	**8.7%**	**5%**
X	Tele Nordeste Celular BCP	TIM Bell Canada, Safra	Incumbent Attacker	65.0% 35.0%	9.9%	8%

[a]Based on number of mobile telephony subscribers as of December 2001.
[b]Number of mobile subscribers over total inhabitants as of December 2001.
[c]GDP of the region served over total Brazilian GDP.
[d]Consolidated figures; segregated data not available.

EXHIBIT 12
Major Mobile
Telecom
Operators in
Brazil
(continued)

Source: Compiled by
authors from Anatel
Web page,
http://www.anatel.gov.
br/Tools/frame.asp?
link=/telemapa/dados_
brasil_paste.pdf;
Teletime News,
January 31, 2002; and
"Anuário Pay TV
2002," Brazilian Pay
TV Association
(ABTA) Web page,
http://www.abta.com.
br/panorama/indica_
merc.php.

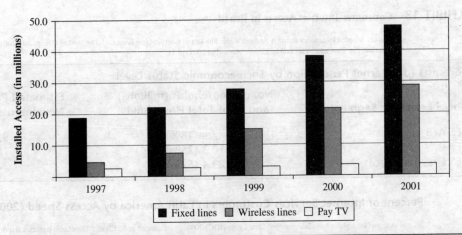

	1997	1998	1999	2000	2001	CAGR
Fixed lines (in millions)	18.8	22.1	27.8	38.3	47.8	26.3%
Teledensity	11.7%	13.6%	16.8%	N/A	27.8%	
Wireless lines (in millions)	4.6	7.4	15	21.5	28.7	58.0%
Teledensity	2.8%	4.5%	9.1%	12.9%	16.7%	
Pay TV (in millions)	2.5	2.7	3.0	3.5	3.6	8.5%
Households penetration	6.0%	6.2%	6.5%	7.7%	7.7%	

EXHIBIT 13 Consumer Internet Access in Brazil

Source: Adapted by authors from "A Second Wave: The Brazil Internet User Forecast," The Yankee Group, July 2001, p. 4; and "The Brazilian Pay TV Case," The Yankee Group, November 2001, p. 11.

Forecasts for Internet Penetration by Socioeconomic Status Level

Social Economic Segments	No. of Households (millions) and % of Total Households	Estimated Percent (%) of New Internet Users Adds
SES A/B	7.4 (18%)	92%
SES C	10.3 (25%)	8%
SES D/E/Rural Areas	23.4 (57%)	—

Percent of Internet Services Customers in Latin America by Access Speed (2000)

Source: Adapted by authors from International Data Corp. (IDC) 2000, as referenced in N. Elkin, "The eLatin America Report," *eMarketer*, July 2001, p. 50.

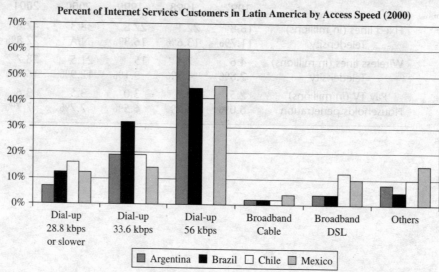

Percent of Internet Services Customers in Latin America by Access Speed (2000)

Source: Adapted by authors from companies' Web sites, www.speedy.com.br, www.telesp.com.br, www.veloxzone.com.br, www.telemar.com.br, www.internetturbo.com.br/residencial, www.virtua.com.br, www.tva.com.br. Note: Access providers had to contract with ISPs to provide access and Internet services to subscribers.

Broadband Access Providers in Brazil

Company	Service	Technology	Broadband ISP Agreements
Telefonica	Speedy	ADSL	UOL, Terra, iG, Ajato
	Multilink	ISDN	Terra
Telemar	Velox	ADSL	Terra, iG, BrTurbo
	DVI Telemar	ISDN	Terra
Brasil Telecom	Internet Turbo	ADSL	UOL, Terra, iG, BrTurbo
Globocabo	Vírtua	Cable	UOL, Terra, Globo.com
TVA	Internet Rápida	Cable	UOL, Terra, Ajato

EXHIBIT 13 **Consumer Internet Access in Brazil (continued)**

Source: Adapted by authors from "Latin America ADSL Update," The Yankee Group, December 2001.

ADSL Offerings in Latin America, 2001

Country	Percentage of Latin American Broadband Subscribers	Monthly Price Range November 2000	Monthly Price Range November 2001	Price Change
Argentina	17%	$47–$50	$30	(36%)–(40%)
Brazil	66%	$26–$41	$14–$30	(26%)–(46%)
Chile	6%	$43	$39	(9%)
Mexico	1%	N/A	$50	N/A

Note: The price of ADSL service offerings was based on 256 Kbps of downstream speed.

Cable TV Subscribers in Brazil

Source: Adapted from Morgan Stanley and World Bank figures in "The eLatin America Report," *eMarketer*, January 2001, pp. 43, 44; and "The eLatin America Report: Demographics, Infrastructure, Usage Patterns and eCommerce Trends," *eMarketer*, June 2001, p. 26.

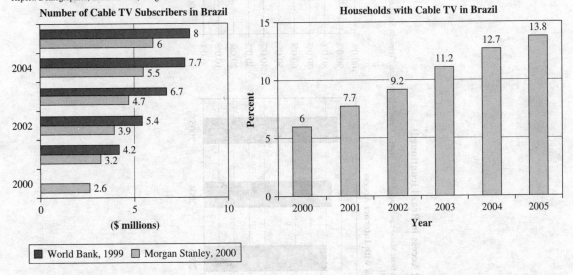

Number of Cable TV Subscribers in Brazil

Households with Cable TV in Brazil

■ World Bank, 1999 □ Morgan Stanley, 2000

Source: Analysis of various forecasts completed by Gretchen Engster, Sean Gass, and Bob Geiman (HBS MBA 2002), "Field Study Report," December 2001, p. 12.

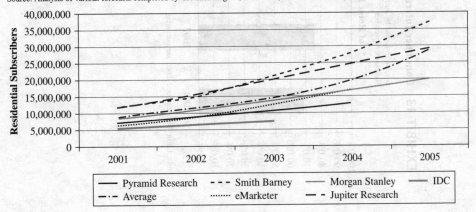

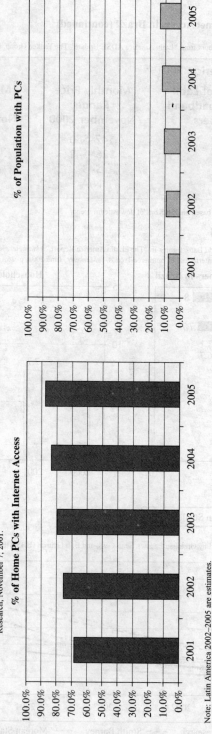

EXHIBIT 13 Consumer Internet Access in Brazil (continued)

Source: Adapted by authors from Mario Epelbaum, Nicolai Sebrell, Camilo Horvilleur, "Telecom Services–Wireline: The November Connection," Morgan Stanley, Latin America Equity Research, November 7, 2001.

% of Home PCs with Internet Access

% of Population with PCs

Note: Latin America 2002–2005 are estimates.

EXHIBIT 14 Major ISP Players in Brazil

Source: Compiled by authors from "Brazilian 2002 Market Liberalization" and "Portugal Telecom: A Busy Year in the Brazilian Internet Industry," The Yankee Group; T. Fuoco, "Projeto Anatel Favorece Provedor," *Valor Online*; "Teles e provedores discutem mudanças nas tarifas de interconexão," *Mundo Digital*, April 2002; and company Web sites.

ISP	Ownership	Communications Infrastructure Partner	Access Modes	Locations Served/No. of Subscribers/ Visitors	Market Share
Internet Group (iG)	GP Investimentos, Telemar acquired access and hosting operations in 2001	Telemar Telesp BrT	Free Dial-up ADSL	Serves 173 Brazilian cities Only operates in Brazil In early 2002, 6.8 percent of the population of Brazil had an account with iG	Leading ISP in Brazil with 34 percent of free ISP market share plus 28 percent of total ISP market share
Universo Online (UOL)	Folhapar, Grupo Abril, and Portugal Telecom (Portugal)	Embratel Telesp Telemar BrT	Dial-up, ADSL, Cable, ISDN	300 cities in Brazil, Argentina, Colombia 1.5 million subscribers 20 million unique visitors/mo. Q3 2001 ARPU = $8.30/user	31 percent market share in Brazil
Terra Networks (formerly Terra Lycos)	Telefonica (Spain)	Telesp Embratel Telemar BrT	Dial-up, ADSL, Cable, ISDN	Largest subscriber base is in Brazil and Mexico 3rd largest ISP in the world with global presence 4.35 million subscribers (1.3 million paid subscriptions)	Leading ISP in Latin America with 15% market share (11% market share for free ISPs) 9 percent market share in São Paulo
America Online	AOL (U.S.), Cisneros Group (Venezuela), and Banco Itaú	Telesp Embratel Telemar BrT	Dial-up	298 cities in Brazil, Argentina, Mexico, Puerto Rico 1.33 million subscribers (included free trial promotions) Q3 2001 ARPU = $3.97/user	6 percent market share in Brazil

ISP	Ownership	Communications Infrastructure Partner	Access Modes
BOL	Folhapar, Grupo Abril, and Portugal Telecom (Portugal)	Embratel	Dial-up
iBest	Brasil Telecom and GP Investimentos	Brasil Telecom	Free Dial-up
BR Free	N/A	Intelig	Free Dial-up
Tutopia	IFX Corporation (U.S.)	N/A	Free Dial-up
Ajato	TVA / Grupo Abril	TVA (Cable and MMDS)	ADSL, Cable
BrTurbo	Brasil Telecom	Brasil Telecom	ADSL
Globo.com	Globo and Telecom Italia	Globo Cabo (Cable)	Cable

EXHIBIT 14   **Major Telecom Infrastructure and Access Services Providers in Brazil**

Source: Developed by authors from interviews and reports by industry analysts, companies' Web sites, companies' annual reports.

Company	Backbone (km)[a]	Control	Remarks
Embratel	70,000	MCI Worldcom	Nationwide backbone
Telefonica Data	**TBA**	**Telefonica Group**	**TBA**
Brasil Telecom	TBA	Telecom Italia Financial investors	TBA
Telemar	TBA	Financial investors	Nationwide backbone, along with Pegasus
AT&T Latin America	340	AT&T Corp.	Metropolitan rings in the cities of São Paulo, Rio de Janeiro, and Belo Horizonte
Engeredes	4,000	Algar[b]	Metropolitan rings in the cities of São Paulo, Rio de Janeiro, and Belo Horizonte
Impsat	3,304	British Telecom and financial investors	Metropolitan rings in the cities of São Paulo, Rio de Janeiro, and Belo Horizonte
MetroRed	1,800	Financial investors	Metropolitan rings in the cities of São Paulo, Rio de Janeiro, and Belo Horizonte
Intelig	15,000	National Grid, Sprint	Nationwide backbone
Pegasus	6,000	Financial investors[c]	Nationwide backbone, along with Telemar
Eletronet	16,000	AES Corp.	Network expected to reach 22,000 km in 5 years
Copel Telecom	9,000	Copel[d]	Strong presence in state of Parana
Diveo	NA	Financial investors	Fixed wireless backbone in the cities of São Paulo, Rio de Janeiro, and Belo Horizonte

[a]1.00 kilometer = 0.63 mile.
[b]Brazilian conglomerate.
[c]Indirect cross ownership with Telemar.
[d]Brazilian electrical utility company.

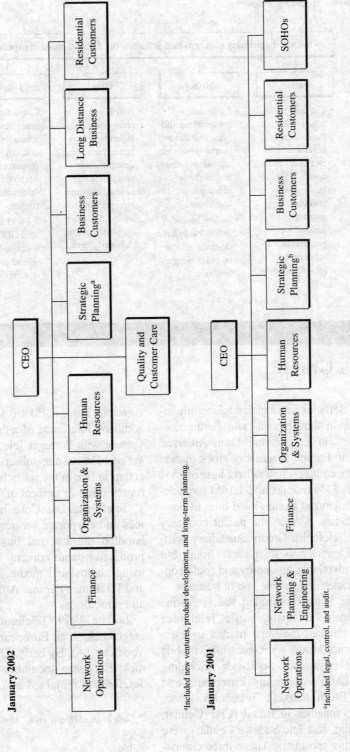

EXHIBIT 15 Telesp Organizational Chart

January 2002

Source: Company internal documents.

[a]Included new ventures, product development, and long-term planning.

[b]Included legal, control, and audit.

January 2001

EXHIBIT 16
Primary Concerns of São Paulo Consumers

Source: Developed by authors from "Brazil: Internet users worry about data protection," *EIU Views Wire, The Economist*, October 25, 2000; data analysis by Gretchen Engster, Sean Gass, and Bob Geiman (HBS MBA 2002), "Field Study Report," December 2001, p. 21.

What are the primary concerns that influence the decision-making process of São Paulo consumers?

Safety
- The high crime rates in São Paulo and the general awareness of the unsafe environment result in a high consumer demand for products and services that provide security.

Money
- Financial concerns are still prevalent due to memories of past inflationary times and unstable economic conditions.
- Income inequality in São Paulo has dramatic effects on purchasing behavior.

Time
- Brazilians recognize that technology may be used to save time but many consumers still have a hard time incorporating technology applications into their daily lives.

Health
- Consistent with many developed countries, a main concern for most consumers is the health of their family and friends.
- 7.3% of household GDP is spent on health-related products or services.

Education
- The low-quality school system and expensive private school alternatives in São Paulo encourage many consumers to seek education through supplementary channels.

Appendix

Telefónica Group

In early 2002, Telefónica was a global telecommunications operator in the Spanish- and Portuguese-speaking markets in Europe and Latin America. Ranked second in Europe in terms of stock market capitalization, the company had a client base of 78M (45M fixed line, 33M mobile, and 1.14M pay television). It was organized along global lines of business with Telefónica, S.A. as the parent company and head of the Telefónica Group. Subsidiary companies reported directly to Telefónica Group, but they operated with relative autonomy and could control other companies in the same line of business.

Telefónica de Espana managed the fixed-line telephony business in Spain, while Telefónica LatinoAmerica handled the same market in Latin America. Telefónica Moviles S.A. controlled mobile communications businesses worldwide, including the Spanish, Latin American, European, and Mediterranean Basin markets. Telefónica's three mobile phone companies in Brazil (CRT Celular, Tele Leste Celular, and Tele Sudeste Celular) were housed within this subsidiary. These three companies contributed 5.2M subscribers to Telefónica's customer base, 3.4M of which were prepaid.[46] In addition, Telefónica Moviles had solidified a joint venture with Portugal Telecom that ensured a market of 11M cellular subscribers, "with market leadership in five of the six richest areas in the country," representing 71 percent of GDP.[47]

Telefónica DataCorp managed the data services and corporate services business, while Terra handled the Internet business. Admira covered production and content dissemination services using audiovisual media; Atento, CRM services; and Telefonica Paginas Amarilla, telephone guides and directories.

In late 1999, Telefonica's credit rating (A+) lagged behind all European incumbents except for Vodafone (A). By early 2002, the credit ratings of most European incumbents fell below A, while Telefonica's remained at A+.[48]

[46] "Telefonica/Telesp Fixa," Unibanco Research, March 4, 2002.
[47] Ibid.
[48] Ibid.

Appendix

	Ownership	Revenue		EBITDA	
	Percent	**2001**	**2000**	**2001**	**2000**
Telefonica de Espana	100.0%	10,220.4	10,182.9	4,508.1	4,448.4
Telefonica Moviles	92.7	8,411.1	7,401.2	3,333.7	2,451.4
Telefonica LatinoAmerica	100.0	10,137.4	10,371.3	5,163.0	5,359.3
Telefonica DataCorp	100.0	1,849.7	1,123.7	23.6	75.0
Terra Lycos	37.6	690.0	304.0	(232.0)	(359.3)
TPI	59.9	511.7	413.0	128.8	121.2
Admira Media	100.0	1,403.1	723.9	152.5	13.6
Atento	100.0	643.6	526.9	53.8	25.2
Other Subsidiaries		1,574.8	1,668.5	(120.2)	(267.2)
Deletions Group		(4,389.5)	(4,229.9)	(207.7)	51.1
Total Group		31,052.3	28,485.5	12,803.6	11,918.7

Appendix (continued)

Telefonica Group Key Statistics

Source: Telefónica Annual Report, 2001.

	1997	**1998**	**1999**	**2000**	**2001**
Fixed telephone lines (thousands)	28,159.9	36,792.8	40,199.1	42,263.5	44,955.8
Spain	16,798.3	18,205.2	19,226.2	20,317.8	20,646.9
Other countries	11,361.6	18,587.6	20,972.9	21,945.7	24,308.7
Mobile customers (thousands)	5,053.5	10,514.4	19,582.1	24,920.3	32,355.6
Spain	3,198.7	4,894.3	9,052.3	13,669.0	16,793.4
Other countries	1,865.8	5,620.1	10,530.8	11,251.3	15,462.2
Pay TV customers (thousands)	1,751.9	2,369.8	2,489.5	982.5	1,148.1
Spain	200.0	282.1	440.1	633.1	806.4
Other countries	1,551.9	2,087.7	2,049.4	349.4	341.7
Total customers (millions)	35	49	62	67	78
Serving employees[a]	92,151	103,662	118,778	145,730	161,029
Operating revenues (millions of euros)	14,202.5	17,465.5	22,957.0	28,485.5	31,052.6
Financial debt[b] (millions of euros)	13,755.1	18,837.4	20,472.1	26,951.4	28,941.6
Investment[c] (millions of euros)	4,122.3	4,417.9	7,185.6	21,128.6	8,420.9
Cash flow (millions of euros)	5,778.3	6,515.7	8,985.0	10,466.4	10,554.1
Net income (millions of euros)	1,142.3	1,307.7	1,804.8	2,504.8	2,106.8

[a]Average number in the year.
[b]Financial debt: Long-term creditors (not including minority shareholders) + issues and debts with credit institutions − Temporary financial investments − cash.
[c]Tangible fixed and intangible, includes advances to suppliers and installation materials.

(continued)

Appendix (continued)

	Vodafone	BT	SBC	Telmex	KPN	PT	TI	AT&T	Verizon	TF	NTT	MCI	Sprint	FT	DT
Rev. growth (%)	134%	10%	4%	−2%	30%	60%	7%	5%	11%	24%	23%	9%	3%	24%	15%
EBITDA growth (%)	114%	1%	2%	−4%	72%	26%	6%	9%	3%	21%	7%	1%	25%	32%	373%
NP growth (%)	−24%	−31%	−2%	−3%	126%	9%	17%	36%	43%	39%	35%	3%	25%	32%	373%
Net debt (€ millions)	9,363	12,263	25,319	7,016	17,319	3,227	14,485	62,811	54,959	22,403	−840	24,135	4,386	52,742	48,509
Firm value/EBITDA	90.84	10.40	9.18	4.50	6.12	8.77	8.68	5.69	8.51	9.35	70.68	5.11	4.39	15.72	9.96
P/E	438.91	28.85	20.78	0.08	7.21	21.65	42.65	10.79	11.69	30.42	233.03	9.40	9.16	28.60	16.24
Price/book value	1.52	3.76	5.43	3.90	0.92	2.68	4.76	0.49	3.99	3.01	25.02	0.70	1.46	3.16	2.51
EBITDA margin %	31.0%	50.2%	39.8%	55.3%	54.5%	36.7%	43.1%	32.7%	39.0%	41.8%	32.8	33.3%	28.8%	31.7%	33.9%
Debt/total cap	4.6%	41.1%	46.0%	61.0%	63.0%	41.9%	50.7%	38.7%	62.4%	56.4%	20.1%	31.0%	26.7%	65.6%	61.0%
EBITDA/debt	35.8%	59.8%	78.9%	76.1%	23.1%	44.9%	66.7%	33.2%	44.0%	36.4%	140.4%	52.3%	113.2%	16.9%	26.2%

Case 3-5

Outsourcing IT: The Global Landscape in 2004

Companies use *outsourcing* (see Exhibit 1 for definition) to reduce cost and to increase quality, reliability, and predictability of product and service offerings. Outsourcing involves aggregating specific tasks or entire processes and moving them to *other organizations*—often in locations where a lower wage or more appropriate business structure exists. Contracts specify mutually agreed upon levels of service and can run for a decade or more. *Offshoring* is a form of outsourcing where aggregate activities are moved to *other countries*. Companies can establish offshore operations through a foreign subsidiary, joint venture, or by contracting with an established firm. The list of companies doing outsourcing is growing.

Manufacturing has long outsourced individual components of production and final product assembly. For more than 70 years, Hollywood outsourced filming to Canada and other film-friendly locations. A key area of outsourcing has involved information technology (IT.) Barclays outsourced management of a 3,900 ATM network in the United Kingdom.[1] London-based HSBC outsourced call center and back-office jobs to China, Malaysia, India,[2] and the Philippines.[3]

John Schmidlin, J. P. Morgan Chase & Co. CTO, managed their $5 billion outsourcing deal: "Don't underestimate the complexity," he said. "It's complicated and intricate. And don't build expectations too high. Stay open-minded and fact-based."[4] His biggest regret? He wishes he'd outsourced sooner.

One study championing the benefits observed, "For every dollar of spending on business services that moves offshore, U.S. companies save 58 cents, mainly in wages. Offshore services are identical to those they replace—and at times better."[5] The potential benefits of outsourcing can't be ignored, but it can be a complex transformation of the business. Consultants exist to assist and advise organizations moving towards outsourcing (e.g., TPI served as advisor on 41 percent of the 2003 outsourcing deals with a total contract value of more than $200 million,[6] Bain, Deloitte Consulting, and McKinsey also consult, largely on offshoring, as does Equaterra which is a start-up founded by former employees of TPI.[7]) Some consultancies specialize in advice specifically related to offshoring.[8]

At the end of the twentieth century, many companies invested in process reengineering to make their businesses more efficient.[9] This led to a *process* view of business. *Business Process*

This case was prepared by Professor F. Warren McFarlan and Research Associate Brian J. DeLacey. Copyright © 2004 President and Fellows of Harvard College. Harvard Business School Case No. 304-104.

[1] Barclays outsources ATM management, February 26, 2004, Financial Services Distribution. From Factiva, 3/3/04.

[2] Offshore rewards are not without their risks, eFinancialNews.com, November 16, 2003 LENGTH: 761 words, eFinancialNews, Phillipa Leighton-Jones.

[3] Eileen A. Mencias, "HSBC to Open Call Center in Alabang," *Manila Standard,* April 14, 2004.

[4] Brian Deagon, "Buying IT Becoming Pay-As-Go," July 8, 2003, Investor's Business Daily. Date accessed on Factiva: April 30, 2004.

[5] Reaping the Benefits of Business Process Outsourcing, McKinsey and Co., Michael Bloch and Stephan Spang, http://www.bto.mckinsey.de/_downloads/themen/mckonit_bpo.pdf. Accessed on April 29, 2004.

[6] See http://www.tpi.net/about. Accessed on April 28, 2004.

[7] Smart Timing; Outsourcing advice for sale, Lisa Dicarlo, *Forbes,* April 26, 2004. Accessed on April 14, 2004.

[8] One firm in Cambridge, Massachusetts helps others establish a "global delivery center" offshore—see a full description at http://www.i-vantage.com. Another firm in San Ramon, California, neoIT deals extensively with firms in Silicon Valley (see http://www.neoit.com) its mission: "To help clients achieve superior results through advice and management of offshore IT and BPO services." Accessed on March 29, 2004.

[9] Thomas H. Davenport, Laurence Prusak with H. James Wilson, *What's the Big Idea? Creating and Capitalizing on the Best Management thinking.* (Boston: Harvard Business School Press, 2003), p. 155

EXHIBIT 1 Glossary of Terms

Insourcing. Attracting foreign companies to establish operations based in the United States. (See also *Onshoring*.)

Micro-multinational. "A company that from its inception is based in the U.S. but maintains a less-costly skilled work force abroad."[a] This is Silicon Valley's dream start-up—where firms are small but follow the model of large multinationals who have led the way in global outsourcing (See also *Outsource from the get-go*.)

Offshoring. Moving business processes to other countries—either by establishing an offshore subsidiary or contracting with an established firm to handle the outsourced process.

Onshoring. (See also *Insourcing*.) When global companies establish corporate offices outside of their own country, with the objective of putting in place a globally distributed value chain where work can be done anywhere in the world based upon relative advantage and efficiency.

Outsourcing. Contracting independent third parties to agreed-upon and execute well-defined business processes. The third parties may be in the same city, state, or country or they may be abroad in a country with a lower wage or where a more appropriate business structure exists.

Outsource from the get-go. In April 2004, VC portfolios typically had about half of their companies using offshoring in India. That was expected to climb to 90 percent in the future. (See also *Micro-multinational*.)[b]

[a] Ann Grimes, "Venture Firms Seek Start-Ups That Outsource," *The Wall Street Journal*, April 2, 2004.
[b] *The Wall Street Journal* proclaimed the overall message in Silicon Valley, April 2, 2004.

Outsourcing (BPO) became possible because of key advances in information technology (IT). The digital foundation of a globally connected knowledge economy was formed by standardization and commercialization of the Internet, the rapid evolution of World Wide Web technologies including XML for data interoperability, along with an unprecedented build-out of communications bandwidth. Business processes are no longer constrained by physical, geographic, or organizational bounds when IT can tie these processes together.

Background on IT Outsourcing

The focus of this paper is on IT outsourcing. Increasingly, work can migrate to wherever it can be completed most effectively for the organization. In some cases this may lead to a shared-service or centralization, but in other cases it leads to outsourcing.

IT outsourcing began with ADP payroll processing in 1949.[10] A major expansion of outsourcing occurred when Kodak decided to outsource its entire IT operations in 1990. Other companies followed Kodak's lead. By "1995, more than half of midsize to large firms had outsourced or were considering outsourcing significant IT activities."[11]

Some specific benefits include avoiding technology obsolescence, leveraging cutting-edge technologies and skills, benefiting from economies of scale, and taking advantage of best practices provided by outsourcing vendors. There are many risks, but also the promise of significant savings. (See Chapter 10.)

Some 2003 outsourcing examples include a 10-year, $2.4 billion deal CSC reached with United Kingdom's Royal Mail to provide network, voice, data, mobile, and Internet services.[12] In April 2003, Hewlett-Packard Co. won a 10-year contract for $3 billion with Procter & Gamble to manage "IT infrastructure, data center operations, desktop and end-user support, network management, and some applications

[10] L. M. Applegate, Robert D. Austin, and F. Warren McFarlan. *Corporate Information Strategy and Management: Text and Cases*. 6th ed. (New York: Irwin/McGraw Hill, 2003), p. 563.

[11] Ibid., p. 564.

[12] Computer Sciences Corporation, April 21, 2004, Hoover's Company Profiles. From Factiva, April 28, 2004.

development and management for P&G operations in 160 countries."[13]

The continuing outsourcing momentum was evident in April 2004, when the BBC announced plans to outsource its BBC Technology division which "employs some 1,400 people, and generates over 220m pounds ($374m) in revenue every year with an operating profit of 19m pounds ($32.3m). The deal itself, which will cover the entire IT infrastructure and Web site and support services, is likely to run for some 10 years from the end of 2004 and be worth around 2bn pounds ($3.4bn) to the eventual supplier."[14] This would include existing, smaller outsource contracts rolled up into a larger outsourcing deal.

The BBC's final list of outsourcing providers included CSC, Fujitsu, EDS, Capita, Accenture, IBM, Logica, and Hewlett-Packard. The contract included provisions that help desk support and other services must remain in the United Kingdom although application development could move offshore. "By outsourcing IT the BBC expects to realize an annual savings of between $35.8 and $53.8 million."[15]

What IT Processes Are Companies Outsourcing?

Many diverse areas of corporate organizations were being outsourced in 2004, including:

- Call centers providing support (e.g., American Express Co., Dell Inc. and Citigroup Inc[16]).

- Payment processing (e.g., HP took on payment processing for P&G's major geographies[17]).
- Check clearing (e.g., EDS handled digital payments and transfers for the Western Payments Alliance, which handles 7 million checks per day).
- Systems and software development (by 2004, there were more IT engineers in Bangalore—150,000 than in Silicon Valley—120,000).
- Desktop support (e.g., Gartner concluded Boeing could outsource their desktop support function and save 37 percent over in-house staff[18]).
- Data and voice networking infrastructure, data center operations.
- Technology design (Apple outsourced much of the design work for its blockbuster iPod to a number of engineering firms in Silicon Valley).[19]

A new book, from Massachusetts Institute of Technology and Harvard University authors, suggests many more jobs could be outsourced, or eliminated, in the future. The authors argue that a key trait of jobs that will disappear "is whether a job can be 'routinized,' or broken down into repeatable steps that vary little from day to day. Such a job is easier to replace with a clever piece of software or to hand over to a lower-paid worker outside the U.S." These routine jobs will be outsourced or turned into a software program: "If you can really write the whole job down on paper, then someone else can do it."[20]

[13] Paula Musich, HP, Procter & Gamble Sign $3 Billion Deal, April 11, 2003, eWeek, at http://www.eweek.com. Accessed April 28, 2004.

[14] BBC Unveils Outsourcing Shortlist. February 9, 2004, *ComputerWire News.* Accessed on April 30, 2004.

[15] Ephraim Schwartz, "BBC to sell off IT," *InfoWorld,* April 20, 2004. Accessed on April 27, 2004. http://www.infoworld.com/article/04/04/20/HNbbc_1.html.

[16] Joanna Slater, Call of the West: For India's Youth, New Money Fuels a Revolution—As Foreign Goods, Jobs Flood the Country, Young People Are Spurning Tradition. January 27, 2004. *The Wall Street Journal.* Accessed on Factiva April 29, 2004.

[17] Hewlett-Packard Wins First Business-Process Outsourcing Deal, It reached a multiyear deal to provide finance and administration services for Procter & Gamble, Paul McDougall, *InformationWeek,* March 16, 2004, http://www.informationweek.com/story/showArticle.jhtml?articleID=18400459.

[18] Boeing may outsource desktop-support jobs to computer giant Dell, Dominic Gates, *Seattle Times* aerospace reporter, March 26, 2004.

[19] Electronics Design Chain, Summer 2002 Issue, Inside the Apple iPOD Design Triumph, Erik Sherman, available from http://www.designchain.com/coverstory.asp?issue=summer02. Accessed on April 27, 2004.

[20] The future of work: Flexible, creative, and good with people? You should do fine in tomorrow's job market, by Peter Coy with William C. Symonds in Boston, Stephen Baker in New York, Michael Arndt in Chicago, Robert D. Hof in San Mateo, Calif., and bureau reports. March 22, 2004, *BusinessWeek.* From Factiva, April 28, 2004.

What activities shouldn't be outsourced? First, there needs to be an economic payback. Certainly, outsourcing core competencies can be a dangerous undertaking,[21] so finding the right mix of activities to outsource is key to maximizing productivity and overall capabilities of the modern firm. The Apple iPod story is especially interesting because the company has been very successful with the product despite being known for proprietary design work as a major core competence.

Who is Outsourcing?

Outsourcing IT has become a common practice from the smallest to the largest firms. The largest outsourcing projects have initially been undertaken by huge multinationals, providing critical mass and momentum to the outsourcing industry.

To be most effective, outsourcing needs to be considered in the strategic thinking of a firm—especially when it comes to dealing with core competencies of the firm—and integrated into the overall execution of a company's operating plan. Outsourcing may be right for one firm, but not for another in the same industry.

Some of the most successful and innovative financial services firms have considered outsourcing and reached different conclusions: J. P. Morgan Chase has a $5 billion outsourcing contract, while E*TRADE has reserved outsourcing for narrow areas such as help desks. Mellon is working toward a goal of offshoring one-quarter of development by the end of 2004 but has presently limited outsourcing to recordkeeping at Dreyfus and hasn't found sufficient economic benefit for outsourcing their infrastructure.[22] All of these plans are regularly re-evaluated in light of new developments.

Rapid technological developments[23] and increasing competition in a down economy made outsourcing attractive to even the smallest companies. Consider the following examples:

1. In early 2004, nearly every Silicon Valley start-up receiving funding included outsourced engineering resources (from India) as part of their business plan.[24]
2. DFS Group, which runs airport shopping around the world worked with a consulting firm to outsource most of its 265-person IT operation to India in 2002, saving 40 percent of their operating costs.[25]
3. Best Buy, despite strong revenues and earnings, announced plans to outsource much of its 820-person IT department to Accenture—retaining 40 people to oversee the relationship, transferring 650 people to Accenture, and laying off 130 workers.[26, 27] (At the same time, Best Buy, like Wal-Mart, was eliminating outsourcing in purchasing and instituting a direct procurement

[23] Falling hardware prices and increasing power, the development of software interface standards and packaged systems, virtually unlimited and inexpensive global communications bandwidth—it's an ideal recipe for outsourcing.

[24] Hunt begins for millions of missing jobs as United States recovers: Smaller companies choosing to outsource abroad could be to blame for the slow rate of growth in employment, says Dan Roberts. February 17, 2004 Tuesday, London Edition 1, Section: Back page—First Section; Pg. 24, 803 words, Copyright 2004 The Financial Times Limited. Financial Times (London, England).

[25] Is Your Job Going Abroad? As the debate about exporting work from America dominates the presidential campaign, voters need to separate myth from reality. A *Time* guide to how we got here—and why short-term pain might translate into long-term gain, Jyoti Thottam; With reporting by Barbara Kiviat/New York, Sara Rajan/New Delhi, Cathy Booth Thomas/Dallas, and Karen Tumulty/Washington. March 1, 2004. *Time.*

[26] Best Buy Is Expected to Eliminate Jobs, Gary McWilliams, March 26, 2004, *The Wall Street Journal.* Accessed from Factiva on 3/26/04.

[27] Carol Sliwa, Best Buy to Outsource IT to Accenture; IT head count expected to drop from 820 to 40 as retailer stresses agility over customization. April 19, 2004, *Computerworld.* Accessed from Factiva April 29, 2004.

[21] An Unseen Peril of Outsourcing, David Gumpert, *BusinessWeek,* March 3, 2004. http://www.businessweek.com/smallbiz/content/mar2004/sb2004033_0420.htm. Accessed on April 16, 2004.

[22] Innovative Institutions—These six Wall Street firms tapped into technology and let their inner innovation sing. Jessica Pallay, December 1, 2003, Wall Street + Technology. Accessed through Factiva April 30, 2004.

operation at a global purchasing center in China. Direct procurement was expected to improve overall profitability since 70 percent of Best Buy's $25 billion in 2003 sales were made in China.[28] All of this required a global chain of information to map to procurement.)

How Much IT is Outsourced?

Investor's Business Daily reported that "Global spending on major outsourcing projects—in which a customer hires an outside company to design, implement, and run a computer network or other information technology endeavor—rose 44 pecent from 2002 . . . up from a 32 percent increase in 2002 vs. 2001."[29]

According to Gartner, "Outsourcers already manage . . . 769,171 servers and 28.4 million desktop PCs."[30] Gartner projects: "The worldwide outsourcing market is expected to grow from $161.9 billion in 2002 to just over $235.6 billion in 2007 at a compound annual growth rate (CAGR) of 7.8 percent." This is broken down into four large segments of outsourcing: data center, network, enterprise applications, and desktop.[31]

Another measure is the size of megadeals valued at over $1 billion: "Two-thirds of the 15 [IT outsourcing] megadeals (contracts worth $1 billion or more) in 2003 were awarded by European organizations. Until 2003, Europe accounted for just 14 of the 78 publicly announced megadeals. Cap Gemini Ernst & Young (CGE&Y) joined the megadeal ranks, HP won its second megadeal, Accenture won three, and for the first time since 1992, EDS did not win a megadeal during the calendar year. IBM won six and Computer Sciences Corp. (CSC) won four deals."[32] Data Monitor found that "deals valued at more than $100 million rose 49 percent in 2003 to 244 contracts."[33]

Many firms are extending their information technology outsourcing agreements, focused mostly on infrastructure, into business process outsourcing, focusing on higher level operations and applications.

The growth in outsourcing certainly has sufficient momentum to continue, and perhaps accelerate. *The Wall Street Journal* suggests that a large range of activities could be outsourced or sent offshore: "Jobs that can be reduced to a series of rules are likely to go—either to workers abroad or to computers. The jobs that stay in the United States or that are newly created in the decade ahead are likely to demand the more complex skill of recognizing patterns or require human contact."[34]

Given the increase in outsourcing and offshoring, what will be the long-term impact? One indicator is that "Offshore deals made up just 1.4 percent of total outsourcing contracts last year . . . but the value of offshore contracts rose 890 percent from 2002 to $1.66 billion."[35] Some reports indicate that as many as "3.3 million jobs representing $136 billion in wages" could move offshore to India by the end of the decade.[36]

---

[28] Best Buy Seeks Direct Procurement in China. April 23, 2004. SinoCast China IT Watch. Accessed from Factiva April 29, 2004.

[29] J. Bonasia, Outsourcing Contracts Soared in 2003—Trend Still Picking Up Steam—Gov't agencies, businesses hiring, January 21, 2004, Investor's Business Daily, from Factiva March 3, 2004.

[30] Bruce M. Caldwell, Flexibility Is Key Trend in 2003 IT Infrastructure Outsourcing (Executive Summary), March 16, 2004, Research Report: ITSV-WW-EX-0433.

[31] Forecast for IT Outsourcing Segments Shows Strong Growth, March 10, 2004, Bruce M. Caldwell, Robert De Souza, Allie Young, Ron Silliman, Eric Goodness, Report # ITSV-WW-DA-0225.

[32] Bruce M. Caldwell, Flexibility Is Key Trend in 2003 IT Infrastructure Outsourcing (Executive Summary).

[33] J. Bonasia, Outsourcing Contracts Soared in 2003—Trend Still Picking Up Steam—Gov't agencies, businesses hiring.

[34] Barbell Effect—The Future of Jobs: New Ones Arise, Wage Gap Widens—Outsourcing, Technology Cut Need for Rote Workers; Brainpower Is in Demand—Hot Area: Massage Therapy, David Wessel, April 2, 2004, *The Wall Street Journal*.

[35] J. Bonasia, Outsourcing Contracts Soared In 2003—Trend Still Picking Up Steam—Gov't agencies, businesses hiring.

[36] Jon E. Hilsenrath, Data Gap—Behind Outsourcing Debate: Surprisingly Few Hard Numbers—Counting Jobs Moving Abroad Is a Complicated Task; Benefits Are Less Tangible, April 12, 2004, *The Wall Street Journal*.

EXHIBIT 2 Leading IT Outsourcing in Companies in the United States

The leading companies are EDS, IBM Global Services, Computer Sciences Corporation (CSC), and Hewlett-Packard. To get a flavor of these leading businesses it's helpful to look at how a few of the companies describe themselves.

EDS sees itself as "the world's most experienced outsourcing services company, delivers superior returns to clients through its cost-effective, high-value services model. EDS' core portfolio comprises information technology and business process outsourcing services, as well as information technology transformation services."[a]

IBM Global Services reports:

"Outsourcing has for years helped organizations trim costs. Our Business Transformation Outsourcing (BTO) services go beyond that limited role and make outsourcing a strategic element in business transformation. We can operate your business processes, applications and infrastructure, enabling you to focus on your core strengths, and pursue new opportunities. We can help you become an on demand business.

The value-creation approaches of the past two decades have largely been exploited: cost reduction and competitive positioning in the 1980s, process improvement and reengineering in the early 1990s and the enterprise, CRM and Web technologies of the late 1990s—all have run their course.

Creating value now increasingly involves transforming an organization into a networked, on demand e-business. That means outsourcing noncore activities, focusing on strategic capabilities and collaborating with partners and suppliers."[b]

CSC draws the critical distinction between *IT Outsourcing* and *Business Process Outsourcing:*

"A step beyond IT outsourcing, business process outsourcing (BPO) is increasingly becoming the strategic choice of companies looking to achieve cost reductions while improving their service quality, increasing shareholder value, and focusing on their core business capabilities.

CSC's breadth of capabilities, proven program management skills, and ability to integrate technology with business processes makes us your natural choice as BPO partner. With a comprehensive menu of BPO services across a range of functions—including claims processing, invoicing, human resources and payroll, finance, procurement, and customer support—CSC is already providing BPO services to many clients, generating significant revenues. As our BPO offerings grow, we commit to bringing operational excellence to reengineer your business processes for optimal service, quality, and cost."[c]

[a] http://www.eds.com/about_eds/en_about_eds.shtml, accessed on March 3, 2004.
[b] http://www-1.ibm.com/services/bcs/bto_home.html, accessed on March 3, 2004.
[c] http://www.csc.com/solutions/businessprocessoutsourcing, accessed on March 3, 2004.

Leading Outsourcing Vendors

A number of United States companies provide global outsourcing services. The biggest leaders are CSC, IBM, EDS, and HP. A number of prominent companies with consulting traditions also compete in this same space—Accenture, Deloitte Consulting, Booz Allen Hamilton, and Keane. (See Exhibit 2 for an overview of several companies.)

Some companies in India are outsourcing their IT work to American companies. IBM, for example,

won a big contract to "look after the hardware, software, datacentres, customer billing, CRM, helpdesks, and disaster recovery facilities of Bharti Tele-Ventures, India's largest private telecoms carrier. Over 10 years, IBM will earn $750 million for this outsourcing deal."[37]

[37] IT Week Comment—New players on the IT stage. April 5, 2004, VNU Business Publications, 2004. Accessed on April 2, 2004.

EXHIBIT 3
The Biggest U.S. Players in India

Source: *BusinessWeek*, December 8, 2003.

Company reports, Nasscom, Evalueserve. Many other examples are available at http://www.wipro.com as well as Web sites of other companies specializing in outsourcing.

Company	Purpose	India Staff
GE Capital Services	Back-office work	16,000
GE's John Welch Tech Center	Product R&D	1,800
IBM Global Services	IT services	10,000[a]
Oracle	Software, services	6,000[b]
EDS	IT services	3,500[c]
SAP	Staff	2,000[d]
Texas Instruments	Chip design	900
Intel	Chip design	1,700
J.P. Morgan Chase	Back-office	1,200

[a] By 2005.
[b] Unspecified.
[c] By 2004.
[d] The Economist: IT industry's location shifts, July 17, 2003, The Economist Intelligence Unit Ltd.

IBM subsequently acquired Daksh eServices Ltd. of India, adding to their staff of 9,000 in early 2004. Daksh eServices (revenue of $15 million in FY02, and estimates ranging from 2,300 to 6,000 employees) offers call center; Web-based customer service, and e-mail response for companies like Amazon.com, Paypal, Yahoo!, and Sprint PCS. Some believe this is the first in a wave of acquisitions of BPO providers in India, driven by the need of large outsourcing firms to remain cost competitive by obtaining low-cost services in India.

India: Global Leader in Providing Outsourced Solutions

India has become the leading country outside of the U.S. to provide global outsourcing. India's well-educated, English-speaking workforce, operating in areas of the country where robust technological infrastructure has been established, competes favorably with the world's best information technology professionals. As an indication of supporting infrastructure, fiber optic connections increased seven times between 2001 and 2002; voice calls across the Pacific cost one-fourth what they did two years ago.[38]

Driving this growth is the fact that staff salaries for engineers in India are one quarter of a similarly skilled worker in the United States. Salaries for call center workers have an even greater economic differential. According to the *Wall Street Journal,* "An Indian call center worker earns about $200 to $300 a month, about a tenth of the comparable U.S. wage."[39]

In "The Rise of India," *BusinessWeek* reports that the number of business process outsourcing (BPO) employees in India was estimated at 400,000 for 2001, growing to 4 million by 2008. During this same period, the BPO contribution to India's economy is expected to grow from 1.4 percent of GDP to 7 percent of GDP.[40] For India, this is an important area of economic growth, and numerous companies are working in the area of outsourcing (see Exhibits 3 and 4 for a list of the leading companies in India).

According to *Forbes,* $1.5 billion of India's IT-enabled services were exported in 2002; that is expected to increase more than tenfold by 2008.[41]

New firms in India are reshaping the competitive outsourcing landscape. An example is Hexaware

[38] Jesse Drucker, Global Talk Gets Cheaper—Outsourcing Abroad Becomes Even More Attractive as Cost of Fiber-Optic Links Drops, March 11, 2004, *The Wall Street Journal.*

[39] Jay Solomon in New Delhi and Elena Cherney, Outsourcing to India Sees a Twist, April 1, 2004, *The Wall Street Journal.*

[40] Manjeet Kriplani, Pete Engardio, and Steve Hamm, "The Rise of India," *BusinessWeek,* December 8, 2003.

[41] A Tale of Two Cities; From techie to truck driver in Silicon Valley. From tea broker to techie in Bangalore. The two sides of offshoring, Kerry A. Dolan and Robyn Meredith, April 12, 2004, *Forbes.* From Factiva April 1, 2004.

EXHIBIT 4
The Biggest Outsourcing Companies Based in India

Source: December 14, 2003, Hoover's Company Capsules. Based upon casewriter research, smaller outsourcing companies from India include MphasiS BFL, Ltd., Datamatics Technologies Ltd. (purchased Detroit-based CorPay Solutions Inc.), vCustomer Corp., Allserve Systems PLC, eServe, Infotech Enterprises.

Infosys

2003 Sales ($mil.): $753.8 — 1-Yr. Sales Growth: 38.3%
2003 Net Inc. ($mil.): $194.9 — 1-Yr. Net Inc. Growth: 18.5%
2003 Employees: 15,940 — 1-Yr. Employee Growth: 48.4%

Tata

2003 Sales ($mil.): $1,041.0 — 1-Yr. Sales Growth: 18.3%
2003 Employees: 24,000 — 1-Yr. Employee Growth: 26.3%

Wipro

2003 Sales ($mil.): $904.1 — 1-Yr. Sales Growth: 29.9%
2003 Net Inc. ($mil.): $170.9 — 1-Yr. Net Inc. Growth: 0.2%
2003 Employees: 23,300 — 1-Yr. Employee Growth: 68.8%

Satyam Computer Services, Ltd.

2003 Sales ($mil.): $459.2 — 1-Yr. Sales Growth: 10.8%
2003 Net Inc. ($mil.): $79.8 — 1-Yr. Net Inc. Growth: 208.1%
2003 Employees: 9,838 — 1-Yr. Employee Growth: 3.2%

Technologies in Mumbai, helping to transform not only the IT industry, but also the city previously known as Bombay:

> Hexaware's headquarters, the workplace of some 500 programmers (another 800 work at a development center in the southern city of Chennai, and 200 more are in Bangalore), is a silvery four-story glass building chock-full of blond-wood cubicles and black Dell computers . . . it's the talent—coupled with the ridiculously low salaries, of course—that's luring big clients from Europe and North America. The coders here work for the likes of Citibank, Deutsche Leasing, Alliance Capital, Air Canada, HSBC, BP, Princeton University, and several other institutions that won't permit Hexaware to reveal their names.[42]

The rapid development of this industry is amazing. Consider that, only a decade ago, Wipro was:

> . . . selling cooking oil and personal computers, mostly in India. Today, it is a $903 million-a-year global company, and most of its business comes from information-technology services. Since 1997, Wipro's revenue has grown by an average of 26 percent a year while profits have grown by 69 percent. Its 15,000 technologists write software,

integrate back-office solutions, design semiconductors, debug applications, take orders, and field help calls for some of the biggest companies in the world. They are as good at doing all of that as anyone in the world. Perhaps better. And they are cheaper—on average about 40 percent cheaper—than comparable American companies.[43]

Five years ago, Wipro had one-tenth the revenue, and one-ninth the number of employees. They were focused on engineering and IT consulting.[44] Today, the company is providing real competition for the industry's outsourcing leaders—Wipro is now able to compete on price and capabilities.

For the 4th quarter ending April 2004, Wipro reported $73.3 million in profit. The 43 percent increase in quarterly profit was "driven by higher outsourcing orders, higher prices, and measures to damp the impact of a strong rupee on its export

---

[42] "The New Face of the Silicon Age: How India became the capital of the computing revolution." http://www.wired.com/wired/archive/12.02/india.html, Issue 12.02. February 2004.

[43] Keith H. Hammonds, "The New Face of Global Competition: Not so long ago, India's Wipro Ltd. sold cooking oils and knockoff PCs. Now its 15,000 technologists cook up vital software applications and research for Ericsson, GM, the Home Depot, and other giant customers. Are you prepared to go head-to-head with the best the world has to offer?" *Fast Company*, February 1, 2003.

[44] Jesse Drucker, "Global Talk Gets Cheaper—Outsourcing Abroad Becomes Even More Attractive as Cost of Fiber-Optic Links Drops."

earnings."[45] *The Wall Street Journal* noted, "For the full fiscal year, Wipro's net profit rose 23 percent . . . with revenue jumping 36 percent . . . [despite the fact that] some clients have deferred orders until the completion of U.S. elections in November."[46]

BusinessWeek notes the increasing strength of the outsourcing providers in India:

> Their ability to offer prices that undercut Western adversaries by as much as 70 percent is just the start. They're also amassing the skills to handle complex consulting projects . . . Three years ago, just 125 of the top 500 U.S. companies placed work with Indian companies, according to Nasscom, India's software-services trade association. Last year, that number hit 285, including Boeing, Cisco Systems, and Lehman Brothers.[47]

In India, outsourcing strength goes beyond IT—people are turning to India for health care and even hip replacements at a quarter of the cost charged in the United States and the United Kingdom. India has "capitalized on the high cost of health care administration in the U.S."[48] IT plays a key role with India providing "billing services and processing insurance claims for U.S. hospitals and insurers . . . (as well as) clinical trials for Western drug companies."[49] Communication and coordination capabilities of IT facilitate all forms of modern-day outsourcing "from the back-office to the operating room."[50]

Beyond India

Outsourcing is expanding to other countries. The Philippines expects 2004 revenues of $800 million from outsourcing activities. With unemployment over 10 percent, a slower growing economy, and average household income in 2000 at $2,600, they have strong economic incentives. HSBC announced plans to bring their back-office operations to the Philippines due to the country's "language . . . and intellectual skills."[51]

Some suggest China will quickly push that country to the forefront of global outsourcing. Tata Consultancy Services, of India, established a base of operations in China.

By early 2004, in order to garner more business, international outsourcing companies had begun expanding their corporate presence outside of their home countries. Call centers in the Philippines have attracted investments from some of the oldest outsourcing firms, SPI Technologies (based in the Philippines) announced plans to establish new offices in India.[52]

Sales pressure began intensifying. "Infosys, Tata, Satyam, and Wipro: India's most successful outsourcing contractors are bolstering their bases in Canada. Their goal: To hunt down outsourcing contracts in the United States."[53] Infosys announced plans to invest $20 million for offices and staff in California and other regions, establishing a new level of competition with IBM, EDS, and others.[54]

Hiring and retaining qualified workers remains a challenge in all countries hoping to establish a base in outsourcing. *BusinessWeek* cited the example of Business Processing Services Inc., where half the staff on some projects quit during the first year[55] for better opportunities. The company had

[45] "Wipro Ltd.: India-Based Software Maker Posts 43% Surge in Net Profit, April 19, 2004," *The Wall Street Journal.* Accessed from Factiva April 27, 2004.

[46] Ibid.

[47] Manjeet Kripalani in Bombay and Steve Hamm in New York, with Spencer E. Ante in New York and Andy Reinhardt in Paris. Scrambling to Stem India's Onslaught; Now big Western service outfits have to fight back on both the high and low ends. *BusinessWeek.* January 26, 2004.

[48] Jay Solomon, Traveling Cure: India's New Coup in Outsourcing: Inpatient Care—Facing Expense, Long Waits at Home, Westerners Fly in; A Hospital Empire Grows—Mr. Salo Has 'Real Doubts', April 26, 2004, *The Wall Street Journal.* From Factiva 4/26/04.

[49] Ibid.

[50] Ibid.

[51] Eileen A. Mencias, "HSBC to Open Call Center in Alabang." April 14, 2004, *Manila Standard.*

[52] Singapore Leads India Charge—Southeast Asian Nations Hope to Avert Overreliance on China, Phillip Day, April 5, 2004, *The Wall Street Journal.*

[53] Chris Sorensen, India's new beachhead: Several of the world's outsourcing giants are targeting U.S. contracts from new bases—in Canada, *Financial Post,* April 14, 2004, National Post.

[54] Joanna Slater, Infosys Plans U.S. Investment of $20 Million, April 9, 2004, *The Wall Street Journal.*

[55] David Rocks, with Girlie Linao, in Manila, A mighty river of well-paying jobs? Outsourcing could give the Philippines economy a big boost, but there are major obstacles to overcome, March 22, 2004.

to revise its recruiting plans to identify candidates better suited for the jobs.

The Challenges of Outsourcing

Outsourcing can be complex even for experts, whether it is done onshore or offshore. The most visible example is EDS, which won a $7 billion military contract in 2000 to "design and install a single, hacker-proof network linking 345,000 computers at 4,000 Navy and Marine Corps locations."[56] On the surface it sounds easy enough. Quickly, though, problems began to snowball. EDS soon realized it might lose as much as $2 billion or more on the deal due to underestimating performance requirements, excessive customizations, and poor administrative and cost controls. EDS has renegotiated terms of the contract and struggled to regain its operational credibility and seems to be making progress, but it has been at great financial and reputational expense. (EDS won no megadeals over $1 billion in 2003.)

McKinsey recommends obtaining affirmative answers to these questions before outsourcing:[57]

- Can the outsourcer drive costs lower?
- Can it capture the benefits earlier?
- Can it further increase the quality of the service?
- Can it leverage an existing IT platform to reduce new investments?
- Will it contractually commit to the benefits it promises?
- Can it regularly bring the most relevant innovations to bear on the process and continuously improve performance and quality?

Some practical advice is available on where to pay particular attention to the details:

1. Training new workers with the outsourcing provider, and dealing with existing workers impacted by the transfer of the work process, is one of the most vexing challenges.
2. For medical records, financial records, and other sensitive information, privacy loss remains a worry. There may be laws governing the flow of sensitive information across country borders.[58]
3. Where transaction processing is involved, original data quality is critical to avoid rework and gain full benefit of efficiency in operations: "Thirty percent of all purchase orders are incorrect, and 70 percent of all documents have data discrepancies, according to . . . the head of Exonomy, Standard Chartered Bank's trade finance portal."[59]
4. Scope creep, performance and service level standards, handling intellectual property (e.g., trademarks) and confidentiality issues (e.g., around employment agreements), and even foreign regulatory requirements and taxation need to be explicitly addressed.[60]
5. "Soft issues"—regional job loss, customer reaction, and "cross-cultural friction"—also need attention.

Once a contract is in place, it is crucial to have metrics and good management systems to measure the state of the relationships and progress against deliverables.[61] Gartner recommends annual

[56] Gary McWilliams, "Sink or Swim: After Landing Huge Navy Pact, EDS Finds It's in Over Its Head—Mired in Big Computer Job, Company Loses $1.6 Billion; Jordan Tries a Turnaround—Plea for Staff to Ask for Help," *The Wall Street Journal*, April 6, 2004, A1. Accessed on Factiva April 28, 2004.

[57] Michael Bloch and Stephan Spang, "Reaping the Benefits of Business Process Outsourcing," McKinsey and Co., http://www.bto.mckinsey.de/_downloads/themen/mckonit_bpo.pdf. Accessed on April 29, 2004.

[58] Michael M. Phillips, "Outsourcing Fears Land in Congress's Lap—Legislators Debate a Number of Measures That Respond to Political Hot Potato," *The Wall Street Journal*, March 5, 2004. Accessed on Factiva April 29, 2004.

[59] Stephen Lange Ranzini, "For Interoperability, XML Is the Best Game in Town," *American Banker* 169, no. 78, April 23, 2004. Accessed on Factiva April 30, 2004.

[60] Offshoring begins to reveal hidden costs that reduce its benefits, April 28, 2004, *Palm Beach Daily Business Review*, 50, 172. Accessed on Factiva April 29, 2004.

[61] Larry Dignan, Outsmarting Outsourcers; Deals with computing service providers are still murky. The best negotiators are insisting on performance goals. July 1, 2003, *Baseline*, 1, 20. Accessed from Factiva, April 28, 2004.

benchmarking and making sure that the company and outsourcing provider are aligned on vision, contract, pricing and service level, and customer satisfaction.[62]

Offshoring is Even More Complex

Two examples of well-known institutions that pulled back some of their initial commitment to offshoring are Dell and Lehman Brothers Holdings.

Dell decided to reduce some of its commitment to offshoring when enterprise support customers complained about language difficulties and response times. Dell quickly rerouted calls and established procedures to limit the amount of time frontline customer support personnel were allowed to search for a solution prior to escalating the most sensitive enterprise calls to higher levels of support.[63, 64] (Dell continues to successfully use extensive offshore resources in other areas.)

Lehman Brothers Holdings Inc. experienced problems with outsourcing their IT help desk—some suggest "Lehman underestimated the complexity of internal help desk calls, and the training and process documentation involved."[65] Nevertheless, Lehman decided to continue, and eventually increase the amount they outsource: "Lehman now outsources about 20 percent of its IT operations to India, . . . Eventually that proportion should reach about 40 percent . . . [I]t costs about 40 to 50 percent less to outsource IT functions to India, compared with performing those tasks in-house. The combined value of the Lehman IT contracts to Tata and Wipro will eventually reach between $50 million and $70 million annually."[66]

A number of case examples exist and provide guidelines on what does and doesn't work when it comes to offshoring. Several examples of companies in Massachusetts, headed by technologists of Indian heritage, highlighted case examples where outsourcing and offshoring was attempted but failed. [67, 68, 69] Across a number of test cases, potential problem areas include the following:

1. Salary in India might be one-third the United States, but the resource could be one-sixth as productive.

2. Fast-changing requirements make it impossible for a distant group (e.g., India) to keep up with the rate of change.

3. Going beyond rote instructions to active problem identification and resolution can be problematic, yet the additional time to write detailed instructions and specifications runs counter to the software culture of quick and interactive design chats across cubicle walls.

4. Familiarity with customer needs and proximity to customer and final end user can be important towards understanding, interpreting, and implementing customer requirements.

5. Currency fluctuations could cause rapid changes and eliminate cost advantages; international

[62] Benchmarking Helps to Ensure Success in IT Outsourcing Deals, March 16, 2004, Business Issues. Gartner Research Reports Number: R-21-8516.

[63] Is Your Job Going Abroad? As the debate about exporting work from America dominates the presidential campaign, voters need to separate myth from reality. A TIME guide to how we got here—and why short-term pain might translate into long-term gain. Time Cover Story/Nation/'04 The Issues, See http://www.time.com/time/covers/1101040301/story.html, Jyoti Thottam; With reporting by Barbara Kiviat/New York, Sara Rajan/New Delhi, Cathy Booth Thomas/Dallas and Karen Tumulty/Washington, 4,490 words, March 1, 2004.

[64] Ed Frauenheim, Dell drops some tech calls to India, November 24, 2003, CNET, News.com, http://att.com.com/2100-7342_3-5110933.html. Accessed April 5, 2004.

[65] How To OffShore Call Center Ops The Right Way, April 20, 2004, CMP TechWeb. Accessed through Factiva, April 30, 2004.

[66] Lehman Plans to Continue India Outsourcing, December 18, 2003, *The Wall Street Journal.*

[67] Eduardo Porter, Send Jobs to India? U.S. Companies Say It's Not Always Best, April 28, 2004, *New York Times*. From Factiva.com, April 28, 2004.

[68] Stephanie Armour, Workers asked to train foreign replacements; 'It was hideously awkward,' ex-worker says of situation, April 6, 2004, *USA Today*, B.01. Accessed on Factiva April 28, 2004.

[69] Scott Thurm, Tough Shift—Lesson in India: Not Every Job Translates Overseas—ValiCert Learned Key Roles Must Remain in U.S. for Outsourcing to Work—E-Mails Across 14 Time Zones, March 3, 2004, *The Wall Street Journal.*

political relationships can also complicate operational stability, as can travel restrictions.[70]

The Wall Street Journal noted that differences in work styles, communications norms, and even basic time zones make offshoring difficult but manageable. By structuring work in such a way as to reduce the need for continual interaction and assign appropriate tasks based on locational strengths, the benefits seem to outweigh the costs for perhaps all but the smallest projects.[71]

Despite the difficulties and challenges, large companies remain determined to gain the benefits of outsourcing and offshoring, integrating these approaches into their overall organizational design.

The Backlash?

Some companies already felt a backlash as outsourcing decisions involve eliminating large numbers of American workers—500 or more from a company—and re-skilling takes time.

Newsweek described the dynamic change taking place in California's Silicon Valley, which are similar to some of the reactions in other technology intensive regions like New England:

Four years ago tech executives lobbied for visas for high-tech immigrants; now they are far more likely to export jobs than to import workers. Outsourcing has opened a deep rift in the Valley, where top brass appreciate the cost savings, and midlevel employees dread losing their jobs.[72]

eFunds (an outsourcing firm working in financial services) is one such company that felt the backlash. When eFunds won a "seven-year, $326,000-per-month contract to process electronic welfare-benefits transfers and food stamp cards for about 200,000" people in New Jersey, a state senator noted the irony of having a customer service center in Mumbai, India dealing with unemployed Americans. As a result,

eFunds is building a call center in Camden, N.J., at the request of the Department of Human Service's Division of Family Development . . . [A]s a result of changes in the contract, costs incurred by the state will increase about 20 percent . . . this works out to additional costs of about $8.6 million per year, and that figure could increase.[73]

A cover story of *Time*—"Is Your Job Going Abroad?"—underscores the widespread concerns around job loss. Although many jobs have moved offshore, statistics suggest more jobs have been created domestically: "A recent study commissioned by the Information Technology Association of America found that the offshoring of IT services and software led to the creation of 90,000 U.S. jobs last year."[74] These additional points are worth noting:

1. "High-tech hardware would have been 20 percent more expensive in the 1990s if not for offshoring. This spurred investment in more high-tech gear, boosting productivity and freeing up cash to plow into still more innovation. Plus, for every dollar spent on offshoring, the U.S. gets back $1.12 (and the global economy reaps another 33 cents.)"[75]

2. Department of Labor statistics indicate that large layoffs (of 50 people or more) are occurring at about the same rate during the past five

---

[70] As one example, this article describes the immediate closing of visa assistance offices, against the strong wishes of U.S. government officials: China Shuts Help Center for U.S. Visas, by Phelim Kyne, April 28, 2004, *The Wall Street Journal*. Accessed through Factiva 4/29/04.

[71] Scott Thurm, Tough Shift—Lesson in India: Not Every Job Translates Overseas—ValiCert Learned Key Roles Must Remain in U.S. for Outsourcing to Work—E-Mails Across 14 Time Zones, March 3, 2004, *The Wall Street Journal*.

[72] Karen Breslau, Valley of Power; Like Hollywood, Northern California's tech corridor is a hot spot of politics—and money. Some movers and shakers. March 29, 2004, *Newsweek*.

[73] Saving jobs, raising costs, Marc Ferranti, IDG News Service, April 28, 2003. Accessed http://www.computer-world.com on March 3, 2004.

[74] Kerry A. Dolan with David Whelan, The Great Offshore Wimp-Out; The offshoring story has two sides. Guess which one Lou Dobbs wants to talk about? April 26, 2004, *Forbes*, Volume 173 Issue 9. Date accessed on Factiva, April 30, 2004.

[75] Kerry A. Dolan and Robyn Meredith, A Tale of Two Cities; From techie to truck driver in Silicon Valley. From tea broker to techie in Bangalore. The two sides of offshoring, April 12, 2004, *Forbes*. From Factiva, April 1, 2004.

years, as during the mid- to late 1990s (prior to the outsourcing boom.)[76]

Fearing a backlash, many companies will not allow their name to be identified as a customer on Web sites and in brochures of offshoring businesses. One company allows the customer to choose whom they would speak with—a call center person from the United States or from India. The customer is informed that service from India may lead to a quicker response, by as much as two days.[77] It may be this kind of selectivity will not remain a necessity for long, as the customer benefits become clear and the outcomes viewed more positively, but for the time being it is all part of a complex political and societal debate.

The political debate around outsourcing is heated. In the 2004 race for president, outsourcing had been an important topic of debate.

Conclusion

Outsourcing is proving to be an important approach for dealing with time-to-market and cost pressures leading many companies to redefine how they deliver products and services. Planning for outsourcing needs to go well beyond just counting the cost of salaries involved.

Contracts need to factor in flexibility, staff transition plans, and cultural fit. In addition, it remains important to make ongoing arrangements for continued ownership and responsibility for the delivery and governance of the overall outsourcing operation. According to the former group IT director at Royal Mail, company resources must continue to lead the IT strategy[78] and manage the outsourcing agreement (this may cost 5 to 10 percent of the overall outsourcing budget).

Calculating the relative costs and benefits of offshoring is a complex equation. Labor rates around the world continue changing. A country's currency stability and political climate can have an impact—a rising rupee cuts into profits of Indian outsourcers. Competition will lead to new business processes and may increase or reduce the benefits of outsourcing.

The outsourcing landscape will remain dynamic and change dramatically in the years ahead as IT continues to help redefine the organization.

Outsourcing is essentially a modern day extension of the division of labor, and could have an impact no less than that described in Adam Smith's 1776 classic *Wealth of Nations:* "The greatest improvement in the productive powers of labour, and the greater part of the skill, dexterity, and judgment with which it is anywhere directed, or applied, seem to have been the effects of the division of labour."[79]

"Today, the division of labor is going global . . . We have been here before. In 1900, 40 percent of Americans worked on a farm, declining to 20 percent by 1940, and 5 percent by 1970."[80] Just as the division of labor and Frederick Taylor's process analysis played a large role in Henry Ford's transformation of manufacturing at the beginning of the twentieth century,[81] similar forces are at work as we begin the twenty-first century.

Outsourcing results from the interacting forces of IT, a global division of labor and the recognition of businesses as being comprised of well-defined processes. The continued advances in IT will ensure its important role in shaping how organizations are defined in the twenty-first century.

[76] Data Gap—Behind Outsourcing Debate: Surprisingly Few Hard Numbers—Counting Jobs Moving Abroad Is a Complicated Task; Benefits Are Less Tangible—One Report: 'A Little Wobbly', Jon E. Hilsenrath, April 12, 2004, *The Wall Street Journal.* (Factiva: 4/13/04)

[77] Jesse Drucker and Ken Brown, Press 1 for Delhi, 2 for Dallas—Latest Wrinkle in Jobs Fight: Letting Customers Choose Where Their Work Is Done, March 9, 2004, *The Wall Street Journal.*

[78] Management Week—Outsourcing Interview—Tips for better outsourcing. By Madeline Bennett, April 26, 2004, VNUnet. Date accessed on Factiva, April 29, 2004.

[79] Adam Smith, *Wealth of nations, Inquiry into the nature and causes of the wealth of nations* (Buffalo, NY : Prometheus Books, 1991), p. 9.

[80] Tim Kane, The New Economy recovers, April 11, 2004, *The San Diego Union—Tribune.* Accessed through Factiva April 27, 2004.

[81] Division of labor, interchangeable parts, continuous flow, and reducing wasted effort were cornerstones of the Ford manufacturing process, as described at http://world-information.org/wio/infostructure. Accessed on April 27, 2004.

CONCLUSION

The Challenges of Managing in a Network Economy Revisited

Prediction is hard, especially of the future.

Yogi Berra, Hall of Fame baseball player and manager

In 1943, Thomas Watson, the venerable chairman of the IBM Corporation, predicted that there would be a world market for "maybe five computers." Today there are hundreds of millions of computers worldwide. The magnitude of the error in this "expert's" forecast stands as a reminder that it is difficult to see far into the future. A quick glance backward reinforces the point. In 1992, there were no Web browsers. Before 1995 Amazon.com was but a glimmer in Jeff Bezos's eye. Much has changed very quickly, and nothing has happened to suggest that the IT industry is on the verge of slowing down its pace of evolution and change. There is surely more excitement ahead.

The objective of this book has been to provide its readers with a better understanding of the influence of twenty-first-century technologies on executive decisions. While this kind of understanding may help sharpen our predictions, our aim has not been to arm you to engage in future thinking for prediction's sake alone. Instead, we have focused on providing analytic frameworks and an overview of the issues involved in using those frameworks to identify opportunities, design and deploy new technology-based businesses, and create business value in the Network Economy. These frameworks are based on concepts and theory that have withstood the test of time and remain relevant despite radical changes in the business and technology environment. We have dealt with enduring practical questions from the point of view of the executives who are grappling with them. Not long ago, many predicted the death of traditional economic and management principles. The subsequent fall in technology market stocks suggests that we should not be too quick to throw out fundamental management principles as we embrace the new.

Markets and models, capabilities and organization, networked infrastructure and operations, and leadership of the IT organization are core subject areas that can be used to organize the management issues discussed in this book. Within these subject areas we explored the following key themes:

1. The continuous pace of technology evolution requires that we confront new choices for designing and building industries, markets, and organizations.

2. The business models that dominated the Industrial Economy are evolving to take advantage of the new technologies and business practices of the Network Economy, giving rise to new sources of power and differentiation.

3. The types of opportunities pursued and the technology employed strongly influence the approach to developing, operating, and managing IT.

4. As IT infrastructure becomes more standardized, modular, and scalable, we are seeing a shift in IT investment priorities and decisions from a cost-avoidance, project-centered approach to an asset-based, strategic option approach.

5. The time required for successful organization learning and assimilation of rapidly changing technologies limits the practical speed of change.

6. External industry, internal organizational, and technological changes are increasing the pressure on organizations to buy rather than make IT applications and services.

7. The ability to exploit twenty-first-century technology demands high levels of engagement and cooperation among four key constituencies: Business executives, IT executives, users, and technology providers/partners.

8. The ability to ensure high levels of security, privacy, reliability, and availability is a core capability that determines an organization's ultimate success and survival.

9. Over the last decade there has been a fundamental shift in IT that has dramatically changed the way people access and use technology, the way organizations exploit it, and the way it is developed and managed.

As we have demonstrated, the effect of the new technologies on markets and industries will be to alter competitive positions and frame new strategic imperatives that require new capabilities. The new technologies have enabled new business models and improved the viability of old ones; executives in established firms that do not seize the opportunities presented by new technologies will find their market positions threatened.

New networked infrastructures interweave complex business-technical issues that general managers dread but that ultimately make the difference between a rigid and constraining IT capability and a flexible and dynamic one. These infrastructures come with many layers of relationships, technology models, and risk management processes that ultimately determine the IT possibilities that dramatically affect the ability to compete today and the business opportunities that can be pursued in the future. Finally, there are the challenges of executing technology-based strategic initiatives, an area that many companies cannot seem to master. The projects grow larger and harder, and decisions must be made ever more quickly. Most executives express concern that this relentless pace of change is occurring much too fast to enable them (and their organizations) to learn. Yet this is an area that must be mastered if disasters are to be averted and returns are to be realized from IT investments.

We conclude this book with two integrative cases that enable an analysis of issues discussed throughout the book.

UCB: Managing Information for Globalization and Innovation (A)

UCB is a Belgian chemical and pharmaceutical company and a midsized player in an industry of global giants. The case explores the IT initiatives and challenges facing executives as they struggle to develop a practical IT development portfolio and reliable IT operations in a resource constrained world. This is a holistic IT strategy and operations case that can be viewed from the perspective of both the CEO and CIO.

Enabling Business Strategy with IT at the World Bank

This case provides an overview of IT management in a global institution, which has transformed its IT strategy in the past five years and is pursuing numerous new initiatives. Operating in 109 offices, the World Bank, through a satellite-enabled system, delivers highly sophisticated knowledge management data to some of the poorest parts of the world. The case raises very important issues about the dimensions of the digital divide between rich and poor countries and provides for an in-depth discussion on the issues involved in a turnaround IT organization.

As you review these final cases, consider the many opportunities and challenges that confronted these executives and the approaches they used to address them. How can you address the same challenges as you lead your organization in the turbulent yet exciting and energizing Network Economy? We hope you have gotten useful guidance from the frameworks and ideas presented in this book, and we wish you success.

Case C-1

UCB: Managing Information for Globalization and Innovation (A) (Abridged)

In October 2002, Vincent Damien was updating the IT/IS plan for 130 subsidiaries and 10,000 employees of UCB spanning three sectors: Chemicals, Films, and Pharma. UCB had just completed an analysts' meeting, maintaining a 10 percent growth projection for profit before tax and exceptional items. Pharma business remained strong, led by its fast-growing drug Zyrtec. Films opened a new R&D facility in August but was in the midst of a price war, and Chemicals was completing an acquisition while benefiting from strong margin improvements. Despite the good news, the stock price had been trading at its lowest level since January 1998. (Refer to Exhibit 1 for a description of recent business developments.)

Damien faced the challenge of bringing the IT/IS plan in line with the overall business plan. As Damien prepared for his budget meeting for the members of the executive committee[1], he contemplated:

1. Are cost and service enhancement opportunities being appropriately addressed throughout UCB's supply chain?
2. Was the company interface to the customer appropriate for its industry in 2002? Were customers being fully supported with appropriate information, ordering capabilities, and services?

This case was prepared by Professor F. Warren McFarlan and Research Associate Brian DeLacey. Copyright © 2004 President and Fellows of Harvard College. Harvard Business School Case No. 304-096.

[1] Executive committee members include Georges Jacobs (chairman), Edouard Croufer (director-general, pharmaceutical sector), William Lowther (director-general, films sector), and Ben Van Assche (director-general, chemical sector).

3. Did systems give UCB information to react at least as fast as competitors to new challenges? (This was important given the role of innovation, speed, and flexibility in UCB's success.)
4. Were the costs of software maintenance and upgrades being driven down? Was the computing capacity being efficiently utilized?
5. Were the right priorities being set for the numerous demands on the IT/IS budget? Which projects should be the central focus? Was the priority setting process adequate?
6. Was UCB appropriately organized to address the varied geographic and organizational demands being placed on the information architecture of the company?

Vincent Damien: Administrative and IT Director

Vincent Damien graduated with a degree in applied economics and European studies from the University of Louvain. Damien joined UCB in May 1991 as a corporate auditor. In January 1993, he was appointed management controller of Pharma, where he experienced firsthand how operations and business groups depended upon information technology. In 1996, Damien assumed responsibilities for Pharma MIS where he saw significant need for improvement in the way information technology/information systems (IT/IS) was managed. At that time, there were no standards between any of UCB's three operating sectors which, Damien felt, led to tremendous redundancy, inconsistency, and inefficiency.

In 1997, Damien was given responsibility for central services across Belgium, including coordination of human resource matters common to the various Belgian sites. He also took on information technology (IT) infrastructure at the corporate level.

EXHIBIT 1   Recent Business Developments

Source: UCB, "Statement by the Chairmen—2001," http://www.ucb-group.com/corp/default.htm, accessed November 18, 2002.

For the eighth consecutive year, the growth in the ordinary profits before taxation of the UCB Group was above 20 percent. In 2001, this growth was 25 percent.

The Pharma Sector continued to expand in the two therapeutic fields it has chosen: Allergy and neurology. The successive launches of Keppra (United States and Europe) and of Xysal (Europe), together with the arrival of Zyrtec-D (United States), all resulting from UCB's own research, have just completed the range of the main medicines of the Group in the world. Sales of Keppra exceeded expectations and confirmed the excellent reception, from which this new medicine has benefited.

The success of the strategy of innovation and expansion worldwide of the Pharma Sector can be measured by the following elements: An average growth rate in sales amounting over the last five years to more than 20 percent and a profit margin of 28 percent.

In the field of allergy, the performance of Zyrtec has been excellent . . .

In neurology, the turnover of the new anti-epileptic Keppra reached €96 million in the United States in its first full year of being marketed there . . .

In the Chemical Sector, sales only fell by 2 percent, despite the difficult economic climate faced during 2001. Margins were below the level of the previous year . . .

Sales in the Film Sector increased slightly. The profits were affected by the less favorable climate and by the losses suffered on Cellophane in the United States . . .

The ordinary profits before taxation for the whole Group exceeded expectations; they reached €462 million, compared to €370 million in 2000, an increase of 25 percent . . .

The prospects for 2002 are good . . . To support the ambitious projects, which it has for the three sectors, the board of directors approved last December a programme of R&D and investments of €434 million for 2002. The research programme is growing by 16 percent.

Georges Jacobs, Chairman of the Executive Committee and Mark Eyskens, Chairman of the Board of Directors.

Damien also coordinated the successful finalization of UCB's stunning new headquarters in Belgium—a critical corporate project. Upon completion of the new offices, Damien oversaw the relocation of all people and equipment into the new headquarters.

In 1998, Damien became administrative and group IT director, reporting directly to Georges Jacobs, chairman of the executive committee. In addition to IT, Damien was responsible for the follow-up of UCB's investments[2] and all issues related to site management of the new headquarters. From 1999, Damien added responsibility for

all information systems (IS). In 2000, Damien's title changed to administrative and IT/IS director of the UCB Group. Along the way, Damien took on responsibility for headquarters' site management in Brussels. By the end of 2000, Damien had become a member of the senior management team for the 10,000-person company. (See Exhibit 2, describing the organization of UCB SA.)

Damien saw enormous corporate growth during his 10 years at UCB: By the end of 2001, the UCB Group had eight consecutive years of profits before tax of at least 20 percent—with a 25 percent increase to sales for 2001[3] (see Exhibit 3 for a financial summary of UCB).

[2] By means of a global capital asset allocation system developed by Damien's team; a capital asset expenditure request can be approved within a few minutes by 10 people or more spread all over the world via a Web interface application.

[3] Revenue in 2001 exceeded $2B for the first time. One euro (€) was worth approximately $0.884.

EXHIBIT 2
Organization of UCB SA

Source: Adapted from interviews and http://www.ucb-group.com, accessed October 16, 2002.

Executive Committee

Georges Jacobs	Chairman
Edouard Croufer	Director-General Pharma Sector
William Lowther	Director-General Film Sector
Ben Van Assche	Director-General Chemical Sector

Central Services

Vincent Damien	Director Administration & IT
Jean-Pierre Pradier	Director Corporate Human Resources
Jettie Van Caenegem	Director Legal Affairs & Intellectual Property
Marc Wiers	Finances, Adviser to the Executive Committee

Pharma Sector

Edouard Croufer	Director-General
Thomas Beck	Director R&D
Simon Looman	Director Europe
Bruno Strigini	Director Asia
Anthony Tebbutt	Director USA and Canada
Werner De Prycker	Director Global Technical Operations
Gerd Johnscher	Director Medical & Regulatory Affairs

Chemical Sector

Ben Van Assche	Director-General
Jan Vandendriessche	Director Research & Technology
Frank Aranzana	Director Specialties
Pol Vanderhaeghen	Director Methylamines and Derivatives
Frank Coenen	Director Asia
André Jordens	Director Europe
Richard Kemmerer	Director Americas

The Company[4]

The UCB Group was one of the largest concerns in Belgium. Formed under the name of Union Chimique Belge in January 1928, it had since grown by acquisition of other companies. One of these had been the owner of the oldest chemical factory in Belgium, which had been built in the 18th century on a site at Drogenbos (which was still occupied by Chemicals).

UCB prided itself on its flexibility and ability to adapt. "Speed of action" was a key theme when it came to developing a new information system

[4] Description of the company and its sectors is adapted from http://www.ucb-group.com.

(the intranet, e-mail and PeopleSoft all took less than a year to implement) or acquiring a company (some taking as short as 30 days from concept to close). There was an air of practicality about the company, looking for "quick wins" and clearly identifiable business value in all that it did.

The Group employed more than 10,000 people, of whom half were in Pharma and the rest in Chemicals and Films. More than one-third worked in Belgium—which was home to several key production sites as well as general management of the three sectors, and the major R&D center in the pharmaceutical (Braine) and chemical (Drogenbos) fields. (R&D for Films was located in Wigton, Great Britain and another R&D group for Pharma was in Cambridge, Massachusetts in the United States.)

EXHIBIT 3   Financial Summary of UCB Group (in million euros and dollars*)

Source: UCB.

	1999 €	2000 €	2001 €	2001 $	2000 to 2001
Group turnover	€1,842	€2,204	€2,475	$2,188	12%
Capital expenditure during the year	106	177	194	171	10%
R&D expenditure	173	182	218	193	20%
Personnel employed at December 31	9,214	9,910	10,013		1%

Exchange rate used on 31.12.2001: 1€ = 0.884 $.
*http://www.ucb-group.com/corp/reports/2001/#nb.

Consolidated Turnover by Sector (in million euros) Sector	2000 €	2001 €	Increase (%)
Pharma	€1,149	€1,427	+24%
Chemical	664	652	−2%
Film	391	396	+1%

Group Research Expenditure (in million euros)

	2000 €	Percent Total Expenditure	Percent of Turnover	2001 €	Percent of Total Expenditure	Percent of Turnover
Pharma	€139	76%	12%	€168	77%	12%
Chemical	31	17	5	35	16	5
Film	12	7	3	15	7	4

UCB planned to grow by leveraging their research-based activities and acquiring companies where it made sense. UCB eventually sold their mature €187M Methylamines and Derivatives business in September 2003; two small acquisitions were finalized in 2002[5] and some major other ones were under discussion.

UCB Films

Films was a global business dedicated to developing specialty and high-performance film for selected markets including the food and bever-

ages, labels, security products, industrial membranes, health, and pharmaceutical industries. Films had €396 million in sales in 2001 and spent €15 million on research, both slightly ahead of the prior year.

UCB Chemicals

Chemicals developed, manufactured, and marketed specialty chemicals with a high added value. This sector generated "about 40 percent of its sales from Radcure resins—resins that are cured by radiation as opposed to heat in order to polymerize or harden. Chemicals' Radcure resins, sold under the Ebecryl brand, are used in inks, coatings, and powder paints. The company also produced polyester resins (under the Crylcoat name), and acrylic resins (under the Ucecryl, Ucefix, and

---

[5] UCB's Chemical Sector acquired a small specialty chemical company in Korea. UCB Pharma acquired the technology and intellectual property of a pre-clinical anti-cough program from a company in Canada.

Solucryl brands). Roughly half of Chemicals' sales come from Europe; about 30 percent come from the Americas."[6] With Radcure, UCB was a world leader with 35 percent of the market. Chemicals had a small number of customers—a few hundred for Radcure products, about 20 for Powders, and about 20 for Adhesives.

The corporate strategy was to integrate UCB Films and Chemicals activities into a new sector known as **Surface Specialties** by June 2003, with sales of €677 million.

UCB Pharma

Pharma concentrated on products and research in the respiratory (cough, allergy, and asthma) and neurology areas. Pharma's principal products included Zyrtec (with €1.7 billion of sales worldwide, this fast-growing antihistamine was also approaching blockbuster revenues in the United States in a copromotion relationship with Pfizer Inc.), Keppra (anti-epileptic), Nootropil (cerebral function regulator), and Atarax (tranquilizer).

UCB's strategy was to be present in the three major world pharmaceutical markets: Europe, the United States, and Japan. World sales of Pharma amounted to €1,427 million, compared with €1,149 million in 2000, an increase of 24 percent. The increase was 17 percent in Asia-Pacific and 50 percent in America. The main drivers of growth were Zyrtec and the new anti-epileptic drug Keppra. A profitable subsidiary of Pharma, UCB-Bioproducts, was the global leader in peptide[7] contract manufacturing services in Belgium and the United States used by leading pharmaceutical and biotechnology companies.

Pharma had its own sales forces in Europe and the United States, in addition to a very strong marketing relationship with Pfizer in the United States. Pfizer reported U.S. sales increases for Zyrtec from $699 million in 2000 to $1.1 billion in 2002. U.S. Zyrtec sales grew 25 percent to $347 million in the third quarter of 2003, compared to

the same period in 2002 (with 2003 year-to-date turnover of $980 million).

Pharma R&D employed approximately 750 people throughout the world, with 380 in research and 370 in development. The R&D staff was geographically distributed: 590 were based in Europe (primarily in Belgium), 130 in the United States (Cambridge, Massachusetts, and Atlanta, Georgia), and 30 in Japan. The company built its R&D organization through acquisition and internal growth (historically this has been in Braine, Belgium.) (Exhibit 4 provides a breakdown of Pharma Sector finances.)

Evolution of Damien's IT/IS Organization

The graphic timeline in Exhibit 5 depicts some of the major IT/IS milestones from 1997 to 2002. Damien created and retained a longstanding distinction between IT and IS:

The role of *information technology operations* (IT) was:

- To develop, manage, operate, and support the information technology infrastructure, including communication networks, computer hardware and software, as well as the central help desk. For IT, Damien wanted "to establish an efficient, robust, and strong motorway" of information that would help support business processes, improve end users productivity, and facilitate management decision with a view to transforming the business.

The role of *information systems development* (IS) was:

- To understand, with the business users, the business requirements and priorities;
- To develop, implement, maintain, and support the information systems (applications) to meet the business requirements.

Damien established global IT/IS standards:

1. To share experience and develop synergies across the Group.

---

[6] Hoovers profile of UCB Chemicals.

[7] Peptides are active ingredients in new medicines.

EXHIBIT 4 Pharma Sector Finances (in euros million)

Source: UCB.

		1999 €	2000 €	2001 €
Consolidated turnover		€ 903	€1,149	€1,427
Operating profit (EBITDA)		381	444	614
Depreciation		−162	−160	−200
Operating profit (EBIT)		€ 219	€ 284	€ 414
Net financial charges		−10	−10	−11
Profits before taxation	ORDINARY	209	274	403
	EXCEPTIONAL	8	15	8
	Total	217	289	411
Cash flow		179	283	353
Value Add	Remuneration	238	301	351
	Depreciation*	36	38	47
	Finance charges	10	10	11
Ordinary profit	Before taxation	209	274	403
		€493	€ 623	€ 812
Turnover per employee		0.19	0.22	0.24
Value added per employee		0.10	0.12	0.14
Capital expenditure		38	54	75
R&D expenditure		133	139	168
ROCE		40	42	53
Numbers employed at December 31		4,895	5,603	6,047

*Not including depreciation on R&D costs, http://www.ucb-group.com/corp/reports/2001/#nb.

2. To reduce heterogeneity, inconsistencies, and hidden costs.

3. To improve communication and cost effectiveness.

4. This global vision concerns the infrastructure, hardware, software, and communications.

Prior to 1996 all IT/IS activities were independently initiated from within the three main business areas—Film, Chemical, Pharmaceutical—which are referred to as *sectors*. Historically, there had been no central IT planning function. Each sector and geography had hired their own staff to manage IT operations and IS development. After Damien's arrival, there was a consistent move towards a more coordinated effort, and gradually IT/IS staff all moved to report into Damien.

E-mail, Internet/Intranet

Damien's group experienced a high-visibility "quick win" when they implemented a single e-mail system during 1997 and 1998. One of Damien's team members, Philippe Baudoux, "spent six months of the year flying with a mail server as carry-on luggage" installing Exchange mail at every UCB location. Baudoux installed e-mail in 65 countries in just 4 months time. (Prior to this, there had been different e-mail projects in process.)

Standardized Desktop Environment

In 1997, soon after establishing a central IT/IS organization, Damien looked for opportunities to improve the level of information services while also finding cost savings across all the geographies

EXHIBIT 5   **Major IT/IS Milestones (1997–2002)**

Source: UCB.

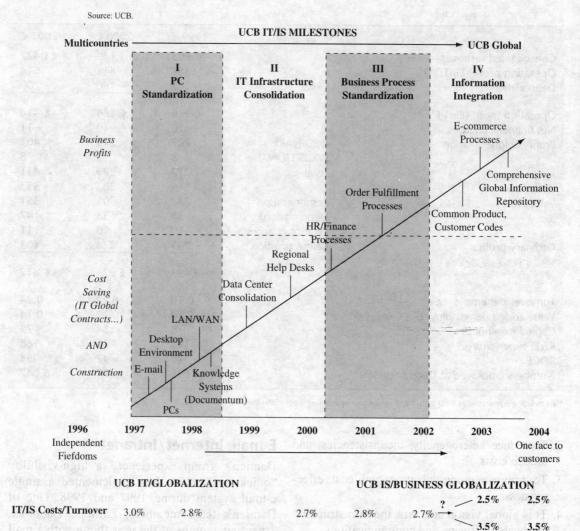

and sectors of the business. Damien saw standardization critical to benefiting the cost of acquisition as well as ongoing maintenance, support, and interoperability.

With the support of the executive committee, Damien focused considerable efforts on the implementation of companywide standard hardware and software systems (e.g., Compaq for desktop PCs—with laptops for sales representatives and business travelers, Microsoft Office for desktop productivity,

NT 4 for the operating system,[8] and Oracle for database applications). Damien's IT/IS budget had been given funds for sectors to upgrade hardware and systems to meet these standards across the company.

[8] Microsoft Office '97 and NT 4 running on Compaq remained the standard for five years avoiding expensive interim upgrades. Only recently had Damien's group begun looking at moving to newer versions of software and alternate PC vendors.

Contract Savings

Damien promoted Michel Hautfenne, a long-time colleague from Pharma, as Group IT/IS contracts manager. Hautfenne systematically went through each area of technology in search of cost efficiencies. By 1999, Hautfenne had squeezed €2.7 million *annual* savings from the budget. He consolidated smaller, individual purchases that had previously been made by the sectors and negotiated them at the group level. Hautfenne also tactfully created competitions among vendors (e.g., Compaq was selected as the PC provider, over strong competition from others), now that he had much greater leverage for savings at the group level.

Hautfenne added *one-time* savings of another €5.5 million by renegotiating contracts already in place for voice and data telecommunications as well as high-priced application software in wide use throughout UCB.

Damien described a recent success in the "globalization" of contract negotiations: "When we began talking about negotiating a large software contract for Braine and Cambridge R&D, there was initial concern because the teams had previously negotiated the contract by themselves. However, we're just about to conclude negotiations at the UCB group level and we're looking at a €2.5 million savings that will include a closer working partnership with the software vendor."

The New Data Center

Damien began his push for a new state-of-the-art data center with the construction of a lights-out central computer room in 1999. His goal was to replace the antique system that was in place.

The new computer room was truly a data fortress, constructed below ground with special consideration for maximum physical and data security. Network and electricity were fully redundant, and key servers were mirrored, providing data integrity in the event of a catastrophic failure. The new facility and data center became the hub of the UCB global network.

Close to 300 servers ran production applications from all sectors and all geographies. Staff rarely needed to access the computer room except to give a visitor tour; even backups were handled automatically by a new robot-driven system. Server operations and monitoring were outsourced—managed remotely from a distance of several miles away from the nearest UCB facility.

Annie Antoine—site IT manager at Braine—had worked for 11 years at UCB (she originally joined UCB to work at the help desk). Antoine was responsible for the new data center as well as IT support for the 2,000-person Braine campus, which consisted primarily of R&D and manufacturing workers. The campus had 2,156 PCs, 725 printers, and 120 databases (mostly Oracle). Antoine's staff consisted of 40 people, 30 percent were UCB employees and 70 percent were external contractors. Antoine and her group reported into Damien through the regional operations (shown in Exhibit 6).

Numerous servers, which previously were spread across all corners of UCB facilities, were moved into the new facility but no consolidation of applications and servers took place. Historically, the rule-of-thumb had been one new server for each application that came on line. However, except for HP critical UNIX systems, no systematic monitoring or analysis of CPU utilization was done. Consequently, it wasn't clear how much computer capacity UCB actually had, nor was it clear how much of the available capacity was being utilized, except also for HP critical UNIX systems.

Overall, the nature of the UCB's operations at Braine was such that a 24-hour downtime would not be a disabling event—if the network would go down for 24 hours, it would be an irritating but not an end-of-the-world event. Still, key backup was needed and existed just a short distance away. The original computer room, on the second floor of an aging, stone farm building, was located 1.5 kilometers from the new data center, on the far side of the Braine campus. Test and development computers still hummed away in the high-tech, reinforced floors of the old building. These systems served as backup and were connected by fiber optic cable to the new data center.

From farm to fortress, UCB had made clear progress with operational support.

EXHIBIT 6 UCB IT/IS

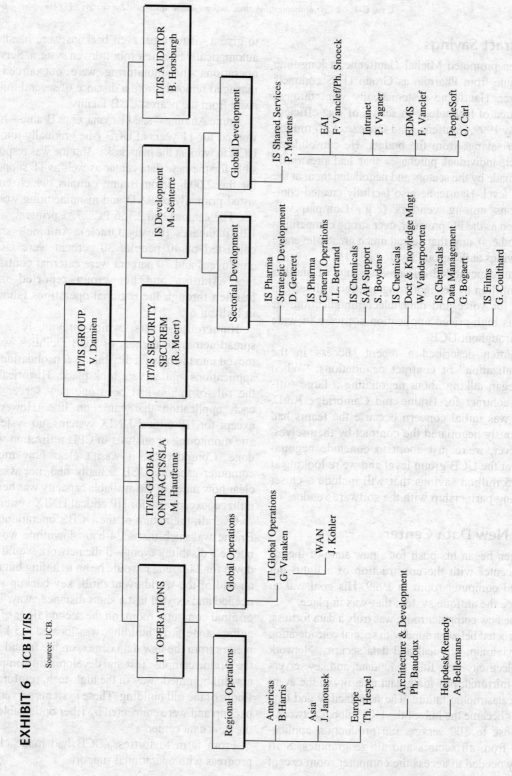

Source: UCB.

602

Help Desk Support

Anne Bellemans, manager of the help desk for UCB Belgium, had been with the company 10 years. She reported in through the regional operations (as shown in Exhibit 6). Prior to UCB she had worked as a sales representative before taking time off to raise children. She returned to the workforce to join UCB in customer support. She soon began working on a centralized database system to help track calls into the center.

By 2002, the help desk supported 200 applications—some of these were crucial applications with as few as five users, while others were corporatewide applications (e.g., Outlook). In addition to knowledge of many applications, call center staff needed to speak multiple languages. A typical call center in Europe provided support in 7 to 10 spoken languages. (In Belgium, it was common to find individuals who were fluent in speaking three languages.)

The help desk began in 1993, with paper, pencil, and only one person covering half of the Braine site (600 clients) with only one language spoken. In 1998 the Belgian help desk employed six people, covering five sites, 2,800 clients, with two spoken languages, French and Dutch. Soon after, there was a rapid regional expansion—leveraging the Remedy software system that was in use and rolling it out to different geographies.

The help desk was so successful they were seeing increasing demands for more novel applications—for instance, it was used to track computer assets and software licenses. Chemicals were interested in using the technology, and possibly even the support people, to assist in providing technical product assistance to customers. The group was disciplined in obtaining feedback from their clients and adjusting services to better meet customer needs.

One of the challenges Bellemans faced was staff turnover, since many people on her team had moved on to other good jobs in the company: "We use the help desk as a trampoline; it is a place where people can get started at UCB but, to stay professionally challenged they need to move into another job after two or three years."

Human Resources

In the early stages of planning for systems support of human resources, some staff argued strongly that the existing SAP installation should be extended to provide the needed functionality. On the one hand, extending the use of SAP for this purpose could have helped to solidify a "privileged partnership" with the vendor, but Damien's team concluded that the functionality of PeopleSoft better met the company's needs.

The implementation of PeopleSoft across the globe moved forward with strong support from managers and executives in the human resources area. The initial modules were implemented to track and record personnel information in addition to providing a system for managing the annual employee review process.

A new director of corporate human resources was hired in 1997, at the same time as Damien took additional responsibilities in IT/IS at corporate level, and pledged strong support for Damien's IT/IS initiatives. The implementation of PeopleSoft took a year and a half but the full benefit of the package was accelerated when Amy Barrett, from UCB's Atlanta office joined the HR team in Belgium. Barrett managed the successful implementation of PeopleSoft in UCB's Atlanta office. She then joined the central HR staff in Belgium to support and roll out the system across the company. Barrett and the IS PeopleSoft team spent the next six months flying to every location and providing personalized instruction on how to use the system.

In 2002, building on the success of the implementation, human resources added an "eRecruiting" module to assist with recruiting over the Web.

Security

There were basic guidelines for e-mail usage in place, which had been endorsed by UCB's legal affairs department. Rudy Meert, who advised the UCB Group on IT/IS security matters since September 2000, established information security policies to put in place across the global enterprise. Meert felt that: "Eighty percent of bad security is due to bad practices. Security is not just a technical solution. It takes organizational management and awareness with a systematic approach. Just one person out of 10,000 can compromise the security of the firm by nonrespecting our policy." Opening the network to the outside, for e-commerce or to give customers and partners extended access to internal information sources, requires appropriate security.

Organization

Damien's management team was quite young; it had been developed through carefully planned rotations among the different IT units in the company, which served to keep people challenged and refreshed. By 2002, Damien's organization (as described in Exhibit 6) had grown to a headcount of 368 people; half this number was accounted for by outsourced contracts. (For selected projects, which were well-defined and clearly specified in advance, such as the development of their corporate Web sites, Damien hired contractors in India. Damien believed the contractors from India developed very high quality software at a fraction of the cost than he would have paid anywhere else.)

Damien's direct reports (as shown in Exhibit 6) were responsible for IT operations, IT/IS global contracts/service level agreements (SLA), IT/IS security, IS projects, and IT/IS auditing. Most of Damien's direct reports and senior managers had longevity with the company of 12 years or more. Many had come from operational roles in the three main sectors prior to joining IT/IS. Thus, they had working familiarity with both the people and the processes in the various parts of the company. Their teams, in turn, were largely comprised of "young" people (e.g., the IS group that supported Pharma had 42 people, where 75 percent were under 35 and 25 percent were 35 years or older).

IT Operations

IT Operations split into **regional and global operations. Regional IT** staff was located around the world (such as Atlanta providing support for the Americas and Malaysia for Asia): They reported directly to Damien and in a dotted-line fashion to the country business manager. **Global operations** staff concentrated on infrastructure (such as the WAN and corporate network standards), which applied to all sectors and regions.

The regional IT operations performed an essential job facilitating the use of corporate standards when appropriate in geographically remote divisions. In addition to the local needs of various business groups, they also had to deal with variations in the technology environment around them, such as the access to the Internet.

The individuals leading these regional operations were a combination of leading-edge technology consultants and leading-edge standards implementers. One concern was that the career paths of these individuals be carefully managed, as in other organizations, these have been high burnout jobs. Jiri Janousek, regional IT/IS manager, Asia Pacific, was based in Malaysia. Janousek described his job this way:

> I'm somebody to complain to, I am a liaison. I know everybody in Belgium, so I am a helper. I am always on call. One time, when I was attending a group IT/IS meeting in Belgium, the general manager from China called me just after I arrived. He had a problem and needed help: "You have a ticket," he told me, "fly back now." In Asia, there are a large number of IT/IS people who effectively work for the GM there—even though they are counted in Vincent's headcount. In Asia, the GMs are bosses. The two other regional IT managers (Brian Harris for the Americas and Thierry Hespel for Europe) have just like Janousek the sense for self-abnegation and were driven by one fixed idea: How can I help my customers.

Janousek was responsible for UCB in Shanghai. When he arrived in 2001, they had 80 computers—which could only run two applications and were constantly crashing. It was continual rebooting. Janousek found funding and initiated a project to replace 79 out of the 80 computers with modern systems—at the same time he upgraded them to Windows XP as a prototype for the next generation standardized desktop. It took six months, running from the end of 2001 into 2002. When this project was done, the crashes were a problem of the past.

By 2002, there were 8,000 PCs, spread through Europe (5,736), Americas (1,418), and Asia (846).

EXHIBIT 7   Support for the Pharma Value Chain

Source: Casewriter compilation.

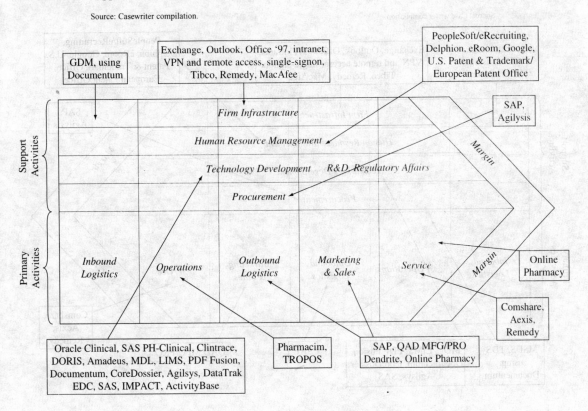

IS Development

The IS development fell under the leadership of Marc Senterre. The group was split into **global development** (e.g., developing and delivering technological solutions in use by all sectors and regions, such as PeopleSoft) and **sectorial development** (e.g., developing and delivering applications for specific sectors, such as knowledge management for Pharma).

Senterre's group had a high level of interaction with personnel in the various business groups. Senterre, who had been with UCB for 15 years, was responsible for a group of 42 people (75 percent under 35 years, 25 percent over 35 years). Pascale Martens reported to Senterre, and led IS global development with responsibility for shared services. Martens' past responsibilities included

the implementation of PeopleSoft; current projects included the corporate intranet and Web portal as well as the electronic document management system (EDMS), which was based on Documentum—a development environment that enabled "enterprise content management software solutions . . . to intelligently create and manage all types of content—documents, Web pages, XML files, and rich media—using one common content platform and repository."[9] EDMS was a critical system that would serve as the backbone of the knowledge management systems and PeopleSoft. (Exhibit 7 describes how the UCB application portfolio impacted various areas of the Pharmaceutical

[9] From http://www.documentum.com, accessed November 18, 2002.

EXHIBIT 8 **IS Support for Chemicals' Value Chain**

Source: Case writer compilation.

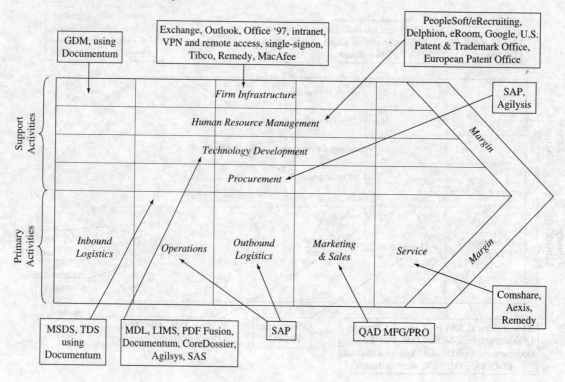

value chain. Exhibit 8 does the same for the Chemical business.)

Major IS Projects

The 3R Portal Project: Bringing the Right Information to the Right Person at the Right Time

The 3R project was designed to provide access to key information through a customizable, personalized Web portal. The 3R portal would gather internal and external information, giving transparent access. There were two key layers being planned: One was the corporate level of information (e.g., HR information) and the second was the sectorial and functional layer (e.g., including site-specific information relevant to specific job responsibilities).

This project required two new capabilities for the corporate network: One was a single username/password logon, where only one username and password was required for access to all network applications; second, was the ability to personalize a Web portal to deliver appropriate information based on the identity of each person who visited and deny access to inappropriate information.

The 3R implementation would give direct access to a personal view of the corporate portal—tailored to the specific username and password each individual used to log onto the system. Corporate "eFlashes," intranet and Internet links, as well as press releases, articles, job postings, PowerPoint presentations, and other content would be customized to the needs of the individual based upon their department, sector, and individual job responsibilities. In addition, this Web portal would be customizable by each individual user.

Martens' group had reviewed a beta release with a group of senior executives. Support for the beta release included a 50-page user manual, which was introduced with an intensive schedule of face-to-face training sessions. Early feedback indicated the system was too complicated to use. Damien observed, "This has been one of the most important, but hardest, projects. Quick wins have been hard to find. Chemicals is our first likely customer. We learned from prototyping that we must predesign the portal, rather than leaving it up to each individual to customize. We think of it as bringing to UCB staff 'the power of now'—and information from all the key systems as needed."

Knowledge Management

Dr. Martine Draguet and Frédéric Vanclef initiated UCB's first knowledge management project at the beginning of 1997, when they began working with Documentum to build a system that would store a large number of documents for regulatory affairs in Pharma. This area had recently become a critical area of investment for Damien's group.

In the past, 60 percent of all documents were in foreign languages, now all of them are in English. In the past, all documents were on paper, now almost all the critical documents are digital. A small group of staff members was dedicated to indexing (and sometimes translating—such as notes from physicians) the following: (1) UCB documents—all official reports and research analysis; (2) scientific quality published papers related to drug development initiatives—including competitor information, papers published; and (3) a formal record—of scientific quality—of in house research reports and findings.

"This has broad application, beyond just submissions," said Draguet, "the idea is to have a repository of all formal records." By the end of 1998, UCB's Knowledge Management system for regulatory affairs had robust security as well as an easy-to-use folder organization for storing and retrieving the 90,000 documents they had stored in the system. Knowledge was a significant source of value across the UCB businesses

Throughout the pharmaceutical industry, more money was being spent on the creation of knowledge than on the equipment used to produce the products developed from that knowledge. This was particularly important to Pharma, which was fundamentally a knowledge building process requiring the retention and continual application of knowledge spanning a number of years.[10] In addition, there were regulatory considerations: Laws related to pharmaceuticals, which varied somewhat by country, generally required companies to keep documents associated with a drug for the life of product plus five years.

Extended Enterprise for Chemicals

Ben Van Assche was a member of the executive committee and director-general of Chemicals. Van Assche had previously been responsible for Pharma, so he spoke from experience when he said: "Pharma and Chemicals have a number of things in common, in particular our focus and global vision for innovation, with an emphasis on coming up with new products and technologies." One manager described Chemicals much the way researchers would describe Pharma: "We have to be inventing molecules."

Van Assche was aware of some of the technologies offered by B2B exchanges and through e-commerce portals, but he still wasn't convinced of the value and benefits of this:

We haven't had much customer demand for purchasing and selling via extranets. Either my people in the U.S. can't feel the (customer) pressure or I don't hear it. If they were hearing it—in the U.S. for instance—I'd expect to have had more push from them. And the cost estimates are high for doing this. We are open to these ideas, but up to now I just haven't seen the cost/benefit payback.

---

[10] The drug development process needed to be supported on a global scale. For instance, "the world's leading drugmakers: Pfizer, AstraZeneca, Bristol-Myers Squibb, GlaxoSmithKline, Novartis, Abbott, Merck, and others are cutting costs by moving research or manufacturing" to India according to "As Economy Expands, India on 'Verge of Something Big'," *USA Today*, February 9, 2004. Accessed on Web, February 9, 2004.

Ideally, Chemicals would like to provide delivery information online but they had no system for fully tracking the shipment of orders. As Van Assche described it, "DHL and UPS work well for keeping track of shipments on small items. Bigger orders, which require shipment as partial truckloads and may be transferred onto multiple trucks during the delivery route, were virtually impossible to track at this time. UCB hadn't been able to find shippers who could track even the delivery status of their own contract shippers at each point in the delivery process.

SAP

SAP had proven difficult to standardize across the company. Initial SAP installations began in October 1996—and the team was successful installing six countries in 12 months. However, there were different versions in use across the Pharma and Surface Specialties sectors. Surface Specialties had five people working on SAP in Belgium, covering purchasing, production, materials management, quality, finance, and distribution.

Surface Specialties was to begin piloting "work at home" offices for sales representatives—with a pilot program for 20 people in the United States, France, and Germany. The hope was that some sales representatives could leave the office and work from home, allowing UCB to "redefine the size" of its regional sales offices. A technical stumbling block was the inability to electronically deliver all the needed customer information to sales representatives prior to making a visit. The sales process relied on many manual systems, and integrating data in from several sources. Van Assche described it this way: "Sales can't easily get profiles of customers. We need ways to get customer sales history—we need a CRM (customer relationship management) portal, a specific customer Web site driven from internal sources with all the customer's information. We don't want to risk information overload though."

The Need for Innovation in Chemicals IT/IS

Frank Aranzana, director of Chemicals Specialties, joined UCB in 1999 after 15 years of extensive and directly relevant experience with Dupont and Dow Chemical, where he had been a business and sales manager. He had extensive involvement with the global deployment of SAP R1, as well as an upgrade to R3. At UCB, Aranzana was responsible for €500 million of revenue in the Specialty Chemicals area. Recently, UCB had sold off one activity and acquired another company in their pursuit of driving Specialty Chemicals revenue above €1 billion by 2006. Explaining the rationale for their recent acquisition Aranzana emphasized, "Scale matters—we want to grow."

Aranzana wanted more information tools for managing all parts of the Chemicals business at UCB. Specifically, Aranzana was looking for business reporting assistance: Which product is making money? Which region is doing well? What does the P&L statement look like? What tools would help maximize the bottom-line? According to Aranzana, "Business was pushing for knowledge management. And we needed material safety data sheets, another issue with a different technical solution."

Transforming the Pharma Sales Force

Luc Vermeesch was a general manager for Pharma. He was responsible for 150 sales representatives in Belgium and Holland. Sales were split 70 percent wholesale and about 30 percent directly to hospitals. Sales representative visits were 10 percent at the pharmacy, 25 percent at the hospitals, and 65 percent directly at physicians' offices. The average rep profile was someone who had been with UCB for 11 years—UCB employees retire at 65 and many reps were close to 55; the average is 41.

All of the representatives worked from a virtual office, working from their homes and needing no dedicated office space to do their work. Still, as late as August 2001, their PCs were merely expensive typewriters. Increasingly, however, they were able to take advantage of the benefits of inventory management, data about doctor office visits, order entry, call planning, event scheduling (e.g., information sessions for physicians), and sharing information across teams of reps calling on the same physician ("We have six products, people learn very fast if they don't work together—they all get hurt."). Vermeesch had an ongoing e-mail exchange with reps—sending approximately 20 or 30 each week to his team of representatives (e.g., highlighting product updates and other market-related activity).

Pharmaceutical Research (Cambridge, Massachusetts)

UCB Pharma research took place in Belgium and the United States. Dr. Thomas Beck, president and director, global research and development, headed the group's activities; he split his time between the two locations. The research groups in Belgium and the United States were focused on different clinical areas but still maintained a high level of communication and transfer of information (e.g., descriptions of chemical compounds and results of laboratory tests were replicated between locations up to four times a day). Research collaboration between the sites was crucial to the successful launch of Keppra, a successful anti-epileptic drug approved by the FDA in November 1999.

Beck felt this information challenge from the day he arrived: "One of the missions when I joined was 'we need to know what we know' (e.g., database of chemicals we've made, gene analysis in the research lab, toxicology for the regulatory audit trail)." Beck also believed innovations in genomics[11] could help improve the drug discovery process.

Pharma Research Computing

Dr. Anna Toy-Palmer had worked with Beck for five years and managed four teams at the Cambridge lab. All of Toy-Palmer's teams made heavy use of computers in their work with molecular modeling, a global database of UCB chemical compounds, pharmacy (which dealt with the overall logistics of compounds), and structural chemistry (utilizing state-of-the-art nuclear magnetic resonance tools to better understand the structures of molecules). In the case of the molecular modeling team, which was staffed by PhDs in science and physical chemistry, the dependence was evident as Toy-Palmer described their work: "Our lab bench is a computer; we depend on the computers for our work."

Planning the 2003 Budget

Damien was just days away from his next 2003 budget planning discussion with the members of the executive committee. The business environment clearly had changed from the past eight years of unbroken growth in revenues and profitability. Pricing pressures were growing in Pharma while demand was rising for technology and applications to accelerate the drug discovery process. The entire chemical industry had "an extremely difficult year in 2001"—industry sales had risen by 5 percent over 2000 but net income had fallen by nearly two-thirds.[12] Firms saw 2001 ordinary profits fall by 61 percent, to €9 million, tracking a general reduction in worldwide industrial activity. Alignment between the business needs and IT/IS was key.

The 2002 IT/IS budget had been just under €71 million. Damien typically analyzed his budget by region, function, and sector. The 2002 Budget (in euros) was 55,522,346 for Europe; 11,466,963 for the Americas; and 3,706,936 for Asia. This was divided nearly evenly, with a third going to R&D, product development, finance/admin. The largest dollar total amount spent on IS was accounted for in Pharma, followed by Chemicals, and Films.[13]

---

[11] Genomics is "the study of genes and their function."

[12] Standard & Poor's Industry Surveys on Chemicals: Specialty, April 11, 2002, p. 1.

[13] There was no central accounting or finance system to track project or resource level expenditures, such as might be generated from a centralized purchasing system; so, Damien maintained his own.

IT, being primarily infrastructure, was allocated across the sectors based upon relative revenue; IS projects were fully accounted for by sector, except for global projects (e.g., human resources with PeopleSoft). Damien estimated 2002 funding was spent as follows:

IT/IS Budget 2002—Operating Expenses (in euros)

Source: UCB.

	IT	IS	Total	Turnover	% vs. Turnover
Pharma	24,022,514	26,943,717	50,966,231	1,501,137,739	3.40%
Chemicals	7,262,690	7,179,353	14,442,043	670,852,580	2.15%
Films	2,438,826	2,849,145	5,287,971	404,280,681	1.31%
Total	33,724,030	36,972,215	70,696,245	2,576,271,000	2.74%

Damien had changed a great deal about how the company operated. Over the span of this time, the IT/IS group had centrally delivered a robust set of high-value intranet services built around strong, able IT architecture standards, using highly viable mainstream suppliers. UCB had the foundational building blocks for a next generation knowledge management system built on top of Documentum. One area, however, where there had been little progress made was in the development of extranet, and e-commerce capabilities.

Damien had a long list of activities to choose from for inclusion in his 2003 budget plans:

1. The 3R Portal: Bringing the right information to the right person at the right time

EXHIBIT 9

2002 Group IT/IS Expenses: Split

Source: UCB.

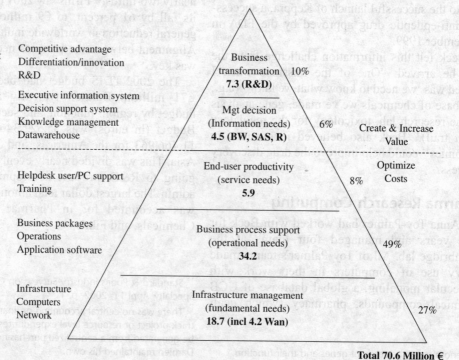

Competitive advantage
Differentiation/innovation
R&D

Executive information system
Decision support system
Knowledge management
Datawarehouse

Helpdesk user/PC support
Training

Business packages
Operations
Application software

Infrastructure
Computers
Network

Business transformation
7.3 (R&D) — 10%

Mgt decision (Information needs)
4.5 (BW, SAS, R) — 6% — Create & Increase Value

End-user productivity (service needs)
5.9 — 8% — Optimize Costs

Business process support (operational needs)
34.2 — 49%

Infrastructure management (fundamental needs)
18.7 (incl 4.2 Wan) — 27%

Total 70.6 Million €

2. Knowledge management

3. Extended enterprise for Chemicals

4. The need for innovation in Chemicals IT/IS

5. Transforming the Chemicals sales force and support

6. Transforming the Pharma sales force

7. Pharmaceutical research software management and computing

The Belgian character, some would say, is one of tremendous pragmatism and a determination to solve problems one by one. For projects in the 2003 budget plan, however, Damien felt there was a need for a longer-term commitment. Past projects had focused heavily on the part of the expense pyramid (see Exhibit 9) he called "optimize costs." In 2003, he felt more investment needed to be made in the "create & increase value" tip of the pyramid. It became essential for Damien to convince the meeting participants that the projects he

planned would bring improvements to help the business and that they weren't, as one executive questioned, simply "taking a cannon to kill a fly."

In the back of his mind, Damien worried, "What is the best role for a CIO in this heavily matrixed, diversified, global company?" Sector-specific applications had grown in number and cost, and their contribution to the business became ever more critical. Damien wanted to make recommendations to the members of the executive committee that would identify and prioritize key business solutions to help meet business and human resource needs.

Finally, as UCB became more active in acquisitions, a major question for IT/IS was: "How best can we integrate new satellite operations and offices? How shall we deal with the challenges of autonomy vs. globalization?" Damien believed that effective integration was essential to gain full advantage of smaller groups becoming part of the larger UCB group.

Case C-2

Enabling Business Strategy with IT at the World Bank

In the spring of 2003, CIO Mohamed Muhsin prepared for his annual review of information technology (IT) strategy and performance with the management committee of the World Bank (the Bank). The group of managing directors chaired by the president of the World Bank, James D. Wolfensohn, had set aside the day to discuss how IT could further enable the Bank's business.

As Muhsin contemplated the key topics for discussion, he gazed through the glass walls of his office at a 50-inch plasma display on the lobby wall. The screen flickered a steady stream of color-coded, real-time information relaying the status of all activities of the Bank's global IT infrastructure—clear evidence of the organization's reliance on 24×7 support for videoconferencing, enterprise applications, and Web services around the globe. Muhsin began to shape his presentation around the two key questions he would be addressing: Now that we have the foundation in place, how can IT help the core business serve our clients better? How do we measure and communicate the value that IT contributes to the business?

The CEO's Vision

When Wolfensohn arrived from the private sector as the new president of the World Bank Group in 1995, he took time to listen to staff, analyze the Bank's business, and especially to travel extensively visiting the Bank's clients. Within two years, he made a strategic compact with his board of directors to implement broad reforms based on what he observed to be two powerful trends:

The development business is undergoing dramatic change: surging private capital flows and declining support for official aid; greatly diversified sources of advice and technical assistance; and recognition of a broader development paradigm—with greater emphasis on local capacity and social, environmental, and governance dimensions.

At the same time, a powerful technological revolution is facilitating access to knowledge, a crucial factor for development. It is also having profound effects on how all organizations do business: more competitive, faster, flatter in their structures; more networked and eager to partner; and more learning-oriented, with knowledge recognized as a key driver of effectiveness.[1]

Wolfensohn's assessment was translated into a business strategy leveraging IT.

The IT Mission

Two fundamental shifts in business strategy took place:

1. *Decentralization.* Moving the Bank's business operations closer to the clients by decentralizing staff and decision making to local offices in more than 100 client countries.

2. *Creation of a knowledge bank.* Delivering more comprehensive and integrated (and therefore more effective) development solutions by increasing collaboration, consultation, and knowledge sharing both within the organization and with partners and stakeholders at all points in the development process—especially in the design stages to ensure buy-in and capacity for successful implementation.

Wolfensohn turned to his newly appointed CIO, Muhsin, and told him to revamp the information systems and build a global network. IT

This case was prepared by Professor F. Warren McFarlan and Research Associate Brian DeLacey. Copyright © 2003 President and Fellows of Harvard College. Harvard Business School Case No. 304-055.

[1] World Bank, "The Strategic Compact: Renewing the Bank's Effectiveness to Fight Poverty," February 13, 1997.

staff from around the Bank were consolidated into Muhsin's group. Their goal was to achieve two competing objectives:

1. Enable a global decentralized organization close to the customer.
2. Provide the collaborative tools and global development knowledge that would help the far-flung Bank staff and stakeholders work more closely and effectively than ever before to scale up the impact of the Bank's work.

Muhsin's responsibilities spanned the globe (see Exhibit 1 for a view of the Bank's global communications network). Wolfensohn then announced to his shareholders and the public:

> My goal is to make the World Bank the first port of call when people need knowledge about development. By the year 2000, we will have in place a global communications system with computer links, videoconferencing, and interactive classrooms, affording our clients all around the world full access to our information bases—the end of geography as we at the Bank have known it.[2]

Muhsin's organization (shown in Exhibit 2) was named the Information Solutions Group (ISG). By 2003, ISG had a staff of 415 individuals. Muhsin worked closely with individuals throughout the World Bank (see Exhibit 3 for biographies of a few of these senior leaders) establishing IT plans and strategies.

The Business of International Economic Development[3]

The World Bank Group included the International Bank for Reconstruction and Development (IBRD), the International Development Association (IDA), the International Finance Corporation (IFC), the Multilateral Investment Guarantee Agency (MIGA), and the International Centre for Settlement of Investment Disputes (ICSID). Together, IBRD and IDA were referred to as "the Bank." (See Exhibit 4.)

This was no ordinary bank, as seen from its mission statement:

- Our dream is a world free of poverty.
- To fight poverty with passion and professionalism for lasting results.
- To help people help themselves and their environment by providing resources, sharing knowledge, building capacity, and forging partnerships in the public and private sectors.
- To be an excellent institution able to attract, excite, and nurture diverse and committed staff with exceptional skills who know how to listen and learn.

The Bank was owned, financed, and run by 184 member countries (all of which were also members of the United Nations). As one of the world's largest sources of development assistance, the Bank supported efforts including building schools and health centers, providing water and electricity, fighting disease, protecting the environment, and helping to create a better investment climate and more efficient public sector. In 2003, the Bank financed 240 projects in 92 countries divided between:

- $7.3 billion for 141 projects as **assistance** to 55 low-income countries unable to borrow money in open markets. Low-income countries were eligible to receive interest-free loans and technical assistance from the World Bank. Countries had 35–40 years to repay loans, with a 10-year grace period.
- $11.2 billion in 99 projects as **loans** to 37 middle-income developing countries. Some of these countries could borrow from commercial sources but generally only at very high interest rates. They received loans from the IBRD at more favorable terms than from a commercial bank—15–20 years with a three- to five-year grace period before the repayment of principal began. Loans could be used for specific programs related to poverty reduction, social services, environmental protection, and economic growth.

---

[2] James D. Wolfensohn, World Bank Group president, annual meeting address, 1997.

[3] Descriptive information for the World Bank is adapted from www.worldbank.org—an exhaustive Web site providing detailed and multimedia information about Bank projects throughout the world.

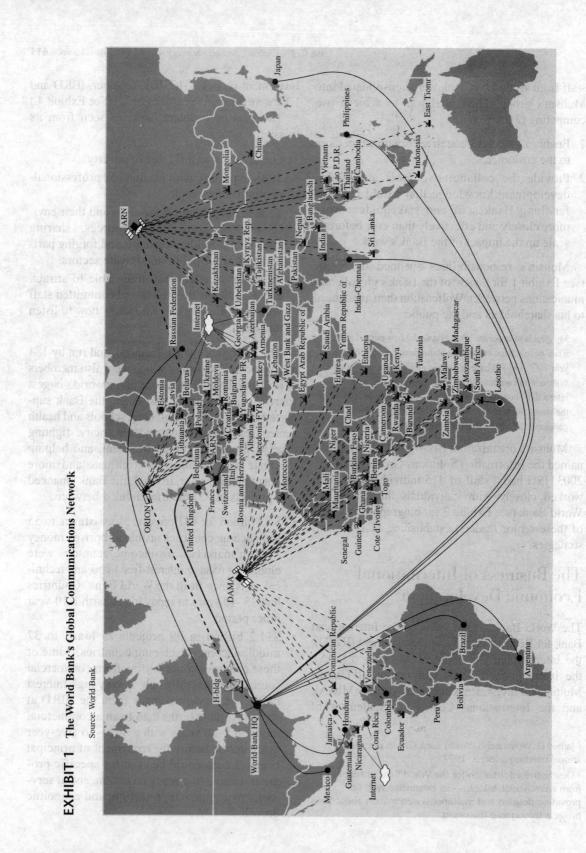

EXHIBIT 1 The World Bank's Global Communications Network

Source: World Bank.

EXHIBIT 2 **Organizational Structure of the Information Solutions Group at the World Bank**

Source: World Bank.

**Position of IT Function in the
World Bank Organization**

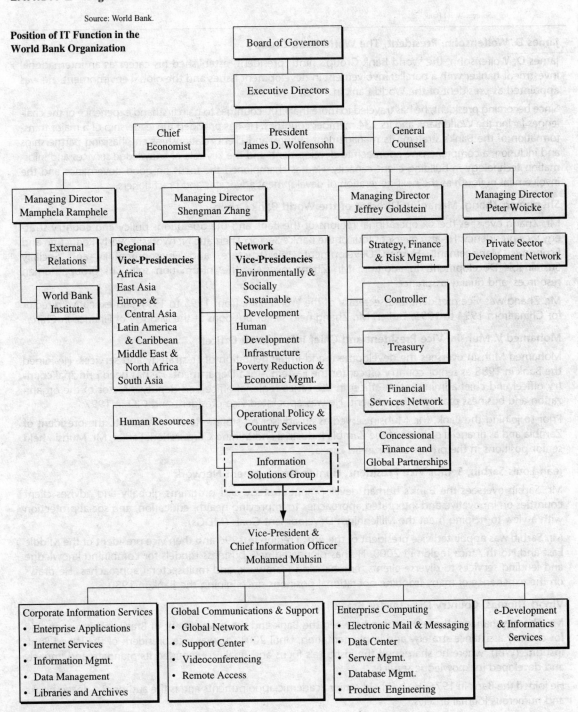

EXHIBIT 3   World Bank Biographies

Source: World Bank.

James D. Wolfensohn, President, The World Bank Group

James D. Wolfensohn, the World Bank Group's ninth president, established his career as an international investment banker with a parallel involvement in development issues and the global environment. He was appointed as president of the World Bank in 1995.

Since becoming president, he has traveled to more than 100 countries to gain firsthand experience of the challenges facing the World Bank and its 184 member countries. He has provided the leadership of a major transformation of the Bank's strategy, its management culture, and client relationships emphasizing partnerships and inclusion, a comprehensive approach to development, and the key role of knowledge services and information technology in building client capacity. He has championed the focus on good governance and the involvement of youth as the next generation of development advocates and practitioners.

Shengman Zhang, Managing Director of the World Bank Group

Mr. Zhang oversees the six operational regions of the Bank and the operations policy and country strategy vice presidency. He also oversees four of the Bank's Sector/Thematic Networks: Poverty Reduction and Economic Management, Human Development, Infrastructure, and Environmentally and Socially Sustainable Development. In addition, Mr. Zhang oversees the information solutions group, human resources, and quality assurance.

Mr. Zhang was vice president and secretary of the World Bank from 1995 to 1997 and executive director for China from 1994 to 1995. Earlier, Mr. Zhang held senior positions at the Ministry of Finance in China.

Mohamed V. Muhsin, Vice President and Chief Information Officer

Mohamed Muhsin oversees the development and implementation of IT strategy and services. He joined the Bank in 1988 as senior country officer for the Eastern Africa Department. He has been principal country officer and chief administrative officer in the Africa regional office and deputy director of the organization and business practices department. He was appointed vice president and CIO in 1997.

Prior to joining the Bank, Mr. Muhsin served as an advisor on state enterprise reform to the president of Zambia and as financial director of the Zambia Industrial and Mining Corporation. Earlier, Mr. Muhsin held senior positions in the private sector in Sri Lanka.

Jean-Louis Sarbib, Senior Vice President, Human Development Network

Mr. Sarbib oversees the Bank's human development strategy and programs globally and advises client countries on innovative and integrated approaches to improving health, education, and social protection with a view to helping meet the Millennium Development Goals (MDGs).

Mr. Sarbib was appointed vice president of the Africa region in 1996 and then vice president of the Middle East and North Africa region in 2000. He has pioneered new business models for combining knowledge and lending services to diverse clients, emphasizing teamwork, and multisectoral approaches. He draws on the experience of many frontline operational positions since joining the Bank in 1980.

Vinod Thomas, Country Director for Brazil

Mr. Thomas manages the relationship between the Bank and the government of Brazil and is responsible for country assistance strategy and implementation. Until 2001, he was vice president of the World Bank Institute (WBI), where he sharpened the institute's focus and quality, expanded its mandate and impact, and developed its knowledge services.

He joined the Bank in 1976. He has held senior academic appointments and is the author of a dozen books and numerous journal articles.

EXHIBIT 3 World Bank Biographies (continued)

Frannie A. Leautier, Vice President, World Bank Institute

Frannie A. Leautier is the vice president of the World Bank Institute. She was appointed to this position in December 2001. Prior to that, Ms. Leautier was the chief of staff for the president of the World Bank Group where she was responsible for providing oversight and guidance to the staff of the president's office in all aspects of their work as well as helping to enhance coordination of the president's office with other units throughout the Bank. Prior to this, Ms. Leautier held senior positions in the Bank's operational vice presidencies.

EXHIBIT 4 Five Agencies, One Group

Source: Adapted from Web site, www.worldbank.org, accessed September 18, 2003.

The World Bank Group consists of five associated institutions owned by member countries with ultimate decision-making power. Each institution plays a distinct role in the mission to fight poverty and improve living standards for people in the developing world. The term "World Bank Group" encompasses all five institutions. The term "World Bank" refers specifically to two: IBRD and IDA.

The International Bank for Reconstruction and Development (IBRD)

- Established 1945 184 members; Cumulative lending: $360 billion
- Fiscal 2002 lending: $11.5 billion for 96 new operations in 40 countries

IBRD aims to reduce poverty in middle-income and creditworthy poorer countries by promoting sustainable development through loans, guarantees, and nonlending. IBRD does not maximize profit but has earned a net income each year since 1948.

The International Development Association (IDA)

- Established 1960 164 members; Cumulative lending: $135 billion
- Fiscal 2002 lending: $8.18 billion for 133 new operations in 62 countries

Contributions to IDA enable the World Bank to provide $6 billion–$7 billion per year in interest-free credits to the world's 78 poorest countries, home to 2.4 billion people. In most of these countries incomes average under $500 a year per person, and many people survive on much less. IDA helps provide access to better education, health care, and clean water and sanitation.

The International Finance Corporation (IFC)

IFC's mandate is to further economic development through the private sector. Working with business partners, it invests in sustainable private enterprises in developing countries and provides long-term loans, guarantees, and risk management and advisory services to its clients.

The Multilateral Investment Guarantee Agency (MIGA)

MIGA helps encourage foreign investment in developing countries by providing guarantees to foreign investors against losses caused by noncommercial risks, such as expropriation, currency inconvertibility and transfer restrictions, and war and civil disturbances.

The International Centre for Settlement of Investment Disputes (ICSID)

ICSID helps to encourage foreign investment by providing international facilities for conciliation and arbitration of investment disputes, in this way helping to foster an atmosphere of mutual confidence between states and foreign investors.

In addition to financing, knowledge services had grown in importance—including policy advice, poverty-reduction strategy, aid coordination, project design, supervision, technical assistance, and capacity building through training programs for public officials. Known originally as a funder of large infrastructure projects, the Bank now financed many more projects in the social sectors. For example, the Bank committed more than $1.6 billion in the last few years to combat the spread of HIV/AIDS around the world as one of the largest financial supporters of HIV/AIDS programs in developing countries.

Transforming the Bank's Business

In March 1997, the Bank's executive board voted in favor of the strategic compact—"to lower the institution's costs, raise productivity, and improve the quality of the projects and programs it supports."[4] Part of this initiative included a major information systems-renewal effort to streamline administrative and operational processes including Y2K compatibility. Key objectives of the strategic compact included decentralization, creation of the knowledge bank, and a matrix of regions and networks.

Decentralization

A key objective was to move the Bank's operations and activities closer to clients to improve responsiveness and strengthen collaboration and country ownership of development programs. Before decentralization, about 38 percent of frontline staff were in field offices; afterwards, about 50 percent were located in full-service country offices. About one-third of the Bank's staff members worked from one of the 110 country offices around the globe. This entailed a radical rethinking of the Bank's systems to become more effective delivering programs for achieving the basic mission of reducing poverty.

[4] From Web site www.worldbank.org, accessed September 15, 2003.

Creation of the Knowledge Bank

Wolfensohn envisioned a "knowledge bank." To that end, a specific objective in the strategic compact was the establishment of a robust knowledge-management system. This required "a sound knowledge base to support nonlending (as well as lending) activities" of the Bank.[5]

By 2003, this vision became reality as client countries wanted to work with the Bank as much for its *development knowledge* (e.g., the expertise of specialized staff skills and ability to transfer learning and experience from projects in one part of the world to another) as for its *money and financing*. In 1980, 21 percent of the Bank's lending went toward the construction of power projects. By 2003, that had fallen closer to 7 percent. In the same period, social services lending (health, nutrition, social safety nets) grew from 5 percent to 22 percent. Knowledge was becoming more critical than physical development.

A Matrix of Regions and Networks

Guided by the strategic compact, the Bank reorganized from a hierarchical organization (with staff organized primarily around regional geography) to a matrix of networks and regions (with emphasis on professional networks of staff from related areas of expertise). These networks were created to encourage greater knowledge sharing and collaboration across regions. Various thematic groups[6] emerged around development issues such as gender, poverty monitoring, and government decentralization. More and more Bank projects took on multisectoral dimensions, working across

[5] The strategic compact was described in the 1997 annual report, from Web site, http://www.worldbank.org/html/extpb/ annrep97/overview.htm, accessed September 11, 2003.

[6] "Thematic Groups (TGs), also known as communities of practice, are groups of people who are passionate about a common subject. Leadership and membership in any Thematic Group is voluntary and open to all staff. TGs also have external partners, and knowledge sharing becomes seamless across the group through the e-mail distribution lists and Web sites." From www.worldbank.org, accessed November 4, 2003.

EXHIBIT 5

Matrix at the Intersection of the Infrastructure Sector and Africa Region

Source: World Bank.

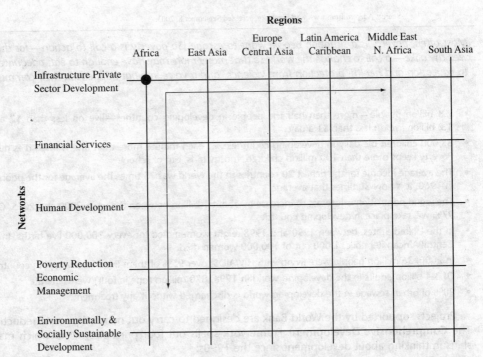

World Bank Organizational Matrix

old "stovepipes" of specialization. IT was considered a key enabler of the matrix.

Country managers negotiated overall assistance strategy for a country "contract"; specialists from various networks would work on specific projects. The largest networks were human development; environmentally and socially sustainable development; finance, private sector, and infrastructure; and poverty reduction and economic management.[7]

One example of how the organization operated in practice was evident in a project with the government of Nigeria. Initially, Nigeria requested assistance developing a global best practice for its transport-sector strategy. The Bank's task team leader (TTL) was in the matrix at the intersection of the infrastructure sector and the Africa region (see Exhibit 5). The TTL e-mailed the 170-person transport-sector thematic network (a thematic group within the infrastructure network) seeking help with best-practice examples. The first response came within minutes from a Bank staff member in Beirut. Eleven country examples were obtained, and the most relevant replies were shared with the government of Nigeria.

Leveraging the World Bank's knowledge expertise, the Nigerian government was able to save significantly on technical assistance costs and improve the timeliness of its own transport-sector strategy. Bank staff concluded, "Thematic networks, combined with modern communication tools, make knowledge sharing an efficient new tool for improving the quality of Bank assistance. Knowledge sharing and learning are two sides of the same coin—everybody within a thematic group stands to gain through such exchanges."

Bank projects addressed numerous challenging global issues (see Exhibit 6) and relied on groups operating increasingly in multisectoral ways. For example, the TTL might also consult with other groups, such as the environmental and socially

---

[7] Learning and knowledge sharing were the two primary objectives of thematic groups. The Bank established and fully supported 80 different thematic groups.

EXHIBIT 6 Global Challenges for the World Bank

Source: Adapted from www.worldbank.org, accessed September 8, 2003.

Most often, poverty is a situation people want to escape. So poverty is a call to action—for the poor and the wealthy alike—a call to change the world so that many more may have enough to eat, adequate shelter, access to education and health, protection from violence, and a voice in what happens in their communities.

World Bank

- 2.8 billion people—more than half the people in developing countries—live on less than $2 a day. Of these, 1.2 billion live on less than $1 a day.
- 33,000 children die daily in developing countries . . . each minute more than one woman dies during childbirth. Poverty keeps more than 100 million children, mostly girls, out of school.
- The average income for the richest 20 countries in the world was 15 times the average for the poorest 20 countries in 1960. It is now 30 times that average.
- The world population is forecast to increase by about 1 billion between the years 2000 and 2015. Of that increase, 97% will take place in developing countries.
- In the United States, between 1990 and 1998, eight women died for every 100,000 live births. In Eritrea and the Central African Republic, 1,000 out of 100,000 women died.
- In 2000, 36 million people were living with HIV/AIDS; over 95% of them lived in developing countries.
- Of 3.4 billion adults in the developing world in 1998, 870 million (one in four) were illiterate.
- 90% of urban sewage in the developing world is discharged without any treatment.

Projects supported by the World Bank are designed to carry out national poverty-reduction strategies. The **Comprehensive Development Framework** spells out four principles, all of which mark significant shifts in thinking about development since the 1990s:

Development strategies should be comprehensive and shaped by a long-term vision. In the past, development strategies emphasized short-term macroeconomic stabilization and balance-of-payment corrections. The CDF stresses longer-term structural and social considerations.

Each country should devise and direct its own development agenda based on citizen participation. The CDF view is when countries "own" reforms, governments and their citizens are more committed to them.

Governments, donors, civil society, the private sector, and other stakeholders should work together in partnership led by recipient countries to carry out development strategies. Partnerships built on transparency, mutual trust, and consultation can increase the efficiency and effectiveness of aid.

Development performance should be evaluated on the basis of measurable results. Traditionally, the Bank tended to concentrate on disbursement levels and project inputs in evaluating development efforts, an approach that measured only resource allocation and consumption.

sustained development group, for environmental impact input.

Knowledge sharing through networks was viewed as more effective in meeting client needs than had been possible in a hierarchy organized primarily around geography. In addition, these networks helped address one of the biggest knowledge-sharing challenges the Bank faced: Knowledge retention. Typical Bank projects took

years, if not decades, to complete. Even with loyal long-term staff, it was difficult to sustain continuity of knowledge throughout the life of a project. These networks helped sustain the knowledge of the project teams through the years as increased efforts were made in assessing the long-term effectiveness across the entire life of the project.

Wolfensohn viewed IT as "the central nervous system of the institution" and consistently supported

EXHIBIT 7   IT Expenditures

Source: World Bank.

	Last Four Years				Next Three Years		
	FY99	**FY00**	**FY01**	**FY02**	**FY03**	**FY04**	**FY05**
Total Bank admin. expenses[1]	1,532.0	1,587.0	1,575.0	1,686.8	1,686.8	1,686.8	1,686.8
Total Bank IT expenses	160.1	182.0	162.8	168.4	180.2	187.8	187.0
Percent of Total for IT	**10.5%**	**11.5%**	**10.3%**	**10.0%**	**10.7%**	**11.1%**	**11.1%**
Work Bank estimates for comparison							
Industry average of 500 companies	5.8%	5.6%	5.6%				
Federal government	10.1%	10.0%	12.0%				
Investment banking	10.2%	11.8%	12.0%				

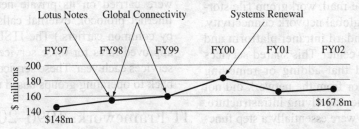

5-Year Trend in Bank IT Expenditures

$19.8 million increase over 5 years, 2.7% per year

All amounts in FY01 dollars.

the budget for IT: "We're not spending in a profligate way but rather in a measured way, as rational investment to generate organizational leverage." He believed in the linkage between a global communications network and the intensive consultations and knowledge sharing inherent in the Bank's new business strategy. Wolfensohn connected the role of IT to the Bank's overall strategy in his speech at the 1996 World Bank annual meeting:

> We have been in the business of researching and disseminating the lessons of development for a long time. But the revolution in information technology increases the potential value of these efforts by vastly extending their reach. To capture this potential, we need to invest in the necessary systems in Washington and worldwide, that enhance our ability to gather development information and

experience, and share it with our clients. We need to become, in effect, the Knowledge Bank.[8]

Aligning IT to Enable the Bank's New Business Strategy

When Muhsin became CIO, high-priority IT issues included Y2K, delivering round-the-clock global support, and building a foundation for global knowledge sharing. To meet a temporary increase in budgetary needs, additional funds were provided during a five-year period. (See Exhibit 7 for IT expenditures.)

[8] World Bank internal correspondence.

The funding mechanisms were an impenetrably complex mix of individual service chargebacks with rebates and nontransparent rate setting combined with direct administrative budgets for some systems units and oversight of dedicated overhead accounts for things like the central libraries. In the last five years, Muhsin substantially simplified the funding and strengthened the governance process so that it became more transparent. There was clearer accountability for the IT function for service delivery and clear accountability for the governance groups as they made investment decisions with long-term impacts.

There were now three main categories of IT services available to all Bank offices:

1. **Basic-service package.** These were fixed-cost, standard underlying network infrastructure services that provided the platform all users needed to access information—enterprise desktop software, e-mail, workgroup file storage, all local and global network connectivity, as well as the standard intranet platform and the global support center. This shared-services model recognized that adding or removing even 100 users to or from the network did not alter the cost of the underlying infrastructure. These investments were essentially a step function where an e-mail server cluster, for example, was added or removed only if there was a swing of 1,400 users. The basic package was generally viewed as a "common good." In fiscal-year 2004, the Information Technology Services Board (ITSB)—which oversaw the IT chargeback system—proposed to the Information Policy Council (IPC)[9] that network links to all country offices should be rolled into the basic package rather than paid locally by each country office. This was the last step in creating a truly *global master service-level agreement* where all staff no matter where they were got the same package at the same per capita cost. The total cost for providing these services was shared among all units proportionally to their headcount.

2. **Corporate information services.** These services provided systems and applications infrastructure to support enterprise functions such as financial and human resource management, frontline operations, and back-office administration. Each year, the IPC looked at the investment plan for supporting corporate systems. The cost for these services was centrally budgeted and not charged back—allocations were part of the annual budgeting process.

3. **Optional IT services.** These included the purchase of desktop and notebook PCs, videoconferencing activity, remote access, wireless devices, and long-distance telephone calls. (Point-to-point calls within the World Bank were carried on its private network over the Internet protocol; external calls were handled by common carriers.) The ITSB reviewed and approved rates for these services and any new services each year. These services were charged back to operating groups based upon usage.

IT Framework, 1996–2002

With strong support from senior management, ISG established a "Five-Point Program" as the Bank's IT strategy (see Exhibit 8). As the foundation of this strategy, global connectivity—built on standards—would provide a global customer base a high degree of reliability and service. To provide a reliable and cost-effective foundation, Muhsin's team standardized and integrated the IT infrastructure, including desktop and laptop computers and software, along with workgroup, storage, and database servers. A robust information management architecture was created to provide a solid foundation for the next generation of Web services and portal applications.

Exhibit 9 contrasts IT before the Five-Point Program was implemented and after. The IT group accomplished a great deal over six years and, with senior management support, they were pushing

---

[9] The council represents operations (e.g., end users in regions and network vice presidencies) and owners of systems and processes (e.g., the controller represents controls and finance, the director of resource management represents the budgeting process, etc.).

EXHIBIT 8   **IT Framework, 1996–2002: Building the Reliable IT Foundation**

Source: World Bank.

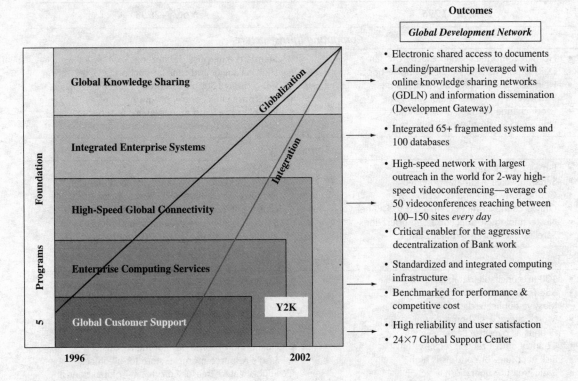

Outcomes

Global Development Network

- Electronic shared access to documents
- Lending/partnership leveraged with online knowledge sharing networks (GDLN) and information dissemination (Development Gateway)

- Integrated 65+ fragmented systems and 100 databases

- High-speed network with largest outreach in the world for 2-way high-speed videoconferencing—average of 50 videoconferences reaching between 100–150 sites *every day*
- Critical enabler for the aggressive decentralization of Bank work

- Standardized and integrated computing infrastructure
- Benchmarked for performance & competitive cost

- High reliability and user satisfaction
- 24×7 Global Support Center

the frontiers of how IT could help the Bank achieve its mission.

A Unique Network Solution

Although all aspects of the Five-Point Program became critical to delivering on the president's vision, the global communications network was clearly the essential highway on which everything else rode. As such, it continued to be a critical lever in transforming the organization. Upgrading of the network was an ongoing process with annual investments to improve performance, reliability, and coverage.

The Bank was able to provide voice, data, and videoconferencing services to country staff and clients from 110 country offices and related distance-learning centers, many where local telecommunications infrastructure was not reliable

or available. The network was monitored in real time in a modern control room (built in 1999) staffed with 30 support personnel.

Country offices varied considerably in size and design, but an average office environment had from 20 to 50 staff members. Offices were typically freestanding buildings, though they might also be a few floors in a shared office building. Power generators were located nearby and relied on regularly. An uninterruptible power supply (UPS) safeguarded the office intranet and network servers. Staff offices had PCs.

Videoconferencing facilities were available and increasingly utilized, as described in the sidebar. Additional office space with PCs was available for anyone visiting on a "mission" from the Bank. Clients visited country offices about as often as staff members visited the client offices.

EXHIBIT 9　IT Before the Five-Point Program Was Implemented (1996) and After (2003)

Source: World Bank.

Then—1996	Now—2003
Computing Infrastructure	
• No two computers set up exactly the same • Daily problems with freeze-up and re-boot • Help desk is 6 people, phone #, 1 shift • Viruses emerging as a major problem • Every change required a visit to the PC • Unnecessary complexity driving costs	• Standard enterprise desktop package • High reliability and user satisfaction • 24×7 Global Support Center • Enterprise virus control program • Remote install and management of service • Benchmarked standardization and competitive cost
Connectivity	
• E-mail is weak substitute for actual network • Separate voice and data, no video • Connectivity slow and capacity low • Only 3 country offices connected to HQ network • No technology for decentralized operations • Satellite licensing is a major barrier	• Global enterprise network with 109 sites • Integrated voice, data, and videoconferencing • HQ LAN speed increased by a factor of 1,000 • Global link capacity increased by a factor of 15 • 84 videoconference (VC)-equipped rooms • Average 50 VCs/day with 120 country links
Systems and Data	
• 100 irreconcilable databases • 65+ fragmented systems • Massive duplicate data entry • Most systems are "homegrown" • IS units all over the Bank • Country offices rely on local systems • Risk exposure for controls is high • Basic Treasury operation	• Consolidated corporate data store • Commercial integrated software packages • Control risks reduced (also Y2K compliance) • Executive financial management tools • Foundation in place for Web services • Offshoring of some development costs • Single resource mgmt. system for all offices • Sophisticated Treasury products—global bonds, hedging products
Information Management and Sharing	
• Almost entirely paper based • Large gaps in official business records • Information only in people's heads • Photocopying is a major industry • Libraries—traditional services only • No concept of knowledge management • Manual updating of the few electronic documents • No Bank reports delivered online • Primitive intranet and Bank Web page • Hard-copy publications only for clients • *No collaborative information solutions*	• Electronic capture, storage, and retrieval • Business records captured in electronic form • Enterprise electronic information warehouse • Electronic shared access to documents • Electronic library sources widely available • Knowledge communities developed • Central cataloguing of all kinds of information • 43,000 Bank reports online • Lending /partnership leveraged with online knowledge-sharing networks (GDLN) and information dissemination (Development Gateway) • External Web; 16 million page views per month; 2,800 visits per hour; 120,000 content pages

A Day in the Life of the Videoconferencing Service

On a Thursday in October 2003, the Bank conducted 67 videoconferences reaching a total of 215 sites worldwide. The conferences started at a little after midnight Washington time and ran throughout the next 24 hours. Conferences included distance-learning sessions, project-coordination meetings, conferences of government officials from different countries with shared issues and concerns, regular staff meetings, and meetings of teams that gathered virtually, as they were located all over the world. A sample listing of the topics for the day included:

- Strategies to Alleviate Rural Poverty
- Religion and Health
- Lebanon Hydrocarbon Study

- Uganda Poverty Strategy Credits
- Indonesia Catchment Protection
- Tajikistan Public Expenditure Review
- Judicial Reform Improving Governance in Kenya
- UNICEF/UNDP Partners Meeting
- Argentina Country Assistance Strategy
- Peru Decentralization Adjustment Loan
- HR Issues Consultation with the Indonesia Office
- Decentralization in Madagascar
- Ghana Urban Water
- Consultative Group on Agriculture

Source: World Bank.

In some countries a distance-learning center was colocated with the Bank office. In those cases, a second videoconference facility shared network infrastructure with the office but had its own dedicated bandwidth. (Most office locations operated on highly reliable service at 786 kilobits per second, or kbps.)

About three-fifths of the country offices were connected by geostationary satellite—a dish sat on the roof or out in the yard. The remaining two-fifths of the country offices were connected with fiber-optic cables. The World Bank partnered with IntelSat as well as various private-sector vendors for satellite services and link maintenance, but given the challenges of local conditions, the mesh network connecting the 110 offices was managed as a private global network.

Over the years, many vendors had suggested the Bank could outsource its global network needs. As the Bank evaluated these offers, a routine question was asked: "Do you provide network service in Ouagadougou?[10] Do you know where it is? We need to enter transactions from virtually anyplace in the world, including Ouagadougou." For many vendors, "global" meant Pacific Rim, Europe, and North and South America. Muhsin said with a smile, "We sometimes refer to this as the Ouagadougou factor."

Network connections to the country offices enabled Bank staff members to speed consultation and decision making, to share knowledge and experience, to process transactions, and to conduct business via videoconferencing as well as e-mail and other network-based applications. In some cases, the offices were able to communicate over equally modern communication infrastructure with their clients, but just as often that was not possible. Virtually all countries were looking to advance their IT infrastructure at a rapid rate.

Network Architecture

The Bank's network integrated capacity from three satellites that—together with a few dedicated terrestrial links—covered all World Bank offices worldwide. The network used a number of different technologies to optimize utilization: Demand assigned multiple access (DAMA) allowed flexible allocation of bandwidth among sites; single channel per carrier (SCPC) allowed dynamic sharing between voice, data, and video services; and time division multiplexing/time

[10] Ouagadougou (pronounced Wah-ga-do-goo) is located in Burkina Faso, a country located in West Africa north of Ghana. The country gained independence from France in 1960.

TABLE A   Technical Attributes of the Global Communications Network at the World Bank

Source: World Bank.

	Latin America, Africa, and Middle East Network	Eastern Europe Network	Asia Network
Number of nodes	64	19	26
Satellite bandwidth	96 Mhz	16 Mhz	36 Mhz
Satellite bandwidth provider	Intelsat	Orion	Intelsat
Satellite	342 degrees Global Beam—C band	Orion 3 Hemi Beam Ku-Band	64 degrees Hemi Beam—C band
Number of simultaneous voice channels	320	114	130
Number of simultaneous video channels (256 kbps)	64	19	26
Data-handling capacity	50 Mbps	14 Mbps	20 Mbps
Data-handling capacity per office	768 kbps	768 kbps	768 kbps

division multiplexing assigned (TDM/TDMA) allowed sharing of satellite capacity.

In 2003, the Bank completed conversion of its full network—voice, video, and data—to run over a single protocol, IP. Working closely with cutting-edge technology, the Bank was one of the first in the world to optimize all its traffic across a single protocol data stream, increasing the efficiency of utilization of the total network bandwidth and further standardizing the technology to enhance reliability and support new functionality.

The Bank's network dynamically allocated satellite resources, gaining time-zone efficiencies; it automatically distributed capacity between voice, data, and video services to maximize utilization of bandwidth. Not only was the same standard quality of service available to every office, it was easily scalable and upgradeable and could be reengineered as business requirements evolved (see Table A).

Network Costs

Because the network was a critical lever in transforming the organization, its implementation and upgrading became an ongoing process with annual investments to improve performance, reliability, and coverage. The Bank had invested $4 million a year since 1997 on development and upgrades

to the global communications network (Table B details the annual operating cost of $12.3 million).

One assessment of the global communications network by industry analysts found that World Bank unit costs per gigabyte of data transmission were lower than those of all comparison organizations in its database; cost efficiency normalized for workload was about twice as good as the peer average.

Business Benefits of the Global Network

The global network achieved many of the benefits envisioned by Wolfensohn. The rest of the Five-Point Program strategy improved the cost-effectiveness and productivity of the Bank

TABLE B   World Bank IT Operating Costs for Its Global Network

Source: World Bank.

Labor (management fee)	$1.393 million
Satellite bandwidth + satellite equipment maintenance	$10.295 million
Network and video equipment maintenance	$0.604 million

TABLE C   **IT-Enabled Business Changes between 1996 and 2002**

Source: World Bank.

	1996	2000	2002
1. Decentralized Global Organization			
Country directors in the field	0%	48%	66%
Regional staff in the field (out of 4,700 total)	38%	45%	50%
Projects involving civil society	50%		70%
Travel (in number of trips)	37,000		35,800
Travel (in days)	405,000		354,800
Videoconferences with country offices	None		9,678
2. Standardized and Streamlined Business Processes			
Project preparation time	24 months	15 months	15 months
Cycle time for project approval	9 months	5 months	5 months
Satisfactory project outcomes	66%	77%	68%
Projects at risk	29%	15%	15%
3. Capacity Building and Development Knowledge Sharing			
Distance-learning centers	0	16	37
Distance-learning conferences	0		875
Communities of practice	30	110	110

(Table C captures the scope and scale of IT-enabled business changes between 1996 and 2002).

The network had multiple benefits, according to Vinod Thomas, formerly vice president of the World Bank Institute and presently country director, Brazil:

The use of technology in the country offices not only provides connectivity among the staff and gives the vital link to headquarters but also is an instrument for dialogue with the clients. Indeed, technology initiatives in the Brazil office are designed to allow seamless interactions among country-based and headquarters staff and government authorities. Through the use of high-speed satellite links to country offices, regional staff have real-time access to key information and maintain close collaboration with headquarters colleagues.

Videoconferences take place on a daily basis, often connecting several sites simultaneously, and allow broad participation among staff and government authorities. Decision-making abilities by the country director, sector leaders, and task managers, an increasing number of whom are in the field, have been strengthened by the close contact with HQ-based senior managers. For example, key meetings for the country assistance strategy

are now conducted across Brazil and the U.S., with decisions made and implemented more swiftly than before. Also, staff are increasingly able to improve efficiencies in their responsibilities and in their interaction with clients—be it in procurement, disbursement, or economic and sector work.

The chief knowledge officer for the Latin America and Caribbean region, David Gray, recounted the following example of improved performance as a direct result of leveraging the Bank's network to do business differently:

As well as being home to over 50 percent of Brazil's poor, the northeast of Brazil is characterized by large wealth inequalities [human, physical, and social] among its states and its people. The World Bank has been working with these states for over three decades both supplying loans and technical assistance. A review found that the Bank's traditional approach was both failing to deliver timely advice and that the capacity to absorb and apply this advice was generally lacking. Based on this, a new approach has been developed, based on the use of a videoconference network. By working with partners, the Bank has convened stakeholders from across the region through NÓS—The North and Northeast Network for

Social Inclusion and Poverty Reduction. The network, which can connect many hundreds of participants over nine states, has extended participation to areas and groups normally excluded from dialogue and allowed open and transparent policy debate between actors, including the federal government, local government, the international community, and civil society. This is resulting in new levels of trust and cooperation and renewed hope in the fight against poverty.

Standardized and Streamlined Global Business Processes

Prior to the deployment of the global communications network, each local office was a disconnected island with its own stand-alone information system and custom business processes. World Bank staff in the field were cut off from the rest of the World Bank, and managers often felt they were "flying blind" because they did not have access to information they needed to manage the country office work program. Project team leaders could not collaborate with team members in the Washington office and with other country offices. Budget information was centralized and country teams had no access, with the result that budget management was very difficult. The business strategy of decentralizing World Bank staff and decision making to the field was not feasible under these conditions.

With the deployment of the global communications network, the Bank was able also to standardize and centralize the World Bank's information systems, which brought standardized business processes to each country office and reduced the World Bank's cost of doing business. Some examples included:

1. The SAP system consolidated 65 disparate business systems into one and standardized the processes for project-cycle work, reducing cycle time with electronic approval of project steps.

2. Real-time project status reports from field-based project staff, central to the analysis of project portfolio risk and proactive project management of risky projects, became accessible to team leaders in the country offices. This included information on project and country budgets—no matter where the expense was incurred and booked. Budget management and forecasting improved to make the Bank better able to deploy resources to high-priority areas.

3. The World Bank's knowledge systems and documents were readily searched and accessed on the intranet from any access point in the global communications network, by users with appropriate access and secured connections.

4. Global payroll operations and standardized HR processes helped the Bank deal with complex retroactive payroll adjustments, benefit processing, and learning programs and protected the Bank from the consequences of inconsistent application of complex policies in each office.

5. Electronic workflow approvals could be accessed from any remote location, improving processing cycle time for project work as well as administrative and budgetary approvals.

Standardized processes in country offices helped the World Bank to ensure better fiduciary controls in remote offices and to use staff more productively for value-added work instead of struggling with idiosyncratic processes invented by each office. For example, the country office procurement process was now identical to that used by the Washington headquarters office, allowing transparency in procurement contracting, reduced cycle time of procurement and, more importantly, fungibility of staff between Washington and country offices.

The global communications network and systems enabled the World Bank to make its decentralization strategy work—enabling improved client responsiveness and improved project success indicators. "As elegant as all this may seem now, getting to this point and getting people to accept standardization was like a real battle," Muhsin quipped.

Offshoring

A review by external consultants determined that indeed there was a strong business case for locating work in different parts of the world and leveraging highly skilled staff and providing better client service while being cost effective.

The World Bank established an accounting office in Chennai, India for all account-related back-office processing. Invoices were scanned in Washington and processed overnight in the Chennai office. Payroll operations, travel accounting, loan accounting, and disbursement functions were other processes moving to the Chennai office. Help-desk 24×7 support of worldwide operations was becoming a viable proposition. Experts were added through contractors working on new systems requested by the owners of various business processes—budgeting, accounting, human resources, and so on. With a global model and standardized business processes and systems, transactions no longer needed to be processed at headquarters but could be positioned at any location that offered comparative advantage over Washington.

The offshore model provided rapid delivery of business systems leveraging a cadre of highly skilled resources and a quick project ramp up and taking advantage of a 24-hour development cycle—all enabled by the World Bank's global communications network. Muhsin supplemented his staff of 415 full-time World Bank employees with between 150 and 250 contractors depending on current projects, about half of which were offshore. A few Bank IT staff located offshore to facilitate the contract management.

As a result of offshoring, the World Bank improved client services with highly qualified staff. This sourcing strategy helped the Bank reduce costs and deliver on its IT strategy.

Responding in a Crisis

Not surprisingly, the global network proved indispensable immediately after the events of September 11, 2001. Restrictions on staff travel made reliance on the voice, data, and video traffic over the network critical to continued operations. Again, during the SARS crisis, key members of a project team were unable to travel to China to negotiate a huge and critical agreement. Instead of just canceling everything and stopping the negotiation until a team could be sent, the Bank suggested—and China representatives agreed—to negotiate by videoconference. Local IT staff from the China country office arranged for a network connection to be established in the finance minister's offices and the meetings went on—often at night for one of the parties, given the 12-hour time difference.

Frannie A. Léautier, the newly appointed vice president of the World Bank Institute (WBI), was involved in the negotiation with China: "Even though we weren't able to sit down and look at each other in the eyes, in a face-to-face sense, the technology let you zoom in and read someone's body language. People felt quite comfortable by the second day of negotiations, and by the third day they were actually more efficient than if people had been face-to-face."

Spurring the Knowledge Revolution in Developing Countries

WBI had a strong outreach program, increasingly relying on technology leverage to accomplish its goals. WBI's overall vision was to "spur the knowledge revolution in developing countries to be a global catalyst for creating, sharing, and applying cutting-edge knowledge necessary for poverty reduction and economic development."

WBI was a 160-person organization responsible for learning and knowledge programs supporting a wide range of areas: Poverty reduction, environmentally and socially sustainable development, financial and private-sector development, human development, and infrastructure.

WBI faced a number of IT challenges. First, there were many *global differences* in connectivity, affordability, and access to technology. Another challenge was the nature of *tacit knowledge*—unique knowledge in the heads of the individual experts and professionals who delivered services throughout the world. Tacit knowledge was immensely difficult to document and share. (One example of tacit knowledge was how to approach a tough negotiation—a common activity for World Bank staff members, and an especially important area of learning for new staff members.) It was widely recognized by WBI and others at the Bank that technology alone would not be sufficient. The power of IT could be best leveraged when other nontechnical issues were addressed at the same time, such as management support, staff behavior, and incentives.

WBI and regional vice presidents became active in a project called "tacit downloading." A manager returning from an important mission (e.g., a trip to a client country) was debriefed in a journalist-styled interview. A few key questions were asked: (1) What was the most important element of this mission? (2) What did you learn? (3) What were the challenges? The tacit downloading session was videotaped, digitized, and immediately made available over the Bank's intranet for use by other staff members. The online video was linked to related project documents, project evaluations, and client feedback to aid future projects.

WBI ran 500 to 600 learning programs for clients annually. It worked with 48,000 client participants in more than 150 countries. WBI arranged formal partnerships with more than 115 organizations and informal ones with 250 more. The global development learning network (GDLN)—a network of some 60 distance-learning centers—leveraged the World Bank's global network.

The launch in November 2002 of the GDLN along with the municipalities network (MUNINET) was marked by the participation of the World Bank president, Wolfensohn, from Brasilia. Eleven interactive sites (including Washington, DC) plus points distributed in some 2,300 municipalities in the country were connected through the GDLN bridge, allowing Wolfensohn to interact with over 2,000 mayors.

Léautier described a fundamental shift made possible by communication technologies:

> By 2003, country directors were responsible for creating the three-year country assistance strategy.[11] Previously, a staff member in Washington, DC prepared this. The world changed: We moved toward having much more inclusiveness in the decision making at the country level.

---

[11] The poverty reduction strategy plan (PRSP) is the country's overall plan for progress. The Bank's role is defined in the country assistance strategy. The comprehensive development framework (CDF), as described in Exhibit 6, is the overall approach the World Bank advocates for helping countries reduce poverty.

Improving client service required putting together a strategy with much more teamwork between the professionals in the Bank and the country team.

Lessons Learned

Muhsin's experiences since becoming CIO were many. He had been through numerous change programs utilizing IT as a key business lever—and in each case the technology interacted with changes in business processes, systems, and applications. Several important lessons stood out:

Keep the Business Leaders Fully Engaged on Major Change Initiatives Leveraged with IT

The IT platform moved from custom applications to a $50 million systems-renewal effort relying on commercial off-the-shelf software (e.g., PeopleSoft, SAP). This happened despite a commonly held belief that the Bank's operations were unique and could only be administered with proprietary systems. To make this transformation successful, Muhsin reached out to other leaders in the organization to help.

Muhsin asked Jean-Louis Sarbib, who was vice president of the Africa region at the time (and presently senior vice president and head of the human development network), to chair a "systems renewal steering committee" where business users could bring their "questions, doubts, nagging feelings, and problems." Sarbib set forth with an objective to get project concerns out on the table for discussion, with the ultimate goal being to create consensus around the project. Sarbib recalled:

> The decision was made to go for the "big bang" approach; this would totally revamp all the systems. It would also require different behavior and much more ownership taking by people for their transactions. As with any effort of this magnitude, it generated a lot of advocates and a lot of antibodies. Mohamed decided to create the systems renewal steering committee, which was a way for all the stakeholders to come together on a regular basis, to be made aware of the progress, and also to have a way of managing the political economy of the transformation.

Muhsin reported to Shengman Zhang, one of the Bank's managing directors. At one point, the systems renewal project was coming under fire for costing too much. Zhang, who reported directly to Wolfensohn, protected the IT organization from "getting too many arrows." According to Zhang: "We start out saying, 'These projects will save us money.' But, the fact of the matter is the savings they generate are mostly indirect and difficult to capture—they make work easier and better, but they don't generate savings directly. This [systems renewal project] enables us to do work faster, better, and more efficiently."

Another area in which Zhang helped was implementation. Systems renewal created dramatic change; even basic processes such as expense reporting and new-hire reference checking changed. This led to considerable resistance and nearly derailed the implementation. ISG established a "war room" to deal with complaints and confusion. Zhang helped here as well:

> First and foremost I was in a position to tell them, when they complained, that the decision has been made. Their job is to help get it done! Another key was making timely decisions when issues did arise; we would analyze, assess, and decide on them quickly. Initially, we met in the war room on a daily basis, relaxing that to weekly and eventually monthly as the systems were installed.

Managing Expectations Can Save Your Program

Major initiatives like the Five-Point Program IT strategy implemented by the Bank inevitably resulted in a huge challenge for managing change. Staff and clients were asked to change the way they did business and often to use new interfaces and systems. Even if there were clear benefits to the new services, there was a period of adjustment that could not be avoided and should not be underestimated.

For Muhsin, one of the most useful pieces of advice he got during the last few years of intensive implementation was from Michael Hammer, who warned of the need to manage the "emotional timeline" during the system-driven changes that were being made. Hammer described the emotion

of participants in these changing systems as moving from *shock and disbelief* at the time of the system's going live to more general *skepticism* and eventual *acceptance*. It often took a long time after the initial implementation for staff to recognize the *true power* and *benefit* of transformative business systems.

Muhsin's experience confirmed Hammer's advice: Right at the time of "go live," IT people were relieved and excited to be on the home stretch, while end users were being pushed to the limits of their capacity for change. "It is important to be out there talking with your clients and sponsors about what to expect and warning your staff that there will be push-back," said Muhsin. "We referred to it as 'the dip.' You actually go down in productivity right after 'go live' before you really begin to get the benefits."

Sustained Support from the Top Makes All the Difference

Muhsin attributed the IT group's success to several key factors, but most critical was the strong support of the World Bank Group's top management. One meeting with Wolfensohn was most memorable. In 1997, shortly after Muhsin became CIO, implementation delays, scope changes, and training demands increased projected costs of the enterprise resource planning (ERP) SAP system by $10 million over the original budget. Wolfensohn was upset. Muhsin brought in Ken Thornton—general manager of IBM's global public sector practice and strategic partner in the ERP implementation—to discuss the problem. Thornton assured Wolfensohn that overruns occured in 80 percent of ERP implementations. Wolfensohn made it clear he wanted to be in the other 20 percent! As the meeting came to a close, Thornton implored Wolfensohn not to lose faith and to keep pressing on with the project. As he left the meeting, his parting message to Wolfensohn was a simple one: "Don't blink." Later that day, Muhsin ran into Wolfensohn at the elevator. "Don't worry," Wolfensohn said, "I won't blink!"

Muhsin noted, "As the Bank has gone through many stages of IT-enabled transformation with their attendant trials and tribulations, Wolfensohn has not blinked." Indeed, Wolfensohn has kept his eyes on the progress. "My biggest worry," said Wolfensohn, "is to maintain the pace of IT systems development—which has been quite extraordinary." A deeper worry was utilization.

According to Wolfensohn:

We are ahead of our culture's willingness and ability to utilize and absorb the technology. Although we are way ahead of any other international development organization, we still have a gap in adoption. The gaps between availability and usage are major. How do we close that gap?

At my level, you have to keep talking it up. Using it. Talking about it intelligently. These are not just toys but knowledge tools enabling a change in scale and effectiveness in our efforts. I believe in a knowledge-based organization. Knowledge can drive organizational direction—if you present people with information, I think they will act rationally.

Wolfensohn viewed communication technology as the key to scale, not just for internal use but also for reaching outside the organization. To fully benefit from this, widespread usage was key.

Assemble a First-Rate IT Team

Muhsin came from the business side of the Bank to take over leadership of the IT function. His business perspective helped to get the IT function a seat at the table. But Muhsin was the first to point out that you need world-class IT talent and an IT senior leadership team with unquestioned commitment to deliver. He explained, "At every opportunity I told the president about the quality of my staff and their long hours and dedication. The president always made time for us. When we had meetings of the IT function, he could be counted on to stop by and show his appreciation. It made a huge difference."

IT Framework, 2002–2006

Building on the Foundation and Meeting the New Challenges

By 2003, the basic IT foundation was in place to support 7,000 staff members in Washington and 3,000 more staff members in country offices, including 16,000 desktop and laptop PCs. Managers

throughout the Bank could look at the same data—whether from Washington headquarters or as a country director in South Africa.

In planning for the future, Muhsin and his staff consulted with various stakeholders throughout the areas of operations, regions, and networks. The consensus was that over the next three to four years, the IT function needed to leverage the investments in the technology and systems platforms described in the 2002–2006 plan to enable key Bank business strategies (see Exhibit 10 for IT framework, 2002–2006).

Strategy for Customer Relationship Management Portals

Web portals were increasingly being used to convey information (e.g., project status, expenses, cash flows, and financial/loan agreements) to clients in developing countries, train new staff, help share information between projects and connect staff experts across areas of expertise, and also contribute to lifelong learning (constant learning was needed, and having access to the information and expertise was key; in addition, the convenience of online learning was important). Progress on portals was being made quickly (the overall architecture is shown in Exhibit 11).

In many ways, the Client Connection was emblematic of the implementation of Wolfensohn's vision. Wolfensohn had been pushing for systems investments to go beyond internal processes and really deliver value to the Bank's clients. "Why," he asked, "shouldn't it be possible for clients of the Bank to see and manage their relationship with the Bank online just like customers of, say, Citibank? We need to give them a card that gives them access to their disbursement information, their lending activities, whatever we are engaged in providing them" (see Exhibit 12).

Wolfensohn said he frequently provided these ideas to the Bank's IT team. IT and the business units with which they worked in partnership figured out how to do it and often came back with something even better. At the 2003 Bank annual meetings in Dubai, Wolfensohn announced the Client Connection as a key element in the overall

EXHIBIT 10   **IT Framework, 2002–2006: Enabling the Business Strategy**

Source: World Bank.

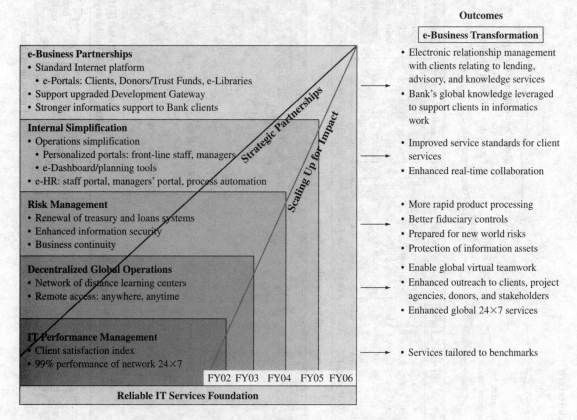

Outcomes

e-Business Transformation

e-Business Partnerships
- Standard Internet platform
  - e-Portals: Clients, Donors/Trust Funds, e-Libraries
- Support upgraded Development Gateway
- Stronger informatics support to Bank clients

- Electronic relationship management with clients relating to lending, advisory, and knowledge services
- Bank's global knowledge leveraged to support clients in informatics work

Internal Simplification
- Operations simplification
  - Personalized portals: front-line staff, managers
  - e-Dashboard/planning tools
- e-HR: staff portal, managers' portal, process automation

- Improved service standards for client services
- Enhanced real-time collaboration

Risk Management
- Renewal of treasury and loans systems
- Enhanced information security
- Business continuity

- More rapid product processing
- Better fiduciary controls
- Prepared for new world risks
- Protection of information assets

Decentralized Global Operations
- Network of distance learning centers
- Remote access: anywhere, anytime

- Enable global virtual teamwork
- Enhanced outreach to clients, project agencies, donors, and stakeholders
- Enhanced global 24×7 services

IT Performance Management
- Client satisfaction index
- 99% performance of network 24×7

- Services tailored to benchmarks

Strategic Partnerships

Scaling Up for Impact

FY02 FY03 FY04 FY05 FY06

Reliable IT Services Foundation

strategy to increase e-business partnerships. The Client Connection was a new secure Web site offering government officials and project-implementing agencies quicker access to information related to their lending activities as well as the Bank's country analytic work. The main objectives of the Client Connection were to support better-informed decision making and to simplify the process of doing business with the Bank.

The Client Connection gave clients access to confidential information about their projects and loan portfolio including:

- The status of individual loans, credits, grants, and trust funds
- Disbursements, loan charges, debt service, and bills

- Related legal agreements and project documents
- Model forms for financial transactions
- Details of procurement transactions

It also gave clients access to World Bank knowledge resources including:

- Country-specific research, statistical data, economic, and sector studies
- World Bank lending instruments and financial products
- World Bank news, reports, publications, policies, procedures, forms, and templates
- World Bank-supported projects and programs

Client Connection was the World Bank's answer to online portfolio management. The new

EXHIBIT 11 Internet Services Program Architecture

Source: World Bank.

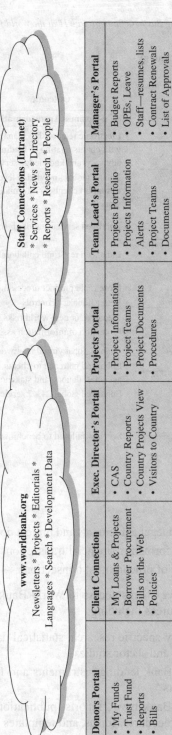

www.worldbank.org
Newsletters * Projects * Editorials *
Languages * Search * Development Data

Staff Connections (Intranet)
* Services * News * Directory
* Reports * Research * People

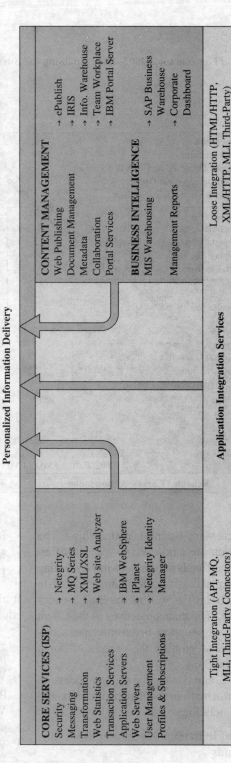

Donors Portal	Client Connection	Exec. Director's Portal	Projects Portal	Team Lead's Portal	Manager's Portal
• My Funds • Trust Fund • Reports • Bills	• My Loans & Projects • Borrower Procurement • Bills on the Web • Policies	• CAS • Country Reports • Country Projects View • Visitors to Country	• Project Information • Project Teams • Project Documents • Procedures	• Projects Portfolio • Projects Information • Alerts • Project Teams • Documents	• Budget Reports • OPEs, Leave • Staff –resumes, lists • Contract Renewals • List of Approvals

Core Common Features * Workflow * View Calendar * View E-mail * Alerts * Reports * News

Personalized Information Delivery

CONTENT MANAGEMENT
Web Publishing → ePublish
Document Management → IRIS
Metadata → Info. Warehouse
Collaboration → Team Workplace
Portal Services → IBM Portal Server

BUSINESS INTELLIGENCE
MIS Warehousing → SAP Business Warehouse
Management Reports → Corporate Dashboard

CORE SERVICES (ISP)
Security → Netegrity
Messaging → MQ Series
Transformation → XML/XSL
Web Statistics → Web site Analyzer
Transaction Services → IBM WebSphere
Application Servers → iPlanet
Web Servers → Netegrity Identity Manager
User Management
Profiles & Subscriptions

Application Integration Services

Tight Integration (API, MQ, MLI, Third-Party Connectors)

Loose Integration (HTML/HTTP, XML/HTTP, MLI, Third-Party)

R/3	People Soft	Loans DB	Other DB	BW	IW

Structured Content

Documents IRIS	Lotus DB	Intranet Web sites

Unstructured Content

EXHIBIT 12
World Bank
Card

Source: World Bank.

Web site was fully integrated with the Bank's business systems. "Clients want to make well-informed business decisions," said Jan Wright, loan department director. "By providing accurate, up-to-the-minute information online, Client Connection will help clients plan and manage better, and it will also be a place where they can initiate financial transactions with the Bank online and track their status."

Consultations and testing sessions were held with clients and staff during the development phase. A high level of attention was paid to security and access. The Client Connection was scheduled to launch in 10 countries beginning in October 2003. A full-scale rollout was planned beginning in January 2004. Over the next several months, a communications and training campaign would help designated Bank staff become versed in the Client Connection so that they would help clients begin using this powerful new tool.

IT and the Frontline Business

Muhsin saw the need to refocus IT investment from modernization of internal backroom business functions to delivering information to the frontline business process and out into the field in support of client interactions. One way of doing this was through information portals improving work efficiency and effectiveness for managers and teams while also improving services for clients and partners. At the same time, it was critical to maintain seamless integration of the diverse portals to make the user experience—external to the Bank as well as internal—as productive as possible.

One unanticipated result of the Bank's experience with the use of IT in its transformation had been that governmental organizations in client countries were now looking to the Bank for direct assistance and advice on IT components of their development projects. The Bank's experience in implementing its own comprehensive IT strategy had given it substantial credibility with clients in this arena.

They were especially interested in the Bank's implementation experiences. The Information Solutions Group now included informatics services to provide expertise to clients through the Bank's frontline country programs as they attempted to address the digital divide.

For example, as Afghanistan emerged from the war, one of the first things Wolfensohn did when he met with President Karzai was to offer to set up a global communications capacity with a distance-learning center. Karzai recognized immediately the power and the potential of information communications technology. The satellite-based distance-learning and videoconferencing center in Kabul now connected Afghans, helped them share ideas, and transacted business globally. It provided them with their first-ever robust government e-mail system. At the beginning, money for the banking system had to be transported in suitcases under escort to Dubai. Now, their connectivity provided them an electronic money-transfer system.

It was not only global scale and connectivity to bridge the digital divide that interested Wolfensohn. He was continually pushing the envelope for the application of appropriate technology in international development. One of his favorite examples was a blue plastic hand-cranked and solar-powered radio on display in his office. It costs $40, was simple to use, and was indestructible and reliable in widely varying environments. Given the excellent sound quality, 40 people could hear it clearly, making it a cost-effective tool. Two minutes of cranking powered the radio for two hours—fully charged, the radio played nonstop for 24 hours. Expensive batteries were not needed. Language instruction, education, and medical information would be delivered via radio throughout developing nations. Without these kinds of simple devices, "When the batteries die, learning stops," said Freeplay Foundation

EXHIBIT 13
A Lifeline Radio

Source: Freeplay
Foundation.

(www.freeplayfoundation.org), creator of the Lifeline radio (see Exhibit 13).[12] Inspired by this example, Wolfensohn asked, "Why not a hand-cranked PC?"

Conclusion

The expectations placed on the Bank's IT function had steadily expanded in the five years since the function was consolidated and resources aligned to business needs. Indeed, Muhsin reported that when he went to conferences with other CIOs, most complained that their main problem was lack of support from the top management. Muhsin recalled, "My problem is somewhat different. I have more support from top management than I know what to do with. My problem is managing expectations!"

---

[12] See www.freeplayfoundation.org for more information on the Freeplay organization, whose "sole mission is to enable sustained delivery of radio information and education to the most vulnerable populations via self-powered radios."

Managing director Zhang believed that business strategy and IT strategy were intertwined, and he commented:

> Decentralization continues. Internally we are working on building capability and capacity. We are also focusing more on the client side to make it easier to become integrated with clients [for disbursements, payments, and status of project implementation]. A key part of our client relationship is knowledge sharing. Sometimes knowledge is embedded in the relationship. Sometimes it comes in the form of a loan. Other times it is in the form of a study or simply a conversation. A challenge is how to capture, package, and disseminate this to all parties.
>
> We continue to look for ways to link costs to benefits. The benefits of the technology are constantly changing; we started with the ability to have a videoconference between two people, and that expanded to five. Before you know it, you'll be able to have a videoconference with the whole world. The question is, where do you cut off? Where does the cost versus benefit make the most sense?
>
> Information technology is very important to our strategy. These days we can't work without it. By enabling speed of communication and parallel operations and global finance, IT innovation allows us to build in support for our work, including transparency of the organization.

Muhsin thought to himself about Wolfensohn's view that "IT is the key to scale; our clients and especially the world's poor are depending on us to scale up our impact." As Mushsin prepared for the annual IT review discussion with Wolfensohn and the management committee, he challenged himself to think of new and innovative ways the Bank could increase the leverage of IT. Muhsin believed that the creative and productive utilization of IT by staff presented numerous opportunities to support clients and directly assist developing countries in using IT to accelerate development.

Annotated Bibliography

General Management Bookshelf

Ackoff, Russell L. *Creating the Corporate Future: Plan or Be Planned For.* New York: Wiley, 1981. An important book that provides a broad context for IT planning.

Anthony, Robert N. *The Management Control Function.* Boston: Harvard Business School Press, 1988. This book introduces the framework of operational control, management control, and strategic planning relative to the area of IT application and its management problems.

Argyris, Chris. *On Organizational Learning.* Cambridge, MA: Blackwell Business, 1993. Explores how to achieve organizational effectiveness by managing through improved communication processes.

Austin, Robert A., and Lee Devin. *Artful Making: What Managers Need to Know about How Artists Work.* Upper Saddle River, NJ: Prentice Hall, 2003. A thoughtful book that compares the issues involved in developing software with those of producing a play and finds a surprising number of commonalities.

Austin, Robert D., and Stephen P. Bradley. *The Broadband Explosion.* Boston: Harvard Business School Press, 2004. A collection of essays focusing on the new potential and problems posed by the explosion of broadband.

Bartlett, Christopher A., and Sumantra Ghoshal. *Managing across Borders: The Transnational Solution.* Boston: Harvard Business School Press, 1991. A succinct and mind-expanding discussion of the impact, true costs, and strategic value of computer systems and their notable future influence.

Beer, Michael, Russell A. Eisenstat, and Bert A. Spector. *The Critical Path to Corporate Renewal.* Boston: Harvard Business School Press, 1990. Through an in-depth analysis of six companies that have undergone fundamental changes, the authors describe what works and what does not in corporate renewal.

Benko, Cathleen, and F. Warren McFarlan. *Connecting the Dots: Aligning Projects with Objectives in Unpredictable Times.* Boston: Harvard Business School Press, 2003. A hands-on book on how to do a better job of aligning an IT portfolio with corporate strategy.

Bower, Joseph L. *Managing the Resource Allocation Process: A Study of Corporate Planning and Investment.* Boston: Division of Research, Harvard Business School Classics, 1986. This in-depth analysis of corporate planning and capital budgeting provides critical insights relevant to both the role of steering committees and how IT planning can be done effectively.

Bradley, Stephen P., and Richard L. Nolan, eds. *Sense and Respond: Capturing the Value in the Network Era.* Boston: Harvard Business School Press, 1998. This book captures the tremendous shift in the adaptiveness of management control systems and organizations in an information-mediated world.

Brealey, Richard, and Stewart C. Myers. *Principles of Corporate Finance,* 6th edition. New York: McGraw-Hill, 2000. Describes the theory and practice of corporate finance. Discusses why companies and financial markets behave the way they do.

Brynjolfsson, Erik, and Brian Kahin, eds. *Understanding the Digital Economy: Data, Tools and Research.* Cambridge, MA: MIT Press, 2000. Considers new types of data collection and research that might help public and private organizations analyze the economic impact of the Internet and electronic commerce in the United States and internationally. Main areas of discussion include market structure, competition, and organizational change.

Bunnell, David, and Adam Brate. *Making the Cisco Connection: The Story behind the Real Internet Superpower.* New York: Wiley, 2000. A detailed story of the most Internet-enabled company in the world. It both describes its accomplishment in great detail and identifies what it did to get there.

Burgleman, Robert A., and Modesto A. Maidique. *Strategic Management of Technology and Innovation.* New York: McGraw-Hill Higher Education, 1992. Using a combination of text, readings, and cases, this book discusses how general managers can augment and develop a firm's capabilities for managing technological innovation.

Burt, Ronald S. *Structural Holes: The Social Structure of Competition.* Cambridge, MA: Harvard University Press, 1992. The basic element in this account is the structural hole: a gap between two individuals or organizations that have complementary resources or information. When the two are connected through a third individual, an entrepreneur, or an organizational market, the gap is filled, creating important advantages for the intermediary. Competitive advantage is a matter of access to structural holes in relation to market transactions.

Cairncross, Francis. *The Death of Distance: How the Communications Revolution Will Change Our Lives.* Boston: Harvard Business School Press, 1997. This far-reaching book describes the societal transformation that is being enabled by cheap, ubiquitous global bandwidth.

Carr, Nicholas G. *Does IT Matter: Information Technology and the Erosion of Competitive Advantage.* Boston: Harvard Business School Press, 2004. A controversial book that suggests that IT's role as a source of competitive advantage in the past no longer exists.

Champy, James, and Michael Hammer. *Reengineering the Corporation.* New York: Harper Collins, 1993. This pathbreaking book discusses the practical barriers and problems in achieving reengineering success.

Chandler, Alfred D., and James W. Cortada, eds. *A Nation Transformed by Information: How Information Has Shaped the United States from Colonial Times to the Present.* New York: Oxford University Press, 2000. A 250-year history of the information revolution. It is perhaps the most thoughtful book written on the roots of the information economy.

Christensen, Clayton M. *The Innovator's Dilemma: When New Technologies Cause Great Firms to Fail.* Boston: Harvard Business School Press, 1997. An explosive best-seller that highlights the perils of slow-moving change-resistant corporate cultures in a fast-moving technical world.

Copeland, Tom, Tim Koller, and Jack Murrin. *Valuation: Measuring and Managing the Value of Companies.* New York: Wiley, 2000. Provides insights and information on value creation and measurement, valuing start-ups and other hypergrowth companies, valuing cyclical companies and companies in emerging markets, and calculating the cost of capital and option pricing methods to value flexibility.

Davenport, Thomas H., and John C. Beck. *The Attention Economy: Understanding the New Currency of Business.* Boston: Harvard Business School Press, 2001. A thoughtful book that captures the importance of knowledge management in an information-overloaded world.

Gladwell, Malcom. *The Tipping Point.* Boston: Little Brown & Company, 2000. This book persuasively describes the multiple sources that suddenly lead to a massive adaptation of a technology in a short period of time.

Hamel, Gary, and C. I. Prahalad. *Competing for the Future.* Boston: Harvard Business School Press, 1994. How to develop core competencies to implement a future-oriented strategy.

Kuhn, Thomas S. *The Structure of Scientific Revolution.* Chicago: University of Chicago Press, 1970. Thomas Kuhn (1922–1996) argued that scientific advancement is not evolutionary but rather is a "series of peaceful interludes punctuated by intellectually violent revolutions." In those revolutions "one conceptual world view is replaced by another."

Leonard, Dorothy A. *Wellsprings of Knowledge: Building and Sustaining the Sources of Innovation.* Boston: Harvard Business School Press, 1998. Focuses on the knowledge-creating activities and behaviors that managers guide, control, and inspire: developing problem-solving skills, experimenting to build for the future, integrating information across internal project and functional boundaries, and importing expertise from outside the firm.

Nolan, R. L. *Dot Vertigo: Doing Business in a Permeable World.* New York: John Wiley & Sons, 2001. Discussions of the different kinds of organization structure challenges that have been created in an information-enabled world, where the boundaries of an organization are no longer clear.

Nolan, Richard L., and David C. Croson. *Creative Destruction: A Six-Step Process for Transforming the Organization.* Boston: Harvard Business School Press, 1995. This book analyzes the very different organization structures that are made possible by new information technology and the problems involved in implementing those structures.

Perlow, Leslie. *When You Say Yes, but Mean No: How Silencing Conflict Wrecks Relationships and Companies.* New York: Crown Business, 2003. A very insightful analysis of the interpersonal issues found in an ultimately failed dot-com. Very useful for project managers.

Porter, Michael. *Competitive Advantage: Creating and Sustaining Performance,* New York: Free Press, 1985. A complement to *Competitive Strategy,* this book explores the underpinnings of competitive advantage in the individual firm. Now an essential part of international business thinking, *Competitive Advantage* takes strategy from broad vision to an internally consistent configuration of activities. Its powerful framework provides the tools needed to understand the drivers of cost and a company's relative cost position.

Porter, Michael. *Competitive Strategy.* New York: Free Press, 1995. This widely read book provides a disciplined structure to the question of how firms achieve superior profitability. Porter's rich frameworks and deep insights provide a sophisticated view of competition.

Shapiro, Carl, and Hal R. Varian. *Information Rules: A Strategic Guide to the Network Economy.* Boston: Harvard Business School Press, 1998. The first book to distill the economics of information and networks into practical business strategies.

Shell, G. Richard. *Bargaining for Advantage: Negotiation Strategies for Reasonable People.* New York: Viking Penguin, 1999. This book provides a realistic, powerful framework for business and consumer negotiations that will help everyone from the inexperienced anxious negotiator to the seasoned veteran.

Simons, R. *Performance Measurement and Control Systems for Implementation Strategy.* Upper Saddle River, NJ: Prentice Hall, 2000. A thoughtful analysis of the new kind of control systems for implementing strategy.

Simons, Robert. *Levers of Control.* Boston: Harvard Business School Press, 1995. Provides a refreshing and new way to think about management control.

Slywotsky, A., and D. Morrison. *Profit Patterns: 30 Ways to Anticipate and Profit from Strategic Forces Reshaping Your Business.* New York: New York Times Business, 1999. Extrapolating from the painter Pablo Picasso's work, the authors theorize that by recognizing industry patterns—by seeing the order beneath the surface chaos—managers, investors, and entrepreneurs can prepare for change before it occurs.

Tapscott, Don, David Ticoll, and Alex Lowy. *Digital Capital: Harnessing the Power of Business Webs.* Boston: Harvard Business School Press, 2000. A book on the implications of a digitized, totally wired world.

Timmons, Jeffry A. *New Venture Creation: Entrepreneurship for the 21st Century.* New York: McGraw-Hill/Irwin, 1999. Covers the process of getting a new venture started, growing the venture, successfully harvesting it, and starting again.

Treacy, Michael, and Fred Wiersema. *Disciplines of Market Leaders: Choose Your Customers, Narrow Your Focus, Dominate Your Market.* Reading, MA: Addison-Wesley Publishing Co., 1994. This book presents a view of what needs to be done for firms to be successful in the market.

Williamson, O. E., and Sidney G. Winter, eds. *The Nature of the Firm: Origins, Evolution, and Development.* New York: Oxford University Press, 1993. Develops Ronald H. Coase's theory, first presented in his 1937 article "The Nature of the Firm," that raised fundamental questions about the concept of the firm in economic theory. The book contains the original article as well as a series of lectures by Williamson and Coase's Nobel Prize in Economics acceptance speech.

Yoffie, David B., ed. *Competing in the Age of Digital Convergence.* Boston: Harvard Business School Press, 1997. An important set of essays on the implications for corporate strategy of computing in a digitized world.

Technology Management Bookshelf

Baldwin, Carliss Y., and Kim Clark. *Design Rules: The Power of Modularity.* Cambridge, MA: MIT Press, 2000. Argues that the computer industry experienced previously unimaginable levels of innovation and growth because it embraced the concept of modularity, building complex products from small subsystems that could be designed independently yet function together as a whole.

Beck, Kent. *Extreme Programming: Embrace Change.* Reading, MA: Addison-Wesley, 1999. Provides an intriguing high-level overview of the author's Extreme Programming (XP) software development methodology, a controversial approach to software development which challenges the notion that the cost of changing a piece of software must rise dramatically over the course of time.

Brooks, Frederick. *The Mythical Man-Month: Essays on Software Engineering.* Reading, MA: Addison-Wesley, 1995. One of the classics in the field of program management. The author draws on his experience as the head of operating systems development for IBM's famous 360 mainframe computer and distills his wisdom in an easily accessible form.

DeMarco, Tom, and Timothy Lister. *Peopleware: Productive Projects and Teams.* New York: Dorset House, 1999. Using a conversational and straightforward style, the authors assert that most projects fail because of failures within the teams running them.

Feghi, Jalal, Jalil Feghi, and Peter Williams. *Digital Certificates: Applied Internet Security.* Reading, MA: Addison-Wesley, 1999. An excellent reference on the subject of encryption and digital certificates.

Forcht, Karen A. *Computer Security Management.* Danvers, MA: Boyd & Fraser, 1994. A practical book that describes the multiple aspects of computer security and the steps to be taken to gain good results.

Highsmith, James III. *Adaptive Software Development: A Collaborative Approach to Managing Complex Systems.* New York: Dorset House, 1999. Provides a series of frameworks to help an organization employ adaptive principles, establish collaboration, and provide a path toward using an adaptive approach on large projects.

Hoch, Detlev J., Cyriac R. Roeding, Gert Purkett, and Sandro K. Lindner. *Secrets of Software Success: Management Insights from 100 Software Firms around the World.* Boston: Harvard Business School Press, 1999. A practical book that focuses on the issues that must be resolved for a successful software implementation.

Lawrence, Paul R., and Jay W. Lorsch. *Organization and Environment: Managing Integration and Differentiation.* Boston: Harvard Business School Classics, 1986. This classic presents the underlying thinking of the need for specialized departments and how they should interface with the rest of the organization. It is relevant for all IT organizational decisions.

Lucas, Henry C., Jr. *Information Technology and the Productivity Paradox: Assessing the Value of Investing in IT.* New York: Oxford University Press, 1999. An interesting analysis of how one goes about justifying IT investments.

McKenney, James L. *Waves of Change: Business Evolution through Information Technology.* Boston: Harvard Business School Press, 1995. This book captures the long-term dynamics of an evolving information architecture as it traces more than 30 years of the history of information technology in four organizations.

Perrow, Charles. *Normal Accidents: Living with High Risk Technologies.* Princeton, NJ: Princeton University Press, 1999. Looking at an array of real and potential technological mishaps—including the Bhopal chemical plant accident of 1984, the *Challenger* explosion of 1986, and the possible disruptions of Y2K and genetic engineering—Perrow concludes that as our technologies become more complex, the odds of tragic results increase.

Raymond, Eric S., and Bob Young. *The Cathedral and the Bazaar: Musings on Linux and Open Source by an Accidental Revolutionary.* Sebastapol, CA: O'Reilly and Associates, 2001. A text defining the open source revolution in computing, discussing the advantages of open source computing with such technologies as Perl, Linux, and Apache. Offers a glimpse into the future of these types of technologies and their uses in the digital age.

Smith, H. Jeff. *Managing Privacy Information Technology and Corporate America.* Chapel Hill: University of North Carolina Press, 1994. A very practical book that talks about information technology privacy, current practices, and issues for the future.

Upton, David. *Designing, Managing, and Improving Operations.* Upper Saddle River, NJ: Prentice-Hall, 1998. An example of Upton's writings on the benefits of incremental improvement strategies and especially the need to design operational infrastructures so that they can be improved incrementally.

Utterback, James. *Mastering the Dynamics of Innovation: How Companies Can Seize Opportunities in the Face of Technological Change.* Boston: Harvard Business School Press, 1994. An analysis of the forces to manage in developing new products and processes as a strategic force.

Wheelwright, Steven C., and Kim B. Clark. *Leading Product Development.* New York: Free Press, 1995. A focused view on senior management's role in shaping strategy based on continuous product development as a competitive means. Time from concept to market is the critical success factor.

Yates, Joanne. *Control through Communication: The Rise of System in American Management.* Baltimore: Johns Hopkins University Press, 1993. Traces the evolution of internal communication systems through the late 19th century and into the 20th century through a focus on innovative companies such as DuPont.

Zwicky, Elizabeth D., Simon Cooper, and D. Brent Chapman. *Building Internet Firewalls,* 2nd edition. Sebastapol, CA: O'Reilly, 2000. An excellent reference on firewalls and their capabilities.

Index